|H|A|C|K|E|R|S|

TOEFL

WRITING

해커스 어학연구소

Hackers TOEFL Writing (iBT Edition)

초판 1쇄 발행 2006년 6월 10일
초판 4쇄 발행 2006년 9월 15일

저자 David Cho 언어학 박사/ 前 UCLA 교수
펴낸곳 (주)해커스 어학 연구소
펴낸이 해커스 어학 연구소 출판팀
주소 서울시 강남구 삼성동 168-21 석광빌딩
전화 02-3454-0010
팩스 02-563-0622
홈페이지 www.goHackers.com
등록번호 89-90700-21-3 13740
정가 19,500원

P·R·E·F·A·C·E

토플이 단순히 시험 준비뿐 아닌 실제의 영어 실력 향상을 통해 사회에 공헌을 한다는 마음으로 집필을 시작했던 해커스 토플 시리즈가 이제는 10권이 넘어섰습니다. 이 모든 학습교재가 모든 서점의 토플 학습 분야에서 1위~10위를 점하며 베스트셀러를 넘어 스테디셀러로 당당히 입지를 굳히고 있음은 해커스 토플 교재에 내재하는 교육 철학의 방향이 옳음을 증명하기에 기쁩니다.

또한, 해커스 가족들과 함께한 초기의 작은 정보나눔터 goHackers.com은 엄청난 속도로 발전하는 인터넷 시대를 선도하는 최고의 사이트로 자리매김하고 있습니다. 이러한 해커스의 발전은 시간의 흐름에 의해 저절로 이루어졌거나 한순간의 우연이 아닌, 수많은 해커스 가족들이 잠 못 이루고 흘린 땀과 눈물의 결실이기에 더더욱 뿌듯하고 자랑스럽게 생각됩니다

'원리와 공식'으로 대표되는 해커스 토플 그래머나, '논리적 사고 발달을 위한 토론식 독해서'인 해커스 토플 리딩을 비롯한 해커스 토플 시리즈로 학습한 많은 분들이 원하는 점수를 획득했을 뿐 아니라, 실제 유학 생활의 실력으로도 이어져 도움을 받았다고 합니다. 시험 성적 상승을 위한 단순 수험서가 아닌 제대로 된 영어 학습의 고전서를 세상에 선보이겠다는 꿈을 가지고 해커스를 일궈 온 것이 제대로 검증받고 있다는 생각입니다.

iBT 토플에서는 기존의 문법(Structure) 섹션이 폐지되고 Speaking 섹션이 추가됨과 더불어 여러 영역을 통합적으로 평가하여 기존 시험의 부족한 점을 보완하고 있습니다. 기존에 실행되던 CBT 토플시험에는 언어의 4영역인 Reading, Listening, Writing, Speaking 중 Speaking, 즉 말하기 영역을 평가하는 부분이 빠져 있어 안타깝던 차에 이러한 변화에 발맞추어 오랜 기간 과학적이고 심층적인 분석을 통해 기존 CBT 해커스 시리즈들을 언어 학습을 위해 더욱 통합적이며 효율적인 방향으로 업그레이드하였습니다.

특히 해커스 iBT 토플 라이팅은 최신 토플 경향의 실전 문제들을 최다 수록하고 있으며, 핵심적인 라이팅 전략을 제시함으로써 고득점 달성과 실제 영작문 실력의 향상을 동시에 얻을 수 있도록 하였습니다. 또한 각 문제 유형을 단계별로 학습할 수 있도록 체계적 구성을 갖추고 있으며, 실제 대학 생활에서 접할 수 있는 리딩과 강의 주제들을 다양하게 다루어 학습자들이 이 책 한 권으로 완벽하게 실전을 대비할 뿐 아니라 유학 생활에 도움이 되도록 하였습니다.

오랜 연구와 시도로 새로운 갑옷을 두른 또 하나의 고전 해커스 토플 iBT 라이팅 책이 여러분이 낯설어 할지도 모를 새로운 시험의 확실한 해결책이 되어 주리라 믿으며, 나아가 여러분이 꿈을 이루어나가는 길에 밝은 빛과 길잡이가 되기를 기원합니다.

David Cho

Contents

Intro

Integrated Section

Independent Section

토플 출제기관인 ETS에서는 2005년 9월부터 미국을 시작으로 차세대 토플 (Next Generation TOEFL)인 iBT TOEFL (Internet-based test)을 시행하고 있다. iBT TOEFL이란 인터넷을 통해 실시되는 시험으로 유학생들이 토플 시험에서 고득점을 얻음에도 불구하고 실제 미국 대학 생활에서 영어 구사 능력이 떨어진다는 기존 테스트의 문제점을 보완하고자 한 것이다.

iBT TOEFL의 특징

1. 문법 영역이 사라지고 말하기 영역이 평가된다.
   듣기(Listening), 말하기(Speaking), 읽기(Reading), 쓰기(Writing)의 네 개 영역이 두루 평가됨에 따라 문법(Structure)영역이 없어지고 기존에 없었던 말하기(Speaking) 영역이 새로 추가되었다.

2. 통합 평가 영역이 출제된다.
   iBT TOEFL에서는 듣기(Listening), 말하기(Speaking), 읽기(Reading), 쓰기(Writing) 각 영역의 한 가지 능력만을 평가하는 유형의 문제 외에 '읽고 들은 후 질문에 대한 답변 말하기', '들은 후 질문에 대한 답변 말하기', '읽고 들은 후 질문에 대한 답을 글로 쓰기'와 같은 신개념의 통합형 문제가 출제된다.

3. Note-taking이 허용된다.
   네 개 시험 영역 모두 시험 도중 Note-taking을 허용하고 있어, 문제를 풀 때 Note-taking 내용을 참고할 수 있다. 단, Note-taking 용지는 시험이 끝나면 모두 수거된다.

4. 온라인 성적 확인이 가능하며 성적표에 실력 평가와 피드백 항목이 주어진다.
   시험일로부터 15일(주말, 공휴일 제외)이 지나면 온라인상에서 본인의 성적을 확인할 수 있다. 이때 iBT TOEFL 성적표에는 총점과 함께 각 영역별 수험자의 실력 정도가 표시되며, 시험 성적에 근거하여 수험자가 실제로 어느 정도의 영어를 구사할 수 있는가에 대한 설명이 함께 주어진다.

5. CAT(Computer Adaptive Test) 출제 방식이 아니다.
   응시자의 실력에 따라 난이도가 컴퓨터상에서 조절되어 출제되는 CAT(Computer Adaptive Test) 방식이 아니라, 정해진 문제들이 일정한 조합에 따라 출제된다. 따라서 기존 CAT 방식에서 가졌던 시험 초반 문제를 반드시 잘 맞추어야 고득점을 얻는다는 부담감이 없다.

iBT TOEFL의 구성

시험영역	출제 지문 및 문항 수	시험 시간	점수 범위	iBT TOEFL상의 변화 및 특징
Reading	• 3-5개 지문 출제 • 1지문당 길이: 700단어 • 각각 12-14문항 출제	60-100분	0 - 30	• 지문 길이가 길어졌으며, 다양한 구조(multiple-focus)의 지문이 출제됨 • 문장 간략화하기(sentence simplification), 전체 요약문 완성하기(summary), 정보를 분류하여 표의 빈칸 채우기 (category chart) 문제 추가
Listening	• 2-3개 대화 출제 • 1대화당 길이: 3분 • 각각 5문항 출제 • 4-6개 강의 출제 • 1강의당 길이: 3-5분 • 각각 6문항 출제	60-90분	0 - 30	• 대화 및 강의의 길이가 길어지고, 실제 상황에 더욱 가까워짐 • 들으면서 Note-taking하는 것이 허용됨 • 화자의 태도, 목적 및 동기를 묻는 문제 추가 • 미국 이외의 영어권 국가 네이티브의 발음 도입
휴식		10분		
Speaking	2개 독립 문제 (independent tasks) 4개 통합 문제 (integrated tasks)	20분 준비시간: 15~30초 답변시간: 45~60초	0 - 4점 (총점은 0 - 30점)	• 독립형 문제(1-2번) 익숙한 주제에 대해 의견 말하기 • 통합형 문제(3-6번) 읽고 들은 내용에 기초하여 말하기
Writing	1개 통합 문제 (integrated task)	20분	0 - 5점 (총점은 0 - 30점)	• 통합형 문제가 추가됨 • 반드시 타이핑 해야 함
	1개 독립 문제 (independent task)	30분		

iBT 토플 관련 제반사항

시험 소요 시간	약 4시간
총점	120점
진행 순서	읽기(Reading), 듣기(Listening), 말하기(Speaking), 쓰기(Writing) 순으로 진행
실시일	시험은 1년에 30~40회 정도 실시되며, 각 나라와 지역별로 시험일의 차이가 있음
시험장소	시험은 전용 컴퓨터 단말기가 마련된 ETS의 Test center에서 치러짐

접수 방법	• 인터넷 접수
	  시험 응시일로부터 최소 7일 전까지 인터넷상에서 등록. 신용 카드 및 전자 수표로 결제 가능. 상시 등록 가능. 등록 확인 e-mail 발송됨 (www.etskorea.or.kr)
	• 전화 접수
	  시험 응시일로부터 최소 7일 전까지 전화로 등록. 신용 카드가 필요하며 접수 번호(registration number), 시험 일자, 리포팅 횟수, 시험장 주소를 전화상에서 알려줌. (Tel. 82-2-3211-1233)
	• 우편 접수
	  iBT TOEFL Bulletin에 있는 등록 신청서(registration form)을 작성하여, 지불 결제 수단(수표 및 우편환만 허용, 현금을 보내면 추가 비용이 있음)과 함께 우편으로 시험응시일로부터 최소 4주 전까지 등록 (주소: 서울시 마포구 염리동 168-15번지 한미 교육 위원단, 프로메트릭 풀브라이트 빌딩 121-874)

시험 비용	• iBT TOEFL 시험 비용: US $170 • 시험 일자 조정 비용: US $40 • 취소한 성적 복원 신청 비용: US $20 • 추가 리포팅 비용: US $17 (1 대학 당)
지불 수단	• 신용 카드 • 전자 수표(e-check) (미국 구좌 소지자에 한함) • 미국 달러 수표를 비롯한 기타 통용 수표 • 우편환
시험 등록 취소	• 등록 센터를 직접 방문하거나 웹사이트에 접속하여 등록을 취소, 우편이나 E-mail로는 불가능 • 시험일로부터 최소 4일 전까지 등록을 취소해야 85$를 환불받을 수 있음
시험 당일 주의사항	• 반드시 공인된 신분증(여권, 운전 면허증, 주민등록증, 군인 신분증) 원본 지참 • 접수 번호(Registration Number) 지참
시험 관련 절차	• 각 영역에서 최소 한 개 이상의 질문에 답해야 공식 성적표가 발송됨 • 10분간의 휴식 시간이 주어지며, 주어진 시간 초과시 퇴장 당하거나 성적이 취소될 수 있음
성적 및 리포팅	• 시험 응시일로부터 15일(주말, 공휴일 제외) 후에는 온라인상에서 성적 확인 가능 • 시험일 자동적으로 4개 기관까지 성적 리포팅 가능. 시험 응시일로부터 15일 후 응시자와 리포팅 장소로 성적이 발송되며 소요일은 7~10일 정도 • 성적표의 유효기간은 2년 • 시험이 끝날 때 성적을 취소할 수가 있으며 만약 취소한 성적을 다시 받아보고자 한다면 시험 응시일로부터 10일 이내로 주최기관측에 연락을 취해야 함 • 추가로 리포팅을 하고자 할 때에는 www.ets.org/toefl로 접속하여, 토플 성적 리포팅 신청서(TOEFL Score Report Request Form)을 작성하면 됨

* www.goHackers.com의 토플길라잡이를 참고하시면 업데이트 되는 iBT TOEFL관련 정보를 얻을 수 있으며, 각종 시험 접수와 결과 확인 등 관련 링크가 정리되어 편하게 이용할 수 있습니다.

iBT와 CBT의 비교

시험 영역	iBT	CBT
	Listening	Listening
	Speaking	Structure (Grammar)
	Reading	Reading
	Writing	Writing
시험 시간	4시간	3.5시간
Note-taking	허용됨	허용 안됨
Computer 적응 방식	CAT 방식이 아님	CAT 방식
총 점수 범위	0 - 120	0 - 300

iBT와 CBT의 점수 비교

iBT Total	CBT Total	iBT Total	CBT Total	iBT Total	CBT Total
120	300	86–87	227	53	153
120	297	84–85	223	52	150
119	293	83	220	51	147
118	290	81–82	217	49–50	143
117	287	79–80	213	48	140
116	283	77–78	210	47	137
114–115	280	76	207	45–46	133
113	277	74–75	203	44	130
111–112	273	72–73	200	43	127
110	270	71	197	41–42	123
109	267	69–70	193	40	120
106–108	263	68	190	39	117
105	260	66–67	187	38	113
103–104	257	65	183	36–37	110
101–102	253	64	180	35	107
100	250	62–63	177	34	103
98–99	247	61	173	33	100
96–97	243	59–60	170	32	97
94–95	240	58	167	30–31	93
92–93	237	57	163	29	90
90–91	233	56	160	28	87
88–89	230	54–55	157	26–27	83

iBT Writing에 대해

iBT Writing 영역은 크게 통합형 영역(Integrated Section)과 독립형 영역(Independent Section)의 두 가지 영역으로 이루어져 있다. 에세이 작성을 요구하는 한 가지 문제밖에 없었던 기존의 시험에서, 강의와 지문의 내용을 요약하는 한 가지 문제가 더 추가된 것이 새로운 점이다.

iBT Writing의 구성

- 라이팅 시험은 약 55분간 진행되며, 총 2개의 문제에 답하게 된다.
- 첫 번째 문항은 통합적 언어 구사 능력을 평가하는 것으로, 한 가지 주제에 대한 읽기 지문과 강의가 주어지면 읽고 들은 정보를 통합, 연관시켜서 답안을 작성해야 한다.
- 두 번째 문항은 독립적 언어 구상 능력을 평가하는 것으로, 특정 입장을 제시하고 이것에 대한 찬성 또는 반대의 입장을 묻는 문제가 주어진다. 자신의 입장을 정하고 적절한 이유를 들어 그 이유를 밝히는 에세이를 작성해야 한다.

iBT Writing 문제 유형 분석

문제 유형			유형 분석	소요 시간
통합형	읽기 → 듣기 → 쓰기	지문 읽고 강의 들은 후 요약하여 쓰기	• 지문 읽기: 학술/비학술적 주제 (250-300단어) 읽기 • 강의 듣기: 지문에서 다룬 토픽에 대해 지문과 다른 방식으로 접근한 강의 (250-300단어) 듣기 • 요약문 쓰기: 지문 내용에 대해 강의에서 어떻게 접근하고 있는지 요약	읽기 시간 3분 듣기 시간 약 2분 작성 시간: 20분
독립형	쓰기	찬반 입장 정하여 에세이 쓰기	• 문제 제시: 특정 입장을 제시하고 찬반 여부를 묻는 질문 제시 • 에세이 쓰기: 자신의 찬성/반대 입장을 밝히고 그 이유를 설명하는 에세이 작성	작성 시간: 30분
				총 55분

iBT Writing 점수 평가 요소

통합형 영역(Integrated Section)

통합형 영역은 요약문의 전개와 구성뿐만 아니라 적절한 어휘 및 문법 사용 여부, 내용의 정확성 등의 요소를 평가하여 채점한다. 채점 기준은 아래의 표에 각 점수대별로 명시되어 있다.

	통합형 영역 채점 기준표
5점	강의로부터 중요한 정보를 매우 잘 선별하고 독해 지문에 제시된 정보와 관련지어 조리 있고 정확하게 정보를 나타낸다. 요약문이 체계적으로 구성되어 있고 약간의 언어상 실수는 있으나 글의 내용이나 맥락을 애매하게 만들거나 거스르지 않는다.
4점	강의로부터 중요한 정보를 대체로 잘 선별하고 제시된 정보와 관련지어 조리 있고 정확하게 정보를 제시한다. 그러나 간혹 사소한 정보가 일부 생략되었거나, 부정확하거나, 모호한 경우가 있다. 또한 이 점수를 받은 요약문에는 문법적 구조와 어법에 있어 사소한 실수가 보이지만, 이는 논점을 이루는 전후 맥락에서 사소하게 일어날 수 있는 실수 정도에 지나지 않는다.
3점	강의로부터 중요한 정보를 포함하고 있으며 지문에 제시된 정보와 관련지어 논점을 전달하지만 다음과 같은 사항에 하나 이상 해당된다. • 전체적인 요약문이 문제에서 벗어나 있지는 않으나, 요점이 모호하거나 광범위하고, 다소 부정확하다. • 강의에서 언급된 핵심 논점 하나가 빠져 있는 경우가 있다. • 강의와 읽기 지문의 일부 핵심 사항들, 혹은 이 둘 사이의 관련 정보가 불완전하거나 부정확하거나 애매할 수 있다. • 강의와 읽기 지문 간의 개념과 관련 사항을 전달하는 데 있어 어법 및 문법에서 자주 실수가 눈에 띄거나 모호한 표현이나 부정확한 의미를 초래할 수 있다.
2점	강의와 관련된 정보를 포함하고 있지만 상당한 언어적 어려움을 보인다. 또는 강의와 읽기 지문을 연관짓는데 있어 빠뜨린 것이 있거나 부정확하다. 이 수준의 글은 다음과 같은 사항에 하나 이상 해당된다. • 상당히 부정확하거나 강의와 지문의 전반적인 관계를 완전히 생략하고 있다. • 강의의 핵심 내용의 상당 부분을 누락하거나 잘못 전달하고 있다. • 요점을 이해하는 데 있어 문제를 야기하는 언어적 오류나 표현을 포함하고 있으며, 읽기 지문과 강의의 내용을 알지 못하는 독자로 하여금 핵심 내용을 이해하기 어렵게 만든다.
1점	다음과 같은 사항에 하나 이상 해당된다. • 강의 내용과 관련하여 거의 의미가 없거나 관련성이 없는 내용을 담고 있다. • 글의 언어적 수준이 매우 낮아 의미를 파악하기가 어렵다.
	단지 독해 지문의 문장을 그대로 사용하거나 주어진 주제와 관련 없는 내용이거나, 영어가 아닌 다른 언어로 쓰여진 글이거나, 단순히 문자를 나열한 경우이거나, 글을 전혀 쓰지 않은 경우이다.

독립형 영역(Independent Section)

독립형 영역도 마찬가지로 전반적인 글의 전개와 구성, 적절한 어휘의 선택과 명확한 문법 사용 여부가 채점의 기준이 된다. 아래의 점수대별 기준표를 잘 읽고 주의해야 할 점을 살펴보자.

독립형 영역 채점 기준표
5점 해당 점수의 글은 다음과 같은 사항 대부분에 부합한다. • 효과적으로 주제와 문제를 서술한다. • 명료하게 적합한 설명, 예시 및 세부 사항을 사용하여 체계적이고 자연스럽게 구성되고 전개된다. • 일관성, 연속성, 통일성을 보여 준다. • 사소한 어휘와 문법적 실수가 있을 수 있으나 다양한 문장 구성 능력을 보여 주며 적절한 어휘와 관용어구를 사용하여 전체적으로 유창한 언어 구사력을 보여 준다.
4점 해당 점수의 글은 다음과 같은 사항 대부분에 부합한다. • 부분적으로 글이 완벽하게 정교하지 않지만 주제와 문제를 비교적 잘 서술한다. • 적절하고 충분한 설명, 예시 및 세부 사항을 사용하여 전반적으로 글의 체계가 잘 잡혀 있고 자연스럽게 전개된다. • 일관성, 연속성과 통일성은 있으나 간혹 불필요한 중복된 표현을 사용하거나 주제를 벗어나거나 불분명한 문맥을 포함한다. • 다양한 문장 구성력과 어휘력을 나타내어 유창한 어휘 구사력을 보여 주지만 간혹 뜻에 맞지 않는 문장 구조, 어형, 또는 관용어 표현에 대한 눈에 띄는 사소한 실수가 있다.
3점 해당 점수의 글은 다음과 같은 사항 중 하나 이상에 해당된다. • 주제와 문제를 어느 정도 자세한 설명, 예시 혹은 세부 사항을 사용하여 서술한다. • 간혹 문맥이 명료하지 않지만 일관성, 연속성, 통일성을 보여 준다. • 일관적이지 못한 문장 구성과 어휘 선택으로 간혹 의미가 분명하지 않으며 명확성이 떨어진다. • 틀리진 않으나 범위의 문장 구성력과 어휘력이 제한되어 있다.
2점 해당 점수의 글은 다음과 같은 결점을 하나 이상 포함한다. • 주제와 문제에 대한 글의 전개 능력이 부족하다. • 구성과 논점의 연결이 부적절하다. • 질문에 대한 대답에 사용된 예문, 설명 혹은 세부 사항이 부적절하거나 불충분하다. • 눈에 띄는 부적절한 단어나 어형을 사용한다. • 문장 구조 및 어법에서 실수가 잦다.
1점 해당 점수의 글은 다음과 같은 결점 하나 이상을 포함하여 매우 수준이 낮다. • 글이 전혀 체계적이지 않거나 완성되어 있지 않다. • 문제에 대한 세부 사항이 거의 혹은 아예 없거나 문제에 대하여 불확실한 태도를 보인다. • 문장 구조와 어법의 사용에 있어 중대한 실수가 잦다.
해당 점수의 글은 주제의 단어를 그대로 베껴 사용하거나, 주제와 상반되는 혹은 관련 없는 글을 쓰거나, 영어가 아닌 언어로 쓰였거나, 단순히 문자를 나열했을 뿐이거나, 혹은 전혀 글을 쓰지 않은 경우에 해당된다.

iBT Writing 점수 환산표

Writing 문제의 답은 ETS의 시험관이 직접 채점하며, 통합형 영역(Integrated Section)과 독립형 영역(Independent Section) 두 개의 영역을 각각 0점-5점 사이의 점수로 매긴 후 각 점수의 평균 점수를 0점-30점 사이의 점수로 환산한다.

Writing 평균 점수	환산된 점수
5.00	30
4.75	29
4.50	28
4.25	27
4.00	25
3.75	24
3.50	22
3.25	21
3.00	20
2.75	18
2.50	17
2.25	15
2.00	14
1.75	12
1.50	11
1.25	10
1.00	8
	7
	5
	4
	0

예) 통합형 영역에서 3점을 받고 독립형 영역에서 4점을 받은 경우

(3 + 4) / 2 = 3.5 → Rubric Mean Average (평균 점수)

3.5점을 환산표를 이용하여 Scaled Score (환산 점수)로 변환하면 22점이 된다.

What to Practice First

1. 문장 표현력을 기른다

간단한 구조의 문장과 누구나 쓸 수 있는 표현만 사용해서는 고득점을 받기 어렵다. 무조건 어려운 어휘와 표현을 외우려 하지 말고 실제 에세이에 사용할 수 있는 주요 표현들을 학습한다. 이 책의 유형별·주제별 표현을 통해 다양한 표현을 학습할 수 있다.

2. 듣기 능력을 기른다

기존의 CBT TOEFL과 달리 iBT TOEFL의 Integrated Section에서는 강의를 듣고 요약할 수 있는 능력을 필요로 하며 작문 능력만큼이나 듣기 실력이 중요하다. 따라서 토플 Listening 교재나 기타 영어 듣기 자료를 활용하여 장문의 대화나 강의를 듣고 이해하는 능력을 키우도록 한다.

3. 노트를 이용한 요약 능력을 기른다

250~300자 정도의 글을 읽거나 듣고 자기말로 요약하는 연습을 한다. 평소에 영자 신문을 읽거나 영어 뉴스를 듣고 이해한 내용을 요약해서 적어 보는 연습을 한다. 같은 소재에 관한 신문 기사와 방송 보도로 연습하면 상호 간 상승 효과를 볼 수 있다. 이때 시간을 제한해 두고 쓰는 연습을 하는 것이 좋다.

4. 영문 타자 연습을 한다

CBT TOEFL의 Writing에서는 Handwriting과 Typing 중 하나를 선택을 할 수 있었으나 새로이 시행되는 iBT TOEFL에서는 Typing만이 가능하다. 영문 타자에 익숙하지 않은 경우 시간을 낭비할 수 있으므로 미리 영문 타자를 연습해 두도록 한다.

5. 다양한 토픽에 대한 배경 지식을 쌓는다

전혀 들어 본 적이 없는 생소한 분야에 대한 글을 읽고 들은 뒤 그 내용을 통합해서 요약해 쓴다는 것은 쉬운 일이 아니다. 따라서 통합형 문제에 대비해 평소에 다양한 분야의 학술·시사적인 내용의 영어 텍스트를 읽어 두고, 주요 아이디어를 머리 속으로 정리해 보는 연습을 하는 것이 좋다.

6. 여러 가지 에세이 토픽에 대한 자신의 입장을 정리한다

독립형 문제에서는 토픽 자체는 어려운 것이 아니라 하더라도, 해당 문제에 대해 별로 생각해 본 적이 없어서 자신의 입장을 정하는 데 곤란을 겪을 수 있다. 다양한 에세이 토픽에 대한 자신의 입장을 간단하게 정리해 보는 연습을 통해 토픽과 아웃라인 정리에 익숙해 지도록 한다.

7. 모델 에세이를 많이 접한다

모델 에세이를 통해 좋은 표현도 배울 수 있을 뿐만 아니라 글의 구성 및 논리를 전개하는 법 등을 익힐 수 있으므로 이는 고득점을 위한 하나의 전략이라고 할 수 있다. 이때 단순히 Model Essay를 비슷하게 외워서 그대로 쓰려고 하기 보다는 전반적인 글의 구성과 논리의 흐름을 익히고, 자신이 쓸 수 있는 핵심 표현을 눈여겨 보는 것이 좋다. 이 책에 수록된 "30일 완성 모델 에세이"를 통해 하루에 Model Essay 한 개씩 학습할 수 있다.

How to Improve Your Score

1. Note-taking과 Outline을 효과적으로 작성한다

Integrated Section의 경우 필기를 하느라 강의 내용을 놓치지 않도록 주의한다. 이때, 하고자 하는 말 전부를 적는 것이 아니라 말할 때 기억의 단서가 될 정도로 간단하게 적는다. Independent Section의 경우에는 본격적으로 에세이를 작성하기 전에 미리 아웃라인을 작성해 놓는 것이 도움이 된다.

2. 시간 분배를 적절히 한다

전체 답안을 작성하는 시간은 20분이다. 첫 1-2분은 노트를 보충하고 전체 답안 구조를 잡는데 쓰고, 15분 가량 동안 실제 요약문을 작성한다. 그리고 나머지 2-3분간 답안을 검토하도록 한다. 평소에 요약문을 쓸 때 시간을 재면서 연습을 해두어 익숙해 지도록 한다.

3. 강의 흐름을 예상하며 듣는다

지문과 강의는 반드시 밀접하게 관련된 내용이 나오므로, 지문과 강의의 기본적인 포인트는 서로 일치하게 되어 있다. 따라서 지문을 읽은 후 강의를 들을 때는 지문에서 나온 핵심 포인트에 따라 다음 강의의 내용을 예상하면서 능동적으로 듣도록 한다.

4. 위기에 침착하게 대처한다

강의를 듣다가 놓친 내용이 있더라도 동요하지 말고 끝까지 집중한다. 초조해하거나 지나간 내용을 생각하면 전체 강의의 흐름을 완전히 놓치게 된다. 전체 흐름을 이해하면 특정 부분을 놓쳤더라도 전후 문맥을 이용하여 무리 없이 요약할 수 있다.

5. 강의의 주요 포인트를 중심으로 요약한다.

요약문을 작성하는 데 있어서 가장 큰 비중은 강의에 있으므로, 강의의 주요 포인트를 잘 살려서 요약하는 것이 가장 중요하다. 그리고 이 강의의 내용과 연계된 지문의 내용을 각각 언급해 주도록 한다.

6. 최종 검토를 꼼꼼히 한다

아무리 잘 쓴 글이라도 틀린 철자가 자주 나오거나 문법적 실수가 많으면 신뢰감이 떨어지고 점수에 나쁜 영향을 미치게 된다. 따라서 답안을 검토할 시간을 따로 할애해 놓고 전체적으로 꼼꼼이 확인하도록 한다.

7. 마지막까지 집중력을 잃지 않는다

약 4시간 정도 진행되는 전체 시험에서 라이팅 영역은 가장 마지막에 이루어지기 때문에 체력적으로 지치고 집중력이 흐려지기 쉽다. 그러나 라이팅 영역에서는 단 두 문제로 다른 영역과 같은 비중의 점수를 얻게 되기 때문에, 마지막까지 집중력을 잃지 않고 최선을 다하는 것이 중요하다.

iBT Writing 화면 구성

1. Writing Section 전체 Direction 화면

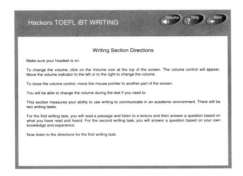

라이팅 시험의 전반적인 시험 진행 방식에 대한 설명이 제시된다. 통합형 문제와 독립형 문제의 2가지 유형에 대해 설명하며, 이 설명을 듣는 동안 볼륨을 조절할 수 있다.

2. 통합형 영역(Integrated Section)

Direction 화면

통합형 영역의 진행 순서에 대해 설명한다. 읽기 지문과 듣기 지문이 차례대로 제시되면 그 내용을 요약해서 작성해야 한다고 씌어 있다.

읽기 지문이 제시되는 화면

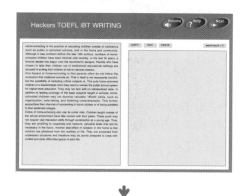

읽기 지문이 제시되고, 화면 상단에 3분간 시간이 카운트다운된다. 오른쪽에 답안을 작성하는 곳은 비활성화되어 활용할 수 없다. 3분이 지나면 자동으로 다음 단계로 넘어간다.

강의를 들을 때 제시되는 화면

강의를 듣는 동안은 화면 중앙에 교수가 강의를 하는 사진이 나온다. 강의가 끝나면 다음 단계로 넘어간다.

답안 작성 화면

답안을 작성하는 화면이다. 화면 상단에 Direction과 문제가 주어지고, 하단 좌측에는 앞서 본 읽기 지문이 다시 제시된다. 하단 우측에는 답안을 작성할 수 있도록 되어 있다. Copy, Cut, Paste 아이콘을 활용할 수 있고 Word count로 자신이 쓴 글의 단어 수를 확인할 수 있다. 화면 상단에 20분이 카운트다운되는데, 시간 이전에 답안 작성을 마칠 경우 Next 버튼을 눌러 계속 진행할 수 있다.

3. 독립형 영역(Independent Section)

Direction 화면

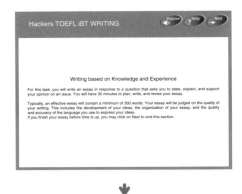

독립형 영역의 진행 순서에 대해서 설명하는 화면이다. 주어진 토픽에 대해 300자 정도로 자신의 의견을 펼치라는 내용의 direction이다.

답안 작성 화면

독립형 영역의 답안을 작성하는 화면이다. 좌측에 Direction과 문제가 주어지고, 우측에서 답안을 작성하게 되어 있다. 통합형 답안 작성시와 마찬가지로 Copy, Cut, Paste 아이콘을 활용할 수 있고 Word count로 단어 수를 확인할 수 있다. 화면 상단에 30분의 시간이 카운트다운되며, 시간 전에 답안 작성을 마치고 넘어가기를 원할 경우 Next 버튼을 눌러 앞으로 진행할 수 있다.

4. 화면 상단 Tool Bar

화면 상단에 시험 진행 과정을 보여 주는 도구 창이 화면 상에 나타난다. 볼륨을 조절하거나 남은 시간을 확인하는 등의 기능을 지원한다.

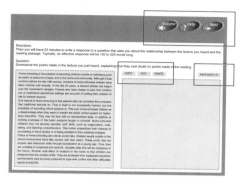

 Volume 버튼을 누르면 좌우로 움직이는 아이콘이 등장하며 이것을 움직여서 사운드의 음량을 조절할 수 있다

Help 버튼을 누르면 시험 진행에 관련된 정보를 알 수 있다. 이 때 시간은 계속해서 카운트된다.

정해진 시간 내에 답안 작성을 마치고 앞으로 진행하기를 원할 때에는 NEXT 버튼을 눌러 다음 단계로 넘어 갈 수 있다

COPY 답안 작성시 복사 기능을 지원한다

CUT 답안 작성시 잘라 내기 기능을 지원한다

PASTE 답안 작성시 붙여 넣기 기능을 지원한다

word count = 0 작성 중인 답안의 단어 수를 보여 준다

Hackers TOEFL iBT Writing 특징

1. **기본에서 실전까지 iBT 토플 라이팅 완벽 대비**

   iBT 토플 라이팅을 위한 첫걸음부터 실전 준비까지 완벽히 대비할 수 있도록 했다. 기본 다지기에서 노트 테이킹 및 요약 연습, 기본 표현 연습으로 기초 체력을 다진 후, 실전 익히기에서는 실제 시험에 대비하는 전략을 제시하고 다양한 문제로 실전감을 익히게 했다.

2. **iBT 토플 라이팅 실제 시험 유형 및 출제 경향 분석**

   현재까지 시행된 iBT TOEFL Writing의 분석 자료를 토대로 실전에 가장 가까운 문제를 출제하였으며, 시험이 출제되는 전반적인 경향을 분석하였다.

3. **iBT 실전 문제 최다 수록**

   각 유형별 문제를 충분히 접할 수 있도록 각 영역의 Hackers Practice와 Hackers Test에서 많은 실전 문제를 제공하였다. 뿐만 아니라 실제 시험과 유사한 Actual Test를 두 세트 수록하여 다양한 문제들을 통해 실질적인 실력 향상을 꾀할 수 있다.

4. **효과적 교재 학습 플랜 제시**

   책의 내용을 효과적으로 학습할 수 있도록 짜여 있는 '학습 플랜'을 제공하여 학습의 효율성을 더한다.

5. **고득점 달성을 위한 최적의 전략제시**

   각 문제의 패턴과 그에 따른 전략을 익혀 여러 가지 형태의 실전 문제에서 이 룰을 그대로 적용하여 풀어 볼 수 있다.

6. **에세이 작성의 단계적 공략**

   브레인스토밍부터 서론–본론–결론으로 이어지는 단계적 방식으로 구성하여, 에세이 작성의 각 단계에 맞는 전략을 차근차근 익힐 수 있도록 하였다.

7. 에세이 작성을 위한 필수 표현 연습

독립형 영역(Independent Section)의 기본다지기에서는 상황별, 주제별 필수 표현을 수록하여, 에세이 작성에 앞서 기본적인 표현력을 기르고 풍부한 에세이를 작성할 수 있는 기초를 튼튼히 하게 했다.

8. 새로 도입된 통합형 문제에 대한 전략 제시

iBT 시험에서 새롭게 도입된 통합형 문제를 해결해 나가기 위한 단계별 접근법 및 전략을 제시하여, 새로운 시험 유형에도 체계적으로 대처해 나갈 수 있는 프로그램을 마련하였다.

9. 노트 테이킹과 요약 스킬 제시

iBT 시험에서 새로이 요구되는 노트 테이킹과 요약에 대한 능력을 기를 수 있도록 스킬과 전략을 제시하고 충분한 연습을 할 수 있도록 구성하였다.

10. 실전 모델 에세이 최다 수록

기출 문제를 포함하여 30개의 주제로 구성된 모델 에세이를 매일 한 개씩 30일 동안 공부할 수 있게 하였고, Review page를 통해 주요 표현과 어구를 스스로 복습할 수 있도록 했다.

11. iBT 실전 CD 포함

실제 시험과 동일한 환경에서 실전 문제를 풀어볼 수 있는 CD를 제공한다. 책에 수록되지 않은 새로운 실전 문제 두 세트를 수록하였고 강의 스크립트와 해석, 해설까지 꼼꼼하게 담았다.

12. 음성 파일 CD 포함

책에 수록된 문제의 모든 사운드 자료를 들을 수 있는 음성 파일을 오디오 CD에 담아 무료로 제공한다.

13. www.goHackers.com을 통한 자료 이용 및 상호 피드백

해커스 홈페이지(www.goHackers.com)에 마련된 게시판을 통하여 책 내용에 관해 궁금한 점을 질문하고 서로 정보를 교환할 수 있으며, 학습 방법에 대한 조언을 구할 수 있다.

Hackers TOEFL iBT Writing 구성

1. 진단고사 (Diagnostic Test)

iBT TOEFL Writing 시험 유형을 그대로 따른 통합형 문제와 독립형 문제 한 세트를 풀어봄으로써 시험에 대한 학습자의 전반적인 이해를 도울 수 있다. 자신의 현재 쓰기 실력에 대해 스스로 진단해 보고 유형 및 난이도에 대해 감각을 잡아 볼 수 있는 기회로 활용할 수 있다.

2. 기본다지기

각 영역의 실전 연습으로 들어가기 전에 먼저 기본 실력을 탄탄히 쌓을 수 있도록 했다. 통합형 영역 에서는 짧은 지문과 강의로 노트 테이킹, 요약 연습을 하면서 실전에 필요한 기본적인 스킬을 익히 도록 구성하였다. 독립형 영역에서는 에세이 작성시 꼭 필요한 기본적인 표현들을 상황별, 주제별로 정리하고 문제를 통해 자신의 것으로 만들 수 있게 하였다.

3. 실전익히기

앞서 쌓은 기초 실력을 바탕으로 실제 시험의 유형을 익히고 각 단계별 전략을 배운다. 통합형 영역 에서는 읽기-듣기-쓰기로 이어지는 각 단계에서의 대처 방안과 전략을 제시하고, 독립형 영역에서는 아웃라인 쓰기에서부터 서론-본론-결론을 작성하는 방법을 각각 익힌다.

4 실제 스텝

실전에서 시험이 진행되는 방식과 그에 따라 문제를 해결해 나가는 과정을 단계별로 한눈에 보고 쉽 게 익힐 수 있도록 구성하였다.

5. Hackers Practice

실전 익히기의 각 단계에서 공부한 전략과 내용을 바탕으로 풍부한 연습을 해볼 수 있다. 수준별 점 진적 구성으로 문제를 풀며 책의 진도를 따라가다 보면 실력이 붙어가도록 하였다.

6. Hackers Test

문제 풀이의 단계별 필요한 전략과 Practice를 학습한 후, 실전과 같은 난이도의 문제를 Hackers Test에서 집중적으로 풀어봄으로써 각 문제 유형에 대한 실전감을 기르도록 했다.

7. Power Test

각 영역의 실전 문제 2세트로 지금까지 배운 내용을 실전에 적용해 보고 자신의 실력을 점검해 볼 수 있도록 하였다. 실제 iBT 시험 문제들을 기본으로 한 구성으로, 최근의 시험 경향과 출제 유형을 반영하였다.

8. Actual Test(책 + CD)

책을 모두 학습한 후 라이팅 영역 전반에 대한 종합적인 이해도와 실력을 측정할 수 있는 Actual Test가 책과 CD를 통해 각각 두 세트씩 제공된다. 실제 시험을 치르기 전에 자신의 실력을 점검해 보고, 실제 시험과 동일한 환경에서 구현되는 실전 CD로 실전 대비 마무리를 할 수 있다.

9. 30일 완성 모델 에세이 부록

학습자가 하루에 모델 에세이 한 개씩을 공부할 수 있도록 구성되어 있으며 Review page의 문제 풀이를 통한 복습으로 에세이에 등장한 주요 표현들을 효과적으로 학습할 수 있다.

10. 해설집

모든 문제들에 대한 모범 답안이 제공되며, 이를 바탕으로 자신의 답안을 보완, 개선할 수 있다. 또한 강의 내용의 스크립트도 모두 수록하였으며 이에 대한 한글 해석과 답안도 함께 제공하였다.

p.31의 진단고사를 풀어 본 후 자신의 현재 실력을 파악하여, 아래에서 적합한 학습 방법을 찾아 공부하면 효과적입니다.

Integrated section

Level 1. 기초 단계: 지문과 강의를 읽고 들을 때는 이해했는데 잘 정리가 안 돼요.
문제 내용을 이해는 했지만 금방 잊어버리고 정리가 안 된다면 [기본다지기]의 노트 테이킹 연습을 통해서 들은 내용을 체계적으로 정리하는 연습부터 해보세요.

Level 2. 중급 단계: 지문과 강의 내용을 읽고 잘 정리했는데 요약하기가 힘들어요.
문제를 잘 정리했지만 요약문을 작성하는 데 어려움을 겪는다면 [기본다지기]의 요약 연습을 통해서 요약문 작성의 기본 실력을 길러 보세요. Check-up 문제를 풀고 나면 모범 답안과 자신의 답안을 비교해보고, 좋은 표현은 꼼꼼이 익힌 뒤 넘어가세요.

Level 3. 상급 단계: 지문과 강의 내용을 그럭저럭 요약해 낼 수 있었어요.
자기 나름대로 요약문을 완성해 낼 수 있었다면, [기본다지기]는 간단히 마스터하고, 이제 [실전익히기]를 통해서 문제 유형을 익히고 Hackers Practice, Hackers Test를 철저히 공부하세요. 그리고 Power Test 와 Actual Test를 통해서 마무리를 하도록 합니다.

Independent section

Level 1. 기초 단계: 하고 싶은 말은 많은데 문장을 어떻게 써나가야 할 지 모르겠어요.
기본 표현들을 몰라 문장을 구성하기가 힘들다면, [기본다지기]의 상황별, 주제별 표현부터 공부하세요. 표현을 열심히 외우고 Check-up 문제를 통해서 철저히 자신의 것으로 만들도록 합니다.

Level 2. 중급 단계: 문장은 쓸 수 있는데 문단을 어떻게 구성해야 할지 모르겠어요.
문장력은 있지만 문단 구성에서 망설였다면, [실전익히기]의 에세이 기본 구조 익히기를 먼저 공부하세요. 에세이의 기본 구조가 어떤 것인지 배우고, 글쓰기의 뼈대인 아웃라인 잡는 방법을 Hackers Practice, Hackers Test를 통해 연습해 보세요.

Level 3. 상급 단계: 내 생각을 어느 정도 자유롭게 쓸 수 있었어요.
자신의 생각을 에세이로 표현할 수 있다면, [기본익히기]는 짧은 기간 동안 소화해내고, [실전익히기]의 에세이 쓰기를 공부해 고득점을 노려보세요. Hackers Practice, Hackers Test를 공부하면서 모범 답안의 좋은 표현을 익혀두었다가, Power Test, Actual Test에서 최대한 활용해 만점 에세이를 작성해보세요.

학습자가 공부할 수 있는 상황에 따라 아래의 방법을 활용하여 공부하면 효율적입니다.

1. 개별 학습

❶ 본 교재에서 제시하는 학습 플랜에 따라 매일의 학습 분량의 미리 계획하고, 이 계획에 맞추어 학습 속도를 적절히 조절해 나가는 것이 좋습니다.

❷ 본문의 내용을 숙지하고 본문에서 제시하는 문제 풀이의 단계별 전략을 Hackers Practice와 Hackers Test를 풀면서 적용해 봅니다.

❸ 통합형 영역에서는 문제를 풀고 나면 강의 스크립트를 확인하여 자신이 놓친 부분을 확인합니다. 모범 노트와 답안을 자신의 답안과 비교하면서 빠진 내용이나 더 좋은 표현을 쓴 부분을 눈여겨 보고, 빠진 부분 및 표현을 보강해서 다시 한 번 답안을 작성해 봅니다.

❹ 독립형 영역에서는 주어진 문제에 대한 답안을 혼자 힘으로 작성해 보고, 모범 답안을 자신의 답안과 비교하면서 좋은 예시나 표현을 확인하고 익힙니다. 모범 답안에서 취한 장점을 활용해서 다시 한 번 답안을 작성해 봅니다.

2. 스터디 학습

❶ 본 교재에서 제시하는 학습 플랜에 따라 매 회의 스터디 분량을 미리 계획합니다. 본문의 내용과 Hackers Practice는 숙제로 각자 공부해 온 후 어려운 문제 등을 스터디 시간에 함께 논의합니다.

❷ 통합형 영역에서는 Hackers Test를 예습 없이 다 함께 시간을 정해 실전감을 가지고 풀어 본 후, 서로의 답안을 비교해 보고 각자의 답안에서 빠진 부분이나 부족한 표현 등을 지적해 줍니다. 마지막으로 교재에 나와 있는 모범 노트와 답안을 함께 읽어 보고, 빠진 내용과 좋은 표현을 확인합니다.

❸ 독립형 영역에서는 교재에 주어진 아웃라인뿐 아니라 새로운 아웃라인의 아이디어를 떠올리기 위해 자유롭게 아이디어를 교환하는 브레인스토밍 연습을 하도록 합니다. Hackers Test는 시간을 정해 실전감 있게 풀어 본 후, 서로의 답안을 비교해 보고 어색한 표현이나 예시 등을 지적해 줍니다. 그리고 교재에 나와 있는 모범 답안을 함께 읽어 보고, 좋은 표현과 논리 전개 방식 등을 확인합니다.

3. 학원/동영상 강의로 학습

❶ 기본적으로 학원이나 동영상 강의의 진도에 맞추어 학습합니다. 주어진 진도를 따라가기 위해 과제를 확실히 준비해 가는 것이 중요합니다.

❷ 다음 강의로 넘어가기 전에 기존의 수업분을 개인적으로 철저히 복습해야 합니다. 학원의 경우에는 수업이 없는 주말 등에 부족한 부분을 보충해서 복습하고, 동영상 강의의 경우에는 기존 수업 내용을 다 복습한 후에야 다음 강의로 넘어가도록 합니다.

❸ 공부하다가 의문점이 생기면 꼭 선생님에게 질문하여 확인하고 자신의 것으로 만드는 것이 좋습니다. 또한 자신이 작성한 요약문이나 에세이를 선생님에게 보일 수 있으면 가능한 자주 제출하고 첨삭을 받도록 합니다.

1. 4주 완성형 – 통합형(INT)과 독립형(IND) 개별 학습 플랜

	Day	1st	2nd	3rd	4th	5th	6th	7th
1st week	본문	진단고사	INT 기본 I-1	INT 기본 I-2	INT 기본 II-1	INT 기본 II-2	INT 실전 I + HP	
	부록	Essay 1	Essay 2	Essay 3	Essay 4	Essay 5	Essay 6	Essay 7, 8
2nd week	본문	INT 실전 I HT	INT 실전 II + HP	INT 실전 II HT	INT PT	IND 기본 I-1	IND 기본 I-2	
	부록	Essay 9	Essay 10	Essay 11	Essay 12	Essay 13	Essay 14	Essay 15, 16
3rd week	본문	IND 기본 I-3	IND 기본 II-1	IND 기본 II-2	IND 기본 II-3	IND 실전 I + HP, HT	IND 실전 II + HP, HT	
	부록	Essay 17	Essay 18	Essay 19	Essay 20	Essay 21	Essay 22	Essay 23, 24
4th week	본문	IND 실전 III + HP, HT	IND 실전 IV + HP, HT	IND PT	AT I	AT II	CD test 1	CD test 2
	부록	Essay 25	Essay 26	Essay 27	Essay 28	Essay 29	Essay 30	

＊ CU: Check-up / HP: Hackers Practice / HT: Hackers Test / PT: Power Test / AT: Actual Test

2. 4주 완성형 – 통합형(INT)과 독립형(IND) 혼합 학습 플랜

	Day	1st	2nd	3rd	4th	5th	6th	7th
1st week	**통합형 (INT)**	진단고사	INT 기본 I-1 + CU 01-05	INT 기본 I-1 CU 06-10	INT 기본 I-2 + CU 01-05	INT 기본 I-2 CU 06-10	INT 기본 II-1 + CU 01-05	
	독립형 (IND)		IND 기본 I-1 + CU 전반	IND 기본 I-1 CU 후반	IND 기본 I-2 + CU 전반	IND 기본 I-2 CU 후반	IND 기본 I-3 + CU 전반	
	부록	Essay 1	Essay 2	Essay 3	Essay 4	Essay 5	Essay 6	Essay 7, 8
2nd week	**통합형 (INT)**	INT 기본 II-1 CU 06-10	INT 기본 II-2 + CU 01-05	INT 기본 II-2 CU 06-10	INT 실전 I + HP 01-06	INT 실전 I HP 07-12	INT 실전 I HT 01-02	
	독립형 (IND)	IND 기본 I-3 CU 후반	IND 기본 II-1 + CU 전반	IND 기본 II-1 CU 후반	IND 기본 II-2 + CU 전반	IND 기본 II-2 CU 후반	IND 기본 II-3 + CU 전반	
	부록	Essay 9	Essay 10	Essay 11	Essay 12	Essay 13	Essay 14	Essay 15, 16
3rd week	**통합형 (INT)**	INT 실전 I HT 03-04	INT 실전 II + HP 01-03	INT 실전 II HP 04-06	INT 실전 II HT 01-02	INT 실전 II HT 03-04	INT PT I	
	독립형 (IND)	IND 기본 II-3 CU 후반	IND 실전 I	IND 실전 II	IND 실전 III	IND 실전 IV	IND PT I	
	부록	Essay 17	Essay 18	Essay 19	Essay 20	Essay 21	Essay 22	Essay 23, 24
4th week	**통합형 (INT)**	INT PT II	AT I	AT II	CD test 1	CD test 2	전체 복습	
	독립형 (IND)	IND PT II						
	부록	Essay 25	Essay 26	Essay 27	Essay 28	Essay 29	Essay 30	

* 8주 완성 계획시에는 4주 계획표의 하루 분량을 이틀에 걸쳐 공부하면 됩니다.

3. 6주 완성형 – 기본 다지기 선행 학습 플랜

	Day	1st	2nd	3rd	4th	5th
1st week	본문	진단고사	IND 기본 I-1	IND 기본 I-1 CU	IND 기본 I-2	IND 기본 I-2 CU
	부록	Essay 1	Essay 2	Essay 3	Essay 4	Essay 5
2nd week	본문	IND 기본 I-3	IND 기본 I-3 CU	IND 기본 II-1	IND 기본 II-1 CU	IND 기본 II-2
	부록	Essay 6	Essay 7	Essay 8	Essay 9	Essay 10
3rd week	본문	IND 기본 II-2 CU	IND 기본 II-3	IND 기본 II-3 CU	INT 기본 I-1	INT 기본 I-2
	부록	Essay 11	Essay 12	Essay 13	Essay 14	Essay 15
4th week	본문	INT 기본 II-1	INT 기본 II-2	IND 실전 I + HP, HT	IND 실전 II + HP, HT	IND 실전 III + HP, HT
	부록	Essay 16	Essay 17	Essay 18	Essay 19	Essay 20
5th week	본문	IND 실전 IV + HP, HT	INT 실전 I + HP	INT 실전 I HT	INT 실전 II + HP	INT 실전 II HT
	부록	Essay 21	Essay 22	Essay 23	Essay 24	Essay 25
6th week	본문	PT INT I + IND I	PT INT II + IND II	AT I	AT II	CD test 1, 2
	부록	Essay 26	Essay 27	Essay 28	Essay 29	Essay 30

4. 4주 완성형 – 실전 중심 학습 플랜

	Day	1st	2nd	3rd	4th	5th	6th	7th
1st week	본문	진단고사	INT 기본 I	INT 기본 II	IND 기본 I-1	IND 기본 I-2	IND 기본 I-3	
	부록	Essay 1	Essay 2	Essay 3	Essay 4	Essay 5	Essay 6	Essay 7, 8
2nd week	본문	IND 기본 II-1	IND 기본 II-2	IND 기본 II-3	INT 실전 I + HP	INT 실전 I HT	INT 실전 II + HP	
	부록	Essay 9	Essay 10	Essay 11	Essay 12	Essay 13	Essay 14	Essay 15, 16
3rd week	본문	INT 실전 II HT	IND 실전 I + HP, HT	IND 실전 II + HP, HT	IND 실전 III + HP, HT	IND 실전 IV + HP, HT	PT INT I + IND I	
	부록	Essay 17	Essay 18	Essay 19	Essay 20	Essay 21	Essay 22	Essay 23, 24
4th week	본문	PT INT II + IND II	AT I	AT II	CD test 1	CD test 2	전체 복습	
	부록	Essay 25	Essay 26	Essay 27	Essay 28	Essay 29	Essay 30	

Diagnostic Test

Diagnostic Test

 Track 1

Directions You have 20 minutes to plan and write your response. Your response will be judged on the basis of the quality of your writing and on how well your response presents the points in the lecture and the relationship to the reading passage. Typically, an effective response will be 150 to 225 words.

The old adage "The early bird gets the worm" has been proven time and time again throughout human history. In the modern world, the early birds are considerably more productive.

Rising just a little earlier in the mornings creates time that can be used for constructive purposes. If the hours that humans spend working and taking care of their basic needs like sleeping and eating are added up, very little time remains for other activities. Many people sleep more than their bodies require. Getting up just two hours earlier on a daily basis would amount to an extra 730 waking hours per year. This time can be used for self-improvement, such as acquiring skills helpful in furthering one's career, or relaxing in preparation for the day. These sorts of activities would improve the quality of life overall.

There are other, more specific reasons to wake up early. The morning hours are typically the most productive for people because there are fewer distractions. Early birds may relax or work in peace without a constant stream of interruptions. Family and friends are still blissfully asleep. Therefore, there are no questions to answer, and no one calls "just to chat." Only in the early hours is it possible to be surrounded by silence, when it is still inside the home and in the streets since the TV is off, and the roads are empty. The quiet of the morning allows early risers to focus on the task at hand before constant interruptions make concentration impossible.

Now listen to part of a lecture on the topic you just read about.

Question   Summarize the points made in the lecture you just heard, explaining how they cast doubt on the points made in the reading.

COPY   CUT   PASTE

word count : 0

Hackers TOEFL iBT Writing

Directions Read the question below. You have 30 minutes to plan, write, and revise your essay. Typically, an effective response will contain a minimum of 300 words.

Question Do you agree or disagree with the following statement?

Movies tell a lot about a country.

Use specific reasons and examples to support your answer.

COPY   CUT   PASTE

word count : 0

정답 p.402

www.goHackers.com

Integrated
Section

Writing Based on Reading and Listening

Hackers iBT TOEFL Writing

Introduction

Overview

읽기와 듣기, 쓰기가 결합된 통합형 문제(Integrated Task)가 주어지는 단계이다. 읽기-듣기-쓰기의 순으로 진행되며, 지문을 읽은 후 강의를 듣고, 읽고 들은 내용을 요약하는 글을 쓰게 된다. 문제는 하나만 주어진다.

지문과 강의는 학술적인 내용이 나오기도 하고 실생활과 가까운 내용이 나오기도 한다. 지문은 한 가지 토픽에 대해 설명을 제시한다. 이어지는 강의에서는 교수가 앞서 읽은 지문의 토픽을 반박하거나 다른 관점에서의 의견을 제시하게 된다.

테스트 진행 방식

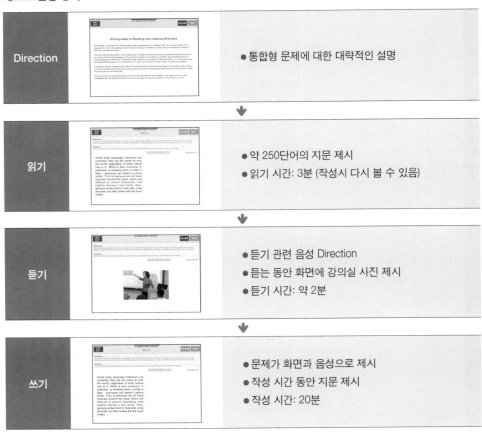

질문의 핵심 포인트

지문과 강의가 끝나면 읽고 들은 내용을 요약하라는 질문이 주어진다. 강의의 내용을 중심으로 요약하되, 강의가 지문의 내용에 대해 어떤 의문을 제기하고 있는지를 지문의 내용과 연결하여 설명해야 한다.

Example

> **Question**
>
> Summarize the points made in the lecture, — 강의 요약
> explaining how they cast doubt on the points made in the reading. ···· 지문에 대한 강의의 의문 제기
>
> 방금 들은 강의의 내용을 요약하시오. 이 때 강의의 논점이 지문의 논점에 어떻게 의구심을 제기하는지를 설명하시오.

STEP별 문제풀이 전략

STEP 1

지문을 읽고 강의를 들으면서 내용을 정리한다 (3분 소요)
처음에 지문이 주어지면 어떤 토픽에 대한 글이며 어떤 입장을 취하고 있는지를 파악하며 노트에 내용을 정리한다. 그 다음 이어지는 강의에서는 같은 토픽에 대해 지문과 어떻게 다른 접근을 하고 있는지에 유의하고, 핵심적인 내용만 노트 테이킹을 하면서 듣는다.

STEP 2

정리한 노트를 연결하고 이에 따라 답안을 구상한다 (약 2분 소요)
강의가 끝나면 주어진 문제에 따라 읽기 노트와 듣기 노트 중 내용상 연관된 부분을 연결해 둔다. 그리고 주어진 문제에 답하기 위해 어떻게 답안을 구성할지 전반적으로 구상한다.

STEP 3

구상한 답안에 따라 실제 요약문 쓰기 (15~18분 소요)
이제 실제 요약문을 작성한다. 앞서 구상한 답안 구조를 기본으로 하여, 지문과 강의의 내용을 노트에 기반해 문장으로 풀어서 쓴다.

STEP 4

전체 요약문을 다시 읽고 문법, 철자, 문장 구조 등을 수정한다 (2~5분 소요)
전체 작성 시간 20분 중 마지막 2~3분 정도는 요약문을 다시 읽어보고 검토 및 수정할 수 있는 시간을 갖도록 한다. 이 때는 더 이상 내용을 추가하기보다는 문법, 철자, 문장 구조 등의 형식적인 면을 중심으로 확인하도록 한다.

기본다지기 ▪ ▪ ▪ ▪

Integrated Section에서 가장 핵심이 되는 것은 주어진 지문과 강의를 소화하여 자신의 언어로 요약해 내는 것이다. 즉, 정보가 주어지면 이것을 이해해서 정리하고 다시 설명할 수 있는 능력이 필요하다. 이를 위해서는 읽고 들은 내용의 중심 내용을 정리하고, 그 내용에 대해 요약문을 써보는 연습을 통해 기본적인 요약 능력을 기르는 것이 필요하다.

따라서 '기본다지기'에서는 먼저 노트 테이킹 연습을 통하여 주어진 지문과 강의의 핵심 내용을 정리하는 효과적인 방법을 익힌 후, 주어진 질문에 서술식으로 답하는 연습을 통하여 요약하는 능력을 기르도록 한다.

I 노트 테이킹 연습

읽고 듣는 중에 노트 테이킹을 하면 정보를 기록할 수 있을 뿐 아니라, 또한 노트 테이킹을 하는 것 자체가 지문과 강의를 체계적으로 이해하는데 도움이 된다.

노트 테이킹의 방법

❶ 요점만 적기
읽고 들은 것을 그대로 받아 적지 말고, 중요한 것만 구별해서 적는다.

원문
Some body language indicators are universal; they are the same all over the world, regardless of what culture one is in.

좋은 노트 (O)

•	Body language – universal, same
•	

나쁜 노트 (X)

•	some body language indicators,
	universal, same all over the world,
•	regardless of culture

➜ 좋은 노트는 원문의 내용에서 가장 중요하다고 생각되는 내용만 선별해서 간단하게 적은 반면, 나쁜 노트는 원문에서 언급한 단어를 순서대로 나열만 하였고 중요도에 상관 없이 군더더기 내용도 적었다.

❷ 간단히 적기
가능한 간단한 문장과 어휘를 사용한다. '절'보다는 '구'를 사용하고, 불필요한 수식어구 등은 피한다. 나중에 내용을 기억해 내는데 단서가 될 수 있을 정도면 충분하다.

원문

Drinking a glass or two of wine a day may help to improve memory because drinking causes new nerve cells to grow in the brain.

좋은 노트 (O)

Drinking wine → improve memory
∵grow new nerve cells
↓
CO_2

나쁜 노트 (X)

Drinking a glass or two of wine may help to improve memory, it causes new nerve cells to grow in the brain

➡ 좋은 노트는 핵심만 '구' 단위로 간단히 적은 반면, 나쁜 노트는 조동사나 수식어 등을 불필요하게 포함했고 '절' 단위의 문장으로 작성하여 지나치게 길어졌다.

❸ 약어 및 기호 사용하기

자주 쓰이는 표현이나 개념은 약어나 기호를 활용하면 효율적이다. 일반적으로 쓰이는 방법을 익혀서 활용하거나, 자신에게 편한 방법을 직접 개발하여 쓰는 것도 좋다.

원문

The practice of monopoly results in higher prices and lower quality.

좋은 노트 (O)

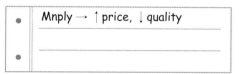

Mnply → ↑price, ↓quality

나쁜 노트 (X)

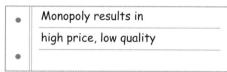

Monopoly results in
high price, low quality

➡ 좋은 노트는 긴 단어를 약어로 줄여서 표현하고, 개념을 화살표를 이용해 나타낸 반면, 나쁜 노트는 긴 단어를 모두 다 적어 넣었고 기호로 활용할 수 있는 개념도 본문에서 쓰인 단어를 모두 그대로 써 놓아 비효율적이다.

❹ 편한 언어 사용하기

노트 테이킹을 할 때는 효율성이 가장 우선이므로, 영어든 한글이든 그때그때 편리한 언어를 적절히 섞어서 활용한다.

원문

Sign language is a method of communication using hands, body and facial expressions to replace sound.

영어 노트의 예

Sign lang. → communicating
w/ hands, body, face
: 2 replace sound

영어 · 한글 노트의 예

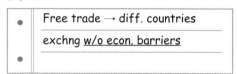

수화 → 소리 대신 손, 몸, 표정으로
communicate

➔ 영어만으로 노트를 작성할 경우 받아들이는 언어를 그대로 적으면 되므로 한글로 바꾸는 시간이 걸리지 않아 효율적이고, 한글을 섞어서 사용할 경우 더 익숙한 언어로 빠르게 작성할 수 있으므로, 두 가지를 편한대로 함께 활용하는 것이 좋다.

❺ 덧붙이기 (Listening)

들은 내용을 노트 테이킹할 때는 시간에 쫓겨 들은 내용도 미처 다 적지 못할 수 있다. 이 때는 밑줄을 긋거나 빈칸을 띄워 두었다가, 듣기 자료가 끝나자마자 쓰지 못한 내용을 덧붙여 적어둔다.

원문

Free trade is a policy where different countries can exchange goods and services with one another without economic barriers.

1차 노트

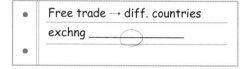

Free trade → diff. countries
exchng _____

2차 노트

Free trade → diff. countries
exchng w/o econ. barriers

➔ 1차로 노트를 작성할 때 들었는데 기억이 갑자기 안 나는 부분이나 제대로 적지 못한 부분은 빠뜨리고 넘어갈 수 있으므로, 빈칸이나 밑줄 등으로 표시해 두었다가 2차로 내용을 첨가하도록 한다.

노트 테이킹의 예

원문

Some body language indicators are universal; they are the same all over the world, regardless of what culture one is in. What is also universal, in particular, is knowing when a smile is fake – everyone can detect a phony smile. This is because we all have muscles around the eyes, which are difficult to control. They tighten during a real smile. Also, genuine smiles tend to fade after a few seconds, but fake smiles will last much longer.

노트

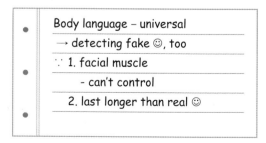

Body language - universal
→ detecting fake ☺, too
∵ 1. facial muscle
- can't control
2. last longer than real ☺

기호 및 약어

❶ 기호

자주 쓰이는 개념은 기호로 만들어 놓고 쓰면 효과적이다. 아래와 같이 일반적으로 쓰이는 기호를 익혀서 사용해도 좋고, 자신만의 방법을 개발하여 활용해도 좋다. 단, 나중에 무슨 뜻인지 알아볼 수 있도록 뜻을 확실히 익혀두도록 한다.

↑↗	증가/ increase	∵	왜냐하면/ because, since
↓↘	감소/ decrease	⊥	사이에/ between, in the middle of
＿(밑줄)	강조/ very, especially	cf	비교/ compare, confer
+, &	그리고/ and, plus	B	그러나/ but
＞	더 큰/ greater than, more, larger	@	~에서/ at
＜	더 작은/ less than, smaller, fewer than	大	큰/ large, big
⟶	~로 되다/ lead to, produce, result in	小	작은/ small, tiny
⟵	~에서 오다/ come from	少	어린/ young
/	당/ per, for each	中	중간/ middle
∴	그러므로/ therefore, so, consequently	人	사람/ man, human

❷ 약어

긴 단어를 다 적는 것은 비효율적이므로, 자주 쓰이는 말의 약자를 정해두거나 자신만의 약자를 만드는 방법을 개발하여 활용하면 시간을 절약할 수 있다.

- ●앞부분만 쓰기
  Korea ☞ Kor   lecture ☞ lec   professor ☞ prof   regular ☞ reg
- ●자음만 쓰기
  passage ☞ pssg   background ☞ bkgrd   page ☞ pg
- ●중간 빼고 쓰기
  government ☞ gov't   improvement ☞ impv't   environment ☞ env't
- ●발음이 비슷한 다른 것으로 대체하기
  to ☞ 2   for ☞ 4   you ☞ U   through ☞ thru

bc	왜냐하면/ because	w/o	없이/ without
b4	전에/ before	w/in	안에/ within
b/t	사이에/ between	imprt	중요한/ important
etc.	등등/ and so on	ppl	사람들/ people
e.g.,ex	예/ for example	rt	오른쪽, 바른/ right
max	최대/ maximum	diff.	다른/ different
min	최소/ minimum	yr	년/ year
w/	같이/ with	i.e.	즉/ that is

1. 읽고 노트 테이킹하기

읽기 지문을 읽을 때에도 핵심 내용을 간략하게 노트 테이킹을 하는 것이 좋다. 흔히 지문을 읽을 때는 노트 테이킹이 필요 없다고 생각하기 쉽지만, 노트 테이킹을 하면 단순히 정보를 기록할 수 있을 뿐만 아니라 글의 구성과 중심 내용을 파악하는 데도 도움이 되므로 적절히 활용하는 것이 좋다.

읽기 지문을 노트 테이킹할 때는 지문을 보면서 동시에 노트 테이킹을 하는 것이므로 자세한 내용을 다 적을 필요 없이 가장 핵심이 되는 내용만 간략히 적도록 한다. 먼저 글의 주제는 대부분 초반에 제시되므로 주제를 맨 위에 적는다. 이어서 나오는 뒷받침하는 내용은 번호로 매기고 들여쓰기로 정리한다.

다음 예제를 통해 읽고 노트 테이킹하는 방식에 대해 간단히 알아보도록 하자.

Example

Good parents share some similar qualities. First of all, they spend time with their children, and give them love and attention. Time spent together often includes playing and studying. On top of that, good parents guide their children. They allow their kids to be independent and make their own mistakes, but provide advice and basic guidelines.

> Good parents - similar qualities
> 1. Spend time 2gether: play & study
> 2. Guide children: allow indep. but advise & guide

● 주제 쓰기
첫 문장에 주어진 'good parents'의 'similar qualities'를 맨 위에 제목으로 정리

● 뒷받침 내용 쓰기
좋은 부모의 특성 두 가지를 각각 1, 2로 번호를 매기고, 들여쓰기해서 하위 개념임을 표시
1. 좋은 부모의 특징 1
   They spend time with their children, and give them love and attention. Time spent together often includes playing and studying. (본문)
   → Spend time 2gether: play & study (노트)
2. 좋은 부모의 특징 2
   Good parents guide their children. They allow their kids to be independent and make their own mistakes, but provide advice and basic guidelines. (본문)
   → Guide children: allow indep. but advise & guide (노트)

해석
좋은 부모들은 몇몇 비슷한 특성을 공유한다. 먼저, 그들은 아이들과 함께 시간을 보내며, 사랑과 관심을 준다. 같이 시간을 보내는 것은 함께 놀이와 공부를 하는 것을 포함한다. 그뿐 아니라, 좋은 부모는 아이들을 이끌어 준다. 좋은 부모는 아이들이 독립적이 되고 실수를 하도록 허용하지만, 충고와 기본적인 지침을 준다.

다음 지문을 읽고 핵심어를 채워 넣어 노트를 완성하시오.

1

Many university students decide to dine in their residence halls. This is very advantageous. Students do not have to waste time cooking food and cleaning up afterwards. Thus, they have more time for their studies. What's more, they can socialize with other students and enjoy eating together.

- Dine in residence hall – advantageous

  1. _____

     → more time 2 study

  2. Socialize, enjoy eating 2gether

2

Although many parents choose to travel with their young children, it's not recommended. Young children are often overwhelmed by the physical hardships of travel, and don't have a good time or even remember their experiences. Parents, on the other hand, often do not fully enjoy their travels as they have to attend to their kids' needs, who often just want to go back to the hotel and watch TV.

- Traveling w/ young children – not recommended

  1. Kids

     – physical hardship

     – _____

  2. Parents

     – _____

     – attend kids' needs

---

3 Even though processed foods are cheap, convenient, and tasty, people should avoid eating these products. Processed foods are very dangerous to people's health. They cause many diseases because of their numerous additives and preservatives. Not only that, they make people overweight. They contain empty calories and high fat content, resulting in obesity, the number one cause of death in the U.S.

- Processed foods – should avoid

  1. _____

    – cause disease

      ← additives, preservatives

  2. _____

    – empty calories, high fat

      → obesity: No.1 cause of death in U.S.

4 Countries that host big sporting events such as the World Cup or Olympics benefit in two major ways. First, revenue from sporting ticket sales, hotels, and restaurants directly boost the economy of the host nation. In addition, media attention on the country helps promote tourism and boost its public image, helping it gain prominence on the world scene.

- Hosting sporting events – benefits

  1. Revenue from tickets, hotel, etc.

    : _____

  2. Media attention

    : _____

5

Parents often scold their children and tell them to clean their rooms. Although this may seem unnecessary and burdensome to kids, clean surroundings have many beneficial effects. First of all, it's easier to study in a clean room because one can easily find materials such as pencils and books. Also, having neat surroundings will help one's mind feel organized, clear, and ready to learn.

- Clean surroundings – beneficial effects
  1. _____ : easily find materials
  2. _____ , ready 2 learn

6

Many people put radar detector in their cars to notify them when their speed is being checked. These devices are harmful for several reasons. They allow people to speed, which is dangerous to other people on the road. Next, they encourage a cheating mentality in which it's OK to do things as long as one isn't caught.

- Radar detector – harmful
  1. _____
  2. Encourage _____
     : OK when not caught

7

While it may be easier to make friendships with people from the same culture because of shared values and language, it is <u>rewarding</u> to develop <u>cross-cultural relationships</u>. People's minds become <u>more open</u> as they make friends from other cultures. In addition, they get to experience new things they wouldn't normally be able to. For instance, they are exposed to <u>new foods</u>, games, traditions, and holidays that add to their pleasure in life.

- Cross-cultural relationship – rewarding

  1. _____

  2. _____

  - – new foods, games, holidays, etc

8

Some parents discipline their children by "grounding," which is not allowing them to leave the house for a certain period of time. This is an <u>effective</u> punishment because kids cannot join their friends in fun, which is <u>very painful</u> for them. They will then <u>reflect</u> on the consequences of <u>their actions</u>. Furthermore, putting a child under house restriction <u>prevents them</u> from going out and getting into more trouble until they have learned the error of their ways.

- Grounding: _____

  - – effective

  1. Painful → _____

  2. _____

9

As many societies move towards love marriages, the status of arranged marriages has declined. However, recent studies show arranged marriages have a much higher rate of success. One, families are deeply involved in selecting suitable mates and making marriages work. They, therefore, provide numerous forms of support in these cases. What's more, couples go into arranged marriages with the idea that they must make them work, and they do! They do not waste time divorcing looking for the ever elusive Mr. or Ms. Right.

- Arranged marriages – higher rate of success

    1. Families

    - _____

    - _____

    2. Couples

    - _____

    - _____

10

Millions of dollars are allotted every year to space exploration. However, surveys show that people do not regard space exploration as a high priority. Most people are frankly not interested in exploring outer space, and said they don't care about the latest discoveries about the moon or other planets. In addition, many respondents think that money should be spent solving problems on Earth. They want quality jobs, education, and health care as well as a sustainable planet to live on.

Space exploration – not high priority for ppl

    1. _____

    - _____

    2. _____

    - _____

정답 p.406

강의를 들을 때 노트 테이킹의 중요성은 매우 크다. 속도와 진행을 스스로 조절할 수 있는 읽기 지문과 달리 강의는 반복해 들을 수 없고 주어진 속도를 따라가야 하기 때문이다. 따라서, 들으면서 적절히 노트 테이킹을 하면 최대한 내용을 기억해 낼 수 있고, 강의의 흐름을 따라가는 데도 도움이 된다.

듣고 노트 테이킹할 때 가장 중요한 것은 '듣기'에 집중하는 것이다. 적는 것에 치중해서 강의의 흐름을 놓쳐서는 안 되므로, 듣는데 방해가 되지 않을 정도로 간략하게 핵심만 적어야 한다. 강의 역시 주제는 대부분 초반에 제시되므로 먼저 맨 위에 적고, 이어서 나오는 뒷받침하는 내용은 번호로 매기고 들여 쓰기로 정리한다.

다음 예제를 통해 듣고 노트 테이킹하는 방식에 대해 간단히 알아보도록 하자.

Example

So, anyway, let's examine all-you-can-eat buffets. You think they're a great deal, right? Well, buffet food is not good for your health. Food that sits under hot lights for hours loses its freshness and, um, nutritional content. In addition, this type of dining arrangement encourages overeating, which as everyone knows, causes numerous health problems including indigestion.

> • Buffet – not good for health
>
> 　1. Food under lights for long: not fresh/nutri.
>
> • 2. Encourage overeating
>
> 　　→ health problems e.g. indigestion

● 주제 쓰기
　초반에 언급한 'buffet'가 'not good for health'하다는 내용을 맨 위에 제목으로 정리

● 뒷받침 내용 쓰기
　뷔페 음식이 건강에 나쁜 이유 두 가지를 각각 1, 2로 번호를 매기고, 들여 쓰기해서 하위 개념임을 표시

　1. 뷔페 음식이 나쁜 이유 1
　　Food that sits under hot lights for hours loses its freshness and nutritional content. (본문)
　　→ Food under lights for long: not fresh/nutri. (노트)
　2. 뷔페 음식이 나쁜 이유 2
　　Encourages overeating, which causes numerous health problems including indigestion. (본문)
　　→ Encourage overeating → health problems e.g. indigestion (노트)

해석
그럼, 마음껏 먹을 수 있는 뷔페에 대해서 알아볼까요? 여러분은 이것이 굉장히 좋은 조건이라고 생각하겠죠? 뷔페 음식은 건강에 좋지 않습니다. 뜨거운 조명 아래 오랫동안 놓아 둔 음식은 신선도와 영양분이 떨어지거든요. 게다가, 이런 식의 식사 방식은 과식을 하도록 조장합니다. 다들 알다시피 과식은 소화 불량을 비롯한 많은 건강상의 문제를 일으키죠.

다음 강의를 듣고 핵심어를 채워 넣어 노트를 완성하시오. 🎧 *Track 2*

1 | Listen to the lecture. 🎧

- Gardening – benefits

  1. Emotionally stabilizing & calming

- 2. _____

2 | Listen to the lecture. 🎧

- Giving children allowance

  1. _____

- 2. Become responsible in spending

3 | Listen to the lecture. 🎧

- _____ – not good

  1. _____

- 2. Ez 2 cheat ← work together

4 Listen to the lecture. 🎧

- _____
  1. _____
  2. _____
  3. Decide 2 pursue career or not

5 Listen to the lecture. 🎧

- Overpopulation – not a problem
  1. _____ : just not distributed well
  2. _____ : more children encouraged

6 Listen to the lecture. 🎧

- Carpooling – great
  1. _____
  2. _____

7 Listen to the lecture. 🎧

- Resident assistant in dorm – pros
  1. _____
  2. _____

8

Listen to the lecture. 🎧

1. _____
2. _____

9

Listen to the lecture. 🎧

1. _____
2. _____

10

Listen to the lecture. 🎧

1. _____
2. _____

정답 p.409

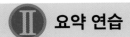

요약은 원문의 주요 내용을 자신의 말로 간단히 설명하는 것이다. 이 때 원문의 내용을 전혀 모르는 사람도 요약문을 읽고 쉽게 이해할 수 있도록 요지를 분명히 나타내는 것이 핵심이다. Integrated Section에서는 지문과 강의의 내용을 요약할 것을 요구하므로, 요약하는 능력이 가장 관건이라고 할 수 있다.

중심 아이디어 풀어서 쓰기

먼저 원문의 중심 아이디어를 파악하는데 주력하며 핵심적인 내용을 노트 테이킹한다. 그리고 이 노트를 중심으로 해서 자신이 이해한 내용을 다시 풀어서 설명하듯이 요약문을 작성한다.

❶ 원문의 핵심 내용 파악 및 노트 테이킹하기

먼저 요약할 원문의 핵심 내용을 노트 테이킹해야 한다. 앞서 배운 노트 테이킹 방법을 활용하여 원문의 중심 포인트를 간단히 정리한다.

원문

> Boycotting is an <u>effective</u> way to <u>protest</u> by <u>not buying certain products</u>. First, it <u>hurts a</u> company <u>financially</u> because their overall <u>sales go down</u>. What's more, boycotting generates <u>negative press</u> and <u>ruins</u> a business's <u>public image.</u>

노트

> • Boycott: not buy certain products
> - effective protest
> • 1. Hurt financially: sales ↓
> • 2. Negative press → ruin public image

➔ 'boycott'이 효과적인 항의 방법이라는 원문의 주제와 그것이 효과적인 이유 두 가지를 파악하고, 핵심적인 내용만 노트로 간략히 정리했다.

❷ 노트를 문장으로 풀어 쓰기

앞서 작성한 노트를 중심으로 해서 자신이 이해한 내용을 다시 풀어서 설명하듯이 요약문을 작성한다. 원문에 나온 복잡한 구문이나 어려운 표현을 쓰려고 애쓰지 말고, 이해한 내용에 기반해서 쉽고 간단한 문장으로 풀어서 쓴다.

노트

> • Boycott: not buy certain products
> - effective protest
> • 1. Hurt financially: sales ↓
> • 2. Negative press → ruin public image

요약

> Boycotting is an effective protesting method because (not only) it hurts the company financially with sales decreases (but also) ruins public image with negative press.

➔ 앞서 정리한 노트에 기반하여 원문의 내용을 다시 자신의 언어로 풀어서 설명했다. 이 때 원문의 문장 구조나 표현을 그대로 따라서 쓰지 않고, 노트를 길잡이로 하여 이해한 내용을 새로운 문장으로 바꾸어 썼다.

표현 바꾸어 쓰기

원문에서 나온 표현이나 문장 구조를 그대로 사용하기보다는 가능한 다르게 바꾸어서 쓰는 것이 좋다.

❶ 능동태/수동태 바꾸기

원문의 문장에서 주어와 목적어의 자리를 바꾸어 능동태를 수동태로, 또는 수동태를 능동태로 바꾼다.

원문

> So the altruistic sentinel's behavior ensures the survival of other members of the meerkat's group.

바꾸어 쓰기

> So the survival of other members of the meerkat's group is ensured by the altruistic sentinel's behavior.

➡ 능동태로 쓰인 원문의 문장에서 주어와 목적어의 위치를 바꾸고 능동으로 쓰인 동사를 수동으로 바꾸어 문장 구조에 변화를 주었다.

❷ 주어 바꾸기

원문의 문장에서 의미상 초점이 되는 부분을 주어로 내세워 문장의 구조를 바꾼다.

원문

> An example that is often cited is the meerkat, which is a mammal that dwells in burrows in grassland areas of Africa.

바꾸어 쓰기

> The meerkat, which is a mammal that dwells in burrows in grassland areas of Africa, is often cited as an example.

➡ 원문에서 내용상 초점이 되는 'meerkat'을 주어로 삼고 문두로 가져옴으로써 문장 구조도 바뀌고 문장의 의미도 더욱 정확해졌다.

❸ 동의어 쓰기

원문에서 쓴 표현을 같은 뜻을 가진 다른 말로 바꾼다. 이 때는 알고 있는 동의어나 동의 표현을 활용할 수도 있고, 원문의 명사를 적절히 대명사로 지칭할 수도 있다.

원문

> In fact, many species of animals appear willing to sacrifice food, or even their lives, to assist other members of their group.

바꾸어 쓰기

> As a matter of fact, various kinds of animals seem to happily give up food or even their lives to help other members of their group.

➡ 'In fact → As a matter of fact', 'willing to sacrifice food → happily give up food' 와 같이 원문의 표현을 같은 뜻을 지닌 다른 표현으로 바꾸어 썼다.

1. 읽고 질문에 답하기

지문을 읽고 그 내용을 요약하는 것은, 지문의 핵심 내용에 대해 물어보는 질문에 서술식으로 대답하는 연습으로부터 시작할 수 있다. 질문에 답할 때는 먼저 지문을 읽으며 노트 테이킹하고 이 노트를 기반으로 대답을 완성한다. 그러나 지문에 있는 표현이나 문장 구조를 그대로 똑같이 따라 쓰는 것보다는, 동의어나 다른 문장 구조를 활용하여 원문과 다르게 쓰는 것이 좋다.

앞서 노트 테이킹을 한 지문의 예제를 통해 읽고 질문에 답하는 방식에 대해 간단히 알아보도록 하자.

Example

Good parents share some similar qualities. First of all, they spend time with their children, and give them love and attention. Time spent together often includes playing and studying. On top of that, good parents guide their children. They allow their kids to be independent and make their own mistakes, but provide advice and basic guidelines.

> Good parents - similar qualities
> 1. Spend time 2gether: play & study
> 2. Guide children: allow indep. but advise & guide

Q According to the passage, what are the qualities that good parents share?

Here are two qualities that good parents share. They ① enjoy doing activities such as playing and studying with their children. Good parents also ② give guidance to their children while encouraging them to be independent.

● 질문 파악
  지문의 주제인 '좋은 부모의 특성'에 대해 묻고 있음을 파악

● 노트 풀어서 쓰기
  뒷받침 내용으로 정리한 좋은 부모의 특성 두 가지를 문장으로 풀어서 쓰기
  1. Spend time 2gether: play & study (노트)
    → They enjoy doing activities such as playing and studying with their children. (답안)
  2. Guide children: allow indep. but advise & guide (노트)
    → Good parents also give guidance to their children while encouraging them to be independent. (답안)

● 표현 바꾸어 쓰기
  원문의 표현을 비슷한 의미의 다른 말로 바꾸어 쓰거나 문장 구조를 바꾸어서 쓰기
  1. 비슷한 말로 바꾸기
    They spend time with their children. Time spent together often includes playing and studying. (본문)
    → They enjoy doing activities such as playing and studying with their children. (답안)
  2. 문장 구조 바꾸기
    They allow their kids to be independent and make their own mistakes, but provide advice and basic guidelines. (본문)
    → Good parents also give guidance to their children while encouraging them to be independent. (답안)

다음 지문을 읽으며 노트 테이킹하고 주어진 질문에 대한 대답을 완성하시오.

1 Many people start their mornings by drinking coffee. Unfortunately, coffee is not good for people's physical or psychological health. One, coffee irritates the digestive system, causing cramping and pain. Next, coffee is highly addictive and causes people to feel irritated if they can't drink it.

Q According to the passage, why is drinking coffee not recommended?

First, coffee ① _____. It can cause

pain and cramping in one's stomach. In addition, ② _____.

People can easily feel unstable without drinking it.

2 Chocolate is a delicious food that is beneficial to health in many ways. One, it is highly nutritious and contains important vitamins such as B, D and E. In addition, chocolate stimulates the secretion of chemicals in the brain that cause a feeling of happiness.

Q According to the passage, why is chocolate beneficial?

Chocolate is very nutritious and ① _____.

Also, it makes the brain ② _____

_____.

3 Studies have shown that children who learn languages early in life have a better chance of attaining and retaining fluency throughout their lives. This is because they closely observe speakers around them, and imitate them freely. At the same time, children seem to have some kind of natural mental programming that allows them to learn grammar quickly and easily.

Q Why do children who learn languages early in life become fluent?

First, children watch other speakers and ① _____ .

Secondly, kids have ② _____

_____ .

4 Wine is very beneficial for people's health. First of all, it is a mild relaxant and reduces anxiety and tension. As part of a normal diet, wine provides the body with energy, with substances that aid digestion. On top of that, it has been known to reduce the risk of heart disease and cancer.

Q According to the passage, what are the benefits of drinking wine?

Wine helps you by ① _____ .

It also ② _____ .

In addition, ③ _____ .

5 Although standardized test scores should be considered in college applications, their importance should be minimized. These tests measure only a narrow aspect of a person's reasoning and thinking abilities. In addition, some people simply don't perform well on tests. As a result, test scores cannot predict a student's performance or success in college and life.

Q Why does the passage say standardized test scores should not be given much weight in college applications?

These tests only measure ① _____ .

Also, some students ② _____ . Therefore,

test scores don't indicate how successful a student will be in college and life.

6 Although many people no longer live together with grandparents, parents, children, and other relatives, it's advantageous to live in extended families. Living with many relatives spreads parenting responsibilities around, no longer solely burdening parents as in the nuclear family. In addition, kids benefit from a more relaxed atmosphere and have more sources of love to draw from.

Q According to the passage, what are the advantages of living in extended families?

Firstly, ① _____ ,

so parents don't carry the whole burden. Secondly, kids benefit from ② _____

_____ .

7 Esperanto is a created language that doesn't belong to any country or culture. While people all over the world are frustrated due to the lack of a common language, Esperanto is a good choice as a secondary universal language for several reasons. First, it is neutral language which makes everyone equal because it is no one's mother tongue. Furthermore, it's very easy to learn because of its simple structure.

> -
> -
> -

Q According to the passage, why is Esperanto a good choice as a secondary universal language?

First, ① _____

_____. It makes everyone equal because it's no one's first language.

Second, ② _____.

8 Although meat is widely popular, a vegetarian diet is good for a number of reasons. First, vegetarian foods are healthful and low in saturated fats. In addition, many animals we eat today are given many growth hormones and other toxic substances that are harmful for human consumption. Next, a vegetarian diet ensures that we are not harming animals. Many chickens and cows are kept in inhumane conditions by the meat industry. A vegetarian diet thus reduces animal cruelty.

> -
> -
> -

Q According to the passage, what are the advantages of having a vegetarian diet?

First, ① _____.

Secondly, ② _____.

Lastly, ③ _____.

9 Group psychology theorizes that people think and act differently in groups than alone. That is, a person in a crowd may lose his or her sense of individuality in favor of the group. Often, the negative aspects of group psychology are emphasized. Such effects include violent behavior, like riots, that may not be normal behavior for any one individual. Crowds can also be positive entities, in which an individual might become infected by a crowd's excitement or anticipation at a concert, party, or election rally.

Q What are the negative and positive aspects of group psychology?

Negative effects of group psychology include ① _____,

_____. Positive aspects, on the other hand,

② _____.

10 Mobile phones are actually detrimental for a few reasons. First, they do not allow people any privacy from being contacted at all times. This means that people cannot concentrate fully on their tasks, but are constantly interrupted. Second, when riding public transportation or going to a performance, one is always interrupted by phones ringing and loud private conversations. This is a highly annoying form of a noise pollution.

Q According to the passage, why are mobile phones disadvantageous?

① _____.

② _____.

_____.

정답 p.413

강의를 듣고 그 내용에 대한 질문에 답할 때도 마찬가지로, 강의를 듣고 노트를 정리한 후, 그 노트의 흐름을 따라서 듣고 이해한 내용을 풀어서 쓴다. 이 때 유의해야 할 점은 단순히 노트에 정리한 단어를 문장으로 바꾸는 것이 아니라, 노트를 길잡이 삼아 자신이 이해한 내용 자체를 풀어서 써야 한다는 것이다.

앞서 노트 테이킹을 한 예제를 통해 듣고 질문에 답하는 방식에 대해 간단히 알아보자.

Example

So, anyway, let's examine all-you-can-eat buffets. You think they are a great deal, right? Well, buffet food is not good for your health. Food that sits under hot lights for hours loses its freshness and, um, nutritional content. In addition, this type of dining arrangement encourages overeating, which as everyone knows, causes numerous health problems including indigestion.

> - **Buffet – not good for health**
>   1. Food under lights for long: not fresh/nutri.
> - 2. Encourage overeating
>   - → health problems e.g. indigestion

Q Why doesn't the professor recommend eating at buffets?

The professor doesn't recommend eating at buffets for two reasons. One, buffet food is ① not fresh and does not have much nutritional value. What's more, people ② at buffets often overeat, which causes many health problems such as indigestion.

- ●질문 파악
  강의의 요점인, '뷔페 음식이 좋지 않은 이유'를 묻고 있음을 파악
- ●노트 풀어서 쓰기
  뒷받침 내용으로 정리한 뷔페가 좋지 않은 이유 두 가지를 문장으로 풀어서 쓰기
  1. Food under lights for long: not fresh/nutri. (노트)
     → One, buffet food is not fresh and does not have much nutritional value. (답안)
  2. Encourage overeating → health problems e.g. indigestion (노트)
     → What's more, people at buffets often overeat, which causes many health problems such as indigestion. (답안)

다음 강의를 들으며 노트 테이킹하고 주어진 질문에 대한 대답을 완성하시오. 🎧 *Track 3*

1 Listen to the lecture. 🎧

Q According to the professor, how do pets help their owners?

🖉 Pets make their owners ① _____.

Pets also teach their owners ② _____

_____.

2 Listen to the lecture. 🎧

Q According to the lecture, how are cold weather and catching colds related?

🖉 Cold weather can make us catch colds indirectly by forcing us to ① _____

_____.

It also makes us ② _____.

3 | Listen to the lecture. 🎧

Q According to the lecture, what are the benefits of moderate alcohol consumption?

🖉 Drinking moderately helps you ① _____

_____ .

In addition, ② _____ .

---

4 | Listen to the lecture. 🎧

Q According to the lecturer, what are the advantages of digital media?

🖉 It's easy to ① _____ in digital media.

In addition, digital media provides ② _____ .

5

> Listen to the lecture. 🎧

> **Q** According to the lecture, what are the advantages of personal communication over e-mail?

🖉 Discussing in person ① _____ .

Not only that, in person, ② _____

_____ .

6

> Listen to the lecture. 🎧

> **Q** According to the lecture, what does the recent survey show about single-sex schools?

🖉 A survey showed that ① _____

_____ . Also, it showed co-ed schools helped students

② _____ .

7

Q Why does the professor cast doubts on computerized testing?

Students who ① _____ find the test stressful, not to mention making and running programs is costly. Also, ② _____

_____.

8

Q According to the lecture, how does winning the lottery alter people's lives?

Lottery winners were ① _____ because

② _____

_____.

9

Listen to the lecture.

Q According to the professor, in what order should a performer present, and why?

A performer should present ① _____

_____ . This also allows him to ② _____

_____ .

10

Listen to the lecture.

Q How does air conditioning affect the environment and people?

Air conditioning ① _____ .

In addition, it causes ② _____

_____ .

정답 p.418

실전익히기

I 읽고 듣고 내용 정리하기

Integrated Section이 시작되면 먼저 읽기 지문과 강의가 주어진다. 통합형 문제는 지문과 강의의 내용을 요약하여 쓸 것을 요구하므로, 첫 단계에서 읽고 듣게 되는 내용을 잘 이해하고 적절히 정리해 두는 것이 매우 중요하다.

지문과 강의 관계의 예

읽기 지문과 강의는 기본적으로 같은 토픽을 다른 관점에서 다룬다. 읽기 지문에서 어떤 토픽에 대한 이론을 설명하고 강의에서는 이 이론에 대해 반론을 펼치거나, 지문에서 일정 관점을 가지고 주장을 하면 강의에서는 지문과 다른 관점의 의견을 제시한다. 아래의 세 가지 예를 통해 지문과 강의의 관계에 대해 좀 더 자세히 알아보자.

❶ 새로운 시스템의 이론과 실제 도입시 결과

읽기 지문에서 새로 고안된 시스템에 대해 설명하고 그것의 장점을 나열한다. 그리고 이어지는 강의에서는 그 시스템을 실제로 도입했을 때 일어나는 예상치 못한 단점들을 제시하여 지문에서 설명한 장점에 대해 반박한다.

관계	예
지문 • 새로운 시스템의 장점 1 • 새로운 시스템의 장점 2 • 새로운 시스템의 장점 3	팀 근무제는 효과적이다 • 여러 사람이 힘을 합치므로 일이 빨리 해결된다 • 여러 사람의 재능을 합쳐 창의적인 결과가 나온다 • 팀 단위로 성취하는 결과가 크므로 공을 더욱 크게 인정받는다
강의 • 실제 도입시 단점 1 • 실제 도입시 단점 2 • 실제 도입시 단점 3	실제로 팀 근무제를 실시했더니 비효과적이었다 • 많은 사람의 의견 일치에 걸리는 시간 때문에 일이 빨리 진행되지 않았다 • 소수의 주도자가 생겨서 여러 사람의 의견이 제대로 반영되지 않았다 • 무임 승차를 하는 팀원이 생겨서 크게 공헌을 한 팀원도 제대로 인정받지 못했다

❷ 현재의 문제점과 가능한 해결 방안

읽기 지문에서 현재 사회 문제로 떠오르고 있는 이슈에 대해 이야기하고 그 현상의 원인을 몇 가지 설명한다. 이어지는 강의에서는 지문에서 설명한 현상의 원인을 각각 해결할 수 있는 방안을 제시한다.

관계   예

| **지문**
• 현재의 문제점 1
• 현재의 문제점 2
• 현재의 문제점 3 | 젊은층이 저조한 투표율을 보이고 있다
• 오늘날의 젊은이들은 개인적이어서 나라 전체의 일보다 자신의 일에 관심이 많다
• 학업 관계상 주소지를 떠나 있는 젊은이는 투표를 위해 돌아오기가 힘들다
• 진보적 사상을 가진 젊은층은 기성세대의 보수적 정치인들에 염증을 느낀다 |
| **강의**
• 문제 해결 방안 1
• 문제 해결 방안 2
• 문제 해결 방안 3 | 젊은층이 정치에 참여하게 하는 방안
• 젊은이들의 삶에 직접적으로 연관되는 문제에 대한 정책을 제시한다
• 주소지가 아닌 곳에서도 투표할 수 있도록 부재자 투표를 실시한다
• 젊은이들의 진보적인 사상을 반영하는 정당의 발전을 장려한다 |

❸ 기존의 과학적 이론과 반론

읽기 지문에서 어떤 토픽에 대한 이론을 설명하고 그러한 이론이 성립되는 이유를 설명한다. 그리고 이어지는 강의에서는 그 이론에 대해 반대되는 증거를 제시하며 그 이론이 틀린 것을 증명한다.

관계   예

| **지문**
• 기존의 과학적 이론 1
• 기존의 과학적 이론 2
• 기존의 과학적 이론 3 | 이타주의는 있다
• 파수꾼 미어캣은 다른 미어캣들이 먹이를 먹는 동안 굶어가며 보초를 선다
• 파수꾼 미어캣은 위험을 무릅쓰며 보초를 선다
• 아무 보상 없이 다른 사람에게 장기를 기증하는 사람도 있다 |
| **강의**
• 기존 이론에 대한 반론 1
• 기존 이론에 대한 반론 2
• 기존 이론에 대한 반론 3 | 이타주의는 없다
• 파수꾼 미어캣은 보초를 서기 전에 먼저 먹이를 먹는다
• 파수꾼 미어캣은 경고음을 내고 도망가 버리며, 오히려 살 확률이 높다
• 장기 기증자는 감사와 존경 등 사회적인 보상을 받는다 |

1. 읽고 내용 정리하기

먼저 읽기 지문이 주어지면 구성이 어떠하며 주요 포인트가 무엇인지를 파악하며 읽고, 지문의 주요 내용을 노트로 정리해 두어야 한다.

❶ 지문의 구성과 읽기 포인트

지문은 주제와 근거, 세부 사항으로 이루어졌음을 알고 이 포인트들을 중심으로 지문을 읽고 정리한다.

● 주제 (Main point)

주제는 글에서 글쓴이가 전달하고자 하는 중심 생각이다. 주로 지문의 앞부분에 나오므로 먼저 이 글이 무엇에 관한 것이며 글쓴이가 내세우는 중심 생각이 무엇인지를 파악하면서 글을 읽기 시작한다.

ex) There are a number of advantages for franchise owners, and among them, many opt for this choice mainly for three reasons.

가맹점 사업을 하는 사람들에게는 수많은 이점이 있으며, 그 중에도 많은 사람들이 주로 세 가지 이유로 가맹점 사업을 선택한다.

● 근거 (Supporting points)

근거는 주제의 중심 생각을 뒷받침하는 항목이다. 주로 주제에서 나타나는 글쓴이의 주장에 대한 근거 세 가지로 구성된다. 흔히 각 문단의 앞부분에 제시되므로 문단의 첫 문장에 주목한다.

ex) First of all, a franchise offers reliable products to first-time business owners.

첫째로, 가맹점은 사업을 처음 하는 사람에게 믿을 수 있는 상품을 제공한다.

● 세부 사항 (Details)

근거로 주어진 내용을 부연 설명하는 내용이다. 따라서 각 근거로 제시된 포인트들의 연장선상으로 생각하면서 읽도록 한다.

ex) The merchandise sold has been tried and tested at other branches; therefore, the new owners can be assured that they will be able to sell them at their locations.

팔게 되는 상품들은 다른 점포에서 이미 테스트를 받은 것들이며, 따라서 새로 사업을 하는 가맹점 주인은 자신의 점포에서도 이 상품들을 팔 수 있으리라는 데에 확신을 가질 수 있다.

❷ 읽기 노트 정리하기

읽기 지문의 노트를 정리할 때는 주제를 큰 제목으로, 각 근거들을 번호를 매긴 작은 제목으로 적는다. 읽기 지문은 답안 작성시 다시 볼 수 있으므로 핵심적인 내용만 간단히 노트하도록 한다.

- **주제 적기:** 노트의 맨 위에 큰 제목으로 적는다
- **근거 적기:** 번호를 매기고 작은 제목으로 적는다.
- **세부 사항 적기:** 근거를 적어 둔 아래에 칸을 들여 적는다.

A popular business decision today is whether to open one's own businesses or purchase a franchise from an established company. There are a number of advantages for franchise owners, and among them, many opt for this choice mainly for three reasons.

주제
가맹점 사업의 세 가지 이점

First of all, a franchise offers reliable products to first-time business owners. The merchandise sold has been tried and tested at other branches; therefore, the new owners can be assured that they will be able to sell them at their locations.

근거 1
믿을 수 있는 상품

세부 사항 1
검증된 상품으로부터 오는 확신

Franchisees also save on advertising. They do not have to spend a lot of time and resources advertising unknown businesses and products. Larger, well-established franchise operations will often have national marketing campaigns and a solid trading name.

근거 2
광고 비용 절약

세부 사항 2
가맹점에서 전국적 광고 실시

Most importantly, franchisees have business security. They have a lower rate of failure because the franchisor helps them set up the business, which has been tested to be successful. Business owners also receive continual assistance in the form of comprehensive training programs in sales and other business skills.

근거 3
사업 안정성 보장

세부 사항 3
가맹 본점의 도움을 통한 낮은 실패율

읽기 노트의 예

• Franchise – advantages 가맹점 사업의 이점   ] 주제

•   1. Reliable products 믿을 수 있는 제품   ] 근거 1
     – tried, tested 실험, 검증을 거침
•   → assured 보증   ] 세부 사항 1

•   2. Save on ad 광고비 절감   ] 근거 2
     – save time & $ to ad 광고에 소비되는 시간과 돈을 절약
•   – national marketing 전국적 마케팅   ] 세부 사항 2

•   3. Business security 사업 안정성   ] 근거 3
     – ↓ fail: fran. help to set up 낮은 실패 확률; 개업을 도와줌
•   – training in business skills 사업 기술을 교육   ] 세부 사항 3

Integrated Section

Independent Section

2. 듣고 내용 정리하기

지문을 읽은 후에는 지문의 내용에 대해 반박하는 강의 내용을 듣게 된다. 실제로 대답해야 할 질문의 초점은 지문보다는 강의에 더 맞추어져 있으므로 강의가 Integrated Section의 핵심이라고 할 수 있다.

❶ 강의의 구성과 듣기 포인트

강의는 읽기 지문과 같은 토픽에 대해 다른 입장에서 접근하는 방식으로 구성되어 있음을 알고, 이러한 포인트들을 중심으로 들으면서 정리한다.

> **●도입 (Introduction)**
> 강의의 도입부에서는 교수가 읽기 지문에서 접근한 토픽에 대해 의문을 제기하거나, 반대하는 뜻을 보인다. 그러나 지문과는 달리 직접적으로 주장을 드러내기보다는 예시나 실험 결과 등을 들어서 간접적으로 제시한다.
>
> ex) One survey of franchise owners showed that they faced some unexpected challenges.
> > 가맹점주들을 상대로 한 조사에서 그들이 예상치 못한 상황에 부딪혔음이 밝혀졌습니다.
>
> **●반론 (Contradicting points)**
> 강의의 반론에서는 읽기 지문에서 나온 근거들을 각각 반박하는 내용이 나온다. 지문에서 읽은 내용 중 어느 부분과 직접 관련된 내용인지 생각하면서 듣도록 한다.
>
> ex) Becoming a franchise owner means giving up control over goods and services.
> > 가맹점 사업을 한다는 것은 제공하는 상품이나 서비스에 대한 통제권을 포기해야 한다는 뜻입니다.
>
> **●세부 사항 (Details)**
> 해당 반론의 내용에 대한 예시나 부연 설명으로, 앞서 제시된 반론의 주장을 어떻게 보강하고 있는지 주의하며 듣는다.
>
> ex) Franchise owners are not free to decide what products to offer. Instead, they're forced to sell what their parent company tells them to.
> > 가맹점주들은 어떤 상품을 제공할 것인가를 자유롭게 정할 수 없습니다. 대신에, 모회사가 지정해 주는 것만을 팔도록 강요당하죠.

❷ 듣기 노트 정리하기

강의의 노트를 정리할 때는 주제에서 제시된 입장을 맨 위에 간단히 적고, 각 반론의 포인트들을 번호를 매긴 작은 제목으로 적는다. 강의는 반복해 들을 수 없으므로, 노트 테이킹보다는 듣고 이해하는 것에 집중하고 노트는 나중에 강의의 흐름을 상기할 수 있을 정도로만 간단히 정리한다.

> **●도입 적기:** 토픽에 대한 강의의 입장을 맨 위에 큰 제목으로 적는다.
> **●반론 적기:** 번호를 매기고 작은 제목으로 적는다.
> **●세부 사항 적기:** 반론 아래에 칸을 들여 적는다.

For those of you dreaming of being your own boss one day, franchising might be a way to go... but be warned. One survey of franchise owners showed that they faced some unexpected challenges. Becoming a franchise owner means giving up control over goods and services. Franchise owners realized that they are not free to decide what products to offer instead they're forced to sell what their parent company tells them to.

> 도입
> 가맹 사업의 예상치 못한 결과
>
> 반론 1
> 상품 선택권 박탈
>
> 세부 사항 1
> 모회사가 정한 상품만 판매

OK, what else? Many surveyed franchise owners felt frustrated about their company's approach to marketing. A lot of the time, franchisees have to fork as much as 6% of their total income over to advertising. The franchisor uses this money to promote the franchise company itself, not the individual business. On top of that, many franchise owners disagreed with the national marketing schemes and had better ideas for local promotions that they could not carry out.

> 반론 2
> 광고 방식에 대한 불만
>
> 세부 사항 2
> 수입의 일부를 광고비로 지불

But we haven't even come to the biggest drawback yet! Here it is... the worst part, according to franchise owners, was how unprofitable the whole enterprise wound up being. They had to pay the franchisor for the services provided and for the use of the system: that is, the initial franchise fee and continuing ones. These charges, um, seemed too high without enough returns. So as you can imagine, a majority stated that they would rather start their own businesses and keep more of the profits.

> 반론 3
> 낮은 수익률
>
> 세부 사항 3
> 높은 가맹비용으로 인한 손해

강의 노트의 예

- **Franchise – drawbacks** 가맹점 사업의 단점 〕 도입

- 1. **Giving up control** 선택권 포기 〕 반론 1
  - **not free: what 2 sell** 무엇을 팔지 마음대로 정하지 못함
  - **forced by parent comp.** 모회사에게 강요 당함 〕 세부 사항 1

- 2. **Frustrated about marketing** 마케팅 방식에 대해 좌절 〕 반론 2
  - **pay 6% of income** 수입의 6%를 지불
    - **→ not directly benefit** → 직접적 혜택이 아님
  - **can't do individ. marketing** 개별적 마케팅을 실행할 수 없음 〕 세부 사항 2

- 3. **Unprofitable** 이윤이 별로 없음 〕 반론 3
  - **pay fee 4 services, system** 서비스와 시스템에 대한 비용을 지불
  - **too high w/o return** 수익 없이 비용이 지나치게 높음 〕 세부 사항 3

Integrated Section

Independent Section

다음은 강의에 잘 쓰이는 표현으로, 예시, 인용, 강조할 때 등의 경우에 단서가 되므로 주의 깊게 듣는다.

예시를 들 때

1. For example: 예를 들어

For example, kids at this stage may believe a block is a car or a boat.
예를 들어, 이 시기의 아이들은 블록이 차나 배라고 생각할 수도 있다.

2. For instance: 예를 들어

For instance, old people who live alone enjoy the companionship of pets.
예를 들어, 혼자 생활하는 노인들은 애완동물을 기르는 것을 좋아한다.

3. To illustrate: 예컨대, 이를테면

To illustrate, biologists believe that problems such as obesity are not a simple genetic matter.
예컨대, 생물학자들은 비만과 같은 문제들이 단순한 유전적 문제가 아니라고 생각한다.

인용할 때

4. The researchers found that ~: 연구원들은 ~임을 알아냈다

The researchers found that bigger babies did better overall on intelligence tests.
연구원들은 덩치가 큰 아기들이 전체적으로 지능검사에서 더 높은 점수를 받는다는 **것을 알아냈다**.

5. A recent study discovered that ~: 최근의 조사에 의하면 ~라고 한다

A recent study discovered that men need physical activity twice as much as women do.
최근의 조사에 의하면 남성들은 여성에 비해 두 배나 많이 육체적 활동을 해야 한다고 **한다**.

6. Through the experiment: 이 실험을 통해

Through the experiment, they found that Internet retailers don't pay much attention to marketing and customer service.
이 실험을 통해, 그들은 인터넷 소매 상인들이 마케팅과 고객 서비스에 별로 관심을 기울이지 않는다는 것을 발견했다.

7. According to ~: ~에 의하면

According to researchers, eating chocolate lowers cholesterol levels.
연구원들에 의하면, 초콜릿을 섭취하는 것이 체내 콜레스테롤 수치를 낮춘다고 한다.

강조할 때

8. Furthermore: 더욱이, 게다가, 더군다나

Furthermore, scientists are now designing robots that look like humans.
게다가, 과학자들은 이제 사람을 닮은 로봇을 개발하고 있다.

9. In fact: 사실상, 실제로, 사실은

In fact, money developed for many reasons, not just the inconvenience of the barter system.
사실상, 돈은 단지 물물교환의 불편 때문만이 아니라, 기타 여러 가지 이유로 발달하였다.

10. **Actually:** 실제로

Actually, an apple falling from a tree caused Newton to think about acceleration.
실제로, 나무에서 떨어지는 사과는 뉴턴이 가속도에 대해 생각하도록 만들었다.

11. **Even though:** ~인데도, ~임에도 불구하고

Even though competition is one key to success, ape studies show that cooperation is more important.
경쟁이 성공에 중요한 한 가지 요인**임에도 불구하고**, 유인원에 대한 연구는 협력이 더 중요한 것이라는 사실을 입증한다.

12. **Moreover:** 게다가, 더욱이

Moreover, home-schooled students are actively involved in their education.
게다가, 자택 학습을 받은 아이들은 자신의 교육에 적극적으로 임한다.

반대 의견을 나타낼 때

13. **However:** 그러나, 그렇지만

However, psychologists believe that memories can be taught.
그렇지만, 심리학자들은 사람들의 뇌리에 기억을 심어주는 것이 가능하다고 생각한다.

14. **On the contrary:** 이에 반하여, 그러하기는커녕

On the contrary, some animals attract mates by how they look.
이에 반하여, 특정 동물들은 자신들의 외모로 상대의 관심을 끈다.

15. **On the other hand:** 다른 한편, 그 반면, 이에 반해서

On the other hand, the left brain is dominant in logical areas such as math and language.
그 반면, 좌뇌는 수학과 언어와 같은 논리적 영역을 지배한다.

16. **In contrast:** ~와 대조를 이루어

In contrast, Erickson looked at kids' social and emotional growth.
이와 대조적으로, 에릭슨은 어린이들의 사회적, 정서적 성장을 고찰했다.

결론을 이끌어 낼 때

17. **Therefore:** 그러므로, 그 결과

Therefore, bicycle lanes help reduce pollution and congestion in cities.
그러므로, 자전거 전용도로는 도심의 공해와 교통체증을 줄이는데 이바지한다.

18. **In short:** 간단히 말하자면, 요컨대

In short, vegetable oil and natural gas could replace fossil fuels.
요컨대, 식물성 기름과 천연가스가 화석 연료를 대체할 수도 있다.

19. **So:** 그래서, 따라서

So, discoveries from Napoleon's expedition taught us a lot about Ancient Egypt.
그래서, 나폴레옹의 원정에서 발견된 것들은 우리에게 고대 이집트에 관해 많은 것을 알려 주었다.

다음 지문을 읽고 주어진 빈칸을 채워 노트를 완성하시오.

01

Cancer is the third highest cause of death among all diseases. Surprisingly, people in particular countries are more prone to certain types of cancer. The main reason for this is genetic factors, that is, traits passed down from generation to generation.

There are a few groups that demonstrate that cancer is hereditary particularly well. Research shows that Japanese men are seven times more likely to get stomach cancer than American men. On the other hand, Japanese men are five times less likely to suffer from prostate cancer than Americans.

Another group that proves that genes affect cancer rates are the Native Americans. They have the lowest rates of contracting any form of cancer compared to all other ethnic groups in the United States. These two examples clearly show that it is heredity that causes the discrepancy in cancer rates among different nationalities.

Note-taking

읽기 노트

- 주제 Cancer – genetic factor

  근거 1 Jap. men

  - _____

    – 5x ↓ prostate canc. than Amer.

  근거 2 Native Amer.

  - _____

02

The "Green Revolution" describes successful agricultural experiments in various countries. More recently, it refers to an international effort to reduce world hunger by improving crop performance. Common methods include irrigation, using fertilizers and pesticides, and introducing genetically-improved seeds.

The Green Revolution is no myth; new seeds planted under this ideology yields tens of millions of extra crops per year, a testament to the success of this development strategy. These techniques more than tripled wheat and other food crop harvests in some developing countries. It was particularly successful in India, establishing it as one of the world's biggest agricultural producers. Its yield increase from 12.3 million tons in 1965 to 76.4 million tons in 2000 allowed it to become an exporter of food grains.

Due to the effectiveness of these improvements in agriculture, global hunger rates, in percentage terms, have dropped since the beginning of the Green Revolution. That is to say, a smaller proportion of the world's population lacks food security. In fact, it has been credited with saving over a billion people from starvation worldwide.

Note-taking

읽기 노트

- 주제 Green Revolution
    : agricul. experiments & intl. effort 4 world hunger
- 근거 1 _____
    – success in India: yields ↑ , became exporter
- 근거 2 _____
    – saving ppl from starvation

03

Smart cars are a much-needed economical and fuel-efficient transportation option in an age when clogged highways and skyrocketing fuel costs are salient social concerns. With the price of gasoline soaring in the US, people can no longer afford to buy vehicles with low gas mileage. As a result, American consumers are embracing smart cars that boast fifty to sixty miles per gallon.

Another advantage of smart cars is their small and streamlined size, which makes them easier to maneuver in crowded cities and reduces traffic congestion. They are about half the size of mid-size cars, meaning roads could potentially accommodate twice the number of drivers with little or no increase in congestion.

Finally, they are safer than other vehicles. Smart car drivers cannot go faster than 85 miles per hour, and thus are involved in fewer accidents caused by reckless or high-speed driving. Moreover, in collisions, smart cars also react differently because they have been designed with a safety-cage that holds its shape in accidents, much like the crash-cage of a racecar.

Note-taking

읽기 노트

주제 Smart car

근거 1 _____

     – gas price ↑

     – Amer. embracing smart car

근거 2 _____

     – ez 2 maneuver

     – ↓ congestion

근거 3 _____

     – not fast : ↓ accident

     – safety-cage

04

The concept of the multinational corporation is a long-established one, dating from the early 17th century. However, the number of these companies, that have branches or franchises in multiple countries, has dramatically increased post-World War II. This ability to span the globe benefits consumers in numerous and varied ways.

Multinationals' costs decrease as a result of economies of scale from increased output. They pass those savings on to their customers, resulting in prices that reflect their reduced costs. Prices are also lowered due to global competition among firms, an effect that wouldn't be possible with only local companies.

Another advantage to consumers is that multinationals allow access to an increased selection of products. No longer are populations limited to the items produced locally, but instead, can choose among products from all over the world. In addition to a wider variety, companies with world-wide reach offer high-quality goods regardless of the consumers' location. Well-known brands guarantee a well-made product, no matter where it is purchased.

Lastly, multinationals help local economies as they open offices and factories overseas. They provide employment for local workers, raising income, and thus, improving the local consumers' standard of living, especially in those areas involved in production. They provide local economies new opportunities to grow and develop when they introduce new technology and train the workers in new skills. In turn, this promotes economic stability.

Note-taking

읽기 노트

> - 주제 Multinat. corp.: branches in many countries
>
>   – benefits consumers
>
> - 근거 1 Costs ↓
>
>   – _____
>
>   – _____
>
> - 근거 2 Select. of prods ↑
>
>   – _____
>
>   – _____
>
> - 근거 3 Help local econ.
>
>   – _____
>
>   – _____

05

A brain drain is the emigration of trained and talented individuals for other nations due to lack of opportunity in their home countries. This expression was coined in the 1950s to describe European scientists moving to the United States. Almost half a million European science and technology graduates now live in the US, and only a small percentage of them intend to return home. Several reasons exist for the continuing brain drain of scientists to the US.

One cause of the brain drain is that the EU invests in a much smaller amount of money in science than the US does. Half the amount of money on research and development results in a corresponding lack of resources, funding, and poor facilities in Europe. Not surprisingly, lower salaries drive many scientists to the US.

Furthermore, the EU suffers from rigid bureaucracy. The complex, detailed paperwork for grant applications results in rejections for minor details. Thus, European scientists feel discouraged about the prospects of obtaining financial assistance and finding work in their home countries.

Lastly, hierarchical attitudes lower morale. Scientists often have to work for older professors for ten years before they get the same opportunities they would initially receive in the US. This also plays out in authorship, where older colleagues claim juniors' work.

Note-taking

읽기 노트

- 주제 Brain drain – talented ppl emigrating

  Eur. scientists → US

- 근거 1 Invest $ ↓

  - _____

  - _____

- 근거 2 Rigid burcrcy

  - _____

  - _____

- 근거 3 Hierarchy: ↓ morale

  - _____

  - _____

06

Ever since Darwin first presented his Theory of Evolution, scientists have been trying to find the missing link that would explain how birds emerged. Based on dinosaur fossils discovered in the last two centuries, they hypothesize that birds evolved from dinosaurs, a theory that is supported by a number of characteristics shared by the two groups.

Anatomically, some dinosaurs were quite similar to modern birds. Some fossil skeletons show light, air-filled bones, which evolved to make today's birds lighter, and eventually allow them to fly. Members of the branch of dinosaurs from which birds descended exhibit another avian characteristic; a wishbone, the part of the breastbone that connects to the wing muscles in birds. In all, birds and dinosaurs share over a hundred anatomical traits.

Dinosaur-to-bird evolution is also supported by the fact that many excavated dinosaur fossils show evidence of feathers of various kinds, and in several stages of development. The first feathered dinosaur to be discovered was covered in featherlike hairs that resembled tubes. Further research has led researchers to believe that many, possibly even all, of the smaller species may have had feathers for a brief period after hatching, in the early stages of development.

Note-taking

읽기 노트

- 주제 Birds evolved from dinos.

  근거 1 _____

-     – _____

-     – _____

- 근거 2 _____

      – _____

-     – _____

07
Listen to the lecture.

Note-taking

듣기 노트

- 도입 *Cancer – cause*

  반론 1 _____

  - salty fish, pickled food → canc.

  - Jap. immigrt. on Amer. diet: ↓ stomach canc.

  반론 2 _____

  - use plants, herbs → natural med.

  - root attacking canc. cell

08
Listen to the lecture.

Note-taking

듣기 노트

- 도입 *Green Revolution – true result*

  반론 1 _____

  - China: out of GR → econ. policy

  - exclud. China, hunger ↑

  반론 2 _____

  - food not effectively distrib.

  - India: half of ppl in poverty, malnourished

09

Listen to the lecture.

Note-taking

듣기 노트

- 도입 Smart cars – 1yr after
  반론 1 _____
  - ↓ mpg than promised
  반론 2 _____
  - vehicles ↑ after new model
  - only 2 seats → more cars
  반론 3 _____
  - too small: can't see, unsafe
  - crushed in accident

10

Listen to the lecture.

Note-taking

듣기 노트

- 도입 Multinat. corp. – recent survey
  반론 1 Effects on pop.
  - _____
  - _____
  반론 2 Loss of unique culture
  - _____
  - _____
  반론 3 Destroy local econs.
  - _____
  - _____
  - _____

11

Note-taking

듣기 노트

도입 Brain drain – changing trend

반론 1 Funding ↑

   – _____

   – _____

   – _____

반론 2 Bureaucracy ↓

   – shorter process 4 grant

반론 3 _____

   – _____

   – _____

12

Listen to the lecture.

Note-taking

듣기 노트

도입 _____

반론 1 _____

   – _____

   – _____

반론 2 _____

   – _____

   – _____

정답 p.424

다음 지문을 읽고 강의를 들으며 주어진 빈칸을 채워 노트를 완성하시오. Track 5

01

As fossil fuels rapidly dwindle, people are starting to explore alternative energy sources for the 21st century and beyond. Hydrogen energy is increasingly viewed as an attractive new source with many fuel and energy applications including powering vehicles, running turbines or fuel cells to produce electricity, and generating heat and electricity for buildings.

One major reason for hydrogen's potential is that it is the third most abundant element on the earth's surface, where it is found primarily in water. That is, hydrogen is produced by using electricity or sunlight to split water into hydrogen and oxygen. Thus, its widespread availability means hydrogen energy would be a much cheaper alternative energy source to nonrenewable fossil fuels, which are projected to be depleted as early as forty years from now.

In addition, hydrogen energy is very environmentally friendly, barely producing any emissions or by-products. It can also be isolated by using renewable sources of energy such as the wind and the sun to split water, a method that is eco-friendly as well.

Another benefit of hydrogen is that it is easy to store and transport. Hydrogen can be compressed into a liquid or gas and then transported in a tank. In addition, with the advent of new technology to store hydrogen in the form of a solid using a hydrogen storage alloy, transport concerns of this volatile resource disappear. In this way, we can simply combine metal and hydrogen, transport the alloy in a stable condition, and then heat up the alloy to get the hydrogen back for use.

Listen to the lecture.

Note-taking

읽기 노트

- 주제 Hydrogen – attractive new source

  근거 1 _____

  - – split water to produce H

  - – wide avail.: cheaper

  근거 2 _____

  - – no emission

  - – renewable source to split water

  근거 3 _____

  - – liquid, gas

  - – storage alloy

듣기 노트

- 도입 Hydrogen – not pass test

  반론 1 _____

  - – cost: hydro > gas

  반론 2 _____

  - – renewable sources: not feasible ← weather

  반론 3 _____

  - – liquid, gas hydro: volatile

  - – alloy: too heavy → unfeasible

02

Educational institutions use a variety of ways to evaluate and improve their services. They have found that student evaluations are an effective method of assessing teacher competence in the classroom. Most often, students are asked to anonymously fill out a form and add a few comments. Their input is valuable for several reasons.

First of all, students are in an ideal position to judge teachers. The youth who see their teachers on a regular basis are much better equipped than anyone else to measure how well an educator answers questions or motivates his students. Pupils themselves are most qualified to rate their own comprehension and learning gains. On top of that, because students are consumers of the educational service, their satisfaction levels should be noted. In this way, their concerns can be recognized and their needs better met.

Furthermore, student evaluations promote higher standards for education. Because they may be used as a basis for teacher promotions and salary increases, many instructors count on them to provide evidence of professional progress. Administrators also rely on these evaluations to measure success within the classroom. As a result, these assessments encourage educators to develop their abilities. Teachers who want to improve are eager to know how students view them. Regular reports inform teachers of their strengths and weaknesses, and thus help them track their progress. This fosters professional growth as pupils point out areas that need improvement.

Listen to the lecture.

Note-taking

읽기 노트

- 주제 Student evaluation – effective
- 근거 1 _____
    - _____
    - _____
    - _____
- 근거 2 Promote ↑ edu. standard
    - promotion & salary: administrator measure
    - encourage tchrs 2 develop
    - inform strnth, wkness

듣기 노트

- 도입 Student evaluation – study
- 반론 1 _____
    - _____
    - _____
    - _____
- 반론 2 Not taken seriously
    - not figured into promotion, salary
    - tchrs disregard report → no change 4 few complaints

03 Advertisements, in one form or another, have existed for centuries. But in the last hundred years, they have reached a new level of pervasiveness. Today numerous types of promotions are visible on nearly every surface, from newspapers to bus stop benches to newspapers to T-shirts. They serve several purposes in society, benefiting both individuals and the nation as a whole.

First of all, advertisements are informational. They notify consumers of newly available products and services. They also instruct consumers where they can be found and how to use them. For example, ads in health magazines and on television often announce the arrival of new, ground-breaking medicines that can help individuals afflicted with any number of illnesses. Often, these people wouldn't find out about these options if it weren't for advertising.

Another frequently overlooked societal benefit of advertisements is that they allow the population to have cheap, or even free, access to certain media, such as television, radio, or newspapers. As providers of these entertainment and informational services create a substantial income from offering space or airtime for sale, they can afford to distribute their news and programming services at substantially lower prices.

Furthermore, advertisements are good for the national interest. Advertisements stimulate consumer spending, which is essential to the healthy functioning of economies. In addition, as many products are advertised internationally and exported, increased sales abroad strengthen the domestic economy. All in all, advertisements provide a valuable service to individuals, society, and the state.

Listen to the lecture.

Note-taking

읽기 노트

- **주제** Advertisement – benefit to indiv. & nation
  - **근거 1** _____
    - _____
    - _____
  - **근거 2** Cheap access to media
    - income from ad → afford prgrms at ↓ price
  - **근거 3** _____
    - _____
    - _____

듣기 노트

- **도입** Advertising – critical approach
  - **반론 1** _____
    - _____
    - _____
    - _____
  - **반론 2** Expensive
    - big cost of ad → pass 2 consumer, ↑ price
    - free TV → pay extra for products
  - **반론 3** _____
    - _____
    - _____

Integrated Section

Independent Section

04

After numerous employee complaints about the restrictive nine-to-five work schedule, a number of companies have begun instituting a flexible working arrangement. This allows staff to work whenever they want, as long as they work their allotted 40 hours a week. This schedule has many benefits for both employers and employees.

First of all, employers who have flexible working hours are able to hire the best workers. Many employees have long, inconvenient commutes that dissuade them from working far from home. A flexible schedule allows employees to travel in non-rush hours, saving a lot of time. On top of that, some workers are simply more productive during certain times of the day, and want to schedule accordingly. For whatever reason, employers who are able to accommodate people's scheduling needs are able to hire and retain the most talented staff, and thus increase their companies' productivity.

In addition, employees who get to work when they want are happy and productive. A flexible working arrangement allows employees to work fewer hours on days when they are not focused, and longer on days when they feel attentive. What's more, flex time gives them the option of sleeping in late one day, or leaving early so that they can attend a class. All in all, this increased flexibility makes people feel free and in control of their lives.

Finally, families benefit from flex time as they are able to coordinate schedules to spend time together. Often, parents have no time to spend with their children in the morning as they must go off to work. A flexible working arrangement would mean that families can enjoy a nice breakfast together. Alternatively, it could mean that people go to work early so that they can come home and spend quality time with their children. In any case, family life improves when members can schedule time to be together.

Listen to the lecture.

Note-taking

읽기 노트

- 주제 _____
- 근거 1 _____
  - _____
-          – _____
- 근거 2 _____
  - _____
-          – _____
  - _____
-          – _____

듣기 노트

- 도입 _____
- 반론 1 _____
  - _____
-          – _____
  - _____
- 반론 2 _____
  - _____
-          – _____

정답 p.434

II 읽고 들은 내용 연계해서 쓰기

앞서 읽고 들은 내용을 합쳐서 요약문을 쓰는 단계로, 이 때 작성한 답안을 통해서 지문과 강의 내용을 이해한 정도와 작문 능력을 동시에 평가받게 되므로 가장 중요한 단계라고 할 수 있다.

1. 노트 연결하고 답안 구상하기

문제를 받으면 지문과 강의의 내용이 관련된 부분을 연결해서 재구성한다. 노트를 연결하면서 머리 속으로 구상하는 답안은, 아래 그림처럼 강의를 중심으로 하되 지문과 연계된 부분은 부가적으로 가져와서 언급하는 것을 기본으로 한다.

노트와 답안의 관계

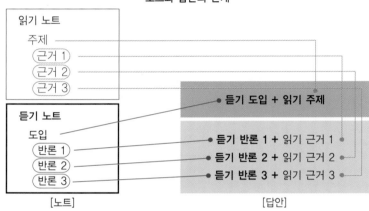

[노트]　　　　　　　　　[답안]

기본 답안의 구조

The lecturer *discusses* 듣기 도입
This *contradicts* the reading passage's claim that 읽기 주제

●First, 듣기 반론 1
　This *casts doubts on* the reading passage's claim that 읽기 근거 1

●Next, 듣기 반론 2
　This *rebuffs* the reading passage's claim that 읽기 근거 2

●Finally, 듣기 반론 3
　This *refutes* the reading passage's claim that 읽기 근거 3

2. 실제 답안 쓰기

답안 구상까지 마치면 이제 실제로 답안을 작성한다. 앞서 익힌 답안 구조를 기본으로 서로 연계된 듣기의 반론과 읽기의 주장을 노트에 기반해 문장으로 풀어서 쓴다.

Integrated Section

Independent Section

❶ 요약문 주제 쓰기 (듣기 도입 + 읽기 주제)

지문과 강의의 전반적인 내용을 제시하며 답안을 시작한다. 먼저 강의의 도입부에 대해 설명한 후, 이것이 지문의 주제와 어떻게 연관되어 있는지를 밝힌다.

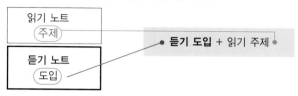

요약문 주제 쓰기의 예

Q Summarize the points made in the lecture you just heard, explaining how they cast doubts on the points made in the reading.

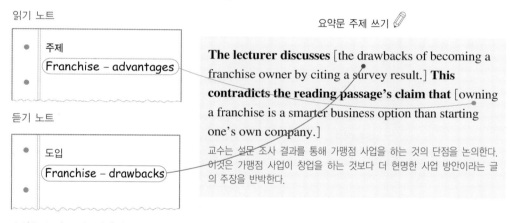

읽기 노트

- 주제
  (Franchise – advantages)

듣기 노트

- 도입
  (Franchise – drawbacks)

요약문 주제 쓰기 ✎

The lecturer discusses [the drawbacks of becoming a franchise owner by citing a survey result.] **This contradicts the reading passage's claim that** [owning a franchise is a smarter business option than starting one's own company.]

교수는 설문 조사 결과를 통해 가맹점 사업을 하는 것의 단점을 논의한다. 이것은 가맹점 사업이 창업을 하는 것보다 더 현명한 사업 방안이라는 글의 주장을 반박한다.

요약문 주제 쓰기에서 활용할 수 있는 표현 구문

> 듣기 도입 쓰기의 기본 구문
> The lecturer <u>discusses</u> ~
>   (= talks about ~/describes ~/explains ~/explores ~ / addresses ~/examines ~/asserts that ~/argues that ~)
>
> 읽기 주제 쓰기의 기본 구문
> This contradicts the reading passage's claim that ~

T I P

먼저 지문의 전반적인 내용을 쓰고, 이어서 강의의 내용을 설명하면서 답안을 시작할 수도 있다.

ex) The reading passage argues that ~. On the other hand, the lecture asserts the opposite by looking at ~
지문은 ~라고 주장한다. 반면에 강의에서는 ~를 통해 반론을 펼친다.

❷ 반론 및 읽기 지문과의 관계 쓰기 (듣기반론 + 읽기 근거)

이제 지문–강의의 세부적인 포인트로 들어가서 강의가 어떻게 반론을 펴고 있으며 그것이 지문과 어떤 관계를 가지고 있는지 설명한다.

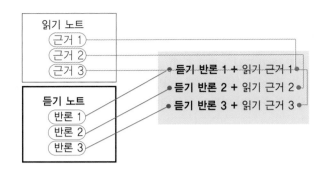

● 강의의 반론과 세부 사항 쓰기

강의에서 반론을 제시하는 각 포인트 별로 한 문단씩 작성한다. 먼저 강의의 반론 내용을 간략히 밝히면서 문단을 시작하고, 이어서 강의에서 제시된 반론의 세부 사항을 설명한다.

반론과 세부 사항 쓰기의 예

읽기 노트

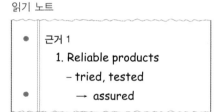

듣기 노트

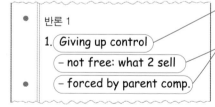

반론과 세부 사항 쓰기 ✎

First, franchise owners have to [give up control over their business.] They are [not free to choose their own products or services.] They are also [forced to comply with their parent company's desires about how to market and sell these goods.]

첫째로, 가맹점 사업자들은 사업 통제권을 포기해야 한다. 그들은 스스로 제품이나 서비스를 선택할 수 없다. 또한 마케팅 방법과 이러한 제품들을 판매하는 방식에 대해서도 모회사의 요구를 따라야만 한다.

반론과 세부 사항 쓰기에서 활용할 수 있는 연결어 구문

1. First / Second / Third
2. Firstly / Secondly / Thirdly
3. To begin with / On top of that / Finally
4. For one / Next / Last

● 읽기 지문과의 관계 쓰기

강의의 세부 사항을 설명하고 난 후에는 여기에 연결지어 표시해 둔 지문의 내용을 합쳐서 쓴다.
이 때 읽기 지문의 노트에서 나온 내용은 지문의 상세한 내용을 참조하되 표현을 그대로 가져다
쓰기 보다는 적절히 다른 말로 바꾸어 쓰는 것이 좋다.

읽기 지문과의 관계 쓰기의 예

읽기 노트

읽기 지문과의 관계 쓰기 ✎

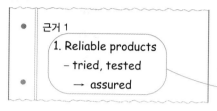

근거 1
1. Reliable products
   - tried, tested
   → assured

This thus refutes the reading passage's argument that franchises are preferable because owners are able to [sell their parent company's reliable products.]

따라서 이것은, 모회사의 믿을 만한 제품을 판매할 수 있기에 가맹점 사업이 바람직하다는 글의 주장을 반박하는 것이다.

듣기 노트

반론 1
1. Giving up control
   - not free: what 2 sell
   - forced by parent comp.

읽기 지문과의 관계 쓰기에서 활용할 수 있는 표현 구문

읽기 지문과의 관계 쓰기 기본 구문

This contradicts the reading passage's claim that ~

= This strongly contradicts the reading passage's support of ~

= This finding effectively rebuts the reading passage's argument that ~

= This fact directly opposes the reading passage's assertion that ~

= These points refute the reading passage's explanation that ~

TIP

답안을 작성할 때 해당 정보가 지문이나 강의 중에 어디에서 나왔는지를 직접 언급하여 밝히면서 쓰는 것이 좋다.

ex) **While the passage** suggested it's beneficial to become a franchise owner, **the lecturer** doubts the idea.
지문에서는 가맹점 사업을 하는 것이 이득이 된다고 주장하는 **반면**, **교수**는 이 생각에 대해 의문을 제시한다.

실제 Step별 샘플

Question Step ⏺ *Track 6*

Step 1 지문 읽기

> Narrator: Now you will see the reading passage for three minutes. Remember it will be available to you again when it is time for you to write. The lecture will begin, so keep your headset on until the lecture is over.

Reading Time: 3 minutes

A popular business decision today is whether to open one's own business or purchase a franchise from an established company. The number of risks is lower for franchise owners; thus, many opt for this choice for three main reasons.

First of all, a franchise offers reliable products to first-time business owners. The merchandise sold has been tried and tested at other branches; therefore, the new owners can be assured that they will be able to sell them at their locations. For example, a McDonald's franchise owner knows what goods he or she will be investing in, and that the public already likes products with that name. They are, therefore, assured that the items they will be selling are already high quality and popular.

Franchisees also save on advertising. They do not have to spend a lot of time and resources advertising unknown businesses and products. That is, larger, well-established franchise operations will often have national marketing campaigns and a solid trading name. For example, KFC franchise owners do not have to worry about promoting an unknown product and doing publicity blitz campaigns. As a result, they do not have to flyer neighborhoods, give out free samples, or pay for expensive advertisements. The amount of time and money saved on advertising is consequently enormous for franchise owners.

Most importantly, franchisees have business security. They have a lower rate of failure because the franchisor helps them set up the business, which has been tested to be successful. Business owners also receive continual assistance in the form of comprehensive training programs in sales and other business skills. The franchisee is thus a part of a support network and receives help from the franchisor in a number of areas.

Step 2 강의 듣기

Narrator: Now listen to part of a lecture on the topic you just read about.

For those of you dreaming of being your own boss one day, franchising might be a way to go... but be warned. One survey of franchise owners showed that they faced some unexpected challenges. Becoming a franchise owner means giving up control over goods and services. Franchise owners realized that they are not free to decide what products to offer... instead they're forced to sell what their parent company tells them to. In addition, they resented the franchisor retaining control over the way in which products and services are marketed and sold.

OK, what else? Many surveyed franchise owners felt frustrated about their company's approach to marketing. A lot of the time, franchisees have to fork as much as 6% of their total income over to advertising. The franchisor uses this money to promote the franchise company itself, not the individual business... which of course causes many owners to grit their teeth at an expenditure which often does not mean direct payback for them. On top of that, many franchise owners disagreed with the national marketing schemes and had better ideas for local promotions that they could not carry out. So, you can see how marketing can be a source of contention between the franchisees and the main owner.

But we haven't even come to the biggest drawback yet! Here it is... the worst part, according to franchise owners, was how unprofitable the whole enterprise wound up being. They had to pay the franchisor for the services provided and for the use of the system: that is, the initial franchise fee and continuing ones. These charges, um, seemed too high without enough returns. So as you can imagine, a majority stated that they would rather start their own businesses and keep more of the profits.

Step 3 요약문 작성하기

Narrator: Summarize the points made in the lecture you just heard, explaining how they cast doubt on the points made in the reading.

Answer Step

Step 1 지문과 강의 내용 정리하기

읽기 노트

• Franchise – advantages	] **주제** 가맹점 사업의 이점
1. Reliable products	] **근거 1** 믿을 수 있는 상품
– tried, tested	] **세부 사항 1** 검증된 상품으로부터 오는 확신
→assured	
2. Save on ad	] **근거 2** 광고 비용 절약
– save time & $ to ad	] **세부 사항 2** 가맹점에서 전국적 광고 실시
– national marketing	
3. Business security	] **근거 3** 사업 안정성 보장
– ↓ fail: fran. help to set up	] **세부 사항 3** 가맹 본점의 도움을 통한 낮은 실패율
– training in business skills	

듣기 노트

• **Franchise – drawbacks**	] **도입** 가맹점 사업의 단점
1. **Giving up control**	] **반론 1** 상품 선택권 박탈
– **not free: what 2 sell**	] **세부 사항 1** 모회사가 정한 상품만 판매
– **forced by parent comp.**	
2. **Frustrated about marketing**	] **반론 2** 광고 방식에 대한 불만
– **pay 6% of income**	] **세부 사항 2** 수입의 일부를 광고비로 지불
→ **not directly benefit**	
– **can't do individ. marketing**	
3. **Unprofitable**	] **반론 3** 낮은 수익률
– **pay fee 4 services, system**	] **세부 사항 3** 높은 가맹 비용으로 인한 손해
– **too high w/o return**	

읽기 노트

```
• │ Franchise – advantages ①'
  │
  │   1. Reliable products ②'
• │      – tried, tested
  │        → assured
  │
  │   2. Save on ad ③'
• │      – save time & $ to ad
  │      – national marketing
  │
  │   3. Business security ④'
• │      – ↓ fail: fran. help to set up
  │      – training in business skills
```

듣기 노트

```
• │ Franchise – drawbacks ①
  │
  │   1. Giving up control  ②
  │      – not free: what 2 sell
• │      – forced by parent comp.
  │
  │   2. Frustrated about marketing ③
  │      – pay 6% of income
• │        → not directly benefit
  │      – can't do individ.
  │        marketing
  │
• │   3. Unprofitable ④
  │      – pay fee 4 services,
  │        system
• │      – too high w/o return
```

도입 The lecturer discusses the ① [drawbacks of becoming a franchise owner by citing a survey result.] These include not having control over one's products, problems with marketing, and lowered profit. 주제 ①' [This contradicts the reading passage's claim that owning a franchise is a smarter business option than starting one's own company.]

반론 1 First, franchise owners ② [have to give up control over their businesses. They are not free to choose their own products or services. They are also forced to comply with their parent company's desires about how to market and sell these goods.] 근거 1 This lack of freedom over product choice thus refutes the reading passage's argument that ②' [franchises are preferable because owners are able to sell their parent company's reliable products.]

반론 2 Next, many franchise owners ③ [feel frustrated about marketing. They have to pay a significant percentage of their income to advertising costs, which don't directly benefit their businesses. Furthermore, they are not able to carry out individual marketing schemes but are under the umbrella of their parent company's advertising efforts.] 근거 2 This refutes the reading passage's viewpoint that ③' [franchise owners benefit by not having to do all their own advertising.]

반론 3 Finally, the biggest reason why becoming a franchise owner is not recommended is that ④ [one cannot maximize on profit. Franchise owners have to pay the parent company many fees for continual training and support. Consequently, their earnings are reduced.] 근거 3 This point counters the reading passage's argument that ④' [franchises are better because of business security in the form of lifetime assistance from the parent company.]

지문 해석 · 답안 해석

지문 해석

오늘날 사업상 많이 하게 되는 결정은 직접 개업을 하느냐 아니면 안정된 기업의 가맹점이 되느냐 하는 것이다. 위험 부담은 가맹점의 경우가 더 낮다. 따라서, 많은 사람들은 세 가지 중요한 이유 때문에 가맹점 가입을 선택한다.

첫째로, 가맹점 사업은 사업을 처음 하는 사람들에게 믿을 수 있는 상품을 제공한다. 팔게 되는 상품들은 이미 다른 가맹점에서 시도해 보았고 검증된 것들이다. 따라서, 새로운 사업주들은 자신들의 영업점에서도 그 상품을 팔 수 있을 것이라는 확신을 가질 수 있다. 예를 들어, 맥도날드 가맹점주들은 그들이 어떤 상품에 투자하게 되는가를 알 수 있고, 대중이 이미 해당 브랜드의 상품을 좋아한다는 것을 알고 있다. 따라서 그들은, 자신들이 판매할 상품이 이미 품질이 좋고 인기가 있다는 사실을 확신할 수 있다.

또한 가맹점주들은 광고비를 절약할 수 있다. 그들은 알려지지 않은 상호와 상품을 광고하는데 많은 시간과 비용을 투자할 필요가 없다. 보다 규모가 크고, 기반이 잡힌 가맹점들은 종종 전국적인 마케팅 캠페인을 벌일 것이며, 믿을 만한 상호명을 가지고 있을 것이다. 예를 들어, KFC 가맹점주들은 알려지지 않은 상품을 판촉하거나 대대적인 홍보 캠페인을 벌일 필요가 없다. 그 결과, 그들은 동네마다 전단지를 돌리거나, 무료 샘플을 나눠 주거나, 값비싼 광고에 돈을 들이지 않아도 된다. 결과적으로 가맹점주들은 광고에서 막대한 비용을 절약할 수 있다.

가장 중요한 것은 가맹점주들이 사업 안정성을 지니고 있다는 것이다. 그들은 실패할 확률이 낮은데, 이것은 가맹 본점에서 사업을 시작하는데 도움을 주기 때문이고, 이것은 성공적인 것으로 입증되었다. 또한 가맹점주들은 판매 및 기타 영업 기술과 관련해 전반적인 교육 프로그램의 형태로 지속적인 도움을 받게 된다. 각 가맹점은 후원 네트워크의 일부분이며, 가맹 본점으로부터 다양한 분야에서 도움을 받는다.

franchise [frǽntʃaiz] 가맹점 사업   established [istǽbliʃt] 확립된, 정평이 있는   opt for~ ~하는 쪽을 택하다
reliable [riláiəbl] 믿을만한   merchandise [mə́ːrtʃəndàiz] 상품   branch [bræntʃ] 지점
assure [əʃúər] 확신시키다   blitz [blits] 대공세   flyer [fláiər] 전단지를 돌리다
consequently [kánsəkwèntli] 그 결과, 따라서   continual [kəntínjuəl] 계속적인   assistance [əsístəns] 원조, 도움
comprehensive [kàmprihénsiv] 전반적인

강의 해석

여러분들 중 언젠가 자기 사업을 하기를 꿈꾸는 사람들이 있다면, 아마 가맹점을 운영하는 것도 한 가지 방법일 것입니다. 하지만, 주의해야 합니다. 가맹점주들을 대상으로 한 설문 조사에서는 그들이 예상치 못한 문제점에 부딪치게 되었다는 것을 밝혀내었습니다. 가맹점 사업을 한다는 것은 상품과 서비스에 대한 통제권을 포기하는 것을 의미했거든요. 가맹점주들은 어떤 상품을 팔 것인가에 대해서 마음대로 결정할 수 없다는 것을 알게 되었습니다. 그 대신, 모회사에서 허가한 상품만 팔도록 강요받았어요. 게다가, 가맹점주들은 상품과 서비스를 홍보하고 판매하는 방식에 있어서도 가맹 본점이 통제를 한다는 것에 대해 분개했습니다.

자, 또 뭐가 있을까요? 설문 조사에 참여한 많은 가맹점주들은 모회사의 마케팅 방식에 대해 불만을 느꼈습니다. 많은 경우, 가맹점주들은 많게는 총 수입의 6퍼센트를 광고비로 지불해야만 합니다. 가맹 본점은 본점 자체를 홍보하는 데에만 이러한 돈을 쓰지, 개개의 가맹점들을 홍보하는 데 쓰지는 않습니다. 물론, 이것은 가맹점주들로 하여금 직접적으로 비용 회수가 되지 않는 지출을 해야 한다는 데 대해 분노하도록 만듭니다. 게다가, 많은 가맹점주들은 전국적인 마케팅 전략에 대해 불만족스러워 했으며, 해당 지역에서의 홍보를 위해 보다 나은 아이디어를 가지고 있어도 실행할 수가 없었지요. 그러니까, 마케팅이 가맹점주와 본점 사이에서 어떻게 분쟁의 씨앗이 되는지를 알 수 있겠죠.

하지만, 가맹점 사업의 가장 큰 단점이 아직 남아 있어요! 가맹점주에 따르면, 가장 큰 단점은 바로, 전반적으로 사업이 얼마나 수익성이 없는가 하는 것입니다. 그들은 제공된 서비스와 시스템 이용, 즉 초기 가맹점 가입비와 유지비에 대해 모회사에게 돈을 지불해야만 했습니다. 이러한 비용은 충분한 수익률도 없이 너무 높아 보였지요. 따라서, 예상할 수 있다시피, 대부분의 가맹점주들은 차라리 독자적인 사업을 시작해 더 많은 이윤을 보는 것이 나을 것이라고 언급했습니다.

unexpected [ʌnikspéktid] 예상치 못한   resent [rizént] 분개하다   frustrate [frʌ́streit] 좌절케 하다
fork over 마지못해 비용을 내다   grit one's teeth at 이를 갈다, 분노하다   expenditure [ikspénditʃər] 비용
payback [péibæ̀k] (자본) 회수   drawback [drɔ́ːbæ̀k] 단점   unprofitable [ʌnpráfitəbl] 수익성 없는   wind up ~ing ~하게 되다

문제

방금 들은 강의의 논점들이 지문의 논점에 어떻게 의구심을 제기하는지를 설명하며 전체 강의 내용을 요약하시오.

노트 해석

가맹점 사업 - 이점
 1. 믿을 수 있는 제품
  - 실험, 검증을 거침 → 보증
 2. 광고비 절감
  - 광고에 소비되는 시간과 돈을 절약
  - 전국적 마케팅
 3. 사업 안정성
  - 낮은 실패 확률: 개업을 도와줌
  - 사업 기술을 교육

가맹점 사업 - 단점
 1. 선택권 포기
  - 무엇을 팔지 마음대로 정하지 못함
  - 모회사에게 강요당함
 2. 마케팅 방식에 있어서 좌절
  - 수입의 6%를 지불 → 직접적 혜택이 아님
  - 개별적 마케팅을 실행할 수 없음
 3. 이윤이 별로 없음
  - 서비스와 시스템에 대한 비용을 지불
  - 수익 없이 비용이 지나치게 높음

답안 해석

교수는 설문 조사 결과를 통해 가맹점주가 되는 것의 단점을 알아본다. 이 단점들에는 제품에 대한 통제력 상실, 마케팅 문제, 그리고 이윤 감소가 포함된다. 이것은 가맹점주가 되는 것이 직접 창업을 하는 것보다 더 현명한 사업 방안이라는 지문의 주장을 반박한다.

첫째로, 가맹점주들은 사업 통제권을 포기해야 한다. 그들은 스스로 제품이나 서비스를 선택할 수 없다. 또한 이러한 제품들을 홍보하고 판매하는 방식에 대해서도 모회사의 요구를 따르도록 강요받는다. 그러므로, 이러한 제품 선택에 대한 자유의 부족은 모회사의 믿을 만한 제품을 판매할 수 있기에 가맹점 사업이 바람직하다는 글의 주장에 의문을 제기하는 것이다.

다음으로, 많은 가맹점주들이 마케팅 방식에 대해 실망감을 느낀다. 그들은 광고비로 그들 수입 중 상당한 액수를 지불해야 하는데, 이것은 그들의 사업에는 직접적인 혜택을 주지 않는다. 게다가, 그들은 개별적인 마케팅 안을 실행할 수가 없고 모회사의 광고 산하에 있어야 한다. 이것은 가맹점주들이 직접 광고를 할 필요가 없으므로 이득을 본다는 글의 견해를 반박한다.

마지막으로, 가맹점 사업이 권장되지 않는 가장 큰 이유는 이윤을 최대화할 수 없기 때문이다. 가맹점주들은 계속적인 훈련과 지원에 대해 모회사에게 많은 비용을 지불해야만 한다. 그 결과, 그들의 수입은 줄어든다. 이러한 요점은 모회사로부터 받는 평생 지원 형태의 사업 안정성 때문에 가맹점 사업이 더 낫다는 글의 주장에 반하는 것이다.

comply with~ ~에 따르다, 응하다 parent company 모회사 preferable[préfərəbl] 바람직한
frustrated[frʌ́strèitid] 좌절감이 드는, 실망한 scheme[ski:m] 계획, 안 maximize[mǽksəmàiz] 최대화하다
lifetime[làiftáim] 평생의

다음 지문을 읽고 강의를 들은 후, 주어진 빈칸을 채워 노트와 요약문을 완성하시오. *Track 7*

01

A growing number of students are studying in groups. This has definite advantages for everyone involved. First of all, some students do not have motivation to study alone, but being with others gives them inspiration and encouragement to study. Group studying can benefit some people who are, for instance, intimidated by certain subjects and would not study them on their own.

Secondly, all the members in the group benefit by supporting each other. Members share knowledge, explain unclear aspects of topics to each other, and learn cooperatively. Teaching others can be an effective way to learn, and students can more fully comprehend subjects when they study together and pass along information.

Finally, studying together saves time searching for information. Members split the burden of doing research by investigating individual topics and later reporting back to each other. This saves time that would have been wasted by duplicating each others' efforts.

Listen to the lecture.

Note-taking

읽기 노트

> • Group study – advantages
>
>   1. _____
>
>   – more motiv.
>
>   – helps ppl intimidated by a subj.
>
>   2. _____
>
>   – share, explain: cooperate
>
>   – teach: best way 2 learn
>
>   3. _____
>
>   – split research
>
>   – save time, effort

듣기 노트

- Group study – S's experience

  1. _____

     – some don't do assign. or show up

     – morale ↓

  2. _____

     – freeloading

     – weak students rely on better ones

  3. _____

     – waste time reviewing easy concept

     – chat → socialize

Summary 🖉

단락 1 쓰기

듣기 도입

① _____ the actual experiences of people who studied in groups.

읽기 주제

This casts doubt on the reading passage's claim that group study is an encouraging, supportive, and time-saving process.

단락 2 쓰기

듣기 반론 1

② _____, it often turned out in group study that many students did not do their parts properly, which brought down morale. Members felt discouraged and less motivated when others in the group complained or didn't show up.

읽기 근거 1

③ _____

group study is encouraging and motivating.

단락 3 쓰기

듣기 반론 2

④ _____, the help was not reciprocal. The group study system created freeloaders who were carried on smarter students' shoulders.

읽기 근거 2

⑤ _____

_____ all participants benefit from group study by supporting each other.

단락 4 쓰기

듣기 반론 3

⑥ _____, time was wasted in group study. Students either chatted or spent unnecessary time reviewing concepts for unprepared participants.

읽기 근거 3

⑦ _____

_____ group study is a beneficial activity.

정답 p.443

02

The world is increasingly becoming more technologically advanced. Digital libraries continue this trend by offering users a number of benefits.

First of all, anyone can easily access books wherever they are located. If people have mobility issues which make going to the library and finding books difficult, digital libraries solve this problem. People who are disabled or live far away from libraries can easily access information from digital libraries.

Next, digital libraries are time-saving and convenient. You don't have to spend time going to the library building and painstakingly searching through book shelves. Digital libraries provide whole books to read online, so you can sit in the comfort of your home and read books on your computer.

Finally, digital libraries help make the intellectual world more vigorous. Now that an astounding amount of information is available on-line, authors share information easily and write higher-quality books. They are further encouraged to create their work more enthusiastically, knowing that they can impact a much greater number of readers.

Integrated Section
Independent Section

Listen to the lecture.

Note-taking

읽기 노트

- Digital library – benefits
    1. _____
       – ppl disabled, live far
    2. _____
       – saves time 2 go & search
       – can read online at home
    3. _____
       – share info → book quality ↑
       – encouraged ∴ impact more readers

```
•   │   Digital library – drawbacks

•       1. _____

            – poor w/o comp.: left out

•           – benefit only rich w/ comp.

        2. _____

•           – books online, endless results 4 one info

                → time-consuming, demanding

•       3. _____

•           – ppl not buy book → authors: no profit, discouraged
```

Summary ✎

단락 1 쓰기

듣기 도입

① _____ some of the negative features of digital libraries.

읽기 주제

This casts doubts on the reading passage's claim that digital libraries are beneficial.

단락 2 쓰기

듣기 반론 1

② _____, digital libraries cannot be endorsed because people need to have access to computers in order to use them. This means that the poor are unable to use them and that only the rich with computers at home benefit.

읽기 근거 1

Thus, the lecturer's point contradicts the reading passage's assertion that everyone can easily access digital libraries.

듣기 반론 2

③ _____ , digital libraries provide so much information that it overwhelms people. It is actually time-consuming and wearying to wade through search results or an entire book online to find one piece of information.

읽기 근거 2

④ _____

_____ digital libraries are time-saving and convenient.

듣기 반론 3

⑤ _____ , intellectual property issues come to the forefront because of digital libraries. People don't buy books much anymore because whole books are available on-line. This discourages authors who don't receive the profits from their hard work.

읽기 근거 3

As a result, digital libraries discourage intellectuals, ⑥ _____

_____ they make the intellectual world more vigorous with the ease of sharing of ideas and an increased number of readers to impact.

정답 p.445

Integrated Section

Independent Section

03

The Internet gives students of any discipline easy access to more information than they've ever had before, making the web an invaluable learning tool. The speed and reach of the Internet lends itself particularly well to organized classes. Thus, as educators are realizing its value, they are making more and more courses available online.

These classes allow students to study without the constraints of time and distance. They may take courses offered by universities thousands of miles away. As long as they have access to the Internet, they may listen to lectures at their leisure. If they have too little time to keep up with the work-load, they may stop the class temporarily and resume when it is convenient.

Internet classes offer other benefits over traditional classes, as well. In a crowded lecture hall, there is simply not enough time to devote to individual students, whereas online courses allow the teacher to respond to each student in turn. Communication is not limited to class time; therefore, all students are guaranteed to have their questions answered. Since discussion between students is also possible outside of class, online courses further encourage the exchange of ideas between students through the use of message boards and e-mail.

Listen to the lecture.

Note-taking

읽기 노트

- Internet – good learning tool → more online courses

  1. Can study regardless of time & distance

  - _____

  - _____

  2. Comm. benefits

  - _____

  - _____

듣기 노트

- Online class – survey by S

  1. No limit → too much freedom

     – _____

     – imposs. to eval.

  2. Hard to maintain discussion

     – prof. not always avail.

     – _____

Summary ✏️

단락 1 쓰기

듣기 도입

① _____ .

읽기 주제

He offers evidence to show that online courses are not beneficial for students, ② _____
_____ .

단락 2 쓰기

듣기 반론 1

③ _____ online classes offer
too much freedom. There is no sense of urgency. Thus, students don't take them
seriously and often procrastinate or drop out. This lack of limitations can also lead to
difficulties in assessing or testing students.

읽기 근거 1

④ _____
_____ .

듣기 반론 2

⑤ _____

discussion is hard to maintain online. Professors don't have time to respond to each student's questions. This often frustrates students, who end up not asking questions because they know they will not get a response. Furthermore, students often do not have good online discussions with each other. This lack of interaction between students and teachers, not to mention among students, is a major frustration for online course takers.

읽기 근거 2

⑥ _____

_____

_____.

정답 p.448

04

A "lie detector" or polygraph instrument is a combination of medical devices that are used to monitor certain changes that occur in the body. While an individual is questioned about a certain event or incident, an examiner observes how that person's heart rate, blood pressure, respiratory rate, and perspiration rate change in comparison to normal levels. Fluctuations may indicate that a person is being deceptive.

Studies reveal that lie detectors are accurate in almost 90% of all cases. Certain physiological responses such as sweating in the hands and increased heart rate occur when people lie. Lie detectors pick up on these common signals, thus revealing deception with high accuracy. These biological fluctuations often signal deception because most of them are involuntary. This is especially the case when a person displays similar responses to a question that was asked repeatedly.

Lie detector tests are highly objective, with questions designed in a way to pinpoint the truth. Examiners pose questions skillfully, taking into careful consideration cultural and religious beliefs. Commonly they ask ten questions, only three or four of which are actually relevant to the issue or crime being investigated. The others are clever control questions that help examiners learn more about a person's honest behavior. Afterwards, examiners analyze data of physiological responses to determine if lying occurred.

Listen to the lecture.

Note-taking

읽기 노트

- Lie detector: fluctuation → deceptive
- 1. _____
  - − _____
  - − _____
- 2. Objective
  - − skillful Q
  - − related Q & control Q

```
•    Lie detector – research
          1. _____
•         – _____
          – _____
•         – _____
•    2. Subjective, biased agnst. trthfl. ppl
          – e.g. topic itself cause responses
•         – examiners' too big influence: not prepared / misread data
```

Summary ✎

단락 1 쓰기

듣기 도입

① _____ the accuracy and objectivity of lie detectors.

읽기 주제

② _____ lie detectors

are a reputable means of determining if a person is lying or not.

단락 2 쓰기

듣기 반론 1

③ _____ they don't

measure truth but physiological changes that can be mistaken for lying. These changes

can occur because people are nervous taking the test. On the other hand, it's easy to

cheat the test by a variety of measures.

읽기 근거 1

④ _____

_____ lie detector tests are highly accurate.

단락 3 쓰기

듣기 반론 2

⑤ _____

the tests are very subjective and already biased against truthful people: a large number of errors occur. This is also due to examiners, whose behavior affects the results greatly when they don't prepare properly or misread the data.

읽기 근거 2

The lecturer thus provides information that is ⑥ _____

_____ .

정답 p.451

Integrated
Section

Independent
Section

05

Fast disappearing are the days of little mom and pop stores. Small specialty shops are being replaced by giant superstores. These megastores help both consumers and local economies.

The first benefit of megastores is that they offer cheaper products than smaller shops do. Because they possess a large amount of capital, they can afford to produce or buy a large number of goods and sell them at much lower prices than family stores. This obviously benefits consumers, who are able to buy at reduced costs and save money.

Another advantage of giant superstores is that they are very convenient. They offer an enormous selection of quality products in one place. Therefore, consumers can get a wide range of popular items without expending much time and energy. For instance, people previously went to separate shops to buy clothes, shoes, electronic appliances, sporting goods, and food. Now, they are able to buy all of these items in one big superstore.

Lastly, megastores provide many benefits for the local economy. A large number of positions, such as cashiers, stockers, and managers, become available when these giant stores open. What's more, megastores mostly recruit and train people from the local area. The resulting job creation, employment of locals, and increased consumer spending revitalize the regional economy.

Listen to the lecture.

Note-taking

읽기 노트

> • Megastore – benefits
>
>   1. _____
>
>   • – _____
>
>   • – _____
>
>   • 2. _____
>
>   • – _____
>
>   • – _____
>
>   • 3. Good 4 econ.
>
>   – many jobs avail.
>
>   • – job, spending ↑ : econ. ↑

```
• Megastore – drawbacks
  1. No saving
•    – product on sale ↓ but others ↑
       → spend more
•  2. _____
•    – _____
     – _____
•  3. _____
     – _____
•    – _____
```

Summary ✎

단락 1 쓰기

듣기 도입

The lecturer examines the negative aspects of megastores.

읽기 주제

① _____

_____ .

단락 2 쓰기

듣기 반론 1

② _____

_____ . In fact, people end up paying more at superstores

than they would at smaller shops because non-sale products are more expensive.

읽기 근거 1

③ _____

_____ .

단락 3 쓰기

듣기 반론 2

④ _____

_____ .

Trying to find unique items is impossible there because they provide only standardized products. What's more, you can't find original products anywhere because small shops that stocked these items couldn't compete with giant superstores and closed down.

읽기 근거 2

⑤ _____

_____ .

단락 4 쓰기

듣기 반론 3

⑥ _____ .

They create undesirable, low-paying jobs. Unfortunately, people don't have other options because other stores with decent jobs went out of business competing with megastores. Worse yet, these stores also don't hire people full-time. As a result, employees don't receive benefits and can't form unions.

읽기 근거 3

⑦ _____

_____ .

정답 p.453

06

In the last 20 years or so, the conversion of wind power into a renewable source of energy has begun. Modern wind turbines harness the power of the wind by using rotors fitted with aerodynamic blades to produce electricity. Unfortunately, wind farms have many negative features that do not make them a viable option.

The first drawback to wind farms is that they kill many birds and bats. A study at one site in California revealed that over 4,700 birds were killed by wind turbines. The birds are attracted by the warning lights for planes and get killed by the blades. In addition, most bird migration paths are unknown, so it is difficult to position wind farms.

Another negative aspect of wind farms is their noise and sight pollution. Many individuals who live near them have complained about the noise produced by operating wind turbines. On top of that, people often oppose them because they spoil the landscape. All in all, wind farms are commonly regarded as noisy eyesores.

The most limiting feature of wind farms is that they are not economical. They can only be constructed in places with high winds. Unfortunately, many of these sites are not convenient for developing large wind energy facilities, so companies must do extensive and expensive work clearing an area to make them.

Integrated Section

Independent Section

Listen to the lecture.

Note-taking

읽기 노트

> Wind farm: harness wind power 4 electr. – negative
>
> 1. _____
>   - _____
>   - _____
> 2. _____
>   - _____
>   - _____
> 3. _____
>   - _____
>   - _____

- Wind farm – steps to address concern

1. _____

   – _____

   – _____

   – _____

2. _____

   – _____

   – _____

3. _____

   – _____

   – _____

   – _____

Summary 🖉

단락 1 쓰기

듣기 도입

The lecturer describes some of the reasons why wind farms are a viable energy option today.

읽기 주제

① _____

_____ .

단락 2 쓰기

듣기 반론 1

② _____

_____. In fact, wind farms ultimately save more animals than they kill. Moreover, people are now putting red airplane warning lights on wind farms to avoid attracting birds.

읽기 근거 1

③ _____

_____.

단락 3 쓰기

듣기 반론 2

④ _____

_____. Wind farms are also very quiet because of blade improvements.

읽기 근거 2

⑤ _____

_____.

단락 4 쓰기

듣기 반론 3

⑥ _____. Because of the taller turbines and larger blades, they can be installed anywhere regardless of wind strength. In addition, the costs of setting up and running wind farms are earned back in a short time.

읽기 근거 3

⑦ _____

_____.

정답 p.456

Hackers **T** e s **t**

다음 지문을 읽고 강의를 들은 후, 주어진 빈칸을 채워 노트와 요약문을 완성하시오. ⌒ *Track 8*

01

In an increasingly interconnected world, human resources departments all over are deciding how to staff their foreign offices, whether to send expatriates abroad or hire locally. Experience has shown us that companies who hire citizens of their home countries enjoy several different benefits. Those employees transferred abroad are already knowledgeable about the company's operations. They do not require an extensive amount of training about the company's expectations or in language, dramatically reducing costs. They are also able to effectively communicate within the company, as well as to headquarters. Thus, interactions between headquarters and the foreign office are more straightforward because cultural differences and language-based misunderstandings are minimized. Expatriates are loyal to the company, not the host country, and therefore, put the company's interests first. As a result, the company can accomplish its goals more efficiently and expediently.

The employees on assignments abroad also benefit, which results in even higher production for the company. Expatriates based in foreign offices are frequently paid as much as two or three times their regular salaries, possibly more if they are in a dangerous region, in addition to other financial advantages, such as receiving free housing. They are also more stimulated by the foreign environment, as they learn to live in a culture quite different from their own. Many employees also appreciate the opportunity to travel in the region of their foreign office. It has been proven over and over again that happy employees are hard-working employees; thus, even if the company compensates them for their troubles with a higher salary, their increased productivity more than makes up for the added cost.

> Listen to the lecture. ⌒

Note-taking

읽기 노트

- Hiring ppl from home country – benefits
  1. Good for company
     - _____
     - _____

  2. Good for employees
     - _____
     - _____
     - _____

듣기 노트

- Effectiveness of ex-pats – case study
  1. What the company noticed
     - _____
     - _____
  2. What employees found
     - _____
     - _____

Summary ✏️

단락 1 쓰기

듣기 도입

The lecturer discusses the harms of companies hiring citizens of their home countries to work abroad.

읽기 주제

① _____
_____
_____
_____ .

단락 2 쓰기

듣기 반론 1

First of all, ex-pats hinder a company's overall effectiveness because ② _____
_____ .

③ _____
_____ .

읽기 근거 1

④ _____
_____ .

단락 3 쓰기

듣기 반론 2

Secondly, ex-pats experience personal problems living abroad ⑤ _____
_____ .

⑥ _____
_____ .

읽기 근거 2

⑦ _____
_____ .

정답 p.459

02

Bicyclists have long complained about the difficulties of biking in most cities across the U.S. Many would bike to work if there were not such a "car culture." To address their needs, many city councils are considering creating bicycle lanes on major commuter routes. A number of factors make this idea worthwhile to institute.

One major benefit of bike lanes is the effect on the environment. Currently, many people drive vehicles that consume high quantities of gasoline and emit dangerous levels of exhaust. This adds to already high levels of pollution and further lowers general air quality. Fortunately, bicycles are an eco-friendly mode of transportation. Surveys show that more people would bicycle to work if their own passageway existed. This would obviously decrease the number of motor vehicles on the road and the harm done to the environment.

In fact, bicycle lanes are advantageous to everyone on the road. Roads without them force cars to slow down to accommodate cyclists in their paths. Drivers already have long commutes and do not appreciate being stuck behind bikers. Therefore, bike lanes are a welcome addition to clogged streets. They reduce traffic congestion by decreasing the number of cars and keeping the flow of traffic moving in cyclists' and drivers' respective lanes.

Furthermore, they reduce many accidents involving cars and bikes. Currently, many drivers do not know how to share the road with people who cycle. Drivers often don't see cyclists or bump into them as they try to pass. In addition, they often squeeze bikers onto the shoulder of the road, resulting in many dangerous accidents. These incidents would be completely avoidable if bike lanes were created.

Listen to the lecture.

Note-taking

읽기 노트

- Bike lane – worthwhile

  1. _____

     – bike: eco-friendly

     – more ppl bike w/ own lane → car ↓ , good 4 envir.

  2. _____

     – cars slow down 4 cycle

     – B.L. keep traffic moving

  3. _____

     – drivers: cause danger to cyclist

     – avoidable w/ B.L.

```
● │  Bike lane - case study
●   1. _____
       - cycling ppl ↑1%: biking too demanding
●      - no difference to envir.
    2. _____
●      - drivers endured road work
       - drivers angry: losing one lane 4 empty B.L.
●   3. _____
       - bikers: assume safe → oblivious to danger
●      - accidents ↑
●
```

Summary ✎

단락 1 쓰기

듣기 도입

The lecturer describes a case study done in San Francisco after bike lanes were instituted.

읽기 주제

① _____

_____ .

단락 2 쓰기

듣기 반론 1

For one, ② _____

_____ .

③ _____ .

④ _____ .

읽기 근거 1

Thus, bike lanes did not noticeably decrease the number of cars on the road, reduce pollution, or help the environment, contrary to the reading passage's argument.

단락 3 쓰기

듣기 반론 2

Next, ⑤ _____ .

⑥ _____ .

⑦ _____ .

⑧ _____ .

읽기 근거 2

Thus, bicycle lanes did not reduce congestion and provide fast passageway for users of the road, as promised by the reading passage.

단락 4 쓰기

듣기 반론 3

Last, ⑨ _____ .

⑩ _____

_____ .

읽기 근거 3

The reading passage, however, argued that bicycle lanes reduce the number of accidents between cyclists and drivers, which was clearly not the case in San Francisco that the lecturer described.

정답 p.462

03

Although the number of students entering scientific fields has slightly increased over the years, women are still disproportionately underrepresented. Several reasons explain the historical lack of women in science.

The first reason is that gender stereotypes paint women as irrational and not analytical, traits that are unsuitable for science. Women are pushed to go into the caring professions, such as teaching or nursing, while men are encouraged to become scientists or policemen. Those women who do opt into academia are often funneled into literature, languages, anthropology, or psychology. In short, women are often connected with the "soft" or "social" sciences. Thus, from the start, "hard" scientific fields are not presented as viable, attractive options for women to excel in.

Next, the grueling course work and initial low salaries deter women from entering science. This also applies to men, but impacts women more negatively because they are still expected to marry and have their careers be secondary to motherhood. Because becoming a scientist is a long, difficult, financially arduous process, many women opt for less time-consuming and more financially lucrative tracks, such as nursing. Doing this allows them to juggle having a career and raising children.

The third reason relates to science still being a male-dominated field. This is very intimidating for most women, who will hit a "glass ceiling," where they face limits to how high they can rise in the scientific world. They must also be comfortable working primarily around men, who may view them with an air of suspicion and superiority.

Listen to the lecture.

Note-taking

읽기 노트

- Lack of women in science

  1. _____
     - _____
     - _____
  2. _____
     - _____
     - _____
  3. _____
     - _____
     - _____

More women in science

1. _____

  – _____

  – _____

2. _____

  – _____

  – _____

3. _____

  – _____

  – _____

Integrated Section

Independent Section

Summary 🖉

단락 1 쓰기

듣기 도입

① _____ .

읽기 주제

② _____

_____ .

단락 2 쓰기

듣기 반론 1

First, the lecturer describes efforts currently underway in education to lure women into
the field. ③ _____.

④ _____.

읽기 근거 1

⑤ _____

_____

_____.

단락 3 쓰기

듣기 반론 2

Next, ⑥ _____.

⑦ _____.

⑧ _____.

읽기 근거 2

⑨ _____

_____.

단락 4 쓰기

듣기 반론 3

Finally, the lecturer explores some of the measures women are taking to tackle the
sexism in the field. ⑩ _____

_____.

⑪ _____.

읽기 근거 3

⑫ _____

_____.

정답 p.465

04

Difficult economic times and worker dissatisfaction over the traditional forty-hour workweek have brought about a shift in the working landscape. Increasingly, today's companies are turning to a four-day work week of thirty-two hours. This is especially beneficial to employers and employees, as well as improving the general economy.

Integrated Section

Independent Section

First of all, employers suffering from lean financial times can benefit from paying less in salaries; namely, a 20% decrease. As economies can experience recession for years on end, companies need to find areas in which they can trim costs. It makes sound economic sense for businesses to shorten their employees' workweek, as excess funds can be used towards investing in better infrastructure and resources. These factors will attract the most qualified, competitive, productive employees, and encourage companies' further growth.

Furthermore, individual employees benefit tremendously from this new working arrangement. Many workers complain that they have no time for a life outside of work. A four-day workweek would translate into more time to relax with friends or families. The time spent pursuing enjoyable hobbies, meeting with friends, or enjoying one's family would in turn result in improved quality of life. This feeling carries over to people's work, in which they are happier and more productive. Thus, a shorter workweek is directly related to worker satisfaction and happiness.

A four-day workweek is also better for the economy. Currently, most job markets are extremely tight. Reducing employee hours would result in the creation of more jobs. In addition, companies would benefit from a broader workforce. The end result is an economy in full swing with happy, productive workers and profitable, booming businesses. A healthy, diverse, productive job market resulting from the four-day workweek is therefore one more reason to support the move away from the traditional forty-hour working arrangement.

Listen to the lecture.

Note-taking

읽기 노트

- 4-day work – beneficial
  - 1. _____
    - – _____
    - – _____
    - – _____
  - 2. _____
    - – _____
  - 3. _____
    - – _____
    - – _____

4-day work – actual experience

1. _____

    – _____

    – _____

    – _____

2. _____

    – _____

    – _____

    – _____

3. _____

    – _____

    – _____

    – _____

Summary ✏️

단락 1 쓰기

듣기 도입

The lecturer believes that ① _____

_____ .

읽기 주제

② _____

_____ .

단락 2 쓰기

듣기 반론 1

One reason why the four-day workweek is ③ _____.

④ _____.

⑤ _____.

읽기 근거 1

⑥ _____.

단락 3 쓰기

듣기 반론 2

On top of that, this working arrangement has a negative impact on employees. ⑦ _____

_____.

⑧ _____.

⑨ _____.

읽기 근거 2

⑩ _____.

단락 4 쓰기

듣기 반론 3

Lastly, the four-day workweek is not good for the economy. ⑪ _____

_____.

⑫ _____.

⑬ _____.

읽기 근거 3

⑭ _____.

정답 p.469

Integrated Section

Independent Section

Track 9

Directions You have 20 minutes to plan and write your response. Your response will be judged on the basis of the quality of your writing and on how well your response presents the points in the lecture and the relationship to the reading passage. Typically, an effective response will be 150 to 225 words.

Increased computer capabilities and the widespread use of electronic mail systems have all contributed to making telecommuting a possibility for many corporate employees. While the concept is only beginning to appeal to company executives, the work-at-home system is rapidly evolving into an attractive trend among the executive and working classes.

Contrary to popular belief, most benefits of at-home work are enjoyed by the employer. For example, businesses save money in real estate when they have fewer employees to make office space for. With real estate prices in major urban areas higher than ever, the possibility of saving money in that sector is a persuasive incentive for companies to allow work to be done from the home. In addition, recent studies have found that employees are actually more productive when allowed the convenience and comfort of working in their home environment.

However, the employee also enjoys a number of advantages. In general, people who have worked at home report happier familial relationships and personal lives. They have more time to spend engaging in activities that increase their pleasure and contentment in life. Another significant benefit is that they don't have to commute. In today's cities, many who choose to live in the suburbs must travel 1-2 hours for work, which takes up not only time, but also mental and physical energy that could be put to more productive use. Thus, for both the employer and employee, the emerging shift to home-based positions offers a variety of opportunities.

> Now listen to part of a lecture on the topic you just read about.

Question Summarize the points made in the lecture you just heard, explaining how they cast doubts on the points made in the reading.

정답 p.472

Track 10

Directions You have 20 minutes to plan and write your response. Your response will be judged on the basis of the quality of your writing and on how well your response presents the points in the lecture and the relationship to the reading passage. Typically, an effective response will be 150 to 225 words.

The recent surge in video game popularity has parents and researchers worried. Based on recent studies, some psychologists have concluded that gaming, specifically first-person action games featuring violence, are harmful to children.

Researchers have found evidence that the practice is addictive. Many youth spend hours playing in front of the television. When forced to stop, the symptoms of withdrawal are similar to those of other addictions, such as compulsive behavior, loss of interest in other activities, or lying to loved ones. As with all other addictions, video games disrupt normal behavior, and contribute to problems common to addicts, including failure at school. Opponents cite cases where gaming replaced all other priorities in a child's life, leading to the complete destruction of a healthy lifestyle.

Research has also shown that certain notoriously violent video games encourage aggressive tendencies. Recent experiments have found a relationship between time spent playing video games and a higher inclination to act violently. High levels of violent game exposure were linked to fighting at school and criminal behavior. In extreme cases, children accused of murder in high-profile trials have admitted that they were inspired by video games to commit the murders.

Yet, children are allowed to waste huge amounts of their time entertaining themselves glued to the screen. These games serve no useful purpose in society, yet they take up a large proportion of our youth's leisure activities. Their time can be used more constructively than staring at a television and not learning anything beneficial.

Now listen to part of a lecture on the topic you just read about.

Question   Summarize the points made in the lecture you just heard, explaining how they cast doubts on the points made in the reading.

정답 p.475

www.goHackers.com

Independent
Section

Writing Based on Experience and Knowledge

Hackers iBT TOEFL Writing

•••• Introduction

Overview

통합형(Integrated) 문제가 끝나고 나면, 주어진 명제에 대해 찬성 또는 반대의 입장을 주장하는 글을 쓰는 독립형(Independent) 문제가 이어진다. 주어진 내용을 바탕으로 정리해서 요약문을 작성하는 통합형과 달리, 독립형 문제에서는 자신의 생각을 주체적으로 정리하여 글을 쓰는 것이 특징이다. 주로 학술적인 내용을 다루는 통합형 문제와는 달리 독립형에서는 좀 더 일상적인 소재를 다룬다.

테스트 진행 방식

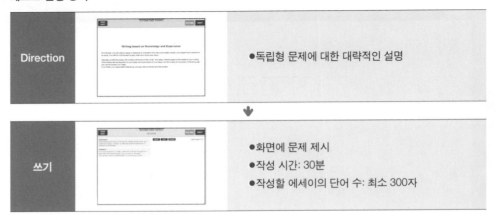

Direction	●독립형 문제에 대한 대략적인 설명

↓

쓰기	●화면에 문제 제시 ●작성 시간: 30분 ●작성할 에세이의 단어 수: 최소 300자

질문의 핵심 포인트

특정한 입장을 제시하고, 이 입장에 찬성하는지 반대하는지의 의견을 물어본다. 이 때 자신의 의견을 뒷받침하기 위한 구체적인 이유와 예를 제시해야 한다.

Example

Question

Do you agree or disagree with the following statement?
Television has destroyed children's ability to read and write.
Use specific reasons and examples to support your opinion.

다음 명제에 찬성하는가 반대하는가? 텔레비전은 아이들의 읽고 쓰는 능력에 해를 끼쳐 왔다. 구체적인 이유와 예를 들어 의견을 뒷받침하시오.

- 찬반 여부를 묻고 있음
- 토픽에 대한 특정 입장을 제시함
- 이유와 예를 제시할 것을 요구

STEP별 문제풀이 전략

STEP 1 **철저한 문제 분석 (1분 소요)**
아무리 잘 쓴 글도 문제에서 묻는 질문에 제대로 답하고 있지 않으면 치명적인 감점을 당하게 된다. 시간에 쫓겨 문제를 대강 읽지 말고, 문제에서 무엇을 물어보고 있으며 어떻게 쓰기를 요구하고 있는지 정확히 이해하도록 한다.

STEP 2 **아웃라인 잡기 (3-5분 소요)**
문제에서 물어보는 사항에 대한 자신의 의견과 그렇게 생각하는 구체적 근거를 적어둔다.

STEP 3 **아웃라인에 따라 각 문단을 작성 (15-20분 소요)**
아웃라인에서 정리한 아이디어를 실제 문장으로 옮겨서 작성한다. 아웃라인의 중심 생각을 기준으로 구체적인 근거를 제시한다.

STEP 4 **검토 및 수정 (3-5분 소요)**
작성을 마치면 에세이를 다시 읽어보고 검토 및 수정할 수 있는 시간을 갖는다. 이때는 내용에 변화를 주려고 하지 말고 형식적인 면을 중심으로 확인하도록 한다.

기본 다지기 ▪ ▪ ▪ ▪

Ⅰ 상황별 표현

영어로 글을 쓰고자 할 때, 그 주제에 대해 평소에 할 말이 많았던 사람이라도 문장을 어떻게 시작하고 구성해 나가야 할지 몰라 당황하는 경우가 많다. 학창 시절 교복에 불만이 많았던 사람이 '중고생의 교복 착용'에 대한 자신의 의견을 밝히는 글을 쓰는 경우를 생각해 보자.

나는 중고생의 교복 착용에 반대한다.	**I object to** requiring students to wear school uniform.
여기에는 여러 가지 이유가 있다.	**There are several reasons for** this.
먼저, 학생들의 표현의 자유가 보장돼야 한다는 것은 분명하다.	First of all, **it is clear that** students' right to express themselves should be protected.
게다가, 사복이 교복보다 편하다는 것에는 의심의 여지가 없다.	Furthermore, **there is no question that** casual clothes are more comfortable than school uniforms.
이러한 이유로, 나는 학생들이 사복을 입을 수 있게 해야 한다고 생각한다.	**For these reasons, I think that** students should be allowed to wear casual clothes.

이때 교복 착용에 대해 아무리 확실한 의견을 가지고 있다고 하더라도, '나는 ~에 반대한다(I object to ~)', '~에는 여러 가지 이유가 있다(There are several reasons for ~)', '~는 분명하다(It is clear that ~)' 등의 적절한 표현을 모르면 좋은 글을 제대로 쓰기가 힘들다.

이렇게 자신의 의견이라는 '음식'을 제대로 담을 수 있는 '그릇'의 역할을 하는 것이 상황별 표현이다. 따라서 평소에 이러한 표현들을 많이 익혀 놓으면 여러 가지 다양한 주제에 대해 글을 쓰더라도 적절히 아이디어를 담아낼 수 있다.

1. 선호, 찬반, 비교, 양보 표현

❶ 나는 B보다 A를 선호한다
I prefer A to B

나는 내가 스스로 룸메이트를 정하는 것보다 나에게 룸메이트가 지정되는 것을 선호한다.
I would **prefer** having an assigned roommate **to** having to choose a roommate on my own.

❷ 내 생각에는, ~이다
In my opinion, 주어 + 동사

내 생각에는, 아이들은 가능한 한 빨리 외국어를 배워야 한다.
In my opinion, children should learn a foreign language as soon as possible.

❸ 나는 ~라고 굳게 믿는다
I firmly believe that 주어 + 동사

나는 굳은 결의가 성공적인 인생의 중요한 요소라고 굳게 믿는다.
I firmly believe that a strong sense of determination is a key factor to a successful life.

❹ ~는 명백하다
It is evident that 주어 + 동사

인터넷의 도입이 인류를 새로운 기술의 시대로 선도했다는 것은 명백하다.
It is evident that the introduction of the Internet ushered humanity into a new age of technology.

❺ 나는 ~에 동의한다
I agree with ~ / I agree that 주어 + 동사

아이들이 필요로 하는 모든 것이 상대적으로 가까이 있기 때문에, 나는 아이들이 도시에서 성장하는 것이 더 낫다는 데 동의한다.

I agree that children are better off growing up in the city because everything they need is relatively close by.

❻ A와 B 중 하나를 선택해야 한다면, 나는 ~을 선택하겠다
Given the choice between A and B, I would choose ~

집을 사는 것과 사업을 인수하는 것 중 하나를 선택해야 한다면, 나는 집을 사는 것을 택하겠다.

Given the choice between buying a house **and** a business, **I would choose** buying a house.

❼ 나는 ~(라는 생각)을 강력히 지지한다
I strongly support the idea of ~

나는 정부가 지원하는 대중교통체제를 강력히 지지한다.

I strongly support the idea of government-funded public transportation systems.

❽ 이 문제에 대한 나의 견해는 ~이다
My view on this issue is that 주어 + 동사

이 문제에 대한 나의 견해는 사람들이 유명인들의 삶에 지나친 관심을 쏟는다는 것이다.

My view on this issue is that people spend too much attention to the lives of celebrities.

❾ 나는 ~에 반대한다
I object to ~ / I object that 주어 + 동사

텔레비전을 통해 공연을 보면서 동일한 수준의 즐거움을 누릴 수 있기 때문에 나는 실황 공연을 보기 위해 많은 돈을 지불하는 것에 반대한다.

I object to paying a large sum of money to watch a live performance because I can experience the same level of enjoyment watching the show on my TV.

❿ 나는 ~인지 의심스럽다, 의문이다
I question whether 주어 + 동사

나는 소득이 직업의 가장 중요한 측면인지 의심스럽다.

I question whether income is the most important aspect of a job.

⑪ 어떤 사람들은 ~에 반대할지도 모른다
Some people may <u>be opposed to</u> ~

어떤 사람들은 자연 환경에의 관심이 절실히 필요한 때에 기업들이 예술 분야에 기부하는 것에 반대할 지도 모른다.

Some people may be opposed to companies donating to the arts when the environment is in great need.

⑫ 나는 ~가 −라고 생각하지 않는다
I don't think it is 형용사 + to 부정사 / that 주어 + 동사

나는 경험이 부족한 직원을 낮은 임금에 고용하는 것이 현명하다고 생각하지 않는다.

I don't think it is <u>wise to</u> hire an inexperienced worker for a low salary.
＊경험이 부족한, 미숙련된 inexperienced

⑬ 나는 ~에 반대한다
I <u>am</u> against ~

안내인을 동반한 관광 여행은 너무 제한적이고 관광 명소만을 포함하기 때문에 나는 그러한 관광 여행에 반대한다.

I am against guided tours because I feel they are too restrictive and include only tourist attractions.
＊제한적, 한정적 restrictive

⑭ 그와 비슷하게, ~이다
<u>Similarly,</u> 주어 + 동사

그와 비슷하게, 광고는 한 국가의 문화, 가치, 그리고 윤리성에 대하여 많은 것을 드러낸다.

Similarly, advertising reveals a lot about a country's culture, values, and morals.

⑮ ~와 비교할 때, −이다
Compared to ~, 주어 + 동사

논픽션과 비교할 때, 소설은 현실로부터의 반가운 기분전환이 될 수 있다.

Compared to non-fiction, fiction can be a welcome distraction from real life.

⑯ A는 B와 비교할 수 없다
A cannot compare with B

집의 다른 공간들은 집에서 내가 가장 좋아하는 방인 나의 침실과 비교할 수 없다.

The rest of the house **cannot compare with** my bedroom, which is my favorite room at home.

⑰ A는 B와 (~가) 비슷하다
A is similar to B

서면으로 불만을 이야기하는 것은 직접 불평하는 것과 비슷한데, 왜냐하면 각각의 경우 모두 고객이 자신의 견해를 표명하는 것이기 때문이다.

Complaining in writing **is similar to** doing it in person because a customer is voicing his opinion in each case.
＊의견을 표현하다 voice

⑱ ~는 장점과 단점을 모두 지닌다
주어 has its (own) advantages and disadvantages

소도시에서 대학을 다니는 것은 장점과 단점을 모두 지닌다.

Attending a small-town university **has its advantages and disadvantages.**

⑲ ~의 장점이 단점보다 훨씬 크다
The advantages of ~ far outweigh the disadvantages

인터넷 뱅킹의 장점이 단점보다 훨씬 크다.

The advantages of Internet banking **far outweigh the disadvantages.**

⑳ 대조적으로, ~이다
In contrast / On the contrary, 주어 + 동사

대조적으로, 부모가 패스트 푸드를 먹지 못하게 하는 아이들은 결국 패스트 푸드를 먹어보긴 하지만 규칙적으로 섭취하지는 않는다.

In contrast, children of parents who forbid them to eat fast food end up trying it but not eating it on a regular basis.

㉑ 반대로, ~이다
Conversely, 주어 + 동사

반대로, 아이가 부모의 충분한 관심을 받기 때문에, 자택 교육을 하는 것은 매우 생산적일 수 있다.

Conversely, home-schooling a child can be very productive because the child receives the full attention of the parent.

＊자택 교육하다 home-school

㉒ 하지만, ~와는 다르게, -이다
However, unlike ~, 주어 + 동사

하지만, 강의식 수업과는 다르게, 토론 그룹은 학생들에게 자신들의 견해를 표현할 수 있는 기회를 제공한다.

However, unlike lecture-style classes, discussion groups give students a chance to voice their opinions.

㉓ ~와는 반대로, -이다
As opposed to ~, 주어 + 동사

집에서 공부하는 것과는 반대로, 도서관에서 공부하는 것은 동기를 부여해주며 주의를 산만하게 하는 것이 없다.

As opposed to studying at home, studying at the library is motivating and free from distractions.

＊주의를 산만하게 하는 것 distraction

㉔ 그럼에도 불구하고, ~이다
Even so / Nevertheless, 주어 + 동사

그럼에도 불구하고, 교복은 학생들이 졸업한 이후로도 오랫동안 학창시절에 대한 즐거운 추억거리를 제공한다.

Even so, school uniforms provide students with fond memories of school long after they have graduated.

㉕ ~에도 불구하고, -이다
In spite of ~, 주어 + 동사

자동차에 의해 발생되는 오염에도 불구하고, 나는 여전히 그것이 금세기 최고의 발명품 중 하나라고 생각한다.

In spite of the pollution that is emitted by cars, I still believe they are one of the greatest inventions of the century.

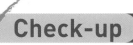

녹색으로 주어진 표현에 유의하여, 다음의 우리말 문장을 영어로 바꾸어 쓰시오.

1 나는 다른 소통 수단보다 직접 대하는 의사소통이 더 낫다는 데 동의한다
＊의사소통 communication　＊직접 대하는 face-to-face

_____

2 도시에서 거주하는 것의 장점이 단점보다 훨씬 크다
＊훨씬 far　＊능가하다 outweigh

_____

3 반대로, 유명인사들은 그들이 결코 보통 사람처럼 취급받지 못하리라고 느낄지도 모른다.
＊유명인사, 연예인 celebrity　＊보통 사람 ordinary person

_____

4 내 생각에는, 사람들은 집이나 차와 같은 큰 구매를 위해 가능한 많은 돈을 모아야 한다.
＊구매 purchase　＊돈을 모으다 save money

_____

5 직업으로 많은 돈을 버는 것은 가족과 친구들과 함께 보낼 수 있는 자유 시간을 갖는 것과 비교할 수 없다.
＊많은, 엄청난 huge　＊돈을 벌다 earn money　＊자유 시간 free time

_____

6 나는 대학을 졸업하는 것이 모든 젊은 학생들의 목표가 되어야 한다고 굳게 믿는다.
  *~를 졸업하다 graduate from *목표 goal

---

7 최상위 대학들의 명성에도 불구하고, 많은 사람들은 여전히 거의 모든 학교에서 수준 높은 교육을 받을 수 있다고 믿고 있다.
  *최상위 대학 top university *명성, 위신 prestige *수준 높은 high-quality

---

8 자택 교육을 받는 아이들과는 반대로, 다른 아이들과 함께 학교를 다니는 아이들은 사교 기술을 발달시킬 기회를 갖는다.
  *자택 교육을 하다 home-school *학교에 다니다 attend school *사교 기술 socialization skills

---

9 대조적으로, 바이러스 프로그래머들은 힘과 수적인 면에서 늘어나고 있다.
  *바이러스 프로그래머 virus programmer *늘다 gain

---

10 나는 회사들이 수익을 내기 위해 할 수 있는 것은 다 하는 것에 반대한다.
  *수익을 내다 make a profit

다음에 주어진 우리말 문장을 영어로 바꾸어 쓰시오.

11 등산과 같은 위험한 활동들과 비교할 때, 테니스 같은 스포츠는 훨씬 덜 위험하지만 마찬가지로 활기를 불어넣을 수 있다.
＊등산 mountain-climbing　＊위험한 hazardous　＊활기를 불어넣는 invigorating

_____

12 서로 다른 학생들이 다른 학습 방식을 갖고 있다는 것은 명백하다.
＊학습 방식 learning style

_____

13 하지만, 다른 기숙사와는 다르게, 이 카페테리아는 학생들에게 식권을 구매할 것을 요구하지 않는다.
＊기숙사 dormitory　＊카페테리아 (셀프 식당) cafeteria　＊식권 meal plans

_____

14 나는 매일 하는 과제가 아이들이 학습할 수 있는 효과적인 방법인지 의문이다.
＊과제 homework assignments　＊효과적인 effective

_____

15 나는 모든 학생들에게 대학 교육이 이용 가능한 것에 반대한다.
＊대학 교육 university education　＊이용 가능함, 유효성 availability

_____

16 인터넷의 발명은 둘 다 세상을 더 작은 곳으로 만들었다는 점에서 비행기의 발명과 비슷하다.
　＊발명 invention　＊~라는 점에서 in that ~

---

17 어떤 사람들은 표준 주간 노동시간을 40시간 이상으로 늘리는 것에 반대할지도 모른다.
　＊표준의 standard　＊주간 노동시간 work week　＊늘리다 extend

---

18 온라인 대학에서 공부하는 것은 장점과 단점을 모두 지닌다.
　＊온라인 대학 online university

---

19 그와 비슷하게, 학생들은 대학에 다니는 동안 자신들이 경험한 교육의 질에 대해 의견을 제공할 수 있어야 한다.
　＊질 quality　＊의견, 반응 feedback　＊제공하다 provide

---

20 나는 일부 학부모들이 자녀들의 스포츠 팀을 감독하는 것이 유익하다고 생각하지 않는다.
　＊감독하다 coach　＊유익한 beneficial

정답 p.478

2. 인과, 주장, 조건, 가정 표현

❶ 그 결과로, ~되다

As a result, 주어 + 동사

그 결과로, 어떤 애완동물들은 가족 구성원만큼 중요하게 여겨진다.

As a result, some pets are considered as important as family members.

❷ ~의 결과로, -되다

As a result of ~, 주어 + 동사

대중 매체의 결과로, 오늘날 사람들이 주의를 지속할 수 있는 시간은 더 짧아지는 경향이 있다.

As a result of mass media, people's attention spans tend to be shorter these days.
＊주의를 지속하는 시간 attention span

❸ 따라서, ~이다

Accordingly, 주어 + 동사

따라서, 여행객들은 날씨가 예상보다 따뜻하면 쉽게 벗을 수 있는 따뜻한 스웨터나 재킷을 하나 가져와야 한다.

Accordingly, travelers should bring one warm sweater or jacket that can be removed easily if the weather is warmer than expected.

❹ 결과적으로, ~이다

Consequently / As a consequence, 주어 + 동사

결과적으로, 부모들은 자녀들과 TV를 함께 시청하는 것이 긴밀한 유대를 쌓을 수 있는 경험이라고 느낄 것이다.

Consequently, parents might find that watching TV with their children can be a bonding experience.
＊유대를 쌓는 bonding

❺ 이러한 이유 때문에, ~이다

For this reason, 주어 + 동사

이러한 이유 때문에, 나는 학교 내에서 지나친 광고를 하는 것에 반대한다.

For this reason, I am against the excessive presence of advertising in schools.
＊지나친 excessive

⑥ 그것이 ~하는 이유이다

That is why 주어 + 동사

그것이 내가 외국 학생들이 자국 학생들에 비해 우대받아서는 안 된다고 생각하는 이유이다.

That is why I feel that foreign students should not get preferential treatment compared to native students.

＊우대, 특혜 preferential treatment

⑦ 이것은 ~을 보여 준다

This reflects ~

이것은 지속적으로 변하고 있는 오늘날의 직장의 특징을 보여 준다.

This reflects the constantly changing nature of today's workplace.

⑧ 이것은 ~의 원인이다

This gives rise to ~

이것은 자원 남용과 지나친 오염에 대한 우려의 원인이다.

This gives rise to concerns about overused resources and excessive pollution.

＊남용된, 과도하게 이용된 overused

⑨ 이러한 점에서, ~이다

In this sense, 주어 + 동사

이러한 점에서, 종신 고용은 많은 직원들에게 바람직한 목표이다.

In this sense, lifetime employment is a desirable goal for many employees.

＊종신 고용 lifetime employment

⑩ 나는 ~에게 -할 것을 권하겠다

I would encourage 사람 + to 부정사

나는 여행객들에게 스스로 장소들을 답사할 것을 권하겠다.

I would encourage travelers **to** explore places on their own.

⑪ ~는 확실하다

It is clear that 주어 + 동사

진보가 종종 해롭다는 것은 확실한데, 특히 그것으로부터 혜택을 얻지 못하는 사람들에게 그렇다.

It is clear that progress is often harmful, especially to people who are unable to benefit from it.

＊~로부터 혜택을 얻다 benefit from~

⑫ ~에는 의심의 여지가 없다
There is no question that 주어 + 동사

사람이 최소한의 적은 위험도 감수하지 않고 성공할 수 없다는 것에는 의심의 여지가 없다.

There is no question that one cannot be successful without at least a little risk.

⑬ ~하는 좋은 방법은 −이다
A good way to 부정사 **is to** 부정사

언어를 배우는 좋은 방법은 원어민들과 가능한 한 많이 연습하는 것이다.

A good way to learn a language **is to** practice whenever possible with native speakers.

⑭ 이러한 이유들 때문에, 나는 ~라고 생각한다
For all these reasons, I think that 주어 + 동사

이러한 이유들 때문에, 나는 학생들이 한 가지 특정 분야를 전공해야 한다고 생각한다.

For all these reasons, I think that students should specialize in a particular field.

⑮ 여러 가지 이유로 ~는 분명해 보인다
It seems clear that 주어 + 동사 **for several reasons.**

여러 가지 이유로 규율 의식이 유용하다는 것은 분명해 보인다.

It seems clear that a sense of discipline is useful **for several reasons.**
*규율 의식 a sense of discipline

⑯ 만일 ~라면 −할 것이다
주어 + **would** + 동사 원형 + **providing that** 주어 + 동사

나는 만일 내가 열정을 갖고 있는 분야의 일이라면 보수를 덜 받는 직업을 갖는 것을 고려해 볼 것이다.

I **would** consider taking a job with less pay **providing that** it was in a field that I am passionate about.
*열정적인 passionate

⑰ 나는 ~라고 가정 / 추측한다
I assume that 주어 + 동사

나는 하루에 5시간 이상씩 TV를 시청하는 사람들이 있다고 가정한다.

I assume that there are people who watch more than five hours of TV a day.

⑱ 만일 그것이 나에게 달려 있다면(나라면), 나는 ~할 것이다
If it were up to me, I would 동사 원형

만일 그것이 나에게 달려 있다면, 나는 모든 1학년 학생들이 모든 수업에 참석하지 않으면 낙제 점수 받는 것을 감수하도록 요구할 것이다.

If it were up to me, I would require all first-year students to attend all their classes or risk failing marks.

＊낙제 점수 failing marks

⑲ 나는 ~라는 조건이라면(만약 ~라면) -할 것이다
I would 동사 원형 on the condition that 주어 + 동사

때때로 내 견해를 드러낼 기회가 여전히 주어진다는 조건이라면 나는 대기업에서 일할 것이다.

I would work for a large company **on the condition that** I would still have a chance to express myself once in a while.

＊내 견해를 드러내다 express myself   ＊때때로 once in a while

⑳ ~하는 것의 이점은 -이다
One advantage of ~ing is that 주어 + 동사

소수의 가까운 친구를 가지는 것의 이점은 한두 사람을 더 잘 알 수 있게 된다는 것이다.

One advantage of having a few close friends **is that** you could get to know one or two people better.

㉑ 만일 나에게 ~할 기회가 주어진다면, 나는 -를 하고 싶다
If I had an opportunity to 부정사, I would want to 부정사

만일 나에게 나보다 어린 사람을 도와줄 기회가 주어진다면, 나는 내가 인생에서 저지른 몇 가지 실수들에 대해서 말해 주고 싶다.

If I had an opportunity to help someone younger than me, **I would want to** tell him/her about some of the mistakes I made in life.

㉒ 만일 나에게 ~을 하라고 한다면, 나는 -할 것이다
If I were asked to 동사 원형, I would 동사 원형

만일 나에게 방문객들을 데리고 내가 사는 도시를 관광하라고 한다면, 나는 그들을 호수의 야간 유람선 순항에 데리고 갈 것이다.

If I were asked to take visitors on a tour of my city, **I would** take them on a night cruise on the lake.

＊유람선 순항 cruise

㉓ 만일 ~가 없다면, -할 것이다
If it were not for 명사, 주어 **would** 동사 원형

만일 비행기의 발명이 없다면, 어떤 도시들은 존재하지 않을 것이다.
If it were not for the invention of airplanes, certain towns **would** not exist.

㉔ 나는 ~라면 좋겠다
I wish 주어 + 동사의 과거형

유년 시절이 내가 책임으로부터 자유로웠던 마지막 시기였기에, 나는 그 시절로 돌아갈 수 있다면 좋겠다.
I wish I could go back to my childhood because that was the last time I was free of responsibility.

㉕ ~라고 가정해 보라
Suppose 주어 + 동사의 과거형

인쇄기가 발명되지 않았다고 가정해 보라. 유럽에서는 어떤 일이 일어났을까?
Suppose the printing press was never invented. What would have happened in Europe?
＊인쇄기 printing press

㉖ ~라고 가정해 보자
Let's assume that 주어 + 동사

시간제 근무를 하는 모든 학생들이 일주일에 20시간 이상을 일하는 것은 아니라고 가정해 보자.
Let's assume that not all students with part-time jobs work more than 20 hours a week.

㉗ 나는 ~라고 생각한다
I suppose 주어 + 동사

나는 프로 운동선수들이 수십만 달러를 받을만큼 그들의 경력에 충분한 돈과 시간을 투자해왔다고 생각한다.
I suppose professional athletes have invested enough time and money in their career to deserve getting paid hundreds of thousands of dollars.

㉘ 만약 ~라면 어떨까? / 어떻게 되었을까?

What if 주어 + 동사?

만약 지구 온난화가 과학자들이 예상하는 것보다 더 빨리 악화되고 있다면 어떨까?

What if global warming is worsening faster than scientists anticipate?

＊지구 온난화 global warming

㉙ 아마도, ~일 것이다

Presumably, 주어 + 동사

아마도, 아이들은 초등학교에서 체육 수업에 의무적으로 참여하는 것으로부터 혜택을 볼 것이다.

Presumably, children benefit from taking mandatory physical education class in elementary school.

＊의무적인 mandatory

㉚ 십중팔구, ~일 것이다

In all likelihood, 주어 + would / will + 동사원형

십중팔구, 도시들은 대중교통에 더 많이 투자함으로써 혜택을 얻을 것이다.

In all likelihood, cities **would** benefit from increased spending on public transportation.

㉛ ~와 무관하게, –이다

Regardless of ~, 주어 + 동사

선천적 재능의 정도와 무관하게, 열심히 노력하지 않으면 결코 성공할 수 없을 것이다.

Regardless of the amount of natural talent one has, if one doesn't work hard, one will never find success.

＊선천적 재능 natural talent

Check-up

녹색으로 주어진 표현에 유의하여, 다음의 우리말 문장을 영어로 바꾸어 쓰시오.

1 이것은 오늘날 소비자들의 높은 기대치를 보여 준다.
＊소비자 consumer ＊기대치 expectations

_____

2 그 결과로, 어떤 부모들은 매일 자녀들이 인터넷을 사용하는 시간을 제한하고 있다.
＊제한하다 limit

_____

3 나는 심지어 담배 회사들도 연구 지원 비용을 받을 자격이 있다고 생각한다.
＊담배 tobacco ＊연구 지원 비용 investment funds ＊~할 자격이 있다 deserve

_____

4 만일 나에게 세계 어디에서든 자원 봉사 활동을 하라고 한다면, 나는 태국에서 자원 봉사하기로 선택할 것이다.
＊자원 봉사하다 volunteer ＊태국 Thailand

_____

5 이러한 이유들 때문에, 나는 사람들이 대학 교육의 경제적 의무를 심각하게 고려해야 한다고 생각한다.
＊경제적인 financial ＊의무 responsibility ＊심각하게 seriously

_____

6 도시권 확대 현상의 결과로, 사람들은 통근할 때 더 멀리 차를 운전하는 경향이 있다.
＊도시권 확대 현상 urban sprawl ＊통근하다 commute ＊더 멀리 farther ＊~하는 경향이 있다 tend to~

_____

7 만일 텔레비전이 없다면, 사람들은 공감대를 훨씬 덜 형성할 것이다.
＊공감대를 형성하다, 공통점을 갖다 have in common

_____

8 학생들이 하루 평균 3시간 인터넷을 사용한다고 가정해 보자.
＊평균 average

_____

9 이것은 범죄율 증가와 한층 높은 신용카드 빚의 원인이다.
＊범죄율 crime rate ＊신용카드 credit card ＊빚 debt

_____

10 여러 가지 이유로 전문인들이 존경을 받는 것은 분명해 보인다.
＊전문인 professional ＊존경하다 respect

_____

다음에 주어진 우리말 문장을 영어로 바꾸어 쓰시오.

11 나는 대학생들에게 전공을 정하기 전에 많은 여러 분야의 사람들과 대화할 것을 권하겠다.
*전공 major *~로 정하다 decide on ~ *분야 field

_____

12 그것이 내가 캠퍼스 밖의 주택에서 사는 것을 선호하는 이유이다.
*캠퍼스 밖의 주택 off-campus housing *선호하다 prefer

_____

13 만일 그것이 나에게 달려 있다면, 나는 고등학교를 졸업하는 학생들에게 그들의 새로운 대학 캠퍼스를 돌아볼 것을 요구할 것이다.
*대학 캠퍼스 college campus *돌아보다, 둘러보다 tour *요구하다 require

_____

14 나의 관심사가 이젠 다르기 때문에, 나의 전공을 바꿀 수 있다면 좋겠다.
*관심사 interest *전공 major

_____

15 우수한 학생들은 자신의 시간을 효율적으로 관리하는 방법을 아는 이들이라는 것에는 의심의 여지가 없다.
*효율적으로 effectively *관리하다 manage

_____

16 새로운 회사에 적응하는 좋은 방법은 다른 직원들이 무엇을 하는지 자세히 관찰하는 것이다.
*적응하다, 익숙해지다 get used to *자세히 closely *관찰하다 observe

_____

17 음주를 하지 않는 것의 이점은 대체로 더 나은 건강 상태를 누릴 수 있다는 것이다.
 ＊대체적으로 in general

_____

18 만일 일주일에 20시간 이상 걸리지 않는다면 나는 대학을 다니는 동안 시간제 근무를 할 것이다.
 ＊걸리다, 차지하다 take up   ＊시간제 근무, 아르바이트 part-time job

_____

19 인생에서 성공하고자 한다면 성실함이 필수적이라는 것은 확실하다.
 ＊성실함 diligence   ＊~에서 성공하다 be successful in ~   ＊필수적인 essential

_____

20 이러한 점에서, 환경을 보호하는 것은 미래의 자연 재해에 대비하는 보험으로 간주될 수 있다.
 ＊자연 재해 natural disasters   ＊~에 대비하는 보험 insurance against ~   ＊간주하다 consider

_____

21 이러한 이유 때문에, 나는 최소한 부모 한 명은 직장 대신 집에 있어야 한다고 생각한다.
 ＊최소한 at least   ＊~대신에 instead of ~

_____

22 나는 사람들이 흡연을 다른 사람들과 어울릴 수 있는 기회로 여긴다고 생각한다.
 ＊흡연 smoking   ＊~와 어울리다 socialize with ~

_____

정답 p.479

3. 예시, 인용, 부연, 요약 표현

❶ ~를 설명하기 위해, -하다
To illustrate ~, 주어 + 동사

이것을 설명하기 위해, 현대 문화에서 춤의 지속적인 인기를 고찰해 볼 수 있다.
To illustrate this, we can consider the continuing popularity of dance in modern culture.

❷ 특히, ~하다
In particular, 주어 + 동사

특히, 서로의 공간을 존중해 주지 않는 것은 룸메이트들 간의 흔한 문제이다.
In particular, not respecting each other's space is a common problem between roommates.

❸ 구체적으로, ~이다
To be specific, 주어 + 동사

구체적으로, 모퉁이에 위치한 방들은 대개 창문을 하나 이상 가지고 있기 때문에 최고이다.
To be specific, corner rooms are the best because they usually have more than one window.

❹ 나의 경험에 따르면, ~이다
From my experience, 주어 + 동사

나의 경험에 따르면, 학생들은 자신들이 필기한 내용을 나중에 복습하면 더 많이 기억하는 경향이 있다.
From my experience, students tend to remember more if they go over their notes later.
＊~을 복습하다 go over ~

❺ 예를 들면, ~이다
For instance, 주어 + 동사

예를 들면, 고등학교 때 항상 TV를 보기 전에 숙제를 끝내는 친구가 있었다.
For instance, I had a friend in high school who always finished her homework before watching TV.

❻ 또 다른 예로, ~이다

In another case, 주어 + 동사

또 다른 예로, 내가 친구에게 조언을 구했을 때 그녀는 어머니께서 하신 말씀과 똑같은 말을 나에게 해주었다.

In another case, I asked a friend for advice and she told me the same thing as my mother had.

❼ 무엇보다도, ~이다

On top of that, 주어 + 동사

무엇보다도, 어떤 이들은 쉽사리 스트레스를 받으며 진정할 시간을 필요로 한다.

On top of that, some people get stressed out easily and need some time to relax.
＊스트레스를 받다 get stressed out

❽ 이해를 돕기 위해, ~하다

To give you an idea, 주어 + 동사

이해를 돕기 위해, 여기 나의 유년 시절의 예가 있다.

To give you an idea, here is an example from my own childhood.

❾ 이러한 예들을 통해 ~를 알 수 있다

I can see that 주어 + 동사 **in these instances**

이러한 예들을 통해 더 나이가 많은 사람의 조언이 유용함을 알 수 있다.

I can see that advice from someone older can be useful **in these instances**.

❿ 어떻게 ~하는지 보여 줄 두 가지 예가 있다

There are two examples to show how 주어 + 동사

어린이들이 그들의 또래들로부터 어떻게 강한 영향을 받는지 보여 줄 두 가지 예가 있다.

There are two examples to show how children are strongly influenced by their peers.
＊또래, 동료 peers

⓫ 그뿐 아니라, ~이다

Not only that, but 주어 + 동사

그뿐 아니라, 아이들의 언어 학습 능력 또한 그때쯤이면 퇴화하기 시작한다.

Not only that, but a child's ability to learn languages also starts to diminish around that time.
＊퇴화하다, 줄어들다 diminish ＊그때쯤이면 around that time

⑫ 연구 결과 ~라는 사실이 지적되어 왔다
Studies have indicated that 주어 + 동사

연구 결과 광고상의 미세한 차이라도 고객들이 특정 상품을 사도록 유도할 수 있다는 사실이 지적되어 왔다.

Studies have indicated that even subtle changes in advertising can induce customers to buy a certain product.

⑬ 전문가들은 ~를 증명해 왔다
Experts have verified that 주어 + 동사

전문가들은 육체적인 활동이 심장 질환의 위험을 상당히 줄여 준다는 것을 증명해 왔다.

Experts have verified that physical activities significantly decrease the risk of heart disease.

⑭ 어떤 사람들은 ~라고 생각한다
Some people presume that 주어 + 동사

어떤 사람들은 학교에서 멀리 사는 학생들이 캠퍼스에서 사는 학생들보다 더 자주 수업에 늦을 것이라고 생각한다.

Some people presume that students who live far away from school are late more often for class than students who live on campus.

⑮ 옛 속담이 말해 주듯, ~이다
As the old saying goes, 주어 + 동사

옛 속담이 말해 주듯, 한 사람의 성격은 그 사람이 친구로 선택한 이들에 반영되어 있다.

As the old saying goes, a person's personality is reflected in the people he or she chooses as friends.

⑯ 다시 말해서, ~이다
In other words, 주어 + 동사

다시 말해서, 혼자 여행하는 것은 고난을 극복하는 법에 대한 교훈이 될 수 있다.

In other words, traveling alone can be a lesson in how to overcome hardship.

⑰ 게다가, ~이다
Moreover / In addition, 주어 + 동사

게다가, 가족들은 자동차의 발전으로 인하여 더 멀리 떨어져 지내는 경향이 있다.

Moreover, families tend to be more spread out due to the wide reach of the car.

⑱ 이런 식으로, ~하다
In this way, 주어 + 동사

이런 식으로, 교사들은 학생들이 더 효과적으로 배울 수 있도록 도와주려는 열의가 더 강력해진다.

In this way, teachers have greater motivation for helping their students learn more effectively.
＊열의, 동기 부여 motivation

⑲ 일반적으로 말해서, ~이다
Generally speaking, 주어 + 동사

일반적으로 말해서, 나는 자동차를 운전하는 것이 환경에 해가 된다고 믿는다.

Generally speaking, I believe driving is harmful to the environment.

⑳ 우리가 알고 있는 것처럼(알다시피), ~이다
As we have seen, 주어 + 동사

알다시피, 사회는 몇몇 중요한 발명품으로부터 많은 혜택을 보았다.

As we have seen, society has benefited greatly from certain significant inventions.

㉑ 실제로, ~이다
As it is, 주어 + 동사

실제로, 잠재적인 지도력을 가진 많은 사람들이 그것을 발달시킬 기회를 전혀 얻지 못한다.

As it is, many people who have potential leadership skills never get a chance to develop them.
＊지도력, 통솔력 leadership skills

㉒ 어느 정도까지는, ~이다
To some extent, 주어 + 동사

어느 정도까지는, 모든 대학들이 학생 모두가 교수들로부터 적절한 관심을 받는 것을 보장해 주려고 한다.

To some extent, all colleges try to ensure that all students receive proper attention from the teaching staff.
＊보장하다, 확실히 하다 ensure

㉓ 간단히 말해서, ~이다
In short, 주어 + 동사

간단히 말해서, 나는 부모들이 자녀들이 TV를 보는 데 얼마 만큼의 시간을 써도 되는지에 대해 분별력이 있어야 한다고 생각한다.

In short, I believe that parents should be selective in how much time their children can spend watching TV.
＊분별력이 있는 selective

㉔ ~를 고려해 볼 때, ~이다.
In view of ~, 주어 + 동사

흡연의 위험성들을 고려해 볼 때, 나는 흡연이 모든 공공장소에서 금지되어야 한다고 믿는다.

In view of the dangers of smoking, I believe that it should be banned from all public spaces.

㉕ 앞서 언급했던 바와 같이, ~이다
As I have mentioned, 주어 + 동사

앞서 언급했던 바와 같이, 알로에는 치료상의 효과가 있는 여러 특성들을 지닌 인기 식물인 것 같다.

As I have mentioned, aloe seems to be a popular plant with many therapeutic qualities.
＊치료상 효과가 있는 therapeutic

㉖ 결론적으로, ~이다
In conclusion, 주어 + 동사

결론적으로, 최고의 직장 동료란 정직하고, 의리가 있으며 협조적인 사람들이다.

In conclusion, the best co-workers are the ones who are honest, loyal, and cooperative.
＊직장동료 co-worker

㉗ 전반적으로, ~이다
Overall, 주어 + 동사

전반적으로, 좋은 이웃들은 믿을 수 있고, 친절하며 자상하다.

Overall, good neighbors are trustworthy, friendly, and caring.
＊믿을 수 있는 trustworthy ＊자상한 caring

㉘ 대체적으로, ~이다
For the most part, 주어 + 동사

대체적으로, 대학의 자금은 모든 학생에게 이익을 주는 도서관에 투자되어야 할 것이다.
For the most part, university funds should go toward library systems that benefit all students.

㉙ 요약하자면, ~이다
To summarize, 주어 + 동사

요약하자면, 컴퓨터 기술이 최대한 효율적으로 존속하게 위해서는 지속적으로 갱신되어야 한다.
To summarize, computer technology must constantly be updated in order to remain as effective as possible.

㉚ 모든 것을 고려해 보면, ~이다
All things considered, 주어 + 동사

모든 것을 고려해 보면, 학생들은 왜 그들이 대학에 다닐 자격이 있는지를 증명할 필요가 있다.
All things considered, students need to prove why they deserve to attend university.

㉛ ~이외에도, 또한 –한다
In addition to ~, 주어 + **also** + 동사

자택 교육을 받은 학생들은 좋은 성적을 받는 것 이외에도 어른을 대하는 데 또한 능숙하다.
In addition to getting good grades, students who are home schooled are **also** highly skilled at dealing with adults.

㉜ 대체로, ~이다
On the whole, 주어 + 동사

대체로, 텔레비전, 전자오락, 인터넷은 사회에 부정적인 영향을 끼쳐 왔다.
On the whole, TV, video games and the Internet have had a negative effect on society.

㉝ 마지막으로 중요한 것은, ~이다
Last but not least, 주어 + 동사

마지막으로 중요한 것은, 전쟁은 누가 옳은가를 결정하는 것이 아니라 누가 남겨지는가를 결정한다는 것이다.
Last but not least, war never decides who is right, but who is left.

녹색으로 주어진 표현에 유의하여, 다음의 우리말 문장을 영어로 바꾸어 쓰시오.

1 앞서 언급했던 바와 같이, 많은 대학생들은 주말 동안 단체 여행을 계획한다.
＊주말 동안 over the weekends ＊단체 여행 group trip

_____

2 간단히 말해서, 나는 어린이들이 건전한 성격을 키우기 위해서는 애정을 필요로 한다고 느낀다.
＊건전한 성격 healtly personality ＊~하기 위해서 in order to ~ ＊애정 affection

_____

3 이러한 예들을 통해, 결단력이 정말 성과를 낸다는 것을 알 수 있다.
＊결단력 determination ＊성과가 나다 pay off

_____

4 실제로, 많은 학생들은 대학의 상담 서비스를 최대한 활용하지 않는다.
＊상담 서비스 counceling service ＊~을 최대한 활용하다 use ~ to one's full advantage

_____

5 그러한 사건들이 어떻게 직원들의 생산력에 영향을 끼치는지 보여 줄 두 가지 예가 있다.
＊생산력, 생산성 productivity ＊영향을 끼치다 affect

_____

6 이런 식으로, 학생들은 자신들이 존경하고 흠모하는 사람들로부터 배울 수 있다.
＊존경하다 respect ＊흠모하다 admire

---

7 요약하자면, 성공적인 학생의 가장 귀중한 도구는 성실함과 시간 관리이다.
＊귀중한 invaluable ＊성실함 diligence ＊시간 관리 time management

---

8 특히, 많은 아이들이 남동생이나 여동생의 탄생을 받아들이는 데 어려움을 겪는다.
＊받아들이다 accept ＊~하는데 어려움을 겪다 have difficulty (in) ~ing

---

9 무엇보다도, 대학에 진학하는 모든 학생들이 실제로 졸업하는 것은 아니다.
＊대학에 진학하다 enter a university ＊실제로 actually

---

10 우리가 알고 있는 것처럼, 핸드폰은 사람들이 서로를 덜 배려하도록 만드는 경향이 있다.
＊핸드폰 mobile phone ＊배려하는, 사려 깊은 considerate ＊~하는 경향이 있다 tend to ~

다음에 주어진 우리말 문장을 영어로 바꾸어 쓰시오.

11 옛 속담이 말해 주듯, "필요는 발명의 어머니이다."
＊필요 necessity ＊발명 invention

---

12 이해를 돕기 위해, 여기 비현실적인 성공담의 예가 있다.
＊비현실적인, 있음직하지 않은 unlikely ＊성공담 success story

---

13 다시 말해서, 때때로 사람은 실수로부터 배우기 위해 실수를 해야 한다.
＊~하기 위해 in order to ~ ＊실수하다 make mistakes

---

14 전반적으로, 내 인생에서 가장 즐거웠던 시간은 내가 고등학교를 졸업한 후의 여름이었다.
＊즐거운 enjoyable ＊~를 졸업하다 graduate from ~

---

15 돈을 버는 것 이외에도, 아버지들이 요리와 집안일을 돕는 것 또한 보기 드문 것은 아니다.
＊돈을 벌다 make money ＊집안일 chores ＊보기 드문 uncommon

---

16 전문직들의 이점들을 고려해 볼 때, 전문직이 각광받는 것은 이상한 일이 아니다.
＊전문직 professional career　＊각광받다 be sought after　＊~이 이상한 일이 아니다 no wonder~

_____

17 일반적으로 말해서, 의학과나 법학과와 같은 전문적인 학부의 입학은 극도로 경쟁적이다.
＊전문적인 professional　＊(대학의) 학부 faculty　＊입학 admission　＊경쟁적인 competitive

_____

18 어느 정도까지는, 모든 여행객들은 숙박시설에 있어서 아늑함과 청결함을 원한다.
＊숙박시설 accommodations　＊아늑함 comfort　＊청결함 cleanliness

_____

19 결론적으로, 나는 좋은 친구란 의리 있고 신뢰할 수 있는 사람이라고 믿는다.
＊의리가 있는 loyal　＊신뢰할 수 있는 trustworthy

_____

20 전문가들은 음식에 사용된 방부제가 암 발생률에 영향을 미칠 수 있다는 사실을 증명
해 왔다.
＊방부제 preservative　＊암 발생률 cancer rate　＊영향을 미치다 affect

_____

정답 p.479

지금까지 상황별 표현을 공부했으니, 어떤 주제에 대해서 글을 쓰더라도 자신 있을 것 같다. 그런데 똑같은 상황별 표현을 활용하더라도 그 안에 담아낼 주제에 대한 표현을 잘 모르면 역시 어려움에 봉착하게 된다. 앞서 살펴본 '중고생 교복 착용'에 대한 글을 그대로 '공공장소 흡연'에 대한 글로 바꾸어 쓴다고 가정해 보자.

나는 **공공장소에서의 흡연**에 반대한다.	I object to **smoking in public**.
여기에는 여러 가지 이유가 있다.	There are several reasons for this.
먼저, **간접 흡연**이 건강에 해롭다는 것은 분명하다	First of all, it is clear that **secondhand smoking** is bad for people's health.
게다가, **비흡연자**의 권리가 보호되어야 한다는 것에는 의심의 여지가 없다.	Furthermore, there is no question that the rights of **non-smokers** should be protected.
이러한 이유로, 나는 공공장소에서 흡연 **금지**가 실시되어야 한다고 생각한다.	For these reasons, I think that a **ban on** smoking in public should be implemented.

이 때 앞서 배운 것과 같이 '나는 ~에 반대한다(I object to~)', '~는 분명하다(It is clear that~)' 등 문장의 틀을 알고 있더라도 '공공장소에서의 흡연(smoking in public)', '간접 흡연(secondhand smoking)', '비흡연자(non-smokers)'과 같은 주제에 관련된 표현을 다양하게 알고 있어야 해당 주제에 대해서 막힘 없이 글을 쓸 수 있다.

이렇게 글이라는 '요리'를 만들 때 그 '식재료'가 되는 것이 주제별 표현이다. 따라서 다양한 분야에서 각각 자주 쓰이는 표현들을 많이 익혀 놓으면 여러 가지 주제에 대해 글을 쓰게 되더라도 자신의 의견을 풍부하게 나타낼 수 있다.

1. 교육, 가정, 사회에 관한 표현

① 청소년 문화
youth culture

반항은 미국 청소년 문화의 중요한 일부분이다.

Rebellion is an important part of **youth culture** in the United States.

② 또래나 동료 간의 압박
peer pressure

긍정적인 동료 간의 압박은 스터디 그룹에서 학생들이 서로를 자극하는데 활용될 수 있다.

Positive **peer pressure** can be applied in study groups to help students motivate each other.
＊자극하다, 동기를 부여하다 motivate

③ 인격 발달
personality development

유치원에서의 인격 발달은 아이에게 한 집단의 일원으로 상호 작용하는 방법을 가르치는데 중점을 둔다.

Personality development in kindergarten is geared towards teaching children how to interact as part of a group.
＊~에 중점을 두다, ~에 맞추다 gear towards ~

④ 동아리 모임
club meeting

동아리 모임은 학생들이 교실 밖에서 서로 만나 사교 활동을 할 수 있도록 한다.

Club meetings allow students to join each other for social activities outside of the classroom.

⑤ 학과 외 활동
extracurricular activities

학과 외 활동에 참가하는 것은 사교 관계를 넓힐 수 있는 좋은 방법이다.

Participating in **extracurricular activities** is a good way to widen their social network.
＊사교 관계 social network

❻ 대입 시험
college entrance exam

학생들이 대입 시험을 준비할 수 있도록 도와주는 수천 개의 웹사이트가 존재한다.

Thousands of websites are available to help students prepare for their **college entrance exams**.

❼ 캠퍼스를 벗어난 생활
off-campus life

사회생활을 시작하기 전에 최소한 일 년간 캠퍼스를 벗어난 생활 경험해 보는 것은 좋은 생각이다.

It is a good idea to experience at least a year of **off-campus life** before moving out into the real world.

❽ 학습 과정
learning process

새로운 일자리에 적응하는 것은 회사 문화에 대한 이해로부터 시작되는 학습 과정이다.

Adapting to a new workplace is a **learning process** that begins with an understanding of the company culture.
＊적응하다 adapt

❾ 팀을 이루어 일하다
work in teams

소규모 공동체의 이웃들은 지역적인 난관들을 해결하기 위해 팀을 이루어 일할 가능성이 더 많다.

Neighbors in small communities are more likely to **work in teams** to overcome local challenges.
＊난관, 문제점 challenges

❿ 어른이 되는 것
growing into adulthood

이전의 세대에서 어른이 된다는 것은 직장을 구하고, 결혼하고, 자녀를 가지는 것을 의미했다.

In previous generations, **growing into adulthood** meant getting a job, getting married and having kids.

⑪ 집안일
household chores / household tasks

집안일을 맡은 젊은이들은 시간을 관리하는 법을 배운다.
Young people who are assigned **household chores** learn how to organize their time.

⑫ 사회적 관례
social customs

사회적 관례는 각국의 국민들이 어떻게 서로를 맞이하고 작별을 고하는지 결정한다.
Social customs determine how each country's citizens greet each other and say goodbye.

⑬ 본보기, 모범
role model

좋은 경영자는 그 자신이 프로답게 행동함으로써 자신의 직원들에게 모범이 되어야 한다.
A good manager should be a **role model** to his employees by conducting himself in a professional manner.

⑭ 엄격한 규정
strict regulation

희귀 야생동물들의 천연 서식지는 엄격한 규정으로 보호되어야 한다.
The natural habitats of endangered wildlife must be protected with **strict regulations**.

⑮ 대중 정서
popular sentiment

금연 지역을 옹호하는 대중 정서가 공공장소에서의 흡연이 금지되어야 하는 이유 중의 하나이다.
Popular sentiment in favor of smoke-free zones is one reason why lighting up should be banned in public places.
＊~을 옹호하는 in favor of~　＊(특히 담배에) 불을 붙이는 것 lighting up

⑯ 특권을 가진 사람들
privileged people

광고주들은 평균적인 소비자들에게 비싼 명품을 구입함으로써 특권을 가진 사람들처럼 느끼도록 장려한다.
Advertisers encourage average consumers to feel like **privileged people** by buying expensive brand name goods.

⑰ **사교 능력**
social skills

사교 능력이 떨어지는 사람은 회사 문화에 적응하는 것을 어려워할 것이다.

A person with poor **social skills** will have a hard time fitting into a company's culture.

⑱ **개발도상국**
developing country

개발도상국에서는 빈부의 격차가 대개 매우 크다.

In a **developing country**, the gap between the rich and the poor is often quite large.
＊격차, 틈 gap

⑲ **선진국**
advanced country

대부분의 선진국에서는 고속 전송을 위한 인터넷 기반이 갖추어져 왔다.

In most **advanced countries**, the Internet infrastructure has been equipped for high-speed transmissions.
＊기반, 기초 구조 infrastructure   ＊전송 transmission

⑳ **~의 모국**
one's native country

자신의 모국이 아닌 해외에서 대학을 다니는 것은 교육적, 문화적, 그리고 언어적 자극을 제공한다.

Attending college outside **one's native country** allows for educational, cultural, and linguistic stimulation.
＊자극, 고무 stimulation

㉑ **잘 차려입다**
dress up

새로운 고객과의 첫 만남을 위해서는 정장으로 잘 차려입는 편이 낫다.

For the first meeting with a new client, it is better to **dress up** in a nice suit.

㉒ **신뢰를 쌓다**
build up trust

이사를 많이 다니는 사람들은 새로운 관계에서 재빠르게 신뢰를 쌓는 경향이 있다.

People who move a number of times tend to **build up trust** quickly in new relationships.

㉓ 장래성 있는 젊은이, 전도 유망한 젊은이
promising youth

불우한 환경에 처한 장래성 있는 젊은이들은 대학 장학금을 받아야 한다.

Promising youth from disadvantaged backgrounds should receive college scholarships.
*불우한, 혜택 받지 못한 disadvantaged

㉔ 잘 교육받은 사람
well-educated person

나의 직장 동료는 잘 교육받은 사람으로, 나는 그의 의견을 존중한다.

My collegue is a **well-educated person** whose views I respect.

㉕ 인성을 함양하다
build strong character

인성을 함양하는 것은 어떤 학문적, 경제적 성공보다 더 중요하다.

Building strong character is more important than any academic or financial success.

㉖ 국제적 위기
international crisis

지구 온난화는 모든 정부에 의해 해결되어야 하는 국제적 위기이다.

Global warming is an **international crisis** that must be addressed by all governments.
*지구 온난화 global warming   *(문제를) 해결하다, 시정하다 address

㉗ 관리직
managerial position

대부분의 사람들은 관리직에 필요한 기술과 지도력을 가지고 있지 않다.

Most people do not have the skills and leadership abilities necessary for **managerial positions**.

㉘ 규칙을 정하다
establish a rule

부모들은 아이들의 행동에 대한 규칙을 정해야 한다.

Parents must **establish rules** for their children's behavior.

또래 집단	a peer group
한 사람의 어린 시절	a person's childhood years
십대가 되다	enter one's teens / reach one's teens
성숙 과정	the maturation process
인생에서 가장 중요한 시기	the most important stage in one's life
인격 발달	personality development
이성	the opposite sex
잠재력	potential
대학 1학년	college freshman
체육	physical education
적성 검사	an aptitude test
수업 출석	class attendance
강제 출석	compulsory attendance
참고서	a reference book
지도 교수	an academic advisor
학습 프로그램	academic programs
입학 지원자	a candidate for admission
입학 지원서	an application form
입학 요건	requirements for admission
초등교육	elementary education
중등교육	secondary education
그룹 과제	group assignment
남녀 공학	co-ed school ↔ single-sex school
야외 활동	outdoor activities
정규 교육	formal schooling
수준 높은 교육	a quality education
교육적인 효과	an educational benefit
전인 교육	a well-rounded education
의견을 공유하다	share ideas
좋은 성적을 받다	get good grades

시험에서 부정 행위를 하다	cheat on tests
나쁜 성적을 기록하다	make poor marks
유학하다	study abroad
실험하다	do experiments
~를 전공하다	specialize in ~
유용한 기술을 배우다	learn valuable skills
개별적인 관심	individualized attention
심한 경쟁	heavy competition
잘못된 생각	misguided belief
타협하다	make a compromise
뒤처지다	fall behind
긍정적인 자아상을 형성하다	develop a positive self-image
잘 연마된	well-cultivated
심층 연구	in-depth research
팀웍을 기르다	build teamwork
경쟁률을 높이다	enhance competitiveness
심하게 다그치다, 독려하다	push hard
주의를 ~로부터 돌리다	divert one's attention from ~
대학 학위	a college degree
학위를 따다	earn a degree
등록금	tuition
시행 착오	trial and error
이력을 쌓다	build up one's resume
많은 분야에서 뛰어나다	excel in many areas
편부모	a single parent
가족 모임	a family gathering
안락한 분위기	a cozy atmosphere
아이를 다그치다	push one's children
정서적인 애착	an emotional attachment
일생의 친구	a lifelong friend

지역 사회의 번영	a community's prosperity
공인	public figures
노인	senior citizens
물려주다	hand down
젊은 세대	the younger generation
세대 차이	the generation gap
미래 세대	future generations
특권을 남용하다	abuse the privilege
일반 대중	the general public
여론을 조사하다	poll the public
여론에 호소하다	appeal to public opinion
협동심	feelings of cooperation
일체감	a sense of unity
소속감	a sense of belonging
상호 신뢰	mutual trust
인접 지역	a neighboring community
벽촌	a remote region
소수 민족 집단	ethnic groups
문명화된 사회	civilized society
빠르게 움직이는 세상	a fast-paced world
늘 변화하는 세상	an ever-changing world
지도자의 책임	leader's responsibility
지도력	leadership skills
사회적 발전	a social progress
사교 모임	social gathering
사회적 규범	social norms
노숙자 수용 시설	a homeless shelter
인구 증가	population growth / a population increase
국가 기반 시설	the country's infrastructure
사회 보장 제도	the social security system

국민의 복지를 증진하다	promote the public good
공무원	a civil servant
국가 정체성	national identity
정책을 실행하다	carry out a policy
공공 시설	public facilities
국제적 차원에서	on a global scale
사기를 북돋우다	boost morale
공통점	common ground
권리를 침해하다	violate a right
유행이 되다	be a growing trend
엄격한 규칙을 부과하다	impose strict rules
논란을 불러 일으키다	provoke controversy
사생활을 침해하다	invade one's privacy
활기찬 주변 환경을 만들다	create a vibrant neighborhood
좋은 모범이 되다	set a good example
환경 문제를 고려하다	consider environmental concerns
상호 교류 기술	interpersonal skills
대화 기술	conversational skills
~와 연락하다	get in touch with ~
공통 관심사를 공유하다	share common interests
나라마다 다르다	vary from country to country
국가적 특징	national characteristics

녹색으로 주어진 표현에 유의하여, 다음의 우리말 문장을 영어로 바꾸어 쓰시오.

1 신입생들은 학교 생활을 하는 동안 자신들의 기숙사 방에 종종 정서적인 애착을 키운다.
＊신입생 freshman ＊기숙사 dormitory(= dorm) ＊키우다 develop

_____

2 대학 시절은 일반적으로 인생에서 가장 중요한 시기로 여겨진다.
＊대학 시절 university years ＊일반적으로, 널리 widely

_____

3 청소년 문화는 지난 50년간 극적으로 변화해 왔다.
＊극적으로 dramatically

_____

4 나는 특히 버스나 기차가 만원일 때 노인들에게 자리를 양보하려고 한다.
＊만원이다 be crowded ＊자리를 양보하다 give one's seat up

_____

5 어떤 대학들은 엄격한 강제 출석 정책을 고려하고 있다.
＊엄격한 strict ＊정책 policy ＊고려하다 consider

_____

6 두 룸메이트는 친구들이 언제 기숙사 방을 방문해도 되는지에 대해 타협했다.
  *룸메이트 roommate *기숙사 방 dorm room

---

7 자전거 동아리 모임에서 회원들은 유지 보수와 타는 기술에 대한 정보를 교환한다.
  *유지 보수 maintenance *타다 ride *정보를 교환하다 exchange information

---

8 미국에서는 소개받은 사람 모두와 악수를 하는 것이 사회적 관례이다.
  *~에게 소개되다 be introduced to *~와 악수하다 shake hands with ~

---

9 교환 학생들은 자신이 공부하게 될 나라의 사회적 규범에 익숙해져야 한다.
  *교환 학생 exchange student *~에 익숙해지다 farmiliarize oneself with ~

---

10 학과 외 활동은 사교 기술을 향상시키는 데 도움이 되고, 교실에서 배울 수 없는 교훈을 가르쳐 준다.
  *사교 기술 social skills *향상시키다, 강화하다 enhance *교훈을 가르치다 teach lessons

---

다음에 주어진 우리말 문장을 영어로 바꾸어 쓰시오.

11 국기와 국가는 국가 정체성의 상징이다.
＊국가 national anthem ＊상징 symbol

_____

12 심층 연구를 시행하지 않고서 어떤 이론이 옳다고 증명하는 것은 불가능하다.
＊시행하다 conduct ＊이론 theory ＊증명하다 prove ＊불가능한 impossible

_____

13 어떤 사람들은 아직도 대학 졸업장이 직장을 보장해 줄 것이라는 잘못된 생각을 가지고 있다.
＊아직도 still ＊대학 졸업장 university degree ＊보장 guarantee ＊(믿음을) 가지다 hold

_____

14 두 사람이 만나면, 그들은 공통점을 찾기 위해 서로에게 질문을 한다.
＊~하기 위해 in order to ~

_____

15 아버지는 아들에게 본보기이므로, 아버지의 태도와 행동은 아들에게 전해질 것이다.
＊태도 attitude ＊행동 behavior ＊~에게 전해지다 pass onto ~

_____

16 대학들은 악명 높은 연설자들을 캠퍼스에 초대함으로써 종종 논란을 불러일으킨다.
＊악명 높은 notorious ＊연설자 guest speaker

_____

17 부모들은 그들이 매우 화가 났을 때라도 고함을 지르지 않음으로써 자녀들에게 좋은 모범이 되어야 한다.
＊화가 나다 be upset ＊고함을 지르다 shout

_____

18 효과적으로 팀을 이루어 일하기 위해서는, 사람들은 타인의 의견을 잘 받아들여야 한다.
＊효과적으로 effectively ＊의견 idea ＊~을 잘 받아들이다 be receptive to ~

_____

19 십대가 되는 것은 모든 아이들의 인생에서 흥분되는 사건이다.
＊흥분되는 exciting ＊사건 event

_____

20 실수하는 것은 학습 과정의 중요한 부분이다.
＊실수하다 make mistakes

_____

정답 p.480

2. 건강, 환경, 생활에 관한 표현

❶ 수명
life span

어떤 사람이 애완동물을 기른다면, 그는 그 애완동물의 수명 내내 돌볼 준비가 되어 있어야 한다.

If a person gets a pet, he should be prepared to take care of it over its entire **life span**.
＊~을 돌보다 take care of ~

❷ 평균 수명
life expectancy

평균 수명은 집안의 (의학적) 내력과 개인의 생활 방식같은 많은 요인에 의해 영향을 받는다.

Life expectancy is influenced by a number of factors, such as family history and personal lifestyle.
＊집안 내력 family history

❸ 의료 서비스, 치료
medical care / health care

의료 서비스의 진보는 의학의 발달과 직접적으로 연관되어 있다.

Improvements in **health care** are directly related to advancements in medical science.
＊발달 advancements

❹ 치명적인 질병
deadly disease

어린이들에게 치명적인 질병에 대한 예방 접종을 하는 것이 선진국에서 사망률을 저하시켰다.

Vaccinating children against **deadly diseases** has lowered mortality rates in advanced countries.
＊예방 접종을 하다 vaccinate ＊사망률 mortality rate

❺ 면역 체계
immune system

규칙적인 운동은 면역 체계를 강화시키고, 따라서 질병을 예방하는 데 도움을 준다.

Regular exercise strengthens the **immune system** and, therefore, helps prevent sickness.

❻ 건강을 유지하다
stay in shape

낮에는 내내 책상에 앉아 있고 밤새 소파에 앉아 있으면서 건강을 유지하는 것은 어렵다.

It is difficult to **stay in shape** when sitting at a desk all day and then sitting on a couch all night.

❼ 범죄율
crime rate

소규모의 지역 사회들은 낮은 범죄율의 이점을 지닌다.

Small communities have the advantage of a lower **crime rate**.
*지역 사회 community

❽ 시골 지역
rural area

시골 지역에서 자라는 것은 혼잡한 도심에서는 불가능한 자연 친화력을 가질 수 있게 한다.

Growing up in a **rural area** allows for a close connection with nature which is impossible in a crowded urban area.

❾ 식량 부족
food shortage

지난 여름의 심각한 가뭄 이후, 이번 겨울의 식량 부족이 예견된다.

A **food shortage** is predicted this winter after a severe drought last summer.
*가뭄 drought

❿ 대규모 파괴
mass destruction

쇼핑몰을 건축하기 위한 지역 자연 환경의 대규모 파괴는 어리석고 무책임하다.

The **mass destruction** of local wildlife to build a shopping mall is ridiculous and irresponsible.

⓫ 신변 안전
personal safety

야간의 캠퍼스 내 신변 안전은 정기적으로 순찰을 도는 24시간 경비 팀에 의해 보장된다.

Personal safety on campus at night is ensured with 24-hour security teams on regular patrol.
*순찰, 순회 patrol

⑫ 환경 문제
environmental concern

지난 여름의 혹서기 동안 지구 온난화의 환경 문제는 새로운 국면에 도달했다.
Environmental concerns over global warming reached new levels during last summer's heat wave.
＊지구 온난화 global warming　＊혹서기 heat wave

⑬ 병에 걸리다
come down with

만약 당신이 병에 걸려 빠른 진단을 원한다면, 인터넷에서 몇 분 이내에 알아낼 수 있다.
If you **come down with** a sickness and want a fast diagnosis, it can be found online within minutes.

⑭ 생활 수준
standard of living / level of lifestyle

각 세대마다 생활 수준은 과학기술의 혁신으로 인하여 개선된다.
In each generation, the **standard of living** improves with new technological innovations.

⑮ 시간이 소모되는 일
time-consuming activity

인스턴트 음식이 많이 있으므로, 오늘날 식사 준비는 더 이상 시간이 소모되는 일이 아니다.
Modern food preparation is no longer a **time-consuming activity**, as many ready-to-eat meals are available.
＊인스턴트 음식 ready-to-eat meals

⑯ 남겨진
left over

스포츠에 너무 많은 에너지를 소비한다면, 공부하기에 충분한 에너지가 남아 있지 않을지도 모른다.
If too much energy is spent on sports, there might not be enough energy **left over** for one's studies.

⑰ 최우선 순위
top priority

오늘날의 젊은이들에겐 평생 직장이 반드시 최우선 순위는 아니다.
For young people today, the **top priority** is not necessarily a lifetime job.

⑱ 내적 가치

intrinsic quality

클래식 음악의 내적 가치를 정의하기는 어렵지만, 음악 자체는 확실히 즐겁다.

While the **intrinsic quality** of classical music is difficult to define, the sounds themselves are certainly pleasing.

＊즐거운 pleasing

⑲ 스트레스 없는 삶

stress-free life

명상, 요가, 그리고 완화 기법은 사람으로 하여금 스트레스 없는 삶으로 인도할 수 있다.

Meditation, yoga, and relaxation techniques can lead a person to a **stress-free life**.

＊완화 기법 relaxation techniques

⑳ ~의 사생활을 존중하다

respect the privacy of ~

룸메이트들은 방에 들어가기 전에 노크를 함으로써 서로의 사생활을 존중해야 한다.

Roommates should **respect the privacy of** others by knocking before entering.

＊노크하다 knock

㉑ 나쁜 습관을 고치다

break a bad habit

흡연 같은 나쁜 습관을 고치기 위한 효과적인 방법은 껌을 씹는 것과 같은 새로운 행동으로 그것을 대체하는 것이다.

An effective way to **break a bad habit** such as smoking is to substitute it with a new behavior, such as chewing gum.

＊대체하다 substitute

㉒ ~에 헌신하다, ~에 전념하다

be dedicated to ~

만일 자녀들이 성공하기를 진심으로 원한다면 부모들은 그들의 교육적인 필요에 헌신할 필요가 있다.

Parents need to **be dedicated to** their children's educational needs if they genuinely want their kids to succeed.

＊진심으로 genuinely　＊교육적 필요 educational needs

㉓ 스트레스를 많이 받는
stressed out

당신이 바꿀 수 없는 일들에 대해 스트레스를 많이 받는 것은 무의미하다.

There is no point in getting **stressed out** about things you cannot change.
＊~하는 것은 무의미하다 there is no point in ~ing

㉔ ~에 대해 까다로운
particular about ~

당신이 만약 숙소의 상태에 대해 까다로운 편이 아니라면, 값싼 숙소는 찾기 쉽다.

If you are not **particular about** the quality of the place, a cheap accommodation is easy to find.
＊숙소 accommodation

㉕ 약점을 극복하다
overcome a weakness

약점을 극복하는데 가장 효과적인 방법은 자신의 사고방식을 바꾸는 것이다.

The best way to **overcome a weakness** is to change one's thoughts.

㉖ 중요한 역할을 하다
play an important role

학과 외 활동은 학생의 사회생활에 중요한 역할을 한다.

Extracurricular activities can **play an important role** in a student's social life.
＊사회생활 social life

㉗ 연 1회의 정기 건강 검진
annual check-up

직장에서는 직원들이 매년 정기 건강 검진을 받도록 요구해야 한다.

Workplaces should require their employees to get **annual check-ups**.

㉘ 대중교통
public transportation

사람들은 대중교통을 이용하고 승용차 사용을 줄이도록 노력해야 한다.

People should try to use **public transportation** and cut back on their automobile usage.
＊~을 줄이다, 삭감하다 cut back on ~   ＊사용 usage

㉙ 교통 체증
traffic congestion / traffic jams

교통 체증은 당장 처리되어야 하는 중요한 문제이다.
Traffic congestion is a major problem that must be addressed now.

㉚ 분별력 있는 사람
level-headed person

분별력 있는 사람은 후회할 만한 말이나 행동을 하지 않는다.
A **level-headed person** does not say or do things that he will regret.

㉛ 성가신 것, 성가신 사람
pain in the neck

성가신 사람을 다루는 최선의 해결책은 그 사람을 무시하는 것이다.
The best solution to dealing with a person who is being a **pain in the neck** is to ignore him.
＊다루다 deal with

㉜ 긍정적인 시각을 유지하다
maintain a positive outlook

인생에서의 성공은 삶에 대한 긍정적인 시각을 유지하는 데 달려 있다.
Success in life depends on **maintaining a positive outlook** on life.

㉝ 내키지 않는 일, 반갑지 않은 일
uninviting task

사람들은 내키지 않는 일을 피하려 하지 말고 그것을 좋은 인격을 발달시키는 한 방법으로써 반겨야 한다.
One should not avoid **uninviting tasks**, but welcome them as a way to improve one's good character.
＊좋은 인격, 성품 good character

㉞ ~에 대해 유난을 떨다, 야단법석을 떨다
make a big fuss over ~

사소한 일에 대해 유난을 떠는 사람들은 다른 사람과 같이 일을 하는데 어려움을 겪는다.
People who **make a big fuss over** small matters have a difficult time working with others.
＊ ~하는 데 어려움을 겪다 have a difficult time ~ing

냉동 식품	frozen food
균형 잡힌 식단	a well-balanced diet
건강에 좋은 음식	healthy food
좋아하는 요리	a favorite dish
중요한 영양소	valuable nutrition
성분, 재료	ingredients
지방 함유와 열량이 높은	high in fat and calories
비위생적인	unsanitary
외국 음식	foreign cuisine
맛있는 음식을 즐기다	enjoy a delicious meal
적절하게 영양이 공급된	properly nourished
필요한 영양소가 결여되다	lack necessary nutrients
식단을 계획하다	plan meals
식료품 구입, 장보기	grocery shopping
음식을 배달시키다	get food delivered
음식 가판대	food stands
의료 시설	medical facilities
최신 의약품	cutting-edge medicine
항생제	antibiotics
의학 기술	medical technology
병이 나다	get sick
충치	cavities
간접 흡연	secondhand smoking
나쁜 시력	poor eyesight
고혈압	high blood pressure
심장 마비	a heart attack
상처로부터 생긴 감염	an infection from a cut
약물 중독	(a) drug addiction
만성 질병	chronic disease
담배를 많이 피우는 사람	heavy-smoker

(환자 등이) 위급한 상태	critical condition
건강에 위협이 되는 요소들	health risks
신체의 건강	physical fitness
평생의 건강	lifelong physical health
스트레스를 해소하다	relieve stress / escape stress
매일의 운동	daily exercise
신체적 능력	physical ability
신체 훈련	physical training
치명적인 사고	a fatal accident
장애인	handicapped people / disabled people
환경 보존	environmental conservation
환경 친화적인 정책	environmentally-friendly policy
생태계를 보호하다	preserve the ecosystem
개발되지 않은 땅	untouched land / undeveloped land
천연 자원	natural resources
재생되지 않는 자원	a non-renewable resource
환경 파괴	environmental destruction
지구 온난화	global warming
공장 폐기물	factory wastes
기업들의 쓰레기 투기	corporate dumping
악순환	a vicious cycle
대중교통	public transportation
운송 시스템	transportation systems
평화롭고 건전한 환경	a peaceful and healthy environment
범죄 예방	crime prevention
교통 혼잡을 완화하다	ease traffic congestion
교통 정체에 갇히다	be stuck in traffic
부산물	a by-product
세심한 결정	a careful decision
깊이 뿌리박힌 편견	a deep-rooted prejudice

중립적인 입장을 취하다	take the middle ground
흔들리지 않는 믿음	an unwavering belief
긍정적인 시각	optimistic view ↔ pessimistic view
인간 본성	human nature
근시안적인 접근	a short-sighted approach
보통 사람	an average person
정당화할 수 있는 이유	a justifiable reason
사고력	thinking ability
상식	common sense
기억력	memory power
의지력	will power
지적 가치가 있는	intellectually rewarding
지적 능력	intellectual capabilities
지각, 자각	a sense of awareness
책임감	a sense of responsibility
돌이킬 수 없는 손상	irreparable damage
순전한 운	pure luck
힘든 하루	an exhausting day
어려움을 극복하다	surmount difficulties
불공평한 비난	unfair criticism
한번에 하나씩 해결하다	take it one moment at a time
조치를 취하다	take steps
다른 의견을 가지다	hold a different opinion
외모	external appearance / physical appearance
인기를 얻다	gain popularity
바른 결단을 내리다	make correct decisions
당황하다, 겁먹다	feel panic
행운을 바라다	keep one's fingers crossed
요구에 부합하다, 수요를 맞추다	meet demand
~을 참다	put up with ~

결론에 도달하다	reach a conclusion
목표에 도달하다	reach one's goals
경험을 나누다	share one's experience
문제로부터 멀리 떨어져 있다	stay out of trouble
행동을 취하다	take actions
신중하게	with discretion
일찍 일어나는 사람	an early bird
늦게 자는 사람	a night owl
충만한 삶	a fulfilling life
신뢰도, 신뢰성	reliability
신뢰할 만한 친구	a reliable friend
무분별한 태도로	in an irrational manner
즐겁고 재미있는 방식	an enjoyable and fun manner
과거의 경험을 떠올리다	recall past experiences
높은 목표를 세우다	set a high goal
자부심	self-esteem
비판적으로 생각하다	think critically
같은 일상을 유지하다	maintain a routine schedule
긴장을 유발하다	generate tension
시간 엄수(하는 성격)	punctuality
안심하다	feel secure
우선 순위를 정하다	set priorities
주의를 끌다	draw one's attention
소송을 걸다	file a suit against
어려운 시기를 겪다	go through a hard time
기력을 회복하다	recharge one's batteries

녹색으로 주어진 표현에 유의하여, 다음의 우리말 문장을 영어로 바꾸어 쓰시오.

1 유독 폐기물은 핵 발전소의 유감스러운 부산물이다.
＊유독 폐기물 toxic waste　＊핵 발전소 nuclear powerplant　＊유감스러운 unfortunate

_____

2 학생들은 대개 교수진과 대학 사이의 노동 분쟁에 있어서 중립적인 입장을 취한다.
＊대개, 보통 usually　＊교수진 teaching staff　＊노동 분쟁 labor dispute

_____

3 노인들은 나이가 들면서 만성 질병에 더 취약해진다.
＊나이 들다 age　＊~에 취약한, 상처 받기 쉬운 vulnerable to ~

_____

4 지구 온난화는 산불을 일으키는 악순환의 일부로서, 이 산불은 지구 온난화를 더욱 초래한다.
＊지구 온난화 global warming　＊산불 forest fires　＊일으키다, 원인이 되다 contribute to　＊초래하다 cause

_____

5 시끄러운 음악이 있는 파티나 콘서트에 참석하는 것은 사람의 청력에 돌이킬 수 없는 손상을 가할 수 있다.
＊시끄러운 loud　＊참석하다 attend　＊청력 hearing

_____

6 지하 주차장을 건설하는 것은 캠퍼스 내 교통 혼잡을 완화할 수 있을 것이다.
*지하 주차장 underground parking lot *건설하다 construct *캠퍼스 내 on campus

---

7 보도에서 20달러 지폐를 발견한다면, 그것은 순전한 운인 경우이다.
*보도 sidewalk *20달러 지폐 twenty-dollar bill

---

8 온라인상으로 재택근무를 하는 것은 장거리 통근 없이 스트레스 없는 삶을 누리게 해 준다.
*온라인상으로 재택근무하다 work online from home *통근 commute

---

9 교내 서점이 추가 주문을 하더라도, 여전히 특정 교재에 대한 수요를 맞추기 어려울지도 모른다.
*교내 서점 campus bookstore *추가 주문하다 order extra copies *특정한 certain *교재 textbook

---

10 규칙적인 운동은 건강을 유지하기 위하여 모든 사람이 따라야 할 기본 공식이다.
*규칙적인 regular *따르다 follow *기본 공식 basic formula

다음에 주어진 우리말 문장을 영어로 바꾸어 쓰시오.

11 범죄율이 증가함에 따라 경찰에 대한 국민의 신용은 하락한다.
＊증가하다 increase　＊국민의 public　＊신용 confidence　＊하락하다, 줄어들다 diminish

_____

12 일부 과학자들은 인간의 수명이 언젠가 200살에 도달할 것이라고 믿는다.
＊언젠가 someday　＊도달하다 reach

_____

13 이 대학은 최신 의약품의 연구와 개발로 유명하다.
＊연구와 개발 research and development (R&D)　＊~로 유명하다 be famous for ~

_____

14 감기에 걸리고 싶지 않으면 옷을 따뜻하게 입어야 한다.
＊감기 cold　＊따뜻하게 옷을 입다 dress warmly

_____

15 아르바이트를 하지 않는 학생들은 자신의 재정 문제를 신중하게 처리해야 한다.
＊아르바이트 part-time job　＊개인적인 personal　＊처리하다 handle

_____

16 연구 결과는 간접 흡연이 직접 들이마시는 담배 연기보다 더 유독하다는 것을 보여 왔다.
＊연구 결과 studies　＊직접 directly　＊(숨/연기를) 들이 마시다 inhale　＊담배 연기 cigarette smoke　＊유독한 toxic

_____

17 효율적인 시간 관리로, 학생들은 자신들의 학업을 소홀히 하지 않으면서도 다양한 활동에 전념할 수 있다.

＊효율적인 effective　＊시간 관리 time management　＊소홀히 하다 neglect　＊다양한 a variety of

_____

18 일찍 도서관에 도착하는 아침형 사람들은 가장 좋은 자리를 얻을 수 있다.

＊도착하다 arrive　＊자리 seat

_____

19 피자와 냉동 식품은 대학생들 사이에서 인기 있는 음식이다.

＊~사이에 among　＊인기 있는 popular

_____

20 그녀의 시간 엄수하는 성격은 그녀가 뛰어난 시간 관리 능력을 가지고 있다는 것을 보여준다.

＊시간 관리 능력 time management skills　＊보여주다 suggest

_____

21 균형 잡힌 식단은 신선한 과일과 채소를 포함해야 한다.

＊포함하다 include

_____

22 그는 다리가 부러진 이래로 어려운 시기를 겪고 있다.

＊다리가 부러지다 break one's leg

_____

정답 p.481

❶ 문맹/컴맹
illiterate people / computer-illiterate people

은행 업무나 쇼핑 같은 간단한 활동도 문맹인 사람에게는 어렵다.
Simple activities like banking and shopping are difficult for **illiterate people**.

❷ 원격 학습
remote learning

인터넷이 연결되어 있으면, 집에서 원격 학습 과정을 시작할 수 있다.
With an Internet connection, people can begin a **remote learning** course at their home.

❸ 풍부한 문화 유산
rich cultural heritage

아시아의 풍부한 문화 유산은 무수한 사원과 사당을 통해 명백히 알 수 있다.
The **rich cultural heritage** of Asia is evident by its myriad temples and shrines.

❹ 모국어
one's first language / mother tongue

스페인어가 그녀의 모국어가 아니기 때문에, 그녀는 말을 할 때 사소한 문법적인 실수를 한다.
Because Spanish is not her **mother tongue**, she makes some minor grammatical mistakes in her speech.

❺ 세계 공용어
global language

많은 사람들은 영어가 세계 공용어가 되어야 한다고 생각한다.
Many people believe that English should become a **global language**.

❻ 최신 정보
up-to-date information

어떤 뉴스 주제의 최신 정보라도 항상 마우스를 몇 번만 클릭하면 얻을 수 있다.
The latest **up-to-date information** on any news topic is always just a few mouse clicks away.

❼ 정보 기술
information technology

인도의 정보 기술 전문가들은 미국의 프로그램 전문가들이 청구하는 비용에 비해 매우 적은 비용으로 복잡한 소프트웨어를 개발한다.

Information technology specialists in India develop complex software at a fraction of the cost that American programmers charge.

＊~의 적은 부분으로 at a fraction of ~

❽ 최첨단 기술, 최신 기술
state-of-the-art technology

몇 년 전만 해도 전화선을 이용한 모뎀은 최첨단 기술로 여겨졌었다.

Just a few years ago, dial-up modems were considered a **state-of-the-art technology**.

❾ 양날의 칼, 이로움을 줄 수도 있고 해를 끼칠 수도 있는 것
double-edged sword

모바일 기술은 시간을 최적으로 이용할 수 있게 해주지만 직원들을 피로하게 할 위험성이 있기에 양날의 칼이다.

Mobile technology is a **double-edged sword** because it makes optimal use of time, but also risks burning emloyees out.

＊최적의 optimal ＊기운을 다 써버리다 burn out

❿ 수정하다, 조정하다
make adjustments

정장이 당신 몸에 잘 맞지 않는다면 재단사가 수정할 수도 있다.

A tailor can **make adjustments** to your suit if it does not fit properly.

＊재단사, 재봉사 tailor ＊잘, 적당히 properly

⓫ 잘 고안된 제도
well-designed system

잘 고안된 제도는 시간과 에너지를 절약해 줄 수 있다.

A **well-designed system** can save time and energy.

⑫ **연간 생산량**
annual output

그 공장은 상품들에 대한 높은 주문 수량을 맞추기 위해 연간 생산량을 늘려야 한다.

The factory must increase its **annual output** to meet the high demand for its products.

⑬ **직업을 구하다**
find employment

만약 학생이 여분의 용돈을 위해 직업을 구하려 한다면, 찾아보기에 적합한 곳은 식당이다.

If a student wishes to **find employment** for extra pocket money, a good place to look is restaurants.
＊용돈 pocket money

⑭ **노동력, 노동 인구**
work force

다양한 노동 인구는 회사가 경쟁사들보다 한발 앞서도록 도와준다.

A diverse **work force** helps a company stay ahead of its competitors.
＊~보다 한발 앞서다 stay ahead of ~

⑮ **구직자**
job seeker

훌륭한 이력서와 긍정적인 태도를 지닌 구직자는 일자리를 찾는 데 어려움이 별로 없을 것이다.

A **job seeker** with a good résumé and positive attitude should have little trouble finding work.
＊이력서 résumé

⑯ **실업률**
unemployment rate

브라질의 실업률은 지난 30년간 높았다.

The **unemployment rate** in Brazil has been high for the last three decades.

⑰ **경제적인 어려움**
financial hardship

경제적인 어려움으로 고민하고 있는 학생들은 긴급 융자를 신청할 수 있다.

Students who suffer from **financial hardship** can apply for emergency loans.
＊신청하다 apply for   ＊긴급 융자 emergency loans

⑱ 은행 계좌
savings account

외국 은행에서 은행 계좌를 개설하려면, 여권과 주소 증명 서류를 보여 주어야 한다.

To open a **savings account** at a foreign bank, you must show your passport and proof of address.

＊여권 passport   ＊주소 증명 서류 proof of address

Integrated Section

Independent Section

⑲ 유지하다, 지속하다
hold down

사교 기술이 부족한 사람들은 안정된 직업을 유지하는 것을 힘겨워할 수도 있다.

People with poor social skills might find it difficult to **hold down** a steady job.

＊사교 기술 social skills

⑳ 손실을 메우다
make up the loss

만약 어느 회사가 판매 손실을 메우기 위해 가격을 올릴 수 없다면, 그 회사는 직원 수를 줄여야 할 지도 모른다.

If a company can't raise prices to **make up the loss** of sales, they might have to cut back on staff.

＊가격을 올리다 raise price   ＊~을 줄이다, 삭감하다 cut back on~

㉑ 빚이 쌓이다
run up debt

사람들은 수중에 돈이 떨어졌을 때 종종 신용카드 빚이 쌓인다.

People often **run up debt** on their credit cards when they are short of cash.

＊돈이 다 떨어지다 be short of cash

㉒ 비용을 분담하다
split the cost

자본이 별로 없는 사람들은 창업 비용을 분담하고 나서 그 후에 벌어들이는 이익을 나누어 갖는다고 알려져 왔다.

People with little money have been known to **split the cost** of starting a new business and then share the resulting benefits.

㉓ 넉넉하게 살다
make a good living

친한 친구가 넉넉하게 산다고 할지라도, 나는 그 친구에게 돈을 빌리는 것이 관계를 상하게 할 것이라고 생각한다.
Even if my close friend **makes a good living**, I think that borrowing money from him will damage the relationship.

㉔ 예산을 초과하여
beyond budget

만일 상사가 여러 개의 사업에 실패해 예산을 초과한다면, 그는 직원들로부터 신임을 잃을 것이다.
If a boss goes **beyond budget** on too many failed projects, he will lose the respect of his staff.

㉕ ~에 투자하다
invest money in ~

만약 어느 고용주가 숙련된 직원에게 더 높은 급료로 돈을 투자한다면, 고용주는 그 직원이 더 많은 성과를 이루기를 기대할 것이다.
If an employer **invests money in** a skilled worker at a higher salary, he should expect a higher standard of performance.

㉖ 부유한
well-off

해외 유학은 비용이 많이 들며 부유한 집안의 사람들만이 그 비용을 부담할 수 있다.
Overseas education is expensive and only those from **well-off** families are able to afford it.

㉗ 비전통적인 방식
non-traditional way

오늘날의 비즈니스 세계에서, 회사들은 비전통적인 방식으로 일을 함으로써 종종 성공을 거둔다.
In today's business world, companies often succeed by doing things in a **non-traditional way**.

㉘ 자동차 산업
auto industry

자동차 업계는 휘발유를 쓰지 않는 자동차 생산을 고려하는 것이 현명할 것이다.
The **auto industry** would be wise to consider making vehicles that do not run on gasoline.

㉙ 우주 탐사
space exploration

우리는 우주 탐사보다는 지구상의 문제들을 해결하는데 더 많은 돈을 써야 한다.

We should spend more money on solving problems on this planet than on **space exploration**.

㉚ 견습생 지위
entry-level position

견습생 지위에서 시작한 대부분의 사람들은 중요한 직위까지 오르게 된다.

Most people who start at **entry-level positions** rise to important positions.

㉛ 직무 내용서
job description

유능한 지원자의 관심을 끌고자 하는 고용주는 상세하고도 정확한 직무 내용서를 작성해야 한다.

An employer who wants to attract good work candidates must write detailed and accurate **job descriptions**.

＊지원자 candidate

㉜ 임시직 직원
temporary worker(=temp)

많은 기업들이 연휴 기간에 임시직 직원들을 고용한다.

Many companies use **temporary workers** during holiday season.

㉝ 고도로 기술이 발달한 사회
high-tech society

고도로 기술이 발달한 사회는 사람들이 더 장수하고 보다 편안한 삶을 살도록 해준다.

A **high-tech society** allows people to live longer and more comfortable lives.

㉞ 세입
tax revenues

정부는 의료 서비스나 교육과 같은 그들의 활동에 필요한 자금을 대기 위해 세입에 의존한다.

Governments rely on **tax revenues** to finance their activities such as health care and education.

＊자금을 조달하다 finance　＊보건 의료 health care

문화적인 활동	a cultural activity
만져 볼 수 있는 전시품	hands-on exhibits
공연 실황	a live performance
영화를 자주 보러 가는 사람, 영화팬	a movie goer
예술을 감상하다	appreciate art
연극을 보러가다	go to the theater
대중음악	popular music
대중매체	mass media
예술 축제	an art festival
유흥 공간	entertainment venues
텔레비전 앞에 달라붙어 있다	glue oneself to the television set
악기	a musical instrument
복장 규칙	a dress code
미술관	an art gallery
여가 활동	leisure activities
예술적 창의력	artistic creativity
진부한 표현	a cliché
전문적이고 과학적인 용어	technical and scientific terms
종교적 박해	religious persecution
통계 분석	statistical analysis
장거리 전화	long-distance phone calls
무선 통신	wireless communications
핵무기	a nuclear weapon
과학적 발견	a scientific discovery
기술적 발전	technological advancements
과학 기술의 기적	a technological miracle
저작권 분쟁	property disagreement
상승과 하강, 좋은 시절과 힘든 시절	ups and downs
중요한 발전	a significant breakthrough
휴양지	recreational areas

기념품	souvenirs
최신 도구	the latest gadget
무선 인터넷	mobile internet
인터넷 컨텐츠	internet content
온라인 모임	online community
온라인 대학	online university / online degree program
파일 공유	file sharing
워드 프로세서, 문서 작성 프로그램	a word-processing program
자동화된 프로그램	computerized programs
시간 소모적 과정	a time-consuming process
중요한 부분을 구성하다	form an integral part
세계화에 발맞추다	keep in step with globalization
국제적 기반 위에	on an international basis
자동차 정비소	a (car) service station / garage
주유소	a gas station
주차장	a parking lot
자동차를 타고 출근하다	drive to work
여행에 휴대하기 좋은	handy on trips
숙박 시설	accommodation(s)
여행 친구	travel buddies
대량 생산 기술	mass-production technologies
유전 공학	genetic engineering
주택 문제	a housing problem
가구, 생활 물품	a living arrangement
연대기순으로	in chronological order
최근의 경향	the latest trend
구식이 되다, 진부하게 되다	become obsolete
노동 시장	the labor market
업계 선두	the market leader
시장의 수요	market demand

자유시장 체제	a free-market system
유망한 직업	a promising job
평생 고용	lifetime employment / lifelong employment
직업적 성취, 만족	career fulfillment
근무 환경	(the) work environment
직무 성과	job performance
직업 요구 조건	a job requirement
직업의 안정성	job security
높은 임금	high wage ↔ low wage
고소득 직업	well-paying job / high-paying job
전문적 업무	professional tasks
번창하는 사업	a prosperous business
대량 생산	mass production
기업 규모 축소, 직원 감축	company downsizing
사업주, 사업가	a business owner
예산 삭감	budget cutbacks
금전적 수입	a monetary gain
생활비	the cost of living / living expenses
생계비를 벌다	earn one's living
비용 효율적인 체계	cost-effective system
소매 가격	retail price
공공 재산	public property
지역 사업	local business
지역 경제에 영향을 미치다	affect the local economy
정부 보조금	a government subsidy
유지 비용	maintenance costs
구호 자금	a relief fund
가치 있는 자산	valuable assets
사업을 일으키다	get a business off the ground
이익을 얻다	reap the benefits

용돈을 아끼다	save (up) one's allowance
전액 환불 받다	get a complete refund
비용만큼 가치가 있다	worth the cost
근무 중인	on duty
소비 습관	spending habits
돈에 의해 좌우되는	money-driven
광고 수익	advertisement revenue
정규직	a full-time position
강한 직업 윤리	strong work ethic
파트 타임으로 일하다	work a part-time job
경기 침체기에	in the slow economy
생산성을 저하시키다	discourage productivity
승진	a promotion
국제 기업	a global company
일에 대한 헌신	commitment to a job
더 큰 수익을 내다	generate more income
수입과 지출을 맞추다	make ends meet
더 높은 가격을 부과하다	charge higher prices
공공 요금	utility bills
수요가 매우 높다	be in great demand
경기 불황	a slow economy
경제 성장을 촉진하다	foster economic growth
금전 거래	a monetary transaction
국제 자본주의	global capitalism
금전적인 상황	a financial situation
경력을 쌓다	build (up) a career

녹색으로 주어진 표현에 유의하여, 다음의 우리말 문장을 영어로 바꾸어 쓰시오.

1 친구들끼리 외식할 때는 종종 각자 무엇을 시켰는지에 관계없이 비용을 공평하게 분담한다.
＊외식하다 eat out　＊시키다, 주문하다 order　＊~에 관계없이 regardless of~　＊공평하게 evenly

_____

2 가장 좋은 이력서는 업무 경력을 가장 최근의 경력부터 가장 오래된 경력까지 시간적인 순서로 나열한다.
＊이력서 résumé　＊업무 경력 work experience　＊나열하다 list

_____

3 에세이 작성은 많은 자료 조사와 수정이 수반되는 시간 소모적인 과정이다.
＊자료 조사 research　＊수정 revision　＊수반하다 involve

_____

4 높은 실업률은 제 기능을 발휘하지 못하는 경제의 한 징후이다.
＊제대로 움직이지 않는 malfunctioning　＊징후 symptom

_____

5 어떤 장학금은 경제적 어려움을 증명할 수 있는 학생들에게만 주어진다.
＊장학금 scholarship　＊증명하다 demonstrate　＊주다, 수여하다 award

_____

6 오늘날의 세상에서, 읽고 쓸 줄 모르는 사람은 넉넉하게 살 수 있는 가능성이 매우 적다.
    *오늘날의 세상에서 in today's world   *~할 가능성이 적다 have a slim chance of ~

_____

7 타자기가 구식이 된 것은 컴퓨터의 도입 후 얼마 지나지 않아서이다.
    *타자기 typewriter   *~의 도입 introduction of ~   *-은 ~후 얼마 지나지 않아서이다 it wasn't long after ~that -

_____

8 값비싼 식당에서 자주 식사를 하는 것은 봉급 생활자로 하여금 예산을 초과하게 할 수 있다.
    *식사 meal   *봉급 생활자 salaried worker

_____

9 내 생각에는, 장거리 전화가 이메일보다 연락을 지속하기에 좋은 방법이다.
    *연락을 지속하다 keep in touch

_____

10 세계화에 발맞추고자 하는 회사들은 다국어로 최신 웹사이트를 유지해야 한다.
    *~하고자 하다 wish to ~   *다국어로 in several languages   *최신의 up-to-date   *유지하다 maintain

_____

다음에 주어진 우리말 문장을 영어로 바꾸어 쓰시오.

11 다른 것들이 모두 그러하듯이, 대학 생활은 좋은 시절과 힘든 시절로 가득차 있다.
＊대학 생활 college life ＊~로 가득차다 be full of ~

_____

12 환율의 급작스러운 변동은 때때로 지역 경제에 영향을 미친다.
＊환율 exchange rate ＊급작스러운 sudden

_____

13 바나나 같은 영양분 가득한 간식거리는 여행에 휴대하기 좋다.
＊영양 많은 nutritious ＊간식거리 snack

_____

14 사업에 돈을 투자하는 것은 안정적인 기업에서 정기적인 봉급을 받는 것보다 위험 부담이 크다.
＊안정된 established ＊정기적인 봉급 regular salary ＊위험 부담이 큰 risky

_____

15 충분히 오랫동안 기다려서 비행기표를 구매하는 여행자들은 막바지 세일의 이익을 얻을 수 있다.
＊비행기표 plane ticket ＊막바지, 최후의 순간 last-minute

_____

16 재정적인 문제를 신중하게 다루지 않는다면 빚이 쌓이게 될 수도 있다.
　＊재정적인 문제 financial matter　＊다루다 handle　＊신중하게 carefully

---

17 만약 팀이 부진한 성적을 보이면 감독은 작전 계획을 수정해야 한다.
　＊부진한 성적을 보이다 perform poorly　＊감독 coach　＊작전 계획 game plan

---

18 어떤 사람들은 수지를 맞추기에 충분한 돈을 벌기 위해 두 가지 일을 해야 한다.
　＊두 가지 일을 하다 work two jobs　＊돈을 벌다 earn money

---

19 고전하는 고용 시장은 대개 경기 침체의 산물이다.
　＊고전하는 struggling　＊고용 시장 employment market　＊산물 product

---

20 많은 젊은이들이 좋아하는 취미는 대중음악을 듣는 것이다.
　＊좋아하는, 선호하는 favorite　＊취미, 기분전환 pastime

정답 p.481

I 에세이 기본 구조 익히기

주제가 확실히 드러나고 일관성과 통일성이 지켜지는 좋은 글을 쓰기 위해서는 처음부터 글 전체의 구조를 잘 잡아두어야 한다. 기본적으로 에세이는 서론-본론-결론의 3단 구조를 갖고 있다.

서론 앞으로 전개할 중심 내용과 주제를 소개하는 부분이다. 글의 토픽을 소개하고(도입) 그에 대한 자신의 의견 (대주제문)을 밝히며 글을 시작한다.

본론 서론에서 밝힌 의견에 대한 이유를 제시하는 부분으로, 주로 두 개의 문단으로 구성된다. 본문의 각 문단은 문단의 핵심 내용(소주제문)으로 시작하며, 그 핵심 내용에 대한 이유와 구체적 근거를 제시한다. 구체적 근거로는 예시나 상세 설명 등을 두 가지 정도 덧붙일 수 있다.

결론 서론과 본론의 내용을 요약하고 정리하는 부분이다. 글 전체 내용을 간단히 정리하고 나서, 강조하거나 여운을 남기는 맺음말로 글을 마친다.

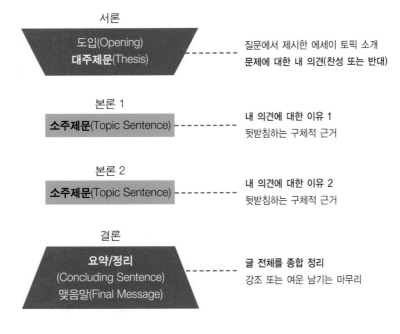

[에세이의 기본 구조]

1. 브레인 스토밍하기 (Brainstorming)

브레인 스토밍이란 한 가지 토픽에 대해서 떠오르는 생각을 자유롭게 전개시켜 나가는 방법으로, 주어진 문제에 대한 자신의 의견과 그 의견의 이유에 대한 아이디어를 얻기 위해 이용할 수 있다.

❶ 찬반 입장 정하기

먼저 주어진 토픽에 대해 자신의 입장이 찬성하는 쪽인지 반대하는 쪽인지를 생각해 본다. 찬반의 입장이 쉽게 정해지지 않으면 찬성하는 쪽의 이유와 반대하는 쪽의 이유를 다 생각해 보고 더 이유가 많이 생각나거나 설득력이 있는 쪽으로 선택한다.

❷ 이유 생각하기

입장이 정해졌으면 그렇게 생각하는 이유를 더욱 다양하게 생각해 본다. 반대하는 입장을 선택한 경우, 주어진 상황에 반대하는 이유를 생각할 수도 있고, 그 상황에 찬성하지 않는 이유도 생각할 수 있다.

브레인 스토밍하는 과정의 예

Do you agree or disagree with the following statement? Volunteer work should be mandatory for college students. Use specific reasons and examples to support your answer.

다음 명제에 찬성하는가 반대하는가? 대학생들에게 의무적으로 봉사 활동을 하게 해야 한다. 구체적인 이유와 예를 들어 의견을 뒷받침한다.

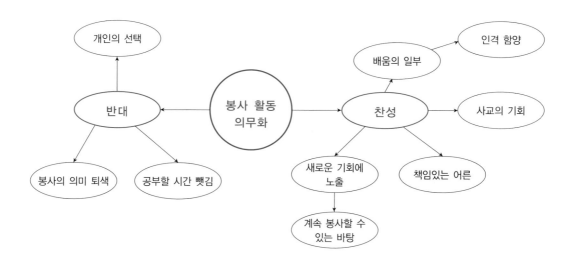

2. 아웃라인 잡기 (Outlining)

아웃라인은 글 쓸 내용의 중심 생각을 정리한 것으로, 앞으로 쓸 글의 뼈대 역할을 한다. 문제의 질문에 대한 나의 의견과, 그 이유 및 구체적 근거를 간단히 정리하면 된다. 서론의 도입부와 결론 부분은 중심적인 내용이 아니므로 아웃라인에는 포함시키지 않는다.

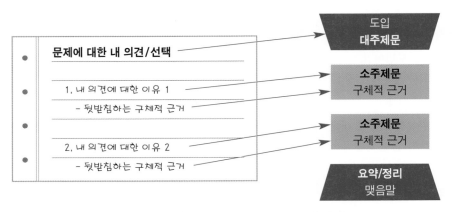

[아웃라인과 실제 에세이 구조의 관계]

ex) Do you agree or disagree with the following statement? Volunteer work should be mandatory for college students. Use specific reasons and examples to support your answer.

다음 명제에 찬성하는가 반대하는가? 대학생들에게 의무적으로 봉사 활동을 하게 해야 한다. 구체적인 이유와 예를 들어 의견을 뒷받침한다.

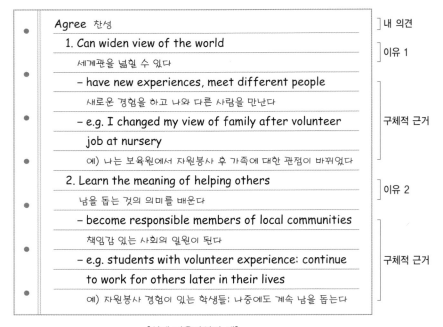

[실제 아웃라인의 예]

❶ 아웃라인 잡기

아웃라인의 본론 부분은 다음과 같이 두 가지 형태 중에 선택해서 잡을 수 있다.

A형) 내 의견의 장점 2개로 구성

기본적인 구성 방식으로, 나의 의견의 장점 두 가지를 각각 본론 1과 본론 2에 넣어 문단을 구성할 수 있다.

> **본론 1** 내 의견의 장점 1
> **본론 2** 내 의견의 장점 2

Integrated Section

Independent Section

ex) Do you agree or disagree with the following statement? Important decisions should not be made without others. Use specific reasons and examples to support your answer.

다음 명제에 찬성하는가 반대하는가? 중요한 결정은 다른 사람들 없이 내려서는 안 된다. 구체적인 이유와 예를 들어 의견을 뒷받침한다.

Agree 찬성

1. Can get help from others' experience and knowledge
   남의 경험과 지식으로부터 도움을 받을 수 있음
   - decisions based on good understanding of the subject
   사안에 대해 잘 알고 나서 내린 결정
   - e.g. when buying a car, get advice from friends who know a lot about cars
   예) 처음으로 차를 살 때 차를 잘 아는 친구의 조언

   본론 1
   다른 사람과 의논하는 것의 장점 1

2. Can make objective decisions
   객관적인 결정을 내릴 수 있음
   - people not involved can give unbiased opinions
   당사자가 아닌 사람은 공정한 의견을 낼 수 있음
   - e.g. introduce your fiancee to close friends before getting married
   예) 결혼할 사람을 친한 친구에게 보여 주는 것

   본론 2
   다른 사람과 의논하는 것의 장점 2

B형) 내 의견의 장점 1개, 반대 의견의 단점 1개로 구성

내 의견과 반대 되는 쪽을 반박하는 내용도 함께 쓰고 싶으면, 본론 1에서는 찬성하는 쪽의 장점을 들어 찬성하는 이유를 쓰고 본론 2에서는 자신이 선택하지 않은 입장의 단점을 들어 반박한다.

> **본론 1** 내 의견의 장점
> **본론 2** 반대 의견의 단점

ex) Do you agree or disagree with the following statement? Important decisions should not be made without others. Use specific reasons and examples to support your answer.

다음 명제에 찬성하는가 반대하는가? 중요한 결정은 다른 사람들 없이 내려서는 안 된다. 구체적인 이유와 예를 들어 의견을 뒷받침한다.

Disagree 반대	
1. Can get help from others' experience and knowledge	
남의 경험과 지식으로부터 도움을 받을 수 있음	**본론 1**
– decisions based on good understanding of the subject	다른 사람과
사안에 대해 잘 알고 나서 내린 결정	의논하는 것의
– e.g. when buying a car, get advice from friends who know a lot about cars	장점
예) 처음으로 차를 살 때 차를 잘 아는 친구의 조언	
2. Can't make objective decisions alone	
혼자서는 객관적인 결정을 내릴 수 없음	**본론 2**
– one can't see the big picture	혼자 결정하는
당사자는 문제의 큰 그림을 보지 못함	것의 단점
– e.g. when in love, some people rush into marriage	
예) 사랑에 빠져 성급하게 결혼하는 경우	

TIP

아웃라인은 글을 쓰기 전에 아이디어를 정리하기 위한 것이므로, 반드시 영어로 써야 하는 것은 아니다. 한글과 영어 중 편리한 쪽을 선택해 쓰거나 두 언어를 함께 사용할 수 있다.

❷ 구조 잡기 연습
에세이의 구조를 단계에 따라 잡아 보자.

Question

Do you agree or disagree with the following statement? Eating homemade food is better than eating out in restaurants or food stands. Use specific reasons and examples to support your answer.

다음의 주장에 찬성하는가 반대하는가? 집에서 만든 음식을 먹는 것이 음식점이나 노점에서 사먹는 것보다 낫다. 구체적인 이유와 예를 들어 대답을 뒷받침한다.

Integrated Section

Independent Section

Step 1 문제 분석
'집에서 만든 음식을 먹는 것이 식당이나 노점에서 사먹는 것보다 더 낫다'는 명제에 찬성하는지 반대하는지를 묻는 문제이다.

Step 2 아웃라인 잡기
1) '찬성한다'로 의견의 방향을 설정한다.
2) 집에서 먹는 음식이 밖에서 사먹는 것보다 낫다고 생각하는 이유를 두 가지 든다.
3) 구체적 근거를 각 두 개 정도 적어둔다.

Agree 찬성	내 의견
1. Much cheaper 훨씬 더 저렴하다	내 의견의 장점 1
– cost of groceries is lower than eating out 식료품 가격이 외식비보다 더 저렴하다 – e.g. my experience – saved a lot by cutting expenses on eating out 예) 내 경험 – 외식비를 줄여 많은 돈을 아꼈다	구체적 근거
2. A more relaxing environment at home 집의 분위기가 더 안락하다	내 의견의 장점 2
– can take your time and don't need to care other customers 느긋한 시간을 가질 수 있고 다른 손님을 신경 쓰지 않아도 된다 – e.g. can have own party or make noise at home 예) 집에서는 나만의 파티를 열거나 시끄럽게 해도 괜찮다	구체적 근거

다음 주어진 질문에 답하는 에세이의 아웃라인을 완성하시오.

01

Do you agree or disagree with the following statement? High school students should be allowed to choose which subjects they will study. Use specific reasons and examples to explain your answer.

guideline

고등학교에서는 학생들이 공부하고자 하는 과목을 배울 수 있도록 허용해야 한다는 입장에 반대하는 쪽으로 의견을 정하고, 정해진 과목들을 듣는 것의 장점 두 가지를 생각해 아웃라인으로 잡아 보자.

outline

- 내 의견 Disagree

    이유 1 _____

- 이유 2 _____

02

Do you agree or disagree with the following statement? A teacher's ability to relate well with students is more important than the ability to give knowledge. Use specific reasons and examples to support your answer.

guideline

선생님은 잘 가르치는 능력보다 학생들과 잘 어울리는 능력이 더 중요하다는 의견에 찬성하는 쪽으로 자신의 입장을 정한다. 그렇게 생각하는 이유를 '(1) 친근한 선생님은 학생들의 학습 의욕을 북돋는다 (2) 선생님과의 상호 작용은 학생들의 사회성을 강화한다' 로 정하고, 각 이유에 대한 구체적인 근거를 아웃라인으로 잡아 보자.

outline

- 내 의견 Agree

    이유 1 Friendly teachers motivate students to study

    – 구체적 근거: 일반적 진술 _____

    – 구체적 근거: 예시 _____

- 이유 2 Interaction with teachers enhance students' social skills

    – 구체적 근거: 일반적 진술 _____

- – 구체적 근거: 예시 _____

03

Do you agree or disagree with the following statement? Young people enjoy life more than older people. Use specific reasons and examples to support your answer.

guideline

젊은이들이 나이 든 사람들보다 인생을 더 즐긴다는 의견에 찬성하는 쪽으로 입장을 정한다. 그 이유로 '(1) 젊은이들은 더 활동적이다 (2) 젊은이에게는 책임이 더 적다'로 정하고, 각 이유에 대한 구체적인 근거를 아웃라인으로 잡아 보자.

outline

- 내 의견 Agree

  이유 1 Young people are physically active

  　– 구체적 근거: 일반적 진술 _____

  　– 구체적 근거: 예시 _____

  이유 2 Young people have fewer responsibilities

  　– 구체적 근거: 일반적 진술 _____

  　– 구체적 근거: 예시 _____

04

It is better for governments to spend their funds on the exploration of outer space than on earthly matters. Do you agree or disagree? Use specific reasons and details to support your answer.

guideline

정부는 우주 탐험에 돈을 많이 투자해서는 안 된다는 쪽으로 입장을 정한다. 그 이유를 '(1) 사람들의 생명을 살리는 더 급한 일에 돈을 써야 한다 (2) 파괴된 환경을 복원하는 것이 더 시급하다'로 정하고, 각 이유에 대한 구체적 근거를 아웃라인으로 잡아 보자.

outline

- 내 의견 Disagree

  이유 1 Saving human lives is more imperative

  　– 구체적 근거: 일반적 진술 _____

  　– 구체적 근거: 예시 _____

  이유 2 Restoring the damaged environment is more pressing

  　– 구체적 근거: 일반적 진술 _____

  　– 구체적 근거: 예시 _____

정답 p.482

다음 주어진 질문에 대한 에세이의 아웃라인을 작성하시오.

01

It is better to have friends who are similar to you than those who are different from you. Do you agree or disagree? Use specific reasons and details to support your answer.

outline

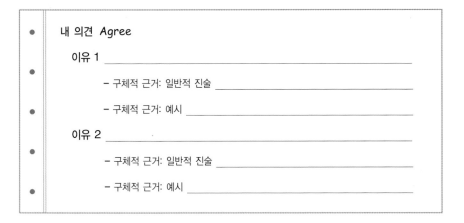

02

Do you agree or disagree with the following statement? Eating homemade food is better than eating out at restaurants or food stands. Use specific reasons and examples to support your answer.

outline

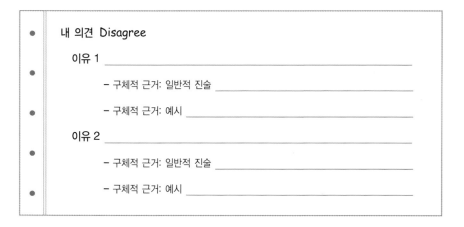

03

Do you agree or disagree with the following statement? University athletic departments should receive the same amount of funding as university libraries. Use specific reasons and examples to support your answer.

outline

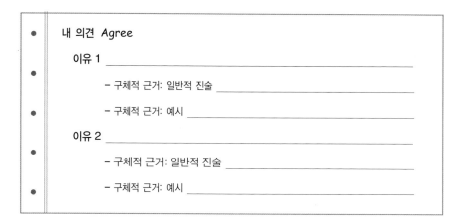

04

Do you agree or disagree with the following statement? Zoos serve no practical function. Use specific reasons and examples to explain your answer.

outline

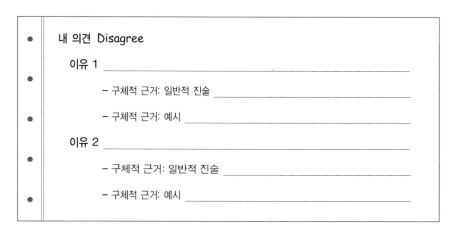

정답 p.484

에세이의 구조에 대해 배웠으니 이제 에세이를 구성하는 단락들을 직접 써 보기로 한다. 글을 쓰려고 시작할 때는 누구나 어떤 이야기부터 시작해야 할지 고민하게 마련이다. 에세이의 첫인상을 결정하는 역할을 하는 서론을 쓰는 방식에 대해 알아보자.

1. 서론의 내용과 구성

서론은 에세이에서 전개할 중심 내용을 소개하는 부분이다. 먼저 무엇에 관한 글인지를 제시하고, 나의 의견과 그렇게 생각하는 이유를 간단히 밝히면서 글을 시작한다.

> ● **도입 (Opening)**
> 도입은 글을 시작하는 문장으로서 주제의 배경을 제시한다. 주어진 질문의 표현을 재진술하여 토픽을 제시하면 쉽다.
>
> ● **대주제문 (Thesis)**
> 대주제문은 글의 전체 주제를 소개하는 문장이다. 질문에 대한 구체적인 자신의 의견을 제시하고 본론의 중심 내용인 이유 두 가지를 함께 소개한다.

ex) 콘서트나 운동 경기 등을 직접 참여해서 실황으로 보는 것이 텔레비전으로 보는 것보다 즐겁다는 진술에 찬성하는지 반대하는지를 밝히고 구체적인 이유와 예를 들어 자신의 견해를 뒷받침한다.

도입　　많은 사람들이 여가 시간을 활용하여 콘서트나 운동 경기 등의 관람을 즐긴다. 어떤 사람들은 직접 그 장소에 가서 실황으로 보는 것을 좋아하고, 다른 사람들은 집에서 텔레비전으로 보는 것을 더 좋아한다. 〈질문을 이용한 토픽의 소개〉

대주제문　나는 직접 가서 공연이나 경기를 관람하는 것이 더 좋다는 의견에 동의한다. 왜냐하면, 더욱 생동감을 느낄 수 있고 또 TV로는 보여지지 않는 부분도 볼 수 있기 때문이다. 〈내 의견 + 이유 두 가지〉

서론에 쓰기 좋은 표현

> 도입
> It is often said that ~ 종종 ~라는 말을 한다　Many people believe that ~ 많은 사람들이 ~라고 생각한다
>
> 대주제문
> I agree/disagree that ~ 나는 ~에 찬성/반대한다　I question whether ~ 나는 ~인지 의문스럽다
> I strongly support the idea of ~ 나는 ~라는 생각에 전적으로 찬성한다　In my opinion 내 생각으로는
> My view on this issue is that ~ 이 문제에 대한 나의 생각은 ~이다　From my point of view 내 관점에서는

T I P

단순히 질문지 문구를 이용한 시작에서 벗어나 독특한 나만의 도입문을 쓸 수도 있다. 주어진 토픽과 관련된 자신의 일화나, 시사적 현안, 속담, 전문가의 발언 등을 인용하여 독자의 관심을 이끌어내는 것이다. '실황 공연 vs. TV 중계'에 대한 에세이의 도입을 독특하게 바꿔 보자. '2002년 월드컵 경기의 결승전 관람권은 판매가 시작된지 5분만에 동이 나고 말았다. 사람들은 TV에서 편안하게 볼 수도 있는 경기의 표를 왜 그렇게 손에 넣으려고 애썼던 것일까?'

2. 서론 쓰기의 예

Question

Do you agree or disagree with this statement? People learn more from their peers than those older than them. Use specific reasons and examples to explain your position.

다음 명제에 찬성하는가 반대하는가? 사람들은 연장자들보다는 자기 또래의 사람들로부터 더 많이 배운다. 구체적인 이유와 예를 들어 자신의 입장을 설명하시오.

Step 1 도입 쓰기
급변하는 세상에서 변화를 따라 잡지 못하는 나이 든 사람에게서는 배울 것이 없다는 일반적인 통념을 배경으로 제시하면서 글을 시작한다.

Step 2 대주제문 쓰기
도입에서 제시한 배경에도 불구하고 여전히 연장자로부터 배울 것이 많다는 자신의 의견을 제시한다. 왜 그렇게 생각하는지 아웃라인에서 정한 두 가지 이유를 간단히 설명하여 앞으로 본론에서 이어질 내용을 미리 밝힌다.

People learn more from their peers than those older than them.

Outline

서론 쓰기

Disagree

1. Elders have more experience
   - know-how, skills to learn from
   - e.g. was able to learn practical skills from a senior worker
2. More comprehensive understanding of the life
   - more mature, have patience and wisdom
   - e.g. when sister worried about her future, advice from friends and parents

도입

As the world is changing faster than ever before, **people** in many cultures, especially the young, **believe that** people learn more from their peers, who are caught up with the latest developments, than from their elders.

대주제문

However, **in my opinion**, no matter how fast the world is changing, [there are always more things to learn from older people than from one's peers.] **This is because** elders [have more life experience] as well as [a more comprehensive understanding of life.]

주어진 아웃라인을 참고하여 빈칸에 적절한 문장을 써서 서론을 완성하시오.

01

Do you agree or disagree with the following statement? Famous athletes and entertainers deserve the million-dollar salaries they earn. Use specific reasons and examples to support your opinion.

guideline

유명인들은 고액의 보수를 받을 자격이 있다는 진술에 동의하는 서론의 도입 문장을 작성해 보자. 유명인들의 보수를 둘러싼 논란을 배경으로 제시하며 시작한다.

outline

- **Agree** 찬성
  1. They do their best to be the finest in their fields
     그들은 자신의 분야에서 최고가 되기 위해 최선을 다한다
  2. They bring in huge incomes for their employers
     그들은 자신의 고용주에게 엄청난 수입을 가져다 준다

서론 쓰기 ✎

도입

① _____

_____

_____.

스포츠와 연예 산업이 그 어느 때보다도 빠르게 증가하면서, 사람들은 종종 유명 인사들이 그들이 벌어들이는 수백만 달러의 수입을 얻을 자격이 있는지에 대해 논쟁을 벌인다.

대주제문

I would argue that the high salaries of famous athletes and entertainers are definitely justifiable. The rationale behind this is that celebrities do their best to be the finest in their respective fields. Furthermore, famous athletes and entertainers bring in huge incomes for their employers.

나는 유명 운동 선수나 연예인들이 받는 높은 수입이 분명 정당하다고 주장한다. 유명 인사들은 자신의 분야에서 최고가 되기 위해 최선을 다한다는 것이 그 근거이다. 게다가, 유명 운동 선수와 연예인들은 자신의 고용주에게 엄청난 수입을 가져다 준다.

02

Do you agree or disagree with the following statement? It is more advantageous for children to grow up in rural areas than in big cities. Use specific reasons and examples to support your opinion.

guideline

어린이들은 도시에서 자라는 것보다 시골에서 자라는 것이 좋다는 진술에 찬성하는 서론의 도입 문장을 작성해 보자. 어린이가 성장하기에 좋은 환경에 대한 논란을 배경으로 제시하며 시작한다.

outline

> **Agree** 찬성
>
> 1. Countryside is safer than city
>   시골은 도시보다 안전하다
> 2. Countryside provides a fun, healthful, and natural environment
>   시골은 즐겁고 건전하며 자연적인 환경을 제공해 준다

서론 쓰기 🖊

도입

① _____

_____

_____.

점점 더 많은 사람들이 도시에서 살기 때문에, 어린이가 도시에서 성장하는 것이 더 좋은지 아니면 시골에서 자라는 것이 더 좋은지에 대한 논란이 일어났다.

대주제문

From my point of view, growing up in the countryside is more beneficial for children because it is safer and provides a fun, healthful, and natural environment.

내 관점에서는, 어린이는 시골에서 자라는 것이 더 유익하다. 시골은 더 안전한데다가, 즐겁고 건전하며 자연적인 환경을 제공해 주기 때문이다.

Do you agree or disagree with the following statement? High schools should require all students to wear school uniforms. Use specific reasons and examples to support your opinion.

guideline

고등학생의 교복 착용 의무화에 대해 찬성하는 서론의 대주제문을 작성해 보자. 교복 착용을 찬성하는 자신의 입장과 그렇게 생각하는 이유 두 가지를 아웃라인을 참고해 한 문장으로 정리한다.

outline

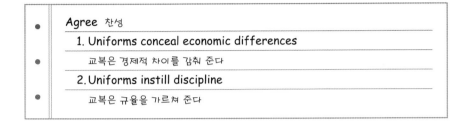

- Agree 찬성
  1. Uniforms conceal economic differences
     교복은 경제적 차이를 감춰 준다
  2. Uniforms instill discipline
     교복은 규율을 가르쳐 준다

서론 쓰기 ✏

도입

As teenagers become more conscious of fashion and self-expression, many students feel that high schools should give them the freedom to choose what they want to wear to school.

십대 청소년들이 옷차림과 자기 표현에 점점 더 신경을 쓰게 됨에 따라, 많은 학생들은 학교측이 학생들에게 학교에 입고 오는 옷을 선택할 자유를 주어야 한다고 생각한다.

대주제문

Although I can understand their position, ① _____

_____

_____ .

학생들의 입장도 이해할 수 있지만, 나는 교복 의무 착용 정책을 지지한다. 왜냐하면 교복은 학생들간의 경제적 차이를 감춰 주고, 학생들에게 규율을 가르쳐 주기 때문이다.

04

Do you agree or disagree with the following statement? Children should wait to begin learning a foreign language until they start school. Use specific reasons and examples to support your opinion.

guideline

아이들은 학교에 들어가서야 외국어를 배우기 시작해야 한다는 입장에 반대하는 서론의 대주제문을 작성해 보자. 취학 전 외국어 학습을 주장하는 자신의 입장과 그렇게 생각하는 이유 두 가지를 아웃라인을 참고해 정리한다.

outline

> - Disagree 반대
>   1. Younger children have an advantage at language acquisition
>   어린 아이들은 언어 습득에 있어서 이점을 가지고 있다
>   2. Children who are not attending school have more free time to study languages
>   학교에 다니지 않는 아이들은 언어를 배울 자유 시간이 더 많다

서론 쓰기 🖋

도입

Everyone recognizes the importance of learning foreign languages in this global era. Unfortunately, the later one waits to begin learning another language, the harder it becomes.

오늘날의 지구촌 시대에는 모든 사람들이 외국어 학습의 중요성을 인정한다. 안타깝게도, 외국어를 늦게 배우기 시작할수록 배우기는 더 어려워진다.

대주제문

① _____

_____ .

② _____

_____ .

따라서, 어린이들은 가능한 한 빨리 외국어를 배우기 시작해야 하는데 이는 어린이들이 언어 습득에 있어서 이점을 가지고 있기 때문이다. 게다가, 아직 학교에 다니지 않는 아이들은 언어를 배울 자유 시간이 더 많다.

정답 p.486

주어진 아웃라인을 참고하여 에세이의 서론을 작성하시오.

01 Do you agree or disagree with the following statement? Classmates are a more important influence than teachers are on a child's success in school. Use specific reasons and examples to support your opinion.

outline

> **Agree** 찬성
>
> 1. Classmates spend more time with each other than with their teachers
>   반 친구들은 선생님보다 더 많은 시간을 함께 보낸다
>
> 2. Children are heavily influenced by peer pressure
>   어린이들은 또래 집단의 압력에 크게 영향을 받는다

서론 쓰기 🖉

도입

_____

_____ .

대주제문

_____

_____

_____

_____ .

02

Do you agree or disagree with the following statement? The government should destroy old, historic buildings and replace them with modern buildings. Use specific reasons and examples to support your opinion.

outline

> Disagree 반대
>
> 1. Old buildings have historical value
>
>   오래된 건물은 역사적 가치를 가지고 있다
>
> 2. It costs too much to replace old buildings with new ones
>
>   오래된 건물을 새 건물로 교체하는 데는 비용이 너무 많이 든다

서론 쓰기 ✏

도입

_____

_____ .

대주제문

_____

_____

_____

_____ .

정답 p.487

III 에세이 쓰기 - 본론

어떤 글에서나 본론은 글쓴이가 말하고자 하는 바의 핵심을 담고 있는 가장 중요한 부분이다. 따라서 좋은 글을 쓰려면 본론에서 자신이 말하고자 하는 바를 효과적으로 전달할 수 있어야 한다. 에세이의 중심축인 본론을 쓰는 방식에 대해 알아보자.

1. 본론의 내용과 구성

본론은 서론에서 제시한 주제를 뒷받침하기 위한 설명으로 이루어진 단락이다. 본론의 각 단락은 소주제문과 구체적 근거로 구성된다.

> ● **소주제문 (Topic Sentence)**
> 소주제문은 서론에서 제시한 자신의 의견에 대한 이유를 각각 설명하는 문장이다. 또한 본론 각 단락의 중심 문장으로서 단락의 맨 앞에 등장한다.
>
> ● **구체적 근거 (Supporting Details)**
> 구체적 근거는 소주제문을 뒷받침하여 설명해주는 상세한 내용이다. 먼저 소주제문에 대해 일반적인 관점에서 추가로 설명을 한다. 그리고 구체적이면서도 사실적인 느낌을 주기 위해 자신의 경험담을 예로 들거나 알고 있는 신문기사, 통계 자료 등을 인용하여 예시를 들도록 한다.

ex) 콘서트나 운동 경기 등을 직접 참여해서 실황으로 보는 것이 텔레비전으로 보는 것보다 즐겁다는 진술에 찬성하는지 반대하는지를 밝히고 구체적인 이유와 예를 들어 뒷받침한다.

단락 1	소주제문 1	직접 공연을 보면 TV로는 느낄 수 없는 생동감을 느낄 수 있다.
	구체적 근거 1	일반적 진술: TV에서는 공연장의 실제 분위기를 느끼기 힘들지만, 현장에서는 무대나 경기장 안팎의 현장감과 열기로 인해 즐거움이 두 배가 된다.
	구체적 근거 2	예시: 한 조사에 따르면 야구팬들의 70%이상이 경기 상황보다도 경기장의 분위기나 관중들의 열기를 느끼기 위해 경기장을 직접 찾는 것을 선호한다고 한다. 〈통계 자료〉
단락 2	소주제문 2	직접 공연을 보면 TV 카메라가 잡을 수 없는 것도 다 볼 수 있다.
	구체적 근거 1	일반적 진술: TV를 볼 때는 카메라가 잡는 화면에 들어오는 것만 수동적으로 볼 수 있는 반면, 현장에서는 TV에서 볼 수 없는 다양한 것들을 다 볼 수 있다.
	구체적 근거 2	예시: 실제로 나는 실황 공연에 갔다가 TV에 시간 관계상 방영되지 않은 앵콜 공연까지 볼 수 있었다. 〈나의 경험담〉

TIP

> 본론 각 단락의 마지막에 한 문단을 끝맺는 마무리 문장을 쓸 수도 있다. 마무리 문장은 소주제문과 의미상 연결되는 내용이어야 한다. 위의 예에서 두 번째 본문 마지막에 '사람들은 이렇게 TV에서는 얻을 수 없는 즐거움을 찾아 현장에 직접 가는 것이다' 라고 쓸 수 있다.

2. 본론 쓰기의 예

Question

Do you agree or disagree with this statement? People learn more from their peers than those older than them. Use specific reasons and examples to explain your position.

다음 명제에 찬성하는가 반대하는가? 사람들은 연장자들보다는 자기 또래의 사람들로부터 더 많이 배운다. 구체적인 이유와 예를 들어 자신의 입장을 설명하시오.

Step 1 소주제문 쓰기

아웃라인에서 정한 자신의 의견에 대한 이유 두 가지를 각 본론 단락의 처음에서 밝히면서 시작한다. 아웃라인에서 '이유 1: 연장자는 경험이 많다' 라고 정했다면, '첫째, 연장자들은 인생의 경험이 많고, 따라서 젊은이들에게 여러 가지 도와줄 수 있는 것이 많다.' 라고 하면서 본론의 첫 번째 단락을 시작한다.

Step 2 구체적 근거 쓰기

해당 단락의 소주제문에서 밝힌 자신의 이유에 대해 좀 더 구체적으로 설명한다. 먼저 연장자가 왜 경험이 더 많은지, 그것이 어떻게 도움이 될 수 있는지를 일반적인 견지에서 더 자세히 설명한다. 그리고 자신이 연장자의 경험으로 인해서 도움을 받았던 경우를 예시로 들어 주장을 뒷받침한다.

Outline	본론 쓰기 - 단락 1

Outline

- Disagree
  1. Elders have more experience
     - know-how, skills to learn from
     - e.g. was able to learn practical skills from a senior worker
  2. More comprehensive understanding of the life
     - more mature, have patience and wisdom
     - e.g. when sister worried about her future, advice from friends and parents

본론 쓰기 - 단락 1

소주제문 1
To start with, [older people have a wealth of experience] in many aspects of life, and are thus able to provide practical assistance to young people.

구체적 근거 1: 일반적 진술
As older people have [accumulated their own know-how in their careers or lives, they have many resources and skills] with which to teach and guide younger people.

구체적 근거 2: 예시
From my personal experience, [I learned much more from my senior employees than from my peers] when I first started working at a motor company. As my peers did not have much work experience, we were not able to learn much from each other, but instead spent time out chatting and socializing. On the other hand, the senior employee in my department taught me many actual skills from doing presentations and writing papers to handling the machinery in the office. He helped me greatly, and thanks to him, I was able to acclimate easily to the workplace.

Hackers **Practice**

주어진 아웃라인을 참고하여 빈칸에 적절한 문장을 써서 본론을 완성하시오.

01

Do you agree or disagree with the following statement? It is good for teenagers to have jobs while they are still students. Use specific reasons and examples to support your opinion.

guideline

십대 학생들이 직업을 갖는 것은 바람직하다는 의견에 찬성하는 쪽으로 입장을 정하고, 학생이 직업을 가지는 것의 장점 두 가지로 본론 각 단락의 소주제문을 작성해 보자.

outline

- **Agree** 찬성
  - 1. Improve a sense of responsibility

    책임감을 증진시킨다
    - working students are required to assume responsibilities

      일하는 학생들은 책임을 져야 한다
    - e.g. students with jobs do better in school: know how to handle multiple tasks

      예) 일하는 학생들은 학교에서도 더 잘한다; 여러 가지 일을 처리하는 법을 안다
  - 2. Encourage appreciation of the value of money

    돈의 가치를 인식하도록 장려한다
    - naturally learn that effort and time is needed to earn money

      돈을 벌기 위해서는 노력과 시간이 필요하다는 것을 자연스레 배운다
    - e.g. my experience of working at restaurant: not easy to make money

      예) 식당에서 일한 경험; 돈을 벌기가 쉽지 않았다

본론 쓰기 ✏️

단락 1 쓰기

소주제문 1

① _____.

우선, 학생들의 일은 십대들의 책임감을 증진시킨다.

구체적 근거 1: 일반적 진술

② _____

_____

_____.

일을 하는 학생들은 제시간에 직장에 도착하고, 현명하게 일정을 관리하고, 마감 시한을 지키고, 업무 규칙을 준수하고, 철저하게 업무를 완수하는 것과 같은 필수적인 책임들을 맡게 된다.

구체적 근거 2: 예시

Studies reveal that students who work fewer than 15 hours a week actually academically outperform their peers who do not work because they know how to handle multiple tasks and responsibilities, and can consequently manage their time well. On the whole, students who juggle work and school are more mature and well-equipped to succeed than their non-working peers. These benefits extend far outside the classroom.

연구 결과는 한 주에 15시간 이하로 일하는 학생들이 실제로 일하지 않는 학생들보다 학업상 뛰어나다는 것을 보여주는데, 이것은 그들이 복합적인 과제와 책임을 처리하는 방법을 알고 결과적으로 자기 시간을 잘 관리하기 때문이다. 전반적으로, 일과 학교를 병행하는 학생들이 일하지 않는 학생들보다 좀 더 성숙하고 성공할 능력을 갖추고 있다. 이러한 장점들은 교실 훨씬 밖까지 영향을 미친다.

단락 2 쓰기

소주제문 2

③ _____.

게다가, 시간제로 일하는 것은 청소년들로 하여금 돈의 가치를 인식하도록 장려한다.

구체적 근거 1: 일반적 진술

④ _____.

_____.

실제 업무 경험은 십대 학생들로 하여금 돈을 벌기 위해서는 의식적인 노력을 기울이고 그들의 소중한 시간을 바쳐야 한다는 것을 자연스레 배우게 한다.

구체적 근거 2: 예시

From my personal experience, I worked at a fast-food restaurant when I was seventeen in order to make money to buy a new computer. I made only four dollars an hour doing exhausting work such as moving heavy boxes of ingredients, washing dirty dishes, and mopping the floors. However, through this work experience, I learned the value of money and became much more careful spending my parents' hard-earned money.

개인적 경험으로는, 나는 17살 때 새 컴퓨터를 살 돈을 마련하기 위해, 패스트푸드 식당에서 일했다. 나는 무거운 재료 상자들을 나르고, 더러운 접시를 닦고, 걸레로 바닥을 닦는 것과 같은 힘겨운 일을 하면서 1시간에 4달러밖에 벌지 못했다. 하지만, 이러한 업무 경험을 통해, 나는 돈의 가치를 배웠고 부모님께서 고생해서 버신 돈을 쓰는 데 좀 더 신중하게 되었다.

정답 p.488

02

Do you agree or disagree with the following statement? University students should be required to attend classes. Use specific reasons and examples to support your opinion.

guideline

대학교의 의무 출석제를 찬성하는 쪽으로 입장을 정하고, 출석을 의무로 할 경우의 장점 두 가지로 본론 각 단락의 소주제문을 작성해 보자.

outline

Agree 찬성

1. Help students become more responsible and self-disciplined

학생들이 좀 더 책임감과 자제심을 지니게 된다

– have to come to class regularly & disciplinary measures for absences

수업에 정기적으로 출석해야 하고 결석에 대해서는 처벌을 받는다

– e.g. my experience in college: skipped classes and faced severe consequences

예) 대학에서 나의 경험: 수업을 빠지고 혹독한 결과를 맞게 됐다

2. Enhance educational environment

교육 환경을 향상시킨다

– professors can effectively teach a regular group

교수들은 일정한 그룹의 학생들을 효율적으로 가르친다

– e.g. class with optional attendance: students not serious about class

예) 선택 출석제의 수업: 학생들이 수업에 대해 진지하지 않다

본론 쓰기 ✏️

단락 1 쓰기

소주제문 1

① _____

_____ .

첫째로, 의무 출석제는 학생들이 좀 더 책임감과 자제심을 갖도록 하는 데 중추적인 역할을 한다.

구체적 근거 1: 일반적 진술

② _____

_____ .

③ _____

_____ .

이는 의무 출석제가 학생들로 하여금 수업에 정기적으로 참석하도록 개인적인 책임을 지게 하기 때문이다. 게다가, 학생들은 결석과 지각에 대해 낙제와 학점 부족, 근신, 심지어는 정학과 같은 징계 처분에 직면하게 된다.

구체적 근거 2: 예시

For example, when I was a freshman in college, I frequently skipped required classes because I was totally free from my parents' and teachers' supervision. However, thanks to the strict mandatory attendance policy, I had to improve my negligent and irresponsible behavior or else I would have to face severe consequences. I received a series of D's on my report card, stayed up several nights to work on make-up assignments, and even had to repeat several courses. Fortunately, I began to take school more seriously and improved my academic performance.

예를 들면, 내가 대학교 신입생이었을 때, 부모님과 선생님의 감독에서 벗어나 철저히 자유로웠기 때문에 나는 종종 필수과목에 빠지곤 했다. 그러나, 엄격한 의무 출석제 덕분에, 나는 태만하고 무책임한 행동을 개선해야 했고, 그렇게 하지 않았다면 나는 혹독한 결과에 직면해야 했을 것이다. 나는 성적표에 줄줄이 D를 받았고, 보충 과제를 하기 위해 며칠 밤을 새워야 했으며, 심지어 몇 과목은 재수강해야 했다. 다행스럽게도, 나는 수업을 좀 더 진지하게 받아들이고 나의 학업 성취도를 향상시키기 시작했다.

단락 2 쓰기

소주제문 2

④ _____ .

의무 출석제는 또한 수업에서 교육적인 환경을 강화하는 데 일조한다.

구체적 근거 1: 일반적 진술

⑤ _____
_____ .

⑥ _____
_____ .

근면한 수업 출석이 단계적으로 지식과 이해를 높이므로 교수들이 일정하고 안정적인 그룹의 학생들을 능률적으로 가르칠 수 있다는 것이 한 가지 이유이다. 반면에, 출석이 선택적이라면 결석으로 인한 학생들 간 수준 차이와 전반적인 학생 수의 부족 때문에 토론과 실습의 전체적인 흐름이 심각하게 방해받는다.

구체적 근거 2: 예시

Studies show that mandatory attendance greatly improves the learning atmosphere in classes. They have found that in optional attendance courses, only a few sincere, hardworking students concentrate and enthusiastically participate in class discussions. The rest of the students who are chronically late or frequently skip class engage in distractive behaviors such as doodling, daydreaming, dozing off, or passing notes during class because they cannot understand the lessons. On the other hand, the studies further demonstrate that students take mandatory attendance classes much more seriously.

여러 연구에서는 의무 출석제가 수업에서 학습 분위기를 크게 향상시킨다는 것을 보여준다. 이 연구에서는 출석이 선택인 수업에서 오직 몇 명의 성실하고 열심히 공부하는 학생들만이 집중하고 의욕적으로 수업 토론에 참여한다는 것을 발견했다. 상습적으로 지각하거나 자주 수업을 빠지는 나머지 학생들은 수업 내용을 이해할 수 없기 때문에, 낙서나 공상을 하고, 졸거나, 수업 중에 쪽지를 돌리는 등 주의 산만한 행동을 일삼았다. 반면 연구 결과는 학생들이 의무 출석제 수업들을 훨씬 더 심각하게 받아들인다는 것을 보여 준다.

정답 p.489

03

Do you agree or disagree with the following statement? It is better to do work by machine than by hand. Use specific reasons and examples to support your opinion.

guideline

일을 손으로 처리하는 것보다 기계를 이용하여 하는 것이 더 낫다는 의견에 찬성하는 쪽으로 입장을 정하고, '(1) 시간이 절약된다 (2) 기계는 정확하다' 라는 소주제문을 뒷받침하는 구체적 근거를 각각 덧붙여 본론을 완성해 보자.

outline

Agree 찬성

1. Saves a lot of time

시간을 많이 절약한다

– can optimize the use of time by using machines

기계를 사용하면 시간을 최대한 활용할 수 있다

– e.g. dishwasher: improved life by saving time to wash dishes

예) 식기세척기: 설거지하는 시간을 절약함으로써 삶을 개선

2. Machines are more accurate

기계가 더 정확하다

– compared to humans, machines are precise and efficient

인간에 비해 기계들은 정확하고 효율적이다

– e.g. thanks to machines, teachers can mark exams without errors

예) 기계 덕분에 선생님은 실수 없이 시험을 채점할 수 있다

본론 쓰기 ✏️

단락 1 쓰기

소주제문 1

① _____ .

첫째로, 기계는 엄청난 양의 시간을 절약해 준다.

구체적 근거 1: 일반적 진술

This is because machines can operate at a constant speed over a long period of time. Conversely, because of their physical limitations, human beings need more time to complete the same tasks. Therefore, in today's busy world, people can optimize the use of their valuable time by using machines such as washing machines, hair dryers, and microwaves.

이는 기계가 일정한 속도로 오랜 시간 동안 작동할 수 있기 때문이다. 반대로, 육체적인 한계 때문에 인간은 같은 업무를 완수하는 데 더 많은 시간이 걸린다. 따라서, 오늘날의 바쁜 세상에서는 사람들은 식기세척기, 헤어 드라이어, 전자 레인지와 같은 기계를 사용함으로써 그들의 소중한 시간을 최대한 활용할 수 있다.

구체적 근거 2: 예시

② _____ .

③ _____ .

④ _____
_____ .

⑤ _____
_____ .

시간을 절약해 주는 기계의 가장 좋은 예는 식기세척기이다. 식기세척기는 많은 사람들의 삶을 극적으로 향상시킨다. 사람들은 싱크대 앞에 서서 설거지하고 행주로 닦으며, 적어도 매일 한 시간씩 귀중한 시간을 낭비하곤 했었다. 그러나, 식기세척기의 등장으로 사람들은 좋아하는 TV쇼를 보거나 가족과 대화를 나누거나 아니면 그냥 휴식을 취하며 시간을 원하는 대로 보낼 수 있다.

단락 2 쓰기

소주제문 2

⑥ _____ .

게다가, 기계는 사람보다 더 정확하게 일을 한다.

구체적 근거 1: 일반적 진술

Compared to humans who naturally make mistakes, machines do assignments very precisely and efficiently. They work at a regular rate, do not make careless mistakes, and do not get tired.

자연히 실수를 범하는 인간에 비해, 기계는 매우 정확하고 효율적으로 일을 처리한다. 기계는 일정한 속도로 일하고 부주의한 실수를 저지르지 않으며 지치지 않는다.

구체적 근거 2: 예시

⑦ _____ .

⑧ _____ .

⑨ _____

_____ .

⑩ _____

_____ .

예를 들면, 선생님들은 학생들의 객관식 시험을 채점하며 많은 실수를 범하곤 했었다. 주의력이 산만해지면 무심코 실수를 하곤 했다. 다행히도, 컴퓨터 방식으로 채점하는 기계의 등장 덕분에, 선생님들은 점수를 잘못 매길 가능성에 대해 더 이상 염려하지 않아도 된다. 그 결과, 학생들과 선생님들 모두 결과에 확신을 갖게 된다.

마무리 문장

As this example shows, machines can more efficiently and accurately take care of tedious details.

이러한 예가 보여 주듯이, 기계는 지루한 일의 세부적인 부분까지 보다 효율적이고 정확하게 다룰 수 있다.

정답 p.490

04

Do you agree or disagree with the following statement? The clothes a person wears affect his behavior. Use specific examples to support your answer.

guideline

사람들은 입는 옷에 따라 다르게 행동한다는 의견에 찬성하는 쪽으로 입장을 정하고, '(1) 옷의 격식에 따라 다르게 행동한다 (2) 옷의 사회적 역할에 따라 다르게 행동한다' 라는 소주제문을 뒷받침하는 각각의 구체적 근거를 제시하여 본론을 완성해 보자.

outline

> **Agree** 찬성
>
> 1. Act differently depending on formality and style of clothes
>   옷의 격식과 스타일에 따라 다르게 행동한다
>   - clothes represent certain characteristics, moods, etc
>   옷은 특정한 성격, 분위기 등을 대변한다
>   - e.g. act professionally with formal suit, or casually with T-shirt
>   예) 정장을 입으면 전문적으로, 티셔츠를 입으면 격식 없이 행동
> 2. Behave differently in line with clothes' social roles
>   옷의 사회적 역할에 따라 다르게 행동한다
>   - act according to expected responsibilities and manners
>   기대되는 책임과 태도에 따라 행동한다
>   - e.g. school uniforms: decreased student misbehavior
>   예) 교복: 학생들의 비행 감소

본론 쓰기

단락 1 쓰기

소주제문 1

To begin with, people act differently based on the formalness and style of their clothes.

첫째로, 사람들은 옷의 격식과 스타일에 근거해서 다르게 행동한다.

구체적 근거 1: 일반적 진술

① _____

_____ .

② _____

_____ .

즉, 옷의 디자인과 색상이 특정한 성격, 분위기, 느낌을 대변하는 것이다. 따라서, 사람들은 자신들의 옷이 얼마나 직업적 혹은 캐주얼하게 보이는가에 따라 자동적으로 행동한다.

구체적 근거 2: 예시

③ _____ .

④ _____ .

⑤ _____ .

⑥ _____

_____ .

개인적인 예를 들자면, 중요한 비즈니스 회의에서 나는 회의의 공식적이고 형식적인 분위기를 나타내는 단순한 디자인의 어두운 색상 정장을 입는다. 그 결과, 나는 직업적으로 행동하고 세련된 말투를 구사한다. 반면에, 야외 활동을 위해 티셔츠와 편한 바지를 입으면, 나는 자연스럽게 행동하고 매우 격식 없이 편안하고 활발해지게 된다.

단락 2 쓰기

소주제문 2

⑦ _____

_____ .

게다가, 사람들은 그들의 옷이 대변하는 사회적인 역할에 따라 다르게 행동한다.

구체적 근거 1: 일반적 진술

⑧ _____

_____ .

따라서 사람들이 교복이나 회사 유니폼과 같은 특정한 옷을 입을 때, 사람들은 그 옷이 상징하는 기대되는 사회적 책임과 의무에 따라 행동하는 경향이 있다.

구체적 근거 2: 예시

⑨ _____ .

⑩ _____ .

⑪ _____ .

예를 들면, 많은 고등학교들이 교복 정책을 채택하는데 이는 학교 관리자들이 교복이 학생들의 행동을 개선하고 방과 후의 범죄를 감소시킨다고 믿기 때문이다. 놀랄 것도 없이, 연구 결과는 의무 교복 정책 채택 후 흡연, 싸움, 절도, 음주와 같은 학생들의 비행 건수가 현저하게 감소하였다고 보고한다. 그 주된 이유는 사람들이 불건전하거나 불법 활동에 참여해서는 안 되는 미성년자로 자신들을 인식할 것이라는 사실을 학생들이 잘 알고 있었기 때문이다.

마무리 문장

As this example shows, clothes assign different social roles to people.

이러한 예가 보여 주듯이, 옷은 사람들에게 각기 다른 사회적 역할을 정해 준다.

정답 p.491

주어진 아웃라인을 참고하여 에세이의 본론을 작성하시오.

01 Do you agree or disagree with the following statement? Reading works of fiction is a more satisfying pastime than watching movies. Use specific reasons and examples to support your opinion.

outline

> Disagree 반대
>
> 1. Movies make the plots more thrilling and exciting
>   영화는 줄거리를 더 긴장감 있고 흥미롭게 만든다
>   – special sound effects & stimulating graphics
>   특수 음향 효과와 자극적인 그래픽
>   – e.g. movie vs. book 'The Lord of the Rings' (or your own example)
>   예) '반지의 제왕' 영화와 책 (혹은 자신의 예)
> 2. Provide families and friends with quality time
>   가족과 친구와 함께 보내는 오붓한 시간을 제공한다
>   – way to gather in one place and enjoy pastime together
>   한자리에 모여서 함께 여가 시간을 즐기는 방법
>   – e.g. families watching movies together (or your own example)
>   예) 가족끼리 모여서 영화를 관람 (혹은 자신의 예)

본론 쓰기 ✏️

소주제문 1

_____

_____ .

구체적 근거 1: 일반적 진술

_____

_____

_____ .

구체적 근거 2: 예시

_____

_____

_____

_____ .

소주제문 2

_____

_____ .

구체적 근거 1: 일반적 진술

_____

_____

_____ .

구체적 근거 2: 예시

_____

_____

_____

_____ .

정답 p.492

02

Do you agree or disagree with the following statement? Knowing how to read and write is more important now than it has ever been. Use specific reasons and examples to support your opinion.

outline

Agree 찬성

1. Ability to read is requisite for obtaining information

지식을 얻기 위해서는 읽기 능력이 필요하다

– libraries connected to the Internet: need reading ability to find information

인터넷에 연결된 도서관: 지식을 검색하기 위해서는 읽기 능력 필요

– e.g. my experience of writing term papers (or your own example)

예) 학기말 보고서를 작성했던 나의 경험 (혹은 자신의 예)

2. Writing competence is important for communication in this global age

세계화 시대에 작문 능력은 의사소통을 위해 중요하다

– Internet allows people around the world to communicate in writing

인터넷은 전세계의 사람들이 글로 의사소통하게 해준다

– e.g. workers trained in writing for business (or your own example)

예) 비즈니스를 위해 작문 훈련을 받는 직장인들 (혹은 자신의 예)

본론 쓰기 🖊

소주제문 1

_____ .

구체적 근거 1: 일반적 진술

_____

_____

_____ .

구체적 근거 2: 예시

_____

_____

_____

_____ .

소주제문 2

_____ .

구체적 근거 1: 일반적 진술

_____

_____

_____ .

구체적 근거 2: 예시

_____

_____

_____

_____ .

마무리 문장

_____

_____ .

정답 p.493

Ⅳ 에세이 쓰기 - 결론

결론은 글의 마무리 단계로, 여기에서 독자에게 강한 인상을 남기면 앞서 자신이 주장한 바가 더욱 설득력 있게 된다. 에세이의 '화룡점정'이라고 할 수 있는 결론을 쓰는 방식에 대해 알아보자.

1. 결론의 내용과 구성

결론은 에세이 전체의 마무리로, 구체적인 주제 설명에서 일반적 개념으로 범주를 넓혀 작성한다. 결론은 요약/정리와 맺음말로 구성된다.

- **요약/정리 (Concluding Sentence)**
  요약/정리는 서론의 대주제문을 재진술하거나, 본론의 내용을 요약하면 된다. 서론과 본론의 내용을 마지막으로 통일성 있게 정리하도록 한다.

- **맺음말 (Final Message)**
  맺음말은 글의 주제에 대한 자신의 최종 의견으로, 효과적이고 강한 메시지를 던질 수 있는 단계이다. 글의 주제에 기초하여 전체를 보는 관점으로 보다 일반적인 개념을 서술한다.

ex) 콘서트나 운동 경기 등을 직접 참여해서 실황으로 보는 것이 텔레비전으로 보는 것보다 즐겁다는 진술에 찬성하는지 반대하는지를 밝히고 구체적인 이유와 예를 들어 자신의 견해를 뒷받침한다.

요약/정리   정리하자면, 나는 보다 생동감 있고, TV가 보여 줄 수 없는 것까지도 볼 수 있기 때문에, 현장에 직접 가서 공연이나 경기를 보는 것이 낫다고 생각한다. 〈대주제문 재진술 or 본론 요약〉

맺음말   결국 TV의 편리함보다는 현장에서 느낄 수 있는 즐거움이 훨씬 크기 때문에 사람들이 공연장에 모이는 것이 아닐까? 〈전체 관점에서의 비교〉

결론에 쓰기 좋은 표현

In conclusion 결론적으로	In short/In brief 간단히 말해서
To sum up/In summary 요약해서 말하면	All in all 대체로
All things considered 모든 것을 고려해 볼 때	On the whole 전반적으로

T I P

독자에게 강한 여운을 남기는 나만의 독특한 맺음말을 써볼 수도 있다. 예를 들어, "화상 전화가 실제 만남을 대신할 수는 없듯이, TV 중계가 현장의 생동감을 대신할 수는 없다"와 같은 인상을 남기는 말 한 마디는 자신의 주장에 더욱 설득력을 실어줄 수 있다.

2. 결론 쓰기의 예

Question

Do you agree or disagree with this statement? People learn more from their peers than those older than them. Use specific reasons and examples to explain your position.

다음 명제에 찬성하는가 반대하는가? 사람들은 연장자들보다는 자기 또래의 사람들로부터 더 많이 배운다. 구체적인 이유와 예를 들어 자신의 입장을 설명하시오.

Step 1 요약/정리 쓰기

전체 내용을 간략히 정리하는 부분으로, 아웃라인에서 정리한 자신의 의견과 두 가지 이유를 간단히 한두 문장으로 요약한다. 이 때 서론의 대주제문을 참조하되 다른 표현을 활용해서 바꾸어 쓰도록 한다.

Step 2 맺음말 쓰기

마지막으로 좀 더 일반적인 관점에서 자신의 의견에 대한 인상을 강하게 남기는 문장을 쓴다. '나이 든 사람들이 어디서나 존경 받는 것은 그들이 지혜의 보고이기 때문이다.' 라고 하면서 연장자로부터 배울 것이 많다는 자신의 의견을 다시 한번 정리할 수 있다.

Outline	결론 쓰기 ✎

Disagree
1. Elders have more experience
  – know-how, skills to learn from
  – e.g. was able to learn practical skills from a senior worker
2. More comprehensive understanding of the life
  – more mature, have patience and wisdom
  – e.g. when sister worried about her future, advice from friends and parents
	요약 / 정리
	To sum up, people learn more from older people than those of the same age group because [elders have more actual experience] as well as [a comprehensive understanding of life.]
	
	맺음말
	All things considered, there is a reason why old people are venerated in all cultures: they are a great source of wisdom.

Hackers **Practice**

주어진 아웃라인을 참고하여 빈칸에 적절한 문장을 써서 결론을 완성하시오.

01

Do you agree or disagree with the following statement? It is better to study alone than in a group of students. Use specific reasons and examples to support your opinion.

guideline

혼자 공부하는 것보다 그룹 스터디를 하는 것이 낫다는 주장을 다시 한번 내세우고 그 이유 두 가지를 제시하여, 전체 에세이의 내용을 요약, 정리해 보자.

outline

- Disagree 반대
  1. Strengthen a sense of responsibility
     책임감을 강화한다
  2. Share ideas and broaden one's point of view
     의견을 교류하고 관점을 넓힌다

결론 쓰기 ✎

요약/정리

① _____

_____ .

② _____

_____ .

요약하자면, 다른 학생들과 모여서 공부하는 것은 혼자 공부하는 것보다 더 나은 선택이다. 학생들은 책임감을 강화할 수 있을 뿐만 아니라, 서로 다른 많은 의견을 교류함으로써 관점을 넓힐 수 있다.

맺음말

All in all, studying in a socially-interactive environment helps students in their overall development, not just academically.

대체로, 사람들 간에 교류가 있는 환경에서 공부하는 것은 학생들이 단순히 학술적으로 뿐만 아니라 전인적으로 성장하는 데 도움을 준다.

02

Do you agree or disagree with the following statement? Children should not make important decisions alone. Use specific reasons and examples to support your opinion.

guideline

아이들이 중요한 결정을 혼자 내려서는 안 된다는 자신의 입장을 다시 한번 강조하고, 아이들이 의사결정 능력이 떨어지는 이유 두 가지를 재언급하면서 에세이의 전체 내용을 정리해 보자.

outline

- Agree 찬성
  - 1. Children have a limited point of view
    - 어린이는 관점이 제한되어 있다
  - 2. Children don't have enough experience
    - 어린이는 충분한 경험이 없다

결론 쓰기 🖉

요약/정리

① _____

_____.

결론적으로, 어린이는 관점이 제한되어 있고 충분한 경험이 없으므로 중요한 결정을 혼자서 내리도록 해서는 안 된다.

맺음말

Thus, parents, who know their children's best interests, need to guide them in making wise decisions.

따라서, 아이들에게 가장 이익이 되는 것이 무엇인지를 알고 있는 부모들이 아이들로 하여금 현명한 결정을 내릴 수 있도록 도와줘야 한다.

03

Do you agree or disagree with the following statement. Watching a performance in person is preferable to viewing it on television. Use specific reasons and examples to support your opinion.

guideline

공연은 실황으로 보는 것보다 텔레비전으로 보는 것이 좋다는 입장의 에세이를 마무리하면서, 텔레비전으로 공연을 보는 즐거움을 간략하게 한 마디로 정리하여 결론의 맺음말을 작성해 보자.

outline

> Disagree 반대
> 1. Can relax in the comfort of home
>   집의 안락함 속에서 편하게 있을 수 있다
> 2. Can save time and money
>   시간과 돈을 절약할 수 있다

결론 쓰기 ✐

요약/정리

In short, I strongly disagree with the view that attending a live performance is better than watching it on TV. Watching a performance on TV allows you to relax in the comfort of your home and saves much time and money.

간단히 말해서, 나는 텔레비전으로 공연을 보는 것보다 현장에서 보는 것이 더 낫다는 의견에 강력히 반대한다. 텔레비전을 통해 중계를 보면 집의 안락함 속에서 편하게 즐길 수 있고, 시간과 돈을 절약할 수 있다.

맺음말

① _____

_____ .

결국, 집을 나서지 않고도 느긋하게 앉아서 자신만의 공연을 즐길 수 있는 것이다.

04

Do you agree or disagree with the following statement? It is better to have a teacher than to learn by oneself. Use specific reasons and examples to support your opinion.

guideline

독학하는 것보다는 선생님에게서 배우는 것이 좋다는 입장을 다시 한번 요약한 결론 문단에서, 선생님의 지도로 학생들이 성장하는 과정을 간단히 묘사하여 에세이를 마무리해 보자.

outline

> **_Agree_** 찬성
>
> 1. Teachers give helpful, time-saving guidance
>   선생님은 도움이 되고 시간을 절약하도록 지도를 해준다
> 2. Teachers are motivating and encouraging
>   선생님은 동기를 부여해 주고 의욕을 북돋아 준다

결론 쓰기

요약/정리

As you can see, I wholeheartedly agree with the idea that it is better to have a teacher. While a few students may prefer learning alone, teachers undeniably give helpful and time-saving tips as well as motivation and encouragement.

이렇게 볼 수 있듯이, 나는 선생님이 있는 것이 더 낫다는 생각에 진심으로 동감한다. 소수의 학생들은 혼자 공부하는 것을 선호할 수도 있지만, 선생님들은 확실히 도움이 되고 시간을 절약할 수 있는 조언을 해주며, 동기를 부여해 주고 의욕을 북돋아 준다.

맺음말

① _____

_____ .

결과적으로, 학생들은 선생님들의 지도와 함께 한걸음씩 내디디며 빠르게 성장하게 된다.

정답 p.494

주어진 아웃라인을 참고하여 에세이의 결론을 작성하시오.

01

Do you agree or disagree with the following statement? The most important period in a person's life is one's twenties. Use specific reasons and examples to support your opinion.

outline

> **Agree** 찬성
> 1. Time to choose a career
>   직업을 선택할 시기
> 2. Time to choose whether to have a life partner
>   배우자를 둘 것인지 선택할 시기

결론 쓰기 ✎

요약/정리

_____
_____
_____ .

맺음말

_____
_____ .

02

Do you agree or disagree with the following statement? Schools should ask students to evaluate their teachers. Use specific reasons and examples to support your opinion.

outline

- Agree 찬성
  1. Encourage students to actively participate in class
     학생들이 수업에 능동적으로 참여하도록 고무한다
  2. Improve teaching performance with constructive criticism
     건설적인 비평으로 교습 능력을 향상시킨다

결론 쓰기 ✎

요약/정리

_____

_____

_____ .

맺음말

_____

_____ .

정답 p.495

실제 Step별 샘플

Directions

Read the question below. You have 30 minutes to plan, write, and revise your essay. Typically, an effective response will contain a minimum of 300 words.

Question

Do you agree or disagree with this statement? People learn more from their peers than those older than them. Use specific reasons and examples to explain your position.

Step 1 문제 분석

사람은 나이 많은 사람보다 자신의 또래로부터 더 많이 배운다는 명제에 찬반의 입장을 묻는 문제이다. 주어진 명제에 대한 자신의 입장과 그렇게 생각하는 이유를 서론에서 간단히 밝히고, 본론에서 보다 구체적으로 설명한다.

Step 2 아웃라인 잡기

● 주어진 명제에 반대하는 쪽으로 방향을 정한다.
● 반대하는 이유로 연장자가 가지는 강점 두 가지와 구체적 근거를 정리해 본다.

Disagree 반대
1. Elders have more experience
연장자가 보다 많은 경험을 가지고 있다
– know-how, skills to learn from
전수 받을 노하우, 기술
– e.g. was able to learn practical skills from a senior worker
예) 직장 선배에게 실제적인 기술을 배울 수 있었다
2. More comprehensive understanding of the life
인생에 대한 보다 폭넓은 이해
– more mature, have patience and wisdom
보다 원숙하고, 인내력과 지혜를 가지고 있다
– e.g. when sister worried about her future, advice from friends and parents
예) 언니가 자신의 미래에 대해 걱정했을 때 친구들과 부모님으로부터 들었던 충고

Step 3 에세이 쓰기
작성한 아웃라인을 바탕으로 서론, 본론, 결론을 각각 작성하여 하나의 에세이를 완성한다.

(도입) As the world is changing faster than ever before, people in many cultures, especially the young, believe that people learn more from their peers, who are caught up with the latest developments, than from their elders. (대주제문) However, no matter how fast the world is changing, there are always more things to learn from older people than from one's peers. This is because elders have more life experience as well as a more comprehensive understanding of life.

(소주제문 1) To start with, older people have a wealth of experience in many aspects of life, and are thus able to provide practical assistance to young people. (구체적 근거 1: 일반적 진술) As older people have accumulated their own know-how in their careers or lives, they have many resources and skills with which to teach and guide younger people. (구체적 근거 2: 예시) From my personal experience, I learned much more from my senior employees than from my peers when I first started working at a motor company. As my peers did not have much work experience, we were not able to learn much from each other, but instead spent time out chatting and socializing. On the other hand, the senior employee in my department taught me many actual skills from doing presentations and writing papers to handling the machinery in the office. He helped me greatly, and thanks to him, I was able to acclimate easily to the workplace.

(소주제문 2) Furthermore, older people tend to have a more comprehensive understanding of life. (구체적 근거 1: 일반적 진술) They are not only more mature, but can also teach us valuable lessons of life such as patience and wisdom. (구체적 근거 2: 예시) For example, after failing twice in a row for an English teaching position, my sister hesitated whether or not to give up studying for the examination. When most of her friends encouraged her to start looking for a different job, she became hopeless and went through a hard time worrying about her future. Meanwhile, my parents advised her to continue studying and try to pass the examination again, knowing that she loves kids and enjoys teaching. On top of that, they told her stories of how they overcame failures in their own lives. Because of their advice, my sister rose to the challenge, passed her exam, and finally became a teacher last year. While her friends could not see the wisdom in continuing to try to become a teacher after already failing the examination twice, my parents knew that people should believe in their dreams and choose careers that make them happy, no matter what obstacles they have to surmount. (마무리 문장) In this respect, older people's understanding greatly affect younger people's lives in positive ways.

(요약/정리) To sum up, people learn more from older people than those of the same age group because elders have more actual experience as well as a comprehensive understanding of life. (맺음말) All things considered, there is a reason why old people are venerated in all cultures: they are a great source of wisdom.

Step 4 전체 검토/수정

에세이를 완성한 후에는 다음의 사항에 유의하여 작성한 글을 다시 한번 읽어 보고 틀린 부분은 수정한다. 감점 요소를 최소화하도록 각각의 유의사항을 염두하여 에세이를 쓰도록 한다.

Essay Organization (에세이의 구성)

서론	도입과 대주제문이 모두 명시되어 있는가?	Yes / No
	문제 유형에 적절한 대답과 입장을 보여주고 있는가?	Yes / No
본론	각 단락은 소주제문으로 시작하고 있는가?	Yes / No
	소주제문은 서론의 주제를 뒷받침하고 있는가?	Yes / No
	소주제문을 뒷받침하는 구체적 근거가 충분한가?	Yes / No
	소주제에서 벗어난 구체적 근거는 없는가?	Yes / No
	다양한 표현과 연결어가 사용되고 있는가?	Yes / No
결론	요약/정리가 대주제문을 반영하고 있는가?	Yes / No
	본론과의 통일성이 지켜지는가?	Yes / No

Sentence Structure & Grammar (문장 구조와 문법 체크)

문장에 주어와 동사가 포함되어 있는가?	Yes / No
주어와 동사의 수가 일치하는가?	Yes / No
동사의 시제가 올바로 사용되어 있는가?	Yes / No
지시어나 소유격이 명사와 일치하는가?	Yes / No
의미가 모호한 문장은 없는가?	Yes / No

에세이 해석

문제

다음 명제에 찬성하는가 반대하는가? 사람들은 연장자들보다는 자기 또래의 사람들로부터 더 많은 것을 배운다. 구체적인 이유와 예를 들어 자신의 입장을 설명하시오.

해석

세계가 과거의 그 어느 때보다도 빠르게 변하고 있기 때문에, 여러 문화권의 사람들, 그 중에서도 특히 젊은이들은 사람들이 나이 든 연장자보다 최신의 유행에 민감한 친구들에게서 보다 많은 것을 배울 수 있다고 믿고 있다. 하지만 세계가 얼마나 급격하게 변하고 있던 간에 상관없이, 항상 웃어른에게서 배울 수 있는 것이 친구들에게서 배울 수 있는 것보다 더 많다. 이는 웃어른들이 보다 긴 인생 경험뿐 아니라 인생에 대해 보다 폭넓은 이해를 가지고 있기 때문이다.

우선 첫째로, 연장자들은 인생의 여러 면에 있어서 풍부한 경험을 갖고 있고, 따라서 젊은 사람에게 실제적인 도움을 줄 수 있다. 연장자들은 그들의 직장이나 인생에 있어서 자신만의 노하우를 쌓아왔기 때문에, 젊은 사람들을 가르치고 지도해 줄 수 있는 지식이나 기술을 많이 가지고 있다. 내 개인적인 경험에 따르면, 내가 처음 자동차 회사에서 일하기 시작했을 때 동료들보다는 직장 선배들에게 보다 많은 것을 배웠다. 동료들은 풍부한 업무 경험을 가지고 있지 않았기 때문에 우리는 서로에게서 많은 것을 배울 수 없었고 대신, 잡담을 나누고 노닥거리면서 시간을 보냈다. 한편, 내가 속한 부서의 직장 선배는 프레젠테이션을 하고 서류를 작성하는 요령에서부터 사무실 내의 기계장치를 다루는 기술까지 많은 실제 실제적인 기술을 가르쳐 주었다. 그는 나에게 큰 도움을 주었고, 그 덕분에 나는 직장에 쉽게 적응할 수 있었다.

그 뿐 아니라, 연장자들은 인생에 대한 보다 폭넓은 이해를 가지고 있다. 이들은 보다 원숙할 뿐 아니라, 우리에게 인내와 지혜 같은 귀중한 인생의 덕목을 가르쳐줄 수 있다. 예를 들어, 우리 언니는 영어교사 임용 시험에 두 번 연달아서 떨어졌을 때 시험 공부를 그만둬야 할지 말지 결정을 내리지 못했다. 대부분의 친구들이 다른 직장을 찾아보기를 권했을 때 언니는 희망을 잃었고 미래에 대해서 걱정하면서 힘든 시간을 보냈다. 그 때, 우리 부모님은 언니가 아이들을 좋아하고 가르치는 것을 즐긴다는 것을 알기에, 공부를 계속해서 다시 한번 시험에 도전해 보라고 조언했다. 이에 덧붙여서, 부모님은 언니에게 자신들이 살아오면서 어떻게 실패를 극복해 왔는지에 대한 이야기를 해주셨다. 부모님의 조언 덕분에, 언니는 도전에 응했고 시험에 합격해서 결국 작년에 선생님이 되었다. 언니의 친구들은 시험에 이미 두 번이나 떨어진 후에도 계속 선생님이 되기 위해 노력하는 것이 현명한 선택이라는 것을 알지 못했던 반면, 부모님은 사람들이 어떠한 어려움을 이겨내야 할지라도, 자신의 꿈을 믿고 자신들을 행복하게 만들어줄 직업을 선택해야 한다는 것을 알고 계셨다. 이런 점에서 볼 때, 연장자의 이해력은 젊은이들의 삶에 큰 긍정적 영향을 미칠 수 있다.

요약해서 말하자면, 사람들은 동년배 집단의 사람들보다 연장자들에게서 보다 많은 것을 배우는데, 이는 연장자들이 삶에 대한 폭넓은 이해뿐 아니라 보다 많은 실제 경험을 가지고 있기 때문이다. 이러한 모든 것들을 생각해 보면, 어느 문화권에서나 연장자들이 존경을 받는 데는 한 가지 이유가 있다. 그들이 지혜의 보고이기 때문이다.

peer[piər] 동배   elder[éldər] 연장자   comprehensive[kàmprihénsiv] 포괄적인, 종합적인   a wealth of 풍부한, 많은
aspect[ǽspekt] 관점   accumulate[əkjúːmjəlèit] 축적하다   senior[síːnjər] 손위의, 선배의   socialize[sóuʃəlàiz] 어울리다
machinery[məʃíːnəri] 기계류   thanks to~ ~덕분에   acclimate[əkláimit] 순응하다   mature[mətʃúər] 원숙한, 분별 있는
patience[péiʃəns] 인내심   in a row 연속적으로   hopeless[hóuplis] 절망적인   meanwhile[míːnhwàil] 그 동안
rise to the challenge 어려움에 잘 대처하다   obstacle[ábstəkl] 장애(물)   surmount[sərmáunt] 극복하다
venerate[vénərèit] 존경하다

P O W E R Test

Directions Read the question below. You have 30 minutes to plan, write, and revise your essay. Typically, an effective response will contain a minimum of 300 words.

Question Do you agree or disagree with the following statement?

People are incapable of being satisfied with what they have; they always want what they don't have.

Use specific reasons and examples to support your answer.

---

outline ✎

- _____
  _____
- _____
  _____
- _____
  _____
- _____
  _____
- _____
  _____
- _____
  _____
-

정답 p.496

Directions Read the question below. You have 30 minutes to plan, write, and revise your essay. Typically, an effective response will contain a minimum of 300 words.

Question Do you agree or disagree with the following statement?

Mobile phones have given people more freedom.

Use specific reasons and examples to support your answer.

outline ✎

- _____
- _____
- _____
- _____
- _____
- _____
- _____
- _____

정답 p.498

Hackers iBT TOEFL Writing

Actual Test

Hackers TOEFL iBT Writing

 Track 11

Directions You have 20 minutes to plan and write your response. Your response will be judged on the basis of the quality of your writing and on how well your response presents the points in the lecture and the relationship to the reading passage. Typically, an effective response will be 150 to 225 words.

The United States' individual income tax was first legislated by the northern states in 1862, during the American Civil War. It was essential in raising funds to cover the high costs of the war. Additional revenue was desperately needed to fund the Union army, on top of the income generated by the usual taxes and customs on imports, since the war had lasted longer and proved more expensive than anticipated. The tax was successful, raising millions for the federal government.

Another aspect of this tax, the first progressive tax in the history of the US, was its fairness. Individuals were charged based on their ability to pay. Therefore, those earning less than $600 per year, the vast majority of the population, were exempt from the tax. People making between $600 and $5,000 were to pay 5% of their income, while those on the upper end, with incomes of upwards of $10,000 per year, had to pay 10% on their earnings. This graduated rate system removed a portion of the tax burden from the poor, who were disproportionately affected by consumption taxes on food, clothes and other essential items.

In addition, the income tax was necessary to consolidate control in the hands of the federal government. This was especially important at a time when federal authority was under attack by the southern Confederate states. For the first time, the Bureau of Internal Revenue made its presence known with an "army of officials" in every corner of the country. This centralized system empowered the government with the authority to enforce the law.

Listen to the lecture

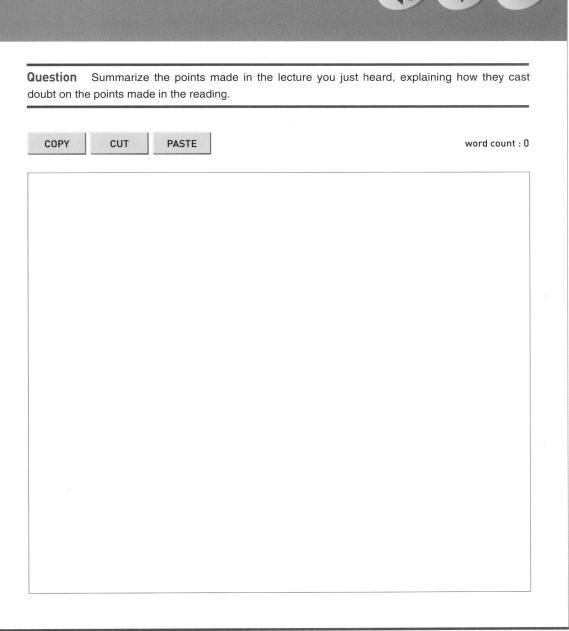

VOLUME

HELP
?

NEXT

Question Summarize the points made in the lecture you just heard, explaining how they cast doubt on the points made in the reading.

COPY   CUT   PASTE

word count : 0

Hackers TOEFL iBT Writing

PAUSE
TEST

Directions Read the question below. You have 30 minutes to plan, write, and revise your essay. Typically, an effective response will contain a minimum of 300 words.

Question Do you agree or disagree with the following statement?

The decisions that people make quickly are always wrong.

Use specific reasons and examples to support your answer.

VOLUME

HELP
?

NEXT

COPY   CUT   PASTE

word count : 0

Hackers TOEFL iBT Writing

Directions You have 20 minutes to plan and write your response. Your response will be judged on the basis of the quality of your writing and on how well your response presents the points in the lecture and the relationship to the reading passage. Typically, an effective response will be 150 to 225 words.

Rural communities in the United States are threatened with the impending shortage of doctors. Most of the current physicians in these areas are elderly. When they retire, there will be a shortage of young doctors to replace them. Unfortunately, this looming crisis does not look like it will be averted; new medical school graduates do not want to work in rural areas for several reasons.

One big deterrent to working in the countryside is the lower pay doctors receive. Many medical school graduates have accrued high levels of debt in school. Thus, they are attracted to high-paying jobs that will help them get out of debt faster. Urban positions offer this higher remuneration they seek. As a result, most doctors avoid working in low-paying rural jobs.

In addition, many young doctors who work in rural areas lack access to experienced doctors. As recent graduates, young doctors don't have enough practical training to feel confident about their abilities to diagnose under difficult conditions. Hence, they prefer being around other experienced doctors and learning from them. Cities provide a wealth of experienced doctors to choose from to serve as guides and mentors. This informal apprenticeship is extremely valuable for young doctors, and the patients they will invariably save.

On top of that, being in the countryside is simply not appealing for many young doctors. Most of them want to enjoy a big-city lifestyle with its cultural and entertainment amenities. The rural areas often seem too slow-paced and boring for recent medical school graduates. Instead, they often seek a stimulating and exciting atmosphere in which to spend this dynamic time in their lives.

Listen to the lecture

VOLUME
◀))

HELP
?

NEXT
➡

Question   Summarize the points made in the lecture you just heard, explaining how they cast doubt on the points made in the reading.

| COPY | CUT | PASTE | word count : 0 |

정답 p.505

Actual Test

Hackers TOEFL iBT Writing

Directions Read the question below. You have 30 minutes to plan, write, and revise your essay. Typically, an effective response will contain a minimum of 300 words.

Question Do you agree or disagree with the following statement?

It is sometimes acceptable to infringe upon people's freedom.

Use specific reasons and examples to support your answer.

COPY   CUT   PASTE

word count : 0

30일 완성
Model Essay

Hackers iBT TOEFL Writing

Model Essay 구성

Question
iBT 기출문제를 포함한 30개 topic

Outline (Agree/Disagree)
질문에 대한 찬성/반대 유형 모범 아웃라인

Model Essay
아웃라인을 바탕으로 찬성/반대 중 하나의 주장을 선택하여 작성한 모범 답안

해석과 어휘
에세이 해석과 어휘 해설

Review
에세이에 사용된 주요 표현을 학습할 수 있는 빈칸 채우기 문제

Model Essay 학습 방법

1st STEP Question & Outline
문제에서 요구하는 의도를 파악하고 찬성과 반대 입장 모두 작성된 아웃라인을 참고한다. 주장을 뒷받침할 수 있는 아이디어가 많은 입장으로 방향을 정하되 *표 되어 있는 아웃라인은 제시된 모델 에세이의 기본 구조가 되므로 사고의 전개를 파악해 본다.

2nd STEP Model Essay
에세이의 전체 내용을 읽으며 글의 구조와 사고의 흐름을 익힌다. Model Essay에 굵게 처리된 표현은 다른 주제의 에세이를 작성할 때도 쓰일 수 있는 유용한 표현이므로 꼼꼼하게 익혀 자신의 것으로 만든다.

3rd STEP Review
에세이의 빈칸을 채우는 연습을 통해 앞서 학습한 주요 표현을 복습한다.

Question

Do you agree or disagree with the following statement? University athletic departments should receive the same amount of funding as university libraries. Use specific reasons and examples to support your answer.

대학에서 학생들의 스포츠 활동은 도서관만큼 재원을 지원받아야 한다는 진술에 찬성하는지 반대하는지를 밝히고 구체적인 이유와 예를 들어 대답을 뒷받침한다.

Outline

Agree*

1. Sports improve students' physical health
   스포츠는 학생들의 신체 건강을 향상시킨다
   - many studies show exercises strengthen bones, muscles, etc.
     많은 연구 결과들이 운동이 뼈, 근육 등을 강화한다는 사실을 보여준다
   - e.g. obese cousin lost weight after started regular walking
     예) 비만인 사촌이 정기적으로 걷기 시작한 이후 체중을 감량하였다

2. Sports activities foster students' social skills
   스포츠 활동은 학생들의 사회적 기술을 양성한다
   - sports activities require collective effort and cooperation
     스포츠 활동은 공동의 노력과 협력을 필요로 한다
   - e.g. soccer game
     예) 축구 경기

Disagree

1. Schools should cover more students' needs
   학교는 더 많은 학생들의 요구를 수용해야 한다
   - money should be spent to help the most students
     자금은 대부분의 학생을 돕는데 쓰여야 한다
   - e.g. provided more scholarships, so more students liked school
     예) 장학금을 더 많이 제공해서 더 많은 학생들이 학교를 좋아하게 되었다

2. Studying outweighs playing sports
   공부를 하는 것이 운동을 하는 것보다 더 중요하다
   - if focused on academics, students perform better
     학업에 집중하면, 학생들은 더 나은 성과를 보인다
   - e.g. a school spent most money on sports, and had low test scores
     예) 한 학교는 대부분의 자금을 운동에 써서 시험 성적이 낮았다

Model Essay

(도입) In order to prepare their students academically and help their graduates find jobs, many universities fund their libraries and other academic facilities **at the expense of** sports activities. In the "real world," sports are considered a waste of time **at worst** and a pleasant diversion **at best**. (대주제문) However, sports improve students' physical health and social skills. Therefore, universities should invest an equal amount of money in both their students' sports activities and school libraries.

(소주제문 1) To start with, sports activities **play a pivotal role** in promoting students' physical health. (구체적 근거 1: 일반적 진술) This is evidenced by a number of clinical studies that clearly show that a variety of physically active aerobic exercises such as cycling, swimming, and running, especially during one's twenties, build and strengthen bones, muscles, and joints. **More importantly**, habitual physical activity **has a positive influence on** circulation of blood and reduces the risk of hypertension and diabetes. (구체적 근거 2: 예시) **To illustrate this point**, my cousin **led a sedentary life** by being glued to the computer for hours on end everyday. Inevitably, he **suffered from** obesity as a result of his inactive lifestyle. However, he began to lose considerable weight after he joined a walkathon club in college and started walking for two hours everyday for five months as his doctor suggested. (마무리 문장) **Likewise**, students can reap numerous health benefits from participating in sports activities.

(소주제문 2) **Also**, sports activities foster students' social skills. (구체적 근거 1: 일반적 진술) This is because sports include a wide variety of group activities such as soccer, football, and basketball that require **collective** effort and cooperation. (구체적 근거 2: 예시) The best example of this is a soccer game. When participating in soccer games, students have the chance to learn how to cooperate and work as a team. They cheer for their teammates, pass the ball to one another through openings, and strive together for the common goal of leading the game to victory, one that a single person cannot attain.

(요약 / 정리) **To summarize**, I definitely believe that universities should give the same amount of funds to students' sports activities as they do to their libraries. (맺음말) **On the whole**, I agree with the saying "**a sound mind in a sound body**." In other words, students' mental fitness from healthy social relationships and physical well-being are the most important factors for their success.

해석

학생들을 학문적으로 준비시키고 졸업생들이 일자리를 찾는 것을 돕기 위해, 많은 대학들은 스포츠 활동을 희생해서 도서관이나 기타 학업 시설에 자금을 지원한다. "현실 세계"에서 스포츠는 최악의 경우 시간 낭비로까지 여겨지고 기껏해야 즐거운 오락으로 여겨진다. 하지만, 스포츠는 학생들의 육체적인 건강과 사회 생활 능력을 배양해 준다. 따라서 대학은 학생들의 스포츠 활동과 학교 도서관에 같은 양의 돈을 투자하여야 한다.

우선 스포츠 활동은 학생들의 신체적인 건강을 증진시키는 데 중요한 역할을 한다. 이는 특히 20대에 하는 싸이클링, 수영, 달리기 등의 다양한 활동적인 유산소 운동이 골격, 근육, 관절 등을 형성하고 단단하게 해준다는 것을 보여준 수많은 임상 연구에 의해서 증명되었다. 보다 더 중요한 것은 습관적인 운동이 혈액순환에 좋은 영향을 미치고 고혈압이나 당뇨병의 위험을 줄여 준다는 것이다. 예를 들면, 내 사촌은 매일 몇 시간 동안 컴퓨터에 붙어서 앉아있는 삶을 살았다. 당연하게도, 그는 활동적이지 않은 생활을 한 결과로 비만으로 고생했다. 하지만, 그가 의사가 권한대로 대학에서 걷기 클럽에 가입해서 5개월간 매일 두 시간씩 걷기 시작한 이래로 상당한 양의 체중을 감량하기 시작했다. 이처럼 학생들은 스포츠 활동에 참여함으로써 많은 혜택을 볼 수 있다.

또한, 스포츠 활동들은 학생들의 사회적 기술을 양성한다. 이는 스포츠가 공동의 노력과 협동을 요구하는 축구, 미식축구, 농구와 같은 다양한 단체 활동들을 포함하기 때문이다. 이것의 가장 좋은 예는 축구 경기이다. 축구 경기에 참여할 때, 학생들은 협력하고 팀으로 일하는 법을 배울 기회를 갖는다. 그들은 팀 동료들을 위해 응원하고 틈새를 통해서 다른 구성원에게 공을 패스하고, 경기를 승리로 이끄는 공동의 목표를 달성하기 위해서 함께 노력한다. 이는 혼자서는 달성할 수 없는 것이다.

요약하자면, 나는 대학이 도서관에 들이는 것과 같은 금액의 자금을 학생들의 스포츠 활동에 지원해야 한다고 확신한다. 전체적으로 볼 때, 나는 "건강한 신체에 건전한 정신"이라는 격언에 동의한다. 다르게 말하면, 건전한 사회 관계와 신체적인 건강으로부터 비롯되는 학생들의 정서적인 건강은 이들의 성공을 위한 가장 중요한 요소이다.

obese[oʊbíːs] 비만의   foster[fɔ́(ː)stər] 양성하다   outweigh[àutwéi] (가치, 중요성, 영향력이) ~보다 크다
play a pivotal role 중추적 역할을 하다   clinical study 임상 연구   aerobic[ɛəróubik] 신체의 산소 소비량을 증대하는
habitual[həbítʃuəl] 습관적인   circulation[sə̀ːrkjəléiʃən] 순환   hypertension[hàipərténʃən] 고혈압
diabetes[dàiəbíːtiːz] 당뇨병   sedentary[sédəntèri] 앉아 있는   obesity[oʊbíːsəti] 비만   inactive[inǽktiv] 활동하지 않는
considerable[kənsídərəbl] 상당한   walkathon[wɔ́(ː)kəθɑ̀n] 장거리 경보   likewise[láikwàiz] 마찬가지로
collective[kəléktiv] 연합된, 단체의   a sound mind in a sound body 건강한 신체에 건전한 정신   fitness[fítnis] 건강

① at the expense of   ② at worst   ③ at best   ④ play a pivotal role   ⑤ More importantly
⑥ has a positive influence on   ⑦ To illustrate this point   ⑧ led a sedentary life
⑨ suffered from   ⑩ Likewise   ⑪ Also   ⑫ collective   ⑬ To summarize   ⑭ On the whole
⑮ a sound mind in a sound body

Review

(도입) In order to prepare their students academically and help their graduates find jobs, many universities fund their libraries and other academic facilities ① a_____ sports activities. In the "real world," sports are considered a waste of time ② a_____ and a pleasant diversion ③ a_____ . (대주제문) However, sports improve students' physical health and social skills. Therefore, universities should invest an equal amount of money in both their students' sports activities and school libraries.

(소주제문 1) To start with, sports activities ④ p_____ in promoting students' physical health. (구체적 근거 1: 일반적 진술) This is evidenced by a number of clinical studies that clearly show that a variety of physically active aerobic exercises such as cycling, swimming, and running, especially during one's twenties, build and strengthen bones, muscles, and joints. ⑤ M_____ _____, habitual physical activity ⑥ h_____ circulation of blood and reduces the risk of hypertension and diabetes. (구체적 근거 2: 예시) ⑦ T_____, my cousin ⑧ l_____ by being glued to the computer for hours on end everyday. Inevitably, he ⑨ s_____ obesity as a result of his inactive lifestyle. However, he began to lose considerable weight after he joined a walkathon club in college and started walking for two hours everyday for five months as his doctor suggested. (마무리 문장) ⑩ L_____, students can reap numerous health benefits from participating in sports activities.

(소주제문 2) ⑪ A_____, sports activities foster students' social skills. (구체적 근거 1: 일반적 진술) This is because sports include a wide variety of group activities such as soccer, football, and basketball that require ⑫ c_____ effort and cooperation. (구체적 근거 2: 예시) The best example of this is a soccer game. When participating in soccer games, students have the chance to learn how to cooperate and work as a team. They cheer for their teammates, pass the ball to one another through openings, and strire together for the common goal of leading the game to victory, one that a single person cannot attain.

(요약 / 정리) ⑬ T_____, I definitely believe that universities should give the same amount of funds to students' sports activities as they do to their libraries. (맺음말) ⑭ O_____, I agree with the saying "⑮ a_____." In other words, students' mental fitness from healthy social relationships and physical well-being are the most important factors for their success.

Question

Do you agree or disagree with the following statement? Being happy with a job is more important than having a high salary. Use specific reasons and examples to support your answer.

업무에 만족하는 것이 높은 보수를 받는 것보다 중요하다는 진술에 찬성하는지 반대하는지를 밝히고 구체적인 이유와 예를 들어 대답을 뒷받침한다.

Outline

Agree*

1. Money can't buy happiness
   돈으로 행복을 살 수 없다
   - stuck in dull jobs
     지루한 직업에 갇히게 됨
   - e.g. brother unhappy with high paying job
     예) 높은 보수의 직장에서 불행했던 형

2. More successful if one enjoys work
   일을 즐기면 더 성공할 수 있다
   - motivation more powerful if one enjoys work
     일을 즐기면 동기 부여가 더 강력하다
   - e.g. Steve Jobs at Apple Computers
     예) 애플 컴퓨터의 스티브 잡스

Disagree

1. Money is necessary for life
   인생에 돈이 필요하다
   - buy food, house
     음식과 주택 구매
   - e.g. parents' preparation for retirement
     예) 부모님의 은퇴 준비

2. High salary means one can do more enjoyable things
   높은 보수로 더 많은 일을 즐길 수 있다
   - have new experiences
     새로운 경험을 한다
   - e.g. take time off to travel
     예) 여행을 떠나 시간을 보낸다

Model Essay

(도입) After graduating from school, people spend the **bulk of** their time at their jobs. Regardless of their salaries, if they dread going to work, then they will **have difficulty enjoying** the rest of their lives. (대주제문) **In this sense**, finding satisfying positions is more important than finding lucrative positions. This is **due to** the fact that money alone cannot make people happy and if they enjoy their jobs, they are more likely to succeed.

(소주제문 1) Making a lot of money will not be sufficient if a person is unhappy. (구체적 근거 1: 일반적 진술) While money is necessary in order to survive, people who choose high salaries often find themselves **stuck in** positions that they aren't satisfied with. The problems they have with their careers then **taint** other aspects of their lives, making them unhappy. (구체적 근거 2: 예시) To illustrate, my brother always hoped to be a writer, but took an administrator position in a high-tech company because it paid him a higher salary. However, whenever he came home from work, he seemed so **stressed out** that he did not talk much or eat properly but just went to bed. Fortunately, after he left his job and started building his career in the literary world, he enjoyed going to work and carried that happiness with him when returning home at night.

(소주제문 2) **Moreover**, if people choose jobs that they are passionate about, then they have a much greater chance for success. (구체적 근거 1: 일반적 진술) This is mainly due to the fact that they put in more effort than people who are merely trying to earn their paychecks. While some believe money to be a great motivator, nothing **compares to** the results of following one's dreams. (구체적 근거 2: 예시) Steve Jobs, the head of Apple Computers, is one of the best examples that demonstrate this point. He had to start his business from his garage, and he spent night and day putting parts together because he was **dedicated to** changing the world with computers. Due to his enthusiasm toward his work, Jobs has improved the world for everyone and won the respect of his peers. He succeeded because he had found his **calling**.

(요약/정리) **For these reasons**, I strongly agree that being happy with a job should come before the benefits of a high salary, since people who find pleasure in their work are happier and do better than people who only value money. (맺음말) Unfortunately, people are **drawn in** by the allure of **high-paying jobs** and do not stop to think of the impact that such positions will have on other aspects of their lives. By choosing careers that they enjoy, people will, **in the long run**, have more balanced lives.

해석

학교를 졸업한 후, 사람들은 대부분의 시간을 직장에서 보낸다. 봉급에 상관없이 만일 그 직장이 출근하기 두려운 곳이라면 업무 외 생활에서도 즐거움을 찾기 힘들게 될 것이다. 이러한 점에서 만족스러운 일자리를 찾는 것이 수입이 좋은 일자리를 찾는 것보다 더 중요하다. 이것은 돈만으로는 사람들이 행복해질 수 없다는 사실 때문이며, 만약 사람들이 일을 즐긴다면 보다 성공할 가능성이 높아지기 때문이다.

만약에 어떤 사람이 불행하다면 돈을 많이 버는 것으로 충분하지 않을 것이다. 돈은 생활을 영위하는 데 있어서 필요하지만 높은 보수를 선택하는 사람들은 종종 자신이 원하지 않는 자리에 갇혀 있는 자신을 발견하게 된다. 직장에서 그들이 겪는 문제는 인생의 다른 측면에 좋지 않은 영향을 미치게 될 것이고, 결국 그들을 불행하게 만들 것이다. 예를 들어, 나의 형은 항상 작가가 되고 싶어 했지만, 높은 봉급을 지급한다는 이유로 첨단기술 회사의 관리직을 맡았다. 그러나 일을 마치고 집에 올 때마다 형은 스트레스로 너무 지쳐서 말도 많이 하지 않고, 제대로 먹지도 않은 채 곧장 잠자리에 들었다. 다행히도 형이 그 직장을 그만두고 문학계로 진로를 바꾸자, 그는 직장에 가는 것을 즐기게 되었고 그 행복감을 밤에 집으로 돌아올 때 가지고 왔다.

게다가, 만약 사람들이 자신이 열정적으로 임할 수 있는 직업을 선택한다면, 그 사람은 성공할 가능성이 훨씬 더 높다. 이것은 단지 봉급만 챙기려는 사람보다 그 사람이 훨씬 더 많은 노력을 기울일 것이기 때문이다. 돈이 큰 동기 부여가 된다고 믿는 사람들도 있지만, 개인의 꿈을 추구하는 것의 결과에 비할 수 있는 것은 아무것도 없다. 이 논지를 가장 잘 설명해주는 예는 애플 컴퓨터의 대표이사인 스티브 잡스이다. 그는 컴퓨터로 세상을 변화시키고자 하는 신념으로 그의 차고에서 사업을 시작해서 밤낮으로 부품을 조립했다. 그는 일에 대한 열정으로 모든 이들을 위해 세상을 발전시켰고 동료들의 존경을 얻어냈다. 그는 그의 천직을 찾았기 때문에 성공할 수 있었다.

이러한 이유로, 일에 대한 만족이 높은 봉급의 장점보다 우선시되어야 한다는 데 나는 강력하게 동의한다. 자신의 업무를 즐기는 사람이 더 행복하고, 돈의 가치만을 중시하는 사람들보다 일을 더 잘할 수 있기 때문이다. 안타깝게도 사람들은 높은 봉급의 유혹에 이끌리고 그런 업무가 인생의 다른 면들에 미칠 영향에 대해서는 생각해 보지 않는다. 자신이 즐길 수 있는 업무를 선택함으로써 사람들은 결국에 더 안정된 삶을 살아갈 것이다.

---

bulk of ~ ~의 대부분   regardless of ~ ~에 관계없이   dread[dred] 두려워하다   have difficulty (in) ~ing ~하는 데 어려움을 겪다
in this sense 이러한 점에서   lucrative[lúːkrətiv] 유리한, 돈이 벌리는   due to ~ ~에 기인하는, ~때문인   be likely to ~ ~할 것 같다
sufficient[səfíʃənt] 충분한   stuck in ~ ~에 처박힌   taint[teint] 더럽히다   to illustrate 예를 들면
administrator[ədmínistrèitər] 관리자   stressed out 스트레스로 지친   be passionate about ~ ~에 열정적이다
paycheck[péitʃèk] 급료 (지불 수표)   motivator[móutəvèitər] 동기를 부여하는 것   nothing compares to ~ ~에 비할 것은 없다
demonstrate[démənstrèit] 설명하다   garage[gəráːdʒ] 차고   be dedicated to ~ ~에 헌신하다, 전념하다
enthusiasm[inθúːziæzəm] 열중   calling[kɔ́ːliŋ] 천직   for these reasons 이러한 이유들 때문에   be drawn in ~ ~에 이끌리다
allure[əljúər] 매혹   high-paying job 보수가 많은 직업   in the long run 결국에는   balanced[bǽlənst] 안정된

---

① bulk of   ② have difficulty enjoying   ③ In this sense   ④ due to   ⑤ stuck in   ⑥ taint
⑦ stressed out   ⑧ Moreover   ⑨ compares to   ⑩ dedicated to   ⑪ calling
⑫ For these reasons   ⑬ drawn in   ⑭ high-paying jobs   ⑮ in the long run

Review

(도입) After graduating from school, people spend the ① b_____ their time at their jobs. Regardless of their salaries, if they dread going to work, then they will ② h_____ the rest of their lives. (대주제문) ③ I_____, finding satisfying positions is more important than finding lucrative positions. This is ④ d_____ the fact that money alone cannot make people happy and if they enjoy their jobs, they are more likely to succeed.

(소주제문 1) Making a lot of money will not be sufficient if a person is unhappy. (구체적 근거 1: 일반적 진술) While money is necessary in order to survive, people who choose high salaries often find themselves ⑤ s_____ positions that they aren't satisfied with. The problems they have with their careers then ⑥ t_____ other aspects of their lives, making them unhappy. (구체적 근거 2: 예시) To illustrate, my brother always hoped to be a writer, but took an administrator position in a high-tech company because it paid him a higher salary. However, whenever he came home from work, he seemed so ⑦ s_____ that he did not talk much or eat properly but just went to bed. Fortunately, after he left his job and started building his career in the literary world, he enjoyed going to work and carried that happiness with him when returning home at night.

(소주제문 2) ⑧ M_____, if people choose jobs that they are passionate about, then they have a much greater chance for success. (구체적 근거 1: 일반적 진술) This is mainly due to the fact that they put in more effort than people who are merely trying to earn their paychecks. While some believe money to be a great motivator, nothing ⑨ c_____ the results of following one's dreams. (구체적 근거 2: 예시) Steve Jobs, the head of Apple Computers, is one of the best examples that demonstrate this point. He had to start his business from his garage, and he spent night and day putting parts together because he was ⑩ d_____ changing the world with computers. Due to his enthusiasm toward his work, Jobs has improved the world for everyone and won the respect of his peers. He succeeded because he had found his ⑪ c_____.

(요약/정리) ⑫ F_____, I strongly agree that being happy with a job should come before the benefits of a high salary, since people who find pleasure in their work are happier and do better than people who only value money. (맺음말) Unfortunately, people are ⑬ d_____ by the allure of ⑭ h_____ and do not stop to think of the impact that such positions will have on other aspects of their lives. By choosing careers that they enjoy, people will, ⑮ i_____, have more balanced lives.

Question

Do you agree or disagree with the following statement? Young people enjoy life more than older people. Use specific reasons and examples to support your answer.

나이 든 사람들보다 젊은 사람들이 인생을 더 즐긴다는 진술에 찬성하는지 반대하는지를 밝히고 구체적인 이유와 예를 들어 대답을 뒷받침한다.

Outline

Agree*

1. Young people are physically active
   젊은 사람들은 육체적으로 활동적이다
   - if not healthy, it's hard to enjoy life to its fullest
     건강하지 않으면 인생을 충분히 즐길 수 없다
   - e.g. grandfather can't enjoy hiking anymore because of physical weakness
     예) 할아버지께서는 건강이 쇠약해지셔서 등산을 더 이상 즐기실 수 없다

2. Young people have fewer responsibilities
   젊은 사람들은 책임이 적다
   - as people age, obligations restrict people from enjoying their lives
     사람들이 나이가 들면서 책임 때문에 인생을 즐기는 것을 제한받는다
   - e.g. older brother can't take vacation whereas I can
     예) 오빠는 휴가를 떠날 수 없지만 나는 떠날 수 있다

Disagree

1. Older people have more time and money
   나이 든 사람들은 시간과 돈이 더 많다
   - enough time and money offers wider range of options to improve quality of life
     충분한 돈과 시간은 삶의 질을 향상시킬 수 있는 보다 넓은 선택의 기회를 제공한다
   - e.g. grandmother volunteers after retirement and feels more satisfied with her life
     예) 할머니께서는 은퇴 후에 봉사 활동을 하시며 삶에 대해 더 만족하신다

2. Older people know how to enjoy life through experience
   나이 든 사람들은 경험을 통해 인생을 즐기는 방법을 안다
   - old people have less stress and know how to deal with it
     나이 든 사람들은 스트레스가 적고 그것을 해소하는 방법을 안다
   - e.g. according to Time magazine, older people are less subject to depression than young people
     예) 타임지에 따르면 나이 든 사람들은 젊은 사람들에 비해 우울증에 빠질 확률이 적다

Model Essay

(도입) It is often said that youth **is wasted on** the young because most young people seem anxious to be older in the mistaken belief that they will be happier when they get older. **In contrast**, older people tend to **look back** with regret and wish they could reclaim the joy they had in their youth. (대주제문) Most adults would agree that young people enjoy their lives much more than older people because they are more energetic and have fewer responsibilities.

(소주제문 1) Young people have more opportunities to enjoy their lives because they are physically active. (구체적 근거 1: 일반적 진술) This gives them **a wider range of** options than older people, offering many more ways to find happiness. That is, unless you are healthy, it is hard to enjoy life **to its fullest**. (구체적 근거 2: 예시) **For instance**, my grandfather was a man of great physical strength and used to love hiking in the mountains when he was younger. Although he has much more leisure time after his retirement, he cannot pursue **physically demanding** activities now. He always misses the days when he went on trekking expeditions to the Himalayas in Nepal and encourages me to fulfill whatever dream I have when I am still young and healthy.

(소주제문 2) Another reason young people are happier is because they have fewer things they have to **care for**. (구체적 근거 1: 일반적 진술) **As people age**, responsibilities such as children to raise and jobs to maintain begin to **burden them down**. These cares restrict the actions they can do and thus limit how much they can enjoy life, whereas young people with no obligations are free to pursue any endeavor that **catches their fancy**. (구체적 근거 2: 예시) For example, my eldest brother who is married with two kids has never taken a whole week off since he **started his own business**. He cannot enjoy his free time as much as he did when he was my age. I, on the other hand, can take a trip whenever I want to, because I am still a student and single. He envied me so much when I took a trip to Europe for two months last summer.

(요약/정리) **In conclusion**, young people's physical health and lack of obligations **lead to** their greater enjoyment of life. (맺음말) Most young people squander their youth in a rush to be older, not realizing the advantages that youth confers. **However**, they need to cherish their youth while they can, since this is the only time that the young will have this invaluable opportunity for happiness.

해석

흔히 말하길 젊은이들은 청춘을 낭비한다고 한다. 대부분의 젊은 사람들이 나이가 들면 더 행복해질 거라는 잘못된 믿음으로 나이가 들기를 갈망하기 때문이다. 그에 반해서, 나이 든 사람들은 후회와 함께 과거를 되돌아보며 젊었을 적 그들이 누렸던 기쁨을 되찾기를 바란다. 대부분의 성인들은 젊은 사람들이 나이 든 사람들보다 인생을 훨씬 더 즐긴다는 데 동의하는데, 그것은 그들이 원기왕성하고 책임을 적게 지기 때문이다.

젊은 사람들은 신체적으로 활동적이기 때문에 인생을 즐길 기회를 더 많이 갖게 된다. 이것은 나이 든 사람들에 비해 행복감을 찾을 수 있는 방법들을 더 많이 제공하며 보다 넓은 선택의 범위를 준다. 즉, 건강하지 않다면 인생을 완전히 즐기기는 어렵다. 예를 들면, 나의 할아버지께서는 젊은 시절에 대단한 체력의 소유자이셨고 등산하는 것을 즐기곤 하셨다. 비록 퇴직 후에 많은 여가 시간을 누리시기는 하지만, 지금은 육체적으로 힘든 활동을 계속 하실 수 없다. 할아버지께서는 항상 네팔의 히말라야 산맥으로 원정 등반 가셨던 시절을 그리워하시고, 아직 젊고 건강할 때 내가 가진 소망들을 실현시키라고 격려하신다.

젊은 사람들이 더 행복한 또 다른 이유는 그들이 돌봐야 하는 일들이 적기 때문이다. 사람들은 나이가 들어감에 따라, 자녀를 양육하고 직업을 유지해야 하는 등의 책임이 부담으로 다가오기 시작한다. 이러한 걱정거리들은 그들이 할 수 있는 행동을 제한하고 따라서 결국 얼마만큼 인생을 즐길 수 있는가를 제한하게 된다. 반면에, 의무가 없는 젊은 사람들은 자유롭게 그들이 좋아하는 것에 노력을 쏟을 수 있다. 예를 들면, 결혼해서 두 자녀를 두고 있는 나의 큰 오빠는 사업을 시작한 이후로 일주일을 통째로 쉬어 본 적이 없다. 오빠는 그가 내 나이였을 때만큼 자유 시간을 누릴 수 없다. 반면에, 나는 내가 원할 때 언제든지 여행을 떠날 수 있다. 나는 여전히 학생 신분이고 미혼이기 때문이다. 그는 내가 지난 여름 두 달간 유럽으로 여행을 떠났을 때 나를 매우 부러워했다.

결론적으로, 젊은 사람들이 육체적으로 건강하고 의무가 적다는 것이 그들을 더 큰 인생의 즐거움으로 인도해 준다. 대부분의 젊은 사람들은 청춘이 주는 이점을 깨닫지 못하고 서둘러 나이를 먹어가면서 그들의 젊음을 낭비한다. 그러나, 젊음은 이 젊은이들이 행복을 얻을 수 있는 소중한 기회를 갖게 되는 유일한 시기이기 때문에, 이들은 젊음을 누릴 수 있을 때 소중히 여겨야 할 것이다.

be wasted on ~ ~에 낭비되다   anxious[ǽŋkʃəs] 열망하는   look back 되돌아보다   reclaim[riːkléim] 되찾다
energetic[ènərdʒétik] 정력적인, 원기 왕성한   a wider range of 더 넓은 범위의   to its fullest 완전히, 충분히   used to ~ ~하곤 했다
hiking[háikiŋ] 하이킹, 도보 여행   physically demanding 육체적으로 큰 노력을 요하는   trekking expedition 원정 등반
care for 돌보다   burden down 부담지우다   restrict[ristríkt] 제한하다   obligation[àbləgéiʃən] 의무   endeavor[endévər] 노력
catch one's fancy ~의 마음에 들다   lead to 이끌다   squander[skwándər] 낭비하다   in a rush 아주 바쁘게
confer[kənfə́ːr] 주다   cherish[tʃériʃ] 소중히 하다   invaluable[invǽljuəbl] 매우 귀중한

① is wasted on   ② In contrast   ③ look back   ④ a wider range of   ⑤ to its fullest
⑥ For instance   ⑦ physically demanding   ⑧ care for   ⑨ As people age
⑩ burden them down   ⑪ catches their fancy   ⑫ started his own business   ⑬ In conclusion
⑭ lead to   ⑮ However

Review

(도입) It is often said that youth ① i_____ the young because most young people seem anxious to be older in the mistaken belief that they will be happier when they get older. ② I_____, older people tend to ③ l_____ with regret and wish they could reclaim the joy they had in their youth. (대주제문) Most adults would agree that young people enjoy their lives much more than older people because they are more energetic and have fewer responsibilities.

(소주제문 1) Young people have more opportunities to enjoy their lives because they are physically active. (구체적 근거 1: 일반적 진술) This gives them ④ a_____ options than older people, offering many more ways to find happiness. That is, unless you are healthy, it is hard to enjoy life ⑤ t_____. (구체적 근거 2: 예시) ⑥ F_____, my grandfather was a man of great physical strength and used to love hiking in the mountains when he was younger. Although he has much more leisure time after his retirement, he cannot pursue ⑦ p_____ activities now. He always misses the days when he went on trekking expeditions to the Himalayas in Nepal and encourages me to fulfill whatever dream I have when I am still young and healthy.

(소주제문 2) Another reason young people are happier is because they have fewer things they have to ⑧ c_____. (구체적 근거 1: 일반적 진술) ⑨ A_____, responsibilities such as children to raise and jobs to maintain begin to ⑩ b_____. These cares restrict the actions they can do and thus limit how much they can enjoy life, whereas young people with no obligations are free to pursue any endeavor that ⑪ c_____. (구체적 근거 2: 예시) For example, my eldest brother who is married with two kids has never taken a whole week off since he ⑫ s_____. He cannot enjoy his free time as much as he did when he was my age. I, on the other hand, can take a trip whenever I want to, because I am still a student and single. He envied me so much when I took a trip to Europe for two months last summer.

(요약 / 정리) ⑬ I_____, young people's physical health and lack of obligations ⑭ l_____ their greater enjoyment of life. (맺음말) Most young people sqander their youth in a rush to be older, not realizing the advantages that youth confers. ⑮ H_____, they need to cherish their youth while they can, since this is the only time that the young will have this invaluable opportunity for happiness.

Question

Do you agree or disagree with the following statement? The news media is a reliable source of unbiased information. Use specific reasons and examples to support your answer.

뉴스미디어는 신뢰할 수 있는 공정한 정보원이라는 진술에 찬성하는지 반대하는지를 밝히고 구체적인 이유와 예를 들어 대답을 뒷받침한다.

Outline

Agree

1. People monitor different media
   사람들은 여러 가지의 미디어를 감시한다
   - under people's watch, media can't be dishonest
     사람들의 감시 아래서 미디어는 부정직할 수 없다
   - e.g. media watchdog agencies
     예) 미디어 감시 기관

2. Media is largely dependent on its reputation
   미디어는 평판에 크게 좌우된다
   - loyalty to a station depends on honesty
     한 방송국에 대한 충성은 정직함에 달려 있다
   - e.g. statistics show media's reputation is closely related to sales
     예) 통계 자료는 미디어의 평판이 판매 기록과 밀접한 관계를 갖는다는 것을 시사해준다

Disagree*

1. News media is related to its own stakeholders
   뉴스미디어는 그들 각자의 이해 관계자들과 연관되어 있다
   - major companies try to make news in favor of them
     대기업들은 자신들에게 유리하게 기사를 쓰려고 한다
   - e.g. different portrayals of Iraq war by media in US and other countries
     예) 미국과 다른 국가들의 미디어에서 이라크 전쟁을 둘러싼 각기 다른 묘사

2. News media attempts to make stories look more colorful and dramatic
   뉴스미디어는 기사를 더 다채롭고 극적으로 보이게 하려고 한다
   - to draw in more viewers and thus maximize profits
     더 많은 시청자를 확보하고 수익을 극대화하기 위해서이다
   - e.g. the case of exaggerated reports about kimchi
     예) 김치에 대한 과장된 보도 사건

Model Essay

(도입) A lot of controversy exists over whether the news media provides people with credible information or not. (대주제문) Although many TV programs and newspapers pretend to be **unbiased and accurate**, I see the distortions in their coverage and reporting. This is because every media company **has its own stakes** and tries to make stories look more sensational in order to gain viewer popularity.

(소주제문 1) **To begin with**, the news media is untrustworthy since it **is related to** its own stakeholders. (구체적 근거 1: 일반적 진술) That is, major corporations own media companies and are obviously interested in portraying reality and **current events** in a way favorable to their own interests. This is especially true when a country or certain political party that the media supports is involved in a story. (구체적 근거 2: 예시) The best example of this is the Iraq War. When the war **broke out**, a majority of the media in the United States portrayed the war as a way to attain world peace. In contrast, countries which were against the United States mainly showed **on-the-spot** broadcasts of brutal scenes that depicted the United States as a ruthless invader. (마무리 문장) The difference in news coverage of the war plainly highlights how partial and biased news companies are.

(소주제문 2) **In addition**, the news media is not reliable as it attempts to make stories look more colorful and dramatic. (구체적 근거 1: 일반적 진술) This is mainly because it wants to draw in more viewers or readers so that it can **maximize profits**. As a result, the media often provide sensationalized information that **catches people's attention** to accomplish these aims. (구체적 근거 2: 예시) For example, one broadcasting station in Korea had to apologize to viewers for its exaggerated report on kimchi. It had reported that kimchi was produced in very filthy and unhealthful environments. The truth was that only a small number of businesses produced kimchi in unclean surroundings, but the broadcasting station **deliberately** exaggerated this incident. Because of this false report, customers stopped buying kimchi for a while, and many kimchi businesses had to **close down**. (마무리 문장) As this incident reveals, the news media often magnifies stories and provides distorted information, sometimes with disastrous results.

(요약/정리) In conclusion, because the news media **is concerned with** its own stakeholders and **tends to** make stories more provocative to earn people's interest, I firmly believe that the news media is an **unreliable source of information**. (맺음말) On the whole, it would be wise for people who follow the news to be more willing to question who is telling them as well as what they are being told.

해석

뉴스미디어가 사람들에게 신뢰할 수 있는 정보를 제공하는지 아닌지에 대해 많은 논쟁이 존재한다. 많은 TV 프로그램들과 신문은 선입견이 없고 정확하다고 자부하지만, 나는 그들의 보도에서 왜곡된 정보를 발견한다. 이것은 모든 미디어 회사들이 각자의 이해 관계를 가지고 있고 독자들의 인기를 얻기 위해 이야기들을 좀 더 선정적으로 보이도록 하기 때문이다.

우선, 뉴스미디어는 각자의 이해 관계자와 연관이 되어있기 때문에 믿을 수 없다. 즉, 대기업들은 미디어 자회사를 소유하고 있고, 현실이나 시사 문제들을 명백히 자신의 이익에 유리한 방식으로 그려내고자 한다. 이것은 그 미디어가 지지하는 나라나 특정한 정당이 내용과 깊이 관련되어 있을 경우에 특히 사실로 나타난다. 이에 대한 가장 좋은 예는 이라크 전쟁이다. 전쟁이 발발했을 때, 대다수의 미국 언론은 그 전쟁을 세계 평화를 달성하기 위한 방법으로 묘사했다. 이와 반대로, 미국에 반대하는 나라들은 주로 미국을 무자비한 침략자로서 그리는 잔혹한 장면들을 현장 중계했다. 이 전쟁에 대한 뉴스 보도의 차이는 미디어 회사들이 얼마나 편파적이고 편견을 지니고 있는지 분명하게 강조해준다.

게다가, 뉴스미디어는 보도 내용을 좀 더 흥미진진하고 극적으로 보이게 하려고 시도하기 때문에 신뢰할 수 없다. 이는 주로 더 많은 시청자와 독자들을 이끌어 이윤을 극대화하고 싶어하기 때문이다. 결과적으로, 미디어는 이러한 목적을 달성하기 위해 사람들의 관심을 끌 수 있는 선정적인 정보를 제공하는 경우가 종종 있다. 예를 들면, 한국에 있는 한 방송사는 김치에 대한 과장된 보도 때문에 시청자들에게 사과해야만 했다. 그 방송사는 김치가 매우 불결하고 비위생적인 환경에서 제조된다고 보도했다. 사실은 매우 소수의 회사들만이 불결한 환경에서 김치를 제조하고 있었으나, 방송국은 이 사건을 고의적으로 과장했다. 이 오보 때문에, 소비자들은 얼마간 김치의 구입을 중단했고 다수의 김치 회사들은 문을 닫아야 했다. 이 사건이 보여주듯, 뉴스미디어는 종종 이야기를 부풀리고 왜곡된 정보를 제공하여, 어떤 경우에는 심각한 결과를 초래하기도 한다.

결론적으로, 뉴스미디어는 각자의 이해 관계자와 관련이 되어있고, 사람들의 관심을 끌기 위해 이야기를 좀 더 자극적으로 만드는 경향이 있기 때문에 나는 뉴스미디어는 신뢰할 수 없는 정보원이라고 확신한다. 전반적으로, 뉴스를 주시하는 사람들은 그들이 보도 받는 내용뿐만 아니라 누가 보도하고 있는지에 대해서도 자발적으로 의문을 제시하는 것이 현명하다.

news media 보도 기관, 뉴스미디어(신문, 라디오, 텔레비전 등)   controversy[kántrəvə̀:rsi] 논쟁
credible[krédəbl] 믿을 만한, 신뢰할 수 있는   unbiased[ʌ̀nbáiəst] 선입견이 없는, 공정한   distortion[distɔ́:rʃən] 왜곡
coverage[kʌ́vəridʒ] (신문·방송의) 보도   have its own stakes 자기 이해 관계를 지니다   sensational[senséiʃənəl] 선정적인
gain popularity 인기를 얻다   to begin with 우선   untrustworthy[ʌ̀ntrʌ́stwə̀:rði] 믿을 수 없는   be related to ~ ~와 관련이 있다
stakeholder[stéikhòuldər] 이해 관계자, 투자자   major corporation 대기업   obviously[ábviəsli] 명백히
favorable[féivərəbl] 호의적인, 유리한   current events 시사 문제   be involved in 깊이 관련되다   break out 발발하다
attain[ətéin] 달성하다   on-the-spot 현장에서의   depict[dipíkt] 그리다, 묘사하다   ruthless[rú:θlis] 무자비한, 냉혹한
plainly[pléinli] 분명히, 알기 쉽게   highlight[háilàit] 강조하다, 두드러지게 하다   partial[pá:rʃəl] 편파적인
biased[báiəst] 편견을 가진   colorful[kʌ́lərfəl] 흥미진진한   dramatic[drəmǽtik] 극적인   broadcasting station 방송국
deliberately[dilíbəritli] 고의적으로   exaggerate[igzǽdʒərèit] 과장하다   filthy[fílθi] 불결한   close down 폐업하다
magnify[mǽgnəfài] 확대하다, 과장하다   provocative[prəvákətiv] 도발적인   be willing to ~ 기꺼이, 자발적으로 ~하다

① unbiased and accurate   ② has its own stakes   ③ To begin with   ④ is related to
⑤ current events   ⑥ broke out   ⑦ on-the-spot   ⑧ In addition   ⑨ maximize profits
⑩ catches people's attention   ⑪ deliberately   ⑫ close down   ⑬ is concerned with
⑭ tends to   ⑮ unreliable source of information

Review

(도입) A lot of controversy exists over whether the news media provides people with credible information or not. (대주제문) Although many TV programs and newspapers pretend to be ① u_____, I see the distortions in their coverage and reporting. This is because every media company ② h_____ and tries to make stories look more sensational in order to gain viewer popularity.

(소주제문 1) ③ T_____, the news media is untrustworthy since it ④ i_____ its own stakeholders. (구체적 근거 1: 일반적 진술) That is, major corporations own media companies and are obviously interested in portraying reality and ⑤ c_____ in a way favorable to their own interests. This is especially true when a country or certain political party that the media supports is involved in a story. (구체적 근거 2: 예시) The best example of this is the Iraq War. When the war ⑥ b_____, a majority of the media in the United States portrayed the war as a way to attain world peace. In contrast, countries which were against the United States mainly showed ⑦ o_____ broadcasts of brutal scenes that depicted the United States as a ruthless invader. (마무리 문장) The difference in news coverage of the war plainly highlights how partial and biased news companies are.

(소주제문 2) ⑧ I_____, the news media is not reliable as it attempts to make stories look more colorful and dramatic. (구체적 근거 1: 일반적 진술) This is mainly because it wants to draw in more viewers or readers so that it can ⑨ m_____. As a result, the media often provide sensationalized information that ⑩ c_____ to accomplish these aims. (구체적 근거 2: 예시) For example, one broadcasting station in Korea had to apologize to viewers for its exaggerated report on kimchi. It had reported that kimchi was produced in very filthy and unhealthful environments. The truth was that only a small number of businesses produced kimchi in unclean surroundings, but the broadcasting station ⑪ d_____ exaggerated this incident. Because of this false report, customers stopped buying kimchi for a while, and many kimchi businesses had to ⑫ c_____. (마무리 문장) As this incident reveals, the news media often magnifies stories and provides distorted information, sometimes with disastrous results.

(요약/정리) In conclusion, because the news media ⑬ i_____ its own stakeholders and ⑭ t_____ make stories more provocative to earn people's interest, I firmly believe that the news media is an ⑮ u_____. (맺음말) On the whole, it would be wise for people who follow the news to be more willing to question who is telling them as well as what they are being told.

Question

Do you agree or disagree with the following statement? It is unrealistic for people to work at the same company for their entire lives. Use specific reasons and examples to support your answer.

일생 동안 한 직장에서 근무하는 것은 비현실적이라는 진술에 찬성하는지 반대하는지를 밝히고 구체적인 이유와 예를 들어 대답을 뒷받침한다.

Outline

Agree*

1. Lifetime employment decreases one's productivity
   평생 고용은 개인의 생산성을 감소시킨다
   - people become weary of the work and can't work to their fullest potential
     사람들은 일에 싫증을 내게 되고 잠재력을 최대한 발휘할 수 없게 된다
   - e.g. study: long-time employees show 30% decrease in productivity
     예) 연구 결과: 장기 근속자들은 30% 생산성 감소를 보임

2. Experiences in many companies help to choose right one
   여러 회사에서의 경험은 적합한 직장을 찾는데 도움이 된다
   - can find the company that best suits them
     그들에게 가장 맞는 회사를 찾을 수 있다
   - e.g. my sister found the best job for her after switching companies
     예) 회사를 옮겨 다닌 후에야 가장 맞는 직장을 찾은 언니

Disagree

1. Ensures stability in careers
   직업 안정성을 보장한다
   - unlikely to be fired or moved around the company
     해고되거나 여기저기 옮겨 다닐 가능성이 적다
   - e.g. my father has worked for one company since he was 20
     예) 나의 아버지는 20세부터 한 회사에서 근무하셨다

2. Easier to climb the ladder when working in the same company
   같은 회사에서 근무하면 출세하기가 더 쉽다
   - long-term workers are more likely to get promoted for their loyalty
     장기 근속자들은 충성도 덕분에 승진할 가능성이 더 높다
   - e.g. executives in Korea worked their way up the ranks
     예) 한국의 임원들은 차근차근 현재의 지위로 올라왔다

Model Essay

(도입) **In this rapidly changing world**, it is becoming clear that those who are inflexible and afraid of change **are unlikely to** succeed. (대주제문) When it comes to jobs, while some argue that it is ideal to work for the same company **for people's entire lives**, I agree that it is unrealistic to remain at one firm because doing so prevents them from performing their best and finding well-suited positions.

(소주제문 1) **First**, working for the same company decreases one's productivity. (구체적 근거 1: 일반적 진술) This is because if people work at the same company too long, they often **become weary of** the work, which makes it difficult to work **to their fullest potential**. (구체적 근거 2: 예시) For example, a recent study showed that employees who have been working for over ten years produce 30 percent less than new employees who have been working for under two years at the same firm. This is because they **become fed up with** the same work, people who they meet, and monotonous **work atmosphere**. The study also mentioned that due to this same daily routine, their work seems very dull and this hinders them from performing their best.

(소주제문 2) **Second**, experiences gained from working in many companies help workers choose the right one for them. (구체적 근거 1: 일반적 진술) This is because they find the company that best utilizes their skills and challenges their abilities. (구체적 근거 2: 예시) For instance, my sister has worked in many different companies, from **a huge conglomerate** to a small company with three employees. My parents were disappointed whenever she told them that she was going to **switch companies**. However, she said that she wants to find the perfect company for her. **In the end**, she found her dream job at a workplace that suited her. If she had chosen to stay at one company, she would not have been able to find the right type of career for herself.

(요약/정리) **In short**, it is impractical to work for the same company since it leads to lower productivity. Furthermore, by experiencing different workplaces, people are better able to choose the right **career path** for their talents. (맺음말) Although the stability of working for one company is appealing, it prevents employees from truly growing in their professional lives.

해석

이렇게 급격하게 변화하는 세상에서는, 유연성이 없고 변화를 두려워하는 사람들은 성공하기 어렵다는 것은 점차 자명해지고 있다. 직장에 대한 문제에 이르게 되면, 어떤 이들은 일생 동안 한 직장에서 일하는 것이 이상적이라고 주장하지만, 나는 한 직장에 머무르는 것은 비현실적이라는데 동의하는데, 이는 이렇게 하는 것이 사람들로 하여금 최선을 다하는 것과 적합한 직장을 찾는 것을 방해하기 때문이다.

첫째로, 같은 직장에서 근무하는 것은 생산성을 감소시킨다. 이는 만약에 사람들이 같은 회사에서 지나치게 오래 근무하면, 그들은 종종 일에 싫증을 내게 되고, 이는 그들이 가지고 있는 잠재력을 최대한 발휘하는 것을 어렵게 만든다. 예를 들면, 최근의 한 조사 결과에 따르면 10년 이상 근무한 직원들은 같은 회사에서 10년 미만 근무한 새 직원들에 비해 30퍼센트 적은 양을 생산한다는 것이 드러났다. 이는 그들이 같은 업무와, 만나는 사람들, 지루한 업무 환경에 싫증이 났기 때문이다. 또한 조사 결과에 따르면 이러한 똑같이 반복되는 일상 때문에, 그들이 하는 업무가 매우 따분하게 느껴지며 이것은 그들이 최선을 다하는 것을 방해한다고 언급했다.

둘째로, 여러 회사에서 얻은 경험이 근로자들이 적절한 일자리를 선택할 수 있게 도와준다. 이는 그들이 자신들의 기술이 가장 잘 활용될 수 있고, 자신들의 능력을 최대한으로 끌어낼 회사를 찾기 때문이다. 예를 들면, 나의 언니는 대기업에서부터 직원 세 명의 작은 회사에 이르기까지 여러 군데의 직장에서 일했다. 나의 부모님께서는 언니가 직장을 옮기겠다고 할 때마다 실망하셨다. 그러나, 언니는 자신에게 완벽하게 맞는 직장을 구하고 싶다고 했다. 결국 언니는 그녀에게 알맞은 자신이 꿈꿔오던 직업을 얻었다. 만약 그녀가 한 회사에 머무르는 편을 선택했다면, 언니는 자신에게 알맞은 종류의 직업을 찾을 수 없었을 것이다.

요약하자면, 같은 직장에서 근무하는 것은 낮은 생산성으로 이어지기 때문에 비현실적이다. 게다가 여러 가지의 일자리를 경험함으로써, 사람들은 자신의 재능에 맞는 진로를 더 잘 선택할 수 있게 된다. 비록 한 직장에서 일하는 것의 안정성은 매력적이지만, 이는 직원들이 직업 면에서 진정으로 성장하는 것을 방해한다.

inflexible[infléksəbl] 유연성이 없는, 경직된   be unlikely to ~ ~할 가망이 없다   when it comes to ~ ~에 대해서라면
prevent A from B A가 B하는 것을 방해하다, 막다   well-suited[wélsjú:tid] 적합한   productivity[pròudəktívəti] 생산성
become weary of 싫증이 나다, 지루해지다   to its fullest 완전히, 충분히   potential[pəténʃəl] 가능성, 잠재력
become fed up with ~ ~에 싫증이 나다, 진절머리가 나다   monotonous[mənátənəs] 단조로운, 변화 없는   due to ~ ~ 때문에
daily routine 일상 업무, 일과   dull[dʌl] 따분한   hinder[híndər] 방해하다, 저지하다   A as well as B B뿐만 아니라 A도
utilize[jú:təlàiz] 이용하다   conglomerate[kənglámərit] (거대) 복합 기업   in the end 결국은   career path 진로
stability[stəbíləti] 안정성

---

① In this rapidly changing world   ② are unlikely to   ③ for people's entire lives   ④ First
⑤ become weary of   ⑥ to their fullest potential   ⑦ become fed up with   ⑧ work atmosphere
⑨ Second   ⑩ a huge conglomerate   ⑪ switch companies   ⑫ In the end   ⑬ In short
⑭ career path

Review

(도입) ① I_____, it is becoming clear that those who are inflexible and afraid of change ② a_____ succeed. (대주제문) When it comes to jobs, while some argue that it is ideal to work for the same company ③ f_____, I agree that it is unrealistic to remain at one firm because doing so prevents them from performing their best and finding well-suited positions.

(소주제문 1) ④ F_____, working for the same company decreases one's productivity. (구체적 근거 1: 일반적 진술) This is because if people work at the same company too long, they often ⑤ b_____ the work, which makes it difficult to work ⑥ t_____. (구체적 근거 2: 예시) For example, a recent study showed that employees who have been working for over ten years produce 30 percent less than new employees who have been working for under two years at the same firm. This is because they ⑦ b_____ the same work, people who they meet, and monotonous ⑧ w_____. The study also mentioned that due to this same daily routine, their work seems very dull and this hinders them from performing their best.

(소주제문 2) ⑨ S_____, experiences gained from working in many companies help workers choose the right one for them. (구체적 근거 1: 일반적 진술) This is because they find the company that best utilizes their skills and challenges their abilities. (구체적 근거 2: 예시) For instance, my sister has worked in many different companies, from ⑩ a_____ to a small company with three employees. My parents were disappointed whenever she told them that she was going to ⑪ s_____. However, she said that she wants to find the perfect company for her. ⑫ I_____, she found her dream job at a workplace that suited her. If she had chosen to stay at one company, she would not have been able to find the right type of career for herself.

(요약/정리) ⑬ I_____, it is impractical to work for the same company since it leads to lower productivity. Furthermore, by experiencing different workplaces, people are better able to choose the right ⑭ c_____ for their talents. (맺음말) Although the stability of working for one company is appealing, it prevents employees from truly growing in their professional lives.

Question

Do you agree or disagree with the following statement? People today pay too much attention to the personal lives of celebrities. Use specific reasons and examples to support your answer.

요즘 사람들은 유명인사의 사생활에 지나치게 관심을 기울인다는 진술에 찬성하는지 반대하는지를 밝히고 구체적인 이유와 예를 들어 대답을 뒷받침한다.

Outline

Agree*

1. Many tabloids and magazines cover celebrities' lives
   많은 타블로이드 신문과 잡지들이 유명인들의 사생활을 다룬다
   - a large percentage of media attention goes to celebrities' lives
     언론의 관심사 중 많은 부분이 유명인사의 사생활에 집중된다
   - e.g. TV shows that cater to the public's curiosity about stars
     예) 스타에 대한 대중의 호기심을 만족시키는 TV쇼

2. Celebrities are invaded of their privacy
   유명인들은 사생활을 침해받는다
   - media spend a lot of money to offer celebrities' private information
     유명인사들의 사생활에 대한 정보를 제공하기 위해 대중매체들은 많은 돈을 쓴다
   - e.g. celebrities' lawsuit against gossip media, JK Rowling
     예) 유명인사들의 대중매체를 상대로 한 소송, JK 롤링

Disagree

1. People were more obsessed with stars in the past
   사람들은 과거에 스타에게 더 집착했다
   - today they are less of an object of interest
     오늘날의 유명인들은 예전보다 덜 관심의 대상이 된다.
   - e.g. Beatles' popularity in America in the past
     예) 과거 미국에서의 비틀즈의 인기

2. Media focuses on world and local news
   대중매체는 세계와 지역 뉴스에 중점을 둔다
   - most people read newspaper to know about political, economic issues, not celebrities
     대부분의 사람들은 유명인사에 대해서가 아니라 정치적, 경제적 이슈에 대해 알기 위해 신문을 읽는다
   - e.g. survey: why people read newspaper and watch TV
     예) 설문 조사: 사람들이 왜 신문을 읽고 TV를 보는가

Model Essay

(도입) Gossip seems to be a trait shared by every culture. It is an inherent human characteristic to **compare oneself to others**, especially to the rich and famous. (대주제문) **Excessive media attention** on celebrities and the invasion of their privacy reflect the fact that the public is engrossed with celebrities' lives.

(소주제문 1) To begin with, many tabloids and magazines **disclose** celebrities' private lives. (구체적 근거 1: 일반적 진술) This is because **gossip about** public figures has become the most alluring way for the media to **make a profit**. The media has become very efficient at gathering the latest and most intriguing stories about celebrities' personal lives. (구체적 근거 2: 예시) For example, these days, the number of reality shows and talk shows that reveal stars' private lives has greatly increased. By disclosing private information about their lives, stars try to **appeal to** readers or viewers with a down-to-earth approach. They introduce their homes, newly purchased items, or even love life **without hesitation or shame** in front of the camera. Because the media caters to the public's fascination with celebrities, these programs or tabloid magazines outsell informative or useful news items.

(소주제문 2) **On top of that**, many celebrities feel their privacy is invaded by the public's interest in their lives. (구체적 근거 1: 일반적 진술) The competition among the gossip media has become so fierce that they pay **huge sums of money** to photographers and reporters to be the first to offer the more private part of celebrities' lives, such as their newest lovers, marriages, and breakups. They even publish stars' home addresses. (구체적 근거 2: 예시) The growing number of multi-million-dollar lawsuits against gossip tabloids best illustrates this phenomenon. As a result, some celebrities are **taking legal action** to protect their personal lives. For instance, JK Rowling, the famous British writer of the Harry Potter stories, sued a British newspaper for **invasion of privacy** when it published a picture of her son last year. She complained that her child's privacy as well as her own was assaulted.

(요약/정리) In summary, **large sales** in gossip media and the violation of celebrities' privacy show the excessive interest in the lives of **the rich and the famous**. (맺음말) As the number of TV programs and magazines **devoted to** famous people's lives increases each year, people can see that this trend of celebrity watching is here to stay, **at least** for now.

해석

가십은 모든 문화가 공유하는 특징처럼 보인다. 자신을 타인과, 특히 부유하고 유명한 이들과 비교하는 것은 인간의 타고난 특징이다. 유명인사에 대한 언론의 과도한 관심 집중과 사생활 침해는 대중들이 유명인사의 삶에 열중한다는 사실을 반영한다.

우선, 많은 타블로이드 신문들과 잡지들은 유명인사들의 사생활을 폭로한다. 이는 대중적인 인물에 대한 소문을 다루는 것이 언론 매체들이 이윤을 창출하는 가장 매혹적인 방법이 되었기 때문이다. 매체들은 유명인사들의 사생활에 대한 최신 정보, 그리고 가장 호기심을 자극하는 이야기들을 매우 효과적으로 수집한다. 예를 들면, 오늘날 유명인사들의 사생활을 드러내는 리얼리티 쇼와 토크 쇼의 수는 크게 증가했다. 인기스타들은 그들의 삶에 대한 사적인 정보를 드러냄으로써, 실제적인 접근을 꾀하며 독자나 시청자들을 매료시키고 있다. 그들은 카메라 앞에서 주저하거나 부끄러워하는 일 없이 그들의 집과 새로 산 물건들, 심지어 연애사까지도 소개한다. 매체들은 유명인사에 매료된 대중들에 영합하므로, 이러한 프로그램이나 타블로이드 잡지들은 유익하고 유용한 뉴스매체들보다 잘 팔린다.

게다가, 많은 유명인사들은 그들의 삶에 대한 대중의 관심으로 인해 사생활이 침해되었다고 느낀다. 가십 매체 사이에서의 경쟁은 너무 치열해져서 새로 만난 연인이나 결혼, 결별과 같은 유명인사들의 가장 사적인 부분을 최초로 공개하기 위해서 엄청난 돈을 사진기자와 보도기자들에게 지불한다. 인기스타의 집 주소를 공개하기조차 한다. 타블로이드 매체를 둘러싸고 고액의 보상금이 걸린 법정소송들이 늘어나고 있다는 것이 이러한 현상을 가장 잘 대변한다. 결과적으로, 일부 유명인사들은 그들의 사생활을 보호하기 위해 법적인 조치를 취하고 있다. 예를 들면, 해리 포터 시리즈의 유명한 영국 작가 JK 롤링은 작년 그녀 아들의 사진을 공개했을 때 사생활 침해를 이유로 영국 신문사를 고소했다. 그녀는 그녀 자신의 사생활뿐만 아니라, 자녀의 사생활까지도 침해받았다고 불평했다.

요약하자면, 가십 매체의 판매고와 유명인사들의 사생활 침해는 부유하고 유명한 이들의 삶에 대한 과도한 관심을 보여준다. 매년 유명인사들의 삶에 열중하는 TV 프로그램과 잡지의 수가 증가함에 따라, 사람들이 유명인사들에게 주목하는 경향이 적어도 지금으로서는 현존한다는 것을 알 수 있다.

gossip[gásəp] 남의 신변, 행동 따위에 관한 가벼운 소문　inherent[inhí(:)ərənt] 고유한, 본래 타고난　excessive[iksésiv] 과도한, 지나친
invasion of privacy 사생활 침해　be engrossed with ~ ~에 열중하다, 몰두하다
tabloid[tǽblɔid] 타블로이드, 대중 신문(주로 연예인의 가십을 다루는 선정적인 신문)　disclose[disklóuz] 드러내다, 폭로하다
alluring[əljú(:)əriŋ] 매혹적인　intriguing[intríːgiŋ] 호기심을 자극하는　reality show 각본 없이 실제 일어나는 상황을 보여주는 프로그램
down-to-earth[dáuntuáːrθ] 현실적인, 실제적인　cater[kéitər] 요구를 들어주다, 비위를 맞추다　outsell[àutsél] ~보다 많이 팔리다
on top of that 게다가　fierce[fiərs] 치열한, 격렬한　breakup[bréikʌp] 결별　lawsuit[lɔ́ːsjùːt] 소송, 고소
illustrate[íləstrèit] 설명하다, 예증하다　phenomenon[finámənàn] 현상　take legal action 법적 조치를 취하다
assault[əsɔ́ːlt] 공격하다, 괴롭히다　devote to ~ ~에 바치다, 헌신하다

① compare oneself to others　② Excessive media attention　③ disclose　④ gossip about
⑤ make a profit　⑥ appeal to　⑦ without hesitation or shame　⑧ On top of that
⑨ huge sums of money　⑩ taking legal action　⑪ invasion of privacy　⑫ large sales
⑬ the rich and the famous　⑭ devoted to　⑮ at least

Review

(도입) Gossip seems to be a trait shared by every culture. It is an inherent human characteristic to ① c_____, especially to the rich and famous. (대주제문) ② E_____ on celebrities and the invasion of their privacy reflect the fact that the public is engrossed with celebrities' lives.

(소주제문 1) To begin with, many tabloids and magazines ③ d_____ celebrities' private lives. (구체적 근거 1: 일반적 진술) This is because ④ g_____ public figures has become the most alluring way for the media to ⑤ m_____. The media has become very efficient at gathering the latest and most intriguing stories about celebrities' personal lives. (구체적 근거 2: 예시) For example, these days, the number of reality shows and talk shows that reveal stars' private lives has greatly increased. By disclosing private information about their lives, stars try to ⑥ a_____ readers or viewers with a down-to-earth approach. They introduce their homes, newly purchased items, or even love life ⑦ w_____ in front of the camera. Because the media caters to the public's fascination with celebrities, these programs or tabloid magazines outsell informative or useful news items.

(소주제문 2) ⑧ O_____, many celebrities feel their privacy is invaded by the public's interest in their lives. (구체적 근거 1: 일반적 진술) The competition among the gossip media has become so fierce that they pay ⑨ h_____ to photographers and reporters to be the first to offer the more private part of celebrities' lives, such as their newest lovers, marriages, and breakups. They even publish stars' home addresses. (구체적 근거 2: 예시) The growing number of multi-million-dollar lawsuits against gossip tabloids best illustrates this phenomenon. As a result, some celebrities are ⑩ t_____ to protect their personal lives. For instance, JK Rowling, the famous British writer of the Harry Potter stories, sued a British newspaper for ⑪ i_____ when it published a picture of her son last year. She complained that her child's privacy as well as her own was assaulted.

(요약/정리) In summary, ⑫ l_____ in gossip media and the violation of celebrities' privacy show the excessive interest in the lives of ⑬ t_____. (맺음말) As the number of TV programs and magazines ⑭ d_____ famous people's lives increases each year, people can see that this trend of celebrity watching is here to stay, ⑮ a_____ for now.

D a y 07

Question

Do you agree or disagree with the following statement? A teacher's ability to relate well with students is more important than the ability to give knowledge. Use specific reasons and examples to support your answer.

교사가 학생과 잘 어울릴 수 있는 능력은 지식을 전달하는 능력보다 중요하다는 진술에 찬성하는지 반대하는지를 밝히고 구체적인 이유와 예를 들어 대답을 뒷받침한다.

Outline

Agree

1. Friendly teachers motivate students to study
   친근한 교사는 학생들이 공부하도록 동기를 부여한다
   - students focus on studying more when given a teacher's attention
     교사의 관심을 받으면 학생들이 공부에 더 집중한다
   - e.g. friend who was a problem child got accepted to top university thanks to a teacher's concern
     예) 문제아였던 친구는 선생님의 관심 덕분에 일류 대학에 진학했다

2. Interaction with teachers enhance students' social skills
   교사와의 상호 관계가 학생의 사회적 기술을 향상시킨다
   - interpersonal communication skills are needed to be successful
     성공하려면 대인관계의 의사소통 기술이 필요하다
   - e.g. my PE teacher helped me to become more outgoing
     예) 체육 선생님이 나를 외향적인 성격으로 변화시켰다

Disagree*

1. The primary role of a teacher is to give students knowledge and skills needed after graduation
   교사의 주된 역할은 학생에게 졸업 후에 필요한 지식과 기술을 전달하는 것이다
   - students need knowledge and skills for their future
     학생들은 미래를 위해 지식과 기술이 필요하다
   - e.g. my math teacher influenced me to pursue a career in engineering
     예) 수학 선생님이 공학으로 진로를 계속하도록 영향을 미쳤다

2. Maintaining the proper class atmosphere helps students learn better
   적절한 학급 분위기를 유지하는 것이 학생들의 학습에 도움을 준다
   - too friendly teachers hinder learning
     지나치게 친근한 교사는 학습을 방해한다
   - e.g. my 6th grade teacher failed to maintain control over the classroom
     예) 6학년 때 선생님은 학급을 통솔하는 데 실패했다

Model Essay

(도입) Education theory has **undergone a revolution** in the past generation, shifting more classroom management responsibility such as relating well with students to the teachers. The effect has been a decrease in the amount of production expected of today's children, unfortunately to the **detriment** of their education. (대주제문) However, **imparting knowledge** to the students is a more significant task for educators than getting along well with them. This is not only because the **essential** task of teachers are to aid students in acquiring potential knowledge required for their futures, but also because maintaining the proper class atmosphere helps them learn better.

(소주제문 1) The primary role of a teacher is to educate students and give them the skills that they will need **upon graduation**. (구체적 근거 1: 일반적 진술) Teachers who are able to equip their students with knowledge will have a much greater impact on their future success in both their further studies and employment. (구체적 근거 2: 예시) **For example**, the teacher who influenced me the most was my math teacher in high school. Even though I did not have as many chances to build **a personal relationship** with him as I did with my other teachers, he **challenged** me to be more than I thought I could be through the classes he passionately taught. Thanks to him, I realized I had an interest in math and decided to pursue a career in engineering.

(소주제문 2) **Moreover**, maintaining a professional distance from their students is necessary for a proper learning environment. (구체적 근거 1: 일반적 진술) Teachers who become too friendly with students actually hinder their learning, since it **disrupts** the classroom atmosphere. (구체적 근거 2: 예시) **For instance**, my 6th grade teacher wanted to be thought of as a friend instead of an authority figure. It seemed that she **crossed the boundary** needed for teachers to maintain control over the classroom by trying to be friends. While we had a lot of fun in class, she had to waste at least an hour of class time every day settling the class down after she played with us during the break times.

(요약 / 정리) **On the whole**, giving information is a more important skill for teachers than being able to relate to their students. This is because the principal role of a teacher is to ensure students are prepared when they leave the school and to maintain a proper class atmosphere that is **conducive to** learning. (맺음말) Students have **plenty of** opportunities to make friends and should learn that the classroom is a time for working. Valuable skills and knowledge for their futures can only be acquired by having teachers who know how to give knowledge to their pupils.

해석

이전 세대에 교육 이론은 혁신적인 변화를 거쳤는데, 이를 통해 학생과 잘 어울리는 것과 같은 학급 운영의 책임은 교사들에게 더 전가되었다. 그 영향으로 오늘날의 아이들에게 기대할 수 있는 학업 성취도는 감소했으며, 안타깝게도 이는 그들의 교육에 해가 되었다. 학생들에게 지식을 전달하는 것이 학생들과 잘 어울리는 것보다 교육자의 중요한 직무이다. 이것은 교사의 필수적인 임무가 학생이 미래에 필요한 잠재적인 지식을 획득하는 것을 돕는 데 있을 뿐만 아니라, 적절한 학급 분위기를 유지하는 것이 학생들로 하여금 더 잘 학습하도록 하기 때문이다.

교사의 주된 역할은 학생들을 교육하고 졸업 후에 필요한 능력을 길러 주는 것이다. 학생들이 지식을 갖추도록 할 수 있는 교사는 계속적인 학업과 취업과 같은 그들 미래의 성공에 훨씬 더 큰 영향을 미칠 수 있다. 예를 들어, 나에게 가장 큰 영향을 미친 선생님은 고등학교 시절 수학 선생님이다. 비록 그분과는 다른 선생님들과 같은 개인적인 관계를 맺을 수는 없었지만, 그분은 열정적인 수업을 통해 내가 할 수 있는 것 이상을 이끌어내도록 자극해 주셨다. 그분 덕분에, 나는 내가 수학에 흥미가 있다는 것을 깨닫고 공학으로 진로를 결정할 수 있었다.

게다가, (교사들이) 학생들로부터 직업적인 거리를 유지하는 것이 적절한 학습 분위기를 위해 필요하다. 학생들과 지나치게 친해진 교사들은 학급의 분위기를 파괴함으로써 사실상 그들의 학습을 방해한다. 예를 들어, 나의 초등학교 6학년 때 선생님은 권위적인 모습이 아닌 친구로 느껴지길 원했다. 그것은 학급의 질서를 유지하기 위해 선생님에게 필요한 경계선을 넘은 것처럼 보였다. 우리는 즐거웠지만 매일 쉬는 시간에 함께 놀고 난 후, 학급을 진정시키는데 적어도 한 시간을 낭비해야 했다.

전반적으로, 학생들과 좋은 관계를 유지하는 것보다 정보를 전달하는 것이 교사들에게 중요한 능력이다. 이것은 교사의 주된 역할이란 학생이 졸업한 후에 준비가 되도록 확실히 하는 것이고, 학습에 도움이 되는 적절한 학급 분위기를 유지하는 것이기 때문이다. 학생들은 친구를 사귈 기회가 많이 있으며, 수업은 공부해야 하는 시간이라는 사실을 배워야 한다. 미래를 위한 귀중한 기술과 지식은 학생들에게 지식을 전해줄 수 있는 교사를 만나야만 이루어질 수 있다.

undergo[ʌ̀ndərgóu] 겪다   shift A to B   A를 B에게로 이동하다   detriment[détrəmənt] 손해   impart knowledge 지식을 전하다
significant[signífikənt] 중요한   get along with ~ ~와 사이좋게 지내다   have an impact on ~ ~에 영향을 주다
challenge[tʃǽlindʒ] 도전하다, 자극하다   hinder[híndər] 방해하다   disrupt[disrʌ́pt] 혼란시키다   authority[əθɔ́ːrəti] 권위
figure[fígjər] (사람의) 모습   cross the boundary 경계선을 넘다   settle down 진정시키다   break time (짧은) 휴식 시간
on the whole 전반적으로, 대체로   relate to 잘 어울리다   principal[prínsəpəl] 주요한
conducive[kəndjúːsiv] 도움이 되는, 이바지하는   pupil[pjúːpəl] 학생

① undergone a revolution   ② detriment   ③ imparting knowledge   ④ essential
⑤ upon graduation   ⑥ For example   ⑦ a personal relationship   ⑧ challenged   ⑨ Moreover
⑩ disrupts   ⑪ For instance   ⑫ crossed the boundary   ⑬ On the whole   ⑭ conducive to
⑮ plenty of

Review

(도입) Education theory has ① u_____ in the past generation, shifting more classroom management responsibility such as relating well with students to the teachers. The effect has been a decrease in the amount of production expected of today's children, unfortunately to the ② d_____ of their education. (대주제문) However, ③ i_____ to the students is a more significant task for educators than getting along well with them. This is not only because the ④ e_____ task of teachers are to aid students in acquiring potential knowledge required for their futures, but also because maintaining the proper class atmosphere helps them learn better.

(소주제문 1) The primary role of a teacher is to educate students and give them the skills that they will need ⑤ u_____. (구체적 근거 1: 일반적 진술) Teachers who are able to equip their students with knowledge will have a much greater impact on their future success in both their further studies and employment. (구체적 근거 2: 예시) ⑥ F_____, the teacher who influenced me the most was my math teacher in high school. Even though I did not have as many chances to build ⑦ a_____ with him as I did with my other teachers, he ⑧ c_____ me to be more than I thought I could be through the classes he passionately taught. Thanks to him, I realized I had an interest in math and decided to pursue a career in engineering.

(소주제문 2) ⑨ M_____, maintaining a professional distance from their students is necessary for a proper learning environment. (구체적 근거 1: 일반적 진술) Teachers who become too friendly with students actually hinder their learning, since it ⑩ d_____ the classroom atmosphere. (구체적 근거 2: 예시) ⑪ F_____, my 6th grade teacher wanted to be thought of as a friend instead of an authority figure. It seemed that she ⑫ c_____ needed for teachers to maintain control over the classroom by trying to be friends. While we had a lot of fun in class, she had to waste at least an hour of class time every day settling the class down after she played with us during the break times.

(요약/정리) ⑬ O_____, giving information is a more important skill for teachers than being able to relate to their students. This is because the principal role of a teacher is to ensure students are prepared when they leave the school and to maintain a proper class atmosphere that is ⑭ c_____ learning. (맺음말) Students have ⑮ p_____ opportunities to make friends and should learn that the classroom is a time for working. Valuable skills and knowledge for their futures can only be acquired by having teachers who know how to give knowledge to their pupils.

Question

First impressions tell a lot about people. Do you agree or disagree? Use specific reasons and examples to support your answer.

첫인상이 사람들에 대해 많은 것을 알려준다는 진술에 찬성하는지 반대하는지를 밝히고 구체적인 이유와 예를 들어 대답을 뒷받침한다.

Outline

Agree*

1. First impressions reveal perspectives and attitudes toward life
   첫인상은 삶에 대한 관점과 태도를 드러낸다
   - outward expressions of minds
     마음의 외적 표현
   - e.g. job interviewers can tell personality in a few minutes
     예) 면접관들은 몇 분 내에 성격을 파악할 수 있다

2. Clothes reveal personal statements
   옷은 개인적인 성향을 드러낸다
   - self-expressive uniform to the world
     세상에 대해 자신을 표현하는 제복
   - e.g. how clothes convey image: ill-coordinated vs. well-coordinated
     예) 옷이 어떻게 이미지를 전달하는가: 잘 입은 사람 vs. 못 입은 사람

Disagree

1. First impressions often mislead
   첫인상은 종종 오해를 불러일으킨다
   - appearance does not reflect inner qualities such as character
     외모는 성격과 같은 내적 가치를 반영하지 않는다
   - e.g. warmhearted colleague with a grim face
     예) 얼굴은 험악하지만 따뜻한 마음을 지닌 동료

2. Initial impressions change over time
   첫인상은 시간이 지나면 변한다
   - people need time to judge others correctly
     다른 이들을 정확하게 판단하려면 시간이 필요하다
   - e.g. survey: how first impressions about spouses changed after marriage
     예) 설문 조사: 결혼 후에 배우자에 대한 첫인상이 어떻게 바뀌었는가

Model Essay

(도입) **A substantial number of** people mistrust their first impressions of people. (대주제문) Even though I agree that first impressions are sometimes **misleading**, I strongly believe that first impressions are usually correct because people's appearances inevitably reveal their personalities and attitudes. On top of that, people's clothes reveal the **personal statements** they are making to the world.

(소주제문 1) **To begin with**, I strongly believe that people's appearances and speech can accurately portray their perspectives and attitudes toward life. (구체적 근거 1: 일반적 진술) This is largely because people's **habitual facial expressions** and speech, which are the outward expressions of their minds, accurately reflect their emotional responses and reactions to life. (구체적 근거 2: 예시) For example, experienced interviewers can accurately judge and evaluate candidates' **characteristics** during the few minutes of an interview. According to their accounts, an **optimistic and outgoing** person has brighter facial expressions, a higher tone of voice, and lively hand gestures. On the other hand, a pessimistic person with low self-esteem has more solemn expressions, a quiet voice, and minimal body motions. (마무리 문장) This proves that people's appearances can reveal their characters.

(소주제문 2) **In addition**, people's style of dress reveals what statements they are making to the world. (구체적 근거 1: 일반적 진술) An important reason is that clothes serve as a self-expressive kind of uniform to the world. (구체적 근거 2: 예시) **To illustrate**, people who wear dirty, torn, or ill-fitting clothes convey the feeling that they are messy, disorganized, and not interested in their appearances. **On the contrary**, people who wear neat, well-coordinated, and stylish clothes express to the world that they care about how they look and want to **make good impressions**. Whether a person underneath his clothes is truly neat and organized or sloppy and scattered, his choice of clothes and general appearance tell the world what image he is interested in conveying. (마무리 문장) **In this respect**, first impressions are very revealing of how people want to represent themselves.

(요약/정리) In conclusion, **initial impressions** are truthful because they reveal people's characteristics and attitudes. **In addition**, people's clothes show what images they are trying to convey to the world. (맺음말) **For this reason**, people can safely trust their first impressions.

Day

08

해석

상당수의 이들이 사람들에 대한 첫인상을 신뢰하지 않는다. 첫인상이 때때로 오해를 불러일으킨다는 것에는 동의하지만, 나는 첫인상이 대체로 정확하다고 확신한다. 왜냐하면 사람들의 외모는 필연적으로 그들의 성격과 태도를 드러내기 때문이다. 더구나, 사람들의 옷은 그들이 세상에 표출하고자 하는 개인적인 주장을 드러낸다.

우선, 나는 사람들의 외모와 말투가 정확하게 그들의 삶에 대한 사고방식과 태도를 나타낸다고 확신한다. 이는 마음의 외적 표현이라 할 수 있는 사람들의 습관적인 표정과 말투가 그들의 삶에 대한 정서적인 반응이나 대응 자세를 정확히 반영하기 때문이다. 예를 들면, 숙련된 면접관은 지원자의 성격을 몇 분의 면접 동안 정확하게 파악하고 평가할 수 있다. 그들의 설명에 따르면, 낙관적이고 외향적인 사람은 더 밝은 표정과 높은 목소리, 활기찬 손동작을 보여준다고 한다. 반면에, 자부심이 낮은 비관적인 사람은 굳은 표정과 조용한 목소리, 최소한의 몸동작을 보인다고 한다. 이는 사람의 외모가 성격을 드러낸다는 것을 보여준다.

게다가, 사람들의 옷차림은 그들이 세상에 대한 개인적인 주장을 드러낸다. 중요한 이유는 옷이 세상에 자신을 표현하는 일종의 제복의 역할을 하기 때문이다. 예를 들면, 더럽고 찢어지거나 잘 맞지 않는 옷을 입은 사람들은 지저분하고 부주의하며 자신의 외모에 관심이 없다는 느낌을 전달한다. 이와 반대로, 단정하고 조화가 잘 된 멋진 옷을 입은 사람들은 그들이 어떻게 보이는지에 대해 신경 쓰고 있으며, 좋은 인상을 주고 싶어한다는 것을 세상에 표현하는 것이다. 옷 아래 감춰진 사람이 진정으로 깔끔하고 조직적이든, 또는 너저분하고 산만하든 간에, 옷의 선택과 전반적인 외모가 세상에 그 사람이 어떤 이미지를 전달하고자 하는지를 보여준다. 이러한 점에서, 첫인상이야말로 사람들이 자신을 표출하고자 하는 방식을 드러내는 것이다.

결론적으로 첫인상은 사람들의 성격과 태도를 드러내기 때문에 정직하다. 게다가, 사람들의 옷차림은 그들이 세상에 전달하고자 하는 이미지를 보여준다. 이러한 이유로, 사람들은 그들의 첫인상을 신뢰해도 무방하다.

substantial [səbstǽnʃəl] 상당한　a substantial number of 상당수의　mistrust [mistrʌ́st] 불신하다　first impression 첫인상
misleading [mislíːdiŋ] 오해시키는　inevitably [inévitəbli] 불가피하게, 필연적으로　statement [stéitmənt] 주장
accurately [ǽkjuritli] 정확히　perspective [pərspéktiv] 사고방식　habitual [həbítʃuəl] 습관적인　facial expression 얼굴 표정
reflect [riflékt] 반영하다　reaction [riǽkʃən] 반응　candidate [kǽndidèit] 지원자, 후보　characteristic [kæriktərístik] 특성, 개성
optimistic [ɑ̀ptəmístik] 낙관적인　pessimistic [pèsəmístik] 비관적인　self-esteem [sèlfestíːm] 자존심, 자부심
solemn [sɑ́ləm] 심각한, 근엄한　minimal [mínəməl] 최소한의　serve as ~ ~의 역할을 하다　ill-fitting 들어맞지 않는
messy [mési] 지저분한, 흐트러진　disorganized [disɔ́ːrgənàizd] 정리되지 않은, 부주의한　well-coordinated 잘 조화된
sloppy [slɑ́pi] 너절한, (옷이) 몸에 맞지 않는　scattered [skǽtərd] 산만한　convey [kənvéi] 전달하다
in this respect 이러한 관점에서

① A substantial number of　② misleading　③ personal statements　④ To begin with
⑤ habitual facial expressions　⑥ characteristics　⑦ optimistic and outgoing　⑧ In addition
⑨ To illustrate　⑩ On the contrary　⑪ make good impressions　⑫ In this respect
⑬ initial impressions　⑭ In addition　⑮ For this reason

Review

(도입) ① A_____ people mistrust their first impressions of people. (대주제문) Even though I agree that first impressions are sometimes ② m_____, I strongly believe that first impressions are usually correct because people's appearances inevitably reveal their personalities and attitudes. On top of that, people's clothes reveal the ③ p_____ they are making to the world.

(소주제문 1) ④ T_____, I strongly believe that people's appearances and speech can accurately portray their perspectives and attitudes toward life. (구체적 근거 1: 일반적 진술) This is largely because people's ⑤ h_____ and speech, which are the outward expressions of their minds, accurately reflect their emotional responses and reactions to life. (구체적 근거 2: 예시) For example, experienced interviewers can accurately judge and evaluate candidates' ⑥ c_____ during the few minutes of an interview. According to their accounts, an ⑦ o_____ person has brighter facial expressions, a higher tone of voice, and lively hand gestures. On the other hand, a pessimistic person with low self-esteem has more solemn expressions, a quiet voice, and minimal body motions. (마무리 문장) This proves that people's appearances can reveal their characters.

(소주제문 2) ⑧ l_____, people's style of dress reveals what statements they are making to the world. (구체적 근거 1: 일반적 진술) An important reason is that clothes serve as a self-expressive kind of uniform to the world. (구체적 근거 2: 예시) ⑨ T_____, people who wear dirty, torn, or ill-fitting clothes convey the feeling that they are messy, disorganized, and not interested in their appearances. ⑩ O_____, people who wear neat, well-coordinated, and stylish clothes express to the world that they care about how they look and want to ⑪ m_____. Whether a person underneath his clothes is truly neat and organized or sloppy and scattered, his choice of clothes and general appearance tell the world what image he is interested in conveying. (마무리 문장) ⑫ l_____, first impressions are very revealing of how people want to represent themselves.

(요약/정리) In conclusion, ⑬ i_____ are truthful because they reveal people's characteristics and attitudes. ⑭ l_____, people's clothes show what images they are trying to convey to the world. (맺음말) ⑮ F_____, people can safely trust their first impressions.

Day 09

Question

Do you agree or disagree with the following statement? University students should take classes in many different subjects. Use specific reasons and examples to support your answer.

대학생들이 많은 다양한 과목들을 들어야 한다는 진술에 동의하는지 반대하는지를 밝히고 구체적인 이유와 예를 들어 대답을 뒷받침한다.

Outline

Agree*

1. Different classes require different skill sets
   각각의 수업이 다른 능력을 요구한다
   - knowledge not as important as learning skills
     지식은 기술 습득만큼 중요하지 않다
   - e.g. college literature class
     예) 대학에서의 문학 수업

2. Meet different kinds of people
   다양한 종류의 사람을 만난다
   - more tolerant about different opinions
     다른 의견을 좀 더 수용하게 된다
   - e.g. sharing opinions in philosophy class
     예) 철학 수업에서의 의견 교환

Disagree

1. Focus on skills needed for work
   직업을 갖는데 필요한 기술에 집중한다
   - prepare for job
     취업에 대비한다
   - e.g. took many classes related to major and it helped in getting a job
     예) 전공 관련 수업을 많이 들었더니 취업에 도움이 됐다

2. Easier to make friends
   친구 사귀기가 더 쉽다
   - see same students regularly, more comfortable
     같은 학생들을 정기적으로 만나므로 더 편안하다
   - e.g. many of my friends are from the same major
     예) 내 친구들 중 다수는 같은 학과에서 만났다

Model Essay

(도입) Attending college is an invaluable opportunity for students to explore their interests. The variety of courses **available** allows them to try different fields and **settle on** a specialization that best serves their life goals. Many people argue that students should focus on their majors while in school. (대주제문) **However**, it is important that students approach many different subjects, since this helps them develop different skill sets and aids in their understanding of other people.

(소주제문 1) One benefit of taking a variety of subjects is that each type of class requires a different skill set; therefore, you can **equip yourself with** various skills. (구체적 근거 1: 일반적 진술) The knowledge acquired in a class can be forgotten later but the skills that you have practiced while taking courses in different fields will confer great advantages **later on**. (구체적 근거 2: 예시) When I was a college student majoring in electrical engineering, I took a literature course, even though it was not required. From the course, I learned how to discuss my opinions and **back them up** with evidence. I did not realize how valuable this skill is until after I graduated from the university, at job interviews. Thanks to the **synthesis skills** I had developed in the literature class, I was able to present my views effectively as well as answer questions precisely. Engaging in a broader field of study helped me to get my job.

(소주제문 2) **Furthermore**, when taking different kinds of classes, a student meets many kinds of people. (구체적 근거 1: 일반적 진술) These encounters expose everyone to new points of view and make them more **tolerant of** others' opinions. (구체적 근거 2: 예시) For instance, I was really surprised by the views of a religious studies major in a philosophy class I took. Our stances on truth were obviously informed from very different angles: I used scientifically verifiable evidence to know, but my classmate drew on faith to believe. Through our discussions, we both had the chance to see philosophical issues **from new perspectives**. (마무리 문장) Since prejudice develops from ignorance, those who meet many types of individuals are less likely to have **preconceived notions** of others they meet in the future.

(요약/정리) **Therefore**, because taking many different subjects provides students a chance to build varied skills and help them **appreciate** the views of other people, I strongly agree that university students should attend a variety of courses. (맺음말) Once they leave college, it becomes less likely that they will have the same access to information and to diverse groups of people. **Consequently**, the time spent in college is the best chance one gets to explore **a broad range of** areas of study and perspectives.

해석

대학에 다니는 것은 학생들이 자신의 관심사를 탐색할 수 있는 귀중한 기회이다. (대학에서) 수강할 수 있는 다양한 수업들은 학생들로 하여금 다양한 분야를 시도해보고 그들의 인생 목표에 가장 적합한 전공 분야를 결정하도록 해준다. 많은 이들이 학생들이 재학 중에는 자신의 전공에만 집중해야 한다고 주장한다. 그러나, 학생들이 다양한 과목을 접해 보는 것이 중요하다. 왜냐하면, 그것은 학생들이 다양한 능력을 함양하고 타인을 이해하는데 도움을 주기 때문이다.

다양한 과목을 듣는 것의 한 가지 이점은 각각의 수업이 다른 능력을 요구한다는 점이다: 따라서, 다양한 기술을 갖출 수 있다. 수업 시간에 획득한 지식은 나중에 잊어버릴 수 있지만 다양한 분야에서 수업을 들으면서 연습한 기술은 후에 아주 커다란 혜택을 주게 된다. 내가 전기 공학을 전공하는 대학생이었을 때, 나는 비록 필수 과목은 아니었지만 문학 수업을 수강했다. 그 수업을 통해, 나는 나의 의견을 논의하고 증거를 들어 뒷받침하는 법을 배웠다. 나는 이 기술이 얼마나 귀중한 것인지 대학 졸업 후의 취업 면접 때까지 깨닫지 못했다. 문학 수업을 통해 계발시킨 종합적 능력 덕분에 나는 질문에 정확히 대답할 수 있었을 뿐만 아니라, 나의 견해를 효과적으로 제시할 수 있었다. 보다 넓은 분야의 학문을 공부했던 것이 내가 일자리를 구하는 데 도움을 주었다.

게다가, 다양한 종류의 과목을 듣게 되면, 학생은 다양한 유형의 사람들을 많이 만나게 된다. 이러한 만남들은 학생들을 새로운 관점에 노출시켜 주고 다른 이들의 의견에 대해 관용적인 자세를 가질 수 있게 해준다. 예를 들어, 나는 철학 수업에서 신학을 전공하는 학우의 견해에 대해 매우 놀랐다. 진리에 대한 우리의 입장은 매우 다른 각도로부터 정해졌다: 나는 알기 위하여 과학적으로 증명할 수 있는 증거를 사용하였지만 내 친구는 믿기 위해 신념에 의지했다. 토론을 통해, 우리 둘은 문제들을 새로운 시각으로 바라볼 기회를 갖게 되었다. 편견은 다른 사람들에 대한 무지에서 비롯되므로, 많은 다른 유형의 개인들과 만나는 이들은 미래에 만나게 될 타인에 대해 선입견을 가지게 될 가능성이 더 적다.

그러므로, 다양한 과목을 듣는 것은 학생들이 다양한 기술을 습득할 수 있는 기회를 제공해주고 다른 이들의 의견을 인정할 수 있게 도와주기 때문에, 나는 대학생들이 다양한 수업을 수강해야 한다는 것에 강력하게 동의한다. 일단 학생이 대학을 졸업하게 되면, 다양한 사회적, 경제적 배경을 지닌 사람들을 만나기가 어려워진다. 결과적으로, 대학에서 보내는 시간이야말로 학생들이 다양한 학문 분야와 시각에 접해 볼 수 있는 최선의 기회인 것이다

---

invaluable[invǽljuəbl] 매우 귀중한   available[əvéiləbl] 이용할 수 있는   settle on 결정하다
specialization[spèʃəlizéiʃən] 전문 과목, 분야   serve[sə:rv] 알맞다, 적합하다   approach[əpróutʃ] 접근하다   a variety of 다양한
equip - with ~ -에게 ~을 갖추게 하다   confer[kənfə́:r] 주다, 수여하다   later on 나중에   electrical engineering 전기 공학
back up 뒷받침하다   thanks to ~ ~ 덕분에   synthesis skill 종합적 능력   precisely[prisáisli] 정확히
engage in 참여하다, 종사하다   encounter[inkáuntər] 만남, 마주침   tolerant of ~ ~를 관용하는, 견뎌내는
biology[baiálədʒi] 생물학   philosophy[filásəfi] 철학   stance[stæns] 입장   verifiable[vérəfàiəbl] 증명할 수 있는
from new perspectives 새로운 시각으로   prejudice[prédʒədis] 편견   ignorance[ígnərəns] 무지   preconceived notion 선입견
appreciate[əprí:ʃièit] 인정하다, 감상하다   have access to ~ ~에 접근하다   diverse[divə́:rs] 다양한   a broad range of 넓은 범위의

---

① available   ② settle on   ③ However   ④ equip yourself with   ⑤ later on   ⑥ back them up
⑦ synthesis skills   ⑧ Furthermore   ⑨ tolerant of   ⑩ from new perspectives
⑪ preconceived notions   ⑫ Therefore   ⑬ appreciate   ⑭ Consequently   ⑮ a broad range of

Review

(도입) Attending college is an invaluable opportunity for students to explore their interests. The variety of courses ① a＿＿＿＿＿ allows them to try different fields and ② s＿＿＿＿＿ a specialization that best serves their life goals. Many people argue that students should focus on their majors while in school. (대주제문) ③ H＿＿＿＿＿, it is important that students approach many different subjects, since this helps them develop different skill sets and aids in their understanding of other people.

(소주제문 1) One benefit of taking a variety of subjects is that each type of class requires a different skill set; therefore, you can ④ e＿＿＿＿＿＿ various skills. (구체적 근거 1: 일반적 진술) The knowledge acquired in a class can be forgotten later but the skills that you have practiced while taking courses in different fields will confer great advantages ⑤ l＿＿＿＿＿. (구체적 근거 2: 예시) When I was a college student majoring in electrical engineering, I took a literature course, even though it was not required. From the course, I learned how to discuss my opinions and ⑥ b＿＿＿＿＿ with evidence. I did not realize how valuable this skill is until after I graduated from the university, at job interviews. Thanks to the ⑦ s＿＿＿＿＿ I had developed in the literature class, I was able to present my views effectively as well as answer questions precisely. Engaging in a broader field of study helped me to get my job.

(소주제문 2) ⑧ F＿＿＿＿＿, when taking different kinds of classes, a student meets many kinds of people. (구체적 근거 1: 일반적 진술) These encounters expose everyone to new points of view and make them more ⑨ t＿＿＿＿＿ others' opinions. (구체적 근거 2: 예시) For instance, I was really surprised by the views of a religious studies major in a philosophy class I took. Our stances on truth were obviously informed from very different angles: I used scientifically verifiable evidence to know, but my classmate drew on faith to believe. Through our discussions, we both had the chance to see philosophical issues ⑩ f＿＿＿＿＿. (마무리 문장) Since prejudice develops from ignorance, those who meet many types of individuals are less likely to have ⑪ p＿＿＿＿＿ of others they meet in the future.

(요약/정리) ⑫ T＿＿＿＿＿, because taking many different subjects provides students a chance to build varied skills and help them ⑬ a＿＿＿＿＿ the views of other people, I strongly agree that university students should attend a variety of courses. (맺음말) Once they leave college, it becomes less likely that they will have the same access to information and to diverse groups of people. ⑭ C＿＿＿＿＿, the time spent in college is the best chance one gets to explore ⑮ a＿＿＿＿＿ areas of study and perspectives.

Question

It is better for governments to spend their funds on the exploration of outer space than on earthly matters. Do you agree or disagree? Use specific reasons and details to support your answer.

정부는 지구상의 문제들보다 우주 탐험에 재원을 투자하는 편이 더 낫다는 진술에 찬성하는지 반대하는지를 밝히고 구체적인 이유와 예를 들어 대답을 뒷받침한다.

Outline

Agree

1. Space exploration makes life more convenient
   우주 탐험은 삶을 좀 더 편리하게 만든다
   - provides useful technology
     유용한 과학 기술을 제공한다
   - e.g. satellites for weather forecasting, GPS, research
     예) 기상 예보와 GPS, 연구를 위해 쓰이는 인공위성

2. Find an alternative habitat for humans
   인류를 위한 대체 거주지를 찾는다
   - overpopulated Earth and depletion of natural resources
     인구 과잉의 지구와 천연 자원의 고갈
   - e.g. spaceships searching for planets with livable conditions
     예) 주거 가능한 조건을 지닌 행성을 찾는 우주선

Disagree*

1. Saving human lives is more imperative
   인류의 생명을 구하는 것이 더 급하다
   - people are dying due to extreme shortage of staples
     생필품이 극도로 부족해 사람들이 죽어가고 있다
   - e.g. UNICEF reports: one-third of African children are undernourished
     예) 유니세프의 보도: 아프리카 아이들의 3분의 1이 영양부족

2. Restoring the damaged environment is a more pressing
   훼손된 자연을 복구하는 것이 더 시급하다
   - clean air and water are indispensable for survival
     깨끗한 공기와 물이 생존을 위해 필수 불가결하다
   - e.g. destruction of woodlands
     예) 산림의 파괴

Model Essay

(도입) Every year, newspapers will flash with news of a latest space exploration triumph or disaster. This **calls into question** whether governments should be spending billions of dollars on exploring outer space. (대주제문) **In my opinion**, governments should not waste their money on space exploration but should spend money **attending to** people's pressing, unfulfilled basic needs and the ravaged environment.

(소주제문 1) **To start with**, saving human lives is definitely more **imperative** than exploring outer space. (구체적 근거 1: 일반적 진술) This is clearly evident when one ponders that a countless number of people are dying **at this very moment** because of an extreme shortage of fundamental **necessities of life**, such as food, medicine, and clean drinking water. Therefore, governments must shoulder their essential responsibility for satisfying people's basic needs on Earth. (구체적 근거 2: 예시) To illustrate, according to a shocking report recently released by UNICEF, nearly one-third of children in southern and eastern Africa are severely malnourished and **dying of illnesses** such as diarrhea which can be easily cured with sufficient provisions of medicine and hospital treatment. (마무리 문장) Therefore, the world should focus its attention on the lives of these innocent children **rather than** exploring unknown lives on other planets.

(소주제문 2) Moreover, restoring the damaged environment is a much more pressing issue than exploring outer space. (구체적 근거 1: 일반적 진술) This is largely because clean air and water are **indispensable** to the survival of both humans and animals. Unfortunately, brutal exploitation and destruction of nature for the building of houses and factories have definitely **resulted in** irreversible environmental pollution. (구체적 근거 2: 예시) For example, people have been mindlessly **cutting down** countless trees for urbanization and industrialization. As a result, deforestation has dramatically changed a great portion of land into deserts and barren land where landslides and floods frequently occur. Unfortunately, governments need to spend an astronomical amount of their funds for several decades in order to restore the damaged forests and woodlands. (마무리 문장) This clearly proves that restoring the natural environment is **far more overarching** than exploring outer space.

(요약 / 정리) **In summary**, without any doubt, governments must spend as much money as possible for our basic needs on Earth. (맺음말) By spending such **an exorbitant sum of** money on space exploration, we inadvertently kill millions of people whose basic needs are not met, and let the Earth's destruction continue unchecked.

해석

매년, 신문은 최근에 있었던 우주 탐사의 성공이나 실패에 대한 소식을 속보로 전하곤 한다. 이는 정부가 수십억 달러에 달하는 돈을 우주 탐험에 써야 하는지에 대한 의문을 제기한다. 나의 의견으로는, 정부는 돈을 우주 탐사에 낭비할 것이 아니라, 국민의 절박하지만 충족되지 못한 기본적 욕구와 파괴된 환경을 돌보는 데 써야 한다고 생각한다.

우선, 인간의 생명을 구하는 것이 우주를 탐사하는 것보다 시급하다는 것은 명백하다. 이는 바로 이순간에도 무수한 사람들이 식량, 약품과 깨끗한 식수와 같은 기본적인 생필품의 극심한 부족으로 인해서 죽어가고 있다는 사실을 생각해보면 분명히 드러난다. 따라서 정부는 지구상의 사람들의 기본적 욕구를 만족시켜 주어야 하는 그들의 근본적인 책임을 짊어져야 한다. 예를 들면, UNICEF에서 최근에 발표된 충격적인 보고에 따르면, 아프리카 아이들의 3분의 1이 극심한 영양 부족 상태에 처해 있으며, 충분한 약품의 공급과 병원 치료를 받는다면 쉽게 치료될 수 있는 설사와 같은 병으로 죽어가고 있다고 한다. 따라서 세계는 다른 행성의 미지의 생명체를 탐험하기보다는 이러한 무고한 아이들의 생명에 관심을 쏟아야 한다.

게다가 파괴된 환경을 복구하는 것이 우주를 탐험하는 것보다 훨씬 시급한 문제이다. 이는 깨끗한 공기와 물이 인류와 동물의 생존에 있어서 필수 불가결하기 때문이다. 안타깝게도, 무차별적인 개발과 주택과 공장을 짓기 위한 자연의 파괴가 되돌릴 수 없는 환경 오염을 초래해왔다. 예를 들면, 사람들은 도시화와 산업화를 위해 아무 생각 없이 수많은 나무들을 베어내고 있다. 그 결과, 산림 파괴는 엄청난 크기의 토지를 극적으로 산사태와 홍수가 빈번하게 일어나는 사막과 불모지로 변화시켰다. 안타깝게도, 정부는 파괴된 숲과 삼림지를 복구하기 위해서는 수십 년간 천문학적인 양의 재원을 들일 필요가 있다. 이는 자연 환경을 복구하는 것이 우주를 탐험하는 것보다 훨씬 더 중요하다는 것을 명백히 보여준다.

요약하자면, 의심할 여지 없이 정부는 지구상에 있는 우리의 기본적인 욕구를 해결하는 데 가능한 많은 돈을 소비해야 한다. 우주 탐험에 터무니 없는 양의 돈을 소모함으로써, 우리는 의도하지 않게 기본적 욕구가 충족되지 못한 수백만 명의 사람들을 죽이고 있으며, 지구의 파괴가 계속되도록 내버려두고 있다.

---

outer space (대기권 외) 우주 공간   flash[flæʃ] 순식간에 전하다   call into question 의심을 가지다, 이의를 제기하다
space exploration 우주 탐험   attend to ~을 보살피다, 돌보다   pressing[présiŋ] 긴급한, 절박한
unfulfilled[ʌnfulfíld] 이행되지 않은   basic needs 기본적 욕구   imperative[impérətiv] 긴급한, 피할 수 없는
necessities of life 생활필수품   shoulder[ʃóuldər] 떠맡다, 짊어지다
UNICEF (United Nations International Children's Emergency Fund) 유엔아동기금
malnourished[mælnə́:riʃt] 영양 부족의   die of illness 병으로 죽다   diarrhea[dàiərí(:)ə] 설사   provision[prəvíʒən] 공급, 지급
rather than ~ ~하기보다 차라리   indispensable[ìndispénsəbl] 필수 불가결한   brutal[brú:təl] 잔인한, 야만적인
exploitation[èksplɔitéiʃən] 개발, 이기적 이용   irreversible[ìrivə́:rsəbl] 되돌릴 수 없는   mindlessly[máindlisli] 무관심하게, 부주의하게
cut down 베어 넘어뜨리다   urbanization[ə̀:rbənizéiʃən] 도시화   deforestation[di:fɔ(:)ristéiʃən] 산림 파괴, 벌채
barren[bǽrən] 메마른, 불모의   landslide[lǽndslàid] 산사태   astronomical[æ̀strənámikəl] 천문학적인
overarching[ðuvərá:rtʃiŋ] 무엇보다 중요한   without any doubt 의심할 여지 없이   exorbitant[igzɔ́:rbitənt] 엄청난, 터무니 없는
inadvertently[ìnədvə́:rtəntli] 의도하지 않게

---

① calls into question   ② In my opinion   ③ attending to   ④ To start with   ⑤ imperative
⑥ at this very moment   ⑦ necessities of life   ⑧ dying of illnesses   ⑨ rather than
⑩ indispensable   ⑪ resulted in   ⑫ cutting down   ⑬ far more overarching   ⑭ In summary
⑮ an exorbitant sum of

Review

(도입) Every year, newspapers will flash with news of a latest space exploration triumph or disaster. This ① c_____ whether governments should be spending billions of dollars on exploring outer space. (대주제문) ② l_____, governments should not waste their money space exploration but should spend money ③ a_____ people's pressing, unfulfilled basic needs and the ravaged environment.

(소주제문 1) ④ T_____, saving human lives is definitely more ⑤ i_____ than exploring outer space. (구체적 근거 1: 일반적 진술) This is clearly evident when one ponders that a countless number of people are dying ⑥ a_____ because of an extreme shortage of fundamental ⑦ n_____, such as food, medicine, and clean drinking water. Therefore, governments must shoulder their essential responsibility for satisfying people's basic needs on Earth. (구체적 근거 2: 예시) To illustrate, according to a shocking report recently released by UNICEF, nearly one-third of children in southern and eastern Africa are severely malnourished and ⑧ d_____ _____ such as diarrhea which can be easily cured with sufficient provisions of medicine and hospital treatment. (마무리 문장) Therefore, the world should focus its attention on the lives of these innocent children ⑨ r_____ exploring unknown lives on other planets.

(소주제문 2) Moreover, restoring the damaged environment is a much more pressing issue than exploring outer space. (구체적 근거 1: 일반적 진술) This is largely because clean air and water are ⑩ i_____ to the survival of both humans and animals. Unfortunately, brutal exploitation and destruction of nature for the building of houses and factories have definitely ⑪ r_____ irreversible environmental pollution. (구체적 근거 2: 예시) For example, people have been mindlessly ⑫ c_____ countless trees for urbanization and industrialization. As a result, deforestation has dramatically changed a great portion of land into deserts and barren land where landslides and floods frequently occur. Unfortunately, governments need to spend an astronomical amount of their funds for several decades in order to restore the damaged forests and woodlands. (마무리 문장) This clearly proves that restoring the natural environment is ⑬ f_____ than exploring outer space.

(요약 / 정리) ⑭ l_____, without any doubt, governments must spend as much money as possible for our basic needs on Earth. (맺음말) By spending such ⑮ a_____ money on space exploration, we inadvertently kill millions of people whose basic needs are not met, and let the Earth's destruction continue unchecked.

Question

Do you agree or disagree with the following statement? Friends are the most important influence on young adults. Use specific reasons and examples to support your answer.

친구는 청소년의 인생에 가장 중요한 영향을 미친다는 진술에 찬성하는지 반대하는지를 밝히고 구체적인 이유와 예를 들어 대답을 뒷받침한다.

Outline

Agree*

1. Spend lots of time with their friends
   친구들과 많은 시간을 함께 보낸다
   - as they get older, spend more time at school with friends, less with parents
     나이가 들면서 학교에서 친구들과 더 많은 시간을 보내고 부모와는 적게 보낸다
   - e.g. in school preparing for exams
     예) 학교에서의 시험 준비

2. Young people feel like they have to fit in
   청소년은 (또래 그룹에) 소속되고 싶어한다
   - want to be popular
     인기를 얻고 싶어한다
   - e.g. friend acted bad to be cool and fit in
     예) 멋지게 보이고 또래에 끼기 위해 문제를 일으킨 친구

Disagree

1. Family influence young adults more
   가족이 청소년에 더 많은 영향을 미친다
   - family members give more attention and love
     가족들은 관심과 사랑을 더 많이 준다
   - e.g. stay on their side even when friends tease or turn their back
     예) 친구들이 괴롭히거나 등을 돌릴 때에도 가족은 편을 들어 준다

2. Teens affected greatly by celebrities
   청소년은 연예인의 영향도 크게 받는다
   - kids try to emulate celebrities they see on TV
     아이들은 TV에서 보는 연예인들을 모방하려고 한다
   - e.g. following fashion trends from TV
     예) TV에 나오는 유행을 쫓는다

Model Essay

(도입) It is said that young adults are a society's most precious resource. As such, parents want to know why some young people succeed, and others have problems. Most parents would argue that they **have the greatest impact**. (대주제문) Yet, **after closer inspection**, it is evident that their friends wield the most impact as they spend most of their time together and exercise **peer pressure**.

(소주제문 1) First, friends significantly **influence** young adults because of the amount of time they spend together. (구체적 근거 1: 일반적 진술) As young adults become older, they spend less time with their parents and more with their friends in school. Especially their junior or senior year in high school, young people spend most of the day with their friends staying out or **hanging out** together. (구체적 근거 2: 예시) **For example**, when I was a senior in high school, I had spent almost half a day in school preparing for the college entrance exam. Since I did not have much chance to talk to my family, I consulted with my friends whenever I had problems and listened to their advice. This was because I thought they understood me better than my parents did as we spent long time together.

(소주제문 2) **Additionally**, friends greatly influence young adults because they exercise peer pressure. (구체적 근거 1: 일반적 진술) As they enter **adolescence**, they want to win more recognition from friends and be popular. Often, they **reluctantly** commit irreversible mistakes because their friends push them to or they think they do not **belong to** the 'right' group. (구체적 근거 2: 예시) For instance, one of my old friends was a good student and athlete, but when he became a high school student, he began to **get into trouble**. The main reason was the group of people that he hung out with. The pressure to 'be cool' was so great that he started **missing classes** and drinking alcohol. (마무리 문장) The incredible pressure that young adults feel to be accepted into the social fold can be an overwhelming force that parents just cannot **compete with**.

(요약 / 정리) Because of the amount of time they spend together and simple peer pressure, it is an inevitable **fact of life** that youth are most influenced by their friends. (맺음말) **As a result**, it becomes important for parents to ensure their children spend time with people who will be a positive influence on their lives.

해석

청소년이 사회의 가장 귀중한 자원이라고들 한다. 이에 따라, 부모들은 왜 어떤 아이들은 성공하고, 다른 아이들은 문제를 겪는지 알고 싶어한다. 대부분의 부모들은 자신이 (자녀에게) 가장 큰 영향을 미친다고 주장할 것이다. 그러나 면밀히 살펴 보면, 청소년들은 친구들과 대부분의 시간을 함께 보내고 또래 집단 간의 압력을 행사하기 때문에, 그들의 친구들이 가장 큰 영향력을 행사하고 있다는 점이 명백하다.

우선, 친구들이 청소년에게 중요한 영향을 끼치는 이유는 이들이 많은 시간을 함께 보내기 때문이다. 아이들은 성장하면서, 차차 그들의 부모와 보내는 시간이 줄어들고 학교에서 친구들과 더 많은 시간을 보내게 된다. 특히 고등학교 2학년이나 3학년 때는 아이들은 친구들과 집 밖에서 함께 어울리면서 하루의 대부분을 보낸다. 예를 들어, 내가 고등학교 3학년이었을 때, 나는 대입 시험을 준비하면서 하루의 거의 절반을 학교에서 보냈다. 가족과 이야기할 기회가 많지 않았기 때문에, 나는 내게 문제가 있을 때마다 친구들과 상의했고 그들의 조언을 구했다. 이것은 그들이 나와 많은 시간을 함께 보냈기 때문에 부모님보다 나를 더 잘 이해한다고 생각했기 때문이다.

게다가, 친구들은 또래 집단의 압력을 행사하기 때문에 청소년들에게 큰 영향을 끼친다. 아이가 사춘기에 접어들면 그들은 친구들로부터 인정을 받고 인기를 얻고 싶어한다. 종종 아이들은 친구들에 의해 떠밀리거나 혹은 자신들이 '올바른' 집단에 속해 있지 않다는 생각 때문에, 마지못해 돌이킬 수 없는 실수를 저지르곤 한다. 예를 들어, 나의 오래된 친구 하나는 모범생에 운동도 잘했었지만 고등학생이 되자 그는 문제를 일으키기 시작했다. 주된 원인은 그가 함께 어울려 다니던 친구들 때문이었다. '멋져 보이고 싶은' 압박감이 너무 커서 그는 수업을 빠지고 술을 마시기 시작했다. 청소년들이 사회적 집단에 받아들여져야 한다고 느끼는 중압감은 부모들에 의한 영향이 필적할 수 없는 압도적인 영향력으로 작용할 수 있다.

함께 보내는 많은 시간과 단순한 또래 집단의 압력으로 인해 청소년들이 그들의 친구들로부터 가장 큰 영향을 받는다는 것은 피할 수 없는 인생의 현실이다. 결과적으로, 부모가 자녀들이 그들의 삶에 긍정적인 영향을 줄 수 있는 건전한 친구들과 시간을 보낼 수 있도록 보장해주는 것이 중요해지고 있다.

impact[ímpækt] 강한 영향   closer inspection 정밀 조사, 정밀 심사   it is evident that ~ ~인 것이 분명하다
wield[wi:ld] (영향을) 미치다   exercise[éksərsàiz] (권력 등을) 행사하다   peer pressure 또래 집단으로부터 받는 사회적 압력
significantly[signífikəntli] 상당히, 두드러지게   influence[ínfluəns] 영향을 주다   hang out 어울리다, 사귀다
college entrance exam 대학 입학 시험   consult with ~ ~와 상의하다   additionally[ədíʃənəli] 게다가
adolescence[ædəlésəns] 사춘기   recognition[rèkəgníʃən] 인식, 인정   reluctantly[rilʌ́ktəntli] 마지 못해
irreversible[ìrivə́:rsəbl] 되돌릴 수 없는   belong to 소속하다   get into trouble 말썽을 부리다, 곤란에 빠지다
incredible[inkrédəbl] (믿기 어려울 만큼) 대단한   social fold 사회 집단   overwhelming[òuvərhwélmiŋ] 압도적인
force[fɔ:rs] 영향력   compete with 겨루다, 필적하다   inevitable[inévitəbl] 피할 수 없는   fact of life 인생의 현실
ensure[inʃúər] 확실히 하다

① have the greatest impact ② after closer inspection ③ peer pressure ④ influence
⑤ hanging out ⑥ For example ⑦ Additionally ⑧ adolescence ⑨ reluctantly ⑩ belong to
⑪ get into trouble ⑫ missing classes ⑬ compete with ⑭ fact of life ⑮ As a result

Review

(도입) It is said that young adults are a society's most precious resource. As such, parents want to know why some young people succeed, and others have problems. Most parents would argue that they ① h_____ . (대주제문) Yet, ② a_____ , it is evident that their friends wield the most impact as they spend most of their time together and exercise ③ p_____ .

(소주제문 1) First, friends significantly ④ i_____ young adults because of the amount of time they spend together. (구체적 근거 1: 일반적 진술) As young adults become older, they spend less time with their parents and more with their friends in school. Especially their junior or senior year in high school, young people spend most of the day with their friends staying out or ⑤ h_____ together. (구체적 근거 2: 예시) ⑥ F_____ , when I was a senior in high school, I had spent almost half a day in school preparing for the college entrance exam. Since I did not have much chance to talk to my family, I consulted with my friends whenever I had problems and listened to their advice. This was because I thought they understood me better than my parents did as we spent long time together.

(소주제문 2) ⑦ A_____ , friends greatly influence young adults because they exercise peer pressure. (구체적 근거 1: 일반적 진술) As they enter ⑧ a_____ , they want to win more recognition from friends and be popular. Often, they ⑨ r_____ commit irreversible mistakes because their friends push them to or they think they do not ⑩ b_____ the 'right' group. (구체적 근거 2: 예시) For instance, one of my old friends was a good student and athlete, but when he became a high school student, he began to ⑪ g_____ . The main reason was the group of people that he hung out with. The pressure to 'be cool' was so great that he started ⑫ m_____ and drinking alcohol. (마무리 문장) The incredible pressure that young adults feel to be accepted into the social fold can be an overwhelming force that parents just cannot ⑬ c_____ .

(요약/정리) Because of the amount of time they spend together and simple peer pressure, it is an inevitable ⑭ f_____ that youth are most influenced by their friends. (맺음말) ⑮ A_____ , it becomes important for parents to ensure their children spend time with people who will be a positive influence on their lives.

Day 12

Question

Higher education should be available only to good students. Do you agree or disagree? Use specific reasons and details to support your answer.

고등 교육은 우수한 학생들에게만 주어져야 한다는 진술에 찬성하는지 반대하는지를 밝히고 구체적인 이유와 예를 들어 대답을 뒷받침한다.

Outline

Agree

1. Only the academically talented have qualification for higher education
   오직 학업적으로 우수한 학생들만이 고등 교육을 받을 능력이 있다
   - academically poor students can't keep up with the curriculum
     학업적으로 뒤떨어지는 학생들은 교과 과정을 따라갈 수 없다
   - e.g. study: correlation between high school marks and academic performance in college
     예) 연구: 고등학교 성적과 대학 학업 성취도 간의 관계

2. Smart students improve academic performance of each other
   우수한 학생들은 서로의 학업 성취도를 향상시킨다
   - competition and discussion challenge and encourage
     경쟁과 토론은 의욕을 북돋고 격려한다
   - e.g. my brother studied harder when he transferred to a top university
     예) 형은 일류 대학으로 편입한 후에 공부를 더 열심히 했다

Disagree*

1. Everyone should be given equal opportunity
   모든 이에게 동등한 기회가 주어져야 한다
   - explore various fields of interest in college
     대학에서 다양한 관심 분야를 탐색한다
   - e.g. my sister who became a fashion designer thanks to open admission
     예) 자유 입학제 덕분에 의상 디자이너가 된 언니

2. Diversity improves understanding of life
   다양성은 삶을 더 잘 이해하게 해준다
   - a goal of higher education is to open people's minds
     고등 교육의 목표는 사람들의 마음을 여는 것이다
   - e.g. survey: open admission colleges students are more tolerant of others
     예) 조사: 자유 입학제를 적용하는 대학의 학생들이 다른 이에 대해 더 포용력 있다

Model Essay

(도입) Many people believe that only highly-qualified students should be **admitted to universities**. (대주제문) Although I admit that a restricted admission policy **has its advantages**, I strongly believe that a university education should be available to all students because every student should be given a fair opportunity to find and develop his or her talents **through higher education**. In addition, a more diverse student body adds to the understanding of life for all students.

(소주제문 1) **For one**, I strongly believe that an open admission policy provides students with an equal opportunity to achieve their dreams. (구체적 근거 1: 일반적 진술) That is, it allows individual students with different talents and aptitudes to freely **explore various fields** of interest in college. (구체적 근거 2: 예시) For example, my sister's high school transcript showed that she had **a low probability of** pursuing higher education. However, **against all expectations**, she entered a college with an open admission policy and discovered her talent for fashion design by taking a fabric design class in college. **If it had not been for** this admission policy, my sister would not have been able to **live out** her dream as a prominent fashion designer today. (마무리 문장) Consequently, college is the optimal place where students can identify and actualize their dreams regardless of grades during high school.

(소주제문 2) Another reason that an open admission policy is beneficial is that the diversity of this environment improves students' understanding of life. (구체적 근거 1: 일반적 진술) One of the goals of higher education is to open people's minds. There is no better way to do this than **in a real-life setting** where people are exposed to **a myriad of** individuals from very different backgrounds. (구체적 근거 2: 예시) A study of colleges with open admission policies revealed that students were very **tolerant of** other opinions, and in fact used these differences to reflect more deeply on life. This shows that learning from experience and contact with other realities, not just reading about different lifestyles is the best kind of learning. (마무리 문장) **Thus**, an open admission policy creates a more diverse, stimulating, and challenging environment that promotes true understanding and growth.

(요약/정리) To summarize, an open admission policy **has a very positive influence on** society. The reasons are that all students can be given chances to identify and nurture their potentials, and they also gain greater understanding from being in this diverse environment. (맺음말) **As you can see**, I believe that nothing should stop people from seeking and acquiring knowledge.

해석

많은 사람들이 오직 우수한 능력의 학생들만이 대학에 입학하는 것이 허용되어야 한다고 생각한다. 비록 입학 허가를 제한하는 제도가 이점을 지니고 있다는 것에는 동의하지만, 나는 모든 학생들에게 대학 교육의 기회가 주어져야 한다고 확신한다. 왜냐하면 모든 학생들에게 고등 교육을 통해 자신의 재능을 탐색하고 계발할 수 있는 공정한 기회가 주어져야 하기 때문이다. 게다가, 더욱 다양한 학생들이 모이면 모든 학생들에게 삶에 대한 이해를 높여 줄 수 있다.

첫째로 나는 자유 입학제가 학생들에게 그들의 꿈을 실현할 수 있는 동등한 기회를 제공한다고 확신한다. 즉, 이는 제각기 다른 재능과 적성을 지닌 각각의 학생들이 대학교에서 자유롭게 다양한 분야의 관심사를 탐색해 볼 수 있도록 해준다. 예를 들면, 나의 언니의 고등학교 성적 증명서는 그녀가 고등 교육을 수행할 가망이 적은 학생이라고 나타냈다. 그러나, 예상과는 달리, 그녀는 자유 입학제를 적용하는 대학교에 진학하여 직물 디자인 수업을 수강하면서 의상 디자인에 대한 그녀의 재능을 발견했다. 이와 같은 입학 허가 제도가 없었더라면, 언니는 오늘날 촉망받는 의상 디자이너로서의 그녀의 꿈을 실현할 수 없었을 것이다. 따라서, 대학교는 고등학교에서의 성적과 상관없이 학생들이 자신들의 꿈을 확인하고 실현할 수 있는 최적의 장소이다.

자유 입학제가 유익한 또 다른 이유는 이러한 환경의 다양성이 학생들의 삶에 대한 이해를 높이기 때문이다. 고등 교육의 목표 중 하나는 사람들로 하여금 개방적인 사고를 갖게 하는 것이다. 자신과 매우 다른 배경을 지닌 무수한 사람들에게 노출되는 실제 환경에서 이를 실행하는 것보다 더 좋은 방법은 없다. 자유 입학제를 적용하고 있는 대학들을 조사한 결과, 학생들이 다른 사람의 의견에 대해 큰 포용력을 가지며, 실제로 이러한 의견의 차이를 인생에 대해 보다 깊이 고찰해 보는데 사용했다는 것이 밝혀졌다. 이는 단지 책에서 다양한 생활 방식에 대해 읽는 것이 아닌, 경험과 다른 현실에의 접촉으로부터 배우는 것이야말로 최고의 학습 방법이라는 것을 보여 준다. 따라서, 자유 입학제는 진정한 이해와 성장을 촉진시키는, 보다 다양하고 활기차며 의욕을 북돋는 환경을 조성해 준다.

요약하자면, 자유 입학제는 사회에 매우 긍정적인 영향을 미친다. 그 이유는 모든 학생들이 자신의 잠재력을 탐색하고 성장시킬 수 있는 기회를 부여받고, 또한 다양한 환경에 속함으로써 보다 폭넓은 이해를 얻을 수 있기 때문이다. 여기서 볼 수 있듯이, 나는 어떤 것도 사람들이 지식을 추구하고 획득하는 것을 방해해서는 안 된다고 믿는다.

highly-qualified 우수한 능력을 갖춘   admit[ədmít] (입학을) 허가하다   restricted[ristríktid] 제한된, 한정된
admission[ədmíʃən] 입학, 허가, 입장   diverse[divə́ːrs] 다양한   student body [집합적] (대학 등의) 학생 총수, 전학생
aptitude[ǽptitjùːd] 소질, 적성   concentration[kànsəntréiʃən] 집중, 집결   transcript[trǽnskript] 성적 증명서
academic performance 학업 성취   probability[prɑ̀bəbíləti] 실현성, 가망
against all expectations 모든 기대에 어긋나게, 예상과는 달리   fabric design 직물 디자인   if it had not been for ~ 만약 ~이 없었다면
live out 실현하다   prominent[prɑ́mənənt] 저명한   consequently[kɑ́nsəkwèntli] 결과적으로   optimal[ɑ́ptəməl] 최적의
actualize[ǽktʃuəlàiz] 실현하다   real-life setting 실제 환경   a myriad of 무수한   be tolerant of ~ ~을 견뎌내다, 관용하다
stimulating[stímjulèitiŋ] 활기를 띠는   challenging[tʃǽlindʒiŋ] (의욕, 흥미를) 돋우는   nurture[nə́ːrtʃər] 기르다, 양성하다

① admitted to universities   ② has its advantages   ③ through higher education   ④ For one
⑤ explore various fields   ⑥ a low probability of   ⑦ against all expectations
⑧ If it had not been for   ⑨ live out   ⑩ in a real-life setting   ⑪ a myriad of   ⑫ tolerant of
⑬ Thus   ⑭ has a very positive influence on   ⑮ As you can see

Review

(도입) Many people believe that only highly-qualified students should be ① a_____.

(대주제문) Although I admit that a restricted admission policy ② h_____, I strongly believe that a university education should be available to all students because every student should be given a fair opportunity to find and develop his or her talents ③ t_____. In addition, a more diverse student body adds to the understanding of life for all students.

(소주제문 1) ④ F_____, I strongly believe that an open admission policy provides students with an equal opportunity to achieve their dreams. (구체적 근거 1: 일반적 진술) That is, it allows individual students with different talents and aptitudes to freely ⑤ e_____ of interest in college. (구체적 근거 2: 예시) For example, my sister's high school transcript showed that she had ⑥ a_____ pursuing higher education. However, ⑦ a_____, she entered a college with an open admission policy and discovered her talent for fashion design by taking a fabric design class in college. ⑧ I_____ this admission policy, my sister would not have been able to ⑨ l_____ her dream as a prominent fashion designer today. (마무리 문장) Consequently, college is the optimal place where students can identify and actualize their dreams regardless of grades during high school.

(소주제문 2) Another reason that an open admission policy is beneficial is that the diversity of this environment improves students' understanding of life. (구체적 근거 1: 일반적 진술) A goal of higher education is to open people's minds. There is no better way to do this than ⑩ i_____ where people are exposed to ⑪ a_____ individuals from very different backgrounds. (구체적 근거 2: 예시) A study of colleges with open admission policies revealed that students were very ⑫ t_____ other opinions, and in fact used these differences to reflect more deeply on life. This shows that learning from experience and contact with other realities, not just reading about different lifestyles is the best kind of learning. (마무리 문장) ⑬ T____, an open admission policy creates a more diverse, stimulating, and challenging environment that promotes true understanding and growth.

(요약/정리) To summarize, an open admission policy ⑭ h_____ society. The reasons are that all students can be given chances to identify and nurture their potentials, and they also gain greater understanding from being in this diverse environment. (맺음말) ⑮ A_____, I believe that nothing should stop people from seeking and acquiring knowledge.

Question

Do you agree or disagree with the following statement? With the help of the Internet, students can learn more effectively. Use specific reasons and examples to support your answer.

인터넷의 도움으로 학생들은 보다 효과적으로 학습할 수 있다는 진술에 찬성하는지 반대하는지를 밝히고 구체적인 이유와 예를 들어 대답을 뒷받침한다.

Outline

Agree*

1. Quick research
   빠른 자료 조사
   - no need to comb through books
     책을 뒤질 필요가 없다
   - e.g. used Internet to research paper on Jazz
     재즈 보고서를 위한 자료 조사에 인터넷 이용

2. Online courses
   온라인 교육 과정
   - allows students without access to learn
     기회가 없는 학생들에게 배움의 기회 제공
   - e.g. research: increasing online enrollment
     예) 조사: 온라인 교육과정 등록 증가

Disagree

1. Too much information
   지나친 정보의 홍수
   - difficult to get through, untrustworthy
     정리하기 어렵고 신뢰할 수 없다
   - e.g. used Internet for term paper, received low mark
     예) 인터넷을 활용해 기말 보고서를 작성했다가 낮은 점수를 받았다

2. Online classes, a waste of time
   온라인 교육 과정은 시간 낭비
   - little feedback, low quality
     피드백이 적고 질이 낮음
   - e.g. friend disappointed after listening to online lecture
     예) 온라인 수업을 수강하고 난 후 실망했던 친구

Model Essay

(도입) In the past, information was a valuable **commodity** and was difficult to obtain for those without money. The **advent** of digital technology has given everyone access to a wealth of information on the web cheaply and conveniently. (대주제문) The Internet is a highly valuable tool because it allows students to conduct research not just quickly but easily and take online courses **in the comfort of** their homes.

(소주제문 1) **First of all**, students are able to do research on the Internet with great ease and in a short period of time. (구체적 근거 1: 일반적 진술) There is no need to drive to libraries, **comb through** scores of books, or rely on the librarians' help. Now they can **go online** to find information on what they want to learn about. (구체적 근거 2: 예시) For instance, when I was a freshman in college, I had to write a report on Jazz history. Since I was not familiar with the genre, I did not know which books I should use as references. Therefore, I accessed the Internet, and **in a matter of minutes**, I was able to view vast amount of material about Jazz from around the globe. When compared to books, the website contained more **up to date** information and music. If I had to find all that information from books or magazines, it would have probably taken me a whole week.

(소주제문 2) Furthermore, online courses open up education to students who are unable to attend **on-campus classes**. (구체적 근거 1: 일반적 진술) Online courses are very useful and can provide a much-needed **alternative** for those with busy lives and inflexible schedules. They thus allow students to learn in the comfort of their homes, at their own pace. (구체적 근거 2: 예시) **According to** a recent research, the number of people choosing to take online courses is greatly increasing. In addition, it has also announced that not only students but also office workers who are not able to attend classes on campus are starting to **take online courses**. (마무리 문장) As life becomes increasingly busy, fast-paced, and complex, the Internet provides a wonderful way to learn outside the traditional bounds of the classroom.

(요약/정리) **To summarize**, the Internet is an extremely helpful tool to students. Because of it, people are able to conduct extensive research **in a fraction of** the amount of time it used to take. They are also able to take online courses in their homes, saving both time and money. (맺음말) The Internet is revolutionizing the way students learn, and launching the 21st century in a new direction.

해석

과거에 정보는 값비싼 상품이었고 돈이 없는 이들이 정보를 획득하기란 어려웠다. 디지털 과학 기술의 등장은 모든 이들이 싸고 편리하게 웹상의 다양한 정보에 접근할 수 있도록 해주었다. 인터넷은 학생들이 빠를 뿐 아니라, 쉽게 자료를 조사하고 집에서 편안히 온라인 수업을 들을 수 있게 해주므로 아주 유용한 도구이다.

우선 첫째로, 학생들은 아주 쉽게 그리고 짧은 시간 안에 인터넷상에서 자료 조사를 할 수 있다. 도서관까지 운전해서 가거나, 많은 책을 샅샅이 뒤지거나, 사서의 도움에 의존할 필요가 없다. 이제 그들은 알고 싶은 정보를 찾기 위해 인터넷에 접속하면 된다. 예를 들어, 내가 대학교 1학년이었을 때 나는 재즈의 역사에 관한 보고서를 작성해야 했다. 내가 그 장르에 대해 아는 것이 별로 없었기 때문에 어떤 책들을 참고해야 할지 알 수 없었다. 그래서, 나는 인터넷에 접속했는데, 몇 분만에 전세계의 재즈에 대한 방대한 분량의 자료를 볼 수 있었다. 책과 비교했을 때, 그 웹사이트는 좀 더 최신의 정보와 음악을 보유하고 있었다. 만약 내가 이 모든 정보를 책이나 잡지에서 찾으려고 했다면, 아마도 일주일 내내 걸렸을 것이다.

더욱이, 온라인 교육 과정은 캠퍼스에서 이루어지는 수업을 수강할 수 없는 학생들에게 교육의 기회를 제공해준다. 온라인 수업은 매우 유용하며, 바쁜 삶을 살거나 변경할 수 없는 일정을 가지고 있는 사람들에게도 꼭 필요한 대안이 될 수 있다. 따라서, 온라인 수업은 학생들이 집에서 편안하게, 자신의 속도에 맞추어 학습할 수 있도록 해 준다. 최근에 시행된 조사에 따르면, 온라인 수업을 수강하는 사람들의 수가 크게 증가하고 있다. 게다가 학생뿐만 아니라 캠퍼스에서 수업을 들을 수 없는 직장인들도 온라인 수업을 수강하고 있다고 한다. 삶이 점차 바쁘게, 빠르게, 복잡하게 돌아가면서, 인터넷은 전통적인 교실의 울타리 밖에서 학습하는 훌륭한 방식을 제공한다.

요약하자면, 인터넷은 학생들에게 매우 유용한 도구이다. 인터넷 덕분에, 사람들은 예전에 자료 조사하는데 걸렸던 시간에 비해 짧은 시간 안에 광범위한 자료 조사를 할 수 있다. 또한 학생들이 집에서 온라인 수업을 들을 수 있기에 시간과 돈이 절약된다. 인터넷은 학생들의 학습 방법에 대변혁을 가져오고 있으며 21세기를 새로운 방향으로 열어가고 있다.

commodity[kəmádəti] 상품   obtain[əbtéin] 얻다   advent[ǽdvent] 출현, 도래   digital technology 디지털 기술
access[ǽkses] 접근   online course 온라인 강좌   with great ease 매우 손쉽게   in the comfort of their homes 집에서 편안하게
comb through 세밀히 조사하다   scores of 무수한   go online 인터넷에 접속하다   reference[réfərəns] 참조, 참고 문헌(도서)
in a matter of minutes 몇 분만에   up to date 최신의, 최근의   much-needed 절실한   alternative[ɔːltə́ːrnətiv] 대안
inflexible[infléksəbl] 변경할 수 없는   fast-paced 빠른 속도의   bounds[bàundz] 범위, 한계   extensive[iksténsiv] 광범한, 대규모의
in a fraction of the time 순식간에   revolutionize[rèvəljúːʃənàiz] 급격한 변화를 가져오다   launch[lɔːntʃ] 착수하다

① commodity   ② advent   ③ in the comfort of   ④ First of all   ⑤ comb through   ⑥ go online
⑦ in a matter of minutes   ⑧ up to date   ⑨ on-campus classes   ⑩ alternative   ⑪ According to
⑫ take online courses   ⑬ To summarize   ⑭ in a fraction of

Review

(도입) In the past, information was a valuable ① c_____ and was difficult to obtain for those without money. The ② a_____ of digital technology has given everyone access to a wealth of information on the web cheaply and conveniently. (대주제문) The Internet is a highly valuable tool because it allows students to conduct research not just quickly but easily and take online courses ③ i_____ their homes.

(소주제문 1) ④ F_____, students are able to do research on the Internet with great ease and in a short period of time. (구체적 근거 1: 일반적 진술) There is no need to drive to libraries, ⑤ c_____ scores of books, or rely on the librarians' help. Now they can ⑥ g_____ to find information on what they want to learn about. (구체적 근거 2: 예시) For instance, when I was a freshman in college, I had to write a report on Jazz history. Since I was not familiar with the genre, I did not know which books I should use as references. Therefore, I accessed the Internet, and ⑦ i_____, I was able to view vast amount of material about Jazz from around the globe. When compared to books, the website contained more ⑧ u_____ information and music. If I had to find all that information from books or magazines, it would have probably taken me a whole week.

(소주제문 2) Furthermore, online courses open up education to students who are unable to attend ⑨ o_____. (구체적 근거 1: 일반적 진술) Online courses are very useful and can provide a much-needed ⑩ a_____ for those with busy lives and inflexible schedules. They thus allow students to learn in the comfort of their homes, at their own pace. (구체적 근거 2: 예시) ⑪ A_____ a recent research, the number of people choosing to take online courses is greatly increasing. In addition, it has also announced that not only students but also office workers who are not able to attend classes on campus are starting to ⑫ t_____. (마무리 문장) As life becomes increasingly busy, fast-paced, and complex, the Internet provides a wonderful way to learn outside the traditional bounds of the classroom.

(요약/정리) ⑬ T_____, the Internet is an extremely helpful tool to students. Because of it, people are able to conduct extensive research ⑭ i_____ the amount of time it used to take. They are also able to take online courses in their homes, saving both time and money. (맺음말) The Internet is revolutionizing the way students learn, and launching the 21st century in a new direction.

Question

It is better to have friends who are similar to you than those who are different from you. Do you agree or disagree? Use specific reasons and details to support your answer.

자신과 다른 친구들보다 공통점이 많은 친구들을 사귀는 것이 더 낫다는 진술에 찬성하는지 반대하는지를 밝히고 구체적인 이유와 예를 들어 대답을 뒷받침한다.

Outline

Agree

1. Have more fun together enjoying activities both like
   둘 다 좋아하는 활동을 함께 즐기면 더 재미있다
   - share same hobbies and interests
     같은 취미와 관심사를 공유한다
   - e.g. survey: people with same hobbies get along better than people with different ones
     예) 조사: 다른 취미를 지닌 사람들보다 같은 취미를 지닌 사람들끼리 더 잘 통한다

2. Similar friends understand each other better
   비슷한 친구들은 서로를 더 잘 이해한다
   - friendship strengthens through sympathy
     공감을 통해 우정이 더 깊어진다
   - e.g. friend who knows me well gave me a helpful advice when I was in trouble
     예) 내가 어려움에 처했을 때 날 잘 아는 친구가 유용한 조언을 해주었다

Disagree*

1. Different friends add diversity to life
   다른 친구들은 삶에 다양성을 더해 준다
   - encourage me to explore a whole new world
     내가 완전히 새로운 세계를 경험하도록 격려한다
   - e.g. friend introduced skiing and tennis to me
     예) 친구가 나에게 스키와 테니스를 소개해 주었다

2. Different friends broaden outlook on life
   다른 친구들은 삶에 대한 견해를 넓혀 준다
   - show new aspects of life by sharing each other's knowledge
     서로의 지식을 공유함으로써 삶의 새로운 측면을 보여 준다
   - e.g. survey: people with dissimilar friends experience expanded perspectives
     예) 조사: 다른 친구와 어울리는 사람들이 보다 열린 사고방식을 경험한다

Model Essay

(도입) **"Opposites attract"** is certainly true for me when I consider the people in my life. (대주제문) My life is definitely enhanced by spending time with friends who **are different from** me. Such friends bring diversity and new activities to my reality. As well, they **expand my horizons** by offering different perspectives.

(소주제문 1) First of all, I strongly believe that friends who are different from me can **add diversity** to my life. (구체적 근거 1: 일반적 진술) This is largely because friends who have different hobbies, tastes, and experiences can encourage me to explore a whole new world **far beyond my mundane existence**. (구체적 근거 2: 예시) For example, thanks to my athletic friend's influence, I changed my sedentary lifestyle and was introduced to skiing and tennis, which are now some of my favorite activities. My life is greatly **enriched with** new hobbies and interests because of all the different friends in my life. This has made me a more **well-rounded person**, as well as allowed me to enjoy **a wealth of** new experiences.

(소주제문 2) **Additionally**, friends who are different from me broaden my outlook on life. (구체적 근거 1: 일반적 진술) The reason is that friends who are specialists in different fields of study or hold **divergent political or social opinions** can dramatically open my eyes to new aspects of life by sharing their knowledge and stories. (구체적 근거 2: 예시) Surveys show that people with dissimilar friends experience expanded perspectives. This is because people become more open-minded when they learn about things they have no knowledge of and are exposed to beliefs that **are contrary to their own**. Likewise, through exposure to new ways of thinking, my views and opinions are challenged, which helps me define who I am. All of this results because of our differences, which force me to reflect on my beliefs.

(요약/정리) **To conclude**, I choose to **associate with** friends who are different from me because they fill my small world with various exciting events and perspectives. (맺음말) Through my experiences **hanging out with** them, our differences constantly **highlight my unique self**. My mind is broadened, and my life is enriched. Like magnets, our friendships prove that opposites do indeed attract.

해석

"서로 다른 사람끼리 이끌린다"라는 말은 내 주위 사람들을 고려해 볼 때 나에게는 틀림없는 사실이다. 나의 삶은 나와 다른 친구들과 함께 시간을 보내면서 확실히 풍요로워졌다. 이런 친구들은 나의 삶에 다양성과 새로운 활동을 가져다 준다. 뿐만 아니라, 그들은 (나와는) 다른 관점을 보여줌으로써 나의 시야를 넓혀 준다.

첫째로, 나는 나와 다른 친구들이 나의 삶에 다양성을 더해 준다는 것을 확신한다. 이는 다른 취미, 취향, 경험을 가진 친구들은 내가 일상적인 생활을 벗어나 완전히 새로운 세계를 경험할 수 있게 해주기 때문이다. 예를 들면, 운동을 즐기는 친구들의 영향 덕분에, 나는 늘 앉아서 지내던 나의 생활 방식을 바꾸어 스키와 테니스를 시작하게 되었고, 이는 내가 가장 좋아하는 활동이 되었다. 내 주위의 다양한 친구들 덕분에 내 삶은 새로운 취미와 관심사들로 훨씬 풍요로워졌다. 이는 나로 하여금 수많은 새로운 경험을 즐기게 해주었을 뿐만 아니라, 보다 더 다재다능한 사람으로 변모시켰다.

게다가, 나와 다른 친구들은 인생에 대한 나의 견해를 넓혀준다. 그 이유는 다른 학업 분야에 전문적인 지식을 지녔거나 각기 다른 정치적 혹은 사회적 의견을 지닌 친구들이 자신의 지식과 경험을 공유함으로써 극적으로 내가 삶의 새로운 측면에 눈을 뜨게 해줄 수 있기 때문이다. 연구 결과에 따르면 자신과 다른 친구와 어울리는 사람들이 보다 넓은 시야를 가지고 있다는 것이 드러났다. 이는 사람들이 알지 못했던 것들에 대해 배우거나 자신의 생각과 상반되는 생각을 접하게 되면, 좀 더 개방적인 사고를 갖게 되기 때문이다. 마찬가지로, 새로운 사고방식을 접하게 됨으로써 나의 사고방식과 의견은 도전을 받게 되고 이것은 나의 정체성을 정의하는 데 도움을 준다. 이 모든 결과는 서로의 차이점이 나로 하여금 내 신념에 대해 다시 한번 생각하게 만들기 때문에 생긴다.

결론을 내리자면, 나는 나와 다른 친구들과 교제하는 것을 선호한다. 왜냐하면 그들이 나의 작은 세계를 다양하고 흥미로운 사건과 사고방식으로 채워 주기 때문이다. 그들과 어울리는 경험을 통해, 우리의 차이점은 끊임없이 나의 독특한 개성을 돋보이게 한다. 나의 마음은 넓어지고, 나의 삶은 풍요로워진다. 나와 친구들과의 우정은, 마치 자석처럼 정반대의 사람들끼리도 정말 이끌릴 수 있다는 것을 잘 보여준다.

Opposites attract 서로 다른 사람끼리 이끌린다 **enhance**[inhǽns] 높이다, 증가시키다 **as well** 게다가
expand one's horizons 시야를 넓히다 **perspective**[pərspéktiv] 사고방식 **mundane**[mʌ́ndein] 평범한, 세속적인
mundane existence 일상 생활 **athletic**[æθlétik] 운동을 즐기는 **sedentary**[sédəntèri] 앉아 있는
well-rounded[wélráundid] 다재다능한, 만능의 **a wealth of** 풍부한 **outlook**[áutlùk] 견해, 전망 **specialist**[spéʃəlist] 전문가
divergent[divə́:rdʒənt] (의견이) 갈라지는, 일탈의 **dramatically**[drəmǽtikəli] 극적으로 **be contrary to ~** ~와 상반되는
way of thinking 사고방식 **exposure**[ikspóuʒər] 노출 **reconsider**[rì:kənsídər] 재고하다 **associate with ~** ~와 교제하다
hang out with ~ ~와 함께 어울려 다니다 **highlight**[háilàit] 돋보이게 하다, 강조하다 **magnet**[mǽgnit] 자석

---

① Opposites attract ② are different from ③ expand my horizons ④ add diversity
⑤ far beyond my mundane existence ⑥ enriched with ⑦ well-rounded person ⑧ a wealth of
⑨ Additionally ⑩ divergent political or social opinions ⑪ are contrary to their own
⑫ To conclude ⑬ associate with ⑭ hanging out with ⑮ highlight my unique self

Review

(도입) ① "O_____" is certainly true for me when I consider the people in my life. (대주제문) My life is definitely enhanced by spending time with friends who ② a_____ me. Such friends bring diversity and new activities to my reality. As well, they ③ e_____ by offering different perspectives.

(소주제문 1) First of all, I strongly believe that friends who are different from me can ④ a_____ to my life. (구체적 근거 1: 일반적 진술) This is largely because friends who have different hobbies, tastes, and experiences can encourage me to explore a whole new world ⑤ f_____. (구체적 근거 2: 예시) For example, thanks to my athletic friend's influence, I changed my sedentary lifestyle and was introduced to skiing and tennis, which are now some of my favorite activities. My life is greatly ⑥ e_____ new hobbies and interests because of all the different friends in my life. This has made me a more ⑦ w_____, as well as allowed me to enjoy ⑧ a_____ new experiences.

(소주제문 2) ⑨ A_____, friends who are different from me broaden my outlook on life. (구체적 근거 1: 일반적 진술) The reason is that friends who are specialists in different fields of study or hold ⑩ d_____ can dramatically open my eyes to new aspects of life by sharing their knowledge and stories. (구체적 근거 2: 예시) Surveys show that people with dissimilar friends experience expanded perspectives. This is because people become more open-minded when they learn about things they have no knowledge of and are exposed to beliefs that ⑪ a_____. Likewise, through exposure to new ways of thinking, my views and opinions are challenged, which helps me define who I am. All of this results because of our differences, which force me to reflect on my beliefs.

(요약/정리) ⑫ T_____, I choose to ⑬ a_____ friends who are different from me because they fill my small world with various exciting events and perspectives. (맺음말) Through my experiences ⑭ h_____ them, our differences constantly ⑮ h_____. My mind is broadened, and my life is enriched. Like magnets, our friendships prove that opposites do indeed attract.

Day 15

Question

Do you agree or disagree with the following statement? Being a leader is better than being a follower. Use specific reasons and examples to support your answer.

한 집단의 지도자가 되는 것이 일원이 되는 것보다 낫다는 진술에 찬성하는지 반대하는지를 밝히고 구체적인 이유와 예를 들어 대답을 뒷받침한다.

Outline

Agree

1. Being in control is satisfying
   통제력을 갖는 것은 만족스럽다
   - chance to control group
     그룹을 통솔하는 기회
   - e.g. was a leader, members followed and felt happy
     예) 내가 지도자 역할을 했을 때 일원들이 나를 따랐고 만족감을 느꼈다

2. Taking a leader's position offers chance to develop skills
   지도자의 위치를 맡는 것은 기술을 계발할 수 있는 기회를 제공한다
   - learn how to organize and plan
     조직하고 계획하는 법을 배울 수 있다
   - e.g. developed confidence and decision making skills
     예) 자신감과 의사 결정 능력을 계발했다

Disagree*

1. Not everyone has skills for leadership
   모든 이가 지도자의 능력을 갖춘 것은 아니다
   - because of glamour, people without capability assume position
     (지도자라는 지위의) 매력 때문에 능력이 없어도 직책을 맡는다
   - e.g. New Orleans shows trouble from failed leadership
     예) 뉴올리언스의 재해와 실패한 지도자의 능력

2. Possible negative consequences
   발생할 수 있는 부정적인 결과
   - criticism and negative impact of failure
     실패로 나타나는 비난과 부정적인 효과
   - e.g. guilty because of group failure
     예) 그룹의 실패로 느낀 죄책감

Model Essay

(도입) It is often said that it is better to be a leader than a follower, and society certainly **tends to** embrace that viewpoint. (대주제문) However, **after some reflection** it seems that on the whole, it is usually better not to be a leader because not everyone is qualified to be one and the potential consequences of failure are too big for one to handle.

(소주제문 1) The primary reason for avoiding the leader's role is that not everyone has what it takes to be a leader. (구체적 근거 1: 일반적 진술) Too often, the glamour of being the person **in charge** can be blinding and people who assume the position are not capable of achieving success because they actually lack the knowledge and experience necessary. (구체적 근거 2: 예시) This can have tragic consequences as seen by the head of the Federal Emergency Management Agency. He did not have the proper experience and so when a major disaster occurred in New Orleans, many people died **because of** the agency's poor response. (마무리 문장) It is true that by **taking on** a principal position, one can actually gain valuable experience, but the potential long-term **ramifications** are not a worthwhile risk if one lacks the essential know-how.

(소주제문 2) **On top of that**, taking a leader's position is too risky because of the possible negative consequences. (구체적 근거 1: 일반적 진술) Although the praise and rewards of successful leadership can be attractive, there can be criticism and negative impacts **in the event of** failure. (구체적 근거 2: 예시) For example, I had the opportunity to lead a project team in my school's physics class. Although I **tried my best** to have a good team project report, we failed to do so. **At the end**, I was the one responsible for the team's failure and so **not only** was my grade affected but also were the grades of my teammates, making me feel guilty. From this incidence, I learned that a leader is viewed as being ultimately responsible for the failure of the group even when the fault **lies in** matters outside of the leader's control. (마무리 문장) **Therefore**, it is important not to underestimate the practical or emotional consequences of unsuccessful leadership.

(요약/정리) In summary, becoming a leader should not be **entered upon** lightly, but avoided in most cases. It is because not everyone is qualified to take such role and the risk followed by a failure is too high. (맺음말) The mere opportunity to be **in the spotlight** or gain experience hardly warrants the personal and professional risks involved in being the leader of a project.

해석

사람들은 흔히 추종자가 되기보다는 지도자가 되는 편이 낫다고 말하고, 사회는 확실히 그러한 견해를 받아들이는 경향이 있다. 하지만 잘 생각해 보면 대체적으로 지도자가 되지 않는 편이 나은데 그 이유는 모든 이가 지도자의 자질을 지닌 것은 아니고 실패로 인해서 잠재적으로 발생될 수 있는 결과가 한 개인이 감당하기에는 지나치게 크기 때문이다.

지도자의 역할을 기피해야 하는 주된 이유는 모든 이가 지도자의 자격을 지닌 것은 아니기 때문이다. 대부분의 경우, 지도자가 된다는 매력은 사람의 판단력을 흐릴 수 있고 (그 매력에 이끌려서) 그 지위를 차지하게 되는 사람은 실제로 필요한 지식과 경험이 부족하기 때문에 성공을 이루어낼 수 있는 능력을 가지고 있지 않다. 이것은 미국 연방 비상관리국의 국장의 경우에서 볼 수 있듯 비극적인 결과를 초래할 수 있다. 그는 적절한 경험을 갖추지 못했기 때문에 뉴올리언스에 큰 재해가 발생했을 때 관리국의 서투른 대응으로 인해 많은 사람들이 생명을 잃었다. 책임자의 지위를 맡음으로써 실제로 귀중한 경험을 얻을 수 있다는 것은 사실이지만, 만일 지도자가 필수적인 전문 지식을 갖추고 있지 않았을 때 잠재적으로 일어날 수 있는 장기적인 결과는 시도해 보기에는 너무나 큰 모험이다.

더구나, 발생할 수 있는 부정적인 결과 때문에 지도자의 역할을 맡는 것은 매우 위험하다. 성공적인 리더십에 따르는 칭찬과 보상은 매력일 수는 있으나, 실패할 경우에는 비난과 부정적인 파장이 뒤따른다. 예를 들면, 나에게는 학교의 물리학 수업에서 프로젝트 팀을 이끌 기회가 있었다. 비록 훌륭한 팀 프로젝트 보고서를 작성하기 위해 최선을 다했지만, 우리는 실패했다. 마침내, 나는 팀의 실패에 대한 책임을 져야 했고 그것은 나의 성적뿐만 아니라 팀 구성원들의 성적에도 영향을 주었고 나는 죄책감을 느꼈다. 이 일로 인해, 나는 지도자의 영향력을 벗어난 사안에 실패의 원인이 있을 때라도 지도자가 궁극적으로 그룹의 실패에 대해 책임이 있는 존재로 여겨진다는 것을 깨달았다. 따라서, 성공적이지 못한 지도자가 다다르게 될 실질적 혹은 감정적인 결말을 과소평가하지 않는 것이 중요하다.

요약하자면, 지도자가 되는 것은 경솔히 받아들이기보다는, 대부분의 경우에 있어 피해야 하는 것이다. 그것은 모든 이가 그러한 역할을 맡을 자격을 갖춘 것은 아니고 실패에 뒤따르는 위험이 지나치게 크기 때문이다. 단순히 주목을 받거나 경험을 쌓을 수 있는 기회라는 점이 프로젝트의 리더가 됨으로써 발생하는 개인적이나 직업적인 면에서 겪게 될 위험들을 정당화해 주지는 못한다.

embrace[imbréis] 받아들이다　reflection[riflékʃən] 숙고, 재고　on the whole 전체적으로　better not to ~ ~하지 않는 편이 더 낫다
potential[pəténʃəl] 잠재적인　consequence[kɑ́nsəkwèns] 결과　glamour[glǽmər] (현혹적인, 신비한) 매력
in charge (of) ~ ~을 맡고 있는　blinding[bláindiŋ] 현혹시키는　assume[əsʤúːm] (역할을) 맡다
Federal Emergency Management Agency(FEMA) 미국 연방 비상관리국　ramification[ræ̀məfəkéiʃən] 결과　take on 맡다
on top of that 게다가　criticism[krítisìzəm] 비판　in the event of (만일) ~의 경우에는　try one's best 최선을 다하다
at the end 마침내　ultimately[ʌ́ltimitli] 궁극적으로　lie in ~ ~에 있다　underestimate[ʌ̀ndəréstəmèit] 과소평가하다
enter upon 얻다, 시작하다　be in the spotlight 주목을 받다　hardly[hɑ́ːrdli] 거의 ~않다　warrant[wɔ́ːrənt] 정당화하다

① tends to　② after some reflection　③ in charge　④ because of　⑤ taking on　⑥ ramifications
⑦ On top of that　⑧ in the event of　⑨ tried my best　⑩ At the end　⑪ not only　⑫ lies in
⑬ Therefore　⑭ entered upon　⑮ in the spotlight

Review

(도입) It is often said that it is better to be a leader than a follower, and society certainly ① t_____ embrace that viewpoint. (대주제문) However, ② a_____ it seems that on the whole, it is usually better not to be a leader because not everyone is qualified to be one and the potential consequences of failure are too big for one to handle.

(소주제문 1) The primary reason for avoiding the leader's role is that not everyone has what it takes to be a leader. (구체적 근거 1: 일반적 진술) Too often, the glamour of being the person ③ i_____ can be blinding and people who assume the position are not capable of achieving success because they actually lack the knowledge and experience necessary. (구체적 근거 2: 예시) This can have tragic consequences as seen by the head of the Federal Emergency Management Agency. He did not have the proper experience and so when a major disaster occurred in New Orleans, many people died ④ b_____ the agency's poor response. (마무리 문장) It is true that by ⑤ t_____ a principal position, one can actually gain valuable experience, but the potential long-term ⑥ r_____ are not a worthwhile risk if one lacks the essential know-how.

(소주제문 2) ⑦ O_____, taking a leader's position is too risky because of the possible negative consequences. (구체적 근거 1: 일반적 진술) Although the praise and rewards of successful leadership can be attractive, there can be criticism and negative impacts ⑧ i_____ failure. (구체적 근거 2: 예시) For example, I had the opportunity to lead a project team in my school's physics class. Although I ⑨ t_____ to have a good team project report, we failed to do so. ⑩ A_____, I was the one responsible for the team's failure and so ⑪ n_____ was my grade affected but also were the grades of my teammates, making me feel guilty. From this incidence, I learned that a leader is viewed as being ultimately responsible for the failure of the group even when the fault ⑫ l_____ matters outside of the leader's control. (마무리 문장) ⑬ T_____, it is important not to underestimate the practical or emotional consequences of unsuccessful leadership.

(요약/정리) In summary, becoming a leader should not be ⑭ e_____ lightly, but avoided in most cases. It is because not everyone is qualified to take such role and the risk followed by a failure is too high. (맺음말) The mere opportunity to be ⑮ i_____ or gain experience hardly warrants the personal and professional risks involved in being the leader of a project.

Question

People should carefully plan activities for their free time. Do you agree or disagree? Use specific reasons and details to support your answer.

사람들은 여가 시간을 위한 활동들을 신중하게 계획해야 한다는 진술에 찬성하는지 반대하는지를 밝히고 구체적인 이유와 예를 들어 대답을 뒷받침한다.

Outline

Agree

1. Carefully planned activities make the best use of free time
   신중하게 계획된 활동은 여가 시간을 최대한 활용할 수 있게 해준다

   – no waste of time deciding what to do
      무엇을 할지 결정하며 시간을 낭비하지 않음

   – e.g. research: people waste free time idly if not scheduled
      예) 설문 조사: 사람들은 여가 계획이 짜여 있지 않을 때 게으르게 시간을 낭비함

2. Prevent unpleasant events
   불쾌한 사건을 방지한다

   – unexpected troubles cause stress
      예기치 못한 문제들은 스트레스를 유발한다

   – e.g. hotels were all occupied on an impromptu trip
      예) 즉흥적으로 떠난 여행에서 호텔이 모두 차 있었다

Disagree*

1. Spontaneity allows me to choose what I want to do at the time
   즉흥적 활동은 내가 그 순간에 하고 싶은 것을 선택하게 해준다

   – scheduling doesn't consider one's mood for it at the time
      계획을 짜두는 것은 그 순간의 기분을 고려하지 않는다

   – e.g. went dancing though I didn't feel like to, just because I planned it
      예) 가고 싶지 않았지만 계획했기 때문에 춤추러 갔다

2. More adventurous and fun
   더 모험적이고 재미있다

   – experience surprising and unanticipated events
      놀랍고 예기치 못한 일들을 경험한다

   – e.g. study: spontaneous activities more fun than planned ones
      예) 연구: 즉흥적인 활동이 계획된 활동보다 더 재미있다

Model Essay

(도입) People's busy schedules often dictate that they carefully plan activities for their free time **far in advance**. (대주제문) Although this is often necessary in today's hectic world, I avoid scheduling **as much as possible** because I prefer spontaneous activities for my free time. **The rationale behind this** is that spontaneity allows me to choose what I want to do at the time. In addition, I find doing things **on the spur of the moment** more adventurous and fun.

(소주제문 1) **First**, I strongly believe that leisure time without a plan allows me the flexibility to follow my moods and whims. (구체적 근거 1: 일반적 진술) From my experience, I take pleasure in going on impromptu trips to places I like in order to relieve my stress from my demanding schedule, without being rushed by a series of appointments and arrangements. **On top of that**, scheduling things far in advance does not **take into account** that the day an event comes, I may not be in the mood to do it. (구체적 근거 2: 예시) For instance, when I make plans to go out dancing with friends, sometimes the night arrives, and I **would rather** sit at home and watch a movie. Canceling, however, is disappointing for my friends, inconsiderate, and often impossible. I then spend the night wishing I did not have to do my planned activity. (마무리 문장) It thus **makes more sense** to take things as they come, and spontaneously do things.

(소주제문 2) Spontaneous activities are also more fun and thrilling. (구체적 근거 1: 일반적 진술) **This is because** when I spend my free time without a plan, I often experience surprising and unanticipated events such as finding new dishes in exotic restaurants, making new friends, discovering scenic attractions, and obtaining unusual information regarding new places. Such incidents are beyond my imagination and my **humdrum day-to-day life**. (구체적 근거 2: 예시) Psychological assessments further show that people rate spontaneous activities more fun than planned ones. This results because people want to **make the most of** their unscheduled time, and allow exciting experiences to present themselves and undreamed-of possibilities to unfold. (마무리 문장) As a result, spontaneous activities **have an air of** mystery and adventure to them.

(요약/정리) To summarize, the benefits of not planning my leisure time **far outweigh** the advantages of planning. The reasons are that spontaneity allows me to follow my moods and gives activities I choose a feeling of adventure and excitement. (맺음말) **All in all**, unplanned free time allows me to enjoy myself to the fullest.

해석

사람들은 바쁜 일정 때문에 종종 여가 시간에 할 활동을 오래 전부터 신중히 계획하도록 강요받는다. 비록 오늘날의 정신없이 바쁜 세상에서는 이렇게 하는 것이 필요한 경우도 종종 있기는 하지만, 나는 여가 시간에 즉흥적인 활동을 하는 것을 선호하기 때문에 되도록 일정을 미리 정하는 것을 피한다. 이에 대한 이유는 계획에 얽매이지 않음으로 인해서 내가 그 순간에 하고 싶은 것을 선택할 수 있기 때문이다. 게다가, 나는 순간의 충동에 의한 활동이 더 모험적이고 재미있다고 느낀다.

첫째로, 나는 계획 없는 여가 시간이 내 기분과 변덕에 따라서 행동할 수 있는 융통성을 부여해 준다고 확신한다. 내 경험상, 나는 빡빡한 일정으로 인한 스트레스를 해소하기 위해 내가 좋아하는 장소로 일련의 일정과 준비에 쫓기지 않고 즉흥적으로 여행을 떠나는 것에서 기쁨을 느낀다. 게다가, 오래 전에 미리 일정을 짜두는 것은 그 일이 닥친 날에, 내가 막상 하고 싶은 기분이 아닐 수도 있다는 사실을 고려하지 않는다. 예를 들어, 내가 친구들과 춤을 추러 가려고 계획을 세웠지만 밤이 되면 차라리 집에서 영화를 보고 싶을 때가 있다. 그러나, 취소하는 것은 친구들에게 실망을 안겨줄 것이고, 배려심 없는 행동이며, 종종 불가능하기도 하다. 그럴 때면 나는 계획된 활동을 할 필요가 없었다면 좋았을 것이라고 생각하며 밤을 보내게 된다. 따라서, 닥치는 상황에 따라서 즉흥적으로 행동하는 편이 좀 더 이치에 맞는다.

즉흥적인 활동은 또한 훨씬 재미있고 스릴 있다. 이는 내가 계획 없이 여가 시간을 보낼 때, 이국적인 식당에서 새로운 음식을 발견하거나, 새로운 친구들을 사귀거나, 풍경이 아름다운 장소를 발견하거나 새로운 장소에 대한 진귀한 정보들을 얻는 등 놀랍고 예기치 않았던 사건들을 종종 경험하게 되기 때문이다. 그러한 사건들은 나의 상상력과 단조로운 일상 생활의 범주에서 벗어난 것이다. 이에 더하여 심리학적 조사 자료에 따르면 사람들이 즉흥적인 활동을 계획된 활동보다 더 재미있어 한다는 것을 보여 준다. 이는 사람들이 계획에 얽매이지 않은 시간을 최대한 활용하고 싶어하고, 재미있는 경험이 일어나고 상상조차 못했던 가능성이 펼쳐지게 하고 싶어하기 때문이다. 그 결과, 즉흥적인 활동들은 신비롭고 모험적인 성격을 가진다.

요약하자면, 여가 시간을 계획하지 않는 것의 장점이 계획을 세우는 것의 장점보다 훨씬 많다. 그 이유는 즉흥적인 선택은 내 기분에 따라서 행동할 수 있게 해주고 내가 선택한 활동에 모험심과 흥분을 느끼게 해주기 때문이다. 대체적으로, 계획이 짜여 있지 않은 여가 시간은 나 자신을 마음껏 즐길 수 있게 해준다.

dictate[díkteit] 지시하다, 명령하다　in advance 미리　hectic[héktik] 몹시 바쁜　as much as possible 가능한 많이, 되도록
spontaneous[spɑntéiniəs] 충동적인　rationale[ræ̀ʃənǽl] 근본적 이유, 이론적 해석　spontaneity[spɑ̀ntəníːəti] 충동성
on the spur of the moment 충동적으로　whim[hwim] 변덕, 즉흥　impromptu[imprɑ́mptjuː] 즉석에서, 준비 없이
demanding[dimǽndiŋ] 큰 노력을 요하는　a series of 일련의, 연속의　arrangement[əréindʒmənt] 준비
take into account 고려하다, 참작하다　be in the mood to~ ~할 기분이 나다　would rather ~ 오히려 ~하고 싶다
inconsiderate[ìnkənsídərit] 남을 배려할 줄 모르는　make sense 이치에 맞다, 말이 되다　unanticipated[ʌ̀næntísəpèitid] 뜻밖의
scenic attractions 경치가 멋진 관광지　regarding[rigáːrdiŋ] ~에 관해서는　humdrum[hʌ́mdrʌ̀m] 평범한, 단조로운
assessment[əsésmənt] 평가, 판단　make the most of 최대한 활용하다
undreamed-of[ʌ̀ndríːmdʌ̀v] 꿈에도 생각지 않은, 전혀 예상 외의　unfold[ʌnfóuld] 펼쳐지다, 전개되다　outweigh[àutwéi] 능가하다
all in all 대체로　to the fullest 완전히, 마음껏

① far in advance　② as much as possible　③ The rationale behind this
④ on the spur of the moment　⑤ First　⑥ On top of that　⑦ take into account　⑧ would rather
⑨ makes more sense　⑩ This is because　⑪ humdrum day-to-day life　⑫ make the most of
⑬ have an air of　⑭ far outweigh　⑮ All in all

Review

(도입) People's busy schedules often dictate that they carefully plan activities for their free time ① f_____ . (대주제문) Although this is often necessary in today's hectic world, I avoid scheduling ② a_____ because I prefer spontaneous activities for my free time. ③ T_____ is that spontaneity allows me to choose what I want to do at the time. In addition, I find doing things ④ o_____ more adventurous and fun.

(소주제문 1) ⑤ F_____ , I strongly believe that leisure time without a plan allows me the flexibility to follow my moods and whims. (구체적 근거 1: 일반적 진술) From my experience, I take pleasure in going on impromptu trips to places I like in order to relieve my stress from my demanding schedule, without being rushed by a series of appointments and arrangements. ⑥ O_____ , scheduling things far in advance does not ⑦ t_____ that the day an event comes, I may not be in the mood to do it. (구체적 근거 2: 예시) For instance, when I make plans to go out dancing with friends, sometimes the night arrives, and I ⑧ w_____ sit at home and watch a movie. Canceling, however, is disappointing for my friends, inconsiderate, and often impossible. I then spend the night wishing I did not have to do my planned activity. (마무리 문장) It thus ⑨ m_____ to take things as they come, and spontaneously do things.

(소주제문 2) Spontaneous activities are also more fun and thrilling. (구체적 근거 1: 일반적 진술) ⑩ T_____ when I spend my free time without a plan, I often experience surprising and unanticipated eventssuch as finding new dishes in exotic restaurants, making new friends, discovering scenic attractions, and obtaining unusual information regarding new places. Such incidents are beyond my imagination and my ⑪ h_____ . (구체적 근거 2: 예시) Psychological assessments further show that people rate spontaneous activities more fun than planned ones. This results because people want to ⑫ m_____ their unscheduled time, and allow exciting experiences to present themselves and undreamed of possibilities to unfold. (마무리 문장) As a result, spontaneous activities ⑬ h_____ mystery and adventure to them.

(요약/정리) To summarize, the benefits of not planning my leisure time ⑭ f_____ the advantages of planning. The reasons are that spontaneity allows me to follow my moods and gives activities I choose a feeling of adventure and excitement. (맺음말) ⑮ A_____ , unplanned free time allows me to enjoy myself to the fullest.

Question

Do you agree or disagree with the following statement? It is better to spend time with one or two close friends than with a large number of friends. Use specific reasons and examples to support your answer.

많은 수의 친구들과 시간을 보내는 것보다 한두 명의 친구들과 시간을 보내는 것이 더 낫다는 진술에 찬성하는지 반대하는지를 밝히고 구체적인 이유와 예를 들어 대답을 뒷받침한다.

Outline

Agree*

1. Easier to deepen connections with a few people
   사람이 적은 편이 관계를 깊이 발전시키는데 용이하다
   - need to spend time together to build true intimacy
     진정한 친밀함을 쌓기 위해서는 함께 시간을 보내는 것이 필요하다
   - e.g. my best friend and I got closer after we joined the same club
     예) 나와 가장 친한 친구는 같은 동아리에 가입한 후부터 더 친해졌다

2. Can have more personal conversations
   더 많은 개인적인 대화를 나눌 수 있다
   - comfortable in a small group
     소규모 그룹이 더 편안하다
   - e.g. can discuss anything with close friend
     예) 친한 친구와는 어떤 것이든 얘기할 수 있다

Disagree

1. The more, the merrier
   더 많을수록 즐겁다
   - can have more fun with different types of people
     여러 부류의 사람들과 있으면 더 재미있다
   - e.g. to have a fun party, need many people
     예) 재미있는 파티를 열기 위해서는 많은 인원이 필요하다

2. Can learn more from various people
   다양한 사람들로부터 더 많은 것을 배울 수 있다
   - you can learn specific skills or values from them
     그들로부터 특정한 기술이나 가치를 배울 수 있다
   - e.g. I learned leadership from Tim, honesty from Heather
     예) 팀에게서 리더십을 배웠고, 헤더로부터 정직함을 배웠다

Model Essay

(도입) Most people think that having many friends is better than having just a few. They mistakenly believe that, due to **time constraints**, it is better to try and meet all their friends at one time. **However**, the quality of the friendships is more important than their quantity. (대주제문) When one has the time to spend with friends, it is better to spend it with just a few instead of with a large group since one can cultivate more profound relationships and have more intimate conversations.

(소주제문 1) When going out with a small number of people, it is easier to deepen connections with them because you can spend a significant amount of time with each person. (구체적 근거 1: 일반적 진술) A certain amount of time spent together, interacting with each other, is needed to **build true intimacy** between friends. (구체적 근거 2: 예시) For example, my best friend and I did not think we **had a lot in common** when we first hung around a large group of friends, because we did not have enough chances to talk to each other. However, when we joined the same club, we **got to know** each other better. The more time we spent sharing our experiences, the stronger our friendship became over time. Although I did not make a lot of other new friends during that time, I had found a close friend for life.

(소주제문 2) **Next**, when **going out with** only a few friends, the content of the conversations can be much more personal. (구체적 근거 1: 일반적 진술) People **tend to** feel more comfortable in a small group, so they can have more private conversations **concerning** their personal lives, not wasting time on **small talk** and other trivialities. (구체적 근거 2: 예시) For instance, in larger gatherings, I feel the discussion of sensitive topics **awkward**, because not everyone is a close friend. In contrast, when I am with my close friends, I know we can discuss anything, from favorite movies to family matters, without **worrying about** being judged because we understand each other so well.

(요약/정리) **As I have shown**, it is much better to meet with just a few friends than to go out with large groups in that it allows us to strengthen relationships and to discuss more **personal matters**. (맺음말) People often do not nurture the relationships they have and prefer to keep trying to develop new ones. In doing so, they miss the opportunity to build a few deep friendships that are much more satisfying than many **superficial** ones.

해석

대부분의 사람들은 많은 친구들을 만나는 것이 단지 몇 명의 친구만 만나는 것보다 낫다고 생각한다. 그들은 시간 제약 때문에, 한 번에 모든 친구들을 만나는 것이 더 낫다는 잘못된 생각을 가지고 있다. 그러나, 우정에 있어서 질이 양보다 더 중요하다. 친구들과 함께 보낼 시간이 있을 때에는, 보다 깊은 관계를 발전시킬 수 있고 보다 친밀한 대화를 나눌 수 있기 때문에, 많은 인원의 그룹과 보내는 것보다 소수의 친구와 함께 보내는 것이 더 낫다.

적은 수의 친구들과 어울릴 때에는 각각의 친구와 많은 시간을 함께 보낼 수 있기 때문에, 그들과의 관계를 보다 깊게 발전시키기 더 쉽다. 친구 간에 진정한 친밀함을 쌓기 위해서는 서로 교류하며 일정한 양의 시간을 함께 보내는 것이 필요하다. 예를 들면, 나의 가장 친한 친구와 나는 처음에 많은 수의 친구들 사이에서 어울렸을 때는 서로 이야기할 기회가 없었기 때문에 별로 공통점이 많지 않다고 생각했다. 그러나 같은 클럽에 가입하게 되자, 우리는 서로에 대해 더 잘 알게 되었다. 경험을 공유하며 더 많은 시간을 보낼수록, 우리의 우정은 시간이 갈수록 더 깊어졌다. 비록 그 기간 동안 나는 다른 친구들을 많이 사귀지는 못했지만, 평생을 함께할 친한 친구를 얻었다.

다음으로, 적은 수의 친구들과 어울릴 때에는 대화의 내용이 좀 더 개인적이 된다. 사람들은 작은 집단에서 좀 더 편안하게 느끼는 경향이 있어서, 잡담이나 다른 시시한 이야기에 시간을 낭비하지 않고, 그들의 개인적인 삶에 대한 보다 긴밀한 대화를 나눌 수 있다. 예를 들면, 많은 사람들의 모임에서는 모든 이들이 친한 친구는 아니기 때문에, 민감한 주제에 대해 의논하는 것이 어색하게 느껴진다. 대조적으로, 내가 친한 친구들과 함께 있을 때는, 우리는 서로를 너무도 잘 알기 때문에 좋아하는 영화에서부터 가족 문제에 이르기까지 비판받을 걱정 없이 어떤 것이든 이야기할 수 있다고 생각한다.

앞에서 밝힌 바와 같이, 관계를 돈독히 하고 보다 개인적인 문제에 대해서 이야기를 나눌 수 있게 해주기 때문에, 많은 수의 무리와 어울리는 것보다 소수의 친구들을 만나는 것이 훨씬 더 낫다. 사람들은 종종 그들이 가진 관계를 진전시키기보다 계속해서 새로운 관계를 만들기 위해 노력하는 것을 선호한다. 그렇게 함으로써, 그들은 다수의 피상적인 우정보다 훨씬 더 큰 만족을 주는 소수의 깊은 우정을 쌓을 수 있는 기회를 놓치고 만다.

mistakenly[mistéikənli] 잘못하여, 실수로   due to ~ ~ 때문에   constraint[kənstréint] 제약, 속박   cultivate[kʌ́ltəvèit] 돈독히 하다
profound[prəfáund] 깊은, 심오한   intimate[íntəmit] 친밀한, 은밀한   significant[signífikənt] 상당한   interact with ~ ~와 교류하다
intimacy[íntəməsi] 친밀, 친교   have a lot in common 공통점이 많다   tend to ~ ~하는 경향이 있다
concerning[kənsə́ːrniŋ] ~에 관하여   small talk 잡담   triviality[trìviǽləti] 사소한 것   gathering[gǽðəriŋ] 모임
awkward[ɔ́ːkwərd] 어색한   in contrast 대조적으로   nurture[nə́ːrtʃər] 키우다, 양육하다   superficial[sjùːpərfíʃəl] 피상적인, 얕은

① time constraints   ② However   ③ build true intimacy   ④ had a lot in common   ⑤ got to know
⑥ Next   ⑦ going out with   ⑧ tend to   ⑨ concerning   ⑩ small talk   ⑪ awkward
⑫ worrying about   ⑬ As I have shown   ⑭ personal matters   ⑮ superficial

Review

(도입) Most people think that having many friends is better than having just a few. They mistakenly believe that, due to ① t_____, it is better to try and meet all their friends at one time. ② H_____, the quality of the friendships is more important than their quantity. (대주제문) When one has the time to spend with friends, it is better to spend it with just a few instead of with a large group since one can cultivate more profound relationships and have more intimate conversations.

(소주제문 1) When going out with a small number of people, it is easier to deepen connections with them because you can spend a significant amount of time with each person. (구체적 근거 1: 일반적 진술) A certain amount of time spent together, interacting with each other, is needed to ③ b_____ between friends. (구체적 근거 2: 예시) For example, my best friend and I did not think we ④ h_____ when we first met in high school, because we did not have enough chances to communicate. However, when we joined the same club, we ⑤ g_____ each other better. The more time we spent sharing our experiences, the stronger our friendship became over time. Although I did not make a lot of other new friends during that time, I had found a close friend for life.

(소주제문 2) ⑥ N_____, when ⑦ g_____ only a few friends, the content of the conversations can be much more personal. (구체적 근거 1: 일반적 진술) People ⑧ t_____ feel more comfortable in a small group, so they can have more private conversations ⑨ c_____ their personal lives, not wasting time on ⑩ s_____ and other trivialities. (구체적 근거 2: 예시) For instance, in larger gatherings, I feel the discussion of sensitive topics ⑪ a_____, because not everyone is a close friend. In contrast, when I am with my close friends, I know we can discuss anything, from favorite movies to family matters, without ⑫ w_____ being judged because we understand each other so well.

(요약/정리) ⑬ A_____, it is much better to meet with just a few friends than to go out with large groups in that it allows us to strengthen relationships and to discuss more ⑭ p_____. (맺음말) People often do not nurture the relationships they have and prefer to keep trying to develop new ones. In doing so, they miss the opportunity to build a few deep friendships that are much more satisfying than many ⑮ s_____ ones.

Day 18

Question

The best way to learn about life is by listening to the advice of friends and family. Do you agree or disagree? Use specific reasons and details to support your answer.

인생에 대해 배우는 최고의 방법은 친구와 가족의 조언을 듣는 것이라는 진술에 찬성하는지 반대하는지를 밝히고 구체적인 이유와 예를 들어 대답을 뒷받침한다.

Outline

Agree

1. One cannot experience all aspects of life on one's own
   혼자서는 삶의 모든 측면을 경험할 수 없다
   - different people have different experiences
     다른 사람들은 제각기 다른 경험을 한다
   - e.g. grandmother as a role model gave me a lot of advice
     예) 할머니께서는 역할 모델로서 나에게 많은 조언을 해주셨다

2. Friends and family can give more useful advice
   친구와 가족은 좀 더 실용적인 조언을 해줄 수 있다
   - they know you well and have similar experiences
     나를 잘 알고 비슷한 경험을 한다
   - e.g. father's advice helped me choose my career
     예) 아버지의 조언이 내가 진로를 결정하는 데 도움을 주었다

Disagree*

1. Personal experience is the best way to learn about life
   직접적인 경험이 인생에 대해 배우는 최고의 방법이다
   - using five senses leaves a lasting imprint on mind
     오감을 사용하는 것이 마음에 지속적인 인상을 남긴다
   - e.g. learned how to make Korean rice cakes with senses
     예) 떡을 만드는 방법을 감각으로 익혔다

2. Experiential learning stimulates a passion for learning
   경험을 통한 학습은 학습에의 열정을 자극한다
   - direct experience with a subject is motivating
     주제에 대한 직접적인 경험이 동기를 부여한다
   - e.g. visiting foreign countries motivates to learn the language
     예) 외국을 방문하면 외국어 학습의 동기가 생긴다

Model Essay

(도입) "Experience is the best teacher." **In other words**, firsthand experience is the best method of learning about life. (대주제문) Although I believe that people should listen to wise people's advice, people ultimately best learn from personal experience. **The rationale behind this is that** people never forget the lessons obtained from firsthand experience. Another reason is that experiential learning is much more motivating.

(소주제문 1) One reason personal experience is the best way to learn about life is that people can easily retain the knowledge. (구체적 근거 1: 일반적 진술) This is due **in large part** to using all five senses of sight, smell, taste, sound, and touch, which leave a lasting imprint on the mind. (구체적 근거 2: 예시) **That said**, I would **have a hard time** writing down directions for making Korean rice cakes, but if given all the ingredients, I would be able to make them. This is because my knowledge is **visceral**, and was learned and remembered in my body by kneading the dough, watching it swell, smelling the delicious aroma, and tasting it. So, I probably could not tell a person accurate ingredient ratios, but I would be able to **figure out** by continual tasting and sensing what ingredients needed to be added, how much longer they needed to cook, and so on.

(소주제문 2) **Furthermore**, people's passion for learning is stimulated by doing things on their own. (구체적 근거 1: 일반적 진술) That is, direct experience with a subject one is trying to learn is very motivating. (구체적 근거 2: 예시) **For example**, people who learn languages through books **find little reason** to memorize endless vocabulary lists and rules of grammar. However, once they visit foreign countries, they suddenly wish that they had studied more diligently at home. This direct experience and contact with foreigners and another language makes learning more practical, fun, and motivational. (마무리 문장) This just shows that learning that remains **on the mental level** can only go so far. In the end, people feel passionate and motivated about subjects when they **put their knowledge into practice**, and experience firsthand what it is they are trying to learn.

(요약/정리) **To sum up**, I strongly believe that the best way of learning about life is through personal experience. The reasons are that the effects of **experiential learning** last longer, and active learning is much more motivational. (맺음말) **At the end of the day**, firsthand experiences surpass a thousand counselors.

해석

"경험이 최고의 스승이다." 바꾸어 말하면, 직접적인 경험은 인생에 대해 배우는 최고의 방법이다. 비록 나는 사람들이 현명한 사람들의 충고를 경청해야 한다고 생각하지만, 사람들은 궁극적으로 개인적인 경험으로부터 가장 잘 배우게 된다. 이에 대한 이유는 사람들은 직접적인 경험으로부터 습득된 교훈은 절대 잊지 않기 때문이다. 또 다른 이유는 경험을 통한 학습이 훨씬 더 큰 의욕을 불러일으키기 때문이다.

개인적 경험이 인생에 대해 학습하는 최고의 방법인 한 가지 이유는 사람들이 쉽게 지식을 기억할 수 있기 때문이다. 이것은 주로 시각, 후각, 미각, 청각, 그리고 촉각의 오감 전부를 사용하기 때문이며, 이는 영속적인 인상을 마음 속에 남기게 된다. 이런 점을 기반해서 생각해보면, 나에게 있어서 떡을 만드는 조리법을 적는 것은 힘든 일이지만, 모든 재료가 주어진다면 나는 떡을 만들 수 있을 것이다. 이것은 나의 지식이 직관적인 것이고 반죽을 만들고, 부풀어 오르는 것을 보고, 맛있는 향을 맡고, 맛을 봄으로써 내 몸에 학습되고 기억되었기 때문이다. 그래서, 나는 다른 사람에게 정확한 재료의 비율을 설명할 수는 없지만, 계속해서 맛을 보면서 어떤 재료가 첨가되어야 하는지, 얼마나 더 오래 조리되어야 하는지 등에 대해 느낌으로써 알아낼 수 있다.

게다가, 스스로 해봄으로써 사람들의 학습에 대한 열정이 고무된다. 즉, 배우고자 하는 대상에 대한 직접적인 경험은 큰 의욕을 불러 일으킨다. 예를 들어, 책으로 언어를 공부하는 사람들은 끝없는 단어 목록과 문법 규칙들을 암기해야 할 이유를 별로 찾지 못한다. 그러나 그들이 한번이라도 외국을 방문하게 되면, 그들은 갑자기 집에서 좀 더 열심히 공부했었더라면 좋았을 것이라고 생각하게 된다. 이러한 외국인과 외국어와의 직접적인 경험과 접촉이 학습을 좀 더 실용적이고 재미있게 해주며, 보다 큰 의욕을 불러일으킨다. 이는 정신적인 수준에 남은 학습만이 오래 지속된다는 것을 보여 주는 것이다. 결국, 사람들은 아는 것을 실전에 옮기고 배우고자 하는 것을 직접적으로 경험할 때, 그 대상에 대해 열정을 느끼고 의욕을 갖게 된다.

요약하자면, 나는 인생에 대해 배우는 최고의 방법은 개인적인 경험을 통한 것이라고 확신한다. 그 이유는 경험으로 인한 학습이 더 오래 지속되며, 능동적인 학습이 훨씬 더 의욕을 불러일으키기 때문이다. 결국에는, 직접적인 경험이 수천 명의 조언자보다 낫다.

in other words 바꾸어 말하면, 즉　firsthand[fə́ːrsthǽnd] 직접의　ultimately[ʌ́ltəmətli] 궁극적으로, 마침내
rationale[ræ̀ʃənǽl] 근본적 이유, 이론적 해석　obtain[əbtéin] 획득하다, 손에 넣다　experiential learning 경험으로부터 배우는 학습
motivating 동기를 부여하는, 흥미를 느끼게 하는　retain[ritéin] 계속 유지하다, 간직하다　due to ~ ~ 때문에
in large part 주로, 대부분　imprint[ímprint] 인상, 자국, 흔적　that said 이런 점을 감안하면
have a hard time ~ing ~하느라 애를 먹다　directions[dirékʃəns] 지시 사항, 사용법　visceral[vísərəl] 본능적인, 내장의
knead[níːd] 반죽하다　ratio[réiʃjou] 비율　figure out 이해하다, 해결하다　and so on 기타 등등
stimulate[stímjəlèit] 자극하다, 격려하다, 고무하다　on one's own 스스로, 혼자 힘으로　diligently[dílidʒəntli] 부지런히, 열심히
motivational[mòutəvéiʃənəl] 학습 의욕을 유발하는　in the end 마침내, 결국　put into practice 실전에 옮기다, 실행하다
to sum up 요약하자면　at the end of the day 결국, 최후에는　surpass[sərpǽs] 보다 낫다, 능가하다

① In other words　② The rationale behind this is that　③ in large part　④ That said
⑤ have a hard time　⑥ visceral　⑦ figure out　⑧ Furthermore　⑨ For example
⑩ find little reason　⑪ on the mental level　⑫ put their knowledge into practice　⑬ To sum up
⑭ experiential learning　⑮ At the end of the day

Review

(도입) "Experience is the best teacher." ① I_____ , firsthand experience is the best method of learning about life. (대주제문) Although I believe that people should listen to wise people's advice, people ultimately best learn from personal experience. ② T_____ people never forget the lessons obtained fromfirsthand experience. Another reason is that experiential learning is much more motivating.

(소주제문 1) One reason personal experience is the best way to learn about life is that people can easily retain the knowledge. (구체적 근거 1: 일반적 진술) This is due ③ i_____ to using all five senses of sight, smell, taste, sound, and touch, which leave a lasting imprint on the mind. (구체적 근거 2: 예시) ④ T_____ , I would ⑤ h_____ writing down directions for making Korean rice cakes, but if given all the ingredients, I would be able to make them. This is because my knowledge is ⑥ v_____ , and was learned and remembered in my body by kneading the dough, watching it swell, smelling the delicious aroma, and tasting it. So, I probably could not tell a person accurate ingredient ratios, but I would be able to ⑦ f_____ by continual tasting and sensing what ingredients needed to be added, how much longer they needed to cook, and so on.

(소주제문 2) ⑧ F_____ , people's passion for learning is stimulated by doing things on their own. (구체적 근거 1: 일반적 진술) That is, direct experience with a subject one is trying to learn is very motivating. (구체적 근거 2: 예시) ⑨ F_____ , people who learn languages through books ⑩ f_____ _____ to memorize endless vocabulary lists and rules of grammar. However, once they visit foreign countries, they suddenly wish that they had studied more diligently at home. This direct experience and contact with foreigners and another language makes learning more practical, fun, and motivational. (마무리 문장) This just shows that learning that remains ⑪ o_____ can only go so far. In the end, people feel passionate and motivated about subjects when they ⑫ p_____ _____ , and experience firsthand what it is they are trying to learn.

(요약/정리) ⑬ T_____ , I strongly believe that the best way of learning about life is through personal experience. The reasons are that the effects of ⑭ e_____ last longer, and active learning is much more motivational. (맺음말) ⑮ A_____ , firsthand experiences surpass a thousand counselors.

Day 19

Question

Do you agree or disagree with the following statement? Exams encourage students to learn. Use specific reasons and examples to support your answer.

시험은 학생들이 학습하도록 장려한다는 진술에 찬성하는지 반대하는지를 밝히고 구체적인 이유와 예를 들어 대답을 뒷받침한다.

Outline

Agree*

1. Encourage students to become involved in their education
   학생들 스스로 교육에 참여하도록 장려한다
   - motivate them to listen to lectures more carefully
     수업에 더 집중하도록 동기를 부여한다
   - e.g. knowing that I would be tested, I studied harder in class
     예) 시험볼 것을 미리 알았기에 수업 시간에 더 열심히 공부했다

2. Force students to review previous lessons
   학생들로 하여금 지난 수업 내용을 복습하도록 한다
   - have to brush up on class materials for better grades
     더 나은 성적을 받기 위해 수업 자료들을 다시 살펴보아야 한다
   - e.g. realize that it's hard to cram, review regularly
     예) 벼락치기하는 것이 어려운 것을 깨닫고 정기적으로 복습하게 된다

Disagree

1. Force to study for exams only, not to truly learn
   진정으로 배우기 위한 것이 아니라 시험만을 위해 공부하도록 강요한다
   - memorize information for exams, not research and analyze
     탐구나 분석을 하는 것이 아니라 시험을 위해 암기만 한다
   - e.g. improve no critical thinking but simple memorizing capability
     예) 비판적 사고는커녕 단순 기억력만 향상되었다

2. Materials learned only for test don't last long
   시험만을 위해 공부한 내용은 오래가지 않는다
   - students try to memorize for tests without enough understanding
     학생들은 충분히 이해를 하지 않고 시험을 위해 외우려고만 노력한다
   - e.g. I crammed for physics exams, but barely remember the material
     예) 물리학 시험을 보기 위해서 벼락치기를 했지만 내용이 거의 기억나지 않는다

Model Essay

(도입) Exams are an important tool to help teachers measure the progress of their students. While educators use them to measure student comprehension, students also **benefit from** the feedback that they give on their studies. (대주제문) I believe exams encourage students to learn, because students are more motivated to **pay attention** in classes and spend time reviewing their lessons.

(소주제문 1) Exams encourage students to **become involved in** their education, rather than act as passive observers. (구체적 근거 1: 일반적 진술) They help students learn primarily by motivating them to listen to professors' lectures more carefully. (구체적 근거 2: 예시) Last semester, for example, I knew that I would be tested on the material presented in class. That is why I spent more time **taking notes** during the lecture and actively **participated in** the discussion instead of just sitting in class. As a result, I not only received a higher grade on my exams, **but also** got a better understanding of the subject. (마무리 문장) **I saw for myself that** when students know that they will be held responsible for the material, they are more likely to **take responsibility for** their own learning.

(소주제문 2) **What's more**, exams force students to review previous lessons in order to improve and maintain their understanding of the subject. (구체적 근거 1: 일반적 진술) Students have to continually **brush up on** what they have learned in class in order to get better grades on their exams. (구체적 근거 2: 예시) For instance, diligent students will realize that it is difficult to **cram** for the entire semester on the night before the exam, so they will regularly go over the material from previous classes in order to retain the information. This will also deepen their understanding of the material, as many insights do not come **at first sight** but after several repetitions. (마무리 문장) **Therefore**, exams work as incentives for students to look over class material repeatedly resulting in verifying their understanding of it.

(요약/정리) Thus, exams encourage students to learn by forcing them to **focus on** lectures and to go back over the material. By preparing for exams, students not only gain more knowledge from the class, but also learn important study skills. (맺음말) **With the rapid increase in technology**, information learned in school is often outdated within a few years, so those students who have the study skills garnered from exams will be able to adapt and be much more successful in an ever-expanding sea of accessible knowledge.

해석

시험은 교사가 학생들의 발달 정도를 측정하도록 도와주는 중요한 도구이다. 교육자들은 학생들의 이해를 측정하기 위해 시험을 사용하고, 이와 동시에 학생들 또한 시험이 그들의 학업에 주는 피드백 작용으로부터 이득을 본다. 학생들이 수업에 집중하고 배운 것을 복습하는데 시간을 쓰도록 보다 큰 동기를 부여받기 때문에 나는 시험이 학습을 장려한다고 생각한다.

시험은 학생들이 수동적인 관찰자로써 임하는 대신 교육에 직접적으로 참여할 수 있게 해준다. 시험은 주로 학생들이 교수의 강의를 좀 더 주의 깊게 들을 동기를 부여함으로써 학습을 돕는다. 예를 들면, 지난 학기에 나는 내가 수업 시간에 제시된 내용에 대해 시험을 보게 된다는 것을 알았다. 그것이 내가 강의 시간에 필기를 더 많이 하고, 단지 수업을 듣고 앉아있기보다, 능동적으로 토론에 참여한 이유이다. 결과적으로, 나는 시험에서 높은 성적을 얻었을 뿐만 아니라, 그 과목에 대해서도 더 잘 이해하게 되었다. 나는 수업 내용에 대해서 책임이 지워진다는 것을 학생들이 알게 될 때, 자신들의 학습에 대해서도 더 책임감을 갖게 된다는 것을 직접 깨닫게 되었다.

게다가, 시험은 학생들이 과목에 대한 이해를 유지하고 증진시키기 위해 지난 수업 내용을 복습하도록 한다. 학생들은 시험에서 보다 좋은 성적을 얻기 위해서는 그들이 수업 시간에 배운 것을 계속적으로 복습해야 한다. 예를 들면, 근면한 학생들은 한 학기 내내 배운 내용을 시험 전날에 벼락치기하는 것은 어렵다는 것을 깨닫고, 그 내용을 기억하기 위해 지난 시간에 배운 내용을 정기적으로 복습할 것이다. 또한, 식견은 대부분 첫눈에 생기는 것이 아니라 수차례의 반복 학습에 의해서 얻어지므로, 정기적인 복습은 이들의 학습 내용에 대한 이해를 깊게 해줄 것이다. 따라서, 시험은 학습 내용을 반복적으로 복습하도록 하는 동기로 작용하여 이에 대해 확실히 이해할 수 있게 해준다.

따라서, 시험은 학생들로 하여금 수업에 집중하고 수업 내용을 복습하게 함으로써 학습을 장려한다. 시험을 준비함으로써, 학생들은 수업으로부터 보다 많은 지식을 습득할 수 있게 될 뿐만 아니라, 학습하는 기술도 배우게 된다. 기술의 급격한 발전으로 인해서 학교에서 배운 정보는 종종 몇 년 안에 시대에 뒤떨어진 것이 되곤 한다. 따라서 시험 공부를 통해 축적된 학습 기술을 가지고 있는 학생들은 계속적으로 팽창하는 지식의 바다에 적응할 수 있고 보다 성공적인 결과를 얻을 수 있다.

spend time ~ing ~하면서 시간을 보내다   become involved in 열중하다, 연루되다   rather than ~ ~라기보다
passive[pǽsiv] 수동적인   motivate[móutəvèit] 동기 부여하다, 자극하다   material[mətíəriəl] 자료   take notes 노트 필기하다
participate in ~ ~에 참여하다   hold responsible for 책임을 지우다   what's more 게다가   brush up on ~ ~을 복습하다
cram[kræm] 벼락 공부하다   go over 복습하다   retain[ritéin] 보존하다, 기억해 두다   insight[ínsàit] 식견, 안식
at first sight 첫눈에, 즉시   incentive[inséntiv] 동기   result in ~ ~로 끝나다   verify[vérəfài] 입증하다, 확증하다
outdated[àutdéitid] 시대에 뒤진   garner[gáːrnər] 얻다, 축적하다   adapt[ədǽpt] 순응하다, 적응하다   ever-expanding 계속 팽창하는
accessible[əksésəbl] 접근할 수 있는

① benefit from   ② pay attention   ③ become involved in   ④ taking notes   ⑤ participated in
⑥ but also   ⑦ I saw for myself that   ⑧ take responsibility for   ⑨ What's more   ⑩ brush up on
⑪ cram   ⑫ at first sight   ⑬ Therefore   ⑭ focus on   ⑮ With the rapid increase in technology

Review

(도입) Exams are an important tool to help teachers measure the progress of their students. While educators use them to measure student comprehension, students also ① b_____ the feedback that they give on their studies. (대주제문) I believe exams encourage students to learn, because students are more motivated to ② p_____ in classes and spend time reviewing their lessons.

(소주제문 1) Exams encourage students to ③ b_____ their education, rather than act as passive observers. (구체적 근거 1: 일반적 진술) They help students learn primarily by motivating them to listen to professors' lectures more carefully. (구체적 근거 2: 예시) Last semester, for example, I knew that I would be tested on the material presented in class. That is why I spent more time ④ t_____ _____ during the lecture and actively ⑤ p_____ the discussion instead of just sitting in class. As a result, I not only received a higher grade on my exams, ⑥ b_____ got a better understanding of the subject. (마무리 문장) ⑦ I_____ when students know that they will be held responsible for the material, they are more likely to ⑧ t_____ their own learning.

(소주제문 2) ⑨ W_____, exams force students to review previous lessons in order to maintain and improve their understanding of the subject. (구체적 근거 1: 일반적 진술) Students have to continually ⑩ b_____ what they have learned in class in order to get better grades on their exams. (구체적 근거 2: 예시) For instance, diligent students will realize that it is difficult to ⑪ c_____ for the entire semester on the night before the exam, so they will regularly go over the material from previous classes in order to retain the information. This will also deepen their understanding of the material, as many insights do not come ⑫ a_____ but after several repetitions. (마무리 문장) ⑬ T_____, exams work as incentives for students to look over class material repeatedly resulting in verifying their understanding of it.

(요약/정리) Thus, exams encourage students to learn by forcing them to ⑭ f_____ lectures and to go back over the material. By preparing for exams, students not only gain more knowledge from the class, but also learn important study skills. (맺음말) ⑮ W_____, information learned in school is often outdated within a few years, so those students who have the study skills garnered from exams will be able to adapt and be much more successful in an ever-expanding sea of accessible knowledge.

Question

Do you agree or disagree with the following statement? It is better to complain in person than in writing. Use specific reasons and examples to support your answer.

불만은 편지상으로보다 직접 표현하는 것이 더 낫다는 진술에 찬성하는지 반대하는지를 밝히고 구체적인 이유와 예를 들어 대답을 뒷받침한다.

Outline

Agree

1. Complaining in person is more effective
   직접 항의하는 것이 더 효과적이다
   - face-to-face correspondence is more persuasive
     일대일 대면이 더 설득력이 있다
   - e.g. better result with complaining in person to landlord
     예) 집주인에 대한 직접적인 항의로 더 좋은 결과를 얻었다

2. Get solution immediately
   곧바로 해결을 볼 수 있다
   - reach settlement on the spot
     즉석에서 해결에 도달한다
   - e.g. got a defective laptop exchanged right away
     예) 결함이 있는 노트북 컴퓨터를 그 자리에서 교환받았다

Disagree*

1. Written complaints deliver displeasure in composed, logical way
   항의 편지는 불쾌함을 차분하고 논리적인 방식으로 전달한다
   - take time to collect emotions and bring anger under control
     감정을 정리하고 분노를 억제할 시간을 갖는다
   - e.g. complaint letter to a Chinese cuisine caterer
     예) 중국 출장 요리사에게 항의 편지를 썼던 일

2. More convenient and time-saving
   편리하고 시간을 절약해준다
   - online consumer complaints center
     온라인 고객 항의 센터
   - e.g. took just three minutes to complain through the Internet
     예) 인터넷을 통해서 불만을 제기하는 데 겨우 3분이 걸렸다

Model Essay

(도입) **On any given day**, it is inevitable to see a long line of people complaining about their poor service or faulty products at stores' customer service desks. (대주제문) As for me, I choose not to join them in line, but prefer complaining in writing. **My reasons for this are** that written complaints allow me to deliver my displeasure in a logical, composed way. Moreover, complaint letters are much more convenient and time-saving.

(소주제문 1) **To start with**, complaining in writing plays an integral role in enabling customers to deliver their opinions in a more composed and logical way. (구체적 근거 1: 일반적 진술) That is, writing allows angry customers to collect their emotions and bring their anger under control by providing them with ample time to reflect on the situation and process their thoughts. (구체적 근거 2: 예시) **To take a personal example**, last month, my father had Chinese cuisine catered for my birthday party. Unfortunately, the dishes were delivered one hour later than the appointed time. **To make matters worse**, the dishes were cold and messily arranged. Even though I was infuriated, I was able to think rationally by selecting appropriate words to best describe the poor service, and **come up with** reasonable reimbursements while writing a complaint letter. If I had complained **in person**, I would have frowned and yelled at the manager using unpleasant and rude words. My poor behavior would **not** have solved the problem **at all**, but caused more conflict.

(소주제문 2) In addition, complaining in writing is the most convenient and the quickest way to **lodge a complaint**. (구체적 근거 1: 일반적 진술) A rapidly growing number of companies, restaurants, and shops encourage customers to file their complaints through the Internet. This technology makes it possible for customers to easily send their letters of dissatisfaction **with a single click of a mouse**. (구체적 근거 2: 예시) The best example of this is an online consumer complaints center. **To be specific**, I purchased a bottle of body lotion last year from a home-shopping channel on television. After I received and opened the package, I **found out** that the bottle was only half full. I was very upset. Therefore, I immediately **logged in to** the company's homepage and wrote my complaint **in detail**. Amazingly, this whole process only took three minutes, and I was reimbursed.

(요약/정리) In summary, I fully believe that complaining in writing is much more effective. The reasons are that written complaints are more logical and composed **as well as** time-saving. (맺음말) All in all, I believe that these are the most important factors for satisfying both sellers and customers.

해석

언제라도, 불충분한 서비스와 결함이 있는 상품에 대해 항의하기 위해 고객 상담 창구에 길게 줄을 늘어선 사람들을 보기란 어렵지 않다. 나의 경우에는, 그 줄에 합류하기보다는 편지로 불만을 제기하는 것을 선호한다. 그에 대한 이유는 항의서가 나의 불만을 논리적이고 차분한 방식으로 전달하게 해주기 때문이다. 게다가, 항의서는 훨씬 더 편리하고 시간을 절약해 준다.

우선, 편지로 항의하는 것은 고객으로 하여금 그들의 의견을 좀 더 차분하고 논리적인 방식으로 전달하게 해주는 중요한 역할을 한다. 즉, 글을 쓰는 것은 화난 고객으로 하여금 상황을 곰곰이 생각하고 그들의 생각을 정리할 충분한 시간을 제공함으로써 그들의 감정을 가다듬고 분노를 억제하게 해준다. 개인적인 예를 들자면, 지난 달 아버지께서 나의 생일파티를 위해 중국 요리를 출장 주문하셨다. 불행히도, 음식은 약속된 시간보다 1시간 늦게 배달되었다. 설상가상으로 음식은 식어 있었고 흐트러져 있었다. 나는 화가 많이 났지만, 항의서를 작성하면서 불만족스러운 서비스를 가장 잘 설명하기 위한 적절한 단어들을 선택함으로써 이성적으로 생각할 수 있었고 합당한 변상을 생각해낼 수 있었다. 내가 만약 직접 불만을 제기했다면, 얼굴을 찌푸리고 불쾌하고 무례한 단어를 사용해서 책임자에게 소리를 질렀을 것이다. 나의 부적절한 행동은 문제를 전혀 해결하지 못하고, 오히려 갈등을 더 불러 일으켰을 것이다.

게다가 항의서를 작성하는 것은 불만을 제기하는 가장 편리하고 빠른 방법이다. 고객에게 인터넷을 통해 불만을 제기하도록 권장하는 회사, 식당 및 상점들의 수가 급격하게 증가하고 있다. 이러한 기술은 고객들로 하여금 그들의 불만이 담긴 편지를 손쉽게 단 한 번의 마우스 클릭만으로 보낼 수 있게 해준다. 이것의 가장 적절한 예는 온라인 고객 항의 센터이다. 구체적으로 말하자면, 나는 작년에 텔레비전 홈쇼핑 채널을 통해 보디로션 한 병을 구입했다. 물품을 받고 포장을 뜯었을 때, 나는 로션이 반밖에 차있지 않다는 것을 알았다. 나는 매우 화가 났다. 그래서, 나는 즉시 그 회사의 홈페이지에 접속해서 자세하게 항의서를 썼다. 놀랍게도, 이 모든 과정은 3분밖에 걸리지 않았으며, 나는 변상을 받았다.

요약하자면, 나는 편지로 불만을 제기하는 것이 훨씬 더 효과적이라고 충분히 확신한다. 그 이유는 항의서가 시간을 절약해 줄뿐만 아니라 좀 더 논리적이고 차분하기 때문이다. 대체로, 나는 이것이 판매자와 고객 모두를 만족시키는 가장 중요한 요인이라고 생각한다.

in person 자기 스스로, 본인이, 직접   on any given day 언제라도   inevitable[inévitəbl] 피할 수 없는   faulty[fɔ́:lti] 결점이 있는
displeasure[displéʒər] 불만   composed[kəmpóuzd] 차분한   play a role 역할을 하다
integral[íntəgrəl] 없어서는 안 될, 절대 필요한   bring under control 억제하다   ample[ǽmpl] 충분한   reflect on 곰곰이 생각하다
process[práses] 정리하다   cater[kéitər] 출장 주문하다, 음식을 조달하다   to make matters worse 설상가상으로
messily[mésəli] 너절하게, 지저분하게   infuriated[infjúərièitid] 격분한, 노발대발한   come up with 생각해내다, 떠올리다
reimbursement[rì:imbə́:rsmənt] 변상   frown[fraun] 눈살을 찌푸리다, 험상궂은 얼굴을 하다   conflict[kánflikt] 갈등, 분쟁, 언쟁
lodge[lɑdʒ] 제기하다   with a single click of a mouse 마우스를 한 번 클릭하기만 하면   specific[spisífik] 구체적인, 뚜렷한
upset[ʌpsét] 당황한   log in to ~ ~에 접속하다   in detail 상세히   reimburse[rì:imbə́:rs] 변상하다, 배상하다   all in all 대체로

① On any given day   ② My reasons for this are   ③ To start with   ④ To take a personal example
⑤ To make matters worse   ⑥ come up with   ⑦ in person   ⑧ not, at all   ⑨ lodge a complaint
⑩ with a single click of a mouse   ⑪ To be specific   ⑫ found out   ⑬ logged in to   ⑭ in detail
⑮ as well as

Review

(도입) ① O_____, it is inevitable to see a long line of people complaining about their poor service or faulty products at stores' customer service desks. (대주제문) As for me, I choose not to join them in line, but prefer complaining in writing. ② M_____ that written complaints allow me to deliver my displeasure in a logical, composed way. Moreover, complaint letters are much more convenient and time-saving.

(소주제문 1) ③ T_____, complaining in writing plays an integral role in enabling customers to deliver their opinions in a more composed and logical way. (구체적 근거 1: 일반적 진술) That is, writing allows angry customers to collect their emotions and bring their anger under control by providing them with ample time to reflect on the situation and process their thoughts. (구체적 근거 2: 예시) ④ T_____, last month, my father had Chinese cuisine catered for my birthday party. Unfortunately, the dishes were delivered one hour later than the appointed time. ⑤ T_____, the dishes were cold and messily arranged. Even though I was infuriated, I was able to think rationally by selecting appropriate words to best describe the poor service, and ⑥ c_____ reasonable reimbursements while writing a complaint letter. If I had complained ⑦ i_____, I would have frowned and yelled at the manager using unpleasant and rude words. My poor behavior would ⑧ n____ have solved the problem _____, but caused more conflict.

(소주제문 2) In addition, complaining in writing is the most convenient and the quickest way to ⑨ l_____. (구체적 근거 1: 일반적 진술) A rapidly growing number of companies, restaurants, and shops encourage customers to file their complaints through the Internet. This technology makes it possible for customers to easily send their letters of dissatisfaction ⑩ w_____ _____. (구체적 근거 2: 예시) The best example of this is an online consumer complaints center. ⑪ T_____, I purchased a bottle of body lotion last year from a home-shopping channel on television. After I received and opened the package, I ⑫ f_____ that the bottle was only half full. I was very upset. Therefore, I immediately ⑬ l_____ the company's homepage and wrote my complaint ⑭ i_____. Amazingly, this whole process only took three minutes, and I was reimbursed.

(요약/정리) In summary, I fully believe that complaining in writing is much more effective. The reasons are that written complaints are more logical and composed ⑮ a_____ time-saving. (맺음말) All in all, I believe that these are the most important factors for satisfying both sellers and customers.

Question

Do you agree or disagree with the following statement? Nowadays people put too much emphasis on personal appearance and fashion. Use specific reasons and examples to support your answer.

요즘 사람들은 외모와 옷차림에 지나친 비중을 둔다는 진술에 찬성하는지 반대하는지를 밝히고 구체적인 이유와 예를 들어 대답을 뒷받침한다.

Outline

Agree*

1. People spend lots of time and money on how they look
   사람들은 외모를 꾸미는 데 많은 시간과 돈을 쓴다
   - spend a lot of money on clothes and cosmetics
     돈과 화장품에 많은 돈을 쓴다
   - e.g. risk injury on plastic surgery
     예) 다칠 위험을 무릅쓰며 성형 수술을 한다

2. People are judged by their appearance
   사람들이 외모로 판단된다
   - people succeed due to looks
     사람들은 외모 때문에 성공한다
   - e.g. untalented but popular good-looking singers
     예) 재능이 없지만 잘생긴 인기 가수들

Disagree

1. People don't spend more time and money on their looks than in the past
   과거보다 사람들이 외모에 돈과 시간을 덜 쓴다
   - old days had very strict rules about fashion
     옛날에는 옷차림에 대한 엄격한 규칙이 있었다
   - e.g. 14th century France, people obsessed over their clothes
     예) 14세기 프랑스의 사람들은 옷에 집착했다

2. Ability is more important than appearance for success
   성공하기 위해서는 외모보다 능력이 더 중요하다
   - technology has made ability more important
     기술의 발전이 능력 위주의 사회를 만들었다
   - e.g. not good-looking but acclaimed singers because of talents
     예) 매력적이지는 않지만 재능 때문에 인정받는 가수들

Model Essay

(도입) People's appearance and dress have always been used to denote **their social status** to others within their community. However, as cultures evolve and people have gained more free time to devote towards grooming, how people look has become increasingly more significant. (대주제문) These days, the rising amounts of money spent on their images, as well as the increasing tendency to judge people by their looks, reflect the fact that people **put too much weight on** fashion and appearance.

(소주제문 1) People waste a greater amount of time and **financial resources** on clothes and improving their outward appearance than ever before. (구체적 근거 1: 일반적 진술) Some people completely replace their wardrobe every year in an effort to **keep up with** current fashion. This trend is also reflected in the cosmetics industry, as new products promising youthful looks **sell out** despite their high price tags. (구체적 근거 2: 예시) However, the most extreme example is plastic surgery. **In an attempt to** regain their youth or fix what are perceived to be flaws, people endure extreme pain and spend lots of money, as well as **risk their lives**, for the benefits of cosmetic procedures. **As a matter of fact**, nowadays, it is not hard to find articles in the newspapers about people who lost their lives during these drastic procedures.

(소주제문 2) **Moreover**, people determine others' worth based on how they look. (구체적 근거 1: 일반적 진술) In our society, there is more and more support for the notion that one has to be attractive in order to be successful. (구체적 근거 2: 예시) For instance, the fact that more attractive people have **a competitive advantage** in careers is reflected by the rise of many mediocre entertainers. These popular singers are **not as skilled as** less famous singers, but have made millions of dollars due to their looks. In today's music industry, for singers, it is quite true that being good-looking is the key element to commercial success rather than their musical talent. This reinforces in people's minds that looks are more important than anything else.

(요약 / 정리) **In summary**, the amount of money spent and the **tendency** to judge others based on their appearance show that people have become too **fixated on** fashion and their looks. (맺음말) Just as one should not **judge a book by its cover**, one should also realize that beauty is only skin deep.

해석

사람들의 외모와 옷차림은 집단 내에서 다른 이들에게 그들의 사회적 신분을 나타내는 데 항상 사용되어 왔다. 그러나 문화가 서서히 발전되어 가고 사람들이 몸치장에 쏟는 자유 시간이 점점 더 많아짐에 따라, 어떻게 보이는가가 점점 더 중요해지고 있다. 오늘날, 사람들을 외모로 판단하는 경향뿐만 아니라, 이미지에 소비되는 증가하는 돈의 양이 사람들이 옷차림과 외모에 지나친 가치를 부여한다는 사실을 반영한다.

사람들은 옷과 그들의 외모를 향상시키는 데 예전보다 훨씬 더 엄청난 양의 시간과 재원을 낭비한다. 어떤 이들은 최신 유행에 뒤떨어지지 않기 위한 노력으로 그들의 옷장을 매년 완전히 갈아치운다. 이러한 경향은 또한 화장품 산업에도 반영되어 있다. 젊어 보이는 외모를 약속하는 새로운 제품들은 높은 가격표에도 불구하고 불티나게 팔린다. 그러나 가장 극단적인 예는 성형 수술이다. 젊음을 되찾고자 하는 혹은 결함이라 인식되는 것들을 고치려는 시도로, 사람들은 생명의 위험을 무릅쓸 뿐만 아니라 엄청난 고통을 감내하고 많은 돈을 쓴다. 사실상, 오늘날 이러한 과도한 시술 중에 목숨을 잃은 사람들에 대한 신문 기사를 발견하기란 어렵지 않다.

게다가, 사람들은 그들이 어떻게 보이는가에 근거하여 다른 이의 가치를 결정한다. 사회에서는 성공하기 위해서는 매력적이어야 한다는 인식이 점점 더 지지를 얻고 있다. 예를 들면, 더 매력적인 사람들이 직업에서 더 경쟁적인 우위를 확보한다는 사실은 많은 2류 연예인들의 성장에 반영된다. 이러한 유명 가수들은 덜 유명한 가수들보다 재능이 더 많은 것은 아니지만, 외모 덕에 수십만 달러의 돈을 번다. 오늘날 음악 산업에서 가수들에게는 훌륭한 외모를 갖추는 것이 상업적 성공의 필수적인 요소이다. 이는 사람들의 마음에 음악적 재능보다는 외모가 다른 어떤 것보다도 중요하다고 북돋는다.

요약하자면, 사람들이 쓰는 돈과 외모를 바탕으로 다른 이들을 평가하는 경향은 사람들이 지나치게 옷차림과 외모에 집착하게 되었다는 것을 보여 준다. 외모로 사람을 판단해서는 안 되며, 또한 외모의 아름다움은 피상적인 것에 불과하다는 것을 깨달아야 할 것이다.

---

denote[dinóut] 나타내다, 표시하다　social status 사회적 신분　evolve[iválv] 서서히 발전하다　devote[divóut] 바치다, 쏟다
grooming[grú(ː)miŋ] 몸치장　B as well as A A뿐만 아니라 B도　tendency[téndənsi] 경향, 풍조
put too much weight on ~ ~에 지나친 가치를 부여하다　financial resources 재원　outward[áutwərd] 외면적인
wardrobe[wɔ́ːrdroub] 옷장　keep up with 뒤떨어지지 않다　cosmetics[kazmétiks] 화장품　despite[dispáit] ~에도 불구하고
price tag 가격표　sell out 다 팔다, 매진되다　plastic surgery 성형 수술　attempt[ətémpt] 시도　regain[rigéin] 되찾다
perceive[pərsíːv] 지각하다, 감지하다　as a matter of fact 사실　drastic[drǽstik] 격렬한, 과격한　base on ~ ~에 근거하다
notion[nóuʃən] 관념　competitive advantage 경쟁적 우위　mediocre[mìːdióukər] 보통의, 2류의　due to ~ ~ 때문에
rather than ~ ~라기보다는　reinforce[rìːinfɔ́ːrs] 북돋다, 강화하다　fixated on ~ ~에 집착하는
judge a book by its cover 표지를 보고 책 내용을 판단하다, 외모로 사람을 판단하다
Beauty is only skin deep 미모는 거죽 한 꺼풀

---

① their social status　② put too much weight on　③ financial resources　④ keep up with
⑤ sell out　⑥ In an attempt to　⑦ risk their lives　⑧ As a matter of fact　⑨ Moreover
⑩ a competitive advantage　⑪ not as skilled as　⑫ In summary　⑬ tendency　⑭ fixated on
⑮ judge a book by its cover

Review

(도입) People's appearance and dress have always been used to denote ① t_____ to others within their community. However, as cultures evolve and people have gained more free time to devote towards grooming, how people look has become increasingly more significant. (대주제문) These days, the rising amounts of money spent on their images, as well as the increasing tendency to judge people by their looks, reflect the fact that people ② p_____ fashion and appearance.

(소주제문 1) People waste a greater amount of time and ③ f_____ on clothes and improving their outward appearance than ever before. (구체적 근거 1: 일반적 진술) Some people completely replace their wardrobe every year in an effort to ④ k_____ current fashion. This trend is also reflected in the cosmetics industry, as new products promising youthful looks ⑤ s_____ despite their high price tags. (구체적 근거 2: 예시) However, the most extreme example is plastic surgery. ⑥ I_____ regain their youth or fix what are perceived to be flaws, people endure extreme pain and spend lots of money, as well as ⑦ r_____, for the benefits of cosmetic procedures. ⑧ A_____, nowadays, it is not hard to find articles in the newspapers about people who lost their lives during these drastic procedures.

(소주제문 2) ⑨ M_____, people determine others' worth based on how they look. (구체적 근거 1: 일반적 진술) In our society, there is more and more support for the notion that one has to be attractive in order to be successful. (구체적 근거 2: 예시) For instance, the fact that more attractive people have ⑩ a_____ in careers is reflected by the rise of many mediocre entertainers. These popular singers are ⑪ n_____ less famous singers, but have made millions of dollars due to their looks. In today's music industry, for singers, it is quite true that being good-looking is the key element to commercial success rather than their musical talent. This reinforces in people's minds that looks are more important than anything else.

(요약/정리) ⑫ I_____, the amount of money spent and the ⑬ t_____ to judge others based on their appearance show that people have become too ⑭ f_____ fashion and their looks. (맺음말) Just as one should not ⑮ j_____, one should also realize that beauty is only skin deep.

Question

Do you agree or disagree with the following statement? Human activities have enhanced and improved the Earth. Use specific reasons and examples to support your answer.

인간의 활동은 지구를 더 발전시켰다는 진술에 찬성하는지 반대하는지를 밝히고 구체적인 이유와 예를 들어 대답을 뒷받침한다.

Outline

Agree

1. Human activity has made the Earth a convenient place to live
   인간의 활동이 지구를 더 살기에 편리한 곳으로 만들었다
   - development of transportation and telecommunications
     교통과 통신의 발달
   - e.g. invention of the Internet
     예) 인터넷의 발명

2. Human activity has solved basic human needs
   인간의 활동은 인간의 기본적 욕구를 해결했다
   - ancient people died from hunger, disease, and natural disasters
     고대 사람들은 배고픔, 질병, 자연 재해로 목숨을 잃었다
   - e.g. the agricultural revolution brought about increase in food supply
     예) 농업 혁명은 식량 생산의 증가를 가져왔다

Disagree*

1. Human activities caused damage to the environment
   인간의 활동은 환경을 손상했다
   - bring life-threatening changes to the earth
     지구에 치명적인 변화를 가져온다
   - e.g. global warming
     예) 지구 온난화

2. Human activities threaten people's lives
   인간의 활동은 사람들의 생명을 위협한다
   - results from human inventions
     인간의 발명품들로부터 기인한다
   - e.g. cars and weapons
     예) 자동차와 무기

Model Essay

(도입) **It seems obvious that** human activity has made the Earth a more convenient place for human habitation. People have electricity, indoor plumbing, and other modern conveniences. (대주제문) However, upon closer examination, there is a dark side to all of this "development." Human activities are seriously threatening the environment as well as people's lives.

(소주제문 1) **Above all**, human activities have caused irreversible damage to the natural environment. (구체적 근거 1: 일반적 진술) In other words, humans' selfish and greedy attempts to enrich their lives have resulted in overexploiting resources, invading **natural habitats**, and polluting water and the air. (구체적 근거 2: 예시) **The best illustration of this is** global warming. This dangerous phenomenon is directly caused by the **greenhouse gases** which are produced when people burn oil and coal to generate electricity, run automobiles, and heat houses. In addition, logging companies cut down numerous trees that are an indispensable **defense mechanism** to absorb harmful gases. **As a result of** these selfish and short-sighted human activities, the earth is suffering from scorching summers, massive flooding, and habitat destruction. (마무리 문장) **In this respect**, the side-effects of human activities have critically harmed the environment.

(소주제문 2) Furthermore, human activities are increasingly threatening people's lives. (구체적 근거 1: 일반적 진술) This largely results from human inventions ranging from seemingly innocuous automobiles to outright destructive **weapons of mass destruction**, such as the atomic bomb. (구체적 근거 2: 예시) To take an example, cars are a highly convenient means to move around. Unfortunately, they are a deadly **form of transportation**, and millions of people die worldwide in car accidents every year. This is coupled by the large number of people who get **respiratory illnesses** from breathing in toxic **exhaust fumes** from motor vehicles. On top of that, millions of people die every year from war machines, including bullets, bombs, chemical weapons, and other sophisticated destructive inventions. (마무리 문장) It should then **come as no surprise** that people's activities are actually bringing about their own demise.

(요약/정리) **To summarize**, I firmly believe that human activities have harmed the Earth. This is because human inventions have endangered both the natural environment and human lives. (맺음말) On the whole, advancements in technology have been more of **a curse than a blessing**.

해석

인간의 활동이 지구를 인간이 살기에 좀 더 편리한 장소로 만들었다는 것은 명백해 보인다. 사람들은 전기와 옥내 수도시설 등의 현대적인 편의 시설들을 갖추게 되었다. 그러나 자세히 살펴보면, 이러한 "발전"에는 어두운 면이 존재한다. 인간의 활동은 사람들의 생명뿐만 아니라 환경까지 심각하게 위협하고 있다.

무엇보다도, 인간의 활동은 자연 환경에 되돌릴 수 없는 피해를 끼쳤다. 다시 말해, 자신의 삶을 풍요롭게 만들고자 하는 인류의 이기적이고 탐욕스러운 시도가 자원을 과도하게 개발하고, 자연 서식지를 침범하고, 물과 공기를 오염시키는 결과를 낳았다. 이에 대한 가장 적절한 예는 지구 온난화이다. 이 위험한 현상은 사람들이 전기를 생산하고, 자동차를 운행하고, 주택을 따뜻하게 하기 위해 석유와 석탄을 태울 때 발생되는 온실 가스에 의해 직접적으로 발생된다. 게다가, 벌목 회사들은 해로운 가스를 흡수하는 필수 불가결한 방어 기제인 수많은 나무들을 베어내고 있다. 이러한 이기적이고 근시안적인 인간의 활동의 결과로 지구는 뜨거운 여름과 대규모의 홍수, 서식지의 파괴로 고통을 겪고 있다. 이러한 점에서, 인간 활동의 부작용은 환경을 심하게 훼손시켰다.

게다가, 인간의 활동은 사람들의 생명을 점점 더 위협하고 있다. 이는 외관상 무해하게 보이는 자동차에서부터 원자 폭탄 같은 명백한 파괴적 대량 살상 무기에 이르는 인간의 발명품들로부터 기인한다. 예를 들자면, 자동차는 이동하는 데 매우 편리한 수단이다. 안타깝게도, 자동차는 치명적인 교통수단이며, 매년 전 세계적으로 수백만의 사람들이 자동차 사고로 목숨을 잃는다. 이에 자동차에서 나오는 유독한 배기가스를 들이마셔서 호흡기 질환에 걸리는 많은 수의 사람들이 더해진다. 게다가, 매년 수백만 명의 사람들이 총탄과 폭탄, 화학 무기 및 기타 정교한 파괴적 발명품을 포함한 전쟁 무기로 인해 목숨을 잃는다. 그리하여 인간의 활동이 실제로는 자신의 종말을 초래하고 있다는 것은 놀라운 일이 아니다.

요약하자면, 나는 인간의 활동이 지구를 훼손시켰다고 확신한다. 이는 인류의 발명이 자연 환경과 인간의 생명을 모두 위험에 빠뜨렸기 때문이다. 전반적으로, 기술의 발전은 축복이라기보다는 저주이다.

habitation[hæ̀bitéiʃən] 거주   indoor plumbing 옥내 수도시설   conveniences[kənví:njənsis] 편리한 설비
upon closer examination 자세히 검토해 보면   dark side 어두운 측면, 비관   irreversible[ìrivə́:rsəbl] 되돌릴 수 없는
result in 결과를 낳다   overexploit[ðuvəriksplɔ́it] 과도하게 개발하다   natural habitat 자연 서식지   global warming 지구 온난화
greenhouse gases 온실 가스   logging[lɔ́(:)giŋ] (산림) 벌채   indispensable[ìndispénsəbl] 필수 불가결한, 없어서는 안될
defense mechanism 방어 기제   short-sighted 근시안적인, 눈앞의 이익만 챙기는   scorching[skɔ́:rtʃiŋ] 몹시 뜨거운
side-effect 부작용   range from A to B A에서 B까지 미치다, 이르다   seemingly[sí:miŋli] 겉으로는, 외관상
innocuous[inɑ́kjuəs] 무해한, 악의 없는   outright[áutràit] 명백한, 완전한   weapon of mass destruction 대량 파괴 무기
atomic bomb 원자 폭탄   means[mi:nz] 수단   deadly[dédli] 치명적인   respiratory illness 호흡기 질환   toxic[tɑ́ksik] 유독한
exhaust fumes 배기가스   sophisticated[səfístəkèitid] 정교한   come as no surprise 놀라운 일이 아니다
bring about 야기하다, 초래하다   demise[dimáiz] 사망   endanger[indéindʒər] 위험에 빠뜨리다

① It seems obvious that   ② Above all   ③ natural habitats   ④ The best illustration of this is
⑤ greenhouse gases   ⑥ defense mechanism   ⑦ As a result of   ⑧ In this respect
⑨ weapons of mass destruction   ⑩ form of transportation   ⑪ respiratory illnesses
⑫ exhaust fumes   ⑬ come as no surprise   ⑭ To summarize   ⑮ a curse than a blessing

Review

도입 ① I_____ human activity has made the Earth a more convenient place for human habitation. People have electricity, indoor plumbing, and other modern conveniences. 대주제문 However, upon closer examination, there is a dark side to all of this "development." Human activities are seriously threatening the environment as well as people's lives.

소주제문 1 ② A_____, human activities have caused irreversible damage to the natural environment. 구체적 근거 1: 일반적 진술 In other words, humans' selfish and greedy attempts to enrich their lives have resulted in overexploiting resources, invading ③ n_____, and polluting water and the air. 구체적 근거 2: 예시 ④ T_____ global warming. This dangerous phenomenon is directly caused by the ⑤ g_____ which are produced when people burn oil and coal to generate electricity, run automobiles, and heat houses. In addition, logging companies cut down numerous trees that are an indispensable ⑥ d_____ to absorb harmful gases. ⑦ A_____ these selfish and short-sighted human activities, the earth is suffering from scorching summers, massive flooding, and habitat destruction. 마무리 문장 ⑧ I_____, the side-effects of human activities have critically harmed the environment.

소주제문 2 Furthermore, human activities are increasingly threatening people's lives. 구체적 근거 1: 일반적 진술 This largely results from human inventions ranging from seemingly innocuous automobiles to outright destructive ⑨ w_____, such as the atomic bomb. 구체적 근거 2: 예시 To take an example, cars are a highly convenient means to move around. Unfortunately, they are a deadly ⑩ f_____, and millions of people die worldwide in car accidents every year. This is coupled by the large number of people who get ⑪ r_____ from breathing in toxic ⑫ e_____ from motor vehicles. On top of that, millions of people die every year from war machines, including bullets, bombs, chemical weapons, and other sophisticated destructive inventions. 마무리 문장 It should then ⑬ c_____ that people's activities are actually bringing about their own demise.

요약 / 정리 ⑭ T_____, I firmly believe that human activities have harmed the Earth. This is because human inventions have endangered both the natural environment and human lives. 맺음말 On the whole, advancements in technology have been more of ⑮ a_____.

Question

When people move to new countries, they should follow the customs there. Do you agree or disagree? Use specific reasons and examples to support your answer.

사람들이 다른 나라로 이민을 가면 그곳의 관습을 따라야 한다는 진술에 찬성하는지 반대하는지를 밝히고 구체적인 이유와 예를 들어 대답을 뒷받침한다.

Outline

Agree*

1. Adopting a new culture's traditions makes life easier and more comfortable
   새로운 문화적 전통을 받아들이는 것은 삶을 더 쉽고 편하게 만든다
   - going against them causes puzzlement or outrage
     (해당 문화를) 거스르는 것은 당황스러움이나 분노를 유발한다
   - e.g. women wearing revealing clothes in the Middle East
     예) 중동에서 몸을 드러내는 옷을 입은 여성

2. Assimilation allows more employment opportunities
   문화에 동화되면 더 많은 취업의 기회를 갖게 된다
   - foreign languages and cultural understanding can be a job requirement
     외국어와 문화적 이해는 취업의 필요 조건
   - e.g. my sister got a good job in Japan by learning the language and custom
     예) 내 여동생은 일본에서 언어와 관습을 배움으로써 좋은 일자리를 얻었다

Disagree

1. Preserving cultural traditions is valuable
   문화적 전통을 고수하는 것은 가치 있다
   - ethnic heritage is important for national identity
     민족적 전통은 국가 정체성을 위해 중요하다
   - e.g. Korean-American football star
     예) 한국계 미국인 미식축구 선수

2. Cultural diversity enriches society
   문화적 다양성이 사회를 풍요롭게 한다
   - retaining own language and culture enhances cultural pluralism
     자기 언어와 문화를 유지하는 것은 문화 다원주의를 증진시킨다
   - e.g. 'salad bowl' model of US
     예) 미국의 '샐러드 보울' 모델

Model Essay

(도입) **In this age of globalization**, a growing number of people immigrate to different countries. Among them, a substantial number believe and practice the saying, "**When in Rome, do as the Romans do**." (대주제문) I believe people should follow this saying and try to adopt their new countries' ways. This allows them to integrate more easily, and also allows immigrants more diverse employment opportunities.

(소주제문 1) To begin with, adopting a new culture's traditions makes life easier and more comfortable. (구체적 근거 1: 일반적 진술) Cultural habits are often deeply-ingrained, and can even function as **de facto** laws for many people. Therefore, going against foreign cultural traditions can cause reactions ranging from puzzlement to outrage, **depending on** the severity of the situation. (구체적 근거 2: 예시) **To take a common situation**, in many Arab countries, women are expected to cover up and be modest. If women from other cultures show too much skin, they will suffer harassment and abuse from locals. (마무리 문장) **As this example demonstrates**, to show proper respect to host countries and also be good ambassadors for their native countries, immigrants should follow their new countries' traditions.

(소주제문 2) Furthermore, **assimilating into** new cultures provides immigrants with diverse employment opportunities. (구체적 근거 1: 일반적 진술) This is because actively associating with natives and following their customs are both helpful when learning foreign languages and understanding other cultures. These are indispensable requirements for obtaining decent jobs in foreign lands. (구체적 근거 2: 예시) **For example**, when my sister moved to Japan five years ago, she tried her best to learn the language and customs. **As a result**, my sister obtained the jobs she wanted, from school teacher to restaurant manager. She was able to do this because she minimized **the language and cultural barriers** between her Japanese co-workers, supervisors, and customers. If it had not been for her adaptation to Japanese culture, my sister would have **had difficulty in** finding good jobs there.

(요약/정리) To sum up, culture is a very sensitive topic. **Accordingly**, immigrants should show proper respect to foreign cultures' traditions and follow them. Doing so makes their own lives easier, as they can **fit in** better. **On a practical level**, immigrants can find jobs easier after they adapt to their new countries' ways. (맺음말) As immigrants in different cultures all around the world can attest, **blending in** is the easiest and best policy.

해석

이 세계화 시대에, 점점 더 많은 사람들이 다른 나라로 이민을 간다. 그들 중, 상당수의 사람들이 "로마에 가면, 로마법을 따르라" 는 속담을 믿고 실천에 옮긴다. 나는 사람들이 이 속담을 따르고 새로운 나라의 방식을 받아들이도록 노력해야 한다고 생각한다. 이는 그들로 하여금 더 쉽게 융합하도록 해주며, 또한 이민자들에게 좀 더 다양한 취업의 기회를 제공한다.

우선, 새로운 문화적 전통을 받아들이는 것은 삶을 더 쉽고 편안하게 만든다. 문화적 관습은 뿌리 깊게 박혀 있는 경우가 많아서, 많은 사람들에게 사실상의 법으로 작용하기도 한다. 따라서, 외국의 문화적 전통을 거스르는 것은 상황의 심각성에 따라, 당황에서 분노에 이르는 반응을 불러 일으킬 수 있다. 흔히 일어나는 상황을 예로 들자면, 많은 아랍 국가에서 여성들은 몸을 가리고 정숙한 태도를 갖춰야 한다. 만약 다른 문화권의 여성이 몸을 지나치게 드러내면, 지역 주민들로부터 희롱과 학대를 겪게 될 것이다. 이러한 예가 보여 주듯이, 이민자들은 새로운 나라에 예의를 표하고 또한 출신 국가를 위해서 훌륭한 외교 사절이 되려면 새로운 국가의 전통을 따라야 한다.

게다가, 새로운 문화에 동화하는 것은 이민자들에게 다양한 취업의 기회를 제공한다. 이는 적극적으로 현지인들과 사귀고 그들의 관습을 따르는 것은 외국어를 배우고 다른 문화를 이해할 때 모두 도움을 주기 때문이다. 이러한 것들은 외국에서 괜찮은 직장을 구하는데 필수 불가결한 요건들이다. 예를 들면, 나의 여동생이 5년 전에 일본으로 이민을 갔을 때, 그녀는 그 언어와 관습을 배우기 위해 최선을 다했다. 그 결과, 내 여동생은 학교 선생님에서부터 레스토랑 지배인까지 그녀가 원하던 일자리들을 구했다. 그녀는 그녀와 일본인 동료와 상사, 고객 사이의 언어와 문화적 장벽을 최소화했기 때문에 이렇게 할 수 있었다. 만약 일본 문화에 대한 그녀의 적응이 없었다면, 내 여동생은 그곳에서 좋은 직장을 구하기가 어려웠을 것이다.

요약하자면, 문화란 매우 까다로운 주제이다. 따라서, 이민자들은 외국 문화의 전통에 예의 어린 존중을 표현하고 그것들을 따라야 한다. 그렇게 함으로써 보다 잘 적응할 수 있게 되어 자신들의 삶을 좀 더 편하게 만들 수 있다. 현실적인 면에서는, 이민자들은 그들이 새로운 나라의 방식에 적응하고 난 후에 일자리를 더 쉽게 구할 수 있다. 전 세계의 여러 문화권에 있는 이민자들에서 볼 수 있듯이, 조화롭게 어울리는 것이 가장 쉬운 최선책이다.

globalization[glòubəlizéiʃən] 세계화   substantial[səbstǽnʃəl] 상당한
When in Rome, do as the Romans do 로마에 가면, 로마 사람들의 풍습을 따르라
integrate[íntəgrèit] 융합하다   de facto laws 사실상의 법   deeply-ingrained 뿌리 깊은, 깊이 배어든
go against 반대하다, 거스르다   puzzlement[pʌ́zlmənt] 당황   outrage[áutreidʒ] 격분, 분개   depending on ~ ~에 따라, ~에 달려
severity[sivérəti] 엄격, 가혹   harassment[hərǽsmənt] 괴롭힘   abuse[əbjúːz] 학대, 욕설   assimilate into ~ ~로 동화하다
associate with ~ ~와 교제하다, 사귀다   indispensable[ìndispénsəbl] 필수 불가결한   requirement[rikwáiərmənt] 필요 조건
decent[díːsənt] 어지간한, 남부럽잖은   if it had not been for ~ 만약 ~이 없었더면   adaptation[æ̀dəptéiʃən] 적응, 순응
have difficulty in ~ing ~하는 데 어려움을 겪다   to sum up 요약하자면   sensitive[sénsitiv] 민감한, 까다로운
bring about 가져오다, 초래하다   attest[ətést] 입증하다, 증명하다   blend in 조화하다, 뒤섞이다, 어울리다

① In this age of globalization   ② When in Rome, do as the Romans do   ③ de facto
④ depending on   ⑤ To take a common situation   ⑥ As this example demonstrates
⑦ assimilating into   ⑧ For example   ⑨ As a result   ⑩ the language and cultural barriers
⑪ had difficulty in   ⑫ Accordingly   ⑬ fit in   ⑭ On a practical level   ⑮ blending in

Review

(도입) ① I_____, a growing number of people immigrate to different countries. Among them, a substantial number believe and practice the saying, "② W_____." (대주제문) I believe people should follow this saying and try to adopt their new countries' ways. This allows them to integrate more easily, and also allows immigrants more diverse employment opportunities.

(소주제문 1) To begin with, adopting a new culture's traditions makes life easier and more comfortable. (구체적 근거 1: 일반적 진술) Cultural habits are often deeply-ingrained, and can even function as ③ d_____ laws for many people. Therefore, going against foreign cultural traditions can cause reactions ranging from puzzlement to outrage, ④ d_____ the severity of the situation. (구체적 근거 2: 예시) ⑤ T_____, in many Arab countries, women are expected to cover up and be modest. If women from other cultures show too much skin, they will suffer harassment and abuse from locals. (마무리 문장) ⑥ A_____, to show proper respect to host countries and also be good ambassadors for their native countries, immigrants should follow their new countries' traditions.

(소주제문 2) Furthermore, ⑦ a_____ new cultures provides immigrants with diverse employment opportunities. (구체적 근거 1: 일반적 진술) This is because actively associating with natives and following their customs are both helpful when learning foreign languages and understanding other cultures. These are indispensable requirements for obtaining decent jobs in foreign lands. (구체적 근거 2: 예시) ⑧ F_____, when my sister moved to Japan five years ago, she tried her best to learn the language and customs. ⑨ A_____, my sister obtained the jobs she wanted, from school teacher to restaurant manager. She was able to do this because she minimized ⑩ t_____ between her Japanese co-workers, supervisors, and customers. If it had not been for her adaptation to Japanese culture, my sister would have ⑪ h_____ finding good jobs there.

(요약/정리) To sum up, culture is a very sensitive topic. ⑫ A_____, immigrants should show proper respect to foreign cultures' traditions and follow them. Doing so makes their own lives easier, as they can ⑬ f_____ better. ⑭ O_____, immigrants can find jobs easier after they adapt to their new countries' ways. (맺음말) As immigrants in different cultures all around the world can attest, ⑮ b_____ is the easiest and best policy.

Question

Do you agree or disagree with the following statement? Games can teach us valuable lessons about life. Use specific reasons and examples to support your answer.

게임이 우리에게 인생에 대해 귀중한 교훈을 가르쳐 준다는 진술에 찬성하는지 반대하는지를 밝히고 구체적인 이유와 예를 들어 대답을 뒷받침한다.

Outline

Agree*

1. Games teach the importance of following social rules
   게임은 사회규범을 지키는 것의 중요성을 가르친다
   - players must strictly observe all the rules and regulations
     경기자는 모든 규칙과 규정을 철저하게 준수해야 한다
   - e.g. learn to respect laws in society through board games
     예) 보드 게임을 통해서 사회에서 법을 지키는 것을 배웠다

2. Games instill a spirit of cooperation
   게임은 협동 정신을 불어넣는다
   - require participants' collective efforts and collaboration
     참가자의 집단적인 노력과 협동이 요구된다
   - e.g. soccer games
     예) 축구 경기

Disagree

1. Waste of time and energy
   시간과 에너지의 낭비
   - no time or energy left for more productive activities
     더 생산적인 일을 하기 위한 시간이나 힘이 남아 있지 않을 수 있다
   - e.g. spent too much time playing tennis, ended up failing mid-term exam
     예) 테니스 치는 데 시간을 너무 많이 써서 결국 중간 고사를 망쳤다

2. Games convey the wrong message about life
   게임은 인생에 대해 잘못된 메시지를 전한다
   - competition, emphasis on winning
     경쟁, 이기는 것에 대한 강조
   - e.g. sports programs on TV focus on the glamour of winners, not on gracious losers
     예) TV의 스포츠 프로그램은 승자의 화려함에만 집중하고 정정당당한 패자의 모습은 비추지 않는다

Model Essay

(도입) Every day, I **look forward to** playing games, which has the curious effect of both relaxing and exciting me. This activity has a deeper purpose, however. (대주제문) **From personal experience**, I strongly believe that playing games teaches people about life. For one, games teach the importance of following social rules. Additionally, they instill **a spirit of cooperation**.

(소주제문 1) First, games teach people, children **in particular**, the significance of following rules in society. (구체적 근거 1: 일반적 진술) This results in large part because **in order to** fairly and orderly play games, all players are required to strictly observe all the rules and regulations. However, when the rules are flawed or circumvented, games will **result in** disorder and chaos, with a lot of cheating and fouls. (구체적 근거 2: 예시) **To take a personal example**, my family has played board games every weekend since when I was little. Through playing these games, I had a valuable opportunity to naturally learn to respect laws in society by thoroughly reading directions, patiently waiting for my turn, and even taking the disciplinary consequences when I cheated or disobeyed the rules. (마무리 문장) Accordingly, games resemble real societies where laws and regulations sustain peace and order.

(소주제문 2) **On top of that**, playing games teaches people the importance of teamwork in life. (구체적 근거 1: 일반적 진술) One important reason is that a wide variety of games, especially sports games **such as** basketball and soccer require participants' collective efforts and collaboration. **Furthermore**, players learn that a person's individual talent and skills alone cannot lead the team to victory. (구체적 근거 2: 예시) **For instance**, in soccer games, teammates must cooperate and work together to win. Accordingly, team members should play **as a united whole** not only skillfully passing the ball to each other and orchestrating complicated formations but also cheering for each other and comforting injured members in order to be victorious. (마무리 문장) In this respect, games can teach people an indispensable **life lesson** on cooperation.

(요약 / 정리) **To conclude**, I strongly believe that playing games instructs us in important life lessons. The reason is that playing games teaches people how to respect social norms and improve their social skills. (맺음말) **As I mentioned above**, I believe that these are vital factors for leading a happy life.

해석

매일 나는 게임하는 것을 고대하는데, 게임은 나의 긴장을 풀어 주고 흥분시키는 신기한 효과를 지닌다. 그러나, 이 활동은 더 심오한 목적을 지니고 있다. 개인적인 경험을 통해, 나는 게임을 하는 것이 사람들에게 인생에 대해 가르쳐 준다는 것을 확신한다. 첫째로, 게임은 사회의 규범을 따르는 것의 중요성을 가르쳐 준다. 게다가, 게임은 협동 정신을 불어넣어 준다.

첫째로, 게임은 특히 어린이들에게 사회에서의 규범을 따르는 것의 중요성을 가르쳐 준다. 이는 대체로 공정하게 규칙을 따라 게임을 하기 위해서는, 모든 참가자가 모든 규칙과 규정을 준수할 필요가 있기 때문이다. 그러나, 그 규칙들에 흠이나 허점이 있을 경우에는, 게임은 많은 속임수와 반칙을 동반하며 무질서와 혼란으로 끝이 난다. 개인적인 예를 들자면, 나의 가족은 내가 어렸을 때부터 주말마다 보드 게임을 해왔다. 이 게임을 통해서, 나는 지시사항을 철저하게 읽고, 참을성 있게 나의 차례를 기다리며, 속임수를 썼거나 규칙을 위반했을 경우에는 이에 수반되는 벌칙을 받아들이기도 하면서 자연스럽게 사회에서 법을 존중하는 것을 배울 귀중한 기회를 얻을 수 있었다. 따라서, 게임은 법과 규제가 평화와 질서를 지속시키는 실제 사회와 공통점이 많다.

게다가, 게임을 하는 것은 협동 정신을 심어 준다. 중요한 이유 한 가지는 다양한 게임들, 특히 농구와 축구 같은 스포츠 경기들은 참가자들의 집단적인 노력과 협동을 요구한다는 점이다. 게다가, 경기자들은 개인의 재능과 기술만으로는 팀을 승리로 이끌 수 없다는 것을 배우게 된다. 예를 들면, 축구 경기에서 팀 동료들은 이기기 위해서는 협동하고 함께 노력해야 한다. 따라서, 팀의 일원들이 승리하기 위해서는 능숙하게 서로에게 공을 패스하고, 복잡한 대형을 구성할 뿐만 아니라, 서로를 격려하고 다친 선수를 돌보며, 하나로 단결된 통일체로서 경기에 임해야 한다. 이러한 점에서, 게임은 사람들에게 협동에 관한 필수 불가결한 인생의 교훈을 가르쳐 준다.

결론적으로, 나는 게임을 하는 것이 우리에게 중요한 인생의 교훈을 가르쳐 준다는 것을 확신한다. 그 이유는 게임을 하는 것이 사람들에게 사회적 규범을 존중하고 그들의 사회적 기술을 증진시키는 방법을 가르쳐 주기 때문이다. 위에서 밝힌 바대로, 나는 이것들이야 말로 행복한 삶을 영위하기 위해 필수적인 요인이라고 생각한다.

look forward to ~ing ~하기를 기대하다, 고대하다   instill [instíl] 불어넣다, 주입하다   orderly [ɔ́:rdərli] 규칙을 따라, 정연하게
observe [əbzá:rv] 준수하다   flawed [flɔ́:d] 흠이 있는   circumvented [sə̀:rkəmvéntid] 허점이 있는   result in ~ ~로 끝나다
disorder [disɔ́:rdər] 무질서   chaos [kéiɑs] 대혼란   cheating [tʃí:tiŋ] 속임수   directions [dirékʃənz] 지시, 사용법
disciplinary [dísəplənèri] 징계의   accordingly [əkɔ́:rdiŋli] 따라서   sustain [səstéin] 유지하다, 지속하다
participant [pɑ:rtísəpənt] 참가자   collective [kəléktiv] 집단적인   collaboration [kəlæ̀bəréiʃən] 협동
orchestrate [ɔ́:rkistrèit] 편성하다, 조직하다   in this respect 이러한 관점에서   indispensable [ìndispénsəbl] 필수 불가결한
norm [nɔ:rm] 규범   as I mentioned above 위에서 밝힌 바와 같이   vital [váitəl] 중대한

① look forward to   ② From personal experience   ③ a spirit of cooperation   ④ in particular
⑤ in order to   ⑥ result in   ⑦ To take a personal example   ⑧ On top of that   ⑨ such as
⑩ Furthermore   ⑪ For instance   ⑫ as a united whole   ⑬ life lesson   ⑭ To conclude
⑮ As I mentioned above

Review

(도입) Every day, I ① l_____ playing games, which has the curious effect of both relaxing and exciting me. This activity has a deeper purpose, however. (대주제문) ② F_____ _____, I strongly believe that playing games teaches people about life. For one, games teach the importance of following social rules. Additionally, they instill ③ a_____.

(소주제문 1) First, games teach people, children ④ i_____, the significance of following rules in society. (구체적 근거 1: 일반적 진술) This results in large part because ⑤ i_____ fairly and orderly play games, all players are required to strictly observe all the rules and regulations. However, when the rules are flawed or circumvented, games will ⑥ r_____ disorder and chaos, with a lot of cheating and fouls. (구체적 근거 2: 예시) ⑦ T_____, my family has played board games every weekend since when I was little. Through playing these games, I had a valuable opportunity to naturally learn to respect laws in society by thoroughly reading directions, patiently waiting for my turn, and even taking the disciplinary consequences when I cheated or disobeyed the rules. (마무리 문장) Accordingly, games resemble real societies where laws and regulations sustain peace and order.

(소주제문 2) ⑧ O_____, playing games teaches people the importance of teamwork in life. (구체적 근거 1: 일반적 진술) One important reason is that a wide variety of games, especially sports games ⑨ s_____ basketball and soccer require participants' collective efforts and collaboration. ⑩ F_____, players learn that a person's individual talent and skills alone cannot lead the team to victory. (구체적 근거 2: 예시) ⑪ F_____, in soccer games, teammates must cooperate and work together to win. Accordingly, team members should play ⑫ a_____ not only skillfully passing the ball to each other and orchestrating complicated formations but also cheering for each other and comforting injured members in order to be victorious. (마무리 문장) In this respect, games can teach people an indispensable ⑬ l_____ on cooperation.

(요약 / 정리) ⑭ T_____, I strongly believe that playing games instructs us in important life lessons. The reason is that playing games teaches people how to respect social norms and improve their social skills. (맺음말) ⑮ A_____, I believe that these are vital factors for leading a happy life.

Day 25

Question

Hard work has more to do with success than luck does. Do you agree or disagree with the statement? Use specific reasons and examples to explain your position.

성공은 운보다는 부지런한 노력 때문이라는 진술에 찬성하는지 반대하는지를 밝히고 구체적인 이유와 예를 들어 입장을 뒷받침한다.

Outline

Agree*

1. Opportunities come only to those prepared
   기회는 준비된 자에게만 찾아온다
   - people can create success regardless of unfavorable situations
     사람들은 불리한 상황에 관계없이 성공을 창조해낼 수 있다
   - e.g. Sumi Jo, famous Korean soprano singer
     예) 조수미, 유명한 한국인 소프라노

2. Success is maintained only through consistent hard work
   성공은 지속적으로 노력해야만 유지된다
   - have to continuously work to stay on top in competitive society
     경쟁 사회에서 정상을 유지하려면 꾸준히 노력해야 한다
   - e.g. scholarship winners' devotion to hard work
     예) 장학금 수여자들의 노력

Disagree

1. Some people get lucky without working for their goals
   몇몇 사람들은 노력하지 않고도 행운이 주어진다.
   - lives change dramatically: lottery, real estate, stocks
     인생이 극적으로 바뀐다: 복권, 부동산, 주식
   - e.g. a lady who found historical relics on her land
     예) 우연히 자신의 땅에서 역사적 유물을 발견해 부자가 된 여인

2. People born rich can become successful without much effort
   부유한 가문에서 태어난 사람은 별다른 노력 없이 성공할 수 있다
   - have promising educational and professional opportunities
     유망한 교육적 그리고 직업적 기회를 가진다
   - e.g. two friends, one from wealthy family and one from poor family
     예) 부자 집안과 가난한 집안 출신의 두 친구

Model Essay

(도입) A great number of people depend on superstitious practices to bring luck into their lives because they believe good fortune can make them successful. (대주제문) However, **in opposition to** this view, I strongly believe that only hard work can result in success. **The reasoning behind this is** that good opportunities come only to those who are prepared. Also, earnest endeavor is indispensable **on the path to success**.

(소주제문 1) To begin with, opportunities for success come only to people who have diligently worked for their dreams. (구체적 근거 1: 일반적 진술) **This is mainly because** people can create and establish the conditions and probability of success regardless of unfavorable situations and adversity **as long as** they **persist in** working hard. (구체적 근거 2: 예시) For example, Sumi Jo, who is the most prominent soprano singer in Korea, endured several years of **intensive and painstaking practice** in foreign countries in order to achieve her dream. Therefore, she was able to win first place in an internationally-renowned competition. Her success in the contest helped her begin a career as an international opera singer, as she was able to seize the opportunity of a lifetime. **On the other hand**, if Jo had been lazy and unprepared, she would not have been able to **capitalize on** the greatest chance of her life.

(소주제문 2) In addition, success is maintained only through consistent hard work. (구체적 근거 1: 일반적 진술) One significant reason is that people who have obtained their goals must invest continuous and conscious effort in order to stay on top amongst tens of thousands of rivals in this competitive society. **Otherwise**, their hard-earned wealth and fame will soon disappear. (구체적 근거 2: 예시) **To clarify**, people who win scholarships are often envied their good fortune. However, most people do not realize that these awardees must work hard and sacrifice many activities by **staying up** nearly every night to study, giving up meeting their friends on the weekends, and even spending their holidays in the library. Not putting in this effort **results in** people losing their grants and reputation. Thus, scholarship winners are not simply lucky.

(요약 / 정리) In summary, **I firmly believe that** only those who work hard can succeed in life, and should not depend on luck. This is because only hard workers can create favorable opportunities and success is maintained only through consistent hard work. (맺음말) As the popular saying goes, **heaven helps those who help themselves**.

해석

많은 수의 사람들이 자신들의 삶에 행운을 불러들이기 위해서 미신적인 관습에 의지하는데 이는 이들이 행운이 자신들을 성공하게 해줄 것이라고 믿기 때문이다. 하지만, 이러한 견해와는 반대되게, 나는 오로지 부지런히 일하는 것만이 성공으로 이어질 수 있다고 확신한다. 이렇게 생각하는 이유는, 좋은 기회는 준비되어 있는 이들에게만 찾아오기 때문이다. 또한 착실한 노력은 성공으로 향하는 길에 있어서 필수적인 것이다.

우선, 성공의 기회는 자신의 꿈을 이루기 위해서 부지런히 노력해 왔던 사람들에게만 찾아온다. 이는 주로 사람들이 어떤 불리한 상황이나 불운에도 상관없이, 계속해서 열심히 일한다면 성공의 여건과 가능성을 만들어내고 굳힐 수 있기 때문이다. 예를 들어, 한국에서 최고로 뛰어난 소프라노 성악가인 조수미씨는 그녀의 꿈을 이루기 위해서 해외에서 수년 간의 고된 집중 훈련을 견뎌냈다. 따라서, 그녀는 세계적으로 유명한 콩쿠르에서 1위를 차지할 수 있었다. 그녀가 이 일생일대의 기회를 움켜쥘 수 있었기에 이 콩쿠르에서의 성공은 그녀가 국제적인 오페라 가수로서의 인생을 시작할 수 있게 도움이 되었다. 반면에, 만약 조수미씨가 게으르고 준비가 되어 있지 않았었다면, 그녀는 일생에 있어서 가장 큰 기회를 이용할 수 없었을 것이다.

게다가, 성공은 지속적으로 열심히 일해야만 유지될 수 있다. 한가지 중요한 이유는 이런 경쟁적인 사회에서는 자신들의 목표를 달성한 사람들도 수만 명의 라이벌 중에서 정상의 자리를 유지하려면 지속적으로 의식적인 노력을 기울여야 하기 때문이다. 그렇게 하지 않는다면, 그들이 어렵게 얻은 부와 명성은 순식간에 사라질 것이다. 예를 들면, 장학금을 탄 사람들은 그들의 행운으로 인해서 종종 부러움을 산다. 하지만 많은 사람들은 이 수여자들이 열심히 공부해야 하며, 공부 때문에 거의 매일 밤을 지새우고, 주말에 친구들을 만나는 것을 포기하고, 심지어는 휴일을 도서관에서 보내는 것으로 인해 많은 활동을 희생해야 한다는 것을 알지 못한다. 이러한 노력을 기울이지 않는다면, 이들은 장학금과 명성을 잃게 될 것이다. 따라서, 장학금 수여자들은 단순히 운이 좋은 것이 아니다.

요약해서 말하자면, 나는 열심히 일하는 자만이 인생에서 성공할 수 있고 운에 기대어서는 안 된다고 굳게 믿는다. 이는 열심히 일하는 자만이 유리한 기회를 만들어낼 수 있고, 이러한 기회를 성공으로 일구어 가는 방법을 알기 때문이다. 속담에서 이르듯이, 하늘은 스스로 돕는 자만을 돕는다.

---

regardless of ~에도 불구하고   unfavorable[ʌnféivərəbl] 불리한   consistent[kənsístənt] 지속적인
devotion[divóuʃən] 헌신, 전념   relic[rélik] 유물   promising[prámisiŋ] 유망한   superstitious[sjù:pərstíʃəs] 미신의
practice[prǽktis] 관습   reasoning[ríːzəniŋ] 추론, 논거   earnest[ə́ːrnist] 성실한   indispensable[ìndispénsəbl] 필수의
diligently[dílidʒəntli] 근면하게, 부지런히   probability[pràbəbíləti] 가망성, 확률   persist in ~을 끝까지 해내다, 관철하다
prominent[prámənənt] 저명한   painstaking[péinstèikiŋ] 힘이 드는, 애쓴   renowned[rináund] 유명한, 명성 있는
conscious[kánʃəs] 의식적인   grant[grænt] 보조금, 장려금   reputation[rèpjə(:)téiʃən] 평판, 세평   awardee[əwɔ̀ːrdíː] 수상자
Heaven helps those who help themselves 하늘은 스스로 돕는 자를 돕는다

---

① in opposition to   ② The reasoning behind this is   ③ on the path to success
④ This is mainly because   ⑤ as long as   ⑥ persist in   ⑦ intensive and painstaking practice
⑧ On the other hand   ⑨ capitalize on   ⑩ Otherwise   ⑪ To clarify   ⑫ staying up   ⑬ results in
⑭ I firmly believe that   ⑮ heaven helps those who help themselves.

Review

(도입) A great number of people depend on superstitious practices to bring luck into their lives because they believe good fortune can make them successful. (대주제문) However, ① i_____ this view, I strongly believe that only hard work can result in success. ② T_____ that good opportunities come only to those who are prepared. Also, earnest endeavor is indispensable ③ o_____.

(소주제문 1) To begin with, opportunities for success come only to people who have diligently worked for their dreams. (구체적 근거 1: 일반적 진술) ④ T_____ people can create and establish the conditions and probability of success regardless of unfavorable situations and adversity ⑤ a_____ they ⑥ p_____ working hard. (구체적 근거 2: 예시) For example, Sumi Jo, who is the most prominent soprano singer in Korea, endured several years of ⑦ i_____ _____ in foreign countries in order to achieve her dream. Therefore, she was able to win first place in an internationally-renowned competition. Her success in the contest helped her begin a career as an international opera singer, as she was able to seize the opportunity of a lifetime. ⑧ O_____, if Jo had been lazy and unprepared, she would not have been able to ⑨ c_____ the greatest chance of her life.

(소주제문 2) In addition, success is maintained only through consistent hard work. (구체적 근거 1: 일반적 진술) One significant reason is that people who have obtained their goals must invest continuous and conscious effort in order to stay on top amongst tens of thousands of rivals in this competitive society. ⑩ O_____, their hard-earned wealth and fame will soon disappear. (구체적 근거 2: 예시) ⑪ T_____, people who win scholarships are often envied their good fortune. However, most people do not realize that these awardees must work hard and sacrifice many activities by ⑫ s_____ nearly every night to study, giving up meeting their friends on the weekends, and even spending their holidays in the library. Not putting in this effort ⑬ r_____ people losing their grants and reputation. Thus, scholarship winners are not simply lucky.

(요약/정리) In summary, ⑭ I_____ only those who work hard can succeed in life, and should not depend on luck. This is because only hard workers can create favorable opportunities and success is maintained only through consistent hard work. (맺음말) As the popular saying goes, ⑮ h_____.

Question

Do you agree or disagree with the following statement? Eating homemade food is better than eating out at restaurants or food stands. Use specific reasons and examples to support your answer.

집에서 만든 음식을 먹는 것이 식당이나 노점에서 외식하는 것보다 낫다는 진술에 찬성하는지 반대하는지를 밝히고 구체적인 이유와 예를 들어 대답을 뒷받침한다.

Outline

Agree*

1. Homemade food is much healthier
   집에서 만든 음식이 훨씬 건강에 좋다
   - can choose healthy ingredients
     건강한 재료를 선택할 수 있다
   - e.g. how my mother cooks
     예) 나의 어머니가 요리하는 법

2. Provide families with quality time together
   가족들에게 오붓한 시간을 제공한다
   - meals at home can serve as an excellent opportunity to gather families
     집에서의 식사는 가족들의 화합에 있어 훌륭한 기회가 된다
   - e.g. eating at home: discuss interesting issues, ask for advice, etc.
     dining out: conversations are disturbed
     예) 집에서의 식사: 흥미로운 주제에 대해 토론, 자문을 구한다 등등
     외식: 대화가 방해를 받는다

Disagree

1. Restaurants provide a variety of flavors
   레스토랑은 다양한 맛을 제공한다
   - different tastes than one's own limited cooking
     자기가 만든 제한된 요리와는 다른 맛
   - e.g. at Greek restaurant, tasted exotic food
     예) 그리스 레스토랑에서 이국적인 음식을 맛보았다

2. Eating out is more convenient
   외식하는 것은 더 편리하다
   - saves time cooking and cleaning
     요리하고 치우는 시간을 절약할 수 있다
   - e.g. friend who saved time for studying by not cooking
     예) 요리하지 않음으로써 공부 시간을 늘린 친구

Model Essay

(도입) These days, a growing number of people prefer to eat at food stands or restaurants **because of** their convenience. (대주제문) **In contrast to** the trend, I definitely feel that eating food at home is better. The rationale behind this is that homemade food is much healthier. Furthermore, eating at home **strengthens family bonds**.

(소주제문 1) **First of all**, eating at home is a much healthier choice for everyone. (구체적 근거 1: 일반적 진술) This is mainly because people can prepare nutritious meals for their families and themselves at home by choosing healthy ingredients. (구체적 근거 2: 예시) For example, when my mother cooks at home, she carefully plans dishes that **tailor to** my family's health needs. Then, she consciously chooses healthy ingredients **ranging from** organic vegetables to low-fat milk, while **cutting down** the use of refined white flour and artificial sweeteners. In addition, my mother regularly sterilizes all the cooking utensils and the kitchen. **Thanks to** my mother's homemade food, my family can maintain our health. On the other hand, a majority of commercial eating places use cheap ingredients and add harmful chemical additives to make their food tastier.

(소주제문 2) **Moreover**, eating at home provides families with quality time together. (구체적 근거 1: 일반적 진술) An important factor is that meals at home can **serve as** an excellent opportunity to gather families in one place and allow them to relax and enjoy delicious homemade food. (구체적 근거 2: 예시) Instead of dining at noisy restaurant, families can **come together** to eat delicious home-cooked dinner every evening after a busy day at school and work. Through preparing and eating together, family members **have a window of opportunity** to bond with one another by talking about what happened throughout the day. Also, they can discuss interesting social issues, share problems, as well as ask for each other's advice while comfortably sitting in cozy dining rooms. Conversely, conversations **are likely to** be constantly disturbed by customers and waiters when families dine out at restaurants.

(요약/정리) In conclusion, **without the slightest hesitation**, I will always choose to eat at home. The reason is that eating nutritious food at home strengthens both my body and my family relationships. (맺음말) **All in all**, I believe that these are the most important factors for leading a healthy physical and mental life.

Day 26

해석

오늘날, 점점 더 많은 수의 사람들이 편리함 때문에 노점이나 음식점에서 식사를 하기를 선호한다. 추세와는 상반되게, 나는 집에서 식사를 하는 것이 분명히 더 좋다고 생각한다. 그 이유는 집에서 만든 음식이 보다 건강에 좋기 때문이다. 그뿐 아니라, 집에서 하는 식사는 가족간의 유대를 강화시켜 준다.

우선, 집에서 식사하는 것은 모든 이에게 훨씬 더 건강에 좋은 선택이다. 이는 주로 사람들이 건강에 좋은 재료를 선택함으로써 집에서 가족이나 자신을 위해서 영양이 있는 식사를 준비할 수 있기 때문이다. 예를 들면, 나의 어머니께서는 집에서 요리를 하실 때 가족의 건강상 필요에 맞는 식단을 계획하신다. 그리고 어머니께서는 정제된 밀가루나 인공 감미료 등의 사용을 줄이면서, 유기농 야채에서 저지방 우유에 이르는 건강에 좋은 재료를 신중하게 고르신다. 게다가, 어머니는 모든 주방기기와 부엌을 정기적으로 소독하신다. 어머니의 집에서 손수 만드신 음식 덕에, 우리 가족은 건강하다. 반면, 대부분의 상업적 식당에서는 값싼 재료를 사용하고 음식을 더 맛있게 하기 위해 해로운 화학 조미료를 첨가한다.

게다가, 집에서 식사하는 것은 가족들이 함께 오붓하게 보낼 수 있는 시간을 마련해 준다. 한 가지 중요한 이유는 집에서 하는 식사가 가족이 한데 모여서 휴식을 취하고 집에서 만든 맛있는 음식을 즐기게 해줄 매우 좋은 기회가 되어 준다는 것이다. 시끄러운 식당에서 식사하는 대신 가족들은 학교나 직장에서 바쁜 하루를 보낸 후에, 매일 저녁 함께 모여서 집에서 만든 맛있는 저녁을 먹을 수 있다. 함께 음식을 준비해서 먹는 것을 통해, 가족 구성원은 하루 동안 무슨 일이 일어났는지에 대해서 이야기하면서 서로 친해질 수 있는 좋은 기회를 갖는다. 또한 그들은 아늑한 식당에 편하게 앉아서 다른 이들의 조언을 구할 수도 있을 뿐만 아니라, 흥미로운 사회 문제에 대해 논하고 서로의 문제를 공유할 수 있다. 반대로, 가족들이 집 밖의 식당에서 식사를 할 때에는 손님들과 웨이터들에 의해 대화가 계속 방해받을 가능성이 높다.

결론을 말하자면, 나는 약간의 주저함도 없이 항상 집에서 식사하는 쪽을 선택할 것이다. 그 이유는 집에서 영양이 있고 깨끗한 음식을 먹는 편이 내 몸과 가족간 유대를 강화시켜 주기 때문이다. 종합해서 말하자면, 나는 이런 것들이 신체적, 정신적으로 건강한 삶을 이끌어 가기 위한 가장 중요한 요인이라고 믿는다.

stand[stænd] 매점, 노점   ingredient[ingríːdiənt] 재료   gather[gǽðər] 모으다   dine out 외식하다
convenience[kənvíːnjəns] 편의   rationale[ræ̀ʃənǽl] 근본적 이유, 이론적 근거   bond[bɑnd] 유대, 결속
nutritious[njuːtríʃəs] 영양분이 풍부한   tailor to ~ ~에 맞게 만들다   organic[ɔːrgǽnik] 무공해의, 유기 농법의
refined[rifáind] 정제된   artificial sweetener 인공 감미료   sterilize[stérəlàiz] ~을 살균하다, 소독하다
utensil[juːténsəl] 기구, 용기   commercial[kəmə́ːrʃəl] 상업의   additive[ǽdətiv] (식품의) 첨가물   conversely[kənvə́ːrsli] 거꾸로
constantly[kánstəntli] 변함없이, 언제나

---

① because of   ② In contrast to   ③ strengthens family bonds   ④ First of all   ⑤ tailor to
⑥ ranging from   ⑦ cutting down   ⑧ Thanks to   ⑨ Moreover   ⑩ serve as   ⑪ come together
⑫ have a window of opportunity   ⑬ are likely to   ⑭ without the slightest hesitation   ⑮ All in all

Review

(도입) These days, a growing number of people prefer to eat at food stands or restaurants ① b_____ ____ their convenience. (대주제문) ② l_____ the trend, I definitely feel that eating food at home is better. The rationale behind this is that homemade food is much healthier. Furthermore, eating at home ③ s_____ .

(소주제문 1) ④ F_____ , eating at home is a much healthier choice for everyone. (구체적 근거 1: 일반적 진술) This is mainly because people can prepare nutritious meals for their families and themselves at home by choosing healthy ingredients. (구체적 근거 2: 예시) For example, when my mother cooks at home, she carefully plans dishes that ⑤ t_____ my family's health needs. Then, she consciously chooses healthy ingredients ⑥ r_____ organic vegetables to low-fat milk, while ⑦ c_____ the use of refined white flour and artificial sweeteners. In addition, my mother regularly sterilizes all the cooking utensils and the kitchen. ⑧ T_____ my mother's homemade food, my family can maintain our health. On the other hand, a majority of commercial eating places use cheap ingredients and add harmful chemical additives to make their food tastier.

(소주제문 2) ⑨ M_____ , eating at home provides families with quality time together. (구체적 근거 1: 일반적 진술) An important factor is that meals at home can ⑩ s_____ an excellent opportunity to gather families in one place and allow them to relax and enjoy delicious homemade food. (구체적 근거 2: 예시) Instead of dining at noisy restaurant, families can ⑪ c_____ to eat delicious home-cooked dinner every evening after a busy day at school and work. Through preparing and eating together, family members ⑫ h_____ to bond with one another by talking about what happened throughout the day. Also, they can discuss interesting social issues, share problems, as well as ask for each other's advice while comfortably sitting in cozy dining rooms. Conversely, conversations ⑬ a_____ be constantly disturbed by customers and waiters when families dine out at restaurants.

(요약/정리) In conclusion, ⑭ w_____ , I will always choose to eat at home. The reason is that eating nutritious food at home strengthens both my body and my family relationships. (맺음말) ⑮ A_____ , I believe that these are the most important factors for leading a healthy physical and mental life.

Day 27

Question

 Do you agree or disagree with the following statement? High school students should be allowed to choose which subjects they will study. Use specific reasons and examples to explain your answer.

고등학생들은 공부하고 싶은 과목을 선택하도록 허용되어야 한다는 진술에 찬성하는지 반대하는지를 밝히고 구체적인 이유와 예를 들어 대답을 뒷받침한다.

Outline

Agree*

1. Electives help students plan for their careers
   선택 과목은 학생들로 하여금 직업을 계획하는 데 도움이 된다
   - valuable opportunities to explore their talents
     선택 과목은 그들의 능력을 시험해 볼 수 있는 소중한 기회이다
   - e.g. sister who wanted to become a veterinarian
     예) 수의사가 되고 싶어했던 누이

2. Students in elective courses show greater interest
   선택 과목을 듣는 학생들은 더 큰 관심을 보인다
   - when students are given freedom, they perform better
     학생들에게 선택의 자유가 주어지면 더 좋은 성과를 나타낸다
   - e.g. study: learn more in elective courses than in mandatory courses
     예) 연구 결과: 의무 과목보다 선택 과목을 들을 때 더 많이 배운다

Disagree

1. By studying many courses you can build knowledge of various fields
   많은 과목을 공부함으로써 다양한 분야의 지식을 쌓을 수 있다
   - these knowledge are helpful for one's life
     이러한 지식들은 인생에 도움이 된다
   - e.g. friend who studied many fields won the quiz contest
     예) 많은 분야를 공부했던 친구가 퀴즈 대회에서 우승하였다

2. Taking different courses provides chance to explore one's potential
   다른 수업을 듣는 것은 개인의 잠재력을 알아보는 기회가 된다
   - should study various fields before going to college
     대학에 가기 전 다양한 분야를 공부해야 한다
   - e.g. did not expect to like history, but decided to major in archaeology at college after taking the class
     예) 역사를 좋아하리라 생각하지 않았지만 수업을 듣고 나서 대학에서 고고학을 전공하기로 결정했다

Model Essay

(도입) For as long as I can remember, people have been debating the **pros and cons** of a **mandatory** curriculum versus elective courses. (대주제문) From personal experience, I strongly feel that elective courses have many positive benefits for students. My two main reasons are **as follows**: electives help students plan for their careers and motivate them to show greater interest in class.

(소주제문 1) To begin with, elective courses **allow** students **to** effectively plan for their future careers. (구체적 근거 1: 일반적 진술) An important benefit is that students have valuable opportunities to **explore** their talents while taking courses that are related to their fields of interests. **As a result**, students can gain an in-depth knowledge and learn about the requirements of career areas that they are considering. (구체적 근거 2: 예시) One person who illustrates this point is my sister, who wanted to become a veterinarian and chose to take several science classes, including biology and anatomy in high school. Thanks to these elective courses, my sister was able to **pursue** her major in animal science in college without hesitation because she was able to discover her passion and love for animals and **solidify** her dream of being a veterinarian in high school.

(소주제문 2) Furthermore, students in elective courses show greater interest in class material. (구체적 근거 1: 일반적 진술) **In support of this**, a number of studies have clearly demonstrated that when people, especially teenagers, are given the freedom to **make their own decisions**, they have higher levels of self-motivation. (구체적 근거 2: 예시) One particular study showed that students who were forced to **take classes** in subjects they had no interest in did not learn anything of appreciable value in these classes. They further stated that taking them was **a waste of time**. This study also showed that students who chose to be in classes demonstrated much enthusiasm and aptitude in them.

(요약/정리) **To sum up**, I strongly support the elective curriculum. **The reasons are that** electives allow students to better prepare for their professional lives as well as improve class involvement. (맺음말) **In general**, I wholeheartedly believe that these are the most important factors for students' successful futures.

Day 27

해석

내가 기억하는 한, 사람들은 선택 과목에 대비한 필수 교과 과정의 장점과 단점에 대해서 논의해 왔다. 개인적인 경험에 따르면, 나는 선택 과목이 많은 이점을 가지고 있다고 절실하게 느낀다. 내가 이렇게 생각하는 두 가지 이유는 다음과 같다: 선택 과목들은 학생들이 자신들의 장래 계획을 세울 수 있게 해주고, 보다 열심히 수업에 참여할 수 있는 동기를 부여해 준다.

우선, 선택적인 교과 과정은 학생들이 효과적으로 미래의 직업을 계획할 수 있게 해준다. 한 가지 중요한 이점은 학생들이 자신의 관심 분야와 관련된 수업을 들으면서 자신의 재능을 탐색할 수 있는 귀중한 기회를 갖게 된다는 것이다. 그 결과로 학생들은 보다 심도 있는 지식을 얻을 수 있고 그들이 고려하고 있는 직업 분야에 필요한 것들에 대해서 배울 수 있다. 이 점을 보여 주는 사람으로 내 누이가 있는데 누이는 수의사가 되고 싶어서 고등학교 시절에 생물학과 해부학 등 몇 개의 과학 수업을 듣는 것을 선택했다. 이러한 선택 과목들 덕분에 내 누이는 대학에서 망설임 없이 동물학을 전공으로 택할 수 있었다. 이는 그녀가 자신의 열정과 동물에 대한 사랑을 발견하고 고등학교 시절에 가졌던 수의사가 되고자 하는 꿈을 굳힐 수 있었기 때문이다.

더욱이, 선택 과목을 듣는 학생들은 수업 내용에 더 큰 관심을 보인다. 이에 대한 근거로, 몇몇 연구 결과에서 사람들, 그 중에서도 특히 10대들은 자신이 스스로 결정을 내릴 수 있는 자유가 주어질 때, 보다 높은 수준의 동기가 유발된다는 것이 증명되었다. 한 특정한 연구 결과를 통해 자신들이 아무런 관심을 가지고 있지 않은 과목의 수업을 듣도록 강요된 학생들은 이러한 수업에서 어떤 가치 있는 것도 배우지 못했다는 것이 밝혀졌다. 더욱이 그들은 이러한 수업들을 듣는 것이 시간 낭비라고 주장했다. 또한 이 연구 결과는 수업에 참여할 것을 선택한 학생들이 그 수업에 대한 열정과 소질을 더 많이 나타낸다는 것을 보여 주었다.

요약해서 말하자면, 나는 선택적인 교과 과정을 전적으로 지지한다. 그 이유는 선택 과목이 학생들의 수업 참여도를 증진시킬 뿐만 아니라, 직업에 대한 준비를 보다 잘 할 수 있게 해주기 때문이다. 대체적으로, 나는 이러한 것들이 학생들의 성공적인 미래에 있어서 가장 중요한 요소라고 진심으로 믿는다.

elective[iléktiv] 선택 과목 explore[iksplɔ́:r] 조사하다, 탐구하다 veterinarian[vètərənέ(:)əriən] 수의사
mandatory[mǽndətɔ̀:ri] 필수의 archaeology[à:rkiálədʒi] 고고학 pros and cons 찬반 양론 versus[vɔ́:rsəs] ~와 대비해서
in-depth 심층의 illustrate[íləstrèit] 설명하다, 예증하다 anatomy[ənǽtəmi] 해부학 concretize[kánkrətàiz] 구체화시키다
appreciable[əprí:ʃiəbl] 평가할 수 있을 만큼의, 인지할 수 있는 enthusiasm[inθjú:ziæ̀zəm] 열성 aptitude[ǽptitjùːd] 소질, 재능
end up 결국 ~이 되다 wholeheartedly[hóulhá:rtidli] 진심으로

---

① pros and cons ② mandatory ③ as follows ④ allow, to ⑤ explore ⑥ As a result ⑦ pursue
⑧ solidify ⑨ In support of this ⑩ make their own decisions ⑪ take classes ⑫ a waste of time
⑬ To sum up ⑭ The reasons are that ⑮ In general

Review

(도입) For as long as I can remember, people have been debating the ① p_____ of a ② m_____ curriculum versus elective courses. (대주제문) From personal experience, I strongly feel that elective courses have many positive benefits for students. My two main reasons are ③ a_____ : electives help students plan for their careers and motivate them to show greater interest in class.

(소주제문 1) To begin with, elective courses ④ a____ students ____ effectively plan for their future careers. (구체적 근거 1: 일반적 진술) An important benefit is that students have valuable opportunities to ⑤ e_____ their talents while taking courses that are related to their fields of interests. ⑥ A_____ _____, students can gain an in-depth knowledge and learn about the requirements of career areas that they are considering. (구체적 근거 2: 예시) One person who illustrates this point is my sister, who wanted to become a veterinarian and chose to take several science classes, including biology and anatomy in high school. Thanks to these elective courses, my sister was able to ⑦ p_____ her major in animal science in college without hesitation because she was able to discover her passion and love for animals and ⑧ s_____ her dream of being a veterinarian in high school.

(소주제문 2) Furthermore, students in elective courses show greater interest in class material. (구체적 근거 1: 일반적 진술) ⑨ I_____, a number of studies have clearly demonstrated that when people, especially teenagers, are given the freedom to ⑩ m_____, they have higher levels of self-motivation. (구체적 근거 2: 예시) One particular study showed that students who were forced to ⑪ t_____ in subjects they had no interest in did not learn anything of appreciable value in these classes. They further stated that taking them was ⑫ a_____ . This study also showed that students who chose to be in classes demonstrated much enthusiasm and aptitude in them.

(요약/정리) ⑬ T_____, I strongly support the elective curriculum. ⑭ T_____ electives allow students to better prepare for their professional lives as well as improve class involvement. (맺음말) ⑮ I_____, I wholeheartedly believe that these are the most important factors for students' successful futures.

Question

Financial loans between friends can harm or damage the friendship. Do you agree or disagree? Use reasons and specific examples to explain your answer.

친구에게서 돈을 빌리는 것이 우정을 해칠 수 있다는 진술에 찬성하는지 반대하는지를 밝히고 구체적인 이유와 예를 들어 대답을 뒷받침한다.

Outline

Agree*

1. Pursuit of money can make people disregard friendships
   돈의 추구는 사람들로 하여금 우정을 경시하게 만든다

   - people in materialistic society believe "money talks"
     물질 만능주의 사회의 사람들은 "돈이면 다 된다"고 믿는다
   - e.g. court cases deal with friends fighting over unpaid debts
     예) 부채를 놓고 다투는 친구들에 관한 재판

2. Loans from friends are not taken seriously
   친구에게서 빌린 돈은 심각하게 생각되지 않는다

   - borrowers care little about punctuality in repayment
     돈을 빌린 사람은 갚을 시간을 엄수하는 것에 대해서는 별로 신경쓰지 않는다
   - e.g. friend who neglected to repay my loan for almost a year
     예) 돈을 빌려가서 일 년 가까이 갚는 것을 꺼린 친구

Disagree

1. Friend in need is a friend indeed
   어려울 때 친구가 진정한 친구이다

   - friends are supposed to help each other
     친구는 서로 도와주어야 한다
   - e.g. had to borrow money to go to the doctor
     예) 의료 진료를 받기 위해 돈을 빌려야 했다

2. Going through a hard time together can solidify relationship
   어려운 시기를 함께 겪는 것은 우정을 돈독히 한다

   - create bonds and find out about real personality
     유대감을 형성하고 참된 인격을 알 수 있다
   - e.g. sister found out her friend was not reliable
     예) 여동생은 그녀의 친구가 미덥지 못한 것을 알아냈다

Model Essay

(도입) An **ongoing debate** exists over whether loaning money to friends can damage the friendships or not. (대주제문) Regarding this **controversial issue**, I strongly support the saying "lend your money and lose your friends." The reasoning behind my thinking is that the pursuit of money can make people disregard friendships. What's more, loans from friends are not seriously considered.

(소주제문 1) **To start with**, money can make people so selfish and greedy that even friendships seem meaningless to them. (구체적 근거 1: 일반적 진술) This largely results from the fact that people believe that "**money talks**." A main reason friends should not borrow money from each other is that when hard-earned money is not paid back on time, lenders become furious and **hold grudges against** borrowers, **regardless of** their friendships. (구체적 근거 2: 예시) **To show this point**, a countless number of court cases deal with hostile friends **fighting over** unpaid money. Lenders often **file lawsuits against** their friends who borrowed from them. In return, borrowers feel extremely betrayed and hurt by their cold-hearted friends who seem to value money more than their friendships. (마무리 문장) **In this respect**, money transactions among friends can unquestionably damage friendships.

(소주제문 2) Another reason is that loans from friends are not taken seriously. (구체적 근거 1: 일반적 진술) This is because relationships based on familiarity and fondness often cause borrowers to **take** the loans **for granted** and to care little about **punctuality** in repayment. **At the same time**, friendships make it difficult for lenders to become formal and businesslike when asking for repayment. (구체적 근거 2: 예시) In my own experience, when I was a freshman in college, my friend asked me to lend him two hundred dollars. Without any hesitation, I lent him the cash without any written agreement or payment plan because I did not want to cloud the friendly relationship. **Unfortunately**, my friend neglected to repay my loan for almost a year. Therefore, whenever I saw my friend, I started to feel bitter and doubted his trustworthiness.

(요약/정리) To conclude, I strongly believe that financial transactions between friends can damage relationships. The reason is that money can make people become blind with greed. Moreover, friends often delay in paying back the money. (맺음말) Consequently, I believe that the best way to solve this problem is by following the saying, "**he that lends, gives**."

해석

친구에게 돈을 빌려 주는 것이 우정을 해칠 수 있는지 아닌지에 대한 계속되는 논란이 일어왔다. 이 쟁점에 대해, 나는 "친구에게 돈을 빌려 주면 친구를 잃는다"라는 속담을 강력하게 지지한다. 내 생각에 대한 이유는 돈을 추구하다 보면 사람들이 우정을 경시하게 될 수 있기 때문이다. 게다가, 친구에게 빌린 돈은 당연시된다.

우선, 돈은 사람들을 지나치게 이기적이고 탐욕스럽게 만들기에 우정조차도 그들에게는 무의미하게 느껴진다. 이는 사람들이 "돈이면 다 된다"라고 믿는 사실에서 비롯된다. 친구들이 서로에게서 돈을 빌리면 안 되는 주된 이유는 힘들여 번 돈을 제때 돌려받지 못하면, 돈을 빌려 준 사람은 그들의 우정에 관계없이 격노하게 되고 돈을 빌려 간 이에게 악의를 품게 되기 때문이다. 이 점을 보여 주는 사례로 수많은 법정 소송들이 빚을 놓고 다투는 적의를 품고 있는 친구들을 다루고 있다. 채권자들은 종종 그들에게서 돈을 빌려간 친구를 상대로 소송을 제기한다. 그 결과, 채무자들은 그들의 우정보다 돈을 더 가치 있게 여기는 것 같은 매정한 친구에 대해 몹시 배신감을 느끼고 상처받는다. 이러한 점에서 친구 사이의 돈 거래가 우정을 해칠 수 있다는데는 의심할 여지가 없다.

또 다른 이유는 친구로부터 빌린 돈은 심각하게 여겨지지 않기 때문이다. 이는 관계가 친밀함과 애정을 기반으로 이루어진 것이기에 빌린 사람이 돈을 제시간에 갚는데 대해서 별로 신경을 쓰지 않게 되기 때문이다. 동시에, 우정은 빌려준 사람이 돈을 갚아달라고 부탁할 때 형식적이고 사무적인 자세를 취하기 힘들게 만든다. 내 경험에 따르면, 내가 대학교 1학년이었을 때, 내 친구는 나에게 200달러를 빌려 달라고 부탁했다. 나는 친밀한 관계를 얼룩지게 하고 싶지 않았기 때문에, 계약서나 지불 방식에 대한 논의 없이 나는 그에게 현찰로 망설임 없이 빌려 주었다. 안타깝게도, 내 친구는 거의 1년이 되도록 내 돈을 갚지 않았다. 그 결과, 나는 그 친구를 볼 때마다, 나는 기분이 상하고 그의 신용을 의심하게 되었다.

결과적으로, 나는 친구 사이의 돈 거래가 관계를 해칠 수 있다고 확신한다. 그 이유는 돈이 사람들로 하여금 탐욕으로 눈이 멀게 하기 때문이다. 게다가 친구들은 종종 돈을 갚는 것을 미룬다. 결과적으로, 나는 이 문제를 해결하는 최선의 방법은 "빌려 주는 사람은 그냥 주는 사람이다"라는 속담을 따르는 것이라고 생각한다.

ongoing [ɑ́ŋɡòuiŋ] 전진하는, 진행 중의 regarding [riɡɑ́ːrdiŋ] ~에 관해서 controversial [kɑ̀ntrəvə́ːrʃəl] 논쟁의 여지가 있는
Lend your money and lose your friends 친구에게 돈을 빌려 주면 친구를 잃는다 reasoning [ríːzəniŋ] 논거, 증명
disregard [dìsriɡɑ́ːrd] 무시하다, 경시하다 loan [loun] 빌려 주기, 대부금 take ~ for granted ~을 당연한 것으로 생각하다
meaningless [míːniŋlis] 무의미한 Money talks 돈이면 다 된다 hard-earned 힘들여 번 on time 시간에 맞게
furious [fjú(ː)əriəs] 격노한 hold grudges against ~에게 악의를 품다 court case 법정 소송 unpaid debts 부채
file lawsuits 소송을 제기하다 transactions [trænzǽkʃənz] 거래 unquestionably [ʌnkwéstʃənəbli] 의심할 여지 없이, 명백히
fondness [fɑ́ndnis] 애정, 기호 at the same time 동시에 punctuality [pʌ̀ŋktʃuǽləti] 시간 엄수
businesslike [bíznislàik] 사무적인 without any hesitation 아무런 주저 없이 written agreement 계약서 cloud [klàud] 더럽히다
trustworthiness [trʌ́stwəːrðinis] 신뢰, 신용 He that lends, gives 빌려 주는 사람은 그냥 주는 사람이다

---

① ongoing debate ② controversial issue ③ To start with ④ money talks
⑤ hold grudges against ⑥ regardless of ⑦ To show this point ⑧ fighting over
⑨ file lawsuits against ⑩ In this respect ⑪ take, for granted ⑫ punctuality ⑬ At the same time
⑭ Unfortunately ⑮ He that lends, gives

Review

(도입) An ① o_____ exists over whether loaning money to friends can damage the friendships or not. (대주제문) Regarding this ② c_____, I strongly support the saying "lend your money and lose your friends." The reasoning behind my thinking is that the pursuit of money can make people disregard friendships. What's more, loans from friends are not seriously considered.

(소주제문 1) ③ T_____, money can make people so selfish and greedy that even friendships seem meaningless to them. (구체적 근거 1: 일반적 진술) This largely results from the fact that people believe that "④ m_____." A main reason friends should not borrow money from each other is that when hard-earned money is not paid back on time, lenders become furious and ⑤ h_____ borrowers, ⑥ r_____ their friendships. (구체적 근거 2: 예시) ⑦ T_____, a countless number of court cases deal with hostile friends ⑧ f_____ unpaid money. Lenders often ⑨ f_____ their friends who borrowed from them. In return, borrowers feel extremely betrayed and hurt by their cold-hearted friends who seem to value money more than their friendships. (마무리 문장) ⑩ I_____, money transactions among friends can unquestionably damage friendships.

(소주제문 2) Another reason is that loans from friends are not taken seriously. (구체적 근거 1: 일반적 진술) This is because relationships based on familiarity and fondness often cause borrowers to ⑪ t_____ the loans_____ and to care little about ⑫ p_____ in repayment. ⑬ A_____, friendships make it difficult for lenders to become formal and businesslike when asking for repayment. (구체적 근거 2: 예시) In my own experience, when I was a freshman in college, my friend asked me to lend him two hundred dollars. Without any hesitation, I lent him the cash without any written agreement or payment plan because I did not want to cloud the friendly relationship. ⑭ U_____, my friend neglected to repay my loan for almost a year. Therefore, whenever I saw my friend, I started to feel bitter and doubted his trustworthiness.

(요약/정리) To conclude, I strongly believe that financial transactions between friends can damage relationships. The reason is that money can make people become blind with greed. Moreover, friends often delay in paying back the money. (맺음말) Consequently, I believe that the best way to solve this problem is by following the saying, "⑮ H_____."

Question

Do you agree or disagree with the following statement? Reading books about real events or people is more beneficial than reading fictional stories and novels. Use specific reasons and details to support your answer.

실제 사건과 실제 인물에 관한 책을 읽는 것이 가상의 소설을 읽는 것보다 유익하다는 진술에 찬성하는지 반대하는지를 밝히고 구체적인 이유와 예를 들어 대답을 뒷받침한다.

Outline

Agree

1. Reading fiction does not help your studies
   소설을 읽는 것은 학업에 도움이 되지 않는다
   - indulging in fiction takes up a lot of studying time
     소설 읽는 것에 빠지면 공부 시간을 많이 빼앗긴다
   - e.g. brother absorbed by fantasy novel failed his exams
     예) 판타지 소설에 빠진 남동생이 시험에서 낙제했다

2. Reading nonfiction helps you understand the real world
   논픽션을 읽는 것은 현실 세계를 이해하는 데 도움이 된다
   - current events and practical information
     시사와 실용적인 정보
   - e.g. newspaper reporting about war on the opposite side of the world
     예) 세계 반대편에서 일어나는 전쟁에 대한 기사를 보도하는 신문

Disagree*

1. Fiction improves readers' mental health
   소설은 독자들의 심적 건강을 개선시켜 준다
   - able to forget about their worries and realities
     걱정과 현실을 잊을 수 있다
   - e.g. reading fiction: positive way of looking at the world
     reading nonfiction: stressful, tiring
     예) 소설을 읽는 것: 세상을 긍정적으로 바라보게 함
     논픽션을 읽는 것: 스트레스가 쌓이고 지루함

2. Fiction develops creativity
   소설은 창의력을 길러 준다
   - readers experience a wonderful and mysterious world
     독자들은 아름답고 신비한 세계를 경험한다
   - e.g. reading The Secret Garden
     예) 비밀의 화원 읽기

Model Essay

(도입) Our society undoubtedly emphasizes "reality": real events, real people, and **established facts**. Despite this focus, or perhaps because of it, many people often want to **take a break** from reality, and love watching fantasy movies or reading fiction. (대주제문) I wholeheartedly believe that both currents need to be supported in our society. Thus, reading should not be limited to nonfiction. **Not only** does fiction improve readers' mental health, but it also develops creativity.

(소주제문 1) First, reading fiction **plays a key role in** improving readers' mental health. (구체적 근거 1: 일반적 진술) This is mostly because people can **relieve** their accumulated **stress** by forgetting about present worries and grim realities while **being engrossed in** a dreamlike world of fantastic and comical characters. Therefore, fiction can be light and easy reading for everyone, young and old alike. (구체적 근거 2: 예시) **For instance**, people who are depressed can escape their dark moods and feel temporarily lighter by reading happy fictional stories. A collection of funny short stories or a novel with an **uplifting ending** can provide humor and a more positive way of looking at the world. In contrast, reading nonfiction, especially newspapers, which **are full of** shocking and gloomy news, can be stressful and tiring.

(소주제문 2) Additionally, reading fictional stories **contributes to** developing people's creativity and stimulating their imaginations. (구체적 근거 1: 일반적 진술) An important factor is that authors of fictional stories, such as poems, romantic novels, and fairy tales, freely create make-believe characters and places in their flights of imagination. Therefore, readers experience a wonderful and mysterious world while reading fictional stories. (구체적 근거 2: 예시) **From my experience**, when I was a freshman in high school, I read *The Secret Garden* by Frances Hodgson Burnett. While reading the book, which is about a friendship that forms in a mystifying mansion, I was able to use my imagination to **vicariously** experience the feelings of the **main characters**, and to create a vivid image of their world. If it had not been for reading novels, I would have not been able to have the inventive and creative mind that I have now.

(요약/정리) To sum up, I am totally **against the opinion that** people should only read nonfiction. The reasons are that fiction books improve mental health and enhance creativity. (맺음말) That is, I believe that reading fiction is to the mind **what exercise is to the body**. In other words, fiction is truly beneficial for people's minds.

해석

우리 사회는 의심할 여지 없이 실제 사건, 실제 인물과 기정 사실과 같은 "현실"을 강조한다. 이러한 현실에 대한 집중에도 불구하고, 어쩌면 아마도 이 때문에, 많은 이들이 종종 현실로부터 휴식을 취하고 싶어하고 판타지 영화나 소설을 읽는 것을 즐긴다. 나는 진심으로 두 가지의 경향이 모두 우리 사회에서 지지되어야 할 필요가 있다고 믿는다. 따라서 독서는 논픽션을 읽는 것으로 한정되어서는 안 된다. 소설은 독자의 정신적 건강을 개선할 뿐만 아니라 창조성을 발전시킨다.

첫째로, 소설을 읽는 것은 독자의 정신적 건강을 개선하는 데 중추적인 역할을 한다. 이는 주로 사람들이 꿈과 같은 환상 세계와 우스꽝스러운 등장인물에 열중해 있는 동안, 현재의 걱정과 냉혹한 현실을 잊음으로써 축적된 스트레스를 해소할 수 있기 때문이다. 따라서 소설은 젊은 사람이나 나이든 사람 모두에게 똑같이 가볍고 쉬운 읽을 거리가 되어줄 수 있다. 예를 들면, 우울한 사람들은 행복한 소설을 읽으면서 우울한 기분을 벗어나서 일시적으로 경쾌함을 느낄 수 있다. 익살스러운 단편 모음집이나 해피엔딩으로 이어지는 소설들은 유머를 제공하고 세상을 향한 보다 긍정적인 방식을 제시할 수 있다. 대조적으로, 특히 신문과 같은 충격적이고 우울한 소식들로 가득찬 논픽션을 읽는 것은 스트레스와 피로를 줄 수 있다.

게다가, 소설을 읽는 것은 사람들의 창조성을 계발하고 상상력을 자극하는 데 기여한다. 중요한 요인은 시, 로맨스 소설, 동화와 같은 소설의 작가들은 그들의 상상의 나래 속의 가상의 등장인물과 장소들을 자유롭게 창조한다는 것이다. 따라서, 독자들은 이러한 작품들을 읽는 동안, 아름답고 신비스러운 세계를 경험한다. 나의 경험에 따르면, 내가 고등학교 신입생이었을 때, 나는 프랜시스 버넷의 비밀의 화원을 읽었다. 신비한 저택에서 벌어지는 우정에 관한 그 책을 읽으면서, 나는 주인공들의 감정을 대신 경험하고 이들의 세계의 모습을 생생하게 그려보는 데 상상력을 이용할 수 있었다. 소설을 읽지 않았다면, 나는 지금처럼 독창적이고 창조적인 감성을 지니지 못했을 것이다.

요약하자면, 나는 사람들이 논픽션만 읽어야 한다는 의견에 전적으로 반대한다. 그 이유는 소설책이 정서적인 건강을 개선하고 창조성을 증대하기 때문이다. 즉, 나는 소설을 읽는 것과 정신의 관계는 운동과 신체의 관계와 같다고 믿는다. 다시 말해, 소설은 진실로 사람들의 정신에 유익하다.

---

undoubtedly [ʌndáutidli] 의심할 여지 없이   established facts 기정 사실   wholeheartedly [hóulháːrtidli] 진심으로, 진지하게
play a key role 중추적인 역할을 하다   accumulated [əkjúːmjulèit] 쌓인, 축적된   grim [grim] 냉혹한
be engrossed in ~ ~에 집중하다, 열중하다   temporarily [tèmpərέ (ː) rəli] 일시적으로, 잠깐
uplifting [ʌplíftiŋ] 사기를 높이는, 격려가 되는   nonfiction [nɑnfíkʃən] 논픽션(소설이나 허구의 이야기가 아닌 전기, 역사, 사건 기록 따위)
contribute to ~ ~에 기여하다   fairy tale 동화   make-believe 가공의, 가상의
vicariously [vaikέ (ː) əriəsli] 상상하여 느껴, 대신하여   vivid [vívid] 생생한, 선명한
A is to B what C is to D A의 B에 대한 관계는 C의 D에 대한 관계와 같다

---

① established facts ② take a break ③ Not only ④ plays a key role in ⑤ relieve, stress
⑥ being engrossed in ⑦ For instance ⑧ uplifting ending ⑨ are full of ⑩ contributes to
⑪ From my experience ⑫ vicariously ⑬ main characters ⑭ against the opinion that
⑮ what exercise is to the body

Review

(도입) Our society undoubtedly emphasizes "reality": real events, real people, and ① e_____ . Despite this focus, or perhaps because of it, many people often want to ② t_____ from reality, and love watching fantasy movies or reading fiction. (대주제문) I wholeheartedly believe that both currents need to be supported in our society. Thus, reading should not be limited to nonfiction. ③ N_____ does fiction improve readers' mental health, but it also develops creativity.

(소주제문 1) First, reading fiction ④ p_____ improving readers' mental health. (구체적 근거 1: 일반적 진술) This is mostly because people can ⑤ r_____ their accumulated _____ by forgetting about present worries and grim realities while ⑥ b_____ a dreamlike world of fantastic and comical characters. Therefore, fiction can be light and easy reading for everyone, young and old alike. (구체적 근거 2: 예시) ⑦ F_____ , people who are depressed can escape their dark moods and feel temporarily lighter by reading happy fictional stories. A collection of funny short stories or a novel with an ⑧ u_____ can provide humor and a more positive way of looking at the world. In contrast, reading nonfiction, especially newspapers, which ⑨ a_____ shocking and gloomy news, can be stressful and tiring.

(소주제문 2) Additionally, reading fictional stories ⑩ c_____ developing people's creativity and stimulating their imaginations. (구체적 근거 1: 일반적 진술) An important factor is that authors of fictional stories, such as poems, romantic novels, and fairy tales, freely create make-believe characters and places in their flights of imagination. Therefore, readers experience a wonderful and mysterious world while reading fictional stories. (구체적 근거 2: 예시) ⑪ F_____ , when I was a freshman in high school, I read *The Secret Garden* by Frances Hodgson Burnett. While reading the book, which is about a friendship that forms in a mystifying mansion, I was able to use my imagination to ⑫ v_____ experience the feelings of the ⑬ m_____ , and to create a vivid image of their world. If it had not been for reading novels, I would have not been able to have the inventive and creative mind that I have now.

(요약/정리) To sum up, I am totally ⑭ a_____ people should only read nonfiction. The reasons are that fiction books improve mental health and enhance creativity. (맺음말) That is, I believe that reading fiction is to the mind ⑮ w_____ . In other words, fiction is truly beneficial for people's minds.

Day 30

Question

Do you agree or disagree with the following statement? Zoos serve no practical function. Use specific reasons and examples to explain your answer.

동물원은 아무런 쓸모가 없다는 진술에 찬성하는지 반대하는지를 밝히고 구체적인 이유와 예를 들어 대답을 뒷받침한다.

Outline

Agree

1. Require space and money for maintenance
   유지 보수에 있어 공간과 자금이 필요하다
   - can better use the space and money
     공간과 돈을 더 나은 데 사용할 수 있다
   - e.g. city that replaced zoo with museum
     예) 동물원을 박물관으로 대체한 도시

2. Harm animals
   동물들에게 해를 끼친다
   - suffer in captivity
     갇혀서 사는 생활에 괴로워한다
   - e.g. unnatural environment for polar bears
     예) 북극곰들에게 자연적이지 못한 환경

Disagree*

1. Play a role in educating people about animals
   사람들에게 동물에 대해 교육하는 역할을 한다
   - children gain hands-on learning experience
     아이들은 체험 학습을 할 수 있다
   - experience in 5th grade visiting the Seoul Children's Zoo
     예) 5학년 때 서울 어린이대공원을 방문한 경험

2. Protect endangered species
   동물원은 멸종 위기에 처한 종을 보호한다
   - provide animals with optimal conditions for survival
     동물들에게 생존에 필요한 최적의 조건을 제공한다
   - e.g. tigers in Korea
     예) 한국의 호랑이

Model Essay

(도입) Today, governments around the world spend a large amount of money developing zoological parks. (대주제문) **I fully support** this because zoos **have positive influences on** both humans and animals. That is, they not only educate people about animals, but also protect endangered species.

(소주제문 1) First, zoos **play a significant role** in providing people with a wide variety of educational opportunities. (구체적 근거 1: 일반적 진술) This results in great part because zoos allow people, especially **children of all ages**, to have the invaluable opportunity to gain active **hands-on experience** by closely observing diverse animal species, such as reptiles, birds, fish, and mammals. (구체적 근거 2: 예시) In my own experience, when I was in fifth grade, I visited the Seoul Children's Zoo. While visiting the zoological park, I **was exposed to** the fascinating world of wildlife by actually watching the animals **up close**, feeding and touching them, and attentively listening to their sounds. **In this way**, visiting zoos unquestionably broadens visitors' knowledge and understanding of the animals and their habitats. If I had not gone to the zoo, I would have had difficulty in understanding the **animal kingdom** in my biology classes in high school.

(소주제문 2) Furthermore, zoos save and protect **endangered species**. (구체적 근거 1: 일반적 진술) That is, zoos provide animals with optimal conditions for survival, including naturalistic habitats, nutritious diets, and **medical treatment**. Therefore, animals that are rapidly **vanishing from the wild** can be protected in zoos. (구체적 근거 2: 예시) The best example of this is the tiger in Korea. As the number of tigers has dramatically decreased because of poaching and habitat destruction, they are **on the verge of** extinction in Korea. Fortunately, zoos are combining efforts to save the tigers and increase their population by hiring nutritionists, zoologists, and veterinarians to keep the animals healthy and encourage them to breed.

(요약/정리) **As mentioned above**, I have no doubt that zoos are very beneficial to society. The reason is that zoos provide people with educational experiences, and animals with safe homes. (맺음말) On the whole, I believe that zoos can open doors for people to understand and love animals **on a deeper level**.

해석

오늘날, 전 세계의 정부들은 동물원을 개발하는 데 많은 돈을 지출한다. 나는 이러한 정책을 전적으로 지지하는데 그 이유는 동물원이 인간과 동물 모두에게 긍정적인 영향을 미치기 때문이다. 즉, 동물원들은 사람들에게 동물에 대해 교육시킬 뿐만 아니라 위험에 처한 종들 또한 보호한다.

첫째로, 동물원들은 사람들에게 매우 다양한 교육의 기회를 제공하는 중요한 역할을 한다. 그 이유는 동물원이 사람들, 특히 모든 연령대의 아이들에게 가까이에서 파충류, 조류, 어류, 그리고 포유류와 같은 다양한 동물의 종을 가까이에서 관찰하면서 적극적인 직접 체험의 기회를 허용하기 때문이다. 나는 5학년 때, 서울 어린이대공원에 갔던 경험이 있다. 동물원을 구경하며 나는 동물들을 코 앞에서 보고, 먹이를 주며 쓰다듬고, 그들이 내는 소리에 귀 기울이면서 흥미진진한 야생의 세계를 접했다. 이처럼 동물원을 방문하는 것은 의심의 여지 없이 동물과 그들의 서식지에 관한 방문객들의 이해와 지식을 넓혀 준다. 내가 만일 동물원에 가지 않았더라면 고등학교 생물학 시간에 동물계를 이해하는데 어려움을 겪었을 것이다.

게다가 동물원은 위험에 처한 동식물 종들을 지키고 보호한다. 즉, 동물원은 동물들에게 자연적인 서식지, 영양이 풍부한 식단, 치료 등 생존에 알맞은 최적의 조건을 제공한다. 따라서 야생에서 급속히 사라져 가고 있는 동물들이 동물원에서 보호받을 수 있다. 이것의 가장 좋은 예는 한국의 호랑이이다. 밀렵과 서식지 파괴 때문에 호랑이의 숫자가 급감하면서 한국에서 그들은 멸종 위기에 처하게 되었다. 다행히, 동물원들은 호랑이들을 보호하고 수를 늘리기 위해 영양사, 동물학자, 수의사들을 고용하여 동물들의 건강을 유지하고 번식을 장려하고 있다.

위에서 언급한 바와 같이, 나는 동물원이 사회에 매우 이롭다는 사실을 확신한다. 그 이유는 동물원들이 사람들에게는 교육의 기회를, 동물들에게는 안전한 보금자리를 제공해주기 때문이다. 전반적으로 나는 동물원이 사람들에게 동물들을 보다 깊이 이해하고 사랑할 수 있는 길을 열어줄 수 있다고 믿는다.

zoological park 동물원   have an influence on ~ ~에 영향을 끼치다   endangered species 멸종 위기에 처한 동식물의 종
result in ~ 귀착하다, 끝나다   children of all ages 모든 연령대의 아동   hands-on experience 실제 체험
reptile[réptil] 파충류   mammal[mǽməl] 포유동물   be exposed to ~ ~에 드러나다
fascinating[fǽsənèitiŋ] 매혹적인, 아주 재미있는   wildlife[wáildlàif] 야생 생물   up close 바로 가까이서
attentively[əténtivli] 주의 깊게   unquestionably[ʌnkwéstʃənəbli] 의심할 나위 없이   animal kingdom 동물계
provide A with B A에게 B를 제공하다   optimal[áptəməl] 최적의   naturalistic[nætʃərəlístik] 자연주의적인
habitat[hǽbitæt] 서식지   vanish[vǽniʃ] 사라지다   poach[poutʃ] 밀렵   destruction[distrʌ́kʃən] 파괴
on the verge of ~ ~하기 직전에, ~에 직면하여   extinction[ikstíŋkʃən] 멸종   veterinarian[vètərənέ(:)əriən] 수의사
breed[briːd] 번식하다

① I fully support   ② have positive influences on   ③ play a significant role   ④ children of all ages
⑤ hands-on experience   ⑥ was exposed to   ⑦ up close   ⑧ In this way   ⑨ animal kingdom
⑩ endangered species   ⑪ medical treatment   ⑫ vanishing from the wild   ⑬ on the verge of
⑭ As mentioned above   ⑮ on a deeper level

Review

(도입) Today, governments around the world spend a large amount of money developing zoological parks. (대주제문) ① I_____ this because zoos ② h_____ both humans and animals. That is, they not only educate people about animals, but also protect endangered species.

(소주제문 1) First, zoos ③ p_____ in providing people with a wide variety of educational opportunities. (구체적 근거 1: 일반적 진술) This results in great part because zoos allow people, especially ④ c_____, to have the invaluable opportunity to gain active ⑤ h_____ by closely observing diverse animal species, such as reptiles, birds, fish, and mammals. (구체적 근거 2: 예시) In my own experience, when I was in fifth grade, I visited the Seoul Children's Zoo. While visiting the zoological park, I ⑥ w_____ the fascinating world of wildlife by actually watching the animals ⑦ u_____, feeding and touching them, and attentively listening to their sounds. ⑧ I_____, visiting zoos unquestionably broadens visitors' knowledge and understanding of the animals and their habitats. If I had not gone to the zoo, I would have had difficulty in understanding the ⑨ a_____ in my biology classes in high school.

(소주제문 2) Furthermore, zoos save and protect ⑩ e_____. (구체적 근거 1: 일반적 진술) That is, zoos provide animals with optimal conditions for survival, including naturalistic habitats, nutritious diets, and ⑪ m_____. Therefore, animals that are rapidly ⑫ v_____ can be protected in zoos. (구체적 근거 2: 예시) The best example of this is the tiger in Korea. As the number of tigers has dramatically decreased because of poaching and habitat destruction, they are ⑬ o_____ extinction in Korea. Fortunately, zoos are combining efforts to save the tigers and increase their population by hiring nutritionists, zoologists, and veterinarians to keep the animals healthy and encourage them to breed.

(요약/정리) ⑭ A_____, I have no doubt that zoos are very beneficial to society. The reason is that zoos provide people with educational experiences, and animals with safe homes. (맺음말) On the whole, I believe that zoos can open doors for people to understand and love animals ⑮ o_____.

HACKERS

TOEFL®

David Cho

해설집

www.goHackers.com

해커스 어학연구소

Hackers iBT TOEFL Writing

Possible Answers & Scripts

해설집

Hackers TOEFL Writing (iBT Edition)

초판 1쇄 발행 2006년 6월 10일
초판 4쇄 발행 2006년 9월 15일

저자 David Cho 언어학 박사/ 前 UCLA 교수
펴낸곳 (주)해커스 어학 연구소
펴낸이 해커스 어학 연구소 출판팀
주소 서울시 강남구 삼성동 168-21 석광빌딩
전화 02-3454-0010
팩스 02-563-0622
홈페이지 www.goHackers.com
등록번호 89-90700-21-3 13740
정가 19,500원

Diagnostic Test 🎧 *Track 1*

1. Note-taking

읽기 노트

- Early birds - productive 아침형 인간 – 생산적
  - 1. Time for constructive purpose 건설적인 시간 활용
    - – extra hrs for self-imprvmnt 자기 계발을 위한 여유 시간
      - → imprv. quality of life 삶의 질 향상
  - 2. Morning: productive 아침: 능률적
    - – no distraction: others sleep, quiet 방해 X: 남들 잘 때, 고요
      - → concentrate 집중 잘됨

듣기 노트

- Early birds - recent study 아침형 인간 – 최근 연구 결과
  - 1. Need 2 sleep for certain hrs, getting less is not healthy
    일정 시간 동안 수면 취해야 함, 적으면 건강에 좋지 않음
    - – get up early, go 2 bed early: gain no time 일찍 일어나려면 일찍 자야함: 시간 벌지 못함
    - – if not enough sleep → get sick 충분히 못 자면 → 병에 걸림
  - 2. Body's natural rhythm 생체 리듬
    - – some don't function well in morning 어떤 사람은 아침에 일이 잘 안됨
    - – tired, not get things done 피곤함, 일을 제대로 할 수 없음

Summary

The reading passage contends that rising earlier is a beneficial activity. On the other hand, the lecturer brings up several points that contradict this argument.

First of all, the lecturer argues that humans need a certain number of hours of daily sleep. Getting less is simply not healthy and will result in getting sick. Thus, night owls should not wake up earlier without going to bed earlier. This point directly contradicts the reading passage's claim that simply rising two hours earlier will improve the quality of all people's lives.

The other main point the lecturer makes is that people have different biorhythms. Some people are naturally early birds, and others are night owls. Getting up earlier for night owls makes them tired, low functioning, and is not beneficial for them. Thus, the lecturer points out that the morning hours are not more productive for everyone, as the reading passage claims.

In conclusion, the lecturer mentions some findings that show humans need a certain number of sleep hours every day. Other research indicates that humans have different natural rhythms which make some more suited to being productive in the morning and others at night. These findings contradict the reading passage's assertion that everyone should wake up two hours earlier to become more productive and concentrated.

해석 지문에서는 아침에 더 일찍 일어나는 것이 이로운 활동이라고 주장한다. 이에 반해, 교수는 이 주장을 반박하는 몇 가지 사항을 언급한다. 우선 첫째로, 사람은 일정한 시간만큼 숙면을 취해야 한다고 교수는 주장한다. (이 시간보다) 숙면을 덜 취하는 것은 건강에 매우 좋지 않으며 결국 병에 걸리게 할 것이다. 따라서, 올빼미형 인간은 더 일찍 잠자리에 들지 않는 이상 더 이른 시간에 기상하지 말아야 한다. 이 주장은 단지 두 시간 더 일찍 기상하는 하는 것이 모든 사람들의 삶의 질을 향상시켜 줄 것이라는 본문의 주장을 정면으로 반박하는 것이다.
교수가 지적하는 또 다른 점은 사람들마다 생체 리듬이 다르다는 것이다. 어떤 사람들은 선천적으로 아침형 인간이고, 다른 사람들은 올빼미형 인간이다. 올빼미형 사람들은 일찍 기상하면 피로해지고, 제대로 기능하지 못하며, 그들에게 이로운 것이 없다. 따라서, 교수는 본문이 주장하는 것처럼 모든 이에게 아침 시간이 더 생산적인 것은 아니라고 지적한다.
결론적으로, 교수는 인간이 매일 일정 시간만큼의 수면을 필요로 한다는 것을 보여주는 몇몇 연구 결과를 언급한다. 다른 연구 결과들은 사람마다 자연적인 생체 리듬이 달라 어떤 이들은 아침시간에 더 능률적이고 어떤 이들은 저녁시간에 더 능률적이라는 것을 나타낸다. 이러한 연구 결과들은 모든 사람들이 생산성과 집중력을 높이기 위해 2시간씩 일찍 일어나야 한다는 본문의 주장을 반박하는 것이다.

어휘 **quality of life** 삶의 질 **biorhythm**[báiourìðəm] 생체 리듬 **early bird** 아침형 인간 **night owl** 올빼미형 인간, 저녁형 인간
more suited to~ ~에 더 적합한 **assertion**[əsə́:rʃ*ə*n] 주장 **concentrated**[kɑ́nsəntrèitid] 집중된

스크립트 및 해석

Reading

"일찍 일어나는 새가 벌레를 잡는다"라는 속담은 인류 역사를 통해 되풀이해서 증명되었다. 현대 사회에서, 아침형 인간은 보다 생산적이다. 아침에 조금만 더 일찍 일어나도 건설적인 목적에 사용될 수 있는 시간이 생긴다. 사람들이 일하고 자고 먹는 것과 같은 기본 욕구를 충족시키는 시간을 합하면, 다른 활동을 할 수 있는 시간은 거의 남지 않는다. 많은 사람들은 자신의 신체가 필요로 하는 것보다 많은 시간을 잔다. 매일 아침에 2시간씩 일찍 일어나면 일 년에 추가로 깨어 있는 시간이 730시간에 달한다. 이 시간은 직업 생활에 도움이 되는 기술 습득이나, 하루를 준비하는 휴식 시간 같은 자기 계발에 이용될 수 있다. 이런 활동들은 전체적인 삶의 질을 향상시켜 줄 것이다.
아침에 일찍 일어나야 하는 보다 구체적인 이유들도 있다. 아침 시간은 주의를 흐트러뜨리는 일이 거의 없기 때문에 대체로 대부분의 사람들에게 가장 생산적인 시간이다. 아침형 인간은 평안함 속에서 계속 방해하는 것이 없이 일을 하거나 휴식을 취할 수 있다. 가족과 친구들은 아직 다행스럽게도 자고 있는 시간이기 때문이다. 따라서, 대답해야 할 질문도 없고, "그냥 수다를 떨기 위해" 전화하는 사람도 없다. 고요함 속에 둘러싸여 있는 것은, 텔레비전이 켜져 있지 않고 도로가 텅 빈 이른 아침에만 가능한 일이다. 그러므로 이러한 아침의 고요함은 아침형 인간들이 지속적인 방해 요인들이 주의를 산만하게 하기 전에 해야 할 일에 집중할 수 있게 해준다.

old adage 옛말, 속담 **constructive**[kənstrʌ́ktiv] 건설적인 **on a daily basis** 매일매일 **self-improvement** 자기 계발
acquire[əkwàiər] 획득하다 **distraction**[distrǽkʃ*ə*ns] 주의를 산만하게 하는 것 **blissfully**[blisfəli] 더없이 행복한

Listening

I'd like to begin by posing the question, are you early birds or night owls? Well, judging by how many are late to class, I can tell you for a fact that most of you are "owls." I am also pretty sure that your parents and teachers have been lecturing you about the benefits of an early start to the day, as mine did. However, recent studies urge us to rethink this assumption.
These studies point out the fact that humans need a predetermined number of hours of sleep daily, and getting less is not healthy. The people pushing you to get up at the break of dawn don't consider the fact that if you do, you must also go to bed earlier. In other words, you don't actually gain any time. And if you don't get the necessary amount of sleep for a long enough period, your body won't be able to cope, and your health will fail.

Maybe some of you have been at that point before, you know, getting sick due to lack of sleep?

Anyway, even if you do manage to get up for the supposed advantages of the quiet morning hours, it's still up for debate whether you'll benefit. You see, scientists have discovered that our bodies have natural rhythms. Uhm... Some people just don't function well in the mornings. It's actually in our genes! They have shown that some people hoping to get their work done before everyone else wakes find themselves groggy and unable to function. They often report regretting having gotten up so early, because they were tired for the rest of the day and didn't get anything done.

오늘 강의는 여러분이 아침형 인간인지 아니면 올빼미형 인간인지 물어보는 것으로 시작하고 싶군요. 여러분 중 지각하는 학생의 수로 미루어 볼 때, 여러분의 대다수가 "올빼미형"이라고 생각됩니다. 저 또한 그랬듯 여러분의 부모님과 선생님들이 아침에 일찍 일어나는 것의 장점에 대한 훈계를 여러분에게 많이 했을 것이라고 생각합니다. 하지만 최근에 발표된 연구 결과는 우리로 하여금 이러한 주장에 대해 다시 한 번 생각해 보게 만듭니다.

이 연구 결과에 의하면 사람은 매일 일정한 시간의 수면을 취해야 하고, 그만큼 수면을 취하지 못하면 건강에 해롭다고 합니다. 여러분에게 새벽에 일어나라고 강요하는 사람들은, 만일 여러분이 정말로 그렇게 하면 보다 이른 시간에 잠자리에 들어야 한다는 점을 고려하지 않습니다. 다시 말해서, 일찍 일어나는 것은 시간을 버는 것이 아닙니다. 그리고 장기간 동안 계속 필요한 만큼의 충분한 수면을 취하지 못한다면, 여러분의 몸이 감당해 내지 못할 것이고, 건강은 나빠질 것입니다. 아마 여러분 중에도, 잠이 부족해 병이 났던 사람이 있죠?

어쨌든, 여러분이 조용한 아침의 이점을 누리기 위해 간신히 일어난다고 하더라도, 그것이 이로운가 하는 것에는 여전히 논쟁의 여지가 있습니다. 사실, 과학자들은 우리의 몸에 생체 리듬이 있다는 사실을 발견했습니다. 어떤 사람들은 아침에 제대로 활동할 수 없다는 것이죠. 이 여부는 사실상 우리의 유전자에 달려 있어요! 어떤 사람들은 다른 사람들이 일어나기 전 할 일을 마치려고 하다가, 지치고 제대로 활동할 수 없게 된다는 사실을 과학자들이 증명한 바 있습니다. 이런 사람들은 종종 일찍 일어난 것을 후회한다고 말했습니다. 그날 하루의 남은 시간 동안 피곤하고 아무 일도 제대로 해낼 수 없었기 때문이죠.

> **lecture about ~** ~에 대해 훈계하다　**assumption** [əsʌ́mpʃən] 가정　**predetermined** [prídìtə́:rmind] 미리 결정된
> **at the break of dawn** 동틀 녘에　**cope (with)~** ~에 대처하다　**groggy** [grági] 비틀거리는, 매우 지친

2. 다음 진술에 찬성하는가 반대하는가? 영화는 한 나라에 대하여 많은 것을 알려 준다. 구체적인 이유와 예를 들어 대답을 뒷받침한다.

Outline

- Agree　찬성
  - 1. Movies show what values are important to a society
    영화는 사회에 있어 어떠한 가치가 중요한지를 말해 준다
    - reveal what a country esteems and looks down upon
      나라가 존중하는 것은 무엇인지 경시하는 것은 무엇인지 드러낸다
    - e.g. heroes and villains in Korean movies and American films
      예) 한국 영화와 미국 영화에서의 영웅과 악당
  - 2. Movies depict social structure　영화는 사회 구조를 묘사한다
    - portray gender, class, and race relations　성별, 계급, 인종 관계를 묘사한다
    - e.g. Indian movies vs. Swedish movies　예) 인도 영화 vs. 스웨덴 영화

Model Essay

Many people see movies as simple escapist entertainment with little redeeming value. However, movies reveal a lot about a society. By viewing them, people learn about a country's values and social structure.

First of all, movies give insight into what values are important to a country. Characters' actions show clearly what societies esteem and what they look down upon. For example, in Korea, family relations are very important. As a result, Korean heroes will sacrifice themselves in order to help other members of their clan. On the other hand, villains will be portrayed negatively as having too much personal ambition. In contrast, heroes in American cinema are often individualistic lone crusaders who succeed in realizing their own dreams. These films conversely depict weaker characters as lacking independence. Movies thus show very clearly what values societies hold dear.

In addition, movies reveal the social structure of a country. This is because they portray gender, class, and race relations. For instance, movies from India show arranged marriages, a majority of women as housewives, and a very pronounced class hierarchy among different castes and tribes. Contrastingly, Swedish films often show love marriages, women working outside the home, and a more egalitarian class society. In addition, the films show a predominately white society. Therefore, watching movies from these cultures gives viewers an idea about how these societies are organized. In other words, one can understand the different social relationships through countries' films.

Since movies mirror the country's values and social structure, they are a great way to learn about other places from the comfort of one's home. Few people have the opportunity to travel around the world, so in order for people to become better versed on the values and social structures of different cultures, they should watch foreign films. This method of global enrichment is both educational and enjoyable.

해석　많은 사람들은 영화를 보완적 가치가 별로 없는 단순한 현실 도피의 오락물로 여긴다. 그러나, 영화는 한 사회에 대해 많은 것을 드러낸다. 영화를 관람함으로써, 사람들은 그 나라의 가치와 사회적 구조에 대하여 배우게 된다.

첫째로, 영화는 한 나라에서 중요한 가치가 무엇인지에 대한 식견을 부여해 준다. 등장인물들의 행동은 사회가 존중하는 것과 경시하는 것을 명백히 보여 준다. 예를 들어, 한국에서는 가족 관계가 아주 중요하다. 그 결과, 한국 영화의 주인공들은 그들 가문의 사람들을 돕기 위해 자기 자신을 희생할 것이다. 반면, 악역은 야망과 같은 개인적 욕망을 지나치게 많이 가진 사람으로써 부정적으로 묘사될 것이다. 반대로, 미국 영화의 영웅은 종종 자신의 꿈을 실현시키는 데 성공한 개인적이고 외로운 개혁가로 나타난다. 이러한 영화들은 거꾸로 독립심이 부족한 인물들을 나약하게 묘사한다. 따라서, 영화는 사회가 소중히 하는 가치들을 명백하게 묘사해 준다.

게다가, 영화는 한 나라의 사회 구조를 드러낸다. 이는 영화들이 성별, 계급, 인종 관계를 그리기 때문이다. 예를 들면, 인도의 영화들은 중매결혼과 가정 주부로서의 대부분의 여성, 다른 카스트와 부족 간의 매우 뚜렷한 계급 제도를 보여 준다. 대조적으로, 스웨덴 영화는 종종 연애결혼과 집 밖에서 일하는 여성, 좀 더 평등적인 계급 사회를 보여 준다. 게다가, 영화는 압도적으로 백인 사회를 그린다. 따라서 이러한 문화의 영화를 보는 것은 관람자에게 이러한 사회들이 어떻게 구성되었는가에 대해 알려 준다. 다시 말해, 사람들은 그 나라의 영화를 통해 서로 다른 사회적 관계를 이해할 수 있다.

영화는 그 나라의 가치와 사회 구조를 반영하기 때문에 집에서 편하게 다른 장소에 대해 배울 수 있는 훌륭한 방법이다. 극소수의 사람들만이 세계를 여행할 기회를 가지므로, 각기 다른 문화들의 미묘한 차이를 보다 잘 알기 위해서는 외국 영화를 봐야 할 것이다. 이렇게 국제적인 식견을 기르는 방법은 교육적이면서도 유쾌할 수 있다.

어휘　escapist[iskéipist] 현실 도피(주의)의　redeeming[ridí:miŋ] 보충하는　esteem[istí:m] 존중하다　look down upon 경멸하다
clan[klǽn] 일족　villain[vílən] 악당　crusader[kru:séidər] 개혁 운동　conversely[kənvə́:rsli] 거꾸로
dear[diər] 소중히　pronounced[prənáunst] 뚜렷한, 현저한　hierarchy[háiərà:rki] 계급 제도
contrastingly[kəntrǽstiŋli] 대조적으로　egalitarian[igælitɛ́(:)əriən] 평등주의적인
predominately[pridámənitli] 압도적으로, 우세하게　verse[və:rs] 정통하다, 숙달하다

Integrated Section

기본다지기

I 노트 테이킹 연습

1. 읽고 노트 테이킹하기

Check-up   p.45

1.

> • Dine in residence hall – advantageous 기숙사에서의 식사 – 이로움
> > • 1. No waste of time 2 cook & clean 요리 & 정리에 시간 낭비 X
> > > → more time 2 study → 공부할 시간 더 많음
> > • 2. Socialize, enjoy eating 2gether 어울리고, 함께 식사

해석 많은 대학생들은 자신들이 묵는 기숙사 내에서 식사를 하기로 결정한다. 이는 매우 이점이 많다. 학생들은 요리를 하고 이후 정리를 하는 데 시간을 낭비하지 않아도 된다. 따라서, 그들에게는 공부할 시간이 더 많아진다. 게다가, 그들은 다른 학생들과 어울리고 함께 식사를 할 수 있다.

어휘 **dine**[dàin] 식사하다 **residence hall** 기숙사 **advantageous**[æ̀dvəntéidʒəs] 이로운, 유리한
clean up 뒷정리하다, 청소하다 **afterwards**[ǽftərwərdz] 후에, 나중에 **what's more** 게다가
socialize with~ (∼와) 교제하다, 사교하다

2.

> • Traveling w/ young children – not recommended 어린 자녀들과 여행하기 – 권장 X
> > • 1. Kids 아이들
> > > – physical hardship 육체적 고충
> > > – don't have good time or remember 유쾌한 시간을 보내거나 여행을 기억하지 못함
> > • 2. Parents 부모
> > > – can't fully enjoy 여행을 만끽하지 못함
> > > – attend kids' needs 자녀들의 바램을 들어줘야 함

해석 많은 부모들이 그들의 어린 자녀들과 같이 여행을 하지만, 이는 권장할 만한 것이 못된다. 어린이들은 종종 여행에 따르는 육체적 고충에 압도되고, 유쾌한 시간을 보내지 못하며, 심지어는 그들이 경험했던 것조차 기억하지 못한다. 반면에, 부모들도 여행을 제대로 즐기지 못한다. 종종 그냥 호텔로 돌아가 텔레비전이나 보기를 원하는 아이들의 바램을 들어주어야 하기 때문이다.

어휘 **recommend**[rèkəménd] 권하다, 추천하다 **overwhelm**[òuvərhwélm] 압도하다, 질리게 하다
hardship[háːrdʃip] 고충, 곤란 **on the other hand** 반면에 **attend to~** ∼에 귀를 기울이다, ∼에 정성을 들이다
needs[niːdz] 욕구, 필요로 하는 것

3.

> - Processed foods – should avoid 가공 식품 – 피해야 함
>   - 1. Dangerous to health 건강에 위험
>   - – cause disease 질병을 유발
>   - ← additives, preservatives ← 첨가제, 방부제
>   - 2. Overweight 과체중
>   - – empty calories, high fat 영양가 없는 칼로리, 고지방
>   - → obesity: No.1 cause of death in U.S. → 비만: 미국 사망 원인 1위

해석 비록 가공 식품이 값싸고, 편리하며, 맛있기는 하지만, 사람들은 이러한 식품의 섭취를 피해야 한다. 가공 식품은 건강에 매우 해롭다. 그 것들은 수많은 첨가물과 방부제 때문에 많은 질병의 원인이 된다. 그뿐 아니라, 가공 식품은 비만을 야기한다. 가공 식품은 영양가 없는 칼로리와 고지방을 함유하고 있어, 미국의 최대 사망 원인인 비만을 초래한다.

어휘 processed food 가공 식품 tasty[téisti] 맛 좋은 additive[ǽdətiv] 첨가물
preservative[prizə́ːrvətiv] 방부제 overweight[óuvərwèit] 비만의 content[kántent] 성분
obesity[oubíːsəti] 비만

4.

> - Hosting sporting events – benefits 스포츠 행사 개최 – 이점
>   - 1. Revenue from tickets, hotel, etc. 매표, 호텔 등의 수익
>   - : economy↑ 경제↑
>   - 2. Media attention 언론 보도 집중
>   - : tourism/public image↑ 관광업/대외 이미지↑

해석 월드컵이나 올림픽 같은 주요 스포츠 행사를 개최하는 국가들은 주로 두 가지 측면에서 이득을 얻는다. 첫째로, 입장권 판매, 호텔, 레스 토랑 등으로 벌어들인 수익은 개최국의 경제에 직접적으로 활력을 불어넣어 준다. 더구나, 개최국에 대한 언론의 집중 보도는 그 나라의 관광 사업을 촉진시켜 주고 대외 이미지를 고양시켜, 세계 무대에서 두각을 나타내도록 도와줄 것이다.

어휘 host[hóust] 개최하다, 주최하다 such as ~와 같은 revenue[révənjùː] 수익, 수입, 세입
tourism[túərizm] 관광 사업 boost[búːst] (경기를) 부양시키다 host nation 개최국
media attention 언론의 집중 보도 public image 대외적 이미지 prominence[prámənəns] 두드러짐
world scene 세계 무대

5.

> - Clean surroundings – beneficial effects 주위가 단정한 것 – 유익한 효과
>   - 1. Ez 2 study: easily find materials 학습 용이: 도구 찾기 쉬움
>   - 2. Help feel organized, ready 2 learn 정돈된 느낌, 공부할 마음가짐

해석 부모들은 종종 자녀들을 꾸짖으며 그들의 방을 정리하라고 시킨다. 비록 이것이 아이들에게는 쓸데없고 성가시게 느껴질 수도 있지만, 주위를 정리하는 것은 여러 유익한 효과를 지닌다. 무엇보다도, 단정한 방에서는 연필이나 책과 같은 도구들을 찾기가 쉽기 때문에 공부 하기가 더 편하다. 또한, 주위가 깨끗하면 정신이 정돈되고, 맑아지며, 공부할 마음이 생기게 된다.

어휘 scold[skóuld] 꾸짖다, 잔소리하다 unnecessary[ʌ̀nnésəsèri] 불필요한
burdensome[bə́ːrdənsəm] 성가신, 부담이 되는, 귀찮은 surrounding[səráundiŋ] 주위, 주변(의 상황)
neat[níːt] 깔끔한, 단정한 organized[óːrgənàizd] 정돈된

6.

> - Radar detector – harmful 레이더 탐지기 – 해로움
>   - 1. Allow ppl 2 speed → dangerous 과속 허용 → 위험
>   - 2. Encourage cheating mentality 부정 행위 심리 장려
>   : OK when not caught : 걸리지만 않으면 괜찮음

해석 많은 사람들은 그들의 차량 속도가 측정되고 있는지를 알려주는 레이더 탐지기를 차에 달아둔다. 이러한 장치들은 몇 가지 이유로 해롭다. 레이더 탐지기는 사람들이 과속을 할 수 있도록 해주는데, 이는 도로상의 다른 사람들에게 위험하다. 다음으로, 레이더 탐지기는 일단 걸리지만 않으면 과속을 해도 괜찮다는 부정 행위 심리를 장려한다.

어휘 **radar detector** 레이더 탐지기 **notify**[nóutəfài] 통지하다 **device**[diváis] 장치
for several reasons 여러 가지 이유로 **cheating**[tʃíːtiŋ] 부정 행위를 하는, 규정을 어기는
mentality[mentǽləti] 심리, 사고방식 **as long as~** ~하는 한

7.

> - Cross-cultural relationship – rewarding 다른 문화권 사람과의 관계 – 보람 있음
>   - 1. More open-minded 포용력 생김
>   - 2. Experience new things 색다른 체험
>   – new foods, games, holidays, etc. 새로운 음식, 놀이, 휴일 등

해석 가치관과 언어가 같기 때문에 같은 문화권의 사람들과 사귀는 것이 더 수월할지는 모르지만, 서로 다른 문화 간에 관계를 형성하는 것은 매우 보람 있는 일이다. 사람들은 다른 문화권의 친구들을 사귈 때 더 포용력이 생기는 경향이 있다. 게다가, 보통은 경험할 수 없는 색다른 경험을 할 수 있다. 예를 들어, 인생에 즐거움을 더해 주는 새로운 음식, 놀이, 전통, 그리고 휴일을 접하게 된다.

어휘 **rewarding**[riwɔ́ːrdiŋ] ~할만한 가치가 있는, ~할 보람이 있는 **cross-cultural** 다른 문화 간의
in addition to 게다가 **get to ~** ~하게 되다 **normally**[nɔ́ːrməli] 보통은
be exposed to ~ ~에 노출되다

8.

> - Grounding: not allowing to leave house 2 discipline – effective
>   외출 금지: 집밖으로 나가지 못하게 함으로써 징계 – 효과적
>   - 1. Painful → reflect on their action 괴로움 → 자신의 행동을 반성
>   - 2. Prevent more trouble 더 잘못을 저지르는 것을 방지

해석 어떤 부모들은 "외출 금지"로써 자녀들을 벌하는데, 이는 일정 기간 동안 아이들이 집밖으로 나가지 못하도록 하는 것을 뜻한다. 이것은 효과적인 처벌인데, (벌 받는 아이는) 친구들과 어울려 재미있게 놀지 못하고, 그것은 아이들에게 매우 고통스럽기 때문이다. 그렇게 되면, 아이들은 그들의 행동을 반성할 것이다. 게다가, 아이를 집안에 가두어 놓는 것은 자신의 잘못을 깨우치기도 전에 아이가 밖에 나가 또 다른 잘못을 저지르는 것을 방지하기도 한다.

어휘 **discipline**[dísəplin] 벌하다 **grounding**[gráundiŋ] 외출 금지 **punishment**[pʌ́niʃmənt] 처벌
painful[péinfəl] 고통스러운 **reflect**[riflékt] 반성하다, 곰곰이 생각하다 **consequence**[kánsəkwèns] 결과
furthermore[fə̀ːrðərmɔ́ːr] 게다가 **restriction**[ristríkʃən] 제한, 구속 **get into trouble** 말썽을 부리다
error of one's ways 잘못한 일, 실수

9.

> Arranged marriages – higher rate of success 중매결혼 – 높은 성공 확률
>> 1. Families 가족들
>>> – involved in selecting good mates 좋은 배필을 구하는데 관여
>>> – provide support 후원해줌
>> 2. Couples 커플
>>> – think they must make it work 결혼 생활 유지할 의지 강함
>>> – not divorcing looking 4 better mate 더 나은 짝을 찾기 위해 이혼 X

해석 여러 문화권이 연애결혼 추세로 옮겨 가면서, 중매결혼의 입지는 좁아져 왔다. 그러나, 최근의 연구 결과는 중매결혼이 성공할 확률이 훨씬 더 높다는 것을 보여 준다. 첫째로 가족들은 적당한 배우자를 정해 주고 결혼을 유지시키는 데 깊이 관여한다. 따라서, 그들은 이러한 경우에 다양한 형태로 후원을 해준다. 또한, 남녀 커플들은 결혼 생활을 반드시 유지해야 한다는 생각을 가지고 결혼하며, 실제로 결혼 생활을 유지한다! 그들은 만나기 힘든 천생연분을 찾기 위해 이혼하며 시간을 낭비하지 않는다.

어휘 love marriage 연애결혼 status[stéitəs] 입지 arranged marriage 중매결혼 decline[dikláin] 쇠퇴하다, 퇴보하다 invest[invést] (시간, 정력 등을) 들이다 elusive[ilúːsiv] (교묘히) 피하는, 잡히지 않는 Mr. Right / Ms. Right 천생연분

10.

> Space exploration – not high priority for ppl 우주 탐험 – 사람들에게 최우선 X
>> 1. Not interested 관심 없음
>>> – don't care about discoveries 발견에 상관 안함
>> 2. Money → 4 problems on Earth 돈 → 지구상의 문제를 위해
>>> – jobs, education, etc. 직업, 교육 등

해석 매년 우주 탐험을 위해 몇 백만 달러가 충당된다. 하지만, 설문 조사는 사람들이 우주 탐험을 최우선 과제로 여기지 않는다는 것을 보여 준다. 대부분의 사람들은 솔직히 우주를 탐험하는 것에는 관심이 없으며, 최근의 달이나 다른 행성에 관한 (과학적) 발견에도 관심이 없다고 말했다. 게다가, 많은 응답자들은 이 돈이 지구상의 문제를 해결하는 데 쓰여야 한다고 생각한다. 그들은 지속적으로 살아갈 수 있는 지구뿐만 아니라, 양질의 일자리와 교육 서비스, 의료 시설을 원한다.

어휘 space exploration 우주 탐험 allot[əlát] 충당하다 priority[praió(ː)rəti] 우선 순위 outer space 우주 공간 respondent[rispándənt] 응답자 health care 의료 sustainable[səstéinəbl] 지속할 수 있는

2. 듣고 노트 테이킹하기

Check-up 🎧 *Track 2*   **p.51**

1.

> Gardening – benefits 정원 가꾸기 – 이점
>> 1. Emotionally stabilizing & calming 정서적으로 안정감 & 차분하게
>> 2. Healthful, nourishing food 몸에 좋고 영양분 많은 음식

script Let me suggest gardening as a wonderful activity with many benefits. First, it's, you know, emotionally

Possible Answers & Scripts

stabilizing and calming to work in nature. In addition, growing your own vegetables ensures that you eat, um, healthful, nourishing food.

해석 저는 정원 가꾸기가 많은 이점을 가지고 있는 훌륭한 활동이라고 제안합니다. 첫째로, 여러분도 알고 있듯이, 자연 속에서 일하는 것은 정서적으로 안정시켜 주고 차분하게 해주지요. 게다가, 직접 채소를 재배하는 것은 몸에 좋고 영양가 있는 음식을 섭취할 것을 보장해 줍니다.

어휘 gardening[ɡáːrdniŋ] 정원 가꾸기 emotionally[imóuʃənəli] 정서적으로 stabilize[stéibəlàiz] 안정시키다
nourishing[nə́ːriʃiŋ] 영양분이 많은

2.

- Giving children allowance 자녀들에게 용돈 주기
  1. Learn how 2 save 저축하는 방법을 배움
  2. Become responsible in spending 소비에 책임감을 갖게 됨

script Uh, some people believe that kids should not get money unless they work, but I really believe that parents should give their children allowances. This helps children learn how to save. Kids also become responsible in their spending habits.

해석 어떤 사람들은 아이들이 일을 하지 않는 한 용돈을 받지 말아야 한다고 생각하지만, 저는 부모들이 자녀들에게 용돈을 주어야 한다고 확신합니다. 이렇게 하는 것은 어린이들이 저축하는 법을 배우게 해주죠. 또한 아이들은 자신들의 소비 습관에 책임감을 갖게 됩니다.

어휘 allowance[əláuəns] 용돈 spending habit 소비 습관

3.

- Take-home exam – not good 자택 시험 – 바람직하지 못함
  1. Goof off & cram later 게으름 & 나중에 벼락치기
  2. Ez 2 cheat ← work together 부정 행위 쉬움 ← 협동해서 품

script Hmm, I really don't think take-home exams are a good idea. They allow students to goof off all semester and then cram one night to answer questions. These exams also make it very easy to cheat, as students can call each other up for answers or, you know, work together.

해석 저는 자택 시험은 정말 좋은 생각이 아니라고 생각합니다. 이 시험은 학생들이 학기 내내 놀다가 시험 전날 문제를 풀기 위해 하룻밤 동안 벼락치기를 할 수 있게 해줍니다. 또한 이러한 시험들은 학생들이 서로에게 연락을 취하여 답을 얻거나 같이 시험 문제를 풀 수도 있으므로 부정 행위를 아주 손쉽게 해주죠.

어휘 take-home 학생이 집에서 하는, 숙제용의 goof off 빈둥거리다, 게으름 피우다 cram[kræm] 벼락치기 공부하다
cheat[tʃiːt] 부정 행위를 하다

4.

- Internship – valuable 인턴쉽 – 가치 있음
  1. Practical training, experience 실용적인 교육, 경험
  2. Gain confidence 자신감을 얻음
  3. Decide 2 pursue career or not 그 분야의 직업을 가질지 결정

script OK, internships are valuable for several reasons. They provide practical, hands-on training and experience in a field of study. This allows students to, let's just say, gain confidence in their abilities as well as decide if they, um, want to pursue a career in this field further or not.

해석 자, 인턴쉽은 여러 가지 이유로 매우 값진 것입니다. 인턴쉽은 해당 학문 분야에서 실용적이고, 직접적인 교육과 경험을 제공해 줍니다. 이는 말하자면, 학생들이 그 분야에서 직업을 갖고 싶은지 아닌지에 대해 결정할 수 있게 해줄 뿐 아니라, 자신의 능력에 대해 자신감을 얻게 해주죠.

어휘 practical[præktikəl] 실용적인 hands-on 실제의 pursue[pərsjú:] 종사하다

5.
- Overpopulation – not a problem 인구 과잉 – 문제 X
  - 1. <u>Enough resources & food</u>: just not distributed well
    자원 & 식량 풍족: 단지 제대로 배분 안될 뿐
- 2. <u>Low birth rate</u>: more children encouraged 낮은 출생률: 더 많은 자녀 두도록 장려

script Despite popular belief, overpopulation is not a problem in the world. One, there are plenty of resources and food for everyone, which are just not being distributed well. Two, many countries actually suffer from too low of a birth rate, and are encouraging couples to have more children!

해석 일반적으로 (사람들이) 생각하는 것에도 불구하고, (현)세계에서 인구 과잉은 문제가 되지 않습니다. 첫째로, 모든 사람을 위한 자원과 식량이 충분히 있으나, 단지 그것들이 제대로 분배되고 있지 않을 뿐입니다. 둘째로, 많은 국가들은 실제로 저조한 출생률 때문에 고생하고 있어서 부부들로 하여금 더 많은 자녀를 두도록 장려하고 있습니다!

어휘 overpopulation[òuvərpàpjəléiʃən] 인구 과잉 distribute[distríbju(:)t] 분배하다 birth rate 출생률

6.
- Carpooling – great 자가용 합승 – 탁월함
  - 1. <u>Save cost & envrmnt</u> 비용 절감 & 환경 보전
- 2. <u>Fun 2 commute 2gether</u> 같이 통근하는 즐거움

script Hmm, carpooling is a great activity. For one, it allows you to save costs on gasoline and save the environment by riding together in one automobile. Not only that, it's a fun way to, you know, hang out with other people by spending time commuting together.

해석 자가용 합승은 탁월한 활동입니다. 첫째로, 합승은 사람들이 자동차를 같이 탐으로써 휘발유 값을 절약하고 환경을 보전할 수 있도록 해줍니다. 그뿐만 아니라, 이것은 함께 통근 시간을 보냄으로써 다른 이들과 어울릴 수 있는 즐거운 방법입니다.

어휘 carpool[ká:rpù:l] 카풀하다, 합승하다 not only that 그뿐 아니라 hang out with~ ~와 교제하다, 친분을 쌓다
commute[kəmjú:t] 통근하다, 통학하다

7.
- Resident assistant in dorm – pros 기숙사의 조교 – 이점
  - 1. <u>Know & help students</u> 학생들을 사귀고 도와줌
- 2. <u>Confidence in leadership, prob. solving ability</u> 지도력, 문제 해결 능력에 대한 자신감

script So, today, let's examine the pros of becoming a resident assistant in a dormitory. It allows you to, um, get to know a batch of students well and help them with any concerns. Oh, in addition, you gain confidence in your leadership and problem-solving abilities.

해석 자, 오늘은, 기숙사의 조교가 되는 것의 이점에 대해서 알아보도록 합시다. 기숙사 조교가 되는 것은 많은 학생들과 가까워지고 도와주게 해줍니다. 게다가, 지도력과 문제 해결 능력에 자신감을 가질 수 있지요.

어휘 **resident assistant** 기숙사 조교 **pro**[prou] 이점 **batch**[bætʃ] 한 때, 무더기 **problem-solving** 문제 해결

8.

> ● T-F exam – not effective 진위형 시험 – 비효과적
> 1. Guess & 50% chance 2 be right 추측해도 맞을 확률 50%
> ● 2. Not test reading / writing 독해 / 작문 실력 평가 X

script All right, true-false exams are often students' favorites. This is not surprising, given how easy they are. For this reason, they are not an effective testing tool because students can guess and still have a 50% chance of being right. In addition, they don't test students' reading comprehension or writing abilities, and are thus not good markers of educational achievement.

해석 자, 진위형 시험은 흔히 학생들이 가장 선호하는 것이지요. 그것이 얼마나 쉬운지를 감안한다면 이는 놀라운 일도 아닙니다. 이러한 이유 때문에, 진위형 시험은 효과적인 측정 수단이 될 수 없습니다. 왜냐하면, 학생들이 추측만해도 맞출 확률이 50%나 되니까요. 게다가, 그 것은 학생의 독해나 작문 능력을 평가하는 것이 아니므로, 교육적 성과를 측정할 수 있는 좋은 지표는 아닙니다.

어휘 **true-false exam** 진위형 시험법, OX 테스트 **comprehension**[kàmprihénʃən] 이해 **marker**[máːrkər] 지표, 표시

9.

> ● Min. age of driver's license: 16 → 18 운전 면허 최소 연령: 16 → 18
> 1. Protect everyone's safety 모든 이의 안전 보호
> ● 2. Insurance rates↓ 보험료 인하

script Now, I know you're going to disagree, but I think the minimum age of getting your driver's license should be raised from sixteen to eighteen. Young people have the highest accident rates. They are reckless, careless, and simply bad drivers! Getting them off the road will protect everyone's safety. Furthermore, insurance rates will go down for everybody if these dangerous young drivers are not allowed on the road.

해석 자, 여러분이 반대할 것을 저도 알고는 있습니다만, 운전 면허를 취득할 수 있는 최저 연령을 16세에서 18세로 올려야 한다고 생각합니다. 젊은이들은 최고의 사고율을 보유하고 있습니다. 그들은 무모하고, 부주의하며, 형편없는 운전자입니다! 그들을 도로에서 몰아내는 것은 모든 이들의 안전을 보호할 것입니다. 더욱이, 이런 위험한 젊은 운전자들이 운전을 못하게 된다면 모든 사람들의 보험료가 인하될 것입니다.

어휘 **driver's license** 운전 면허 **accident rate** 사고율 **reckless**[réklis] 무모한 **insurance rate** 보험료

10.

> ● Taking medicine for small ailments 사소한 질병에 약 복용
> 1. Weaken immune system 면역 체계 약화
>   : more susceptible later 차후 더욱 취약해짐
> 2. Expensive 비쌈
> ● : body naturally cures w/ time & rest 몸은 시간 & 휴식으로 자연 치유

script You know, we live in a pill-popping society that encourages people to take medicine for any and every small ailment. However, this behavior, let's just say, weakens people's immune systems and makes them more susceptible to getting sick again. Not only that, buying medicine for illnesses that the body could naturally cure with time and rest is, well, expensive. The price people pay for their medicine is, hmm, too high for their bodies and pocketbook.

해석 우리는 가벼운 병에도 약을 복용하도록 권장하는, 약에 의존하는 사회에 살고 있습니다. 그렇지만, 이런 습성은 면역 체계를 약화시키고 다시 질병에 걸리기 쉽게 만듭니다. 그뿐만 아니라, 시간과 휴식을 통해 자연적으로 몸이 치료할 수 있는 병 때문에 약을 구입하는 것은 비경제적입니다. 사람들이 약을 위해 지불하는 비용은 신체적으로도 재정적으로도 너무 많습니다.

어휘 pill-popping 툭하면 약에 의존하는   take medicine 약을 복용하다   ailment[éilmənt] 병
immune system 면역 체계   susceptible[səséptəbl] 감염되기 쉬운   get sick 병에 걸리다
not only that 뿐만 아니라   pay for 지불하다   pocketbook[pákitbùk] 지갑, 재력

Ⅱ 요약 연습

1. 읽고 질문에 답하기

Check-up
p.57

1.
| Coffee – harmful   커피 – 해로움 |
| 1. Irritate digestive system   소화기 계통을 자극 |
| – cramping, pain   심한 복통, 고통 |
| 2. Addictive   중독성 |
| – irritated w/o coffee   커피 안 마시면 초조해짐 |

First, coffee ① upsets your digestive system. It can cause pain and cramping in your stomach. In addition, ② coffee is addictive. People can easily feel unstable without drinking it.

해석 많은 사람들은 아침에 커피를 마시며 하루 일과를 시작한다. 유감스럽게도, 커피는 사람들의 신체적, 정신적 건강에 해롭다. 첫째로, 커피는 소화기 계통에 자극을 주며, 심한 복통과 고통을 야기한다. 다음으로, 커피는 중독성이 아주 강하며 커피를 마시지 않으면 초조해지도록 만든다.

질문: 본문에 의하면, 커피를 마시는 것이 왜 권장되지 않는가?
답안: 첫째로, 커피는 소화기 계통을 상하게 한다. 커피는 위에 복통과 경련을 일으킬 수 있다. 게다가, 커피는 중독성이 강하다. 사람들은 커피를 마시지 않으면 쉽게 초조함을 느낄 수 있다.

어휘 physical[fízikəl] 신체적인   psychological[sàikəládʒikəl] 정신적인   digestive system 소화기 계통
cramp[kræmp] 심한 복통   addictive[ədíktiv] 중독성의   irritate[íritèit] 짜증나게 하다, 초조하게 하다
recommend[rèkəménd] 권장하다   unstable[ʌnstéibl] 침착하지 못한

2.

- Chocolate – beneficial 2 health   초콜릿 – 건강에 이로움
    1. Nutritious & contain vitamins   높은 영양가와 비타민 함유
- 2. Stimulate chem. → feeling happy   화학 물질 분비 촉진 → 기쁨을 느낌

Chocolate is very nutritious and ① <u>contains important vitamins</u>. Also, it makes the brain ② <u>release</u> <u>chemicals that cause happy feelings</u>.

해석 초콜릿은 여러 가지로 건강에 이로운, 맛있는 식품이다. 첫째로, 초콜릿은 영양가가 아주 높고 비타민 B, D, E와 같은 중요한 비타민 성분을 함유하고 있다. 게다가, 초콜릿은 두뇌에서 행복감을 느끼게 하는 화학 물질의 분비를 촉진한다.

질문: 지문에 의하면, 초콜릿은 왜 이로운가?

답안: 초콜릿은 영양가가 많으며 중요한 비타민을 함유하고 있다. 게다가, 초콜릿은 행복감을 유발시키는 화학 물질을 두뇌에서 분비하도록 촉진한다.

어휘 nutritious[nju:tríʃəs] 자양분이 많은, 영양이 되는   stimulate[stímjəlèit] 자극하다   secretion[sikrí:ʃən] 분비
chemical[kémikəl] 화학 물질

3.

- Children learning lang. early – fluent   조기에 언어 학습한 아이들 – 유창함
    1. Observe speakers & imitate   다른 사람 말 관찰 & 흉내
    2. Natural mental programming   타고난 지적 프로그램
- : learn grammar quick & ez   문법을 쉽고 빠르게 습득

First, children watch other speakers and ① <u>mimic the sounds they make</u>. Secondly, kids have ② <u>a</u> <u>natural ability to learn grammar easily</u>.

해석 연구 결과는 어린 나이에 언어를 학습하는 아이들이 언어를 유창하게 구사할 수 있는 능력을 획득하고 평생 지속할 수 있는 확률이 더 많다는 것을 보여 주었다. 이것은 아이들이 주변에서 외국어로 말하는 이들을 면밀히 관찰하고, 그들을 자유로이 흉내내기 때문이다. 동시에, 어린이들은 문법을 빠르고 쉽게 배울 수 있게 해주는 어떤 지적 프로그램을 지니고 있는 것처럼 보인다.

질문: 어린 나이에 언어를 학습하는 아이들은 왜 유창해지는가?

답안: 첫째로, 아이들은 다른 화자를 관찰하고 그들이 내는 소리를 모방한다. 둘째로, 아이들은 문법을 쉽게 배울 수 있는 타고난 능력을 가지고 있다.

어휘 attain[ətéin] 달성하다   retain[ritéin] 계속 유지하다, 보유하다   fluency[flú(:)ənsi] 유창함
imitate[ímitèit] 모방하다, 흉내내다

4.

- Wine – beneficial for health   포도주 – 건강에 이로움
    1. Relaxant: ↓anxiety & tension   이완제: 불안 & 긴장감 ↓
    2. Provide energy, aid digestion   에너지 공급, 소화 도움
- 3. ↓heart disease, cancer   심장 질환, 암 ↓

Wine helps you by ① <u>reducing anxiety and tension</u>. It also ② <u>provides energy and aids digestion</u>. In addition, ③ <u>it lowers the risk of heart disease and cancer.</u>

해석 포도주는 건강에 매우 이롭다. 우선, 포도주는 자극성이 적은 이완제이고 불안과 긴장을 완화시켜 준다. 포도주는 통상식의 일부로서, 신체에 에너지를 공급해주고 소화를 돕는 물질도 제공한다. 게다가, 포도주는 심장병과 암의 발병률을 낮춰 준다고 알려져 있다.

질문: 본문에 의하면, 포도주를 마시는 것의 좋은 점은 무엇인가?
답안: 포도주는 불안과 긴장을 덜어 준다. 또한 에너지를 공급해 주고 소화를 도와준다. 게다가, 포도주는 심장병과 암에 걸릴 위험을 줄여준다.

어휘 **relaxant**[rilǽksənt] 완화제, 이완제 **anxiety**[æŋzàiəti] 걱정, 근심 **tension**[ténʃən] 긴장
normal diet 상식 **substance**[sʌ́bstəns] 물질 **digestion**[didʒéstʃən] 소화 (작용), 소화력
heart disease 심장 질환

5.

- Standardized test – should be minimized 정규 시험 – 비중 최소화
  1. Measure only narrow aspects 한정된 부분만 측정
  2. Some students don't do well on test 시험을 잘 못 치는 일부 학생
  → can't predict performance or success → 성과나 성공을 예견 X

These tests only measure ① <u>a small portion of a person's analytical ability</u>. Also, some students ② <u>just don't do well on tests</u>. Therefore, test scores don't indicate how successful a student will be in college and life.

해석 정규 시험 성적이 대학 지원시 반영되어야 하지만, 그 비중은 최소화되어야 한다. 이러한 시험들은 한 사람의 추리력과 사고력의 일부분만을 측정한다. 더구나, 어떤 사람들은 단순히 시험을 잘 치르지 못하기도 한다. 결과적으로, 시험 점수는 대학이나 인생에서 학생의 성과나 성공을 예측해 줄 수 없다.

질문: 지문에서는 왜 정규 시험 성적이 대학 입시에서 많은 비중을 차지해서는 안 된다고 하는가?
답안: 이러한 시험들은 한 사람의 분석력 중 일부분만을 측정한다. 또한, 일부 학생들은 단순히 시험을 잘 치르지 못한다. 따라서, 시험 성적은 학생이 대학과 인생에서 얼마나 성공적일 수 있는지를 예측할 수 없다.

어휘 **standardize**[stǽndərdàiz] 규격하다, 표준화하다 **application**[æpləkéiʃən] 신청, 지원 **minimize**[mínəmàiz] 최소화하다
measure[méʒər] 측정하다 **narrow**[nǽrou] 한정된, 제한된 **reasoning**[ríːzəniŋ] 논리력
thinking ability 사고력 **portion**[pɔ́ːrʃən] 일부, 부분 **analytical**[æn̩əlítikəl] 분석적인
indicate[índikèit] 예측하다

6.

- Extended family – advantageous 대가족 – 이로움
  1. Spread parenting responsibility 자녀 양육 책임 분담
    - no sole burden on parents 부모에 모든 책임 X
  2. Kids benefit 아이들에게 이로움
    - relaxed atmosphere, more sources of love 편안한 분위기, 사랑을 주는 사람들이 더 많아짐

Firstly, ① parenting responsibilities are shared by many relatives, so parents don't carry the whole burden. Secondly, kids benefit from ② relaxed surroundings and more people around to give them love.

해석 많은 사람들이 더 이상 조부모, 부모, 자녀, 그리고 다른 친척들과 다같이 살지 않지만, 대가족 생활을 하는 것은 이롭다. 많은 친지들과 같이 사는 것은 자녀 양육의 책임을 분담해 주며, 핵가족에서와 같이 부모에게만 전적으로 부담을 지우지 않는다. 게다가, 아이들은 보다 편안한 분위기로부터 이익을 얻고 더 많은 사람들로부터 사랑을 받게 된다.

질문: 지문에 의하면, 대가족에서 생활하는 것의 장점은 무엇인가?

답안: 첫째로, 자녀 양육의 책임을 많은 친지들과 분담할 수 있어, 부모들이 모든 짐을 지지 않아도 된다. 둘째로, 아이들은 편안한 분위기와 사랑을 주는 많은 사람들로 인해 혜택을 본다.

어휘 **extended family** 대가족 **parenting**[pέərəntiŋ] 육아, 양육 **burden**[bə́:rdən] (의무, 책임의) 짐, 부담
benefit from ~ ~로부터 이득을 얻다 **nuclear family** 핵가족 **atmosphere**[ǽtməsfìər] 분위기, 환경
source[só:rs] 근원

7.
● | Esperanto: created lang. w/o country, culture 에스페란토: 특정국, 문화에 속하지 않는 인공어
● | - good 4 universal lang. – 공용어로 알맞음
| 　1. Neutral: equal, no one's mother tongue 중립적: 평등, 한 국가의 모국어 X
● | 　2. Ez 2 learn 배우기 쉬움

First, ① Esperanto is a good choice as a universal language because of its neutrality. It makes everyone equal because it's no one's first language. Second, ② you can learn Esperanto easily because it has a simple structure.

해석 에스페란토는 어느 특정한 국가나 문화권에 속하지 않는 인공어이다. 전 세계의 사람들이 공통어가 없어 좌절감을 느끼고 있는데, 에스페란토는 몇 가지 이유로 제2 공통어로써 선택되기에 적합하다. 첫째로, 그것은 어떤 특정한 국가의 모국어가 아니므로 모든 사람에게 공평한 중립적인 언어이다. 게다가, 에스페란토는 간단한 구조로 인해 배우기가 아주 수월하다.

질문: 본문에 의하면, 에스페란토는 왜 제2 공통어로써 적합한가?

답안: 첫째, 에스페란토는 중립성 때문에 공통어로 사용하기 알맞다. 에스페란토는 어떤 한 국가의 모국어가 아니므로 모든 사람들에게 공평하다. 둘째로, 에스페란토는 간단한 구조를 가지고 있어 배우기가 수월하다.

어휘 **Esperanto**[èspərá:ntou] 에스페란토(국제어) **belong to~** ~에 속하다 **common language** 공통어
secondary[sékəndèri] 2차적인, 부가적인 **universal**[jù:nəvə́:rsəl] 전세계의, 보편적인 **neutral**[njú:trəl] 중립적인
mother tongue 모국어

8.
● | Vegetarian diet – good 채식 – 바람직
| 　1. Healthful, fat↓ 건강에 좋음, 지방↓
● | 　2. Meat contains harmful substances 육류 – 해로운 물질 함유
| 　3. Not harm animals 동물들에게 해를 가하지 X
● | 　– animal cruelty↓ 동물 학대↓

First, ① a vegetarian diet is healthful and low in fat. Secondly, ② meat often contains harmful substances like growth hormones. Lastly, ③ being vegetarian ensures that we are not harming or being cruel to animals.

해석 비록 육식이 널리 인기 있는 것은 사실이지만, 채식이 여러 가지 이유로 바람직하다. 첫째로, 채식은 건강에 좋고 포화 지방이 적다. 게다가, 오늘날 우리가 섭취하는 많은 동물에는 사람이 섭취하면 유해한 많은 성장 호르몬과 기타의 독성 물질들이 투여된다. 다음으로, 채식은 우리가 동물들을 해치지 않는다는 것을 보장한다. 많은 닭과 소가 육류업계에 의해 무자비한 환경에서 사육된다. 따라서, 채식은 동물 학대를 감소시킨다.

질문: 본문에 따르면, 채식의 이점은 무엇인가?

답안: 첫째로, 채식은 건강에 좋고 지방 함유량이 적다. 둘째로, 육류는 종종 성장 호르몬 같은 해로운 물질을 함유하고 있다. 마지막으로, 채식주의자가 되는 것은 우리가 동물들에게 해를 끼치거나 학대하지 않는다는 것을 보장해 준다.

어휘 vegetarian diet 채식 saturated fat 포화 지방 growth hormone 성장 호르몬
toxic[táksik] 유독한 substance[sʌ́bstəns] 물질 consumption[kənsʌ́mpʃən] 소비, 섭취
inhumane[ìnhjuːméin] 무자비한, 잔인한 animal cruelty 동물 학대

9.

> • Group psych: ppl think & act diff. in groups 군중 심리: 집단 내에서 다르게 생각 & 행동
>   - lose individuality 4 group 개성을 잃고 집단에 편승
> •   1. Negative: emphasized 부정적 측면: 강조됨
>   - violent behavior, riots 난폭한 행동, 폭동
> •   2. Positive 긍정적
>   - excitement / anticipation @ concert, party, election rally
> •   콘서트, 파티, 선거 운동에서의 흥분 혹은 기대감

Negative effects of group psychology include ① violent behavior, such as rioting, which would be abnormal for individuals acting alone. Positive aspects, on the other hand, ② are being influenced by a crowd's excitement at a concert or party.

해석 군중 심리학은 사람들이 집단 내에 있을 때는 혼자 있을 때와 다르게 생각하고 행동한다고 이론화한다. 즉, 군중 내의 개인이 각자의 개인으로서의 개념을 잃어버리고 집단에 편승할 수도 있다는 것이다. 종종, 군중 심리학의 부정적인 측면이 강조되곤 한다. 그러한 부정적인 영향들은 어떤 한 개인이 하기에는 비정상적일 수도 있는, 폭동과 같은 폭력 행위를 포함한다. 군중은 또한 긍정적으로 될 수도 있는데, 콘서트, 파티, 또는 선거 운동에서 한 개인이 군중의 흥분이나 기대감에 전염될 수도 있는 경우가 그러하다.

질문: 군중 심리의 부정적인 측면과 긍정적인 측면은 무엇인가?

답안: 군중 심리의 부정적인 측면은 폭동과 같이 개개인이 행동하기에는 비정상적일 수 있는 난폭한 행동을 포함한다. 이에 반해, 긍정적인 측면으로는 콘서트나 파티에서 군중의 흥분에 감화되는 것이 있다.

어휘 group psychology 군중 심리학 theorize[θí(ː)əràiz] 이론을 세우다. 이론화하다 that is 말하자면
individuality[ìndəvìdʒuǽləti] 개성, 특성 in favor of~ ~에 편들어, ~에 찬성하여 riot[ráiət] 폭동, 소동
emphasize[émfəsáiz] 강조하다 entity[éntəti] 본체, 실체 infect[infékt] 영향을 미치다
anticipation[æntìsəpéiʃən] 기대, 희망

10.

> Mobile phone – detrimental 휴대폰 – 해로움
> 　1. No privacy: can't fully concentrate, interrupted 사생활 X: 제대로 집중 X, 방해
> 　2. Public places: interrupted by ringing, conversat. 공공장소: 벨소리와 대화로 방해
> 　　→ noise pollution → 소음 공해

① People have no privacy and can't fully concentrate because they are constantly interrupted. ② Also, in public places, mobile phones cause noise pollution when they ring or people have loud conversations.

해석　휴대폰은 몇 가지 이유로 사실상 해롭다. 첫째로, 휴대폰은 사람들이 항시 연락을 받게 해 사생활을 전혀 허락하지 않는다. 이것은 사람들이 하고 있는 일에 제대로 집중할 수 없고 항상 방해를 받는다는 것을 뜻한다. 둘째로, 대중교통을 이용할 때나, 공연을 보러갈 때, 사람들은 울려대는 전화와 크게 떠드는 사적인 대화로 인해 항상 방해를 받는다.
　　　질문: 본문에 따르면, 휴대폰은 왜 이롭지 않은가?
　　　답안: 사람들은 항상 방해를 받기 때문에 사생활이 없으며 제대로 집중할 수가 없다. 또한, 공공장소에서 전화벨이 울려대거나 사람들이 크게 통화를 할 경우 휴대폰은 소음 공해를 유발한다.

어휘　**detrimental**[dètrəméntəl] 해로운, 불리한　**at all times** 늘, 언제나　**interrupt**[ìntər˄pt] 저지하다, 가로막다
　　　public transportation 대중교통　**annoying**[ənɔ́iiŋ] 성가신, 귀찮은　**noise pollution** 소음 공해

---

2. 듣고 질문에 답하기

Check-up　🎧 **Track 3**　　　　　　　　　　　　　　　　　　　　　　　　p.63

1.

> Pet – important 애완동물 – 중요
> 　1. Companion: ↓ loneliness 친구: 외로움↓
> 　2. ppl learn to be responsible and caring 사람들 – 책임감과 보살피는 법 배움

Pets make their owners ① less lonely and keep them company. Pets also teach their owners ② how to become responsible and take care of others.

script　Hmm, so let's explore the importance of pets in the modern world. You know, Westerners no longer live with their families or even with friends anymore. Pets therefore provide companionship and reduce people's loneliness. And you know what else? Pet owners learn about being responsible and caring for other living creatures.

해석　현대 사회에서 애완동물의 중요성을 알아보도록 합시다. 여러분도 알다시피, 서구인들은 더 이상 그들의 가족이나 심지어 친구들과도 같이 살지 않습니다. 따라서 애완동물은 친구가 되어 주고 사람들의 외로움을 덜어 줍니다. 그리고 또 어떤지 아세요? 애완동물 주인들은 다른 생물들을 책임지고 보살피는 법에 대해 배우게 됩니다.
　　　질문: 교수의 말에 의하면, 애완동물들은 주인에게 어떤 도움을 주는가?
　　　답안: 애완동물은 주인들의 외로움을 덜어 주고 그들의 친구가 되어 준다. 또한 애완동물들은 주인들에게 다른 생물들에 대해 책임감을

가지고 돌보는 방법을 가르쳐 준다.

어휘 companionship[kəmpǽnjənʃìp] 동료애 living creature 동물, 생물

2.

> - Cold: cold / wet wealther X, virus O 감기: 춥고 비 오는 날씨 X 바이러스 O
> - – indirect influence 간접적 영향
>   1. Stay indoor → catch a virus ↑ 실내 머무름 → 바이러스 감염 확률↑
>   2. Weaken body: resistance ↓ 몸을 약화시킴: 저항력↓

Cold weather can make us catch colds indirectly by forcing us to ① stay indoors and be close to infected people. It also makes us ② weaker and less resistant to viruses.

script You might think that cold or wet weather gives us colds. This isn't exactly true; cold or wet weather don't make us sick; viruses do. But cold weather often has indirect influences. It causes people to stay indoors more, where they're more likely to catch a virus from someone infected. And cold weather can weaken the body, making us less resistant to diseases.

해석 여러분은 춥거나 비 오는 날씨 때문에 우리가 감기에 걸린다고 생각할지도 모르겠습니다. 이는 정확히 맞는 것은 아닙니다. 춥거나 비 오는 날씨가 우리를 아프게 만드는 것은 아닙니다. 그것은 바이러스가 하는 것이죠. 그렇지만 추운 날씨는 종종 간접적인 영향을 끼칩니다. 추운 날씨는 사람들이 실내에 더 많이 머물게 하고, 실내에 있으면 감기에 걸린 사람으로부터 전염될 확률이 더 높습니다. 그리고 추운 날씨는 몸을 약하게 하여 질병에 대한 저항력을 감소시킵니다.

질문: 강의에 따르면, 추운 날씨와 감기에 걸리는 것의 상관 관계는 무엇인가?
답안: 추운 날씨는 감기에 걸리는 간접적인 원인이 된다. (추운 날씨는) 사람들이 실내에 머물게 하고 감기에 걸린 사람들과 가까이 있도록 만들기 때문이다. 또한 추운 날씨는 몸을 약하게 하고 바이러스에 대한 저항력을 감소시킨다.

어휘 indirect[ìndərékt] (결과, 관계 등이) 간접적인, 이차적인 infect[infékt] (사람에게 병을) 전염시키다, 감염시키다
resistant[rizístənt] 저항력이 있는

3.

> - Drinking moderately – benefits 적당한 음주 – 이점
>   1. Improve memory 기억력 향상
>   - grow new nerve cells 새로운 신경 세포를 자라게 함
>   2. Strengthen bones 뼈를 강화

Drinking moderately helps you ① improve memory by growing new cells in the brain. In addition, ② it makes bones stronger.

script Everyone knows that heavy drinking is unhealthy, but studies have shown that drinking moderately has its benefits! First, drinking a glass or two of wine a day may help to improve memory because drinking causes new nerve cells to grow in the brain. Also, it's been observed that drinking may help strengthen bones.

해석 과음이 건강에 해롭다는 사실은 모두들 알고 있지만, 연구 결과에 의하면 적당한 음주에는 장점도 있다고 합니다! 첫째로, 하루에 한두 잔 정도의 포도주를 마시는 것은 기억력을 향상시켜 줄 수 있습니다. 술을 마시는 것은 두뇌에 새로운 신경 세포가 자라도록 하기 때문 이죠. 또한, 음주가 뼈를 강화시키는데 도움이 될 수 있다는 사실도 알려졌습니다.

질문: 강의에 의하면, 적당한 음주의 이점은 무엇인가?

답안: 술을 적당히 마시는 것은 새로운 두뇌 세포를 자라게 하여 기억력을 향상시킨다. 게다가, 뼈를 강화시킨다.

어휘 **heavy drinking** 폭음, 과음　**moderately**[mάdəritli] 알맞게, 적당히　**nerve cell** 신경 세포
observe[əbzə́ːrv] 알다, 깨닫다

4.

| Adv. of digital media 디지털 미디어의 장점 |
| 1. Ez 2 store & find info 정보 검색 & 저장 용이 |
| 2. Clear, good quality 선명, 좋은 품질 |

It's easy to ① store and find information in digital media. In addition, digital media provides ② clear and good quality.

script So, uh, today let's explore the advantages of digital media. One, it's very easy to store information in this form. This also means that, you know, it's easy to find what you want. Last, digital media boasts very clear and, um, superior quality material.

해석 오늘은 디지털 미디어의 장점에 대해 알아보도록 합시다. 첫째로, 디지털 형태로는 정보를 저장하는 것이 매우 용이합니다. 또한 이것은 원하는 것을 검색해 내기가 수월하다는 것을 의미하죠. 마지막으로, 디지털 미디어는 아주 선명하고 우수한 질을 자랑합니다.

질문: 교수의 말에 의하면, 디지털 미디어의 장점은 무엇인가?

답안: 디지털 미디어로는 정보를 저장하고 검색하기 쉽다. 게다가, 디지털 미디어는 선명하고 우수한 품질을 제공한다.

어휘 **store**[stɔːr] 저장하다, 축적하다　**boast**[boust] 자랑으로 삼다　**superior**[sju(ː)pí(ː)əriər] 뛰어난, 우수한

5.

| Personal comm. better than e-mail 직접 대면하는 의사소통이 이메일보다 나음 |
| 1. Discuss in person 직접 만나서 논의 |
| – avoid misunderstanding 오해 소지 X |
| 2. Response right away in person 대면시 곧장 대답 얻을 수 있음 |
| – e-mail: take time 이메일: 시간이 걸림 |

Discussing in person ① saves you from possible misunderstanding. Not only that, in person, ② you can get a response straight away while e-mail takes time.

script E-mailing is a standard means of communication in today's business world, but there are still some reasons why personal communication should be used. Some business transactions may involve material that is best discussed in person to avoid misunderstandings. It is possible to get a response and reaction right away in person, but e-mail takes time.

해석 이메일은 오늘날 재계에서의 표준적인 의사소통 방식이지만, 아직까지 직접 대면하는 의사소통이 활용되어야 하는 이유가 몇 가지 있다. 일부 사업 거래에는 오해를 피하기 위해 직접 대면하여 논의되어야 하는 자료가 포함되어 있을 수 있다. 직접 만나게 되면 대답과 반응을 바로 얻을 수 있지만, 이메일은 시간이 걸린다.

질문: 강의에 의하면, 이메일과 비교했을 때 직접하는 의사소통의 장점은 무엇인가?

답안: 직접 대면하여 논의하는 것은 오해의 소지를 없애 준다. 뿐만 아니라, 이메일은 시간이 걸리는데 반해, 직접 대면시에는 곧바로 대답을 얻을 수 있다.

어휘 means[miːnz] 수단, 방법 business world 실업계, 재계 transaction[trænsǽkʃən] 업무, 거래
in person 직접 misunderstanding[mìsʌndərstǽndiŋ] 오해

6.

- Single-sex school – good 4 girls → false 여학교 – 여학생들에게 이득 → 사실 아님
  1. No academic imprvmnt over co-ed 남녀 공학 비해 공부 더 잘하지 X
- 2. Learn 2 interact w/ opposite gender at co-ed 남녀 공학에서 이성과 상호 작용하는 법 배움

A survey showed that ① girls in single-sex schools didn't do better than girls in co-ed schools. Also, it showed co-ed schools helped students ② learn how to deal with the opposite sex.

script So, uh, you might've heard that single-sex schools are beneficial for some students. In particular, they say, girls thrive at single-sex schools. But a recent survey showed that girls from single-sex schools didn't actually show academic improvement over girls at co-ed institutions. On top of that, the survey indicated that boys and girls learn, um, to interact with the opposite gender which helps their social development.

해석 자, 여러분은 남학교/여학교가 일부 학생들에게 유익하다는 것을 들어봤을 것입니다. 일반적으로, 특히 여학생들이 (남녀 공학이 아닌) 여학교에 다닐 때 더 (학교 생활을) 잘한다고 합니다. 하지만, 최근의 연구 결과는 여학교에 다니는 여학생들이 남녀 공학에 다니는 여학생들보다 실제로 더 공부를 잘하는 것은 아님을 보여 주었습니다. 게다가, 이 조사는 (남녀 공학에서) 남학생과 여학생들이 이성과 상호 작용하는 법을 배우고, 이것은 학생들의 사회적 발달에 기여한다고 지적했습니다.

질문: 강의에 의하면, 최근 조사 결과가 남학교/여학교에 대해 무엇을 말해 주는가?

답안: 설문 조사는 여학교에 다니는 여학생들이 남녀 공학에 다니는 여학생들보다 공부를 잘하는 것은 아님을 보여 주었다. 또한, 남녀 공학이 학생들로 하여금 이성을 대하는 방법을 배우는데 도움을 준다는 사실을 보여주었다.

어휘 single-sex school 남자/여자학교 in particular 특히, 그 중에서도 thrive[θraiv] 번영하다, 성공하다
co-ed(=co-educational school) 남녀 공학 interact[ìntərǽkt] 상호 작용하다, 서로에게 영향을 끼치다

7.

- Computerized testing – bad 컴퓨터를 이용한 시험 – 나쁨
  1. 4 unfamiliar/not proficient students → stressful 컴퓨터 익숙/능숙 X 학생들 → 스트레스
- 2. Costly 2 make & run test programs 프로그램 제작 & 실행 비용 높음
- 3. Problems in system → ruin results 시스템상 문제 → 시험 결과 망침

Students who ① are not familiar with computers find the test stressful, not to mention making and running programs is costly. Also, ② problems in the system can ruin results.

script   Um, computerized testing is not the best way to test students. Students unfamiliar with computers, or, uh, simply not proficient in using them, find computerized test taking stressful. In addition, it's very costly to devise and implement computer testing programs. Finally, you know what? Problems in the computer system sometimes ruin results.

해석   컴퓨터를 이용한 시험은 학생들을 평가하는 데 있어 최선의 방법이 아닙니다. 컴퓨터에 익숙하지 못하거나, 컴퓨터 사용에 별로 능숙하지 않은 학생들은 컴퓨터로 치는 시험을 보는 것에 매우 스트레스를 받습니다. 게다가, 컴퓨터 시험 프로그램을 고안하고 실행하는 것은 비용이 매우 많이 듭니다. 마지막으로, 컴퓨터 시스템상의 문제는 때때로 시험 결과를 망쳐버리기도 합니다.

질문: 교수는 왜 컴퓨터를 이용한 시험에 의구심을 제기하는가?

답안: 프로그램을 만들고 실행하는 데 비용이 많이 드는 것은 물론이고, 컴퓨터에 익숙하지 않은 학생들은 이런 시험에 스트레스를 받는다. 또한, 시스템상의 문제점은 시험 결과를 망쳐 버릴 수도 있다.

어휘   **computerized**[kəmpjúːtəráizd] 전산화된, 컴퓨터화된   **unfamiliar**[ʌnfəmíljər] 익숙지 못한, 경험이 없는
proficient[prəfíʃənt] 익숙한, 능숙한   **devise**[diváiz] 고안하다, 발명하다
implement[ímpləmənt] (약속, 계획 등을) 이행하다, 실행하다   **ruin**[rú(ː)in] 망치다
cast doubt on~ ~에 의구심을 제기하다   **not to mention~** ~은 말할 것도 없이, ~은 물론이고

8.

> - Lottery winners 복권 당첨자
>   - not more satisfied than non-winners 비당첨자에 비해 더 행복하지 X
>   1. Thrill of winning lottery dulls other experiences 복권 당첨의 흥분으로 다른 경험은 지루
>   2. Less pleasure from ordinary things 일상적 일들로부터 즐거움 적게 느낌

Lottery winners were ① <u>not happier than ordinary people</u> because ② <u>the excitement of winning makes ordinary experiences boring in comparison.</u>

script   Most of you are probably convinced that winning the lottery would make you truly happy, right? Well, you should know that research has shown... within a year or two of winning, lottery winners were no more satisfied than non-winners, and sometimes even less! This is partially because the thrill of winning the lottery dulls other experiences, by contrast. Lottery winners derived less pleasure from ordinary events that would make the rest of us smile... things like seeing a movie, eating out, or having coffee with friends.

해석   아마도 여러분 중 대부분은 복권 당첨이 여러분을 정말로 행복하게 만들어 줄 것이라고 믿겠죠? 그런데, 연구 결과에 의하면, 당첨된 지 1, 2년 이내에, 복권 당첨자들은 비당첨자들과 비교했을 때 (삶에) 더 만족하지 않았고, 심지어 이따금 그들보다 불만족스럽다고 했답니다! 이것은 부분적으로 복권 당첨의 전율에 대조했을 때 다른 경험들이 단조롭고 지루한 것이 되어 버리기 때문이죠. 복권 당첨자들은 평범한 사람들을 미소 짓게 하는 일상적인 일들에 대해 즐거움을 덜 느꼈습니다. 예를 들면 영화를 관람하거나, 외식을 하거나 또는 친구들과 커피를 마시는 것 같은 일들 말입니다.

질문: 강의에 따르면, 복권 당첨은 사람들의 인생을 어떻게 바꾸는가?

답안: 복권 당첨자들은 보통 사람들에 비해 더 행복하지 않았는데, 그 이유는 복권 당첨의 흥분이 대조적으로 일상적 경험들을 지루한 것으로 만들기 때문이다.

어휘   **convince**[kənvíns] 확신시키다   **win the lottery** 복권에 당첨되다   **partially**[páːrʃəli] 부분적으로, 일부분은
dull[dʌl] 둔하게 하다, 시시하게 하다   **by contrast** (~와) 대비하여   **derive**[diráiv] (이익, 즐거움 등을) 끌어내다, 얻다
ordinary[ɔ́ːrdənèri] 평상의, 보통의   **eat out** 외식하다

9.
┌───┐
│ ● │ Order in public presentation 대중 앞에서의 발표 순서   │
│   │ – best to present later 나중에 발표하는 것이 최선   │
│ ● │   1. Time 2 relax & focus 긴장감 늦추고 집중할 시간   │
│   │   2. Watch others: develop competitive edge 다른 사람들 발표 관찰: 경쟁력 계발 │
│ ● │   │
└───┘

A performer should present ① <u>later in a program in order to have time to relax and focus.</u> This also allows him to ② <u>see how other people do and develop his competitive edge.</u>

script When performing, making a speech, or giving some other nerve-wracking public presentation, it's very important to know what order to go in. Ok, many people like going first to get it out of the way and not get nervous watching other competitors. However, it's best to present later in the program. This gives you time to relax and focus. You can also, um, watch other participants to help you develop your competitive edge.

해석 공연을 하거나, 연설을 하거나, 또는 대중 앞에서 매우 긴장되는 발표를 할 때, (자신이) 어떤 순서로 할지를 아는 것은 매우 중요합니다. 많은 사람들은 먼저 하는 것을 선호합니다. 빨리 해치워버리고 다른 경쟁자들을 지켜보며 긴장하지 않기 위해서죠. 하지만, 나중에 발표를 하는 것이 가장 좋은 방법입니다. 이렇게 하는 것은 여러분이 긴장을 늦추고 집중할 수 있도록 해줍니다. 또한 여러분의 경쟁력을 계발하는 데 도움이 되도록 다른 참가자들의 발표를 지켜볼 수도 있습니다.

질문: 교수에 의하면, 발표를 하는 사람은 어떤 순서로 발표해야 하고, 왜 그렇게 해야 하는가?
답안: 발표자는 긴장을 늦추고 집중할 시간을 갖기 위해 프로그램의 후반에 발표를 해야 한다. 이는 또한 발표자로 하여금 다른 사람들은 어떻게 하는지를 보고 자신의 경쟁력을 계발하도록 해준다.

어휘 **make a speech** 연설을 하다 **nerve-wracking**[nə́:rvrǽkiŋ] 신경을 괴롭히는 **nervous**[nə́:rvəs] 겁내는, 불안한 **competitor**[kəmpétitər] 경쟁자 **present**[prézənt] 발표하다 **participant**[pɑ:rtísəpənt] 참가자 **competitive edge** 경쟁력, 경쟁적 우위

10.
┌───┐
│ ● │ Air conditioning – bad 에어컨 – 해로움   │
│   │   1. Destroy envrmnt 환경 파괴   │
│ ● │   : toxic gas, global warming 유독 가스, 지구 온난화   │
│   │   2. Make ppl sick 질병 유발   │
│ ● │   : lung infection, etc. 폐 질환, 기타 등등   │
└───┘

Air conditioning ① <u>emits toxic gases and adds to global warming.</u> In addition, it causes ② <u>lung infections and other sicknesses in humans.</u>

script As temperatures soar in summer, people are inclined to turn on their, you know, air conditioning to cool off and get relief. I have some surprising news for you. Using air conditioning is one of the, um, worst things you could do to the planet. It destroys the environment by releasing toxic gases and actually contributes to global warming. Air conditioning also causes people to get sick with, uh, numerous lung infections as well as chills and the flu.

해석 여름에 기온이 급상승하게 되면, 사람들은 온도를 낮추고 더위를 잊기 위해 에어컨을 사용하는 경향이 있습니다. (그런데) 의외의 사실이

하나 있죠. 에어컨을 사용하는 것은 지구에게 할 수 있는 최악의 행위 중에 하나입니다. 그것은 유독 가스를 방출하여 환경을 파괴시키고, 실제로 지구 온난화 현상에 일조합니다. 또한 에어컨은 사람들로 하여금 오한과 독감은 물론 수많은 폐 관련 질환을 앓게 합니다.

질문: 에어컨의 사용은 환경과 사람들에게 어떤 영향을 미치는가?

답안: 에어컨은 유독 가스를 방출하고 지구 온난화 현상에 일조한다. 더군다나, 그것은 폐 질환과 기타 질병을 유발한다.

어휘 soar[sɔːr] (온도 등이) 급상승하다 be inclined to~ ~하는 성향이 있다 air conditioning 에어컨
cool off 식다, 가라앉다 relief[rilíːf] (고통, 걱정 등의) 제거, 경감 toxic gas 유독 가스
global warming 지구 온난화 현상 lung infection 폐렴, 폐병 chill[tʃil] 한기, 오한
flu[fluː] 유행성 감기, 독감 emit[imít] (빛, 열, 향기 등을) 방사하다, 방출하다

실전익히기

Ⅰ 읽고 듣고 내용 정리하기

HACKERS Practice p.76

1. Note-taking

읽기 노트

Cancer – genetic factor 암 – 유전적 요인
1. Jap. men 일본 남성
– 7x ↑ stomach canc. than Amer. 미국인보다 위암 발생 7배↑
– 5x ↓ prostate canc. than Amer. 미국인보다 전립선암 발생 5배↓
2. Native Amer. 아메리칸 인디언
– lowest rate of any canc. 암 발생률 가장↓

해석 암은 모든 질병 중 세 번째로 높은 사망률이 높은 병이다. 놀랍게도, 특정 국가의 국민들은 일정한 암에 잘 걸리는 경향이 있다. 이것의 주된 원인은 유전적인 요소, 즉 대대로 유전되는 특징들이다.

실제로, 몇몇 집단은 암이 유전적이라는 사실을 증명한다. 연구 결과에 따르면 일본 남성들은 미국 남성들보다 위암에 걸릴 확률이 7배나 높다고 한다. 반면, 일본 남성들은 미국인들에 비해 전립선암에 걸릴 확률이 5배 낮다.

유전자가 암의 발병률에 영향을 끼친다는 것을 증명하는 또 다른 집단은 아메리칸 인디언들이다. 그들은 미국의 어떤 인종 집단들보다 모든 암에 걸릴 확률이 낮다. 이 두 가지 예는 유전적 형질이 각 국가 간의 암 발병률 차이를 유발한다는 사실을 명확히 보여준다.

어휘 cause[kɔ́ːz] 원인 surprisingly[sərpráiziŋli] 놀랍게도 prone to~ ~하는 경향이 있는
genetic[dʒənétik] 유전학적인, 유전상의 factor[fǽktər] 요인 trait[treit] 특성, 특징
that is 즉 pass down 전해지다 generation[dʒènəréiʃən] 세대 demonstrate[démənstrèit] 증명하다, ~의 증거가 되다
hereditary[hərédətèri] 유전성의, 유전적인 stomach cancer 위암 prostate[prásteit] 전립선의
prostate cancer 전립선암 Native American 아메리칸 인디언, 북아메리카 원주민 contract[kántrækt] 걸리다
ethnic group 인종 집단 discrepancy[diskrépənsi] 차이 nationality[næ̀ʃənǽləti] 국적

2. Note-taking

읽기 노트

- Green Revolution   녹색 혁명
  : agricul. experiments & intl. effort 4 world hunger   농업 실험 & 세계 기아 위한 국제적 노력
  1. Yields huge extra crops   방대한 양 농작물 추가 수확
     – success in India: yields ↑, became exporter   인도에서 성공: 수확↑, 수출국 됨
  2. Global hunger ↓ – since GR   녹색 혁명 이래 세계 기아↓
     – saving ppl from starvation   사람들 기근으로부터 구함

해석   "녹색 혁명"이란 많은 국가들에서 일어나는 성공적인 농업 실험들을 일컫는다. 최근에는 이것은 농작물의 수확을 늘려 세계의 기아를 줄이고자 하는 국제적인 운동을 의미하게 되었다. 흔히 쓰이는 방법들로는 관개법, 화학비료와 살충제의 활용, 그리고 유전적으로 개량된 씨앗의 도입 등이 있다.

녹색 혁명은 근거 없는 이야기가 아니다. 이 사상 아래 심은 새로운 종자 씨앗들은 매해 수천 만의 추가 농작물을 생산해내고, 이는 곧 이 개발 전략이 성공했다는 증거이다. 이러한 기법들은 몇몇 개발도상국의 밀과 기타 식용작물의 수확량을 세 배 이상 증진시켰다. 이는 특히 인도에서 성공적이었는데, 이 기법들의 사용으로 인해 인도는 이제 세계적인 농업 생산국으로써 명성을 떨치게 됐다. 농작물 생산량이 1965년 1,230만 톤에서 2000년에 7,640만 톤으로 증가함으로써, 인도는 식용 작물의 수출국이 되었다.

이러한 농업 발전의 효과 덕분에, 세계 기근 인구는 녹색 혁명의 초기 이래 감소하였다. 다시 말하면, 식량 부족 문제를 겪는 세계 인구의 비율이 감소했다. 실제로, 이 녹색 혁명은 전세계적으로 10억 이상의 인구를 기근으로부터 구해낸 공로를 인정받고 있다.

어휘   green revolution 녹색 혁명 (품종개량에 의한 식량 증산)   agricultural[ǽgrəkʌ́ltʃərəl] 농업의, 농사의
world hunger 세계적 식량난   crop[krɑp] 농작물, 수확물   irrigation[ìrəɡéiʃən] 관개, 물을 끌어들임
fertilizer[fə́ːrtəlàizər] 비료, 화학비료   pesticide[péstisàid] 살충제, 농약   genetically[dʒənétikəli] 유전학적으로
myth[miθ] 사회적 통념   ideology[àidiɑ́lədʒi] (사회, 정치상의) 이데올로기, 관념, 의식   yield[ji:ld] 생산량, 수확
testament to~ ~의 증거, ~을 입증하는 것   development[divéləpmənt] (자원 등의) 개발   wheat[hwi:t] (식물) 밀, 소맥
harvest[háːrvist] (작물의) 수확, 추수   developing country 개발도상국   particularly[pərtíkjələrli] 특히
producer[prədjúːsər] 생산자, 생산국   exporter[ekspɔ́ːrtər] 수출국   grain[grein] 곡류, 곡물
due to~ ~때문에   hunger rate 기아 비율, 기근 비율   that is to say 즉, 다시 말하면
proportion[prəpɔ́ːrʃən] 비율   be credited with~ ~의 공로를 인정받다   starvation[stɑːrvéiʃən] 기아, 궁핍

---

3. Note-taking

읽기 노트

- Smart car   스마트 카
  1. Econ., fuel-effic.   경제적, 연료절약형
     – gas price ↑   휘발유 값↑
     – Amer. embracing smart car   미국인들이 스마트 카를 환영함
  2. Small, streamlined   작고 유선형
     – ez 2 maneuver   몰기 쉬움
     – ↓ congestion   교통 혼잡↓
  3. Safer   안전함
     – not fast: ↓ accident   빠르지 않음: 사고율↓
     – safety-cage   안전 장치

해석   차들로 꽉 막힌 고속도로와 천정부지로 치솟는 기름값이 심각한 사회적 문제로 대두되고 있는 이 시대에 스마트 카는 연료 절약형이면
서도 경제적인, 매우 필요한 교통수단 중 하나이다. 미국에서 휘발유 가격이 급상승함에 따라 많은 사람들은 더 이상 연비가 떨어지는
자동차를 구매할 여유가 없다. 따라서, 미국의 소비자들은 이제 갤런당 50에서 60마일을 주행할 수 있는 연비를 자랑하는 스마트 카를
환영하고 있다.
스마트 카의 또 다른 이점은 붐비는 도시에서 작은 유선형 차체로, 이것은 복잡한 도심에서도 차를 손쉽게 몰 수 있게 해주고 교통 혼잡
을 줄여준다. 스마트 카는 중형차의 절반 크기밖에 되지 않아, 교통체증을 거의 증가시키지 않고도 운전자의 수를 잠재적으로 두 배 가
까이 수용할 수 있게 한다는 것을 의미한다.
마지막으로, 스마트 카는 다른 차종에 비하여 더 안전하다. 스마트 카의 운전자들은 시속 85마일 이상의 속도를 낼 수 없으며, 따라서
과속 또는 무모한 운전으로 야기되는 교통사고의 확률이 줄어든다. 뿐만 아니라, 충돌 사고에서, 스마트 카는 경주용 차의 충돌 보호 장
치와 흡사한 사고시에도 원형을 유지하는 안전 장치를 갖추어 고안되었기에, 다른 차종과 다르게 반응한다.

어휘   **clog**[klág] (차들이 정체하여) 길을 막다   **maneuver**[mənúːvər] 조정하다, (차를) 몰다   **mid-sized car** 중형차
salient[séiliənt] 두드러진, 두각을 나타내는   **mileage**[máilidʒ] (특히 자동차) 연비   **fuel-efficient** 연비가 뛰어난
boast[boust] 자랑하다   **embrace**[imbréis] ~을 환영하다   **streamlined**[stríːmlàind] 유선형의, 날씬한
traffic congestion 교통체증   **reckless**[réklis] 무분별한, 무모한   **congestion**[kəndʒéstʃən] 혼잡
high speed driving 과속 운전

4. Note-taking

읽기 노트

- Multinat. corp.: branches in many countries 다국적 기업: 많은 국가에 지사 보유
  - benefits consumers 소비자에게 이익
- 1. Costs ↓ 비용↓
  - economies of scales → benef. 2 consumers 규모의 경제 → 소비자에게 이익
- global compet. → prices ↓ 국제 경쟁 → 가격↓
- 2. Select. of prods ↑ 제품 선택의 다양성 ↑
  - prod. from worldwide 전세계의 제품
  - high-quality, regardless of location 고품질, 장소 불문
- 3. Help local econ. 지역 경제에 이바지
  - provide emplymnt, income ↑, improve stndrd of living 고용 창출, 수입↑, 삶의 질 향상
  - new techno., skills 신 과학 기술

해석   다국적 기업이라는 개념은, 일찍이 17세기 전반부터 시작되어 확립된 지 오래된 것이다. 그러나, 제2차 세계대전 후에, 여러 나라에 걸쳐
지점이나 체인점을 지닌 이 다국적 기업들의 수는 기하급수적으로 늘어나게 되었다. 다국적 기업들이 전세계로 진출할 수 있는 역량은
다양하고도 많은 방법으로 소비자들에게 혜택을 준다.
다국적 기업들의 생산 비용은 생산량의 증가에 따른 규모의 경제에 의해 감소한다. 그들은 이렇게 절감된 비용을 소비자들에게 양도하는
데, 이는 이 기업들의 상품 가격이 낮아지는 결과를 가져온다. 가격은 또한 회사들간의 국제적 경쟁에 의해 더 낮아지는데, 이 현상은 지
방기업들만 존재한다면 불가능한 일일 것이다.
또 한 가지 소비자들에게 유리한 점은 다국적 기업들이 상품 선택의 다양성을 늘려준다는 것이다. 더 이상 사람들은 자신이 사는 지역에
서 생산된 상품들에만 국한되지 않고, 그 대신 전세계적으로 생산되는 상품들 중에서 구매할 상품을 선택할 수 있다. 더욱 폭넓은 선택
권과 더불어, 전세계에 걸쳐 자신들의 상품을 판매하는 회사들은, 소비자의 거주 지역에 상관없이 고품질의 상품을 제공한다. 인지도가
높은 브랜드는, 그것이 어디에서 구매되었는지에 관계없이 품질이 높은 상품을 보장한다.
마지막으로, 다국적 기업들은 해외에 지점과 공장을 개장함으로써 해당 지역의 지역 경제를 돕는다. 그들은 인근 지역 근로자들에게 일
자리를 제공해주고, 그들의 수입을 늘려주며, 따라서, 지역 소비자들의 생활 수준을 향상시켜 준다. 이것은 특히 생산에 직접 관련된 지
역에서 더욱 그러하다. 다국적 기업들은 그 지역에 새로운 과학기술을 도입하고, 인근 지역 노동자에게 새로운 기술을 숙련시킴으로써

지역경제가 성장하고 발전할 수 있는 기회를 제공한다. 이는, 지역 경제의 안정을 촉진한다.

어휘 **multinational corporation** 다국적 기업 **long-established** 설립된지 오래된 **dramatically** [drəmǽtikəli] 극적으로
span the globe 전세계에 걸치다 **economies of scale** 규모의 경제 **savings** [séiviŋ] 저금, 저축
selection of~ 엄선된~ **world-wide** 세계적인 **regardless of~** ~에 상관없이 **well-made** 완성도가 높은, 잘 만들어진
local economy 지역 경제 **standard of living** 삶의 질, 생활 수준 **economic stability** 경제적 안정

5. Note-taking

읽기 노트

- Brain drain – talented ppl emigrating 두뇌 유출 – 인재들의 이주 현상
- Eur. scientists → US 유럽 과학자 → 미국
  1. Invest $↓ 투자비↓
     - half $ → lack resources, funding, facility 비용 미국의 절반 → 자원, 자금, 시설의 부족
     - low salary 낮은 급료
  2. Rigid burcrcy 엄격한 관료주의
     - complx paperwork: rejected apps 복잡한 서류 업무: 지원서 기각
     - discouraged 낙심
  3. Hierarchy: ↓ morale 계급제도: 의욕↓
     - work 4 prof. 4 long time → 4 same opp. given initially in US
       미국에서는 당초에 얻을 기회를 교수 밑에서 오래 일해야 얻음
     - seniors claim juniors' work 선배가 후배의 연구 저작권 주장

해석 두뇌 유출이란 유능하고 잘 훈련 받은 인재들이 자국에서의 기회 부족으로 인해 타국으로 이민을 가는 것을 뜻한다. 이 표현은 1950년대에 유럽의 과학자들이 미국으로 이주한 것을 설명하기 위해 만들어졌다. 거의 50만 명에 달하는 유럽의 과학 및 공학 관련 학과 졸업생들이 현재 미국에서 살고 있고, 그 중 소수의 인원들만이 귀국할 의사를 가지고 있다. 미국으로의 지속적인 과학자 두뇌 유출에는 여러 가지 이유가 존재한다.
두뇌 유출의 한 가지 원인은 유럽연합(EU)이 미국에 비해 훨씬 적은 액수의 돈을 과학에 투자하기 때문이다. 미국과 연구개발 분야를 비교했을 때 미국의 절반 정도만 투자한다는 것은 유럽 내 자금과 자원의 부족, 그리고 미흡한 시설이라는 결과로 이어진다. 낮은 임금이 많은 과학자들을 미국으로 몰아내고 있다는 것은 놀라울 것도 없다.
더군다나, EU는 경직된 관료적인 절차로 고생한다. 연구 보조금의 지원을 위한 복잡하고, 상세한 서류 절차는 사소한 세부 사항으로 인해 기각되는 결과를 낳는다. 따라서, 유럽의 과학자들은 자국에서 재정적인 지원을 받고 일거리를 찾는 것의 전망에 대해 낙담한다.
마지막으로, 계층적인 태도는 사기 진작에 영향을 끼친다. 과학자들은 종종 더 나이 많은 교수 밑에서 10년 일해야 미국에서 당초에 얻을 수 있는 기회를 얻을 수 있다. 또한 이런 문제는 선배가 후배가 업적을 자신의 것으로 발표하는 경우처럼 저작권 문제로 이어지기도 한다.

어휘 **brain drain** 두뇌 유출, 인재의 국외 이주 **emigration** [èməgréiʃən] (타국으로의) 이민, 이주 **coin** [kɔin] (신조어 등을) 만들어내다
graduate [grǽdʒuèit] 졸업생 **EU = European Union** 유럽연합 **research and development** 연구 개발
funding [fʌ́ndiŋ] 자금 조달 **not surprisingly** 놀랄 것도 없이 **drive~ to-** ~을 -으로 몰아내다
suffer from~ ~으로 고생하다, ~으로 해를 입다 **rigid** [rídʒid] 완고한, 엄격한 **bureaucracy** [bjuərάkrəsi] 관료적인 번잡한 절차
paperwork [péipərwə̀ːrk] 문서업무 **grant** [grǽnt] (연구 장학금등) 보조금 **rejection** [ridʒékʃən] 거절, 배제
prospect [prάspekt] 전망 **financial assistance** 재정적 지원 **hierarchical** [hàiərάːrkikəl] 계층제의, 위계조직의
morale [mərǽl] 사기, 의욕 **initially** [iníʃəli] 당초에, 애초에 **play out in~** ~에 적용되다
authorship [ɔ́ːθərʃip] (저작물의) 원작자, 저작권 **colleague** [kάliːg] (직업상의) 동료 **claim** [kleim] (소유권, 사실들을) 주장하다

Possible Answers & Scripts

6. Note-taking

읽기 노트

- Birds evolved from dinos. 공룡에서 진화한 조류
    1. Anatom. similarities 해부학적 유사점
        - light, air-filled bones → 2 fly 가볍고 공기가 채워진 뼈 → 날기 위함
        - wishbone → 2 connect wing muscle like birds 차골 → 조류처럼 날개 근육에 연결됨
    2. Dino. fossils with feather 깃털 달린 공룡의 화석
        - featherlike hairs 깃털 같은 털
        - feathers in early stage of dvlpm. 초기 성장 단계의 깃털

해석 다윈이 진화론을 처음 주장한 이래, 과학자들은 조류가 어떻게 나타났는지를 설명할 수 있는, 사라진 연결고리를 찾으려고 시도해 왔다. 지난 두 세기 동안 발견된 공룡 화석을 토대로 했을 때, 과학자들은 조류가 공룡으로부터 진화했으리라고 가정한다. 이 두 종이 공통적으로 가지고 있는 여러 가지 특성들이 이 가설에 신빙성을 더해준다.

해부학적으로, 몇몇 공룡들은 오늘날의 조류와 꽤 흡사했다. 일부 화석에서는 가볍고 공기를 내포한 뼈가 발견되었는데, 이것이 진화하여 오늘날의 조류가 더 가벼워지고, 마침내 날 수 있게 된 것이다. 조류의 시조가 된 공룡의 부류는 또 다른 조류적 특성을 보인다. 그것은 바로 차골인데, 흉골의 일부로서 조류의 날개 근육으로 이어지는 부분이다. 총괄적으로, 조류와 공룡은 해부학적 특성을 100가지 이상이나 공유한다.

공룡에서 조류로의 진화설은 또한 발굴된 공룡 화석 중 다수가, 또한 여러 발전 단계에서 다양한 깃털을 지녔었다는 흔적을 보인다는 사실로 신빙성이 더해진다. 발견된 최초의 깃털 달린 공룡은 튜브와 같은 모양을 한 깃털 같은 털로 덮여 있었다. 추가적인 연구에 따라 연구원들은 많은 경우 – 혹은 심지어 모든 경우에 – 알에서 부화한 후 성장 초기 단계의 짧은 기간 동안 공룡에게 깃털이 있었을 것이라고 믿고 있다.

어휘 Theory of Evolution 다윈의 진화론 missing link (인류학, 고고학) 사라진 연결고리
emerge[imə́:rdʒ] (새로운 사실 등이) 조사 결과 등에서 나타나다, 밝혀지다 hypothesize[haipάθisàiz] 가설하다, 가정하다
anatomically[æ̀nətάmikəli] 해부학상의 skeletal[skélitəl] 골격의, 해골의 air-filled 공기가 차 있는
branch[brǽntʃ] 분파 be descended from~ ~의 후손이다 avian[éiviən] 새의, 조류의 wishbone[wíʃbòun] (새가슴의) 차골
breastbone[bréstbòun] 흉골, 가슴뼈 excavate[ékskəvèit] 발굴하다 show evidence of~ ~의 흔적, 증거가 있다
stage of development 성장단계, 발전단계 feathered[féðərd] 깃털을 지닌 hatch[hǽtʃ] (알을) 까다, 부화시키다

7. Note-taking 🎧 *Track 4*

듣기 노트

- Cancer – cause 암 – 원인
    1. Jap. – stomach canc.: lifestyle 일본인 – 위암: 생활 양식
        - salty fish, pickled food → canc. 짠 생선, 절인 음식 → 암
        - Jap. immigrt. on Amer. diet: ↓ stomach canc. 일본인 이주자 미국식 식단: 위암 ↓
    2. Native Amer. - lowest canc. rate: diet 아메리칸 인디언 – 암 발생률 최저: 식습관
        - use plants, herbs → natural med. 식물, 약초 사용 → 천연 약효
        - root attacking canc. cell 암세포 공격하는 뿌리

script Many scientists have dedicated their lives to figuring out cancer's causes. Today, we're going to look at cancer incidence in two ethnic groups, and identify relevant factors.

All right, let's take a look at Japanese men. They are especially susceptible to stomach cancer.

Researchers now theorize that this can be traced to their lifestyle. Their food is mostly salty fish dishes and other pickled or smoked foods, which can lead to cancer. A study of Japanese immigrants and their counterparts in Japan confirmed this. It found that those who took on the American diet were less likely to get stomach cancer. Those who stayed in Japan, however, remained at high risk.

Another group that shows how environmental factors affect cancer rates are the Native Americans. They historically have had lower cancer rates than all other ethnicities in the US, but scientists claim this is due to their diet, not genetics. They have a history of using plants and herbs rich in natural medicines. For example, Native Americans often consume this specific root that is rich in chemicals that attack cancer cells in the body.

해석 많은 과학자들은 암의 원인을 규명하는데 자신들의 일생을 바쳐 왔습니다. 오늘은, 두 인종 집단의 암 발병률에 관해 알아보고, 관련 요소들을 확인해 봅시다.

일본 남성들의 경우를 한번 살펴봅시다. 일본 남성들은 특히나 위암에 걸릴 확률이 높습니다. 연구자들은 현재 이것이 그들의 생활 양식에 기인한 것이라는 학설을 내세우고 있습니다. 그들의 음식은 대부분 짭짤한 생선과 기타 절임 또는 훈제 식품으로서, 암을 유발할 수 있는 것들입니다. 일본인 이민자들과 일본에서 생활하는 일본인들 사이의 관계를 조사한 연구 결과는 이를 확증했습니다. 연구 결과에 의하면 미국식 식단을 받아들인 일본인들은 위암에 걸릴 확률이 더 낮았다고 합니다. 그러나 일본에서 거주하는 일본인들은 여전히 위암 발병률이 높았습니다.

환경적 요인이 암의 발병률에 어떤 영향을 끼치는지를 보여주는 또 하나의 집단은 아메리칸 인디언들입니다. 그들은 역사적으로 미국의 다른 어떤 민족들보다 낮은 암 발병률을 지니고 있었지만, 과학자들은 이것이 유전자에 의한 것이 아니라 그들의 식단에 기인한 것이라고 주장합니다. 그들은 천연 약효가 풍부한 식물과 약초를 사용한 역사를 지니고 있습니다. 예를 들어, 아메리칸 인디언들 몸 속의 암세포들을 죽이는 화학 물질이 풍부한 특정 뿌리를 종종 섭취합니다.

어휘 dedicate [dédəkèit] 바치다 incidence [ínsidəns] 빈도, 발병률 relevant [réləvənt] 관련된, 적절한
susceptible to~ ~의 영향을 받기 쉬운, ~에 민감한 theorize [θí(:)əràiz] 이론을 세우다 trace [treis] (원인이 ~에서) 유래하다
pickled [píkld] 절여진 smoked [smóukt] 훈제된 counterpart [káuntərpà:rt] 상대물, 상대방
take on 받아들이다 ethnicity [eθnísəti:] 민족성 rich in~ ~이 풍부한

8. Note-taking

듣기 노트

- Green Revolution – true result 녹색 혁명 – 실제 결과
  - 1. World hunger ↓ : include China 세계 기아 ↓ : 중국 포함
    - China: out of GR → econ. policy 중국: 녹색 혁명 X → 경제 정책
    - exclud. China, hunger ↑ 중국 제외 시, 기아 비율 ↑
  - 2. Success of GR: still many hungry 녹색 혁명의 성공: 여전히 굶주리는 많은 사람들
    - food not effectively distrib. 식량이 효과적으로 분배 X
    - India: half of ppl in poverty, malnourished 인도: 인구 절반이 빈곤, 영양실조

script Although the Green Revolution has been hailed as an immensely successful agricultural experiment, we need to look closer to see the true results. The Green Revolution has been recognized for increasing crop production and reducing hunger world-wide, but perhaps it has received too much credit. Why are 2 billion people still hungry?

First of all, the numbers do show that the average rate of world hunger has decreased since the 1950s. However, this includes the dramatic improvements in China. But China was outside the sphere of the Green Revolution! I mean, the reduction there is attributed to economic policy reform. The actual level of world hunger, excluding China, has increased in the last 50 years, unfortunately.

Furthermore, although more crops are grown, a country which has had successes as a result of the Green Revolution can still have many hungry people. That's because increased food production is not effectively distributed. Let's consider India, which, as you know, experienced a so-called "successful" Green Revolution at the end of the 1960s and 1970s. Yet more than one-half of India's population is still mired in poverty and malnourished, which is evidence that the harvests are not reaching the people.

해석   비록 녹색 혁명이 막대한 성공을 거둔 농업 실험이라는 찬사를 받고 있지만, 우리는 진실된 결과를 알기 위해 더 면밀히 살펴봐야 합니다. 녹색 혁명은 농작물 생산량을 증가시키고 세계의 기근을 감소시킨 것으로 인정 받아 왔지만, 아무래도 과도한 명성을 얻어 온 것 같습니다. 어째서 20억의 인구가 아직도 굶주리고 있을까요?

첫째로, 수치에 따르면 1950년대부터 평균적으로 세계 기근 비율이 감소한 것은 사실입니다. 그러나, 이 수치에는 중국에서의 획기적인 발전도 포함되어 있습니다. 하지만 중국은 녹색 혁명의 영역 밖에 있었습니다! 즉, 중국에서의 기근 감소는 경제 정책의 개혁 때문이었다는 거죠. 중국을 제외한, 국제 기근의 실질적인 수치는, 불행히도 지난 50년간 증가했습니다.

더군다나, 더 많은 농작물이 재배됨에도 불구하고, 녹색 혁명의 결과로 많은 성공을 거두었던 국가에서도 여전히 기근에 시달리는 사람들이 많이 있을 수 있습니다. 이는 증가한 식량 생산분이 효율적으로 배분되지 않기 때문이지요. 1960년대와 1970년대 말에 소위 "성공적인" 녹색 혁명을 겪은 인도의 경우를 고려해 봅시다. 하지만 아직도 인도 인구의 절반 이상은 빈곤과 영양실조에 시달리고 있습니다. 증가한 농작물이 사람들에게 제대로 분배되고 있지 않다는 증거이죠.

어휘   **be hailed as~** ~이라는 찬사를 받다   **immensely**[iménsli] 막대하게   **be recognized for~** ~의 중요성을 인정받다
credit[krédit] 명예, 공, 칭찬   **sphere**[sfiər] 영역   **attribute to~** ~때문이다   **economic policy** 경제 정책
reform[ri:fɔ́:rm] 혁신, 개혁   **excluding**[iksklú:diŋ] ~을 제외한   **unfortunately**[ʌnfɔ́:rtʃənitli] 불행히도
so-called 소위, 이른바   **be mired in~** ~에 빠지다   **malnourished**[mælnə́:riʃt] 영양 부족의

9. Note-taking

듣기 노트

- Smart cars – 1yr after 스마트 카 – 1년 후
  - 1. Not fuel-effic. 연료 효율적이지 않음
    - – ↓mpg than promised 약속한 것보다 연비↓
  - 2. Traffic cong. 교통 혼잡
    - – vehicles↑ after new model 신모델 출시 후 교통량↑
    - – only 2 seats → more cars 좌석 단 2개 → 더 많은 차 필요
  - 3. Deadly 치명적
    - – too small: can't see, unsafe 너무 작음: 보이지 않음, 위험
    - – crushed in accident 사고시 부서짐

script So, ah... Smart cars have been boosting consumers' hopes of reducing fuel costs and doing something positive for the environment. Now, we're going to see whether smart cars lived up to that optimism a year after they came out.

Well, first of all, smart cars are not very fuel-efficient... at least, not as much as manufacturers claim they are. The 60 mile-per-gallon claim that's been promised is actually more like 37, as shown in actual tests. This ranks a lackluster ninth among all cars. So, promises about saving fuel costs seem pretty empty.

As for the effects of smart cars on traffic congestion... did you know that, historically, the number of vehicles on the road increases after the introduction of new models? Look at the SUV boom. We also saw this happen with smart cars, which seat only two passengers. So people had to, uh, use more automobiles to seat the people who previously fit in one sedan. So the introduction of smart cars actually worsened congestion.

And believe it or not, the smart cars' cuteness can be deadly... that's because they might be too small for their own good! Other drivers tend to have more trouble seeing smart cars clearly, and often sideswipe them. So, uh, even smart car owners admitted they felt unsafe driving next to large vehicles on the road. In accidents, smart cars were the ones that, umm, got crushed. So their high accident rate has also added to consumers' misgivings about this so-called miracle automobile.

해석   스마트 카는 연료비를 줄이고 환경에 긍정적인 역할을 하리라는 소비자들의 기대를 높여 왔습니다. 이제는 스마트 카가 출시 1년 후에 그 기대에 부응했는지 살펴봅시다.

첫째로, 스마트 카는 그다지 연료를 절약해 주지 않습니다. 적어도 스마트 카의 제조업체들이 주장하는 것만큼은요. 약속되었던 갤런당 60마일의 연비라는 주장이 실제 실험에서는 37마일로 나타났습니다. 이는 모든 차종과 비교해 보았을 때 보잘것 없는 9위에 그칠 뿐입니다. 따라서 연비가 뛰어나 기름값을 아낄 수 있다는 주장은 빈말인 것으로 추정됩니다.

스마트 카의 교통 체증에 대한 효과에 관해서는... 여러분은, 과거 사실에 비추어 볼 때 새로운 차종이 출시되면 교통 체증이 증가했다는 사실을 알고 계십니까? 스포츠 레저 차량의 급격한 수요 증가 현상을 생각해 보세요. 이러한 현상이 스마트 카의 도입과 함께 또 일어났는데, 이 차종에는 단지 두 명만이 승차할 수 있죠. 그래서, 사람들은 예전에 세단형 자동차에 태울 수 있었던 인원을 태우기 위해 더 많은 차를 몰아야 했습니다. 따라서 스마트 카의 도입은 사실상 교통 체증을 더 악화시켰죠.

그리고 믿거나 말거나, 스마트 카들의 앙증맞음은 치명적일 수 있습니다. 제 역할을 다하기에 너무 작으니까요! 스마트 카는 다른 운전자들이 제대로 확인하는데 어려움을 겪는 경향이 있고, 때때로 옆을 스치고 지나가기도 합니다. 그래서, 스마트 카의 운전자들조차 도로에서 큰 차 옆을 운전할 때 신변의 위협을 느꼈다고 인정했습니다. 교통사고시에, 크게 부서지는 쪽은 스마트 카였습니다. 따라서 그들의 높은 사고율 또한 소위 경이로운 자동차로 불리는 이 스마트 카에 대한 소비자들의 심리를 더욱 불안하게 만들었습니다.

어휘   **optimism**[ɑ́ptəmìzəm] 낙관론, 낙관주의   **SUV = sports utility vehicle** 스포츠 레저 차량
historically[histɔ́(ː)rikəli] 역사적으로   **misgiving**[misɡíviŋ] 불안, 염려   **sideswipe**[sáidswàip] 옆을 스치듯 지나가다

10. Note-taking

듣기 노트

- Multinat. corp. – recent survey   다국적 기업 – 최근 설문 결과
  1. Effects on pop.   인구에 미치는 영향
     - no savings to consumers   소비자 위한 절감 효과 X
     - mnply: price ↑, quality ↓   독점: 가격↑, 질↓
  2. Loss of unique culture   독특한 문화 상실
     - causes homogen.   균질화 유발
     - diverse cultures: become same   다양한 문화: 획일화 됨
  3. Destroy local econs.   지역 경제 붕괴
     - local biz wiped out   지방 기업 파산
     - no choice but to work for multinat.   다국적 기업에서 일하는 것 외엔 선택여지 없음
     - no labor stndrds, don't pay enough   근로기준 X, 충분한 임금 X

script   Let's begin today by posing the question, are multinationals as positive as they would have us believe? Well, that's a complicated issue... but we can begin by looking at some recently taken surveys.

OK, the first questions dealt with their effects on populations. Responders said that although they cut costs and thrive, in reality, it's rare that multinationals pass savings onto consumers. In fact, they're accused of going to the other extreme. What I mean by this is... monopoly, which results in higher prices and lower quality.

Another point mentioned was the high price that comes with the availability of brand-name products world-wide; the loss of unique cultures. People accused multinationals of being a main cause of homogenization across the globe. People everywhere all have to buy the same things, as local products become unavailable. In other words, diverse, remarkable cultures all begin to resemble each other.

We should also consider some of the comments made about their impact on local economies. Uhm...: Some survey-takers actually said that they destroyed them. They saw local businesses wiped out. So... the local populations suffer because they have no other choice but to work for multinationals, even though they don't enforce labor standards, and, often, don't pay their employees enough. Many people expressed that these companies simply don't care about the areas or people they exploit.

해석   오늘의 강의는 다국적 기업은 그들이 주장하는 것만큼 우리에게 이로운 것일까라는 질문으로 시작하도록 합시다. 이것은 복잡한 문제이 기는 하지만, 최근에 시행된 설문 조사들을 살펴보는 것으로 시작해 볼 수 있겠네요.

설문 조사에서 맨 처음 물어본 질문들은 그 지역의 인구에 다국적 기업들이 미치는 영향에 관한 것이었습니다. 설문 조사에 응한 사람들 은 비록 다국적 기업들이 가격을 절감하고 자사의 성장을 이루는 하나, 현실적으로 이 기업들이 비용 절감에 따른 이익을 소비자에게 돌리는 일은 거의 일어나지 않는다고 합니다. 사실상 정반대의 극단으로 치우친다고 비난받는 실정이죠. 다시 말하면, 가격은 높이고 품 질은 저하되게 하는 시장 독점이라는 것입니다.

또 언급된 사항은 세계적인 브랜드 제품의 보급화에 따른 값비싼 희생이었어요. 바로 고유한 문화를 상실했다는 것이죠. 설문 조사를 받 은 사람들은 다국적 기업들을 세계의 균질화의 주된 요인으로 꼽았어요. 사람들은 지역의 상품들을 살 수 없게 됨에 따라 어디에서든 모 두 같은 상품을 구매해야 했습니다. 달리 말하자면, 다양하고, 뛰어난 문화들이 모두 서로 비슷해진다는 것이죠.

또한 다국적 기업들이 지역 경제에 미치는 영향에 관한 몇 가지 비평들을 고려해야 합니다. 설문 조사에 응한 몇몇 사람들은 실제로 이 기업들이 지역 경제를 파괴한다고 대답했습니다. 그들은 지역 사업체들이 전멸당하는 것을 보았습니다. 그래서 비록 다국적 기업들이 종 종 자사의 직원들에게 충분한 임금을 지불하지 않고 근로 기준법을 따르지 않더라도, 그들에게는 다국적 기업을 위해 근무하는 것 이외 의 대안이 없기 때문에, 지역 주민들은 피해를 입게 됩니다. 많은 사람들은 이러한 기업들이, 자사가 착취하는 직원들이나 지역에 대해 전혀 개의치 않는다는 의견을 피력했습니다.

어휘   **pose a question** 질문을 제기하다   **complicated**[kάmpləkèitid] 복잡한, 어려운   **responder**[rispάndər] 응답자
rare[rεər] 희귀한   **accuse of~** (~는 점에서) 비난하다   **extreme**[ikstrí:m] 극단   **monopoly**[mənάpəli] 시장 독점
availability[əvèiləbíləti] 유효성   **brand-name product** 명품   **homogenization**[həmάdʒənaizèiʃən] 동일화, 균질화
across the globe 전세계에 걸쳐   **remarkable**[rimά:rkəbl] 비범한, 뛰어난   **resemble**[rizémbl] ~과 흡사하다
survey-taker 설문조사 응답자   **wipe out** 전멸시키다, 싹 없애다   **have no choice but to~** ~하는 수밖에 없다
enforce[infɔ́:rs] 억지로 시키다, 강요하다   **labor standards** 근로 기준법   **exploit**[éksplɔit] (남을) 부당하게 이용하다

11. Note-taking

듣기 노트

- Brain drain - changing trend   두뇌 유출 - 추세 변화
  1. Funding ↑   자금 제공↑
     - <u>promote, incentives</u>   촉진, 보상
     - <u>tax relief → invest in R&D ↑ salary</u>   세금 감면 → 연구 개발에 투자↑, 급료↑
     - <u>lab, equip ↑</u>   최신 실험실과 장비↑
  2. Bureaucracy ↓   관료주의↓
     - shorter process 4 grant   지원 절차 단축
  3. Promote competitive spirit ← more $ 경쟁심 촉진 ← 더 많은 투자
     - <u>reward 4 innov. & give full credit</u>   기술 혁신에 대한 보상 & 공로 인정
     - → <u>meritocracy</u>   실력사회

script All right, class, for many years, European scientists decided to work in the US, but this trend has changed in recent years.

Right now, the EU is, increasing funding in research and development, promoting science in society, and providing incentives for businesses to invest in research. For example, it offers tax relief for companies that invest in research and development. So, uh, this means that scientists receive higher salaries. Companies are also, you know, making scientists happy by providing state-of-the-art laboratories and equipment.

What's more, foundations now know that their lengthy, complicated grant proposal process deters scientists. So, they are, well, shortening the application process and reducing the amount of bureaucracy to help scientists stay in Europe.

On top of that, councils are promoting a competitive, enterprising spirit by putting more money into promising research. Well, as you can see, the EU today rewards young scientists for their innovations, gives them full credit, and makes science a meritocracy.

해석 여러분, 여러 해 동안 유럽의 과학자들은 미국에서 일하기로 결심했지만, 이 추세는 최근에 바뀌었어요.

현재 유럽연합(EU)은, 연구와 개발에 자금 조달을 늘리고 있고, 사회적으로 과학을 장려하고 있으며, 기업들이 연구에 투자하도록 혜택을 제공하고 있습니다. 예를 들어, EU는 연구와 개발에 투자하는 기업체들에게 세금 공제를 해주고 있어요. 따라서, 이것은 과학자들이 더 높은 임금을 받을 수 있다는 것을 뜻합니다. 회사들은 또한, 과학자들에게 최첨단의 연구소와 연구설비를 제공함으로써 그들을 만족시키고 있습니다.

그 뿐만 아니라, 연구기금 재단들은 이제 그들의 복잡하고, 장황한 연구기금 보조 지원 절차가 과학자들을 단념시킨다는 것을 깨달았죠. 따라서, 그들은 과학자들이 유럽에 남게 하기 위해 지원 절차를 더 간략히 만들고 관료적인 번잡한 절차를 줄이고 있어요.

그 밖에도, 위원회는 전도 유망한 연구에 자금을 더 제공함으로써 경쟁적이고, 진취적인 풍조를 장려합니다. 그래서, 오늘날 EU는 젊은 과학자들을 그들의 혁신 정도에 따라 포상하고, 그들의 공로를 완전히 인정해주며, 과학계를 실력을 기반으로 하는 사회로 만들고 있는 것이죠.

어휘 incentive[inséntiv] 보상금, 혜택   tax relief 세금 공제   state-of-the-art 최신식의   foundation[faundéiʃən] 재단, 협회   deter[ditə́:r] 제지하다, 단념시키다   lengthy[léŋkθi] 긴, 장황한   on top of that 그 밖에   council[káunsəl] 회의, 심의회   enterprising[éntərpràiziŋ] 진취적인   give credit to~ ~에게 공로를 인정하다   meritocracy[mèritákrəsi] 실력 위주 사회

12. Note-taking

듣기 노트

> - Comp. b/t birds & dino. – vital steps missing 새와 공룡 사이 비교 – 중요한 단계 빠져 있음
>   1. Anatomical differences 해부학적 차이
>   - dino.: no collarbone to support wings 공룡: 날개를 받쳐주는 쇄골 없음
>   → must have to fly → 날기 위해선 꼭 필요
>   2. Having feather ≠ bird 깃털 가짐 ≠ 조류
>   - feathers not right for flight: not asymmetrical 날기에 적합한 깃털 아님: 비대칭 아님
>   - to insulate or display 보온이나 장식용

script You have all, no doubt, heard the comparisons between birds and dinosaurs. Today, I'd like you to consider whether the similarities are really substantial enough to proclaim it a fact that birds descended from the dinosaurs. A recent article in a science journal claims that vital steps are missing between the two groups, like, how they learned to fly, for one.

It says that certain anatomical differences between dinosaurs and birds make it highly unlikely that they are related. Even though they have a wishbone, dinosaurs still don't have a collarbone, the skeletal structure that would support wings strong enough to fly. The authors mention that all other flying animals, even bats, have these other features; they're absolutely necessary for flight.

The authors also argue that an animal having feathers does not make it a bird. They point out that dinosaur fossils revealing feather impressions have been discovered, but that does not make them a transitional species. Most often, these feathers were not even the right kind for flight! In order to fly, feathers must be asymmetrical, which the skeletal record simply does not reflect. What the evidence does show is that dinosaurs had other possible reasons for feathers; to help insulate the creatures' bodies in order to maintain a constant temperature, or for display purposes.

해석 여러분은 모두, 아마도 조류와 공룡 사이의 비교에 관해 들어 보았을 것입니다. 오늘 저는 여러분이 이러한 유사점들이 조류가 공룡의 자손이라고 주장할 만큼 정말 중요한지 고려해 볼 바랍니다. 과학 잡지에 실린 최근 한 기사는, 예를 들면, 공룡이 어떻게 나는 방법을 배우게 되었는가와 같은, 두 종류 사이의 매우 중요한 단계가 빠져 있다고 주장합니다.

기사는 공룡과 조류 간 특정 해부학적 차이점들이 이 두 종이 혈연관계를 가지고 있다는 것을 거의 불가능한 일로 만든다고 말합니다. 이 두 종 모두 차골을 가지고 있음에도 불구하고, 공룡들은 여전히 날개가 날 수 있을 정도로 튼튼하게 받쳐주는 골격인 쇄골을 보유하고 있지 않습니다. 이 기사의 저자들은 이 다른 특색인 쇄골을, 날 수 있는 다른 모든 종의 동물들이 보유하고 있음을 지적합니다. 심지어 박쥐까지도 말이죠. 쇄골은 날기 위해 절대적으로 필요한 것입니다.

필자들은 또한 어떤 동물에 깃털이 달려 있다고 해서 그것을 조류로 볼 수는 없다고 주장합니다. 그들은 깃털 흔적을 지닌 공룡의 화석이 발견된 것은 사실이지만, 그렇다고 해서 그것이 과도기적인 종이라는 것을 뜻하는 것은 아니라고 지적합니다. 흔히, 이러한 깃털들은 심지어 날기에 적합한 깃털도 아니었지요! 날기 위해서 깃털은 비대칭이어야 하는데 이 화석들에는 이런 것이 전혀 반영되어 있지 않아요. 화석에 나타난 증거가 나타내는 바는 공룡들이 깃털을 가진 데는 다른 가능성 있는 이유가 있었다는 거죠. 공룡이 일정한 체온을 유지하도록 단열을 돕는다든지, 아니면 장식용으로 보유하고 있을 수도 있었다는 겁니다.

어휘 **substantial**[səbstǽnʃəl] 상당한, 많은 **proclaim**[proukléim] 선언하다, 주장하다 **vital**[váitəl] 절대 필요한, 매우 중요한 **unlikely**[ʌnláikli] 있음직하지 않은 **collarbone**[kálərbòun] 쇄골 **skeletal structure** 골격 **mention**[ménʃən] 언급하다 **absolutely**[ǽbsəlùːtli] 절대적으로, 무조건 **point out** 강조하다, 지적하다 **revealing**[rivíːliŋ] (숨겨진 부분이) 노출된 **transitional**[trænzíʃənəl] 변천하는, 과도기의 **asymmetrical**[èisəmétrikəl] 비대칭의 **insulate**[ínsʃəlèit] 단열하다

HACKERS Test
p.86

1. Note-taking   *Track 5*

읽기 노트

> Hydrogen – attractive new source 수소 – 매력적인 새로운 에너지 원천
>
>   1. Abundant - found in water 풍부 – 물에서 생성
>
>   split water to produce H 물을 분리하여 수소 생성
>
>   wide avail.: cheaper 쉽게 얻을 수 있음: 저렴
>
>   2. Environ. frndly 친환경적
>
>   no emission 방출물질 없음
>
>   renewable source to split water 재생 에너지로 물 분리
>
>   3. Ez 2 store & trnsprt 저장, 운반이 용이
>
>   liquid, gas 액체, 가스
>
>   storage alloy 저장 합금

듣기 노트

- Hydrogen – not pass test 수소 – 적절치 X
  1. Cost of electrcty 전기 비용
     - cost: hydro > gas 비용: 수소 > 가스
  2. Electrcty: not good for environ. 전기: 환경에 이롭지 않음
     - renewable sources: not feasible ← weather 재생가능한 원천: 실행 불가 ← 날씨
  3. Not ez 2 store, trnsprt 저장과 운반 쉽지 않음
     - liquid, gas hydro: volatile 액체, 수소가스: 휘발성
     - alloy: too heavy → unfeasible 합금: 너무 무거움 → 실행 불가능

스크립트 및 해석

Reading

화석 연료가 급속히 줄어들면서, 사람들은 21세기와 그 이후를 대비하여 대체 에너지의 공급원을 찾아 나서기 시작하고 있다. 수소 에너지는 각종 연료와 에너지의 용도로 사용될 수 있는 매력적이고 새로운 에너지 원천으로 점점 더 각광받고 있다. 그 용도에는 운송수단에 동력을 공급하고, 전력을 공급하기 위해 터빈을 돌리거나 연료 전지 역할을 하며, 건물에 난방과 전기를 공급하는 일 등이 포함되어 있다.

수소가 잠재력을 가지고 있는 가장 큰 이유 중 하나는 그것이 물과 유기화합물에서 주로 발견되는, 지구 표면상에서 세 번째로 가장 풍부한 원소이기 때문이다. 즉, 수소는 전기 또는 햇빛을 이용하여 물을 수소와 산소로 갈라 놓음으로써 생산되는 것이다. 따라서 이러한 수소의 널리 구하기 쉬운 특성은, 재생 불가능하고 짧게는 40년 이내에 고갈될 것으로 예상되는 화석 연료에 비해 수소가 훨씬 저렴한 대체 에너지 원천이 될 수 있음을 뜻한다.

게다가, 수소 에너지는, 방출 물질이나 부산물이 거의 없어 매우 환경 친화적이다. 수소는 또한 바람이나 태양열 등의 재생 가능한 에너지원을 사용하여 물을 분열시키는 환경친화적인 방식을 사용하여 분리할 수도 있다.

수소의 또 다른 이점은 저장과 운송이 용이하다는 점이다. 수소는 액체 또는 가스로 압축시켜 탱크에 담아 수송할 수 있다. 게다가, 수소 저장 합금을 사용해 고체 형태로 저장시키는 새로운 기술의 도래로, 쉽게 증발하는 수소를 수송하는 데 대한 걱정은 사라졌다. 이러한 방법으로, 우리는 단순히 금속원소와 수소를 결합시키고, 그 합금을 안정적인 상태로 수송한 후, 그 합금에 열을 가해 수소를 다시 추출하여 사용할 수 있다.

fossil fuel (석유, 석탄, 천연가스 등) 화석 연료 dwindle[dwíndl] 점차 감소하다, 점차 축소하다
alternative energy 대체 에너지 increasingly[inkríːsiŋli] 점점, 더욱더
application[æpləkéiʃən] (특정의 용도, 목적에) 적용, 이용 turbine[táːrbin] (기계) 터빈
fuel cell 연료 전지 hydrogen[háidrədʒən] 수소 element[éləmənt] 원소, 요소
primarily[práimerəli] 본래, 주로 organic compound 유기 화합물 hydrocarbon[hàidrəkáːrbən] 탄화수소
widespread[wáidspréd] 널리 보급된, 광범위한 availability[əvèiləbíləti] (입수) 가능성, 유용성
non-renewable (자원이) 재생 불가능한 project[prèdʒekt] 예상하다 deplete[diplíːt] 고갈시키다
environmentally friendly = eco-friendly 환경 친화적인 barely[bɛ́ərli] 간신히, 가까스로 emission[imíʃən] 배기가스
by-product 부산물 split[split] (분자, 원자등을) 분열시키다 compress into~ ~으로 압축시키다
with the advent of~ ~의 도래로, ~의 등장으로 alloy[ǽlɔi] 합금 volatile[váləti] 휘발성의, 변하기 쉬운
stable condition (분해, 변화하지 않는) 안정적인 상태

Listening

OK, let's take a look at hydrogen energy today. While it may look like a promising source of energy, on closer inspection, it doesn't pass the test. First of all, although water is widely available, the cost of electricity required to obtain hydrogen from water is one huge barrier... in fact did you know that the per-kilogram cost of renewable hydrogen is much higher than the per-gallon cost of gasoline?

Hmmm, what else?... well, when we look at splitting water to obtain hydrogen, we have to take into account that we'll still be relying on electricity, which isn't really environmentally friendly. In other words, the harm to our planet doesn't disappear, but it simply moves somewhere else in the process of producing the energy. On top of that, when we look at using renewable energy sources to split water, it's not always feasible because, well... we can't control the weather! The wind won't blow and the sun won't shine when we need it to.

Another drawback to hydrogen energy is that it's not as easy to store and transport as you might have believed. Not only is transforming hydrogen into a liquid or a gas a difficult task, but hydrogen in these forms is very volatile and dangerous because it ignites fast. When it comes to a hydrogen storage alloy, its extraordinary weight makes it an unfeasible choice. For instance, if you're going to build a hydrogen-fueled car storing the energy in the alloy, the fuel tank alone would weigh more than 300kg!

오늘은 수소 에너지에 대해 살펴보도록 합시다. 그것이 유망한 에너지원인 것처럼 보일지도 모르지만, 정밀 검사를 해보면, 수소는 대체 에너지원으로 적절치 못합니다. 첫째로, 물은 쉽게 입수가 가능하지만, 물에서 수소를 얻기 위해 드는 전기 비용은 하나의 커다란 장벽입니다. 여러분들은 재생 가능한 수소의 킬로그램 당 가격이 휘발유의 갤런 당 가격보다 훨씬 높다는 사실을 알고 있었나요?

또 뭐가 있을까요? 수소 채취를 위해 물을 분해하는 과정을 살펴보면, 우리는 그다지 환경친화적이지 못한 전기에 여전히 의존할 것이라는 사실을 고려해야 합니다. 달리 말하자면, 지구가 입는 피해는 줄어드는 것이 아니라, 단지 에너지의 생산 과정 중 다른 부분으로 옮겨갈 뿐이라는 것입니다. 그밖에 또, 물을 분해하기 위해 재생 가능한 에너지원을 사용하는 것을 검토해보면, 그것은 항상 실행 가능한 것이 아닙니다, 왜냐하면, 우리가 날씨를 조종할 수 없기 때문이죠! 우리가 필요로 할 때 바람이 불고 햇빛이 비추리라는 보장은 없습니다.

수소 에너지의 또 다른 결점은 우리가 알고 있던 만큼 저장하고 수송하기가 쉽지 않다는 점입니다. 수소를 액체나 가스로 변화시킨다는 것은 어려운 작업일 뿐만 아니라, 이 상태에서의 수소는 빨리 발화되기 때문에 휘발성이 많고 위험합니다. 수소 저장 합금의 경우에는, 그것이 너무 무게가 많이 나간다는 점 때문에 실행 불가능한 선택사항 입니다. 예를 들어, 수소를 동력 에너지원으로 하는 차를 제작하는 경우, 연료 탱크만해도 무게가 300kg이 넘어요!

take a look at~ ~을 조사하다, ~을 살펴보다　promising[prámisiŋ] 장래성 있는, 전도유망한　closer inspection 정밀 심사
pass the test 검사를 통과하다, 적절하다고 판명되다　feasible[fíːzəbl] 실행할 수 있는, 가능한
drawback[drɔ́ːbæk] 약점, 결점　ignite[ignáit] ~에 불을 붙이다　when it comes to~ ~인 경우에는, ~의 문제에는
hydrogen storage alloy 수소 저장 합금　extraordinary[ikstrɔ́ːrdənèri] 엄청난, 비상한
unfeasible[ʌnfíːzəbl] 실행하기 어려운, 실시하기 어려운　hydrogen-fueled 수소를 동력 에너지원으로 하는
~alone[əlóun] ~만으로, ~만해도

2. Note-taking

읽기 노트

- Student evaluation – effective 학생 평가 – 효과적
  1. Ideal to judge tchrs 교사 평가에 이상적
    - see regularly 정기적으로 만남
    - rate comprhnsn, learning gain 이해도, 학업성취 평가
    - consumers → satisfctn level 소비자 → 만족도
  2. Promote ↑ edu. standard 교육 수준↑ 촉진
    - promotion & salary: administrator measure 승진 & 급료: 관리자에게 평가 척도
    - encourage tchrs 2 develop 교사들의 발전 장려
    - inform strnth & wkness 강, 약점 알려줌

- Student evaluation – study 학생 평가 – 연구 결과
  - 1. Not trusted 신빙성 없음
    - based on popularity / emotion 인기/감정에 기반
    - edu. service: diff. from other business 교육 서비스: 일반 사업과 다름
    - ┌ studnt: too immature / biased 학생/미숙, 편향적
  - 2. Not taken seriously 진지하게 받아들이지 않음
    - not figured into promotion, salary 승진, 급여에 미반영
    - tchrs disregard report 교사들 평가서 무시
      - → no change 4 few complaints 소수 불만을 위한 개선 없음

스크립트 및 해석

Reading

교육기관들은 서비스 품질을 평가하고 개선하기 위하여 다양한 방법을 사용한다. 그들은 교사의 능력을 평가하는데 있어 학생 평가가 효율적인 방법이라는 것을 발견했다. 종종 학생들은 익명으로 답안을 작성하고 의견을 써달라는 지시를 받는다. 그들의 의견은 여러 가지 이유로 유익하다.

첫째로, 학생들은 교사들을 평가하기에 이상적인 위치에 있다. 교사들과 정기적으로 대면하는 청소년은 그들의 교사가 학생들의 질문에 얼마나 잘 답변하는지 또는 동기부여를 할 수 있게 하는지를 평가하기에 어느 누구보다 나은 자격을 갖추고 있다. 학생들 자신의 이해도와 교육적 성과를 평가하기에는 학생들 자신이 가장 적합하다. 더욱이, 학생들은 교육 서비스의 소비자이기 때문에 그들의 만족도는 주목 받아야 할 것이다. 이런 방법을 통해 그들의 관심사를 알 수 있고 필요로 하는 바를 보다 더 잘 충족시킬 수 있다.

더군다나 학생 평가는 보다 높은 교육 표준을 촉진시킨다. 학생 평가가 교사의 진급과 봉급 인상의 기반으로 사용될 수 있기 때문에 많은 교사들은 이를 전문적 능력의 상승에 대한 증거로 삼는다. 관리자들 또한, 학급내의 성취도를 측정하기 위하여 학생 평가에 의존한다. 그 결과로, 학생 평가는 교육자들로 하여금 자기 계발을 하도록 장려한다. 더 나아지고자 하는 교사들은 학생들이 자신을 어떻게 보는지 알기를 원한다. 정기적인 보고는 교사들에게 그들의 장단점을 알려주고, 따라서 그들의 발전 정도를 확인할 수 있게 한다. 학생들이 개선 사항이 필요한 부분을 지적해 주기 때문에 이는 교사들이 직업적인 성장을 돕는다.

assess[əsés] 가치를 평가하다 competence[kámpitəns] 능력, 적성 on a regular basis 정기적으로
comprehension[kὰmprihénʃən] 이해, 이해력 basis[béisis] 원인, 기반 count on~ ~에 의지하다, ~에 기대하다
administrator[ədmínistrèitər] 관리자, 행정관 foster[fɔ́(:)stər] 촉진하다, 육성하다

Listening

Okay, now, all of you have been asked to fill out evaluation forms for instructors at one point or another in your education. From elementary school onwards, you've been giving feedback about your teachers without really knowing the effects of these assessments. Recent studies of school districts using student evaluations have demonstrated some of their negative aspects.

This might sound harsh, but... student evaluations can't be trusted. They're often based on popularity, not quality. Students, especially younger ones, can't reliably judge their teachers. Their responses are based on emotion; for example, perhaps they did well on the last test, or maybe they were scolded for tardiness and were mad at the teacher. Educational service is different from other types of services. It can't be evaluated using the same methods used in business. Likewise, students are consumers, but they're different from consumers in other markets... they're too immature and biased to properly assess teachers' abilities.

As a result, administrators rarely take student evaluations seriously. In real life, these eval's just don't figure into salary increases, promotions, or anything else that might motivate instructors. Higher-ups hardly ever take action to reward or reprimand teachers. I can tell you from personal experience that I've been getting positive reviews for years, and have yet to see the benefits. Studies also show that negative reports are also usually disregarded by teachers and administrators alike. Few changes to curriculum or teaching methods are made, if any. Educators are seldom pushed to change their ways just because a few kids are unhappy. It's impossible to please everyone, so many teachers, um, don't bother trying.

여러분 모두가 교육 과정 중 단 한번이라도 교사들을 위해 교사능력 평가서를 작성하라는 지시를 받은 적이 있을 거예요. 초등학교 때부터 여러분은 이 평가가 어떤 영향을 미치는지도 정확히 모른 채 교사들에 대한 의견을 제공했을 겁니다. 학생 평가를 이용한 학군들에 대한 최근의 연구는 그것의 몇 가지 단점들을 보여주었습니다.

가혹하게 들릴 수도 있겠지만, 학생 평가는 믿을 만한 것이 못됩니다. 학생 평가는 종종 교육의 질이 아닌 인기에 기반하고 있습니다. 학생들, 특히 나이가 어린 학생들은, 믿을만 하게 교사들을 평가할 수 없습니다. 그들의 대답은 감정에 기반을 두고 있죠. 예를 들어, 아마도 그들이 마지막 시험에서 좋은 성적을 받았다던가 혹은 지각 때문에 꾸지람을 들어 교사에게 화가 났었을지도 모릅니다. 교육 서비스는 다른 형태의 서비스와는 다릅니다. 그것은 상업에서 사용되는 것과 동일한 방법으로 평가될 수 없어요. 마찬가지로, 학생들은 소비자이지만, 그들은 다른 시장에서의 소비자들과 다릅니다. 그들은 너무 미숙하고 편견을 가지고 있어서 교사들의 능력을 올바르게 평가하기 힘들거든요.

결과적으로 관리자들은 좀처럼 학생 평가를 중요하게 여기지 않아요. 현실에서 이 학생 평가는 봉급 인상, 승진, 또는 교사들에게 동기부여를 할 만한 그 어떤 것에도 반영되지 않습니다. 고위 관계자들은 교사들에게 보상하거나 질책하기 위한 어떤 조치도 취하지 않거든요. 개인적인 경험을 토대로, 저는 지난 몇 년간 긍정적인 평가를 받았지만 그것으로 인한 혜택을 보지 못했다는 것을 말씀드릴 수 있습니다. 또한 연구는 부정적 평가 또한 마찬가지로 교사들과 관리자들로부터 경시된다는 것을 보여줍니다. 교육 과정이나 교육 방법에 생기는 변화는 없으며, 설사 있다 해도 매우 미미한 정도입니다. 단지 몇 명의 아이들이 만족하지 못한다고 해서 교육자들이 그들의 교육 방식을 바꾸도록 강요받는 경우는 좀처럼 없습니다. 모두를 만족시킨다는 것은 불가능하기에 많은 교사들은 아예 시도조차 하지 않아요.

fill out ~에 기입하다　at one point or another 단 한번이라도　assessment[əsésmənt] 평가, 판단
demonstrate[démənstrèit] ~의 증거가 되다, 증명하다　reliable[riláiəbl] 믿을 수 있는, 확실한
scold[skould] 꾸짖다, 잔소리하다　tardiness[tάːrdinis] 학업 성취 부족　likewise[láikwàiz] 역시, 마찬가지로
immature[imətjúər] 미숙한, 유치한　biased[báiəst] 편견을 지닌, 편향된　rarely[rέərli] 드물게, 좀처럼 ~하지 않는
figure into~ ~에 반영하다　higher-up (지위가 더) 높은 사람, 고위자　hardly[hάːrdli] 거의 ~않다
take action 행동을 취하다　reprimand[réprəmænd] 징계, 질책　disregard[dìsrigάːrd] 경시하다, 소홀히 하다
if any 설사 있다 해도, 만약 있다면

3. Note-taking

읽기 노트

- Advertisement – benefit to indiv. & nation　광고 – 개인 & 국가에 이득
  1. Informational　정보 제공
     - notify consumer new prod. & serv.　소비자에게 새로운 제품과 서비스 알림
     - e.g. new medicine ad　예) 신약 광고
  2. Cheap access to media　저렴하게 대중매체 이용
     - income from ad → afford prgrms at ↓ price　광고수입 → 낮은 가격으로 프로그램 제공
  3. Good 4 national interest　국익에 보탬
     - stimulate spending → essential 2 econ.　소비 촉진 → 경제에 필수
     - sales abroad ↑ → strengthen domestic econ.　해외 판매 ↑ → 자국 경제 강화

듣기 노트

- Advertising – critical approach 광고 – 비판적 접근
  1. Ad: only to sell 광고: 단순히 판매가 목적
     - not to inform 정보 제공 위함 아님
     - misinformation 잘못된 정보
     - to make ppl desire more 사람들 욕구 유발
  2. Expensive 비쌈
     - big cost of ad → pass 2 consumer, ↑ price 광고의 높은 비용 → 소비자에 전가, 가격↑
     - free TV → pay extra for products 무료 TV → 제품에 추가 지출
  3. Encourage buy more than afford 감당 못할 정도로 소비 장려
     - spur to spend on credit 신용기반 소비 자극
     - economy on borrowed funds: unhealthy 차용 자금 기반 경제: 바람직하지 않음

스크립트 및 해석

Reading

광고는 어떤 형태로든 수 세기간 존재해왔다. 하지만 최근 100년간, 광고는 보급의 정도에 있어 새로운 국면을 맞이했다. 오늘날에는 신문부터 시작해서, 버스 정류장 벤치, 그리고 티셔츠까지 수많은 종류의 판촉물을 거의 모든 곳에서 볼 수 있다. 그들은 사회에서 다양한 기능을 수행하는데, 개인과 국가 전체에 모두 이익을 준다.

우선, 광고는 정보를 제공하는 성격을 띤다. 광고는 소비자들에게 새로 출시된 제품과 서비스에 대해 알려 준다. 광고는 또한 새로 나온 상품이나 서비스를 어디서 구할 수 있는지, 어떻게 사용해야 하는지를 가르쳐 준다. 예를 들어, 건강 관련 잡지나 텔레비전의 광고들은 종종 다양한 질병에 걸린 사람들을 도울 수 있는 혁신적인 약의 출시를 알려 준다. 많은 경우, 이런 사람들은 광고가 아니었더라면 이러한 선택 사항에 대하여 알지 못할 것이다.

자주 등한시되는 광고의 또 다른 사회적 이점은, 전 국민이 저렴한 가격에, 심지어는 무료로 텔레비전, 라디오 또는 신문과 같은 매체에 접할 수 있게 해준다는 점이다. 오락 및 정보 서비스의 공급자들은 지면이나 방송시간을 판매함으로써 상당한 수익을 올린다. 그리하여, 그들은 뉴스와 방송 프로그램을 보다 현저히 낮은 가격에 배급할 수 있게 된다.

게다가, 광고는 국익에 이바지한다. 광고는 소비자 지출을 촉진하는데, 이것은 경제가 건실하게 돌아가게 하는데 필수적이다. 게다가, 많은 상품들이 세계에서 광고되고 수출되므로, 해외에서의 판매 증대는 국내 경제를 더욱 강화시킨다. 결국, 광고는 개인, 사회, 그리고 국가에 중요한 역할을 한다.

pervasiveness[pəːrvéisivnis] 퍼짐, 보급   promotion[prəmóuʃən] 홍보, 판촉
informational[ìnfərméiʃənəl] 정보를 제공하는   ad = advertisement 광고   groundbreaking[gràundbrèikiŋ] 혁신적인
be afflicted with~ ~로 괴로워하다   any number of 얼마든지, 제한없이   overlook[óuvərlúk] 등한시하다
societal[səsáiətəl] 사회적인, 사회의   substantial[səbstǽnʃəl] 상당한   airtime[ɛ́ərtaim] (광고의) 방송시간
programming services 방송 프로그램   substantially[səbstǽnʃəli] 현저히, 충분히   national interest 국익
strengthen[stréŋkθən] 강화하다, 튼튼하게 하다   domestic[dəméstik] 국내의   all in all 대체로, 통틀어 말하면

Listening

Let's take a more critical approach to advertising. The industry tells us that ads do the public real good. But anyone can tell you that the vast majority of ads are intended to do one thing and one thing only: sell a product. Whether that product is a banking service or a new pharmaceutical product is irrelevant. They aren't really meant to inform. In fact, advertisers have been repeatedly accused of using misinformation in their promotions. All this is done just to make people desire more things, most of which they don't actually need.

Another fact of advertising is that it's very expensive. Just think... a 30-second spot during the Super Bowl can cost upwards of $2 million. And how do advertisers cover those costs? Yep, by passing them onto consumers in the form of higher prices. So, you may be happy to watch the Super Bowl on TV for free, but you don't realize you'll end up paying extra for those products advertised during the game.

Another issue associated with advertising stems from these higher prices and the fact that ads encourage people to buy more — more than they can afford, in fact. Advertisements are spurring people to spend, spend, and spend to the point where consumers are paying for everything on credit. Any economist will be happy to tell you that an economy built on borrowed funds is not healthy. As everybody knows, spending money you don't have is not a smart long-term strategy, and the same goes for the general economy.

광고에 대해 좀 더 비판적인 접근을 해 봅시다. 광고업계는 광고가 대중에게 정말 이롭다고 합니다. 하지만 어떤 누구라도 대다수 광고들이 의도하는 바가 단 한 가지 밖에 없다는 것을 압니다. 바로 제품을 판매하는 것이죠. 그 제품이 새로운 은행 서비스인지 새로운 약품인지에 관계 없이 말이죠. 광고는 알려주는 것이 목적이 아닙니다. 사실상, 광고주들은 광고에 잘못된 정보를 사용하는 것에 대해 계속해서 비난을 받아 왔습니다. 이 모든 것들은 단지 사람들로 하여금 대부분 그들이 사실상 필요하지도 않은, 더 많은 것에 욕심을 내도록 하도록 하기 위한 것일 뿐입니다.

광고의 또 다른 점은 그것이 매우 비싸다는 것입니다. 한번 생각해 보세요. 슈퍼볼 경기 도중의 30초짜리 광고의 가격은 2백만 달러를 웃돕니다. 그렇다면 광고주들은 어떻게 이 손실을 메울까요? 맞아요, 바로 소비자들에게 더 높은 가격의 형태로 떠넘기는 것이지요. 따라서, 여러분은 텔레비전에서 무료로 슈퍼볼을 시청할 수 있다고 좋아할 지 모르지만, 여러분이 알지 못하는 것은, 결국엔 여러분이 이 경기 중 광고된 상품들을 사는데 추가로 돈을 내게 되고 말 것이라는 점이지요.

광고와 연관된 또 다른 문제점은 이런 높은 가격과 함께 그것이 사람들에게 더 많이 소비하도록 장려한다는 사실에서 비롯됩니다. 사실, 그들이 비용을 감당할 수 없을 정도까지 말이죠. 광고들은 사람들이 계속해서 소비를 하도록 자극하여 결국엔 그들이 모든 것에 대한 비용을 빌려서 충당하도록 만들고 있습니다. 어느 경제학자라도 빌린 자금을 기반으로 하여 세워진 경제는 바람직하지 못하다고 말할 것입니다. 누구나 알고 있듯이, 자기 것이 아닌 돈을 소비한다는 것은 장기적으로 봤을 때 현명하지 못한 계획이고, 그것은 경제 전반에도 마찬가지로 해당되는 것입니다.

critical[krítikəl] 비평의, 비판적인 **approach to~** (문제 따위의) 접근법 **vast majority** 과반수, 대다수
pharmaceutical[fàːrməsjúːtikəl] 약제의, 조제약의 **irrelevant**[iréləvənt] 관계없는 **advertiser**[ǽdvərtàizər] 광고주
repeatedly[ripíːtidli] 반복적으로 **misinformation**[mìsinfɔːrméiʃən] 오보
the Super Bowl 슈퍼볼 (미국 프로 미식 축구의 왕좌 결정전) **cover**[kʌ́vər] (손실을) 메우다 **pay extra** 비용을 더 지불하다
stem from~ ~에서 비롯되다 **spur**[spəːr] 자극하다, 선동하다 **to the point where~** ~할 지경이 될 때까지
built on~ ~에 기반하여 세워진 **borrowed funds** 빌린 자금 **the same goes for~** ~에도 마찬가지다

4. Note-taking

읽기 노트

- Flexible working arrangement – benefits 자유 시간 근무제 – 혜택
  - 1. Good 4 employers: hire best workers 고용주 이익: 우수 직원 고용
    - travel in non-rush hr: save time 혼잡 시간 피해 출퇴근: 시간 절약
    - accommodate sched. needs: productive workers 일정 관련 요구 충족: 능률적인 직원들
  - 2. Good 4 employees 직원들 이익
    - work when they want : happy, productive 원할 때 근무: 행복, 능률적
    - give options: sleep / class 선택권 부여: 잠/수업
    - family: spend time 2gether 가족: 함께 시간 보냄
      - → family life improves → 가족 생활 개선

듣기 노트

스크립트 및 해석

Reading

9시부터 5시까지로 제한되어 있는 근무시간에 대한 근로자들의 수많은 불평에 따라, 많은 회사들이 자유 시간 근무제를 도입하기 시작했다. 이는 직원들이 할당된 주 40시간의 근무시간을 채우기만 한다면, 언제든지 원하는 시간에 일할 수 있도록 해준다. 이러한 일정은 고용주와 고용자 모두에게 많은 혜택을 제공한다.

첫째로, 자유 시간 근무제를 도입한 고용주는 최고의 직원들을 고용할 수 있다. 많은 근로자들은 오랜 시간이 걸리고 불편한 통근을 하는데 이것은 집에서 거리가 먼 직장에 다니는 것을 단념하게 한다. 자유 시간제는 직원들이 붐비는 시간대를 피해 통근할 수 있도록 해주며 많은 시간을 절약할 수 있게 한다. 더욱이, 어떤 직원들은 하루 중 특정 시간대에 더욱 생산적이므로, 그에 따라 일정을 짜고 싶어한다. 이유를 막론하고, 스케줄에 대한 사람들의 욕구를 충족시켜 줄 수 있는 고용주들은 가장 뛰어난 직원들을 고용하고 계속 보유할 수 있으며, 따라서 회사의 생산력을 향상시킬 수 있다.

게다가, 자신이 근무하고 싶을 때 근무하는 직원들은 행복하고 생산적이다. 자유 시간 근무제는 직원들이 집중력이 떨어지는 날에는 근무시간을 줄이고, 집중력이 높은 날에는 근무시간을 늘릴 수 있도록 해준다. 더욱이, 자유 시간 근무제는 근로자들에게 집에서 늦잠을 자거나, 혹은 수업을 듣기 위해 일찍 퇴근할 수 있는 선택권을 준다. 대체로, 이렇게 융통성을 많이 갖게 되었을 때 사람들은 더 자유롭게 인생을 스스로 통제하고 있다는 느낌을 받는다.

마지막으로, 가족들도 자유 시간 근무제의 이익을 본다. 함께 시간을 보내기 위해 각자의 일정을 조정할 수 있기 때문이다. 흔히, 부모들은 아침에 직장으로 출근해야 하므로 아이들과 함께 보낼 시간이 없다. 자유 시간 근무제는 가족들이 함께 근사한 아침식사를 즐길 수 있도록 해줄 것이다. 아니면, 일찍 출근하고 일찍 퇴근하여 자녀들과 오붓한 시간을 보낼 수도 있다. 어떤 경우든 간에, 가족 일원들이 함께 시간을 보내기 위해 각자의 일정을 조정할 수 있을 때, 가족 관계는 더욱 좋아진다.

restrictive [ristríktiv] 제한적인, 구속성의   institute [ínstitjùːt] 세우다, 제정하다   flexible [fléksəbl] 융통성 있는
arrangement [əréindʒmənt] 조정, 협의   allot [əlát] 분배하다, 배분하다   inconvenient [ìnkənvíːnjənt] 불편한, 귀찮은
dissuade [diswéid] (설득하여) 단념시키다   on top of that 게다가, 무엇보다도   productive [prədʌ́ktiv] 생산적인
accordingly [əkɔ́ːrdiŋli] 그에 따라서, 그에 알맞게, 적절히   accommodate [əkámədèit] 편의를 도모하다, 조절시키다
retain [ritéin] 계속 유지하다, 보유하다   attentive [əténtiv] 주의 깊은, 세심한   sleeping in late 늦잠 자기
all in all 대체로   go off 떠나다, 사라지다   alternatively [ɔːltɔ́ːrnətivli] 번갈아, 교대로
quality time 오붓한 시간, 즐거운 시간

Listening

All right, hmm, let's take a closer look at this flexible hours working arrangement where workers can come and go as they please. Well, studies reveal some interesting findings.

Ok, let's look at employers' experiences first. Many companies lost money because they didn't have enough employees working at times that coordinated with other companies' business hours. And you know what else? Team meetings were almost impossible to schedule because everyone worked at such different times. So, companies had a hard time, you know, getting group projects off the ground. What's more, employers had to stay open at odd hours for a few random employees. This meant, well, let's see, higher building maintenance costs.

Ok, now let's look at flex time's effects on employees. Workers often felt isolated, with no sense of teamwork and group spirit to keep them motivated and happy in their jobs. With people coming and going at different times, there was no sense of working together at one company. As a result, it was often difficult for employees to become friends with each other. Let's just say the working environment felt, um, rather bleak and miserable.

Now, let's turn to the last area related to flex time: family life. Uh, as it turns out, people had less time to spend with their families! Surprising, isn't it? But when we look more closely, we see that people usually come home for dinner at the same time and spend time together. But now with flex time, family members often leave and, well, come home at different times. For instance, some people like to sleep in and work late while their spouses, you know, want to go to work early and enjoy the evening at home. As a result, flex time means that these people won't have much time to spend together. This lack of quality time together creates distance and strain in family relationships.

근로자들이 원하는 시간에 출퇴근할 수 있는 자유 시간 근무제에 대해 더 알아보도록 합시다. 여러 가지 연구는 흥미로운 조사 결과를 밝혀 냅니다.

우선 고용주들의 경험에 대해 먼저 알아봅시다. 많은 기업들은 다른 회사의 근무시간과 같은 시간대에 일하는 직원 수가 부족하여 손실을 겪었죠. 그리고 또 어떤지 아세요? 모든 직원들이 일하는 시간대가 달랐기 때문에, 팀 회의 일정을 짜기란 거의 불가능했죠. 따라서, 회사들은 그룹 프로젝트를 진행하는데 많은 어려움을 겪었습니다. 더군다나, 고용주들은 엉뚱한 시간에 근무하는 몇몇 직원들을 위해 사무실을 열어두어야 했죠. 이로 인해 건물 유지 비용은 더 많이 들게 되었고요.

이제는 자유 시간 근무제가 직원들에게 미치는 영향에 대해 알아보도록 합시다. 일에 있어서 동기를 부여해 주고 만족을 느끼게 하는 팀워크나 공동체 의식이 없었으므로, 근로자들은 종종 고립감을 느꼈습니다. 사람들이 서로 다른 시간에 출퇴근했기 때문에, 그들은 같은 회사에서 근무하고 있다는 동질감을 느끼지 못했습니다. 결과적으로, 흔히 직원들끼리 서로 친해지는 것은 어려웠습니다. 근무 환경은 상당히 삭막하고 비참한 분위기였죠.

이제 자유 시간 근무제와 관련된 마지막 부분인 가족 관계를 살펴봅시다. 사실 사람들은 가족과 같이 보내는 시간이 더 줄어들었어요! 놀랍지 않나요? 하지만 좀 더 주의 깊게 살펴보면, 우리는 사람들이 대체적으로 같은 시간에 귀가하여 저녁을 먹고 함께 시간을 보낸다는 것을 알 수 있습니다. 하지만 자유 시간 근무제로 인해, 가족 일원들은 종종 서로 다른 시간에 출근하고 다른 시간 대에 퇴근했습니다. 예를 들면, 어떤 사람들은 아침에 늦잠을 자고 밤늦게 일하기를 원하는 반면, 그들의 배우자는 아침 일찍 출근하고 저녁시간을 집에서 보내고 싶어할 수도 있습니다. 결과적으로, 자유 시간 근무제는 이러한 사람들이 함께 보낼 수 있는 시간이 많지 않음을 뜻하죠. 이렇게 함께 보내는 오붓한 시간이 부족하면 가족 간에 서로 서먹하게 되며 관계가 상하게 됩니다.

> **as one pleases** 마음대로   **finding**[fáindiŋ] 연구 결과, 조사 결과   **coordinate with ~** ~와 조화되다
> **off the ground** 시작하여, 착수하여   **odd**[ɑd] 이상한   **random**[rǽndəm] 되는 대로의
> **maintenance**[méintənəns] 유지, 보수 관리   **isolated**[àisəlèitid] 고립된   **motivate**[móutəvèit] 동기를 주다
> **bleak**[bli:k] 황량한, 암울한   **miserable**[mízərəbl] 비참한, 불행한   **spouse**[spaus] 배우자, 남편/아내
> **quality time** 가장 재미있고 가치있는 시간   **strain**[strein] 긴장 관계

HACKERS Practice 🎧 *Track 7*   p.104

1. Note-taking

읽기 노트

- Group study – advantages 그룹 스터디 – 이점
  - 1. <u>Encouraging</u> 격려가 됨
    - – more motiv. 동기 부여
    - – help ppl intimidated by a subj. 특정 과목에 겁먹은 학생을 도움
  - 2. <u>Support each other</u> 서로 도움을 줌
    - – share, explain: cooperate 공유, 설명: 협동
    - – teach: best way 2 learn 가르치기: 배우기에 가장 좋은 방법
  - 3. <u>Save time</u> 시간 절약
    - – split research 조사 분담
    - – save time, effort 시간, 노력 절약

듣기 노트

- Group study – S's experience 그룹 스터디 – 학생들의 경험
  - 1. <u>Discouraging</u> 낙담시킴
    - – some don't do assign. or show up 과제를 하지 않거나 아예 빠지는 학생
    - – morale↓ 의욕↓
  - 2. <u>Help: not reciprocal</u> 도움: 비상호적
    - – freeloading 무임승차
    - – weak students rely on better ones 못하는 학생은 잘하는 학생에게 의존
  - 3. <u>Misuse time</u> 시간 낭비
    - – waste time reviewing easy concept 쉬운 개념 복습에 시간 낭비
    - – chat → socialize 수다 → 사교 모임이 됨

Summary

① <u>The lecturer examines</u> the actual experiences of people who studied in groups. This casts doubt on the reading passage's claim that group study is an encouraging, supportive, and time-saving process.

② <u>First,</u> it often turned out in group study that many students did not do their parts properly, which brought down morale. Members felt discouraged and less motivated when others in the group complained or didn't show up. ③ <u>This rebuts the reading passage's claim that</u> group study is encouraging and motivating.

④ Next, the help was not reciprocal. The group study system created freeloaders who were carried on smarter students' shoulders. ⑤ Thus, the lecturer argues against the point made in the reading that all participants benefit from group study by supporting each other.

⑥ Last, time was wasted in group study. Students either chatted or spent unnecessary time reviewing concepts for unprepared participants. ⑦ All of these points refute the reading passage's assertion that group study is a beneficial activity.

해석   교수는 그룹 스터디를 했던 사람들의 실제 경험을 알아본다. 이것은 그룹 스터디가 의욕을 북돋아주고, 보완적이며, 시간을 절약하는 공부 방법이라는 지문의 주장에 의문을 던지는 것이다.

첫째로, 종종 그룹 스터디는 많은 학생들이 자신의 역할을 제대로 하지 않아 사기를 저하시키는 것으로 판명되었다. 일원들은 그룹 내의 다른 이들이 불평을 하거나 모임에 나오지 않을 때면 낙담하게 되고 의욕을 잃게 된다고 느꼈다. 이것은 그룹 스터디가 고무적이고 동기 부여를 해준다는 글의 주장을 반박하는 것이다.

다음으로, (그룹 스터디에서의) 도움은 상호적인 것이 아니었다. 그룹 스터디의 시스템은 무임승차를 하는 사람, 즉 똑똑한 학생들에게 도움을 받기만 하는 이들을 양산했다. 그러므로, 교수는 그룹 스터디의 모든 참가자들이 서로를 도움으로써 혜택을 받는다는 지문의 주장에 대해 반대 의견을 편다.

마지막으로, 그룹 스터디에서는 시간이 낭비되었다. 학생들은 잡담을 하거나 또는 준비가 안된 참가자들을 위해 개념을 복습하는 데 불필요한 시간을 보냈다. 이러한 모든 점들은 그룹 스터디가 유용한 활동이라는 지문의 주장을 반박한다.

어휘   **cast doubt on** 의문을 던지다, 의혹을 제기하다   **encouraging**[inkə́:ridʒiŋ] 고무적인   **supportive**[səpɔ́:rtiv] 지지하는
time-saving 시간 절약해 주는   **morale**[mərǽl] 사기   **discourage**[diskə́:ridʒ] 낙담시키다
show up (모임 등에) 나타나다   **bring down** 떨어뜨리다, 저하시키다   **rebut**[ribʌ́t] 논박하다
reciprocal[risíprəkəl] 상호적인   **freeloader**[frí:lòudər] 무임승차하는 사람   **chat**[tʃæt] 잡담하다
review[rivjú:] 재검토하다, 복습하다   **unprepared**[ʌnpripéərd] 준비가 안된   **refute**[rifjú:t] 반박하다
assertion[əsə́:rʃən] 단언   **beneficial**[bènəfíʃəl] 유용한

스크립트 및 해석

Reading

그룹 스터디를 하는 학생들의 수가 점차 증가하고 있다. 그룹 스터디는 참여한 사람 모두에게 확실한 이점이 있다. 첫째로, 어떤 학생들은 스스로 학습할 의욕을 가지고 있지 않지만, 다른 학생들과 공부를 하는 것은 학습동기 부여를 해줄 뿐만 아니라 격려도 된다. 그룹 스터디는, 예를 들어 특정 과목들에 겁을 먹고 그 과목들을 스스로 공부하지 않는 몇몇 사람에게 이익이 될 수 있다.

둘째로, 그룹 스터디의 일원들은 서로 격려하는 환경 속에서 이득을 얻는다. 그룹학습의 일원들은 지식을 공유하고, 이해가 되지 않는 부분을 서로 설명해 주고, 협동적으로 학습을 하게 된다. 남에게 가르쳐 준다는 것은 효과적인 학습법이 될 수 있고, 학생들은 함께 공부하고 정보를 공유할 때 과목들을 더 깊이 이해할 수 있다.

마지막으로, 그룹 스터디는 정보를 찾는데 소요되는 시간을 절약해 준다. 각 일원들은 각자 맡은 주제를 조사하여 추후 서로에게 알려 줌으로써 조사에 대한 부담을 덜 수 있다. 이것은 서로 같은 조사를 중복함으로써 낭비되었을 시간을 절약해 준다.

   definite[défənit] 명확한   **inspiration**[ìnspəréiʃən] 영감, 격려   **encouragemen**[inkə́:ridʒmənt] 격려
   intimidate[intímədèit] 겁주다   **aspect**[ǽspekt] 양상, 정세   **comprehend**[kàmprihénd] 이해하다
   pass along 전하다   **duplicate**[djú:pləkit] 되풀이하다

Listening

OK, so, let's look at what some students who studied in groups had to say about their experience. Many of them found group study discouraging. Why? Well, some members didn't do their assignments properly or on time, or even at all which obviously brought down group morale. Even worse, some students stopped showing up to group sessions, which also made everyone suffer.

And you know what else? Help was often not reciprocal. Group study seemed to, um, promote a lot of free loading... stronger students tended to carry an unequal workload. Weaker students probably felt they didn't have to study or learn on their own... they could rely on the more capable or prepared members to explain things to them.

Finally, many students complained about the misuse of time in group study situations. Smarter students wasted a lot of time reviewing concepts that everyone should have been familiar with. And uh, let's see, students often chatted instead of getting to the task at hand. So group study often turned into group socializing.

그러면 그룹 스터디를 했던 몇몇 학생들의 견해를 들어보도록 합시다. 그들 중 다수는 그룹 스터디가 의욕을 꺾는다고 생각했다고 합니다. 왜냐구요? 몇몇 일원들이 자신들이 맡은 과제를 충실히 하지 않거나, 제시간에 하지 않거나, 심지어는 아예 하지 않은 경우도 있어 그룹의 사기가 꺾였기 때문입니다. 더 심각한 점은, 몇몇 학생들이 그룹 모임에 아예 참석하지 않기 시작했고, 이로 인하여 모든 일원들이 피해를 보았다는 것입니다.

또한 서로에게 도움을 주는 것은 흔히 상호적인 것이 아니었습니다. 그룹 스터디는, 무임승차를 장려하는 것 같아 보였습니다. 공부를 잘 하는 학생들이 공부 분량을 불리하게 감당하는 경향이 있었거든요. 뒤쳐지는 학생들은 아마도 자신들이 스스로 공부하거나 배울 필요가 없다고 생각했을지도 모릅니다. 그들은 준비를 잘 해 온 사람이나 유능한 사람들이 그들에게 모든 것을 설명해 줄 것이라고 의지할 수 있었으니까요.

마지막으로, 많은 학생들은 그룹 스터디 상황에서 시간이 제대로 활용되지 않은 것에 대해 불평했습니다. 보다 똑똑한 학생들은 모두들 이미 알았어야 하는 개념을 재검토함으로써 많은 시간을 낭비했습니다. 그리고 학생들은 종종 공부를 바로 시작하지 않고 대신 잡담을 하기도 했죠. 그래서 그룹 스터디는 종종 사교 모임으로 변하기도 하였습니다.

discouraging[diskə́:ridʒiŋ] 낙담시키는, 실망스러운 obviously[ábviəsli] 명백하게, 분명히
bring down 떨어뜨리다, 저하시키다 morale[mərǽl] 사기 session[séʃən] 모임
freeload[frí:lóud] 무임승차하다, 공짜로 얻다 unequal[ʌní:kwəl] 불공평한, 동등하지 않은
capable[kéipəbl] 유능한, 역량이 있는 misuse[misjú:s] 오용, 남용 socialize[sóuʃəlàiz] 사교활동을 하다

2. Note-taking

읽기 노트

- Digital library – benefits 디지털 도서관 – 장점
  1. Easy to access 접근이 용이
     - ppl disabled, live far 장애인, 멀리 사는 사람
  2. Time-saving & conven. 시간 절약 & 편리
     - saves time 2 go & search 가고 찾는 시간 절약
     - can read online at home 집에서 온라인상 독서
  3. Intellect. world: vigorous 지식인 세계 – 활발
     - share info → book quality ↑ 정보 공유 → 저서 수준↑
     - encouraged ∵ impact more readers 장려됨: 더 많은 독자에 영향

Possible **Answers** & Scripts

듣기 노트

> - Digital library – drawbacks 디지털 도서관 – 단점
>   1. Need access to computer 컴퓨터에 대한 접근성 필요
>   - poor w/o comp.: left out 컴퓨터 없는 가난한 사람: 소외
>   - benefit only rich w/ comp. 컴퓨터 소지한 부유한 사람에게만 유리
>   2. Overwhelmed with info 정보에 압도당함
>   - books online, endless results 4 one info
>   정보 하나를 위해 온라인책, 수많은 검색 목록 뒤져야 함
>   → time-consuming, demanding → 시간 소모적, 노력 요함
>   3. Intellect. prop. prob. 지적 재산권 문제
>   - ppl not buy book → authors: no profit, discouraged
>   사람들이 책을 사지 않음 → 저자: 수익 없음, 낙담

Summary

① The lecturer discusses some of the negative features of digital libraries. This casts doubts on the reading passage's claim that digital libraries are beneficial.

② First off, digital libraries cannot be endorsed because people need to have access to computers in order to use them. This means that the poor are unable to use them and that only the rich with computers at home benefit. Thus, the lecturer's point contradicts the reading passage's assertion that everyone can easily access digital libraries.

③ In addition, digital libraries provide so much information that it overwhelms people. It is actually time-consuming and wearying to wade through search results or an entire book online to find one piece of information. ④ This rebuts the reading passage's contention that digital libraries are time-saving and convenient.

⑤ Finally, intellectual property issues come to the forefront because of digital libraries. People don't buy books much anymore because whole books are available online. This discourages authors who don't receive the profits from their hard work. As a result, digital libraries discourage intellectuals, ⑥ contrary to the reading passage's assertion that they make the intellectual world more vigorous with the ease of sharing of ideas and an increased number of readers to impact.

해석　교수는 디지털 도서관의 몇몇 부정적인 특성에 대해 토의한다. 이것은 디지털 도서관이 이롭다는 지문의 주장에 의혹을 제기하는 것이다.

디지털 도서관을 지지할 수 없는 이유 중 하나는 사람들이 도서관을 이용하기 위해서 컴퓨터에 접속해야 한다는 것이다. 이것은 가난한 사람들은 디지털 도서관을 이용할 수 없고 오직 집에 컴퓨터가 있는 부유한 자들만이 혜택을 본다는 것을 의미한다. 그러므로, 교수의 논점은 모든 사람들이 쉽게 디지털 도서관을 이용할 수 있다는 지문의 주장을 반박하는 것이다.

게다가, 디지털 도서관은 너무 많은 정보를 제공하여 사람들을 당황하게 한다. 정보 하나를 찾기 위해서 검색 결과나 온라인 책 전체를 뒤져보는 일은 실로 시간 소모적이고 지루하다. 이것은 디지털 도서관이 시간을 절약해주며 편리하다는 지문의 주장을 반박하는 것이다.

마지막으로, 지적 재산권 문제가 디지털 도서관으로 인해 주목받게 된다. 책 내용 전부를 온라인상에서 구할 수 있으므로 사람들은 더 이상 책을 많이 사지 않는다. 이것은 열심히 일한 것에 대한 대가를 받지 못하는 작가들의 의욕을 꺾는다. 그 결과, 디지털 도서관은 지식인들을 낙담시킨다. 이것은 의견 교환이 용이해지고 영향을 끼칠 수 있는 독자가 늘어나 지식 세계를 더욱 활기차게 만든다는 지문의 주장과 상반되는 것이다.

어휘 endorse[indɔ́ːrs] 지지하다, 시인하다 contradict[kὰntrədíkt] 반박하다 assertion[əsə́ːrʃən] 주장, 단언
overwhelm[òuvərhwélm] 압도하다, 당황스럽게 하다 time-consuming 시간이 많이 들어가는 weary[wí(ː)əri] 지치게 하다
contention[kənténʃən] 주장 intellectual property 지적 재산권 come to the forefront 세상의 주목을 받다
intellectual[ìntəléktʃuəl] 지성인, 지식인 vigorous[vígərəs] 활기 있는, 원기 왕성한

스크립트 및 해석

Reading

세상은 점차 기술적으로 더욱 진보하고 있다. 디지털 도서관은 사용자들에게 다양한 혜택을 제공함으로써 이 추세를 이어가고 있다.
첫째로 책이 어디에 위치하든지 간에 누구라도 손쉽게 접근할 수 있다. 만일 사람들이 움직이는 데 불편이 있어서 도서관에 직접 방문하여 책을 찾기 힘들다면, 디지털 도서관이 이 문제를 해결해 준다. 장애를 가진 사람 또는 도서관으로부터 멀리 떨어진 곳에 사는 사람도 손쉽게 디지털 도서관으로부터 정보를 얻을 수 있다.
다음으로 디지털 도서관은 시간을 절약해 주며 편리하다. 도서관 건물까지 가서 고생스럽게 서가를 뒤지는 데 시간을 들일 필요가 없다. 디지털 도서관은 책 전체를 온라인상에서 읽을 수 있게 하므로, 집의 안락함 속에 앉아서 컴퓨터로 독서를 할 수 있다.
마지막으로, 디지털 도서관은 지식인들의 장을 더욱 활기차게 만들도록 돕는다. 이제는 온라인상으로 놀랄 정도로 많은 정보가 제공되므로 저자들은 정보를 쉽게 공유할 수 있고 더 높은 질의 책을 저술할 수 있다. 그들은 훨씬 더 많은 수의 독자들에게 영향을 미칠 수 있다는 사실을 알기에 보다 열성적으로 작품을 창조하는 데 있어 힘을 얻고 있다.

disabled[diséibld] 장애를 가진, 불구가 된 time-saving 시간 절약의 painstakingly[péinstèikiŋli] 힘들여, 힘들게
search through~ ~을 뒤지다 astounding[əstáundiŋ] 몹시 놀라는
enthusiastically[inθjùːziǽstikəli] 열광적으로, 열중하여

Listening

Let's examine what it'd really be like when digital libraries replace traditional libraries. First off, we can't ignore that people need to have access to computers in order to use digital libraries. This means that the poor in the U.S. are, um, often left out of the equation, as well as the majority of the world's population who lack access to computers, in their homes or otherwise. Right now, digital libraries benefit a narrow group: the rich with computers at home.

And you know what else? People are overwhelmed with all the information at their disposal. It's time-consuming and demanding when you have to wade through an entire book online to find one piece of information, not to mention the endless lists of search results.

Finally, the sheer amount of information that is available through digital libraries is raising concerns over intellectual property. Because whole books are available online, few people buy them anymore! Authors thus don't profit anymore from their hard work and end up feeling discouraged.

정말 디지털 도서관이 전통적인 도서관들을 대체한다면 어떠할지 검토해 봅시다. 우선, 우리는 사람들이 디지털 도서관을 사용하기 위해서는 컴퓨터를 사용할 수 있어야 한다는 사실을 잊어서는 안됩니다. 이는 미국의 가난한 빈민들은 종종 이 디지털 도서관의 이용에서 제외된다는 것을 뜻합니다. 집에서도 다른 장소에서도 컴퓨터를 이용할 방법을 갖추지 못한 세계 인구의 대다수는 물론이고 말이죠. 지금 현재 디지털 도서관은 한정된 집단에게만 혜택을 줍니다. 바로 집에 컴퓨터를 보유하고 있는 부유층이죠.
그리고 또 어딘지 아세요? 사람들은 자신들이 마음대로 쓸 수 있는 엄청난 정보의 양에 압도당해 있어요. 정보를 얻기 위해 무수한 인터넷 검색 목록을 뒤져야 하는 것은 말할 것도 없거니와 하나의 정보를 찾기 위해 온라인상으로 책 한 권을 통째로 읽어야 하는 것은 매우 시간 소모적이고 노력을 요하는 일입니다.

마지막으로, 디지털 도서관을 통해 얻을 수 있는 방대한 양의 지식은 지적 재산권에 대한 염려를 불러일으키고 있습니다. 책 전체를 온라인 상에서 입수할 수 있으므로 더 이상 책을 사는 사람들이 거의 없어요! 따라서 저자들은 더 이상 자신들의 힘든 노고에 대한 보상을 받을 수 없고 결국 낙담하게 됩니다.

> be left out of the equation ~에서 제외되다   access[ǽkses] 접근   otherwise[ʌ́ðərwáiz] 다른 방법으로
> be at one's disposal ~의 마음대로 처분할 수 있다, 임의로 쓸 수 있다   demanding[dimǽndiŋ] (일이) 큰 노력을 요하는
> wade through (책을) 힘들여 읽다   not to mention~ ~은 말할 것도 없이   sheer[ʃiər] 순전한, 완전한
> raise concerns over~ ~으로 염려를 불러 일으키다   intellectual property 지적 재산, 지적 소유권
> available[əvéiləbl] 이용할 수 있는

3. Note-taking

읽기 노트

- Internet – good learning tool 인터넷 – 좋은 학습 도구
  - → more online courses → 더 많은 온라인 강의
    - 1. Can study regardless of time & distance 시간, 거리 제약 없이 학습 가능
      - – take courses by univ. far away 멀리 있는 대학의 수업 수강
      - – can stop and resume class 수업 중단, 재개 가능
    - 2. Comm. benefits 의사소통 혜택
      - – online: no limit to time, all stud. get answers 온라인: 시간 제약 X, 모든 학생 답 얻음
      - – discussion between stud. out of class 학생들 간 수업 외 토론

듣기 노트

- Online class – survey by S 온라인 수업 수강생들 설문 조사 결과
  - 1. No limit → too much freedom 제약 X → 지나친 자유
    - – don't take seriously: procrast., drop 진지하지 않음: 시간 끌거나 그만둠
    - – imposs. to eval. 객관적 평가 불가능
  - 2. Hard to maintain discussion 토론하기 힘듦
    - – prof. not always avail. 교수가 항상 있는 것 아님
    - – takes long to get response 응답 얻기까지 오래 걸림
      - : frustrating, discouraged from asking 실망스러움, 낙심

Summary

① The lecturer explores students' responses to online classes. She offers evidence to show that online courses are not beneficial for students, ② which is in opposition to the reading passage's argument.

③ First of all, the lecturer states that online classes offer too much freedom. There is no sense of urgency. Thus, students don't take them seriously and often procrastinate or drop out. This lack of limitations can also lead to difficulties in assessing or testing students. ④ These points directly contradict the reading passage's claim that online classes are valuable because they offer so much freedom to students.

⑤ The other main point that the lecturer makes is that discussion is hard to maintain online. Professors don't have time to respond to each student's questions. This often frustrates students, who end up not asking questions because they know they will not get a response. Furthermore, students often do not have good online discussions with each other. This lack of interaction between students and teachers, not to mention among students, is a major frustration for online course takers. ⑥ The lecturer thus rebuts the reading passage's claim that internet classes promote communication.

해석　교수는 온라인 수업에 대한 학생들의 반응을 탐구한다. 그는 온라인 수업이 학생들에게 유용하지 않다는 것을 보여 주는 증거를 제시하는데, 이는 지문의 주장과는 반대되는 것이다.

첫째로, 교수는 온라인 수업이 지나치게 많은 자유를 허락한다고 언급한다. 온라인 수업에서는 절박감을 찾아 볼 수 없다. 그러므로, 학생들은 수업을 심각하게 받아들이지 않고 종종 미루거나 도중에 그만두어 버린다. 이러한 제한성의 결여는 또한 학생들을 평가하거나 테스트하는 데 어려움을 줄 수 있다. 이러한 요점들은 온라인 수업이 학생들에게 아주 많은 자유를 허락하므로 유익하다는 지문의 주장을 정면으로 반박하는 것이다.

교수가 제시하는 다른 하나의 논점은 온라인상으로는 토론이 지속되기 어렵다는 것이다. 교수들은 각각의 학생들의 질문에 대답할 시간이 없다. 이것은 종종 학생들을 좌절시켜, 학생들은 결국 질문을 하지 않게 된다. 왜냐하면 학생들은 답을 얻지 못할 것이란 것을 알기 때문이다. 게다가, 학생들은 흔히 서로 간에 만족스러운 온라인 토론을 하지 못한다. 학생들 사이의 상호 작용은 물론이고 학생과 교사간의 상호 작용의 부족은 온라인 수업을 수강하는 이들을 좌절하게 만드는 주요인이다. 그리하여 교수는 인터넷 수업이 의사소통을 촉진시킨다는 지문의 주장을 반증한다.

어휘　response[rispáns] 반응　evidence[évidəns] 증거　beneficial[bènəfíʃəl] 유용한
in opposition to ~ ~과 반대되는　urgency[ə́:rdʒənsi] 긴급　procrastinate[proukrǽstənèit] 꾸물거리다, 늑장부리다
drop out 중도에 그만두다　limitation[lìmətéiʃən] 한계　assess[əsés] 평가하다
contradict[kàntrədíkt] 반박하다, 모순되다　valuable[vǽljuəbl] 유익한, 귀중한　maintain[meintéin] 유지하다
frustrate[frʌ́streit] 좌절시키다, 실망시키다　rebut[ribʌ́t] 논박하다　promote[prəmóut] 증진하다, 촉진하다

스크립트 및 해석

Reading

인터넷은 전공을 막론하고 모든 학생들에게 전의 그 어느 때보다도 많은 양의 정보에 쉽게 접근하게 해주며 따라서 귀중한 학습 도구로 사용된다. 인터넷의 속도와 범위는 특히 편성된 수업에 사용하기에 적합하다. 그러므로, 교육자들은 인터넷의 활용 가치를 깨달아가면서, 더 많은 교과목을 온라인 강의로 듣는 것이 가능하도록 조치를 취하고 있다.

온라인 강좌는 학생들이 시간과 거리에 제약받지 않고 공부할 수 있게 한다. 학생들은 매우 멀리 위치한 대학들이 제공하는 강좌를 들을 수도 있다. 인터넷에 접속할 수만 있다면, 학생들은 자신이 한가한 시간에 강좌들을 들을 수도 있다. 만일 학생들이 시간이 너무 없어서 학습 분량을 따라갈 수 없다면, 잠시 수업을 중단했다가 형편이 될 때 다시 들을 수 있다.

인터넷 강좌는 이외에도 일반적인 강의에 비해 많은 혜택을 제공한다. 붐비는 강의실에서는 개별적으로 학생들에게 할애할 수 있는 시간이 절대적으로 부족한 반면, 온라인 교육과정은 교사가 각각의 학생들의 질문에 차례로 답할 수 있게 해준다. 의사 소통은 수업시간만으로 한정되지 않으므로, 각 학생은 질문에 대한 답을 반드시 받을 수 있으리라고 보장받는다. 수업 외의 시간에도 학생들간 토론이 가능하기 때문에, 온라인 강좌는 또한 게시판과 이메일을 활용하여 학생들 간에 의견을 교환할 수 있도록 장려한다.

discipline[dísəplin] 학과, 전공　~ than ever before 전의 그 어느 때보다도 ~하다
invaluable[invǽljuəbl] 매우 귀중한, 값을 헤아릴 수 없는　lend itself to~ ~에 쓸모 있다, 적합하다
constraint[kənstréint] 제약, 제한　at one's leisure 한가한 때에, 느긋할 때에　keep up with~ ~을 따라잡다

work-load 작업량, 학습량 **temporarily**[tèmpərέ(:)rəli] 일시적으로, 잠시 동안 **resume**[rézumèi] 다시 시작하다
simply[símpli] (부정문에서) 전혀, 절대로 **whereas**[hwɛərǽz] ~에 반하여, 그러나 **in turn** 차례로, 번갈아
be guaranteed to~ ~할 것을 보장받다 **message board** 게시판

Listening

Surveys of students and professors that have participated in online courses have brought certain things to light. Hmm, for example... Some professors feel that the absence of limitations gives students too much freedom to be an effective educational tool. I mean, since there is no sense of urgency, many don't take these classes, well... seriously. They procrastinate, or drop just because they don't have the discipline required to keep up. Another concern is, since students can take classes across the world from the institution offering them, progress is nearly impossible to evaluate objectively. Testing is just, sort of, unrealistic, since there's no way to give standardized tests or to control cheating.

And discussion, which we all know is necessary for learning, is really hard to maintain online. Professors simply can't be available to answer questions all the time. And they don't want to type out complicated explanations over and over again for each student. The fact that it takes so long to get a response can be really frustrating for students, and discourage them from even asking. So, uh the lag makes it extremely difficult to keep a vibrant discussion going between teacher and student, or among the students themselves. Let's just say that a frequent complaint of students taking online courses is that there's not enough interaction.

온라인 교육과정에 참여했던 학생들과 교수들에 대한 설문 조사는 특정 문제점들을 밝혀냈습니다. 예를 들어 몇몇 교수들은 전혀 제한이 없는 온라인 교육과정이 효과적인 교육 도구가 되기에는 지나친 자유를 허락한다고 생각합니다. 즉, 꼭 (공부를) 해야 한다는 절박감이 없기 때문에, 많은 학생들이 수업을 진지하게 듣지 않고 시간을 질질 끌거나, 수업을 따라가는 데 필요한 자제력이 없어서 단순히 수업을 그만두어버린다는 것이죠. 또 다른 걱정거리는, 온라인 강좌를 제공하는 교육기관으로부터 전 세계의 학생들이 수업을 들을 수 있기 때문에, 그들의 학업 성취력을 객관적으로 평가하는 것이 거의 불가능하다는 점입니다. 시험을 보는 것은 규격화된 시험을 제공하거나 부정 행위를 제지할 방법이 없기 때문에 비현실적이라는 것이죠.

그리고 우리가 모두 알고 있듯이, 토론은 학습에 있어서 필수적인 것인데, 온라인상으로 토론을 유지하기란 매우 까다롭습니다. 교수들이 언제나 모든 질문에 답변해 줄 수는 없습니다. 그리고 어차피 교수들이 학생들에게 개별적으로 복잡한 설명을 몇 번이고 계속해 타자로 쳐주고 싶어하지도 않고 말이죠. 질문에 대한 대답을 듣기까지 오랜 시간이 걸린다는 사실은 학생들로 하여금 좌절감을 느끼게 하고, 아예 질문하는 것을 단념시킬 수도 있지요. 그래서, 이러한 질문과 답변의 시간차로 인하여 교사와 학생 사이에, 또는 학생들끼리의 활발한 토의가 이루어지는 것이 어려워질 수도 있습니다. 그래서 온라인 학습과정을 이수하는 학생들이 주로 터뜨리는 불만은 상호 작용이 충분하지 않다는 것입니다.

bring ~ to light ~를 규명하다, 폭로하다 **absence**[ǽbsəns] 결여 **limitation**[lìmətéiʃən] 한도, 한계
urgency[ə́rdʒənsi] 긴급, 절박 **take ~ seriously** ~을 진지하게 받아들이다
procrastinate[proukrǽstənèit] 꾸물거리다, 늑장부리다 **objectively**[əbdʒéktivli] 객관적 견지에서
unrealistic[ʌ̀nri:əlístik] 비현실적 **standardize**[stǽndərdàiz] 표준에 맞추다, 규격에 맞추다
cheat[tʃi:t] 부정 행위를 하다, 규정을 어기다 **complicated**[kámpləkèitid] 복잡한, 난해한, 어려운
over and over again 몇 번이고 다시 **frustrate**[frʌ́streit] 좌절시키다, 실망시키다
discourage[diskə́:ridʒ] 용기를 잃게 하다, 낙담시키다 **lag**[læg] (속도 등이) 뒤떨어지다, 지체되다
vibrant[váibrənt] 활기에 넘치는 **interaction**[ìntərǽkʃən] 상호 작용

4. Note-taking

읽기 노트

- Lie detector – fluctuation → deceptive 거짓말 탐지기: 변동 → 거짓말
  1. Accurate 90% 90% 정확성
     – phys. response when lying 거짓말 시 생리적 변화 발생
     – response → involuntary 반응 → 무의식적
  2. Objective 객관적
     – skillful Q 잘 만들어진 질문
     – related Q & control Q 관련 질문 & 대조 표준 질문

듣기 노트

- Lie detector – research 거짓말 탐지기 – 연구 결과
  1. Inaccurate 부정확함
     – not measure truth but phys. change 진실이 아닌 생리적 변화 측정
     – taking test: intimidating → phys. changes from stress
        테스트 받는 것: 위협적 → 스트레스로 인한 생리적 변화 발생
     – ez 2 cheat 속이기 쉬움
  2. Subjective, biased agnst trthfl ppl 주관적, 정직한 사람들에게 편견
     – e.g. topic itself cause responses 예) 주제 자체만으로 반응 유발
     – examiners' too big influence 검시관이 결과에 큰 영향 미침
        : not prepared / misread data 준비가 안 됐거나 결과를 잘못 해석할 때

Summary

① The lecturer is casting doubt on the accuracy and objectivity of lie detectors. ② This refutes the reading passage's claim that lie detectors are a reputable means of determining if a person is lying or not.

③ One reason why polygraphs are inaccurate is that they don't measure truth but physiological changes that can be mistaken for lying. These changes can occur because people are nervous taking the test. On the other hand, it's easy to cheat the test by a variety of measures. ④ This contradicts the reading passage's view that lie detector tests are highly accurate.

⑤ Another reason to view polygraphs with suspicion is that the tests are very subjective and already biased against truthful people: a large number of errors occur. This is also due to examiners, whose behavior affects the results greatly when they don't prepare properly or misread the data. The lecturer thus provides information that is ⑥ contrary to the reading passage's claim that lie detector tests are objective.

해석　교수는 거짓말 탐지기의 정확성과 객관성에 의문을 던지고 있다. 이것은 거짓말 탐지기가 사람의 거짓말 여부를 결정하는 신뢰할 수 있는 수단이라는 글의 주장에 반박하는 것이다.

거짓말 탐지기가 정확하지 않은 이유 중 하나는 그것이 진실을 측정하는 것이 아니라 거짓말로 오해 받을 수도 있는 생리적 변화를 측정한다는 것이다. 이러한 생리적 변화들은 사람들이 검사를 받을 때 긴장하기 때문에 일어날 수도 있다. 반면에, 다양한 방도로 거짓말 테스트를 조작하기도 쉽다. 이것은 거짓말 탐지기 테스트가 아주 정확하다는 지문의 견해를 반박하는 것이다.

거짓말 탐지기를 의혹의 눈길로 바라보는 또 하나의 이유는 테스트가 매우 주관적이고 정직한 사람에 대해서 미리 편견을 가지고 있기 때문이다. 따라서 많은 실수가 일어나게 된다. 이것은 또한 검사관 때문이기도 한데, 검사관이 자료를 제대로 준비하지 않았거나 잘못 해석할 때에는 결과에 상당한 영향을 미치게 된다. 그러므로 교수는 거짓말 탐지기 테스트가 객관적이라는 지문의 주장과 상반되는 정보를 제공하고 있다.

어휘　**cast doubt on~** ~에 의혹을 던지다, 의구심을 제기하다　**accuracy** [ǽkjərəsi] 정확성　**objectivity** [àbdʒektívəti] 객관성
lie detector 거짓말 탐지기　**refute** [rifjúːt] 반박하다　**reputable** [répjətəbl] 훌륭한, 평판이 좋은
determine [ditə́ːrmin] 결정하다　**polygraph** [páligræf] 거짓말 탐지기 (=lie detector)
inaccurate [inǽkjərit] 부정확한　**measure** [méʒərz] 측정하다　**physiological** [fìziəládʒikəl] 생리적인
mistake [mistéik] 오해하다　**occur** [əkə́ːr] 일어나다　**cheat** [tʃiːt] 교묘히 벗어나다, 부정 행위를 하다
a variety of 다양한　**contradict** [kàntrədíkt] 반박하다, 부정하다　**suspicion** [səspíʃən] 의심, 혐의
subjective [səbdʒéktiv] 주관적인　**biased** [báiəst] 편견이 있는　**examiner** [igzǽmənər] 시험관, 조사관
behavior [bihéivjər] 행동　**properly** [prápərli] 제대로　**misread** [misríːd] 잘못 읽다, 해석하다
contrary to ~과 모순되는, 반대되는

스크립트 및 해석

Reading

거짓말 탐지기, 또는 폴리그래프라고 불리는 이 기계는, 생리학적 변화를 감지하는 의료 장비들의 집합체이다. 한 사람이 질문을 받을 때, 검사관은 그 사람의 심장 박동수, 혈압, 호흡 속도, 발한 속도가 정상치에 비해 어떻게 바뀌는지를 측정한다. (이러한 사항들의) 변동은 그 사람이 거짓말을 하고 있다는 것을 나타낼 수 있다.

연구 결과에 따르면 거짓말 탐지기는 모든 사건에서 거의 90%의 정확도를 나타낸다. 손에서 땀이 나는 것이나 심장 박동수가 빨라지는 등의 특정한 생리학적 반응은 사람들이 거짓말을 할 때 나타난다. 검사에서는 이런 일반적인 신호들을 포착하여 높은 적중률로 허위진술의 여부를 나타낼 수 있는 것이다. 통제 불가능한 생물학적 변동이 크게 일어난 다는 것은 종종 허위진술의 신호이며, 특히 그 사람이 반복되는 질문에 비슷한 반응을 나타낼 때 더욱 그러하다.

거짓말 탐지기 검사는 매우 객관적이며, 진상을 밝혀낼 목적으로 질문들이 고안되어 있다. 검사관들은 솜씨 있게 질문을 던지며, 피실험자의 문화적 개념, 신앙적 소신들도 고려한다. 그들은 10개의 질문을 하는데, 그 중 조사되고 있는 범죄사건이나 논쟁점에 관련된 질문은 세 네 개 밖에 되지 않는다. 나머지 대조군 질문들은 검사관들이 피실험자가 정직하게 답하고 있는지를 보여준다. 질문이 끝나면, 검사관들은 생리학적 반응에 관한 자료를 분석하여 허위 진술이 있었는지의 여부를 확실하게 단정지을 수 있다.

physiological [fìziəládʒikəl] 생리학적　**medical device** 의료 장비　**monitor** [mánətər] 측정하다
examiner [igzǽmənər] 조사관, 검사관　**respiratory rate** 호흡 속도　**perspiration** [pə̀ːrspəréiʃən] 발한작용, 땀
fluctuation [flʌ̀ktʃuéiʃən] 오르내림, 변동　**deceptive** [diséptiv] 거짓의, 허위의　**pick up on~** ~을 포착하다
deception [disépʃən] 속임, 사기　**uncontrollable** [ʌ̀nkəntróuləbl] 제어할 수 없는, 통제할 수 없는
designed in a way to~ ~을 하기 위한 목적으로 고안된　**pose a question** 문제를 제기하다
take into consideration~ ~을 고려하다　**relevant to~** ~에 관련된　**control** [kəntróul] (실험의) 대조 표준, 대조구
afterwards [ǽftərwərdz] 그 후에　**analyze** [ǽnəláiz] 분석하다

Listening

Ok, class, today let's examine lie detectors. New research indicates that they are much less accurate than previously thought. Polygraphs don't measure truth telling but physiological changes triggered by a wide range of emotions. For one, taking a test is intimidating. So, people often sweat and have increased blood pressure from the stress of the test, not from lying. What's more, it's easy to cheat the test. People often take sedatives or put anti-perspirant on their fingertips. Some people even press their feet down on tacks in their shoes after every question to have the same body reaction.

So, uh let's just say, the test is very subjective and designed with a bias against truthful people. Simply talking about certain sensitive topics can cause test subjects to become nervous and have body reactions that could be misread as lying. And you know what else? Because polygraph examiners are alone in the room with an examinee, his or her behavior greatly influences the results of the exam. So you see, an examiner who has not, well, prepared properly or misreads the data can give you an incorrect reading.

여러분 오늘은 거짓말 탐지기에 대해 알아보도록 합시다. 새로운 연구 결과에서는 거짓말 탐지기들이 생각했던 것보다 훨씬 부정확하다고 지적합니다. 거짓말 탐지기는 진실을 말하고 있는지 그 자체를 감정하는 것이 아니라 도리어 다양한 감정으로 인해 일어날 수 있는 생리적인 변동 현상들을 감지합니다. 첫째로, 검사를 받는다는 것은 많은 이들에게 겁을 줍니다. 그래서 종종 테스트를 받는 사람들은 땀을 흘리고 혈압이 높아질 수도 있습니다. 거짓말을 해서가 아니라, 검사를 받는 데서 오는 스트레스 때문에 말이죠. 게다가, 검사 결과를 속이는 것은 꽤나 쉬운 일입니다. 테스트 전에 진정제를 복용할 수도 있고 또는 손가락 끝에 지한제를 바를 수도 있습니다. 어떤 사람들은 심지어 질문을 받을 때마다 동일한 신체 반응을 보이기 위해 신발 안에 넣어둔 압정을 발로 밟기도 합니다.

그리고, 검사는 매우 주관적이고, 정직한 사람들에 대한 편견을 바탕으로 고안되었다고 할 수 있습니다. 단순히 특정 민감한 주제에 대하여 이야기 하는 것만으로도 피실험자들을 긴장하게 만들거나 거짓말을 하는 것으로 오인할 수 있는 신체적인 반응을 일으킬 수 있습니다. 또 어떤지 아세요? 거짓말 탐지기 검사관과 피실험자 두 사람만 한 방에 있기 때문에, 검사관의 행동이 검사 결과에 커다란 영향을 미치게 됩니다. 따라서, 준비를 제대로 하지 않거나 잘못 해석한 검사관은 잘못된 결과를 도출해 낼 수도 있습니다.

indicate[índikèit] 나타내다, 지적하다　trigger[trígər] (사건을) 유발하다　intimidate[intímədèit] 겁주다
sedative[sédətiv] 진정제　anti-perspirant 지한제 (땀이 나는 것을 방지하기 위해 바르는 것)
fingertip[fíŋɡərtìp] 손가락 끝　tack[tǽk] 압정　bias[bàiəs] 선입견, 편견
misread[misríːd] 잘못 읽다, 오해하다

5. Note-taking

읽기 노트

- Megastore – benefits　대형 점포 – 이점
  - 1. Cheaper　저렴
    - big capital → low price　많은 자본 → 낮은 가격
    - benefit 2 consumer　소비자에게 이익
  - 2. Conven.　편리
    - selection wide: save time & nrgy　선택의 다양함: 시간 & 에너지 절약
    - buy all items in one store　모든 제품을 한 장소에서 구입
  - 3. Good 4 econ.　경제에 이익
    - many jobs avail.　많은 일자리 창출
    - job, spending↑: econ.↑　직업, 소비↑: 경제↑

Possible **Answers** & **Scripts**

듣기 노트

- Megastore – drawbacks 대형 점포 – 단점
  1. No saving 절약 X
     - product on sale ↓ but others ↑ 세일 제품↓ 기타 제품↑
       → spend more 더 많이 지출
  2. Not conven. 편리 X
     - no unique item: only standard 독특한 상품 사라짐: 표준 상품만 남음
     - can't find anywhere: small shops closed 어디서도 찾을 수 없음: 작은 점포들 폐업
  3. Bad for econ. 경제에 불리
     - low-paying job: no option 저임금 직종: 선택의 여지가 없음
     - no full-time workers → no benefits/union 정규직 채용 안함 → 복리후생 / 노조 X

Summary

The lecturer examines the negative aspects of megastores. ① His information directly contradicts the reading passage's praise of these giant superstores.

② One simple reason that megastores don't pass the test is that they don't offer savings on products. In fact, people end up paying more at superstores than they would at smaller shops because non-sale products are more expensive. ③ This directly rebuts the reading passage's argument that megastores offer cheaper products than other stores.

④ Another reason why shopping at megastores is not recommended is that it's not convenient when you don't want mainstream products. Trying to find unique items is impossible there because they provide only standardized products. What's more, you can't find original products anywhere because small shops that stocked these items couldn't compete with giant superstores and closed down. ⑤ These points contradict the reading passage's claim that megastores are convenient because they offer many products in one place.

⑥ Finally, megastores harm local economies. They create undesirable, low-paying jobs. Unfortunately, people don't have other options because other stores with decent jobs went out of business competing with megastores. Worse yet, these stores also don't hire people full-time. As a result, employees don't receive benefits and can't form unions. ⑦ The lecturer thus refutes the reading passage's claim that superstores help local economies.

해석　교수는 대형 점포의 부정적인 측면을 검토한다. 그의 정보는 이러한 대형 점포에 대한 지문의 칭찬에 정면으로 반박하는 것이다.
　　　대형 점포가 합격점을 받지 못하는 한 가지 간단한 이유는 제품에 대한 할인을 해주지 않기 때문이다. 사실, 사람들은 작은 상점에서 보다 대형 점포에서 더 많은 돈을 지불하게 된다. 왜냐하면 세일을 하지 않는 상품은 더 비싸기 때문이다. 이것은 대형 점포가 다른 상점들보다 더 싼 제품을 제공한다는 지문의 주장을 반박한다.
　　　대형 점포에서의 쇼핑이 권고되지 않는 또 다른 이유는 주류의 제품을 원하지 않을 때 불편하기 때문이다. 대형 점포는 표준화된 제품만을 제공하기 때문에 그곳에선 독특한 제품을 찾기가 불가능하다. 게다가, 우리는 독창적인 제품을 어디에서도 구할 수가 없다. 왜냐하면

이러한 상품을 판매하는 작은 상점들이 대형 점포와 경쟁할 수 없어 문을 닫기 때문이다. 이러한 논점은 대형 점포가 많은 제품을 한 장소에서 판매하므로 편리하다는 지문의 주장을 반박하는 것이다.

마지막으로, 대형 점포는 지역 경제에 해를 끼친다. 대형 점포는 탐탁지 않은 저임금 직종을 양산한다. 불행히도, 사람들은 다른 선택 사항이 없다. 왜냐하면 좋은 일자리를 제공하는 다른 가게들이 대형 점포와 경쟁하다 파산했기 때문이다. 설상가상으로, 이러한 대형 상점들은 사람들을 정규직으로 고용하지 않는다. 그 결과 직원들은 복지 혜택을 받지 못하고 조합을 형성할 수도 없다. 그러므로 교수는 대형 점포가 지역 경제에 이바지한다는 글의 주장을 반박한다.

어휘 **megastore**[mégəstɔ̀ːr] 대형 점포 **contradict**[kɑ̀ntrədíkt] 반박하다, 모순되다 **rebut**[ribʌ́t] 논박하다
convenient[kənvíːnjənt] 편리한 **mainstream**[méinstrìːm] 주류의, 대세의 **standardize**[stǽndərdàiz] 표준화하다
compete with~ ~과 경쟁하다 **close down** 문을 닫다 **local economy** 지역 경제
undesirable[ʌ̀ndizáiərəbl] 바람직하지 못한 **decent**[díːsənt] 좋은, 남부럽지 않은 **union**[júːnjən] 조합
refute[rifjúːt] 반박하다

스크립트 및 해석

Reading

소규모 자영업체의 시대는 급속히 사라져가고 있다. 작은 전문 상점들은 거대한 대형 슈퍼마켓으로 대체되고 있다. 이러한 대형 점포들은 소비자들과 지역 경제 모두에게 도움을 준다.

대형 점포의 첫 번째 이점은 소규모 상점들보다 더 저렴한 가격의 상품을 제공한다는 점이다. 그들은 막대한 자본금을 보유하고 있으므로, 다량의 물품을 생산 또는 구입하여 작은 상점들보다 훨씬 저렴한 가격에 판매할 수 있다. 소비자들은 할인된 가격에 물건을 구매할 수 있고 돈을 절약할 수 있으므로, 이는 분명히 소비자들에게 이로운 것이다.

대형 슈퍼마켓의 또 하나의 이점은 매우 편리하다는 것이다. 그들은 매우 다양하고 품질이 좋은 물건들을 한 장소에서 취급한다. 따라서, 소비자들은 많은 시간과 에너지를 소비하지 않고도 다양한 인기 상품들을 구할 수 있다. 예를 들어, 예전에는 사람들이 옷, 신발, 전자 기기, 스포츠 물품 그리고 식품을 사기 위해 각각 다른 상점에 가야 했지만 이제 그들은 이 모든 물품들을 하나의 대형 슈퍼마켓에서 구매할 수 있다.

끝으로, 대형 점포들은 지역 경제에 많은 혜택을 제공한다. 이러한 대형 상점들이 개점하면, 출납원, 재고 관리인, 지배인과 같은 다양한 직책의 직원들을 필요로 하게 된다. 더군다나, 대형 점포들은 대부분 해당 지역의 사람들을 채용하고 훈련시킨다. 그에 따른 고용 창출, 지역 주민의 채용, 그리고 소비자 지출의 증가는 지역 경제를 활성화시킨다.

days of~ ~의 시대/풍조 **mom and pop store** 소규모 자영업체
specialty[spéʃəlti] (상점 등의) 명물, 특산품 **superstore**[sjúːpərstɔ̀ːr] (교외의) 대형 백화점/슈퍼마켓
can afford to~ ~할 여력이 있다, ~할 능력이 있다 **selection**[silékʃən] 엄선된 것, 선택의 대상이 되는 물품
range[reindʒ] 범위 **expend**[ikspénd] (시간, 노력 등을) 들이다, 소비하다 **previously**[príːviəsli] 이전에는
electronic appliances 가전제품, 전자 기기 **cashier**[kæʃíər] 출납원 **stocker** 재고 관리인
recruit[rikrúːt] 모집하다 **resulting**[rizʌ́ltiŋ] 결과적인, ~의 결과인 **revitalize**[riːváitəlàiz] 부흥시키다, 활력을 불어넣다

Listening

Today, we're going to look at a phenomenon sweeping the country. Megastores, and if they have lived up to their optimistic billing.

First of all, I have some unfortunate news for those of you who believe you save money by buying stuff from megastores. Products on sale for the week are often priced low, but other items are often deceptively more expensive than those at smaller stores. As a result, you ultimately spend more money at superstores than at little shops.

Not only that, megastores are not convenient when you want non-mainstream products. If you wish to buy unique items, superstores won't meet your demands because they only offer standardized products. But, to make matters worse, it won't be easy to find what you desire outside of megastores, either. Why? Well, let's just say, most small shops that stocked original goods were forced to close when large chains came into town.

Finally, giant superstores are really bad for local economies. Megastores create low-paying jobs that, you know, no one wants. Unfortunately, people have no other option than to take them because, uh, superstores run everyone else out of business. As a result, you find scores of teenagers and old people doing dead-end jobs there. And, oh, these stores tend not to hire people full-time, to avoid paying benefits and having unions form.

오늘 우리는 전국을 휩쓸고 있는 대형 점포에 대해 조사해보고, 대형 점포들이 낙관적인 선전에 부응하여 왔는지 알아보도록 합시다.

첫째로, 대형 점포에서 물건을 구매하면 돈을 절약할 수 있다고 믿는 사람들에게 유감스러운 이야기를 해야 겠네요. 그 주의 할인 상품으로 정해진 것들은 종종 가격이 낮게 책정되지만, 다른 물건들은 소규모 상점들과 비교했을 때 교묘하게 더 비쌉니다. 결과적으로, 여러분은 결국 작은 점포에서 보다 대형 슈퍼마켓에서 더 많은 지출을 하게 되죠.

그뿐만 아니라, 대형 점포는 비주류의 제품을 구매하려고 할 때 편리하지 않습니다. 만약 여러분이 독특한 상품을 구매하기 원한다면, 대형 슈퍼마켓은 규격화된 물품만을 취급하기 때문에 여러분의 요구를 충족시키지 못할 것입니다. 하지만, 설상가상으로, 대형 점포가 아니더라도 여러분이 희망하는 독창적인 물건을 찾기는 어려울 겁니다. 왜냐고요? 대규모의 할인 체인점이 들어섰을 때 독특한 물건을 들여놓던 대부분의 소규모 상점들은 어쩔 수 없이 문을 닫아야 했기 때문이죠.

마지막으로, 대형 슈퍼마켓들은 지역 경제에 매우 해롭습니다. 대형 점포들은 아무도 원하지 않는 낮은 임금의 일자리를 생성시킵니다. 불행하게도, 대형 슈퍼마켓들이 다른 모든 상점들을 폐업시키기 때문에, 사람들은 그 일자리를 받아들이는 것 외에는 선택의 여지가 없죠. 그 결과로, 수많은 청소년들과 노인들이 대형 슈퍼마켓에서 장래성 없는 일을 하고 있는 것을 찾아볼 수 있죠. 그리고, 이 대형 상점들은, 복리후생 혜택 제공과 노동조합 형성을 회피하기 위해 직원들을 정규직으로 고용하려 하지 않습니다.

phenomenon[finámənàn] 현상, 사건   sweeping[swíːpiŋ] (장소를) 휩쓸다
live up to~ ~에 부응하다   optimistic[àptəmístik] 낙관적인   billing[bíliŋ] 광고, 선전
deceptively[diséptivli] 현혹시킬 정도로, 헷갈리게   ultimately[ʌ́ltimitli] 마침내, 결국
not only that 비단 그뿐 아니라, 그뿐만 아니라   mainstream[méinstrìːm] (활동, 사상의) 주류
standardize[sténdərdáizd] 표준화하다   to make matters worse 설상가상으로, 엎친 데 덮친 격으로
stock[stɑk] 재고하다, 갖추다   be forced to~ ~하기를 강요당하다
have no other option than to~ ~할 수 밖에 없다, ~외에 선택의 여지가 없다   out of business 폐업하여
scores 다수, 다량   dead-end 장래성이 없는   benefits[bénəfìtʃ] 복리후생   union[júːnjən] 노동조합

6. Note-taking

읽기 노트

•	Wind farm: harness wind power 4 electr. – negative
	풍력 기지: 전기 생산 위해 풍력 이용 – 부정적
•	1. Kill bird, bat 조류, 박쥐 죽임
•	– attracted by light 4 plane 비행기를 위한 빛에 유인됨
	– migration path unknown: hard to position 이동 경로 알려지지 않음: 위치 정하기 힘듦
•	2. Noise, sight pollution 소음 공해, 전망 망침
•	– noise during operation 가동시 소음
•	– spoil landscape → eyesore 경치 망침 → 흉물
•	3. Not econ. 비경제적
•	– need high wind 세찬 바람 필요
•	– extensive & expensive work 광범위하고 비용 많이 드는 작업

듣기 노트

Wind farm – steps to address concern 풍력 기지 – 문제점 해결 위한 조치
1. Bird, bat: negligible 조류, 박쥐: 경미
   - save more animals than kill 죽이는 수보다 구하는 수가 더 많음
   - red light: 4 plane → birds not come 붉은 빛: 비행기 대상 → 새 유인 X
2. Quiet, look better 조용함, 나아진 외형
   - space further apart → pretty 서로간 공간이 멀어짐 → 아름다움
   - better design → quiet 나아진 디자인 → 조용함
3. Econ. 경제적
   - anywhere ← taller turbine, larger blade 어디든지 ← 높은 터빈, 큰 날
   - not confine 2 strong wind 바람의 세기에 구속 받지 않음
   - cost earned back in 3 mo. 3개월 안에 자금 회수

Summary

The lecturer describes some of the reasons why wind farms are a viable energy option today. ① The lecturer's arguments cast doubt on the reading passage's negative portrayal of wind turbines.

② First, wind farms kill a very small number of birds and bats, much fewer than other human activities that harm nature. In fact, wind farms ultimately save more animals than they kill. Moreover, people are now putting red airplane warning lights on wind farms to avoid attracting birds. ③ Thus, the lecturer contradicts the reading passage's argument that wind farms are undesirable because they kill many birds.

④ What's more, recent wind farms space their turbines farther apart, which makes them look less cluttered. Wind farms are also very quiet because of blade improvements. ⑤ Therefore, the lecturer shows that the reading passage's concerns over noise and sight pollution are unnecessary.

⑥ Last, wind farms are economically advantageous. Because of the taller turbines and larger blades, they can be installed anywhere regardless of wind strength. In addition, the costs of setting up and running wind farms are earned back in a short time. ⑦ These findings effectively refute the reading passage's claim that wind farms are not economical.

해석 교수는 풍력 발전 지대가 오늘날 실행 가능한 에너지가 될 수 있는 몇 가지 방식에 대해 설명한다. 그의 주장은 풍력 터빈에 대한 지문의 부정적 묘사에 의문을 제기하는 것이다.
첫째로, 풍력 발전 지대는 아주 적은 수의 새와 박쥐를 죽이는데, 이는 자연을 해치는 인간의 다른 활동에 비하면 아주 적은 것이다. 사실, 풍력 발전 지대는 궁극적으로 동물을 죽이기 보다는 보호해 준다. 게다가, 요즘에는 새가 오는 것을 막기 위해 풍력 지대에 붉은색 비행기 경고등을 세워 놓는다. 그러므로, 교수는 풍력 발전 지대가 많은 새를 죽이므로 바람직하지 못하다는 지문의 주장을 반박한다.
게다가, 최근의 풍력 발전 지대는 터빈을 좀더 떨어지게 배치해 놓아 덜 난잡하게 보인다. 또한 터빈 날이 향상 되어 풍력 발전 지대는 아주 조용하다. 그러므로, 교수는 소음과 시각 공해에 대한 지문의 우려가 불필요하다는 것을 보여준다.
마지막으로, 풍력 발전 지대는 경제적으로 이익이 된다. 더 높아진 터빈과 커진 날 덕분에 풍력 발전 지대는 바람의 세기와 관계없이 어디에나 설치될 수 있다. 게다가, 풍력 발전 설치 비용과 운영 비용은 짧은 시간 내에 회수될 수 있다. 이러한 연구 결과는 풍력 발전 지

Possible Answers & Scripts

대가 경제적이지 않다는 지문의 주장을 효과적으로 반박한다.

어휘 **wind farm** 풍력 발전 지대 **viable**[váiəbl] 실행 가능한 **cast doubt on~** ~에 의문을 던지다, 의혹을 제기하다
portrayal[pɔːrtréiəl] 묘사 **ultimately**[ʌ́ltimitli] 궁극적으로 **warning light** 경고등
contradict[kɑ̀ntrədíkt] 반박하다 **undesirable**[ʌ̀ndizáiərəbl] 바람직하지 않은 **clutter**[klʌ́tər] 어지르다, 흩뜨리다
blade[bleid] 터빈 블레이드, 칼날 **sight pollution** 시각 공해 **economically**[ìːkənámikəli] 경제적으로
advantageous[æ̀dvəntéidʒəs] 이점이 있는 **install**[instɔ́ːl] 설치하다 **regardless of ~** ~에 관계없이
set up 세우다, 설치하다 **refute**[rifjúːt] 논박하다

스크립트 및 해석

Reading

지난 20여년 간, 풍력을 재생 가능한 에너지원으로 바꾸는 작업이 착수되어 왔다. 현대식 풍력 터빈은 공기역학적인 날을 갖춘 축차로 바람의 에너지를 동력화해서 전기를 생산한다. 그러나 애석하게도, 풍력 기지는 많은 결점을 지니고 있어 실용적인 선택이 될 수 없다.

풍력 기지의 첫 번째 결점은 그것이 많은 조류와 박쥐를 죽인다는 점이다. 캘리포니아의 한 풍력 발전소에서의 연구에 따르면, 풍력 기지로 인해 죽은 조류의 수가 4,700마리를 넘는다고 한다. 이 새들은 비행기를 위한 경고등에 유인된 후 풍력 발전기의 날에 치어 죽는다. 게다가, 대부분의 조류의 이동경로가 잘 알려져 있지 않기 때문에, (이를 피해) 풍력 발전소의 위치를 정하기가 쉽지 않다.

풍력 기지의 또 하나의 결점은 그것의 소음 공해와 시각적 오염이다. 풍력 발전소의 인근에 거주하는 많은 사람들은 풍력 터빈을 가동시킬 때 나는 소음에 대해 불만을 토로했다. 그 밖에도, 사람들은 흔히 풍력 기지들이 경치를 망치기 때문에 반대한다. 요약하자면, 풍력 발전소들은 통상적으로 시끄러운 눈엣가시로 여겨진다.

풍력 기지들의 가장 제한적인 점은 그것이 비경제적이라는 것이다. 이것들은 오직 바람이 세차게 부는 곳에만 건설될 수 있다. 유감스럽게도, 대부분의 바람이 세게 부는 부지는 광대한 풍력 설비를 개발하기에 부적합하므로, 기업들은 풍력 기지 건설을 위해 광범위한 노력과 많은 비용을 들여서 지대를 개간해야 한다.

conversion[kənvə́ːrʒən] 변환 **renewable energy** 재생 가능 에너지(태양열, 수력, 풍력 에너지 등)
wind turbine 풍력 터빈 **harness**[háːrnis] (폭포 등의 자연력을) 동력화하다, 이용하다 **rotor**[róutər] (기계) 축차
fitted with~ ~을 갖춘 **aerodynamic**[ɛ̀əroudainǽmik] 공기 역학의 **wind farm** 풍력 기지, 풍력 발전 시설
viable[váiəbl] (계획 등이) 실현 가능한, 실용적인 **drawback**[drɔ́ːbæ̀k] 약점, 결점
warning light 경고등, 봉화 **migration**[maigréiʃən] (새 등이) 철 따라 이동함
position[pəzíʃən] 위치를 정하다, 두다 **on top of that** 더욱이, 그밖에 **oppose**[əpóuz] 반대하다
spoil[spɔil] 망치다, 상하게 하다, 못쓰게 하다 **landscape**[lǽndskèip] 풍경, 경치 **all in all** 대체로
be regarded as ~ ~로서 간주되다 **eyesore**[áisɔ̀ːr] 눈엣가시, 보기 싫은 것

Listening

So, um, you may have heard critics decry wind farms as an unviable energy option for many reasons. Today, let's take a look at some steps that have been taken to address these concerns.

First, studies show that the number of birds and bats killed by wind turbines is negligible when compared to, uh, other human activities doing harm to nature. So, let's just say, by producing energy in an environmentally friendly way, wind farms are ultimately saving more animals than they are killing. For extra precaution, we can, you know, put red lights on wind farms to warn airplanes, but not attract birds.

Next, these wind farms are more silent and better designed than they were beforehand. More recent wind farms have their turbines spaced further apart, due to the higher capacity of the individual wind turbines. Thus, they no longer have the cluttered look of the early wind farms, and some people think they look elegant and beautiful. Also, wind farms today are very quiet because of improvements in the blade design. So, it is possible to hold a conversation directly underneath a modern wind turbine without raising one's voice.

Finally, wind farms are becoming increasingly economical. Now, they can be situated anywhere due to taller turbines with larger blades, and don't have to be confined to regions with strong winds. What's more, production, installation, and operation costs of wind farms are usually earned back within three months of operation.

풍력 기지가 여러 가지 이유로 적절한 에너지원이 될 수 없다고 비평가들이 비난하는 것을 아마 들어 보았을 것입니다. 오늘은 이런 문제점들을 해결하기 취해진 조치들 몇 가지에 대하여 알아보도록 합시다.

우선, 연구 결과에 따르면, 풍력 터빈에 치어 죽는 조류와 박쥐의 수는, 자연을 파괴하는 인간들의 다른 활동들에 비하면 대수롭지 않은 정도입니다. 따라서, 풍력 기지들은 자연 친화적인 방법으로 에너지를 생산함으로써 궁극적으로 죽이는 동물의 수보다 더 많은 수의 동물을 살린다고 할 수 있죠. 추가 예방책으로, 적색 불빛 신호를 풍력 발전소에 달 수도 있습니다. 이런 신호는 항공기들에겐 경고를 주지만 조류를 유인하지는 않거든요.

또한, 이러한 풍력 기지들은 예전보다 더 조용하고 외형이 근사합니다. 최근에 지어진 풍력 기지들은, 개별 터빈의 수용량이 증가한 덕분에, 각 터빈들이 서로 더 멀리 떨어져서 위치해 있습니다. 따라서, 그것들은 더 이상 초기의 풍력 발전소들처럼 빼곡히 붙어있지 않으며, 어떤 사람들은 발전 기지들이 우아하고 아름답다고 생각합니다. 또한, 오늘날의 풍력 기지들은 터빈 날의 디자인이 더 좋아져서 소음을 훨씬 덜 내죠. 그래서, 현대식 풍력 터빈 바로 밑에서는 목소리를 높이지 않고도 대화를 나누는 것이 가능할 정도입니다.

마지막으로, 풍력 기지들은 점점 경제적이 되어가고 있습니다. 이제, 터빈의 길이가 길어지고 날의 크기는 커진 덕분에 풍력 기지는 어느 장소에나 위치할 수 있고, 세찬 바람이 부는 지역에만 한정되지 않습니다. 더욱이, 풍력 발전소의 생산, 설치, 운영에 드는 비용은 대개 운영을 시작한지 3개월 이내에 회수할 수 있습니다.

decry[dikrái] 비난하다, 헐뜯다　unviable[ʌnvàiəbl] (계획 따위가) 실행 불가능한, 발전할 수 없는
take a look 살펴보다　address[ədrés] (어려운 문제 등을) 다루다, 처리하다
negligible[néglidʒəbl] 대수롭지 않은, 하찮은　environmentally friendly 환경 친화적인
ultimately[ʌ́ltimitli] 마침내, 결국　precaution[prikɔ́:ʃən] 주의, 예방책　beforehand[bifɔ́:hǽnd] 미리
further[fə́:rðər] 더 멀리, 더 앞에　capacity[kəpǽsəti] (공장 등의) 최대 생산능력
be confined to~ ~으로 제한되다, ~에 갇히다　installation[ìnstəléiʃən] 설치, 설비

HACKERS Test 🎧 Track 8 p.122

1. Note-taking

읽기 노트

- Hiring ppl from home country – benefits　자국민 채용 – 혜택
  - 1. Good for company　회사에 이득
    - – know well about HQ. & foreign co.　본사와 해외 지사에 정통
    - – loyal to co., put co. first　회사에 충성, 회사가 먼저
  - 2. Good for employees　직원들에게 이득
    - – paid more & financial assist.　더 많은 급료 & 재정 지원
    - – stimulated by new envrmnt　새로운 환경에 자극 받음
    - – chance to travel　여행 기회

Possible **Answers** & **Scripts**

듣기 노트

> - Effectiveness of ex-pats – case study 파견 직원의 효율성 – 사례 연구
>   1. What the company noticed 회사가 발견한 사실
>   - expensive to move back ex-pats when they couldn't cope
>   적응 못해서 돌아오면 비용 낭비
>   - no attachment to host country 머무르는 국가에 애착 없음
>   2. What employees found 직원들이 깨달은 사실
>   - frustrated more than motivated 의욕적이기보다 좌절함
>   - unexpected costs: diff. prod. / poor schools → dissatisfied
>   예상 외의 비용: 다른 제품 / 변변찮은 학교 → 불만족

Summary

The lecturer discusses the harms of companies hiring citizens of their home countries to work abroad. ① By exploring ex-pats' abilities to adjust to the local culture and their decreased efficiency, the lecturer contends that companies should not hire ex-pats, which is in direct opposition to the reading passage's argument.

First of all, ex-pats hinder a company's overall effectiveness because ② they don't know the local language or custom, which made their local dealings difficult, timely, and expensive. ③ They also don't feel dedicated to the host country and often request to be moved back, at great cost to the company. ④ These facts override any familiarity with the company, supposed ease of operations, and benefits for the company as mentioned in the reading.

Secondly, ex-pats experience personal problems living abroad ⑤ that reduce their productivity. ⑥ Their language difficulties and other lifestyle problems such as lack of access to familiar goods or good schools for their kids all contribute to employee unhappiness and decreased efficiency. ⑦ The lecturer's evidence directly contradicts the reading which states that employees abroad are happier living in a foreign environment with all its perks, and thus more productive.

해석　교수는 자국민을 채용하여 해외에서 근무하도록 하는 것에 대한 회사의 손해에 대해서 논의하고 있다. 해외 파견 직원이 해당 지역의 문화에 적응하는 능력, 그들의 능률을 감안할 때, 교수는 회사들이 파견 직원을 채용하지 말아야 한다고 주장하는데, 이는 본문의 주장에 정면으로 대립되는 것이다.
무엇보다도, 해외 파견 직원들은 회사의 전반적인 효율성을 감소시킨다. 그들은 파견 지역의 언어나 풍습을 모르기 때문에 그 지역에서의 거래를 까다롭고, 오랜 시간이 걸리고, 많은 자금이 들게 하기 때문이다. 그들은 또한 파견된 국가에 애착을 느끼지 못하고 종종 본사로 다시 돌아올 것을 요청하는데, 이는 회사에 막대한 비용이 드는 일이다. 이러한 점들은 본문에서 언급된 바와 같이 파견 직원들이 회사 내부사정을 잘 알고 있고, 운영을 수월하게 한다는 점, 그리고 그 이상의 어떤 이점들보다도 큰 문제이다.
둘째로, 해외 파견 직원들은 외국에 거주하면서 그들의 생산력을 저하시키는 개인적인 문제들을 겪는다. 그들의 언어적 어려움이나 익숙한 상품들의 입수 능력 제한이나 자녀들을 위한 좋은 학교 등과 같은 기타 생활 양식의 문제점들은 모두 직원의 불만족과 효율성 감소에 일조한다. 교수가 제시하는 증거는, 해외에서 근무하는 직원들이 외국 환경에서 특전을 누리고 살면서 더욱 만족하고, 따라서 더 생산적이라는 본문의 내용을 정면으로 반박한다.

어휘 **ex-pat = expatriate** 외국 이주민, 해외 파견 직원   **adjust to ~** ~에 적응하다
contend[kənténd] 주장하다   **hinder**[híndər] 방해하다, 저지하다
dealings[díːliŋs] 거래, 매매   **timely**[táimli] 때에 알맞은, 시기 적절한
dedicated[dédəkèitid] (이상, 정치, 목표 등에) 일신을 바친, 헌신적인
override[òuvərráid] 무료로 하다, ~보다 우위에 서다   **familiarity**[fəmìliǽrəti] 잘 앎, 정통
ease[íːz] 수월함   **contribute to ~** ~에 공헌하다   **contradict**[kàntrədíkt] 반박하다
perk[pəːrk] (임직원의) 특전, 혜택

스크립트 및 해석

Reading

점차 상호 연결되는 세상에서, 각 회사마다 인사부에서는 본사 직원을 해외 지사로 파견해 해외 지사를 운영할 것인지 아니면 현지에서 직원을 채용할 것인지 대한 결정을 내리고 있다. 과거의 경험에 비추어 볼 때, 자국민을 직원으로 채용하는 회사들이 여러 가지 다양한 혜택을 누린다는 것이 입증되었다. 해외 지사로 파견되는 직원들은 이미 회사의 운영 방식에 대한 지식을 갖추고 있다. 그들은 회사가 바라는 목표나 언어에 있어 광범위한 교육을 받을 필요가 없기 때문에, 회사는 극적으로 비용을 절감할 수 있게 된다. 그들은 본사와는 물론 사내에서도 효율적으로 의사소통을 할 수 있다. 문화적 차이와 언어기반의 오해가 최소화되기 때문에 본사와 해외 지사 간의 상호 작용이 용이하다. 파견 직원은 회사에 충실한 것인지, 해외 지사의 국가에 대해 충성심을 가지고 있는 것이 아니기 때문에, 회사의 이익을 우선시한다. 따라서, 회사는 목표들을 더 합리적이고 효율적으로 달성할 수 있다.

해외에 파견된 직원들 또한 이득을 얻는데, 이는 회사의 총생산량을 더욱 증가시킨다. 해외 지사에 근무하는 직원들은 종종 보통 그들이 받는 급료의 두 배 혹은 세 배 정도를 받고, 위험한 지역에 근무하면 그보다 더 지급받을 수도 있다. 그뿐 아니라 무료로 주택을 공급받는 등의 기타 재정적 이점도 있다. 많은 직원들은 또한 자신이 근무하는 해외 지사의 지역을 여행할 수 있는 기회를 높이 평가한다. 행복한 직원이 근면한 직원이라는 것은 수도 없이 증명된 사실이고, 따라서, 설령 회사가 그들의 노고를 고려해 더 높은 급료를 지급한다고 해도, 그들의 증가된 생산성은 이 추가적인 비용을 보완하고도 남는다.

increasingly[inkríːsiŋli] 점점, 더욱더   **interconnect**[ìntərkənékt] 서로 연결시키다
human resources department 인사부   **staff**[stǽf] 직원을 두다   **expatriate**[ekspéitrièit] 해외 파견 직원
knowledgeable[nálidʒəbl] 지식이 있는, 식견이 있는   **extensive**[iksténsiv] 광대한, 광범위한
dramatically[drəmǽtikəli] 극적으로, 눈부시게   **headquarter = HQ** (회사나 기관의) 본사, 본관
interaction[ìntərǽkʃən] 상호 작용   **straightforward**[strèitfɔ́ːrwərd] (일이) 간단한
misunderstanding[mìsʌndərstǽndiŋ] 오해, 불화   **host country** 주최국, 해외 지사가 위치한 나라
expediently[ikspíːdiəntli] 편의상, 방편으로   **assignment**[əsáinmənt] (할당된) 직무, 과제
appreciate[əpríːʃièit] 진가를 인정하다, 고마워하다   **compensate**[kámpənsèit] 보상하다, 보수를 지급하다
productivity[pròudəktívəti] 생산성, 생산력   **make up for ~** ~을 보완하다, 만회하다

Listening

Today, let's look at a case study that demonstrates the effectiveness of employing ex-pats in foreign offices. This company evaluated their native employees' performances a year after they were transferred. Those that were left, anyway. All right, let's dive right in.

The first thing that the company noticed was that they needed to be taught how to manage abroad. They didn't know the local language or customs, making dealings with the country's nationals extremely difficult, especially in business. So, relatively simple tasks consumed much more time, and therefore, money, than they should have. They also noted that while it's true that the employees were dedicated to the head office, they didn't necessarily feel the same loyalty to the host country. In fact, a quarter of them demanded to be transferred back for personal reasons after the company had invested a huge sum in moving the employee and their family abroad. Obviously, this makes ex-pats an expensive and unreliable choice.

In this company's experience, many employees said that they'd be happy working and living abroad, but found the reality to be a little different from what they expected. You see, they were frequently more frustrated than motivated. Not being able to communicate with locals led to a sense of profound isolation, affecting performance on the job. These workers also experienced many unexpected non-monetary costs, such as the unavailability of certain familiar products or an appropriate school for their kids. All this resulted in employee dissatisfaction with life, and eventually, reduced efficiency.

오늘은 해외 지사에 자국 직원을 고용하는 것의 효율성을 논증하는 사례 연구를 살펴보도록 합시다. 이 회사는 자국 직원들이 해외 지사로 파견되고 난 1년 후에 그들의 실적을 평가했습니다. 어쨌든 그 중 돌아오지 않고 근무한 직원들 말이죠. 좋아요, 사례를 바로 살펴봅시다. 회사가 맨 처음 알아 차린 것은 해외 지사로 파견된 직원들에게 해외에서 적응하는 방법을 가르쳐야 한다는 것이었습니다. 그들은 해당 국가의 언어나 관습을 알지 못했고, 따라서 그 나라의 자국민들과의 교제, 특히 사업 거래에서 심각한 어려움을 겪었습니다. 그래서, 상대적으로 단순한 직무를 하는데도 시간이 훨씬 더 오래 걸렸고, 그런 까닭에, 비용도 예상보다 많이 들었습니다. 회사는 또한 이 해외 파견 직원들이 본사에 헌신적인 것은 사실이지만, 바로 그들 자신이 근무하는 해외 지사가 있는 국가에는 그와 같은 친밀감을 별로 느끼지 못했습니다. 사실상 그들의 1/4 정도는, 개인적인 사유로 본사에 다시 돌아갈 것을 요청했습니다. 회사가 해외 파견 직원과 그의 가족들을 해외로 이주시키기 위해 많은 비용을 투자한 후에 말이죠. 명백하게, 이는 해외 지사로 본사 직원을 파견하는 것이 비용이 많이 들고 신뢰할 수 없는 방법임을 뜻하죠. 이 회사의 경험에 의하면, 많은 직원들이 기꺼이 해외에서 근무하고 거주하겠다고 말했지만, 그들이 기대한 것과 그들이 실제로 겪은 현실 사이에는 약간의 괴리가 있다고 느꼈습니다. 그들은 의욕이 넘친다기보다는 좌절감을 더 자주 느꼈어요. 지역 사람들과 대화를 나누지 못하는 것은 깊은 고립감을 느끼게 하고, 이는 곧 업무 수행 능력에도 영향을 끼치죠. 이 해외 파견 직원들은 또한 자신들이 애용하던 소비품이나 아이들이 다닐 적절한 학교를 찾는 데 있어서의 어려움 등의 예상 밖의 여러 비금전적인 대가를 치러야 했습니다. 이 모든 것들은 직원들이 생활에 만족하지 못하는 결과를 낳았고 결국에는 효율성을 저하시켰습니다.

effectiveness[iféktivnis] 유효성, 효과적임　　**dive in** (연구, 작업등에) 열심히 착수하다, 몰두하다
custom[kʌ́stəm] (지역적, 문화적) 풍습, 관습　　**dealing**[díːliŋ] 교제, 거래　　**extremely**[ikstríːmli] 매우, 극히
obviously[ábviəsli] 명백하게, 분명히　　**frustrated**[frʌ́strèitid] 실망한, 좌절한　　**motivate**[móutəvéit] 동기가 부여된
profound[prəfáund] 깊은　　**isolation**[àisəléiʃən] 고립감, 고독　　**unavailability**[ʌ̀nəvèiləbíləti] 비유효성, 입수 불가능
appropriate[əpróuprièit] 적당한　　**non-monetary** 비금전적인　　**dissatisfaction**[dissæ̀tisfǽkʃən] 불만, 불평
eventually[ivéntʃuəli] 결국, 마침내

2.　Note-taking

읽기 노트

• Bike lane – worthwhile　자전거 전용도로 – 가치 있음 　　1. Environ.　환경 　　　– bike: eco-friendly　자전거: 친환경적 　　　– more ppl bike w/ own lane → car ↓, good 4 envir. 　　　　전용도로 생기면 자전거 이용증가 → 차량↓, 환경에 이익 　　2. Traffic congestion ↓　교통 체증↓ 　　　– cars slow down 4 cycle　자전거로 인해 차량 서행 　　　– B.L keep traffic moving　자전거 전용도로는 교통 원활하게 함 　　3. Accidents ↓　사고↓ 　　　– drivers: cause danger to cyclist　운전자: 자전거 이용자에 위험 가함 　　　– avoidable w/ B.L.　자전거 전용도로로 방지

듣기 노트

```
● │ Bike lane – case study  자전거 전용도로 – 사례 연구
  │   1. No envir. effect  환경적 효과 없음
● │      – cycling ppl ↑ 1%: biking too demanding  자전거 인구 1% ↑: 너무 고됨
  │      – no difference to envir.  환경에 아무 차이 없음
● │   2. Traffic - worse  교통 – 악화
  │      – drivers endured road work  운전자들 공사 견딤
● │      – drivers angry: losing one lane 4 empty B.L.
  │        화난 운전자들: 빈 자전거 전용도로 때문에 한 차선을 잃음
● │   3. Not safe  안전하지 않음
  │      – bikers: assume safe → oblivious to danger  자전거 이용자: 안전하다고 생각 → 경각심 없음
● │      – accidents ↑  사고 ↑
```

Summary

The lecturer describes a case study done in San Francisco after bike lanes were instituted. ① By showing the study results, the lecturer states that the bike lanes did not have the benefits that the reading passage's arguments would have us believe.

For one, ② the bicycle lane did not have the intended positive effect on the environment by decreasing motor vehicles and pollution as the reading passage contended. ③ After their creation, the number of people cycling to work increased by less than 1%. ④ People found biking to work too physically exhausting. Thus, bike lanes did not noticeably decrease the number of cars on the road, reduce pollution, or help the environment, contrary to the reading passage's argument.

Next, ⑤ bicycle lanes added to traffic congestion problems. ⑥ During and after their creation, road work impeded traffic. ⑦ Later, drivers got angry at losing one of their lanes for the creation of a passageway hardly used by bicyclists. ⑧ In fact, they had longer commutes as their valuable space was taken away. Thus, bicycle lanes did not reduce congestion and provide fast passageway for users of the road, as promised by the reading passage.

Last, ⑨ the number of accidents actually increased after bike lanes were made. ⑩ Bikers assumed that they were safe in their own lane, and were therefore caught unaware when drivers drove in them or opened their car doors in the bike path. The reading passage, however, argued that bicycle lanes reduce the number of accidents between cyclists and drivers, which was clearly not the case in San Francisco that the lecturer described.

해석 교수는 자전거 전용도로가 만들어진 후 샌프란시스코에서 행해진 사례 연구를 설명한다. 샌프란시스코에서는 지문이 주장한 자전거 전용
　　　도로의 혜택을 얻지 못했다고, 교수는 연구 결과를 들어서 이야기한다.
　　　첫째로, 자전거 전용도로는 글에서 주장한 대로 차량 운행 수나 오염을 줄임으로써 환경에 긍정적인 영향을 주지 못했다. 전용도로가 만

들어진 후 자전거로 출퇴근하는 사람의 수의 증가는 1% 미만에 그쳤다. 사람들은 자전거로 출퇴근하는 것이 육체적으로 피로하다는 사실을 알게 되었다. 따라서, 지문의 주장과는 반대로, 자전거 전용도로는 눈에 띌 만큼 도로의 차량 수를 감소시키거나, 오염을 줄이거나, 환경에 도움을 주지 않았다.

다음으로, 자전거 전용도로는 교통 혼잡 문제를 증가시켰다. 자전거 전용도로의 개설 기간 중과 그 후의 도로 공사는 교통을 지연시켰다. 후에, 운전자들은 자전거 이용자가 거의 다니지 않는 통행로의 건설로 인해 차선 하나를 잃었다는 것에 화를 냈다. 사실, 운전자들은 그들의 귀중한 공간이 사라져 버려 통근 시간이 더 길어지게 되었다. 그러므로, 지문에서 약속했던 것처럼 자전거 전용도로는 교통 혼잡을 줄여주지 않았고 도로 이용자들에게 빠른 통행로를 제공해 주지도 않았다.

마지막으로, 자전거 전용도로가 만들어진 후 사고율은 사실상 증가했다. 자전거 이용자들은 자전거 전용도로 내에서 안전하다고 생각했고, 따라서 운전자가 그들에게 다가오거나 자전거 도로 쪽으로 차 문을 열었을 때 이를 제대로 깨닫지 못하였다. 하지만, 지문은 자전거 전용도로가 자전거 이용자들과 운전자 간 사고를 감소시켜 주었다고 주장하는데, 이는 교수가 설명한 샌프란시스코의 경우와는 전혀 맞지 않는 것이다.

어휘　**institute**[ínstitʃùːt] 만들다, 마련하다　**contend**[kənténd] 주장하다　**exhausting**[igzɔ́ːstiŋ] 피로하게 하는
noticeably[nóutisəbli] 눈에 띄게　**traffic congestion** 교통 혼잡　**impede**[impíːd] 방해하다, 지연시키다
passageway[pǽsidʒwèi] 통행로　**unaware**[ʌ̀nəwέər] 눈치채지 못한

스크립트 및 해석

Reading

자전거 이용자들은 미국 대부분의 도시에서 자전거를 타는 것이 어렵다고 오랫동안 불평해왔다. 만일 지금과 같은 "자동차 문화"가 없었더라면 많은 사람들은 직장에 통근할 때 자전거를 이용할 것이다. 그들의 요구에 대처하기 위하여, 많은 시의회들은 주요 통근 도로들에 자전거 전용도로를 마련할 것을 고려하고 있다. 이 안이 시행될 만한 가치가 있는 데는 많은 요인이 있다.

자전거 전용도로의 주된 한가지 이점은 환경에 미치는 긍정적 영향이다. 현재, 많은 사람들은 많은 양의 휘발유를 소모하고 위험 수치의 배기가스를 내뿜는 자동차들을 몰고 다닌다. 이것은 이미 높아져 있는 오염 수치를 악화시키고 공기의 질을 더욱 떨어뜨린다. 다행히도, 자전거는 환경 친화적인 교통수단이다. 설문 조사에 따르면, 만일 자전거 전용도로가 존재한다면 더 많은 사람들이 자전거로 통근할 것이라고 한다. 이렇게 하는 것은 분명히 도로를 사용하는 자동차의 수를 줄이고 환경에 가해지는 피해를 줄일 것이다.

실제로, 자전거 전용도로는 도로를 이용하는 모든 사람들에게 이로울 것이다. 자전거 전용도로가 없는 도로에서는 자전거를 타는 사람들을 수용하기 위해 차들이 속도를 줄여야 한다. 운전자들은 이미 통근시간이 길고, 자전거 타는 사람들 뒤에 막혀 있는 것을 달갑게 여기지 않는다. 따라서, 자전거 전용도로는 이렇게 꽉 막힌 도로에 반가운 손님이다. 자전거 도로는 자동차 수를 줄이고 자전거 이용자와 운전자 각자 전용선의 교통을 원활히 함으로써 교통 혼잡을 감소시킨다.

게다가, 자전거 전용도로는 자동차와 자전거를 둘러 싼 사고를 많이 줄인다. 현재, 많은 운전자들이 어떻게 자전거 이용자와 도로를 함께 이용해야 하는지를 잘 모른다. 운전자들은 종종 자전거 타고 있는 사람을 보지 못하거나, 추월하려고 하다가 그들과 부딪힌다. 게다가, 운전자들은 종종 자전거 타는 사람들을 갓길로 몰아넣는데, 이는 많은 위험한 사고를 초래한다. 이러한 사고들은 자전거 전용도로가 생겨난다면 전적으로 방지할 수 있을 것이다.

　　bicyclist = cyclist 자전거 애호가, 자전거 타는 사람　**address**[ədrés] (문제 등을) 다루다, 처리하다　**city council** 시의회
　　worthwhile[wə́ːrθhwáil] ~을 할 가치가 있는　**institute**[ínstitʃùːt] 설립하다　**emit**[imít] (빛, 열, 향기등을) 방출하다, 내뿜다
　　exhaust = exhaust fumes 배기가스　**fortunately**[fɔ́ːrtʃənitli] 다행히도, 운이 좋게도　**eco-friendly** 환경 친화적인
　　mode of transportation 교통수단　**passageway**[pǽsidʒwèi] 복도, 통로　**obviously**[ábviəsli] 명백하게, 분명히
　　bicycle lane 자전거 전용도로　**advantageous**[ædvəntéidʒəs] 유리한, 이로운　**accommodate**[əkámədèit] 수용하다
　　addition[ədíʃən] 추가물, 증축 부분　**clog**[klɑg] (자동차 등이 정체하여) 길을 막히게 하다　**traffic congestion** 교통 마비
　　respective[rispéktiv] 각자의, 각각의　**shoulder of a road** 갓길, 길섶　**avoidable**[əvɔ́idəbl] 피할 수 있는

Listening

You know, a case study done in San Francisco after bike lanes were instituted on major commute routes revealed some very interesting findings. First off, these lanes clearly did not have the intended environmental effect of more cyclists and less pollution. After their creation, the number of people who cycle to work increased by less than 1%. Why? People found commuting by bike physically too demanding. So, basically the lanes made no big difference, environmentally speaking.

Now, maybe you can guess what drivers felt on the other side of the road. Driving became more stressful during and after the creation of bike lanes. Drivers, you know, impatiently endured months of road work, thinking that the lane would help reduce traffic congestion problems. Afterwards, they became angry at losing one of their much-needed lanes for a marginal number of cyclists. The almost empty bike lane took up space as they sat in traffic longer, adding to their already long commutes.

On top of that, bicycle lanes did not provide the safe passageway that bikers were expecting. When people unwittingly drove in the lanes or opened their car doors into them, bikers, who assumed that the lane was entirely theirs, were often oblivious and got into accidents. So, as it turns out, the number of accidents actually increased after bicycle lanes were made. Well, you can probably imagine the end of this story. The city closed the bike lanes just six months after their grand opening.

주요 도로에 자전거 전용도로가 설치된 후 샌프란시스코에서 실시된 사례 연구는 매우 흥미로운 몇 가지 연구 결과를 드러냈습니다. 우선, 이 자전거 전용도로는 의도했던 바와 같이 자전거 이용자를 늘리고 오염을 줄이는 환경 개선 효과를 명백히 보여주지 못했습니다. 자전거 도로가 생긴 이후, 자전거로 통근하는 사람들의 수는 1% 미만으로 늘어났습니다. 왜 그랬을까요? 사람들은 자전거를 타고 통근하는 것이 육체적으로 너무 고되다고 느꼈습니다. 따라서, 환경적 기준에서 생각할 때, 근본적으로 자전거 전용도로는 아무런 효과도 없었습니다.

이제 운전자들이 도로의 반대편에서 어떤 생각을 했는지 짐작할 수도 있겠네요. 자전거 전용도로의 건설 도중과 그 후, 운전하는 것은 전보다 더 많은 스트레스를 주게 되었습니다. 운전자들은 자전거 전용도로가 교통 혼잡 문제를 줄여줄 수 있으리라 믿고, 도로 공사에 소요된 몇 달을 억지로 견뎠습니다. 그 후에, 그들은 자신들에게 매우 필요한 차선 중 하나가 거의 사용하지도 않는 자전거 전용도로에 쓰이느라 없어져 버렸다는 것에 분개했습니다. 운전자들이 도로에서 더 오래 갇혀 있어야 하는 동안 자전거 전용도로는 거의 텅 빈 채 자리만 차지했으며, 그렇지 않아도 긴 그들의 통근시간을 더 길게 만들었습니다.

그밖에, 자전거 전용도로는 자전거 이용자들이 기대하던 안전한 길을 제공하지 못했습니다. 사람들이 부주의하게 자전거 전용도로로 차를 몰거나 자전거 전용도로 쪽으로 자동차 문을 여는 경우, 자전거 이용자들은 전용도로가 자신들의 전유물이라 여기고 방심하고 있다가 사고를 당했습니다. 그리하여, 사실상 교통사고의 수가 자전거 전용도로의 설치 이후 실제로 더 증가했습니다. 아마도 여러분은 이 이야기의 결말을 짐작할 수 있을 것 입니다. 도시 측은 개장한지 6개월 만에 자전거 전용도로를 폐쇄했습니다.

finding [fáindiŋ] 조사 결과, 연구 결과 demanding [dimǽndiŋ] 큰 노력을 요하는 impatiently [impéiʃəntli] 성급하게 much-needed 많이 필요한 marginal [máːrdʒənəl] 주변적인, 별로 중요하지 않은 take up space 공간을 차지하다 unwittingly [ʌnwítiŋli] 부주의하게 oblivious [əblíviəs] ~이 염두에 없는 as it turns out 실제로는, 실상으로는

3. Note-taking

읽기 노트

- Lack of women in science 과학계 여성 인력 부족
  - 1. Stereotype: unsuitable for sci. 고정관념: 과학에 부적합
    - caring professions 복지 관련 직업
    - soft sci. 수월한 사회과학
  - 2. Grueling course work, low salary 고된 학업 과정, 낮은 임금
    - career vs. motherhood 직업 vs. 육아
    - choose jobs w/ ↓time & ↑money 근무시간↓ & 급료↑인 직업 선택
  - 3. Male-dominated 남성 지배적
    - intimidating 위협적
    - face limits 한계에 부딪힘

Possible **Answers** & **Scripts**

듣기 노트

- More women in science 과학계에 여성 유치
    1. School 학교
        - teachers: encouraging to study sci. 교사들: 과학 공부 장려
        - stressing wom. scienti. 여성 과학자 강조
    2. Financial help 재정 지원
        - foundations: grants 장학 재단: 장학금
        - help women: 2 negoti. b/t career & children 직업과 육아간 조정하도록 도움
    3. Form wom. organization 여성 조직 형성
        - emotional, practical support 정서적, 실무적 도움
        - keep morale high 사기를 높임

Summary

① The lecturer describes some of the steps taken to draw more women into science. ② This casts doubts on the reading passage's argument that science is an unattractive field for females.

First, the lecturer describes efforts currently underway in education to lure women into the field. ③ He mentions that teachers are encouraging girls to pursue biology, chemistry, and physics. ④ Teachers are also stressing women scientists' contributions. ⑤ These two measures are in response to the reading passage's point that gender stereotypes of women hold them back from entering science.

Next, ⑥ the lecturer explains some financial incentives for women to pursue biology, chemistry, and physics. ⑦ The lecturer points out that several foundations give grants to women entering this field. ⑧ This helps them immensely, as many will have to juggle career and children later. ⑨ This effectively rebuts the reading passage which highlighted the grueling course work and initial low salaries as deterrents to women entering science.

Finally, the lecturer explores some of the measures women are taking to tackle the sexism in the field. ⑩ Women are forming their own organizations, which provide emotional and practical support for each other. ⑪ Women's groups also organize social activities to keep morale high. ⑫ All of these efforts undertaken by female scientists are going a long way to address the reading passage's concern over the male domination in the field.

해석 교수는 더 많은 여성을 과학 분야로 끌어들이기 위해 취해진 몇 가지 조치에 대해 설명한다. 이것은 과학이 여성에게는 매력적이지 않은 학문이라는 글의 주장에 의문을 제기하는 것이다.
첫째로, 교수는 여성을 과학 분야로 유인하기 위해 현재 교육계에서 진행 중인 노력을 설명한다. 그는 교사들이 여학생들에게 생물학, 화학, 그리고 물리학을 공부하도록 장려한다고 말한다. 교사들은 또한 여성 과학자의 공헌을 강조한다. 이 두 가지 조치는 여성에 대한 성 고정관념이 그들을 과학 분야에 진출하지 못하도록 한다는 지문의 요지에 대응하는 것이다.
다음으로, 교수는 여성이 생물학, 화학, 그리고 물리학을 공부하도록 하는 재정적 인센티브에 대해 설명한다. 교수는 몇몇 재단들이 이

분야에 진출하는 여성들에게 연구 보조금을 지원해 준다는 것을 지적한다. 이것은 그들에게 상당한 도움을 주는데, 왜냐하면 많은 여성들이 추후에 업무와 육아를 동시에 해나가야 하기 때문이다. 이것은 고된 학업 과정과 낮은 초봉이 여성들로 하여금 과학 분야에 진출하지 못하게 한다고 강조했던 지문을 효과적으로 반박하는 것이다.

마지막으로, 교수는 이 분야에서 성차별을 해결하기 위한 몇 가지 대책들에 대해 알아본다. 여성은 자신들만의 단체들을 형성하는데, 이 단체들은 서로에게 정서적, 실무적 도움을 제공해 준다. 여성 단체들은 또한 사기를 진작시키기 위한 친목 활동을 조직하기도 한다. 여성 과학자들의 이러한 모든 노력은 과학 분야의 남성 지배 현상에 대한 지문의 우려에 대처하는데 큰 도움이 되고 있다.

어휘   **cast doubt on** 의문을 제기하다   **underway**[ʌ̀ndərwéi] 진행 중에 있는   **lure**[ljuər] 유인하다
    biology[baiálədʒi] 생물학   **chemistry**[kémistri] 화학   **physics**[fíziks] 물리학
    stress[stres] 강조하다   **gender stereotype** 성별에 따른 고정관념   **hold back** 만류하다, 보류하다
    financial incentive 재정적 동기   **highlight**[háilàit] 강조하다   **grueling**[grú(:)əliŋ] 엄한, 혹독한
    deterrent[ditə́:rənt] 단념하게 하는, 방해하는   **grant**[grænt] 보조금, 장려금   **immensely**[iménsli] 굉장히, 막대하게
    juggle[dʒʌ́gl] (시간, 일 등을) 잘 조절, 처리하다   **tackle**[tækl] (문제 등을) 해결하다
    sexism[séksizəm] 성차별 주의   **morale**[mərǽl] 사기   **go a long way** 크게 도움이 되다, 큰 영향을 주다
    domination[dàmənéiʃən] 지배, 우위

스크립트 및 해석

Reading

지난 몇 년간 과학 분야로 진출한 학생 수가 다소 증가하긴 했지만, 아직도 이 분야의 여성 수는 적어서 불균형을 이룬다. 역사적으로 과학 분야에 여성의 수가 부족한 점에는 몇 가지 이유가 있다.

첫 번째 이유는 성차별적인 고정관념이 여성들을 이성적이지 못하고 분석적이지 못하다고 묘사하기 때문인데, 이는 과학에는 부적합한 특성이다. 여성들은 교사나 간호사와 같은 복지관계의 직업에 종사하도록 강요받는 반면, 남성들은 과학자나 경찰관이 되도록 장려된다. 학계에서 일하기로 선택하더라도 여성들은 종종 문학, 언어학, 인류학 또는 심리학으로 집중된다. 간략히 말하면, 여성들은 많은 경우에 "수월한" 또는 "사회적인" 과학 분야와 연관지어진다. 따라서, "난해한" 과학 분야는 애초에 여성들이 능력을 발휘할 수 있는 실행 가능하고 매력적인 선택으로 제시되지 않는다.

두 번째 이유는 과학계의 고된 학습 과정과 낮은 초봉이다. 이 제지사항은 남자에게도 적용되나, 여성들에게 더 큰 부정적 영향을 끼친다. 아직까지 여성들은 결혼을 하고 직업은 어머니로서의 역할보다 부차적으로 여겨야 한다는 기대를 받기 때문이다. 과학자가 된다는 것은 길고, 어렵고, 경제적으로 고된 과정이며, 많은 여성들은 간호사와 같이 덜 시간 소모적이고 재정적으로 수지가 맞으면서도 직업과 자녀 양육을 잘 조절할 수 있는 길을 택한다.

세 번째 이유는 과학이 남성 지배적인 분야라는 점이다. 이것은 많은 여성들에게 매우 위협적이고, 그들은 자신들이 과학계에서 얼마나 출세할 수 있는가에 대한 한계에 직면하는 "승진의 최상한선"에 도달하게 될 것이다. 그들은 주로 남성들 사이에서 일하는 것에 익숙해야 하며, 그 남성들은 종종 그들을 의심과 무시의 눈길로 바라볼 것이다.

    disproportionately[dìsprəpɔ́:rʃənitli] 불균형하게   **underrepresented**[ʌ̀ndərrèprizéntid] 불충분하게 표시된
    paint~ as- ~이 -이라고 묘사하다, 표현하다   **unsuitable**[ʌnsú:təble] 부적당한   **caring profession** 복지관계의 직업
    opt into~ ~을 하기로 선택하다   **funneled into~** ~으로 쏟아 부어지다, 모아지다   **anthropology**[æ̀nθrəpálədʒi] 인류학
    soft = easy (속어) 쉬운, 수월한   **viable**[váiəbl] 실행 가능한, 실용적인   **grueling**[grú(:)əliŋ] 엄한, 고된, 녹초로 만드는
    deter[ditə́:r] 방해하다, 단념하게 하다   **be secondary to~** ~보다 부차적, 2차적이다
    arduous[á:rdʒuəs] 힘든, 고된   **time-consuming** 시간 소모가 큰   **financially lucrative** 재정적으로 수지 맞는, 돈이 벌리는
    juggle[dʒʌ́gl] (시간, 일 등을) 잘 조절하다   **raising children** 자녀 양육   **relate to ~** ~에 부합하다
    male-dominated 남성 지배적인   **intimidate**[intímədeit] 위협하다   **glass ceiling** (여성, 소수파의) 승진의 최상한선
    an air of~ ~의 분위기, 눈길   **suspicion**[səspíʃən] 의심, 용의   **superiority**[səpìəriɔ́:rəti] 우월, 우위

Listening

All right, although there is a shortage of women in science, there is hope. We are attracting more women into this field. So, uh, we are starting in schools where teachers are praising girls' analytical and problem-solving abilities and encouraging them to become scientists. More teachers are stressing the importance of women physicists such as Marie Curie and her discovery of curium. In this way, um, teachers are promoting science as a field that is open to women and enriched by their contributions.

In addition to verbally encouraging girls to go into science, we are, you know, offering financial scholarships specifically set aside for them. A number of foundations now give merit-based grants to promising women who are pursuing chemistry, biology, and physics. This financial assistance is greatly appreciated by women who will often negotiate their time-consuming demands of career and children later, and well, simply cannot afford the exorbitant cost of graduate school, not to mention low post-doctorate salaries.

Women are also forming their own organizations to address their concerns and help them combat sexism, especially in hiring practices where, you know, they will most likely be passed over for an equally-qualified or even lesser-qualified man when trying to move to the top positions. Uh, let's just say, when female scientists band together to provide emotional as well as practical support for each other, they survive skewed hiring practices and sexual harassment in the workplace. Women's groups are also organizing fun activities to keep camaraderie high for each other. So anyway, these organizations are going a long way in supporting females in a field that is still heavily biased towards males.

과학 분야에 여성이 부족한 것은 사실이지만, 아직 희망은 있습니다. 우리는 이 분야에 더 많은 여성들을 불러들이고 있어요. 그러니까, 우리는 학교에서부터 시작해서, 교사들이 여학생들의 분석적 능력과 문제 해결 능력을 칭찬하고 그들이 과학자가 되도록 격려하지요. 더욱 많은 교사들이 퀴리부인 같은 인물이나 그녀가 큐륨을 발견한 업적 같은 여성 물리학자의 중요성을 강조하고 있습니다. 이런 식으로, 교사들은 과학분야가 여성에게 개방되어 있고 그들의 공헌으로 인해 강화되는 분야라고 격려하는 것이죠.

여학생들이 과학분야로 진출하도록 말로 장려하는 것 외에도, 우리는 여학생들을 위해 특별히 마련된 장학금을 제공하고 있습니다. 많은 장학 재단이 이제 화학, 생물학, 물리학에 종사하고 있는 장래가 촉망되는 여성들에게 공로 장학금을 수여하고 있습니다. 이러한 재정 지원은 종종 직업과 자녀 양육이라는 시간 소모적인 책임 사이에서 타협해야 하고, 박사학위 취득 후의 낮은 봉급은 물론이고 대학원의 막대한 비용을 감당할 수 없는 여성들로부터 높이 평가받고 있습니다.

여성들은 또한 자신들의 관심사를 제기하고 성차별주의에 맞서 싸울 수 있는 단체를 형성하고 있습니다. 특히나 고용 정책에 있어서, 최고위직으로 인사이동을 할 때 동등한 자격을 지녔거나 혹은 자격이 뒤떨어지는 남성에게 승진의 기회를 박탈당할 가능성이 많은 고용 정책에서 그렇습니다. 달리 말하자면, 여성 과학자들이 서로에게 실무적 도움은 물론 정서적인 지원을 하기 위해 단결할 때, 이들은 직장에서의 왜곡된 고용관행과 성희롱으로부터 살아남을 수 있다는 것이죠. 여성단체는 또한 동지애를 높이기 위해 여가 활동을 계획하고 있습니다. 여하튼, 이 단체들은 아직도 남성에게 심하게 편향된 분야의 여성들을 지지하는데 일조를 하고 있습니다.

shortage of~ ~의 결핍, 부족   **analytical**[ænəlítikəl] 분석적인   **problem-solving ability** 문제 해결 능력
stress[stres] 강조하다, 역설하다   **enrich**[inrítʃ] 비옥하게 하다   **specifically**[spisífikəli] 특별히, 명확히
set aside for~ ~을 위해 마련된   **foundation**[faundéiʃən] 장학 재단   **merit**[mérit] 공적, 공로
grant[grænt] (특정 목적을 위한) 보조금, 조성금   **promising**[prámisiŋ] 장래성 있는   **negotiate**[nigóuʃièit] 협상하다
exorbitant[igzɔ́ːrbitənt] 엄청난, 과대한   **graduate school** 대학원   **post-doctorate** 박사학위 취득자
combat[kəmbǽt] 격투, 논쟁, 맞서 싸우다   **hiring practice** 고용 정책   **equally-qualified** 동일한 자격을 지닌, 동일한 역량의
lesser-qualified 자격이 덜한, 역량이 뒤떨어지는   **band together** 단결하다   **skewed**[skjúːd] 비뚤어진, 잘못된, 왜곡된
sexual harassment 성희롱   **camaraderie**[kæmərǽdəri] 동지애, 우정
biased toward~ ~쪽으로 치우친, 편향된

4. Note-taking

읽기 노트

- 4-day work – beneficial 주 4일 근무제 – 이로움
  1. Employer: pay less salary 고용주: 급료 덜 지급
     - recession: need 2 trim cost 불경기: 비용 절감 필요
     - workweek↓, funds 4 infra, resource↑ 근무시간↓, 하부 구조, 자원 투자 기금↑
     - attract better employee 뛰어난 직원 유인
  2. Employee: ↑time 2 relax 직원: 휴식 시간↑
     - time 4 hobby, friends, family → quality of life↑ 친구, 취미, 가족 위한 시간 → 삶의 질↑
     - happier & more productive 보다 행복 & 더 능률적
  3. Better 4 economy 경제에 이익
     - create more jobs 더 많은 고용 창출
     - broader workforce 폭넓은 인력

듣기 노트

- 4-day work – actual experience 주 4일 근무제 – 실제 경험
  1. Company suffer $ly 기업측 재정적 손실
     - hard 2 complete work → hire more empl. 직무 완수 어려움 → 추가 직원 고용
     - ↑cost: hire & train, computer & space 비용↑: 고용 & 교육, 컴퓨터 & 공간
     - insurance↑: no work day = high risk 보험 비용↑: 휴일 = 사고 위험↑
  2. Employee: bad for career 직원: 경력에 도움 X
     - not enough time 2 improve 능력 개발 시간 부족
     - co. prefer 5 day worker 기업 측 주 5일 근무자 선호
     - unstable > pleasure 불안정 > 만족
  3. Bad for economy 경제에 해로움
     - co. force 2 finish 40hr work in 32hr 기업, 40시간 업무량 32시간 내 완수 강요
       → stressful 4 employee: health↓, not happy 직원들 스트레스: 건강↓, 행복 X
     - work quality↓, productivity↓ 업무 질↓, 생산성↓
     - less $ to fuel economy 경제 활성화 위한 소비 저하

Summary

The lecturer believes that ① the new working arrangement of the four-day workweek is detrimental to businesses, employees, and the economy. ② Her arguments counter the reading passage's support for this practice.

One reason why the four-day workweek is not a good option is that ③ companies suffer financially. ④ Businesses must spend more money hiring and training additional employees as well as providing extra office space and computers. ⑤ On top of that, businesses have to pay more for employee insurance in this working arrangement. ⑥ Thus, the lecturer contradicts the reading passage's argument that the four-day workweek benefits companies monetarily.

On top of that, this working arrangement has a negative impact on employees. ⑦ They are not able to spend enough time in their jobs improving their skills and thus cannot grow professionally. ⑧ Furthermore, companies tend to hire and promote workers who work 40 hours a week. ⑨ As a result, four-day employees feel unstable and uncompetitive, and cannot relax. ⑩ The lecturer's points therefore rebut the reading passage's claims that employees favor this working arrangement because they have more time to enjoy life.

Lastly, the four-day workweek is not good for the economy. ⑪ Companies often force their staff to complete forty hours of work in thirty-two hours. ⑫ This results in increased stress and decreased health for employees. ⑬ Consequently, the overall economy suffers from reduced productivity. ⑭ These facts counter the reading passage's assertion that the four-day workweek benefits the economy by creating more jobs.

해석　　교수는 주 4일 근무제라는 새로운 근무 제도가 기업, 직원, 그리고 경제에 해롭다고 생각한다. 교수의 주장은 주 4일 근무제를 지지하는 지문에 반하는 것이다.

주 4일 근무제가 좋은 선택이 아닌 이유 중 하나는 회사가 재정적으로 손해를 보기 때문이다. 기업들은 추가로 사무실 공간과 컴퓨터를 제공해야 할 뿐만 아니라 직원들을 더 고용하고 교육시키는데 많은 돈을 들여야 한다. 게다가, 기업들은 이런 근무 제도 하에서 더 많은 직원 보험료를 지불해야 한다. 그러므로, 교수는 주 4일 근무제가 재정적으로 회사에게 이익을 준다는 지문의 주장을 반박한다.

게다가, 이러한 근무 제도는 직원들에게도 부정적인 영향을 끼친다. 그들은 그들의 능력을 향상시켜 주는 업무에 충분히 시간을 소비할 수 없고, 따라서 직업적으로 성장할 수 없다. 게다가, 회사는 주당 40시간 근무하는 직원을 고용하고 승진시키려 한다. 그 결과, 주 4일 근무하는 직원들은 불안정하고 경쟁력이 없다고 느끼게 되어 편안한 마음을 가질 수가 없다. 그러므로, 교수의 논지는 직원들이 그들의 생활을 즐길 수 있는 시간을 더 갖게 되어 이러한 근무 제도를 선호한다는 지문의 주장을 논박한다.

마지막으로, 주 4일 근무제는 경제에도 도움이 되지 않는다. 회사는 종종 그들의 직원들에게 32시간 내에 40시간 분량의 일을 완수할 것을 강요한다. 이것은 직원들의 스트레스를 증가시키고 건강을 악화시키는 결과를 초래한다. 결과적으로, 국가 전체의 경제가 생산성의 감소로 인해 피해를 보게 된다. 이러한 사실은 주 4일 근무제가 더 많은 직업을 창출함으로써 경제에 혜택을 가져다 준다는 글의 주장에 반박한다.

어휘　　arrangement[əréindʒmənt] 장치, 제도　four-day workweek 주 4일 근무　detrimental[dètrəméntəl] 해로운, 치명적인
counter[káuntər] 거스르다, 반하다　practice[prǽktis] 관행　monetarily[mànitɛ́:rəli] 재정적으로
unstable[ʌnstéibl] 불안정한　uncompetitive[ʌ̀nkəmpétətiv] 경쟁력이 없는

스크립트 및 해석

Reading

경제 불황과 기존의 주 40시간 근무제에 대한 근로자들의 불만은 노동 시장에 변화를 불러왔다. 점점, 오늘날의 기업들은 주 4일 32시간 근무제를 채택하고 있다. 이것은 경제를 전반적으로 향상시키는 것은 물론이고, 고용주와 직원들에게도 매우 이익이 된다.

첫째로, 재정적으로 힘든 시기를 겪고 있는 고용주들은 급료를 덜 지급함으로써 이익을 얻는다. 즉, 급료의 20%를 절감할 수 있다. 경제는 몇 년이고 불황을 겪을 수 있기에, 기업들은 자신들이 비용을 절감할 수 있는 부분들을 찾아야 한다. 기업 직원들의 근무시간을 단축시키는 것은, 회사가 여분의 자금을 하부 구조와 재원 개발에 투자할 수 있도록 해주기 때문에, 경제적으로 현명한 행동이라고 할 수 있다. 이런 요인들은 가장 적임이고, 경쟁력이 있으며, 생산적인 직원들을 회사로 끌어들일 것이고 회사가 더 성장할 수 있도록 할 것이다.

더군다나, 직원 개개인은 이런 새로운 근무제로부터 엄청난 이득을 얻는다. 많은 근로자들은 직업 외의 삶에 투자할 시간이 없다고 불만을

토론한다. 주 4일 근무제는 친구 혹은 가족들과 함께 더 많이 휴식을 취할 수 있는 시간을 의미한다. 신나는 취미 생활을 하고, 친구들을 만나고, 가족과 즐거운 시간을 보내는 것은 삶의 질이 향상 되는 결과를 가져온다. 이러한 감정은 직장 생활에까지 이어져, 근로자들은 행복한 마음으로 더욱 생산적으로 일한다. 따라서, 근무시간의 단축은 노동자의 만족감과 행복에 직접적인 관련이 있다.

주 4일 근무제는 또한 경제에도 도움이 된다. 현재, 대다수의 인력 시장은 극도로 위축돼 있다. 직원들의 근무시간 단축은 더 많은 일자리 창출이라는 결과를 낳을 것이다. 게다가, 회사들은 더욱 다양한 노동 인구로부터 이득을 볼 것이다. 그 결과 행복하고, 생산적인 근로자와 수익성 높고 급속히 발전하는 기업들로 인해 신바람 나는 경제가 되는 것이다. 따라서 주 4일 근무제의 결과로 빚어지는 튼튼하고, 다각적이며, 생산적인 인력 시장은 기존의 주 40시간 근무제로부터 탈피를 지지해야 하는 또 다른 이유이다.

dissatisfaction[dissӕtisfǽkʃən] 불만, 불평   workweek[wə́:rkwì:k] 1주 노동시간
shift[ʃift] 변화, 이동, 전환   landscape[lǽndskèip] 풍경, 경치
beneficial[bènəfíʃəl] 이익이 되는, 득이 되는   lean[li:n] 수확이 적은   namely[néimli] 즉, 다시 말해서
recession[riséʃən] 불황   on end 연달아   trim[trim] (예산 등을) 깎다, 삭감하다   sound[saund] (재정 상태 등이) 건실한
infrastructure[ínfrəstrʌ̀ktʃər] 내부구조   productive[prədʌ́ktiv] 생산적인
tremendously[triméndəsli] 엄청나게   arrangement[əréindʒmənt] 조정, 협정, 협의   pursue[pərsúi] 추구하다
enjoyable[indʒɔ́iəbl] 유쾌한, 즐거운   carry over to~ ~으로 넘어가다, ~에 영향을 끼치다   job market 인력 시장
workforce[wə́rkfɔ̀rce] 노동인구   booming[bú:miŋ] 급속히 발전하는   diverse[divə́:rs] 여러 가지의, 다양한
profitable[práfitəbl] 이익이 되는, 벌이가 되는

Listening

Well class, today let's examine the four-day workweek, and companies' actual experiences with it. All right... first of all, companies suffered financially. It's just really hard for most people to complete forty hours' of work in thirty-two hours, so companies ended up spending more money hiring additional staff. And uh, well... you know it costs time and money to hire and train more employees... and additional office space and computers for more employees further added to business costs. And you know what else? The cost of employee insurance increased as employees' longer non-working days meant higher risk of accidents.

Of course, the four-day workweek also had many drawbacks for employees. This new working arrangement is, umm, simply not beneficial for workers' careers. Because employees are now spending fewer hours working than before, they aren't able to spend enough time in their jobs improving their skills... they don't experience any professional growth. Not only that, companies would inevitably prefer to hire and promote people who are willing to work five days a week. This, you know, means that four-day employees feel unstable because they know that they are not competitive. So feelings of insecurity like this overrode any pleasure from fewer working hours.

And, oh... this four-day workweek can't be good for the economy. Some companies intent on cutting costs would force their employees to complete forty hours of work in thirty-two hours. This obviously was very stressful for employees, who experienced declining health and happiness. Their work quality later suffered after short bursts of forced productivity or they grew ill, which affected their long-term productivity... And it, of course, impacts the overall economy negatively, as you can imagine. Not to mention... people had a smaller income from working thirty-two hours instead of forty... which means fewer consumer dollars to fuel the economy!

좋아요, 여러분. 오늘은 주 4일 근무제와, 기업들의 실제 경험을 살펴보도록 합시다. 첫째로, 주 4일 근무제를 채택함으로써 기업들은 재정적으로 손실을 입었어요. 대다수의 사람들에게 40시간 안에 해야 될 분량의 일을 32시간 만에 마무리 짓는다는 것은 매우 어려운 일이었고, 따라서 결국 기업들은 추가 직원을 고용하는 데 돈을 더 지출해야 했죠. 그리고, 더 많은 직원들을 고용하고 교육시킨다는 것은 돈과 시간을 투자해야 함을 뜻하죠. 또 이 추가 직원들을 위해 소요되는 사무실 공간과 컴퓨터는 시간과 사업 비용이 더 많이 들게 했고요. 그리고 또 어땠는지 아세요? 직원들이 근무하지 않는 날이 늘어난다는 것은 사고율도 높아짐을 의미했기 때문에 직원 보험 비용도 증가했답니다.

물론, 주 4일 근무제는 직원들에게도 많은 불리한 점을 지니고 있었습니다. 이 새로운 근무제는, 근로자의 이력에 별로 도움이 되지 못합니

다. 직원들이 이제는 전에 비해 근무시간이 줄었기 때문에, 자신들의 경력을 발달시킬 만큼 충분한 시간을 갖지 못합니다. 직업상의 발전을 이루지 못하게 되는 것이죠. 그뿐만 아니라, 기업들은 불가피하게 주 5일 근무를 할 수 있는 사람을 고용하고 승진시키는 것을 선호할 것입니다. 이것은, 주 4일 근무하는 직원들을 불안하게 만듭니다. 자신들이 경쟁력을 갖추고 있지 못하다는 것을 알기 때문이죠. 따라서 근무 시간 단축으로부터 오는 만족감보다 이런 불안감이 더 크게 작용했죠.

그리고 이 주 4일 근무제는 경제에도 득이 될 것이 없습니다. 사내 지출 비용을 삭감하기에 여념이 없는 몇몇 기업들은 40시간 내에 끝내야 할 일을 32시간 이내에 마치도록 강요했습니다. 이것은 명백히 직원들에게 매우 스트레스를 주었고, 그들은 건강이 나빠지고 행복감이 줄어드는 것을 경험했습니다. 그들은 압력을 받아 바짝 효율적으로 일했다가 금방 능률이 떨어지거나 몸이 아프게 되어 버렸으며, 이것은 장기적인 생산성에 영향을 끼쳤습니다. 그리고 이것은, 물론, 상상할 수 있다시피 경제 전반에 부정적인 영향을 끼칩니다. 물론 말할 필요도 없는 것은, 직원들이 40시간 대신 32시간을 일함으로써 수입이 줄어들었다는 거죠. 이것은 곧 경제를 활성화시킬 수 있는 소비가 감소된다는 뜻이고요!

> business costs 사업 비용   drawback[drɔ́:bæk] 약점, 결점   working arrangement 노동 협정, 근무 배치
> inevitably[inévitəbli] 필연적으로, 불가피하게   unstable[ʌnstéibl] 불안정한
> insecurity[ìnsikjú(:)ərəti] 불안감, 불안정   override[òuvərráid] ~보다 우위에 서다, 무효로 하다
> intent on~ ~에 급급하다   declining[dikláiniŋ] 기우는, 쇠퇴하는   burst[bə́:rst] 갑작스러운 활동
> productivity[pròudəktívəti] 생산성, 생산력

POWER TEST

p.134

1. Note-taking ⟲ *Track 9*

읽기 노트

Telecommuting – attractive 재택근무 – 매력적
1. Benefits for employer 고용주의 혜택
– save $ for real estate: ↓ office space 부동산 비 절감: 사무실 공간↓
– employees more productive: comfort at home 직원 능률 제고: 집의 안락함
2. Advantg. for employees 직원들의 혜택
– happy in family, personal life 행복한 가정, 개인 생활
– no commute: save time, energy → productive use 통근 X: 시간, 에너지 절약 → 생산적 사용

듣기 노트

Working from home - unexpected results 재택근무 – 예기치 못한 결과
1. Company 기업
– employ. take excess. break, do other things 직원 과도한 휴식, 개인 용무 봄
– losing $ on wasted time > $ saved on space
낭비된 시간의 손해 비용＞공간 절약에 따른 비용
2. Employees 직원들
– depressed: no interact. 우울함: 상호 작용 X
– no commute: no separation b/t work & home 통근 X: 집과 직장 구분 X

Summary

The lecturer examines one company's experiences with telecommuting. She finds that in actuality, the practice is disadvantageous for both the employer and employees, as opposed to the reading passage's positive claims about working at home.

First of all, the lecturer looks at how an employer of a company that allowed telecommuting fared. The employer ended up losing money on wasted productivity. Workers at home wasted time and took excessive breaks. Furthermore, the money saved in real estate did not make up for the money lost in lower productivity. These findings challenge the reading passage's claim that telecommuting helps employers reduce costs in real estate and increase worker productivity and profits.

The lecturer also describes employee disadvantages of telecommuting. For one thing, those working at home became depressed. They didn't have enough human interaction. Furthermore, work and home started to blend together. They didn't have commuting which mentally separates home from work life. These findings directly contradict the reading passage's assertions that working at home causes employees to have happier personal lives, partly due to not having to commute.

해석　교수는 재택근무와 관련한 한 회사의 경험을 살펴본다. 교수는 재택근무에 대한 본문의 긍정적인 주장에 반해, 현실적으로는, 이 관행이 고용주와 근로자 모두에게 불리하다는 사실을 발견한다.
우선 첫째로, 교수는 재택근무를 허용한 한 기업의 고용주에게 어떤 일이 벌어졌는지를 살펴본다. 결국 고용주는 낭비된 생산력으로 인해 금전적 손실을 겪었다. 재택근무를 하는 직원들은 시간을 허비하고 과도한 휴식을 취했다. 더군다나, 부동산에서 절약한 비용은 생산력 저하로 인해 손해 본 비용을 보충하지는 못했다. 이러한 연구 결과는 재택근무가 고용주들이 부동산 부분의 비용을 절감하고 근로자의 생산성과 수익을 높일 수 있도록 도와준다는 본문의 주장에 이의를 제기한다.
교수는 또한 직원들에게 있어서 재택근무의 단점들에 대해 설명한다. 우선, 재택근무를 하는 직원들은 우울증에 시달리게 되었다. 다른 사람과 접할 일이 별로 없었기 때문이다. 게다가, 직장과 집이 뒤섞이기 시작했다. 그들에겐 심적으로 직장생활과 가정생활을 구분해 줄 통근시간이 없었다. 이런 연구결과는 재택근무가 그들이 통근을 하지 않아도 된다는 부분적인 이유 때문에, 직원들로 하여금 더 행복한 개인 생활을 영위할 수 있게 해준다는 본문의 주장을 정면으로 반박하는 것이다.

어휘　**examine**[igzǽmin] 검토하다　**practice**[prǽktis] 관행　**disadvantageous**[dìsæ̀dvəntéidʒəs] 불리한
fare[fɛər] (일이) 되어가다　**end up~** 마침내는 ~으로 되다　**make up for~** ~을 보완하다
human interaction 사람 간의 상호 작용　**assertion**[əsə́ːrʃən] 주장

스크립트 및 해석

Reading

컴퓨터 기능의 향상과 전자우편 사용의 보급은 많은 직장인들의 재택근무를 가능하게 하는데 일조했다. 이 개념이 기업의 경영진들의 마음에 들기 시작하면서, 재택근무 시스템은 매력적인 하나의 경영 트렌드로 빠르게 발전하고 있다.
보통 생각하는 것과는 달리, 재택근무로 인한 혜택의 대부분은 고용주 몫이었다. 예를 들어, 사무실 공간을 차지하는 직원들의 수가 적어서 회사에서는 부동산 비용을 절약할 수 있다. 주요 대도시 지역의 부동산 값이 그 어느 때보다도 높으므로, 부동산 비용 절감의 가능성은 직원들의 재택근무를 허락하기에 설득력 있는 동기이다. 게다가, 최근 조사 결과에 따르면 직원들이 실제로 자신의 집의 안락하고 편안한 환경에서 일을 할 때 더 능률적이라고 한다.
그러나, 직원 또한 여러 가지 혜택을 누릴 수 있다. 일반적으로, 재택근무를 시도해본 사람들은 개인 생활과 가족관계가 더 행복해진다고 말한다. 그들은 삶의 즐거움과 만족감을 향상시켜 줄 수 있는 활동에 할애할 수 있는 시간이 더 많아진다. 또 하나의 중요한 이점은 더 이상 통근을 하지 않아도 된다는 점이다. 오늘날의 도시에서, 교외 지역에 살기로 선택한 사람들은 직장까지 1~2시간을 통근해야 한다.

이것은 시간을 빼앗을 뿐만 아니라 더 생산적인 용도로 쓰일 수 있는 정신적, 육체적 에너지도 앗아간다. 따라서, 재택근무로 전환하는 추세는 새로이 부상하며 고용주와 직원 모두에게 다양한 기회를 제공한다.

capability[kèipəbílǝti] 능력　appeal to~ ~의 마음에 들다　executive[igzékjǝtiv] (기업의) 임원
work-at-home 재택근무　evolve into~ ~으로 진화하다　contrary to popular belief 보통사람들이 생각하는 것과는 달리
real estate 부동산　sector[séktǝr] (사회, 산업 등의) 분야　persuasive[pǝrswéisiv] 설득력 있는
incentive[inséntiv] 동기　productive[prǝdʌ́ktiv] (직무, 일 등에) 능률적인　convenience[kǝnvíːnjǝns] 안락함
familial[fǝmíljǝl] 가족의　engage in~ ~에 참여하다　contentment[kǝnténtmǝnt] 만족감
suburb[sʌ́bǝːrb] 교외　emerging[imǝ́ːrdʒiŋ] 부상하는　shift to~ ~으로의 전환

Listening

Most so-called "innovative" ideas to improve modern life by, well, adding more conveniences, offer different experiences to the people that try them. That is definitely the case with this new tendency for office employees working from home, rather than, you know, going all the way to the office. Sounds like a great idea, right? Well, actually this system can have some unexpected results for both the employer and the employee.

Alright, let's start by taking a look at how one company fared when they allowed telecommuting. After a couple of years, this telecommunications company found that accountability became an issue. What I mean is that employees working at home often take excessive breaks or do other things while on the clock, since nobody is monitoring them. So the employer ends up losing money on wasted time. This company also saw that although they didn't invest as much in real estate, the money they saved was less than the amount that would've been made from the higher productivity.

But uh, it isn't smooth sailing for the employee, either. While you'd think that everyone would be ecstatic to work at home, many who have tried it say that they became depressed. I mean, think about it... you never get human interaction except with your family, if you even have one! Then there's the fact that a necessary separation between work and home is lacking. No commute exists to provide an important time for mentally separating work from home life. So, those who work at their homes find that everything starts melding together in a really unhealthy way.

새로운 문명의 이기를 만들어내어 현대인의 삶을 향상시키려는 이른바 "혁신적인" 아이디어들은, 그것을 시도하는 사람들에게 각기 다른 경험을 제공합니다. 이는 분명히 사무직원들이 멀리 사무실까지 가지 않고 집에서 재택근무를 하는 새로운 추세의 경우에도 적용됩니다. 좋은 아이디어처럼 들리죠? 사실상 이 시스템은 직원과 고용주 모두에게 예상치 못한 결과를 발생시킬 수 있습니다.

좋아요, 재택근무를 허용한 한 회사가 어떠했는지를 보면서 시작해 봅시다. 재택근무 도입 몇 년 뒤, 이 전자통신 회사는 책임감의 문제가 생긴다는 것을 알아냈습니다. 즉, 그들을 감시할 사람이 아무도 없기 때문에, 재택근무를 하는 직원들은 종종 너무 많이 쉬거나, 근무시간 중에도 다른 볼일을 본다는 것이죠. 따라서 고용주는 낭비된 시간만큼 금전적 손해를 보게 됩니다. 또한 이 기업은 비록 그들이 부동산에는 많이 투자하지 않았지만, 절감한 비용이 직원들의 높은 생산성을 통해 얻었을 수익보다는 적다는 것을 알게 되었습니다.

하지만, 재택근무가 직원들에게도 순조로운 항해는 아닙니다. 여러분은 모든 사람들이 집에서 재택근무를 하는 것을 정말 좋아하리라고 생각할 지도 모르지만, 그렇게 근무를 해본 사람들 중 다수는 우울증에 걸리게 되었다고 합니다. 생각해 보세요. 가족 외에는 사람들과 상호 작용을 할 기회가 없습니다. 가족과 같이 살거나 한다면 말이에요! 그리고, 꼭 필요한 직장 생활과 가정 생활 간의 구분이 없어진다는 점도 있죠. 재택근무에는 직장 생활과 가정 생활을 구분하는 출퇴근시간이 존재하지를 않습니다. 따라서, 재택근무를 하는 사람들은 모든 것들이 부정적으로 뒤섞여 가는 것을 경험하게 됩니다.

innovative[ínǝvèitiv] 혁신적인　convenience[kǝnvíːnjǝns] 편리한 것　tendency[téndǝnsi] 추세
fare[fɛər] 지내다, 살아가다　telecommute[tèlǝkǝmjúːt] 재택근무하다
telecomminucations[telǝkǝmjuinikéiʃǝnz] 전기 전자통신　accountability[ǝkàuntǝbílǝti] 책임
excessive[iksésiv] 과도한　monitor[mɑ́nitǝr] (사람, 일등을) 감시하다　smooth sailing 순조로운 진행
ecstatic[ekstǽtik] 황홀한　meld[meld] 결합시키다　unhealthy[ʌnhélθi] 건강에 해로운

2. Note-taking 🎧 *Track 10*

읽기 노트

- Video games – harmful to children 전자오락 – 아이들에게 해로움
  - 1. Addictive 중독적
    - – when stopped: symptoms like other addiction 멈출 경우: 기타 중독 증세와 유사
    - – disrupt normal behavior, destroying lifestyle 정상 행동에 혼란, 생활 양식 파괴
  - 2. Encourage aggression 공격성 조장
    - – violent game → fighting, criminal 폭력적 게임 → 싸움, 범죄
    - – child. murder: inspired by games 아동 살인범 : 오락 영향 받음
  - 3. Waste of time 시간 낭비
    - – not useful 실용적 X
    - – time can be better spent 더 쓸모 있게 시간 사용할 수 있음

듣기 노트

- Video games – what critics leave out 비평가들이 도외시하는 점
  - 1. Addictive 중독적
    - – 13 hrs of game, 25 hrs of TV 13시간 게임, 25시간 텔레비전 시청
      - → then, anything can be addictive → 그러면, 뭐든지 중독적
    - – obsessive: shown in other aspects 강박 성향: 다른 면에서도 확인됨
      - → games not to blame, but kids → 오락이 아닌 아이가 문제
  - 2. Violence 폭력
    - – violent crime rates: lowest since gaming 폭력 범죄율: 전자오락 도입 이래 최저
    - – games: safety-valve to release aggression 오락: 공격성 방출에 대한 안전 장치
  - 3. Positive effects 긍정적 효과
    - – intelligence: solve problems quickly, multi-task, etc.
      지능: 문제 해결 속도↑, 동시에 여러 가지 일 처리 등
    - – improve reaction time & spatial skills 반응 시간 & 공간 능력 향상

Summary

The lecturer discusses some of the research on gaming. He mentions evidence that shows that video games are beneficial for children, and thus contradicts the reading passage's claim that gaming is harmful for kids.

First of all, the lecturer states that any healthful activity that people enjoy and spend a considerable amount of time doing can be considered addictive. For example, kids spend more time watching TV than playing video games, but this is not criticized. Video games are therefore unfairly accused of being addictive. He further asserts that kids who have addictive tendencies will find anything to become obsessed with; thus, the kids are the problem, not the video games. These points directly contradict the reading passage's claim that gaming is addictive.

Another main point the lecturer makes is that violent crime rates are the lowest among youth than they've been in 30 years since gaming became popular. Therefore, he believes that gaming is an outlet for aggression, whereas the reading passage claims that violent video games encourage aggressive behavior.

Lastly, the lecturer contends that playing video games provides many useful skills for everyday life, and helps with intelligence. In particular, he states that video games help one solve problems quickly, multitask, and improve reaction time and spatial skills. This is in direct opposition to the reading passage's claim that gaming is not beneficial in any way, serving no useful purpose in society and wasting precious time.

해석   교수는 전자오락에 관한 몇 가지 연구 결과에 대해 논의한다. 그는 전자오락이 어린이들에게 이롭다는 것을 나타내는 증거를 제시하고, 그에 따라 전자오락이 아이들에게 해롭다는 본문의 주장을 반박한다.

우선 첫째로, 교수는 사람들이 무언가를 즐기고 그것을 하는데 상당한 시간을 소비한다면 그 어떠한 건강한 활동이라도 중독적으로 간주될 수 있다고 진술한다. 예를 들어, 어린이들은 전자오락보다 텔레비전을 시청하는데 더 많은 시간을 보내지만, 이것은 비난받지 않는다. 따라서 전자오락은 부당하게 중독적이라는 비난을 받고 있다. 그는 더 나아가 중독적인 성향을 지닌 어린이들은 어떤 것이든 탐닉하게 될 수 있다고 주장한다. 따라서, 전자 오락이 아닌 아이들 자신이 문제인 것이다. 이러한 주장들은 본문에서 오락이 중독성을 지니고 있다는 주장을 정면으로 반박한다.

교수가 지적하는 또 다른 점은 전자오락이 각광을 받기 시작한 30년 전 이래로 청소년 범죄율이 최저 수위에 있다는 점이다. 그러므로, 본문에서는 폭력적인 전자오락이 공격적 행동을 장려한다고 주장하는 반면 그는 전자오락을 하는 것이 공격성의 배출구라고 주장한다.

마지막으로, 교수는 전자오락을 하는 것이 일상 생활에 유용한 여러 가지 기술을 키워주고, 지능 발달에 도움이 된다고 주장한다. 특히, 그는 전자오락을 하는 것이 문제를 빨리 풀고, 한꺼번에 여러 가지 일을 처리하고, 반응 시간과 공간 능력을 향상시키는 데 도움이 된다고 진술한다. 이는 전자오락이 어떠한 이점도 가지고 있지 않고, 사회에 유용한 역할을 하지 않으며 귀중한 시간을 낭비하는 것이라고 지문이 주장하는 바와 정면으로 반대되는 것이다.

어휘   **healthful**[hélθfəl] 건강에 좋은   **considerable**[kənsídərəbl] 상당한   **addictive**[ədíktiv] 중독성의
     assert[əsə́ːrt] 단언하다   **tendency**[téndənsi] 경향   **make a point** 주장하다
     outlet[áutlet] (감정 등의) 배출구   **aggression**[əgréʃən] 공격성   **reaction time** 반응 시간   **spatial skill** 공간 능력

스크립트 및 해석

Reading

최근 전자오락의 인기가 급증하면서 부모들과 전문가들이 우려하고 있다. 최근의 연구에 따르면, 몇몇 심리학자들은 게임, 특히 폭력을 특징으로 하는 1인칭 액션게임을 하는 것이 아이들에게 해롭다는 결론을 내렸다.

연구원들은 전자오락 습관이 중독성을 가지고 있다는 증거를 발견했다. 많은 청소년들은 하루에 몇 시간이고 TV 앞에 앉아 게임을 하는데 열중한다. 그들이 게임을 멈추도록 했을 때의 금단 증상은 강박 행동, 게임 이외의 다른 활동에 대한 관심을 잃는 것, 또는 가족에게 거짓말을 하는 것 등 기타 중독 현상에서 보여지는 증상과 유사하다. 모든 중독 현상과 마찬가지로 전자오락은 정상적인 행동에 혼란을 가져오고 학업 부진과 같은 중독자들에게서 흔히 찾아볼 수 있는 문제점들에 일조한다. 전자오락의 반대론자들은 게임을 하는 것이 아이의 인생에서 기타 모든 행위보다 우선시 되어 아이의 건전한 생활양식이 완전히 파괴되는 사례를 들어 보인다.

또한 연구결과는 폭력적인 것으로 악명 높은 특정 전자오락들이 사람들의 공격적인 성향을 부추긴다는 것을 보여주었다. 근래 이루어진 실험들은 전자오락을 하는데 소요된 시간과 난폭하게 행동하는 경향 사이의 관계를 밝혀냈다. 폭력 게임에 대한 높은 노출 수위는 학교에서의 싸움, 그리고 범죄적인 행동 양식과 연관이 있었다. 극단적인 경우로 세인의 관심을 모았던 재판에서 살인 혐의로 기소된 아이들은 그들이 전자오락의 영향을 받아 살인을 저지르게 되었다고 시인했다.

그럼에도 불구하고 아이들은 화면 앞에 바짝 붙어 앉아 즐기며 많은 시간을 낭비하도록 허용되고 있다. 이러한 게임들은 사회에 어떠한 이득도 되지 않지만 우리 아이들의 여가 활동의 큰 비중을 차지하고 있다. TV를 뚫어져라 쳐다보며 유익한 어떤 것도 배우지 않는 것보다. 아이들의 시간을 더욱 건설적으로 활용하는 방법이 있을 것이다.

surge[sə:rdʒ] 급등, 급증   withdrawal symptom (의학) 마약의 금단 증상   addiction[ədíkʃən] (주로 마약, 알코올) 중독
compulsive behavior 강박 행동   disrupt[dìsrʌ́pt] 분열시키다   cite[sait] 인용하다
leading to~ ~으로 이어지는   notoriously[noutɔ́:riəsli] 악명 높게   inclination[ìnklənéiʃən] 성향
exposure[ikspóuʒər] 노출, ~에 접하게 함   accused of~ (~의 혐의로) 기소당한   high-profile 유명한
glued to~ ~에 딱 달라붙은   constructively[kənstrʌ́ktivli] 건설적으로   beneficial[bènəfíʃəl] 이로운

Listening

Today's debate about the dangers video games pose to children has many arguments. I'd like to mention a few things that critics leave out. Sure, kids spend a lot of time playing, but let's look at the figures. They spend about 13 hours a week playing video games, but 25 hours watching TV. By these standards, anything we enjoy is "addictive," like TV, or reading, or skiing. On top of that, studies that say video games promote obsessive tendencies, sort of, uh, forget to mention that these kids show those same tendencies in other aspects of their lives. Video games aren't to blame. As it turns out, these children are simply showing the symptoms of other, unrelated problems.

And as far as violence goes... the truth of the matter is that a few bad apples have claimed that video games made them do it, but over all, violent crime rates, especially among youth, are the lowest they've been since gaming became popular about 30 years ago. If gaming encourages people to act aggressively, shouldn't those have gone up? Isn't it possible that maybe, just maybe, video games act like, kind of, a safety-valve for people to blow off steam? Many experts think so.

Numerous studies also indicate that video games have other positive effects, even the point-and-shoot ones. A positive correlation has been noted with intelligence, for instance. That's because the interactive aspect of gaming requires players to solve problems quickly, multitask, gauge risks and make fast decisions. Research also indicates that it improves reaction time and spatial skills. These are all highly-valued abilities in everyday life!

아이들에게 가해지는 전자오락의 위험에 대한 오늘의 토론에는 많은 주장들이 있습니다. 나는 비평가들이 지적하지 않은 몇 가지 사항을 언급하고자 합니다. 물론, 아이들이 전자오락을 하는데 많은 시간을 보내기는 하지만, 수치를 보도록 합시다. 그들은 대략 1주일에 13시간 정도를 전자오락을 하는데 보내지만 TV를 시청하는 데는 25시간을 보냅니다. 이 기준에 따르자면, TV를 시청하거나 독서를 하거나 스키를 타는 것 등 우리가 즐기는 모든 활동은 "중독성 있는" 것들입니다. 더욱이 전자오락이 강박적 성향을 촉진시킨다는 연구 결과에는, 이 아이들이 생활의 다른 부분에서도 이러한 같은 성향을 나타낸다는 점을 언급하고 있지 않습니다. 전자오락의 탓이 아닙니다. 실제로는, 이 아이들이 단지 전자오락과 무관한 다른 문제점의 증상을 보이는 것뿐입니다.

그리고 폭력에 대해 말하자면 사실상 몇몇 나쁜 아이들이 자신들의 범죄를 전자오락의 탓으로 돌렸지만 전체적으로 볼 때, 특히 청소년들 사이에서의 폭력 범죄율은 전자오락이 유행을 타기 시작한 30년 전 이래 최저입니다. 만일 게임을 하는 것이 사람들로 하여금 공격적인 태도를 취하도록 한다면, 이 범죄율은 증가했어야 하는 것 아닌가요? 만약, 단지 만약에, 전자오락이 일종의 사람들이 스트레스를 풀 수 있는 배출구 역할을 해주는 거라고요? 많은 전문가들은 그렇게 생각합니다.

또한 다수의 연구 결과는 전자오락이 다른 긍정적 효과를 가지고 있다는 것을 보여줍니다 – 심지어 총 쏘는 게임조차도 말이죠. 한 예로, 지능과 전자오락 간에 긍정적인 상관 관계가 밝혀졌습니다. 이는 게임의 상호 작용적인 측면이 플레이어로 하여금 빨리 문제를 풀고, 동시에 여러 가지 일을 하고, 위험을 판단하고 빠른 결단을 내릴 것을 요구하기 때문이죠. 연구 결과는 또한 게임을 하는 것이 반응 시간과 공간 능력을 향상시킨다는 것을 보여줍니다. 이러한 능력들은 모두 일상 생활에서 높게 평가되는 것들이죠!

pose to~ ~에 가하다   obsessive[əbsésiv] 강박 관념의   as it turns out 실제로는   as far as ~ goes ~에 관해서는
bad apples (속어) 악당, 망나니   safety-valve (감정, 정력등의) 무난한 배출구
blow off steam 화를 배출시키다, 스트레스를 풀다   point-and-shoot game 총 쏘는 게임
multitask[mʌ́ltitæsk] 한꺼번에 여러 가지 일을 처리하다   gauge[geidʒ] 측정하다   spatial skill 공간 능력

Independent Section

기본다지기

 I 상황별 표현

1. 선호, 찬반, 비교, 양보 표현

Check-up   p.148

1. **I agree that** face-to-face communication is better than other types of communication.
2. **The advantages of** living in the city **far outweigh the disadvantages**.
3. **Conversely**, celebrities might feel as if they will never be treated like an ordinary person.
4. **In my opinion**, people should save as much money as possible for large purchases, such as a house or car.
5. Earning huge amounts of money in a job **cannot compare with** having free time to spend with family and friends.
6. **I firmly believe that** graduating from a university should be the goal of every young student.
7. **In spite of** the prestige of top universities, many people still believe that a high-quality education can be had at almost any school.
8. **As opposed to** home-schooled children, those who attend school with others have a chance to develop their socialization skills.
9. **In contrast**, virus programmers are gaining in strength and numbers.
10. **I object to** companies doing whatever they can to make a profit.
11. **Compared to** dangerous activities such as mountain-climbing, sports like tennis are much less hazardous, but can be just as invigorating.
12. **It is evident that** different students have different learning styles.
13. **However, unlike** other dormitories, this cafeteria does not require students to purchase meal plans.
14. **I question whether** daily homework assignments are an effective way for children to learn.
15. **I am against** the availability of university education to all students.
16. The invention of the Internet **is similar to** the invention of the airplane in that both made the world a smaller place.
17. **Some people may be opposed to** extending the standard work week to more than 40 hours.
18. Studying at an online university **has its advantages and disadvantages**.
19. **Similarly**, students should be able to provide feedback on the quality of education they experienced while at a university.
20. **I don't think it is** beneficial **that** some parents coach their children's sports teams.

Check-up p.158

1. **This reflects** the high expectations of today's consumers.
2. **As a result**, some parents are limiting the amount of time their children spend on the Internet every day.
3. **I suppose that** even tobacco companies deserve to receive investment funds.
4. **If I were asked to** volunteer anywhere in the world, **I would** choose to volunteer in Thailand.
5. **For all these reasons, I think that** people should seriously consider the financial responsibility of a university education.
6. **As a result of** urban sprawl, people tend to drive farther when commuting.
7. **If it were not for** television, people **would** have much less in common.
8. **Let's assume that** students spend an average of three hours a day on the Internet.
9. **This gives rise to** increased crime rates and higher credit card debt.
10. **It seems clear that** professionals are respected **for several reasons**.
11. **I would encourage** college students **to** talk to people from many different fields before deciding on their majors.
12. **That is why** I would prefer to live in off-campus housing.
13. **If it were up to me, I would** require graduating high school students to tour their new college campus.
14. **I wish** I could change my major because my interests are different now.
15. **There is no question that** good students are the ones that know how to manage their time effectively.
16. **A good way to** get used to a new company **is to** observe closely what other employees do.
17. **One advantage of** not drink**ing is that** you enjoy better health in general.
18. I **would** take a part-time job while in university **providing that** it doesn't take up more than 20 hours a week.
19. **It is clear that** diligence is essential if one is to be successful in life.
20. **In this sense**, protecting the environment can be considered insurance against future natural disasters.
21. **For this reason**, I think that at least one parent should stay at home instead of work.
22. **I assume that** people find smoking a chance to socialize with others.

Check-up p.168

1. **As I have mentioned**, many university students plan group trips over the weekends.
2. **In short**, I feel that children need affection in order to develop healthy personalities.
3. **I can see that** determination really pays off **in these instances**.
4. **As it is**, many students do not use university counseling services to their full advantage.
5. **There are two examples to show how** such events affect workers' productivity.
6. **In this way**, students can learn from people they respect and admire.
7. **To summarize**, a successful student's most invaluable tools are diligence and time management.

8. **In particular**, many children have difficulty accepting the birth of a younger brother or sister.

9. **On top of that**, not all students who enter a university actually graduate.

10. **As we have seen**, mobile phones tend to make people less considerate of each other.

11. **As the old saying goes**, "Necessity is the mother of invention."

12. **To give you an idea**, here is an example of an unlikely success story.

13. **In other words**, sometimes one has to make mistakes in order to learn from them.

14. **Overall**, the most enjoyable time in my life was the summer after I graduated from high school.

15. **In addition to** making money, it is **also** not uncommon for fathers to help with the cooking and the chores.

16. **In view of** the benefits of professional careers, it is no wonder that they are so highly sought after.

17. **Generally speaking**, admissions to professional faculties, like medicine or law, are extremely competitive.

18. **To some extent**, all travelers want comfort and cleanliness in accommodations.

19. **In conclusion**, I believe that a good friend is someone who is loyal and trustworthy.

20. **Experts have verified that** preservatives used in food may affect cancer rates.

Ⅱ 주제별 표현

1. 교육, 가정, 사회에 관한 표현

Check-up   p.182

1. Freshmen often develop an **emotional attachment** to their dorm rooms over the school year.

2. The university years are widely believed to be **the most important stage in one's life**.

3. **Youth culture** has changed dramatically in the last fifty years.

4. I try to give my seat up to **senior citizens**, especially when the bus or train is crowded.

5. Some universities are considering a strict **compulsory attendance** policy.

6. The two roommates **made a compromise** about when friends could visit their dorm room.

7. At bicycle **club meetings**, members exchange information on maintenance and riding techniques.

8. In America, it is a **social custom** to shake hands with everyone to whom you are introduced.

9. Exchange students should familiarize themselves with the **social norms** of the country they will be studying in.

10. **Extracurricular activities** help to enhance social skills and teach lessons not learned in a classroom.

11. Flags and national anthems are symbols of **national identity**.

12. It is impossible to prove a theory correct without conducting **in-depth research**.

13. Some people still hold the **misguided belief** that a university degree will guarantee a job.

14. When two people meet, they ask each other questions in order to find some **common ground**.

15. As a father is a **role model** for his son, his attitudes and behaviors will pass onto him.

16. Universities often **provoke controversy** by inviting notorious guest speakers to campus.

17. Parents should **set a good example** for their children by not shouting, even when they are really upset.

18. To **work in teams** effectively, people must be receptive to the ideas of others.
19. **Entering one's teens** is an exciting event in the life of every child.
20. Making mistakes is an important part of the **learning process**.

2. 건강, 환경, 생활에 관한 표현

Check-up   p.196

1. Toxic waste is an unfortunate **by-product** of nuclear power plants.
2. Students usually **take the middle ground** in labor disputes between teaching staff and the university.
3. Senior citizens become more vulnerable to **chronic disease** as they age.
4. Global warming is part of a **vicious cycle** that contributes to forest fires, which cause even more global warming.
5. Attending parties or concerts with loud music can do **irreparable damage** to one's hearing.
6. Constructing underground parking lots would **ease traffic congestion** on campus.
7. It is a case of **pure luck** if you find a twenty-dollar bill on the sidewalk.
8. Working online from home offers a **stress-free life** without long commutes.
9. Even though the campus bookstore ordered extra copies, it still may be hard to **meet the demand** for certain textbooks.
10. A regular exercise is the basic formula everyone should follow to **stay in shape**.
11. Public confidence in the police diminishes as the **crime rate** increases.
12. Some scientists believe that the human **life span** might someday reach 200 years.
13. This university is famous for its research and development of **cutting-edge medicines**.
14. You should dress warmly if you don't want to **come down with** a cold.
15. Students without part-time jobs should handle their personal finances **with discretion**.
16. Studies have shown that **secondhand smoking** is more toxic than cigarette smoke that is inhaled directly.
17. With effective time management, students can **be dedicated to** a variety of activities without neglecting their studies.
18. **Early birds** who arrive at libraries early can get the best seats.
19. Pizza and **frozen food** are popular food among college students.
20. Her **punctuality** suggests that she has strong time management skills.
21. A **well-balanced diet** should include fresh fruits and vegetables.
22. He's been **going through a hard time** since he broke his leg.

3. 문화, 과학, 경제에 관한 표현

Check-up   p.210

1. When friends eat out, they often **split the cost** evenly, regardless of what each person ordered.
2. The best résumés list work experience in **chronological order**, from the most recent job to the oldest.

기본다지기 Ⅱ. 주제별 표현 • 481

3. Essay writing is a **time-consuming process** that involves a lot of research and revision.

4. A high **unemployment rate** is a symptom of a malfunctioning economy.

5. Some scholarships are only awarded to students who can demonstrate **financial hardship**.

6. In today's world, illiterate people have a very slim chance of **making a good living**.

7. It wasn't long after the introduction of computers that typewriters **became obsolete**.

8. Eating too many meals in expensive restaurants can put a salaried worker **beyond budget**.

9. In my opinion, **long-distance phone calls** are a better way of keeping in touch than email.

10. Companies wishing to **keep in step with globalization** should maintain an up-to-date website in several languages.

11. College life, like everything else, is full of **ups and downs**.

12. Sudden changes in the exchange rate often **affect local economies**.

13. Nutritious snacks, such as bananas, are **handy on trips**.

14. **Investing money in** a business is riskier than collecting a regular salary from an established company.

15. Travelers who wait long enough to buy plane tickets can **reap the benefits** of last-minute sales.

16. You can **run up debt** if you don't handle your financial matters carefully.

17. The coach should **make adjustments** to the game plan if the team performs poorly.

18. Some people have to work two jobs to earn enough money to **make ends meet**.

19. A struggling employment market is usually the product of a **slow economy**.

20. A favorite pastime of many young people is listening to **popular music**.

실전익히기

I 에세이 기본 구조 익히기

HACKERS Practice p.220

1. 다음의 주장에 찬성하는가 반대하는가? 고등학생들은 공부하고 싶은 과목을 선택하도록 허용되어야 한다. 구체적인 이유와 예를 들어 자신의 견해를 뒷받침하시오.

Outline

Disagree 반대
1. By studying many courses one can build knowledge of various fields 많은 과목을 공부함으로써 다양한 분야의 지식을 쌓을 수 있다
2. Taking different courses provides chance to explore one's potential 다른 수업을 듣는 것은 개인의 잠재력을 알아보는 기회가 된다

어휘 **various** [vέ(ː)əriəs] 다양한 **explore** [iksplɔ́ːr] 탐험하다, 탐구하다 **potential** [pəténʃəl] 잠재력

2. 다음의 주장에 찬성하는가 반대하는가? 선생님에게는 학생들과 잘 어울리는 능력이 지식을 전달하는 능력보다 더 중요하다. 구체적인 이유와 예를 들어 자신의 견해를 뒷받침하시오.

Outline

- Agree 찬성
  1. Friendly teachers motivate students to study
     친근한 선생님은 학생들이 공부하도록 동기를 부여한다
     - students focus on studying more when given a teacher's attention
       선생님의 관심을 받으면 학생들이 공부에 더 집중한다
     - friend who was a problem child got accepted to top university thanks to a teacher's concern
       문제아였던 친구는 선생님의 관심 덕분에 일류 대학에 진학했다
  2. Interaction with teachers enhance students' social skills
     선생님과의 상호 관계가 학생의 사회적 기술을 향상시킨다
     - interpersonal communication skills are needed to be successful
       성공하려면 대인관계의 의사소통 기술이 필요하다
     - my PE teacher helped me to become more outgoing
       체육 선생님이 나를 외향적인 성격으로 변화시켰다

어휘 **motivate**[móutəvèit] 동기를 부여하다 **attention**[əténʃən] 관심 **thanks to~** ~ 의 덕택으로
interaction[ìntərǽkʃən] 상호 작용 **enhance**[inhǽns] 강화하다 **social skills** 사회적 기술, 사교 기술
interpersonal[ìntərpə́:rsənəl] 사람 사이의, 대인 관계의 **PE = physical education** 체육 **outgoing**[áutgòuiŋ] 외향적인

3. 다음의 주장에 찬성하는가 반대하는가? 젊은이들은 나이 든 사람들보다 삶을 더 즐긴다. 구체적인 이유와 예를 들어 자신의 견해를 뒷받침하시오.

Outline

- Agree 찬성
  1. Young people are physically active 젊은 사람들은 신체적으로 활동적이다
     - if not healthy, it's hard to enjoy life to its fullest
       건강하지 않으면 인생을 최대한 즐길 수 없다
     - grandfather can't enjoy hiking anymore because of physical weakness
       할아버지께서는 건강이 쇠약해지셔서 하이킹을 더 이상 즐기실 수 없다
  2. Young people have fewer responsibilities 젊은 사람들은 책임이 적다
     - as people age, obligations restrict people from enjoying their lives
       사람들이 나이가 들면서 책임 때문에 인생을 즐기는 것을 제한 받는다
     - older brother can't take vacation whereas I can
       나는 휴가를 떠날 수 있는 반면 오빠는 그럴 수 없다

어휘 **active**[ǽktiv] 활달한, 활동적인 **to the fullest** 최대한으로 **responsibility**[rispὰnsəbíləti] 책임 **age**[eidʒ] 나이를 먹다
obligation[ὰbləgéiʃən] 의무 **restrict**[ristríkt] 제한하다 **whereas**[hwɛərǽz] ~에 반해서

4. 다음의 주장에 찬성하는가 반대하는가? 정부는 지구상의 문제들보다 우주 탐험에 재원을 투자하는 편이 더 낫다. 구체적인 이유와 예를 들어 자신의 견해를 뒷받침하시오.

Outline

- Disagree 반대
  - 1. Saving human lives is more imperative 인류의 생명을 구하는 것이 더 급하다
    - people are dying due to extreme shortage of staples
      생필품이 극도로 부족해 사람들이 죽어가고 있다
    - a number of children dying of hunger in Africa
      굶주림으로 죽어가는 아프리카의 수많은 아이들
  - 2. Restoring the damaged environment is more pressing
    훼손된 자연을 복구하는 것이 더 시급하다
    - clean air and water are indispensable for survival
      깨끗한 공기와 물이 생존을 위해 필수 불가결하다
    - destruction of woodlands 삼림의 파괴

어휘 **imperative** [impérətiv] 피할 수 없는, 부득이한 **due to ~** ~ 때문에 **shortage** [ʃɔ́ːrtidʒ] 부족
restore [ristɔ́ːr] 회복하다 **pressing** [présiŋ] 긴급한, 절박한 **indispensable** [ìndispénsəbl] 필수 불가결한
survival [sərváivəl] 생존 **destruction** [distrʌ́kʃən] 파괴 **woodland(s)** [wúdlænd] 삼림

HACKERS Test   p.222

1. 자신과 비슷한 친구를 사귀는 것이 다른 친구를 사귀는 것보다 낫다. 이 주장에 찬성하는가 반대하는가? 구체적인 이유와 예를 들어 자신의 견해를 뒷받침하시오.

Outline

- Agree 찬성
  - 1. Have more fun together enjoying activities both like
    둘 다 좋아하는 활동을 함께 즐기면 더 재미있다
    - share same hobbies and interests
      같은 취미와 관심사를 공유한다
    - survey: people with same hobbies get along better than people with different ones
      조사: 다른 취미를 지닌 사람들보다 같은 취미를 지닌 사람들끼리 더 잘 통한다
  - 2. Similar friends understand each other better 비슷한 친구들은 서로를 더 잘 이해한다
    - friendship strengthens through sympathy 공감을 통해 우정이 더 깊어진다
    - friend who knows me well gave me a helpful advice when I was in trouble
      내가 어려움에 처했을 때 날 잘 아는 친구가 유용한 조언을 해주었다

---

2. 다음의 주장에 찬성하는가 반대하는가? 집에서 만든 음식을 먹는 것이 식당이나 노점에서 사먹는 것보다 낫다. 구체적인 이유
와 예를 들어 자신의 견해를 뒷받침하시오.

Outline

- Disagree 반대
  - 1. Restaurants provide a variety of flavors 레스토랑은 다양한 맛을 제공한다
    - different tastes than one's own limited cooking
      한계가 있는 자신의 요리와는 다른 맛
    - at Greek restaurant, tasted exotic food
      그리스 레스토랑에서 이국적인 음식을 맛보았다
  - 2. Eating out is more convenient 외식하는 것은 더 편리하다
    - saves time cooking and cleaning 요리하고 치우는 시간을 절약할 수 있다
    - friend who saved time for studying by not cooking
      요리하지 않음으로써 공부 시간을 늘린 친구

3. 다음의 주장에 찬성하는가 반대하는가? 대학에서는 도서관에 지원하는 만큼의 돈을 스포츠 활동에도 투자해야 한다. 구체적인
이유와 예를 들어 자신의 견해를 뒷받침하시오.

Outline

- Agree 찬성
  - 1. Sports improve students' physical health 스포츠는 학생들의 신체적 건강을 향상시킨다
    - many studies show exercises strengthen bones muscles
      많은 연구 결과들이 운동이 뼈와 근육을 강화한다는 사실을 보여준다
    - obese cousin lost weight after started regular walking
      비만인 사촌이 정기적으로 걷기 시작한 이후 체중을 감량하였다
  - 2. Sports activities foster students' social skills
    스포츠 활동들은 학생들의 사회적 기술을 기르는데 일조한다
    - sports activities require collective effort and cooperation
      스포츠 활동들은 공동의 노력과 협력을 필요로 한다
    - soccer game 축구 경기

4. 다음의 주장에 찬성하는가 반대하는가? 동물원은 아무런 쓸모가 없다. 구체적인 이유와 예를 들어 자신의 견해를 뒷받침하시오.

Outline

> **Disagree** 반대
>   1. Zoos play a role in educating people about animals
>   사람들에게 동물에 대하여 가르쳐 주는 역할을 한다
>   – children gain hands-on learning experience   아이들은 체험 학습을 할 수 있다
>   – experience in 5th grade visiting the Seoul Children's Zoo
>   5학년 때 서울 어린이대공원을 방문한 경험
>   2. Zoos protect endangered species   동물원은 멸종 위기에 처한 종을 보호한다
>   – provide animals with optimal conditions for survival
>   동물들에게 생존에 필요한 최적의 조건을 제공한다
>   – tigers in Korea   한국의 호랑이

어휘   **play a role** 역할을 하다   **hands-on** 실제 체험할 수 있는
endangered[indéindʒərd] 멸종 위기에 처한   **optimal**[ɑ́ptəməl] 최적의

II 에세이 쓰기 – 서론

HACKERS Practice

p.226

1. 다음의 주장에 찬성하는가 반대하는가? 유명 운동 선수나 연예인들은 그들이 벌어들이는 수백만 달러의 보수를 받을 자격이 있다. 구체적인 이유와 예를 들어 자신의 견해를 뒷받침하시오.

> [도입] ① As the sports and entertainment industries are growing faster than ever before, people often debate whether or not celebrities deserve the multi-million dollar incomes they earn. [대주제문] I would argue that the high salaries of famous athletes and entertainers are definitely justifiable. The rationale behind this is that celebrities do their best to be the finest in their respective fields. Furthermore, famous athletes and entertainers bring in huge incomes for their employers.

어휘   **celebrity**[səlébrəti] 유명 인사   **multi-million** 수백만의   **income**[ínkʌm] 수입
justifiable[dʒʌ́stəfàiəbl] 정당화되는, 옳다고 증명할 수 있는   **rationale**[ræ̀ʃənǽl] 근본적 이유   **do one's best** 최선을 다하다
respective[rispéktiv] 각자의

2. 다음의 주장에 찬성하는가 반대하는가? 아이들이 자라기에는 대도시보다 시골이 좋다. 구체적인 이유와 예를 들어 자신의 견해를 뒷받침하시오.

[도입] ① <u>Since an increasing number of people live in cities, a controversy has arisen over whether children benefit more from growing up in these urban environments or in rural areas.</u> [대주제문] From my point of view, growing up in the countryside is more beneficial for children because it is safer and provides a fun, healthful, natural environment.

어휘   controversy[kántrəvə̀ːrsi] 논란   urban[ə́ːrbən] 도시의   rural[rú(ː)ərəl] 시골의, 교외의
beneficial[bènəfíʃəl] 이로운   healthful[hélθfəl] 건전한, 건강한

3. 다음의 주장에 찬성하는가 반대하는가? 고등학교에서는 모든 학생들이 교복을 입도록 규정해야 한다. 구체적인 이유와 예를 들어 자신의 견해를 뒷받침하시오.

[도입] As teenagers become more conscious of fashion and self-expression, many students feel that high schools should give them the freedom to choose what they want to wear to school. [대주제문] Although I can understand their position, ① <u>I support mandatory school uniform policies because they conceal students' economic differences and instill discipline in students.</u>

어휘   conscious[kánʃəs] 의식하고 있는, 자각하고 있는   self-expression 자기 표현   mandatory[mǽndətɔ̀ːri] 의무적인, 강제적인
school uniform 교복   conceal[kənsíːl] 감추다   instill[instíl] 주입하다, 서서히 가르치다
discipline[dísəplin] 규율, 훈육

4. 다음의 주장에 찬성하는가 반대하는가? 아이들은 학교에 입학한 후에야 외국어를 배우기 시작해야 한다. 구체적인 이유와 예를 들어 자신의 견해를 뒷받침하시오.

[도입] Everyone recognizes the importance of learning foreign languages in this global era. Unfortunately, the later one waits to begin learning another language, the harder it becomes. [대주제문] ① <u>Accordingly, children should begin learning foreign languages as soon as possible since younger children have an advantage at language acquisition.</u> ② <u>On top of that, children who are not attending school have more free time to study languages.</u>

어휘   recognize[rékəgnàiz] 인정하다, 인식하다   era[í(ː)rə] 시대   accordingly[əkɔ́ːrdiŋli] 따라서
as soon as possible 가능한 한 빨리   advantage[ədvǽntidʒ] 이점   acquisition[æ̀kwizíʃən] 습득

HACKERS Test

p.230

1. 다음의 주장에 찬성하는가 반대하는가? 어린이가 학교 생활을 잘하는 데는 선생님보다는 반 친구가 더 중요한 영향을 미친다.

구체적인 이유와 예를 들어 자신의 견해를 뒷받침하시오.

> [도입] Although teachers play an important role in children's lives, they are involved in their students' lives for a limited time only. [대주제문] Because classmates spend hours together each day, sometimes for years, they are a bigger influence on each other than their teachers are. In addition, children are more influenced by peer pressure than by teachers' instruction.

해석　**도입** 어린이의 삶에 있어서 선생님이 중요한 역할을 하긴 하지만, 그들은 학생들의 인생에 한시적으로 개입할 뿐이다. **대주제문** 반 친구들은 매일 오랜 시간을 함께 보내고, 때로는 몇 년을 함께 지내기 때문에, 선생님보다는 서로가 더욱 큰 영향을 미친다. 게다가, 어린이들은 선생님의 가르침보다는 또래 집단의 압력에 더욱 영향을 받는다.

어휘　**classmate**[klǽsmèit] 반 친구, 급우　**heavily**[hévəli] 몹시, 심하게　**involve**[inválv] 개입하다, 관련시키다
peer pressure 또래 집단의 압력　**instruction**[instrʌ́kʃən] 교육, 가르침; 지시

2. 다음의 주장에 찬성하는가 반대하는가? 정부는 오래된 역사적 건물을 철거하고 현대식 건물로 교체해야 한다. 구체적인 이유와 예를 들어 자신의 견해를 뒷받침한다.

> [도입] Many people often erroneously think new things are always good and believe that governments should destroy old buildings and replace them with new, modern ones. [대주제문] I disagree with their idea, however, because of the historical value of old buildings and the exorbitant cost of replacing them with new ones.

해석　**도입** 많은 사람들은 종종 새로운 것이 항상 좋은 것이라고 잘못 생각하고서, 정부가 오래된 건물을 철거하고 새로운 현대식 건물로 교체해야 한다고 믿는다. **대주제문** 그러나, 나는 오래된 건물의 역사적 가치와 새 건물로 교체하는 데 드는 엄청난 비용 때문에 이러한 생각에 반대한다.

어휘　**erroneously**[iróuniəsli] 잘못되게, 그릇되게　**replace**[ripléis] 교체하다　**exorbitant**[iróuniəsli] 엄청난

Ⅲ 에세이 쓰기 – 본론

HACKERS Practice　　　　　　　　　　　　　　　　　　　　　　　　　p.234

1. 다음의 주장에 찬성하는가 반대하는가? 학생 신분의 십대가 일을 하는 것은 바람직하다. 구체적인 이유와 예를 들어 자신의 견해를 뒷받침하시오.

> [소주제문 1] ① To start with, student jobs improve teenagers' sense of responsibility. [구체적 근거 1: 일반적 진술] ② Working students are required to assume essential responsibilities such as arriving at work on

time, managing their schedules wisely, meeting deadlines, observing work regulations, and thoroughly completing assignments. [구체적 근거 2: 예시] Studies reveal that students who work fewer than 15 hours a week actually academically outperform their peers who do not work because they know how to handle multiple tasks and responsibilities, and can consequently manage their time well. On the whole, students who juggle work and school are more mature and well-equipped to succeed than their non-working peers. These benefits extend far outside the classroom.

[소주제문 2] ③ On top of that, working part-time encourages teenagers to appreciate the value of money. [구체적 근거 1: 일반적 진술] ④ Real work experience allows teenage students to naturally learn that they have to invest conscious effort and dedicate their precious time to earn money. [구체적 근거 2: 예시] From my personal experience, I worked at a fast-food restaurant when I was seventeen in order to make money to buy a new computer. I made only four dollars an hour doing exhausting work such as moving heavy boxes of ingredients, washing dirty dishes, and mopping the floors. However, through this work experience, I learned the value of money and became much more careful spending my parents' hard-earned money.

어휘   assume [əsjúːm] (책임을) 맡다, 지다   appreciation [əprìːʃiéiʃən] (올바른) 인식   essential [əsénʃəl] 본질적인, 필수적인
    observe [əbzə́ːrv] 준수하다   thoroughly [θə́ːrouli] 철저히   academically [æ̀kədémikəli] 학업적으로
    outperform [àutpərfɔ́ːrm] ~을 능가하다, 잘하다   multiple [mʌ́ltəpl] 복합적인, 다수의   juggle [mʌ́ltəpl] 잘 조절하다
    conscious [kánʃəs] 의식적인   dedicate [dédəkèit] 바치다   exhausting [dédəkèit] 피로하게 하는
    mop [map] 닦다   hard-earned 고생해서 번

2. 다음의 주장에 찬성하는가 반대하는가? 대학생들은 수업에 의무적으로 출석해야 한다. 구체적인 이유와 예를 들어 자신의 견해를 뒷받침하시오.

[소주제문 1] ① First of all, required attendance plays a pivotal role in helping students become more responsible and self-disciplined. [구체적 근거 1: 일반적 진술] ② This is largely because a mandatory attendance policy forces students to assume personal responsibility for coming to class regularly. ③ In addition, students face disciplinary consequences for their absences and tardiness, such as course failure, insufficient credit hours, probation, and even suspension. [구체적 근거 2: 예시] For example, when I was a freshman in college, I frequently skipped required classes because I was totally free from my parents' and teachers' supervision. However, thanks to the strict mandatory attendance policy, I had to improve my negligent and irresponsible behavior or else I would have to face severe consequences. I received a series of D's on my report card, stayed up several nights to work on make-up assignments, and even had to repeat several courses. Fortunately, I began to take school more seriously and improved my academic performance.

[소주제문 2] ④ Required attendance also contributes to enhancing the educational environment in class. [구체적 근거 1: 일반적 진술] ⑤ One reason is that professors can effectively teach a regular and stable group of students because their diligent class attendance helps them build knowledge and understanding step-by-step. ⑥ On the other hand, when attendance is optional, the overall flow of discussions and experiments is seriously hampered by the unequal abilities due to skipped classes or general lack of students. [구체적 근거 2: 예시] Studies show that mandatory attendance greatly improves the learning atmosphere in classes. They have found that in optional attendance courses, only a few sincere, hardworking students concentrate and enthusiastically participate in class discussions. The rest of the students who are chronically late or frequently skip class engage in distractive behaviors such as doodling, daydreaming, dozing off, or passing notes during class because they cannot understand the lessons. On the other hand, the studies further demonstrate that students take mandatory attendance classes much more seriously.

어휘 pivotal[pívətəl] 중추적인 self-disciplined 자제하는, 자기 훈련의 mandatory[mǽndətɔ̀:ri] 의무적인
disciplinary[dísəplənèri] 징계의 tardiness[tá:rdinis] 지각 course failure 낙제
probation[proubéiʃən] 근신 suspension[səspénʃən] 정학 supervision[sjù:pərvíʒən] 감독 stay up nights 며칠밤을 새다
academic performance 학업 성취 chronically[kránikəli] 고질적으로 distractive[distrǽktiv] 주의를 산만하게 하는
doodle[dú:dl] 낙서하다 daydream[déidrì:m] 공상하다 doze off 꾸벅꾸벅 졸다

3. 다음의 주장에 찬성하는가 반대하는가? 손보다 기계로 일하는 편이 더 낫다. 구체적인 이유와 예를 들어 자신의 견해를 뒷받침하시오.

[소주제문 1] ① First, machines allow you to save a great amount of time. [구체적 근거 1: 일반적 진술] This is because machines can operate at a constant speed over a long period of time. Conversely, because of their physical limitations, human beings need more time to complete the same tasks. Therefore, in today's busy world, people can optimize the use of their valuable time by using machines such as washing machines, hair dryers, and microwaves. [구체적 근거 2: 예시] ② The best example of a time-saving device is a dishwasher. ③ It improves the lives of many people dramatically. ④ People used to waste their valuable time standing in front of the sink, washing dishes, and drying them with towels for at least one hour every day. ⑤ With the advent of the dishwasher, however, people can spend the time as they choose, watching their favorite TV shows, having conversations with their families, or simply resting.

[소주제문 2] ⑥ Furthermore, machines work more accurately than humans can. [구체적 근거 1: 일반적 진술] Compared to humans who naturally make mistakes, machines do assignments very precisely and efficiently. They work at a regular rate, do not make careless mistakes, and do not get tired. [구체적 근거

2: 예시] ⑦ For example, teachers used to make many mistakes marking students' multiple choice exams. ⑧ Their attention would wander, and they would unintentionally make errors. ⑨ Fortunately, thanks to the introduction of a machine that does computerized marking, teachers no longer have to worry about the possibility of grading errors. ⑩ Consequently, students and teachers alike have confidence in the results. [마무리 문장] As this example shows, machines can more efficiently and accurately take care of tedious details.

어휘 conversely[kənvə́:rsli] 반대로, 거꾸로 optimize[áptəmàiz] 최대한 활용하다 dramatically[drəmǽtikəli] 극적으로 advent[ǽdvent] 출현 careless[kέərlis] 부주의한 multiple choice exams 객관식 (다지선다) 시험 wander[wándər] 방랑하다, 길을 잃다 unintentionally[ʌninténʃənəli] 무심코, 무의식적으로 tedious[tí:diəs] 지루한

4. 다음의 주장에 찬성하는가 반대하는가? 사람들이 입는 옷은 행동에 영향을 준다. 구체적인 이유와 예를 들어 자신의 견해를 뒷받침하시오.

[소주제문 1] To begin with, people act differently based on the formalness and style of their clothes. [구체적 근거 1: 일반적 진술] ① That is, the designs and colors of clothes represent certain characteristics, moods, and feelings. ② Therefore, people automatically act according to how professional or casual their clothes look. [구체적 근거 2: 예시] ③ To take a personal example, for important business meetings, ④ I wear a dark formal suit with a simple design that signifies the official and formal mood of the meetings. ⑤ As a result, I act in a professional manner and use sophisticated language. ⑥ On the other hand, when I wear a T-shirt and sweatpants for outdoor activities, I naturally act and feel very casual, relaxed, and athletic.

[소주제문 2] ⑦ In addition, people behave differently depending on the social roles that their clothes represent. [구체적 근거 1: 일반적 진술] ⑧ Accordingly, when people put on certain clothes such as school or work uniforms, they tend to act in line with the expected social responsibilities and duties that the clothes symbolize. [구체적 근거 2: 예시] ⑨ To illustrate, many high schools adopt school uniform policies because school administrators believe that uniforms improve student behavior and reduce after-school crimes. ⑩ Not surprisingly, studies reported that the number of cases of student misbehavior, such as smoking, fighting, stealing, and drinking, dramatically decreased after adopting mandatory uniforms. ⑪ The main reason was that students were highly conscious of the fact that people would recognize them as minors who should not be engaging in unwholesome or unlawful activities. [마무리 문장] As this example shows, clothes assign different social roles to people.

어휘 formalness[fɔ́:rməlnis] 격식 signify[fɔ́:rməlnis] 뜻하다, 나타내다 sophisticated[səfístəkèitid] 세련된, 정교한 in line with ~ ~에 따라 administrator[ədmínistrèitər] 관리자, 행정관 engage in ~ ~에 참여하다 be conscious of~ ~을 의식하다 unwholesome[ʌnhóulsəm] 불건전한 unlawful[ʌnlɔ́:fəl] 불법의

HACKERS Test p.246

1. 다음의 주장에 찬성하는가 반대하는가? 문학 작품을 읽는 것이 영화를 보는 것보다 더 재미있는 활동이다. 구체적인 이유와 예를 들어 자신의 견해를 뒷받침하시오.

> [소주제문 1] To start with, movies make plots more thrilling and exciting. [구체적 근거 1: 일반적 진술] This is largely because films effectively incorporate special sound effects and visually stimulating graphics. These dramatic impacts and sensations have a great capability to capture viewers' attention and move them emotionally. [구체적 근거 2: 예시] To demonstrate, I saw the movie The Lord of the Rings a few years ago. While watching the movie, I was totally engrossed in the story as I listened to the breathtaking symphony and looked at majestic valleys, horrendous monsters, and mysterious castles. On top of that, cruel war scenes made me sit on the edge of my seat all throughout the movie. However, when I tried to read the book the movie is based on, I soon felt bored by the never-ending, tedious descriptions and details.
>
> [소주제문 2] Another reason I prefer movies to books is that movies provide families and friends with quality time together. [구체적 근거 1: 일반적 진술] Movies serve as an excellent way to gather families and friends together in one place to relax, enjoy a common activity, and eat delicious snacks. [구체적 근거 2: 예시] For instance, many families come together to watch movies every Friday night after a busy week at school and work. Through this shared activity, family members have a rare opportunity to bond together. They can laugh out loud together at funny scenes and share their views on the films. On the other hand, reading is a solitary activity that causes people to retreat to secluded places so that they can be alone to concentrate on their books.

해석 **소주제문 1** 우선, 영화는 줄거리를 좀 더 긴장감 넘치고 흥미롭게 만든다. **구체적 근거 1: 일반적 진술** 이는 영화가 특수 음향 효과와 시각적으로 자극적인 영상을 효과적으로 혼합하기 때문이다. 이러한 극적인 효과와 감흥은 관객의 관심을 사로잡고 감동을 주는 데 커다란 역할을 한다. **구체적 근거 2: 예시** 예를 들면, 나는 영화 반지의 제왕을 몇 년 전에 관람했다. 그 영화를 보는 동안, 나는 숨막히는 교향곡을 듣고 장대한 계곡과 무시무시한 괴물들, 신비한 성을 보며 이야기에 완전히 빠져들었다. 게다가, 잔인한 전쟁 장면은 영화 내내 나로 하여금 긴장되어 제대로 앉아 있을 수 없게 했다. 그러나 영화의 원작을 읽어 보려고 했을 때는, 끝이 없는 장황한 설명과 세부 묘사에 금새 지루해졌다.
소주제문 2 내가 영화를 책보다 선호하는 또 다른 이유는 영화가 가족과 친구간에 함께 오붓한 시간을 보낼 수 있게 해주기 때문이다. **구체적 근거 1: 일반적 진술** 영화는 가족과 친구들이 휴식을 취하고, 같은 활동을 즐기고, 맛있는 간식을 먹을 수 있도록 한자리에 모이게 해주는 훌륭한 역할을 한다. **구체적 근거 2: 예시** 예를 들면, 학교와 직장으로 바쁜 한 주를 보내고 난 후에 많은 가족들이 금요일 밤마다 영화를 보기 위해 모인다. 이렇게 공유된 활동을 통해, 가족들은 유대감을 쌓을 수 있는 좀처럼 없는 기회를 갖게 된다. 그들은 우스운 장면을 보며 크게 웃을 수 있고 영화에 대한 의견을 나눌 수 있다. 반면에, 독서는 사람들로 하여금 책에 집중하기 위해 혼자 외딴 곳에 틀어 박히게 하는 고독한 활동이다.

어휘 plot[plɑt] 줄거리   incorporate[inkɔ́ːrpərèit] 혼합하다   stimulating[stímjulèitiŋ] 자극적인
provide A with B A에게 B를 제공하다   pastime[pǽstàim] 오락, 기분 전환   sensation[senséiʃən] 감흥
capture one's attention 관심을 끌다, 사로잡다   breathtaking[brétèikiŋ] 숨막히는   be engrossed in ~ ~에 몰두하다, 빠지다
majestic[mədʒéstik] 장대한   horrendous[hɔ(ː)réndəs] 무서운, 끔찍한   tedious[tíːdiəs] 지루한, 장황한
sit on the edge of my seat 긴장이 되어 안절부절 못하다   quality time 가장 재미있고 가치 있는 시간
bond together 유대를 형성하다   laugh out 웃음을 터뜨리다   solitary[sɑ́litèri] 혼자만의, 외로운

retreat[riːtríːt] 은둔하다, 틀어박히다   secluded[siklúːdid] 격리된, 외딴

2. 다음의 주장에 찬성하는가 반대하는가? 과거보다 오늘날 읽고 쓰는 능력이 더 중요하다. 구체적인 이유와 예를 들어 자신의 견해를 뒷받침하시오.

[소주제문 1] One, the ability to read is essential for obtaining information in this information era. [구체적 근거 1: 일반적 진술] Almost every significant library and institution in the world is connected to the Internet, which delivers written information at an extremely high speed. Consequently, people with excellent reading abilities can learn about practically any subject from sources located all around the globe at a single click of their mice. [구체적 근거 2: 예시] In my own life, I have several challenging term papers every semester at school. As a result, I often spend several sleepless nights researching on the Internet and reading endless pages of web documents, publications, theses, and government reports. In order to effectively sort through and successfully find necessary information, I have to use diverse reading techniques such as skimming and scanning. Without these reading skills, I would not be able to gain a competitive edge in this information age.

[소주제문 2] What's more, writing competence is extremely important for communication in this global age. [구체적 근거 1: 일반적 진술] An important reason is that the Internet allows people all over the world to write one another effectively and inexpensively through several revolutionary methods including electronic mail and online instant messenger. [구체적 근거 2: 예시] To take one example, when people start working at companies, they have to learn how to compose persuasive and effective letters. They must write innumerable business emails, such as inquiries, confirmations, claim letters, and even contracts. This is because today's world requires a high degree of writing competence, unlike the past when business communication was usually established through telephone calls. [마무리 문장] In this respect, the ability to write is essential in facilitating communication in this global age.

해석 **소주제문 1** 첫째로, 읽기 능력은 정보화 시대에 지식을 얻는 데 있어 필수적이다. **구체적 근거 1: 일반적 진술** 세계 대부분의 주요 도서관과 기관들이 빠른 속도로 문서화된 정보를 전달하는 인터넷으로 연결되어 있다. 그 결과, 우수한 읽기 능력을 지닌 사람들은 실제로 단 한번의 마우스 클릭만으로도 전 세계에 위치한 정보원으로부터, 어떤 주제에 대해서든 배울 수 있다. **구체적 근거 2: 예시** 내 경우, 나는 학교에서 매 학기마다 힘든 보고서를 몇 개씩 작성한다. 그 결과, 나는 인터넷을 검색하고 끝없는 웹 문서, 간행물, 논문과 정부 자료들을 읽으면서 자주 밤을 새우곤 한다. 필요한 정보를 효율적으로 분류하고 성공적으로 찾기 위해서, 나는 대충 읽고 훑어보는 것과 같은 다양한 읽기 기술을 활용해야 했다. 이러한 읽기 능력이 없었다면, 나는 현재의 정보화 시대에 경쟁적 우위를 차지하지 못했을 것이다.
소주제문 2 게다가, 작문 능력은 세계화 시대에 의사소통을 위해 매우 중요하다. **구체적 근거 1: 일반적 진술** 중요한 이유는 인터넷이 전 세계의 사람들이 이메일과 온라인 메신저를 포함한 몇 가지 혁신적인 방법을 통해 효율적으로, 그리고 적은 비용으로 서로에게 글을 쓸 수 있게 해주기 때문이다. **구체적 근거 2: 예시** 한 가지 예를 들자면, 사람들이 회사에 들어가 근무하기 시작할 때, 그들은 설득력 있고 효과적인 서신을 작성하는 방법을 배워야 한다. 그들은 요청서, 확인서, 청구서, 계약서와 같은 수많은 비즈니스 이메일을 써야 한다. 이는 비즈니스 의사소통이 주로 전화를 통해 이루어지던 과거와는 달리, 오늘날의 세상이 높은 수준의 작문 능력을 요구하기 때문이다. **마무리 문장** 이러한 점에서, 작문 능력은 세계화 시대에 의사소통을 원활히 하는 데 있어 필수적이다.

어휘 requisite[siklú:did] 필수의 **term paper** 학기말 보고서 consequently[kánsəkwèntli] 그 결과, 따라서
challenging[tʃǽlindʒiŋ] 힘든 thesis[θí:sis] 논문 sort through 분류하다
diverse[divə́:rs] 다양한 skimming[skímiŋ] 대충 읽기 scanning[skǽniŋ] 훑어보기
competitive edge 경쟁적 우위 competence[kámpitəns] 능력 inexpensive[ìnikspénsiv] 비용이 안드는
persuasive[pərswéisiv] 설득력 있는 innumerable[injú:mərəbl] 무수한 confirmation[injú:mərəbl] 확인서
facilitate[fəsílitèit] 용이하게 하다, 촉진하다

Ⅳ 에세이 쓰기 – 결론

HACKERS Practice p.252

1. 다음의 주장에 찬성하는가 반대하는가? 그룹 스터디를 하는 것보다는 혼자서 공부하는 것이 낫다. 구체적인 이유와 예를 들어
   자신의 견해를 뒷받침하시오.

> [요약/정리] ① To sum up, studying with a group of other students is a better choice than studying alone.
> ② Not only can students strengthen their sense of responsibility, but they can also broaden their
> points of view by sharing many different ideas. [맺음말] All in all, studying in a socially-interactive
> environment helps students in their overall development, not just academically.

어휘 strengthen[stréŋkθən] 강화하다 a sense of responsibility 책임감 broaden[brɔ́:dən] 넓히다
to sum up 요약하자면 all in all 대체로 overall[ðuvərɔ́:l] 전반적인
academically[æ̀kədémikəli] 학술적으로

2. 다음의 주장에 찬성하는가 반대하는가? 아이들은 중요한 결정을 혼자 내려서는 안 된다. 구체적인 이유와 예를 들어 자신의
   견해를 뒷받침하시오.

> [요약/정리] ① In conclusion, children should not be allowed to make important decisions alone because
> of their limited points of view and lack of experience. [맺음말] Thus, parents, who know their children's
> best interests, need to guide them in making wise decisions.

어휘 a point of view 관점 lack of~ ~의 부족

3. 다음의 주장에 찬성하는가 반대하는가? 공연을 현장에서 관람하는 것이 텔레비전으로 보는 것보다 더 즐겁다. 구체적인 이유
   와 예를 들어 자신의 견해를 뒷받침하시오.

[요약/정리] In short, I strongly disagree with the view that attending a live performance is better than watching it on TV. Watching a performance on TV allows you to relax in the comfort of your home and saves much time and money. [맺음말] ① As a result, you can sit back and enjoy your own personal show without leaving your home.

어휘 **performance**[pərfɔ́ːrməns] 공연, 경기   **enjoyable**[pərfɔ́ːrməns] 즐거운   **in the comfort of~** ~의 편안함 속에서
sit back (편하게) 앉다

4. 다음의 주장에 찬성하는가 반대하는가? 독학하는 것보다 선생님으로부터 배우는 것이 더 낫다. 구체적인 이유와 예를 들어 자신의 견해를 뒷받침하시오.

[요약/정리] As you can see, I wholeheartedly agree with the idea that it is better to have a teacher. While a few students may prefer learning alone, teachers undeniably give helpful and time-saving tips as well as motivation and encouragement. [맺음말] ① Consequently, students are able to make rapid progress as they are guided every step along the way by their teachers.

어휘 **by oneself** 혼자서   **time-saving** 시간이 절약되는   **guidance**[gáidəns] 안내, 지도
motivate[móutəvèit] 동기를 부여하다   **encourage**[inkɔ́ːridʒ] 용기를 북돋다   **wholeheartedly**[hóulhá́ːrtidli] 진심으로
undeniably[ʌ̀ndináiəbli] 명백하게, 틀림없이   **tip**[tip] 조언   **consequently**[kɑ́nsəkwèntli] 결과적으로
make progress 성장하다

HACKERS Test
p.256

1. 다음의 주장에 찬성하는가 반대하는가? 사람의 인생에서 가장 중요한 시기는 20대이다. 구체적인 이유와 예를 들어 자신의 견해를 뒷받침하시오.

[요약/정리] In sum, I firmly believe that young people should realize that their twenties are a very precious time. During this period, they must give serious thought to choosing their careers. They must also decide about a life partner at this time. [맺음말] In this regard, the twenties are an important age that should not be wasted.

해석 **요약/정리** 요약하자면, 나는 젊은 사람들이 그들의 20대가 매우 중요한 시기라는 것을 깨달아야 한다고 확신한다. 이 시기 동안, 그들은 자신의 직업을 선택하는 데 있어 심각하게 고려해야 한다. 또한 그들은 이 시기에 배우자에 대한 결정을 내려야 한다. **맺음말** 이러한 점에서 볼 때, 20대는 낭비해서는 안 될 중요한 시기이다.

어휘 **life partner** 배우자   **realize**[rí(ː)əlàiz] 깨닫다   **precious**[préʃəs] 소중한
give serious thought to ~ ~를 심각하게 고려하다   **in this regard** 이러한 관점에서

2. 다음의 주장에 찬성하는가 반대하는가? 학교는 학생들로 하여금 선생님을 평가하게 해야 한다. 구체적인 이유와 예를 들어 자신의 견해를 뒷받침하시오.

> [요약/정리] In brief, student evaluations of teacher quality are very beneficial. They encourage students to participate actively in class as well as provide teachers with constructive criticism to improve their teaching performance. [맺음말] After all, hearing how students rate their performances is a wonderful way for teachers to progress in their fields.

해석　**요약/정리** 요약하자면, 선생님의 자질에 대해 학생들이 평가하는 것은 매우 유익하다. 이는 선생님들에게 그들의 교습 능력을 향상시킬 수 있는 건설적인 비평을 해줄 뿐만 아니라, 학생들로 하여금 수업에 능동적으로 참여하도록 장려한다. **맺음말** 결국에는, 학생들이 선생님의 능력을 어떻게 평가하는가에 귀를 기울이는 것은 선생님들이 자신의 분야에서 발전하게 해주는 훌륭한 방법이다.

어휘　constructive[kənstrʌ́ktiv] 건설적인　progress[prɑ́grəs] 발전, 진보

POWER TEST
p.262

I. 사람들은 소유한 것에 절대로 만족하지 않고 항상 자신이 갖지 못한 것을 원한다는 진술에 찬성하는지 반대하는지를 밝히고 구체적인 이유와 예를 들어 대답을 뒷받침하시오.

Outline

- Agree 찬성
  1. Human nature is insatiable
     인간은 탐욕스러운 본성을 타고났다
     - impossible for people to be truly content with what they have
       자신이 가진 것에 진정으로 만족하기란 불가능하다
     - e.g. small children's greed is innate not learned
       예) 어린 아이들의 욕심스러운 행동: 선천적이지 학습된 것이 아님
  2. Commercials encourage people to crave more
     광고는 사람들로 하여금 더 갈망하기를 장려한다
     - companies try their best to sell new products
       기업들은 신제품들을 팔기 위해 최선을 다한다
     - e.g. brother bought another MP3 player because of commercial
       예) 남동생이 광고에 영향을 받아 또 다른 MP3 플레이어를 샀다

Model Essay

The idea that people are never satisfied with what they have is prevalent in society. From my perspective, I definitely agree with this idea, and therefore, with the saying, "The grass is always greener on the other side of the fence." In other words, people always want what they do not have. What lies behind my reasoning is that human nature is insatiable. Furthermore, in this materialistic society, commercials continually stimulate people's desires.

First, greed is innate to human beings. Therefore, it is impossible for people to be genuinely and truly content with what they have. In other words, it is an undeniable part of a human being's makeup to ceaselessly try to grasp for more and better things in life. This avaricious part of humans can be clearly proven by observing children at very early ages. Toddlers who cannot speak and who have not been taught about greed will display this trait when they play. For instance, small children will cry and fight over toys, food, and attention from adults. Psychologists agree that this behavior is not learned, but innate. In this respect, children's instinctual greediness is proof of humanity's natural acquisitiveness.

In addition, today's business commercials encourage people to crave more possessions. One big reason is that a countless number of companies in the market do their best to come out ahead in sales with their well-made ads. They continually expose vulnerable customers to appealing commercials that show products with new designs and functions. These advertisements imply that buying new products will make them happy and content. To illustrate, last year, my brother bought an MP3 player that he had always wanted. However, a few months later, he saw a commercial for the latest MP3 player with several extra functions, such as a larger memory capacity and a radio. This commercial made my brother desperately want the new MP3 player, so he eventually bought the new device, discarding his former MP3 player, even though it was in perfect condition. This demonstrates how advertisements stimulate people's desire to own the newest and best items on the market.

To conclude, I sincerely believe that people always want what they do not have. The main reason is that human beings are innately greedy. On top of that, materialism continually triggers humans' insatiable desires. Generally, as the old saying goes, "Greed has no limits."

해석　사람들이 결코 자신이 소유한 것에 대해 만족하지 못한다는 생각은 사회에 널리 퍼져 있다. 나는 이 의견에 전적으로 동의하며, 따라서, "남의 떡이 커 보인다"라는 속담에도 동의한다. 다시 말해, 사람들은 항상 자신이 갖지 못한 것을 원한다. 내가 그렇게 생각하는 이유는, 사람은 본성적으로 만족할 줄 모르기 때문이다. 게다가, 오늘날의 물질 만능사회에서 상업 광고들은 계속해서 사람들의 욕구를 자극한다. 첫째로, 탐욕은 인간이라면 타고나는 것이다. 따라서 사람들이 진실로 자신이 소유한 것에 대해 정말 만족하기란 불가능하다. 다시 말해, 인생에서 더 많은 것과 더 좋은 것을 끊임없이 움켜쥐려 하는 것은 인간 기질의 부정할 수 없는 한 부분이다. 이러한 인간의 탐욕스러운 부분은 아주 어린 나이의 아이들을 관찰함으로써 확실히 증명될 수 있다. 말도 못하고 탐욕에 대해 배운 적이 없는 유아들은 놀이할 때 이러한 특징을 보여준다. 예를 들면, 어린 아이들은 장난감, 음식, 어른들로부터의 관심 때문에 울고 싸운다. 심리학자들은 이러한 행동이 학습된 것이 아니라, 타고난 것이라는 데 동의한다. 이러한 점에서, 아이들의 본능적인 탐욕은 인간의 타고난 욕심을 증명한다.
　　게다가, 오늘날의 상업 광고는 사람들로 하여금 더 많이 소유할 것을 갈망하도록 조장한다. 하나의 큰 이유는 시장에 나와 있는 수많은 회사들이 잘 만들어진 광고를 이용해 판매고를 올리기 위해 최선을 다하기 때문이다. 그들은 유혹에 넘어가기 쉬운 소비자들에게 새로운 디자인과 기능을 지닌 상품을 선보이는 매력적인 광고를 계속 내보낸다. 이러한 광고들은 사람들에게 새 상품을 사는 것이 그들을 행복하고 만족하게 해줄 것이라고 암시한다. 예를 들면, 작년에 내 남동생은 항상 갖고 싶어하던 MP3 플레이어를 구입했다. 그러나, 몇 달이 지나고 그는 대용량의 메모리와 라디오 같은 추가적인 기능을 갖춘 최신의 MP3 플레이어 광고를 보았다. 그 광고는 동생으로 하여금

Possible Answers & Scripts

새 MP3 플레이어를 필사적으로 원하게 만들어서, 동생은 이전 MP3 플레이어를 처분하고 결국에는 새 것을 구입했다. 이전 것이 멀쩡했는데도 말이다. 이는 광고들이 최신의 그리고 최고의 물건을 소유하고자 하는 사람들의 욕망을 어떻게 자극하는지를 증명해준다. 결론적으로, 나는 사람들이 항상 자신에게 없는 것을 원한다고 진심으로 믿는다. 주된 이유는 인간이 본질적으로 탐욕스럽기 때문이다. 게다가, 물질 만능주의는 사람들의 만족할 줄 모르는 욕망을 계속해서 자극한다. 대체로, 옛 속담이 말하듯, "탐욕에는 끝이 없다."

어휘   prevalent[prévələnt] 널리 퍼진, 만연한
The grass is always greener on the other side of the fence (속담) 남의 떡이 커 보인다
insatiable[inséiʃiəbl] 만족할 줄 모르는   materialistic[mətìəriəlístik] 물질주의적인   commercial[kəmə́:rʃəl] 상업 광고
innate[inéit] 타고난, 천부의   genuinely[dʒénjuinli] 진정으로   avaricious[ӕvəríʃəs] 탐욕스러운
makeup[méikʌ̀p] 성질, 기질   ceaselessly[síːslisli] 끊임없이   grasp[grӕsp] 움켜잡다
toddler[tádlər] 유아   instinctual[instíŋktʃuəl] 본능적인   acquisitiveness[əkwízitivnis] 욕심
crave[kreiv] 열망하다, 갈망하다   come out ahead 앞서다   vulnerable[vʌ́lnərəbl] (유혹 등에) 넘어가기 쉬운
desperately[déspəritli] 필사적으로   discard[diskáːrd] 버리다, 처분하다   demonstrate[démənstrèit] 논증하다, 설명하다
sincerely[sinsíərli] 진정으로   on top of that 게다가   trigger[trigər] 유발하다

Ⅱ. 휴대폰이 사람들에게 더 많은 자유를 부여해 왔다는 진술에 찬성하는지 반대하는지를 밝히고 구체적인 이유와 예를 들어 대답을 뒷받침하시오.

Outline

> Disagree 반대
> 1. People with mobile phones have to keep in constant contact
> 휴대폰이 있으면 계속 연락을 취해야 한다
>   – People expect a person to always be available
>   사람들이 항상 연락을 받기를 기대한다
>   – e.g. my brother cannot fully relax because of calls
>   예) 우리 형은 전화 때문에 편히 쉬지 못한다
> 2. People are disturbed by noise in public spaces
> 사람들은 공공 장소에서 시끄럽게 한다
>   – cannot escape from phones ringing and people chatting
>   울려대는 전화와 사람들의 수다로부터 피할 수 없다
>   – e.g. nature, theaters, restaurants, even testing centers
>   예) 자연, 극장, 식당, 심지어 시험장

Model Essay

When mobile phones were first invented, they were touted as devices which would liberate people by providing them the opportunity to stay in contact at all times. However, rather than their stated goal of increasing freedom, cell phones have actually imprisoned people in a world where they must be in constant communication. In addition, everyone is disturbed by the noise of cell phones ringing and users' conversations in public spaces.

To begin with, instead of releasing people from their work and social obligations, cell phones have actually put people in constant touch. This is because people, ranging from friends to bosses, expect others to be available at all times. Therefore, people now have difficulty spending free time undisturbed. For example, my brother who works as a salesman could not separate himself from his phone because he did not know when his boss or clients would call. If he missed those calls, it might negatively affect his career, so he always had to be ready. Due to his constantly-ringing cell phone, it is difficult for him to have peaceful weekends, even when he's trying to relax at home.

What's more, people are frequently disturbed by the noise of cell phones in public spaces. Virtually everywhere one goes, one cannot escape hearing ringing phones and people chattering away on their phones. To illustrate, going to hike in secluded nature areas and get away from civilization often means listening to an endless stream of cell phone conversations of fellow hikers. As well, places such as theaters and restaurants are filled with ringing mobile phones. Even at testing centers, which require quiet atmospheres, people have had their concentration disrupted by ringing phones. In this way, cell phone users have interfered with the freedom to silence.

As shown above, rather than offering liberation, cell phones have actually restricted it by making people be in constant contact and disturbing others in public spaces. A new movement to turn off one's cell phone is underway. This just may be the way to increase our freedom.

해석   휴대폰이 처음 발명되었을 당시, 사람들을 사무실로부터 해방시켜 주고 사람들이 원할 때마다 연락을 취할 수 있는 기회를 주는 장비로 각광받았다. 하지만, 보다 많은 자유를 가져다 준다는 휴대폰의 (애초에) 정해진 목표와는 달리, 휴대폰은 사실상 끊임없이 연락해야 하는 세상에 사람들을 가두었다. 게다가, 모든 이들은 휴대폰 벨소리의 소음과 공공장소에서의 사용자들의 대화로 마음이 산란해진다.
     우선, 휴대폰은 사람들을 사무실에서 해방시키기 보다는 사실상 속박하는 역할을 해왔다. 이는, 친구들에서부터 상사에 이르는 사람들이 언제든지 연락이 가능하기를 상대방에게 바라기 때문이다. 따라서, 이제 사람들은 자유 시간을 방해받지 않고 보내기가 힘들다. 예를 들면, 영업사원으로 일하는 우리 형은 언제 그의 상사나 고객이 전화를 할지 알 수 없기 때문에 휴대폰과 떨어져 있을 수가 없다. 만약 그 전화들을 받지 못하면 그의 업무에 부정적인 영향을 미칠지도 모르기 때문에 그는 계속 대기해야만 한다. 끊임없이 울려대는 휴대폰 벨소리 때문에 형은 집에서 편히 쉬고 싶을 때에도 평화로운 주말을 보내기가 힘들다.
     그뿐 아니라, 사람들은 자주 공공장소에서 휴대폰의 소음으로 인해 방해받는다. 사실상 어느 곳을 가더라도, 휴대폰 벨소리와 휴대폰으로 잡담하고 있는 사람들을 피할 수 없다. 예를 들면, 한적한 자연 환경으로 하이킹을 가거나 도시에서 떠나더라도, 하이킹을 온 다른 사람들이 끊임없이 통화하는 소리를 듣게 되는 경우가 많다. 게다가, 극장이나 식당 같은 장소들도 울려대는 휴대폰 소리로 가득 차 있다. 심지어 조용해야 할 시험장에서조차, 사람들은 휴대폰 벨소리 때문에 집중이 흐트러지게 된다. 이런 식으로, 휴대폰 이용자들은 소음으로부터의 자유를 침해해 왔다.
     앞서 말한 바와 같이, 휴대폰은 더 많은 자유를 부여하기보다는 끊임없이 연락을 취하게 하고 공공장소에서 다른 이들을 방해함으로써 사실상 사람들의 자유를 침해한다. 휴대폰을 꺼두는 새로운 움직임이 일고 있다. 이는 우리의 자유를 증강시키는 방법이 되어 줄 것이다.

어휘   **be touted as~** ~라고 크게 선전되다   **liberate**[líbərèit] 자유롭게 만들다   **stay in contact** 연락을 유지하다
stated[stéitid] 공식적인, 명백히 규정된   **imprison**[imprízən] 가두다   **obligation**[àbləgéiʃən] 의무, 책임
undisturbed[ʌ̀ndistə́ːrbd] 방해 받지 않은   **virtually**[vɔ́ːrtʃuəli] 사실상, 실질적으로는, 거의   **secluded**[siklúːdid] 한적한, 외딴
disrupt[dìsrʌ́pt] 혼란시키다   **interfere with ~** ~을 방해하다   **underway**[ʌ̀ndərwéi] 진행 중인

Actual Test Ⅰ

p.268

1. 방금 들은 강의의 논점들이 지문의 논점에 어떻게 의구심을 제기하는지를 설명하며, 전체 강의 내용을 요약하시오.

Note-taking 🎧 *Track 11*

읽기 노트

- US income tax 미국의 소득세
  1. Essential to cover cost of Civil War 남북 전쟁 비용 충당 위해 필수
     - needed additional revenue 부가적 수익 필요
     - war → long, expensive 전쟁 → 장기전, 큰 비용 소요
  2. Progressive tax, fair 누진세, 공정함
     - charged based on ability 능력에 따라 부과
     - no burden 2 poor ppl 가난한 사람에게는 부담 X
  3. Consolidate control of fed. gov't 연방 정부 통제권 강화
     - important: fed. under attack 중요: 연방 정부 공격 받은 상황
     - centralized syst. → power 2 gov't 중앙 집권 체제 → 권한을 정부에 모음

듣기 노트

- Income tax repealed 소득세 폐지
  1. Not necessary 불필요
     - only 3% covered war 단 3%만 전쟁 비용 충당
     - rest from high tariffs & luxury tax 나머지는 높은 관세와 특별 소비세로 충당
  2. Discrim. agnst rich 부유층에게 차별적
     - punish for success 성공에 대해 징벌
     - un-American, inconsist. w/ democracy 비미국적, 민주주의와 불일치
  3. Gave fed. gov't too much power 연방 정부에게 지나친 권력 양도
     - income assess: invasive, insulting 소득 평가: 침해적, 모욕적
     - strong-arm tactics: oppressive, inappropri. 압제적 책략: 억제적, 부적절

Summary

The lecturer explores why the federal income tax was repealed by examining negative aspects of the system. This information contradicts the reading passage's promotion of the tax.

First, the federal income tax was never really necessary. The tax was officially mandated during the Civil War as an attempt to raise money for the war effort, as the reading passage mentions. However, the lecturer points out that only a tiny percentage of the income tax actually covered war expenses. Thus, the lecturer refutes the reading passage's argument of the necessity of this tax.

Second, the tax was discriminatory against the rich, who felt punished for their success because they had had to pay a higher percentage of their income than poorer people. Thus, they found the tax inconsistent with American values of democracy, and felt that they unfairly shouldered the cost of the Civil War. This argument opposes the reading passage's argument that the federal income tax was progressive and fair.

Last, many people rejected the overwhelming power the tax gave the federal government in probing into people's private lives. In particular, some rebelled at the federal government's strong-arm tactics of putting people into jail if they didn't pay their taxes. They found the income tax inappropriate and felt that the government invaded their lives. With these arguments, the lecturer expresses a negative opinion on the reading passage's assertion that the tax was needed to consolidate government power by stressing that it angered many people.

해석   교수는 연방 소득세가 왜 폐지되었는가를 소득세 체계의 부정적 측면을 검토함으로써 알아본다. 이러한 정보는 소득세의 필요를 주장하는 지문의 입장을 반박하는 것이다.

첫째로, 연방 소득세는 꼭 필요한 것이 아니었다. 이 세금은 지문에서 언급한 대로 전쟁 기금을 모으려는 노력의 일환으로 남북 전쟁 기간 동안 공식적으로 지정된 것이다. 하지만, 교수는 소득세의 극히 일부만이 전쟁 비용으로 쓰였다고 지적한다. 따라서, 교수는 이 세금의 필요성에 대한 지문의 주장에 반박한다.

둘째로, 세금은 부자들에게는 차별적이었고, 그들은 이것이 성공에 대해 처벌을 받는 것이라고 느꼈다. 왜냐하면 그들은 가난한 사람들보다 소득의 더 높은 비율을 세금으로 내야 했기 때문이다. 그래서, 그들은 이 세금이 미국의 민주주의 가치와는 맞지 않는다고 생각했고, 그들이 남북 전쟁의 비용을 불공평하게 짊어진다고 느꼈다. 이러한 주장은 연방 소득세가 누진세로서 공평했다는 글의 주장에 반대하는 것이다.

마지막으로, 많은 사람들은 연방 정부로 하여금 사람들의 사생활을 세세히 캘 수 있도록 한 세금의 압도적인 권력을 거부했다. 특히, 몇몇 사람들은 세금을 내지 않으면 사람들을 감옥에 가두는 연방 정부의 압제적 책략에 반발했다. 그들은 소득세가 불합리하다는 것을 알았고 정부가 그들의 생활을 침해했다고 느꼈다. 이러한 주장을 통해, 세금이 많은 이들을 분노하게 했다는 점을 강조함으로써 교수는 세금이 정부의 권력을 강화하기 위해 필요했다는 지문의 주장에 부정적 의견을 제시한다.

어휘   **federal income tax** 연방 소득세   **repeal**[ripí:l] 폐지, 취소하다   **mandate**[mǽndeit] 명령하다, (법을) 제정하다
war expense 전쟁 비용   **discriminatory**[diskrímənətɔ̀:ri] 차별적인, 불공평한   **inconsistent**[ìnkənsístənt] 일치하지 않는
shoulder[ʃóuldər] (부담 등을) 짊어지다   **progressive**[prəgrésiv] 누진적인   **overwhelming**[òuvərʰwélmiŋ] 압도적인
probe[proub] 조사하다   **rebel**[rébəl] 반발하다   **strong-arm**[strɔ́(:)ŋà:rm] 폭력을 쓰는
tactic[tǽktik] 전략   **invade**[invéid] 침해하다, 침범하다   **assertion**[əsə́:rʃən] 주장, 단언
consolidate[kənsálidèit] 강화하다, 굳건히 하다

스크립트 및 해석

Reading

미국의 개인 소득세는 미국 남북 전쟁 당시 1862년에 북부 지역의 주들에 의하여 처음으로 법률로 제정되었다. 그것은 전쟁의 높은 비용을 충당할 기금을 모으는데 필수적인 것이었다. 남북 전쟁이 예상보다 오래 지속되었고 예상했던 것보다 더 많은 비용이 소요되었기 때문에, 북부연방군을 지원하기 위해서는 일반 세금과 수입관세에 더하여 추가적인 세입이 절실히 필요했다. 이 과세법은 성공적이었고, 연방정부에게 수백만 달러를 모아 주었다.

미국 역사상 첫 누진세인 이 관세법의 또 다른 면은, 그것의 공평성이었다. 각 개인들은 자신의 지불 능력에 따라 세금을 부과받았다. 따라서, 전 인구의 대다수였던, 연소득이 600달러 미만인 사람들은 개인 소득세를 공제받게 되었다. 소득이 600달러에서 5,000달러이었던 사람들은 수입 중 5%를 내야 하는 반면 일년 수입이 10,000달러가 넘는 상류층은, 그들의 소득 중 10%를 내도록 하였다. 이 누진세

율 제도는, 옷, 식량 등의 생활 필수품에 대한 소비세로 인해 과잉 관세 적용을 받고 있던 빈곤한 이들의 세금 부담을 줄여주었다. 게다가 소득세는 연방 정부의 수중에 권력을 통합하기 위하여 필요하였다. 이것은 특히 연방 권위가 남부연합군의 공격을 받았던 이 시기에 중요했다. 처음으로, 국세청이 "집행군"을 전국의 방방곡곳에 배치함으로써 자신들의 영향력을 인식시켰다. 이 중앙 집권적 체제는 연방 정부가 법을 집행할 수 있는 권한을 부여했다.

> individual income tax 개인 소득세   revenue[révənjù:] 세입, 수익   desperately[déspəritli] 절실히
> federal government 미국 연방 정부   consolidate[kənsálidèit] 강화하다   be exempt from~ ~으로부터 공제받다
> progressive tax 누진세   upper end 상단   consumption tax 소비세   under attack by~ ~의 비난/공격을 받는
> centralized[séntrəlàizd] 중앙화된   in every corner of~ ~의 방방곡곳에   empower[impáuər] 권한을 부여하다

Listening

So as you know, the federal income tax, written into law during the Civil War, was actually repealed in 1972. If it was so effective, then why didn't it last? Well, first off... those working to abolish the tax said that it was never really necessary. I should mention that the income tax actually covered less than 3% of war expenses. The rest were paid for by higher tariffs and luxury taxes on things like alcohol and cigarettes.

Another reason it was taken off the books is that many of the upper class said it was discriminatory or I should note, against them. They protested that they shouldn't have to pay at a higher rate, because that was punishing them for their success. According to these pillars of society, it was just plain "un-American" and inconsistent with democracy that the cost of the nation's war was more or less squarely on their shoulders.

And the most persuasive argument against the income tax was the overwhelming power it gave the federal government to probe into the private financial lives of American citizens. At the time, many people objected to the invasive procedures necessary to properly assess income. In fact, people were downright insulted that their word wasn't enough and that they had to provide credible information regarding their earnings. They also said that the strong-arm tactics to collect the tax, such as jail-time, were oppressive, not to mention entirely inappropriate for use by the national government.

남북 전쟁 당시 법률 조항에 추가된 연방 소득세는, 사실 1972년에 철회되었죠. 만일 그것이 정말 효과적이었다면, 왜 지속되지 않았을까요? 첫째로, 그 관세를 폐지하려고 활동한 이들은 그 관세가 애초부터 불필요했다고 주장합니다. 소득세는 전쟁 비용의 3% 미만밖에 충당하지 못했거든요. 나머지는 모두 술과 담배와 같은 물품의 높은 관세와 특별 소비세로 충당되었습니다.

법률 조항에서 소득세가 삭제된 또 다른 이유는, 대다수의 상류층이 그 관세법이 차별적이라고 주장했기 때문입니다. 그러니까, 그들에게 불리하게 차별적이라는 것이죠. 그들은 자신들이 더 높은 관세율을 부담해야 할 이유는 없다고 주장했습니다. 왜냐하면 그렇게 하는 것은 자신들의 성공에 대해 벌을 가하는 것이나 마찬가지니까요. 사회의 주축을 이루고 있던 이 계층의 사람들에 의하면, 그들이 국가의 전쟁 비용을 직접적으로 부담한다는 것은 명백히 "비미국적인" 행위이며, 민주주의와 일치하지 않는다는 것입니다.

그리고 개인 소득세에 반대하는 가장 설득력 있는 주장은 개인 소득세가 연방 정부에게 미국 시민들의 사적인 재정 생활을 철저히 수사할 수 있도록 하는 압도적인 권력을 주었다는 것입니다. 그 당시에, 많은 이들은 소득을 제대로 산정하기 위해 필요한 사생활 침해적인 절차들에 반대했습니다. 실제로 사람들은 자신들의 설명으로는 부족하고, 자신들의 소득에 관해 신빙성 있는 정보를 제공해야 한다는 사실에 너무나 모욕을 느꼈죠. 또 그들은 세금을 걷기 위해 수감을 하는 등의 우격다짐 전술은 국민들을 억누르는 것이라고 했습니다. 그러한 방법이 전적으로 정부가 사용해서는 안 될 방법이라는 것은 물론이고 말이죠.

> abolish[əbàliʃ] 폐지하다   tariff[tǽrif] 관세   luxury tax 특별 소비세   discriminatory[diskrímənətɔ̀:ri] 차별적인
> pillar[pílər] 기둥, 중심인물   inconsistent with ~ ~와 일치하지 않는   more or less 다시 말해서, 다소
> squarely[skwɛ́ərli] 정면으로   persuasive[pərswéisiv] 설득력 있는   object[əbdʒékt] 반대하다
> invasive[invéisiv] 침해하는   assess[əsés] 평가하다, 산정하다   downright[dáunràit] 완전히, 철저히
> strong-arm tactics 우격다짐 전술   jail-time 옥살이   oppressive[əprésiv] 압제적인
> inappropriate[ìnəpróupriit] 부적절한

2. 빨리 내린 결정은 항상 옳지 않다는 진술에 찬성하는지 반대하는지를 밝히고 구체적인 이유와 예를 들어 대답을 뒷받침한다.

Outline

- Disagree 반대
  1. Swift decisions help people seize valuable opportunities in business.
     빠른 결정은 사람들로 하여금 사업에 있어서 소중한 기회를 잡을 수 있게 도와준다
     - capitalize on opportunities, such as buying stocks and bidding in auctions
       주식을 사거나 경매에 입찰하는 것과 같은 기회를 이용한다
     - e.g. uncle who bought land through an auction
       예) 경매를 통해 땅을 구매한 삼촌
  2. Crucial in saving people's lives during medical emergencies
     의료상 응급 상황시에 사람들의 생명을 구하는 데 중요하다
     - mean the difference between life and death
       생사를 가르는 차이가 될 수 있다.
     - e.g. when found a person having a heart attack
       예) 심장 마비가 온 사람을 발견했을 때

Model Essay

"Look before you leap" is an aphorism that contains a lot of wisdom. However, there are some circumstances where one must make split-second decisions. These quick decisions, when based on intuition and knowledge gained from previous experiences, can bring about positive results; swift decisions allow people to seize golden opportunities, especially in business. What's more, they are essential in saving lives during medical emergencies.

First of all, swift decisions help people seize valuable opportunities in business. This is largely because our brutally competitive society, with its countless adversaries and rivals, dictates that people make quick decisions in order to capitalize on opportunities. These include selling or buying stocks and bidding in auctions. In my life, my uncle who runs his own business had a great chance to buy a big plot of land through an auction last year. However, he was given only three minutes and ten seconds to make up his mind and bid. Therefore, on the spur of the moment, he made a swift decision to take the chance because he did not want to let the golden opportunity slip by. If it were not for his quick decision, my uncle would not have been able to purchase the property of his dreams at an unbelievably low price. Being able to make up one's mind quickly is clearly advantageous.

In addition, quick decisions are crucial in saving people's lives during medical emergencies. One critical reason for this is that even a fraction of a second can mean the difference between life and death during emergencies such as broken bones, strokes, and heart attacks. Therefore, only a person who can make lightning-fast decisions will be able to save another person's life during life-threatening situations. For instance, passersby must immediately call 911 when they see people having heart attacks. While ambulances are on their way, on-lookers often are called upon to perform CPR. Taking swift, bold action can help heart attack victims regain consciousness and spare them any serious long-term complications.

In conclusion, with absolute conviction, I am against the statement that instant decisions are always wrong. The reason is that immediate decisions can allow a person to seize the chance of a lifetime and can save a person's life during a medical emergency. All in all, I wholeheartedly agree with the saying, "Time and tide wait for no man." In other words, one must be ready to act with lightning speed when the time comes.

해석 "돌다리도 두들겨 보고 건너라"는 많은 지혜가 담긴 격언이다. 하지만 어떤 경우에는 순간에 결정을 내려야 하는 경우도 있다. 직감과 이전의 경험을 통해 얻은 지식에 기반해 내리는 이러한 빠른 결정들은 긍정적인 결과를 가져올 수 있다. 빠른 결정들은 사람들로 하여금 절호의 기회를 포착하도록 한다. 이것은 특히 사업을 할 때 그러하다. 게다가 의료 응급 상황에서 생명을 구하는 것은 필수적이다.

우선, 빠른 결정들은 사람들로 하여금 사업에 있어서 귀중한 기회를 잡도록 도와준다. 그 이유는 수 많은 적과 경쟁자들이 있는 냉혹한 경쟁 사회에서 기회를 잘 이용하기 위해서는 빠른 결정을 내려야 하기 때문이다. 이러한 기회에는 주식을 매각 혹은 매입하거나 경매에서 입찰하는 것이 있다. 내 경험을 얘기하면, 사업을 하셨던 내 삼촌은 작년에 경매를 통해 많은 땅을 사들일 기회가 있었다. 하지만 그에게는 마음을 정하고 입찰하는데 오로지 3분 10초가 주어졌다. 그는 황금의 기회를 놓치기 싫었기 때문에 그 순간, 기회를 잡기로 빠른 결정을 내렸다. 만일 그의 빠른 결정이 아니더라면 내 삼촌은 믿기 힘들 정도로 낮은 가격에 그가 꿈꿔 오던 부동산을 소유하지 못했을 것이다. 마음을 빨리 결정할 수 있는 능력은 분명히 유리한 것이다.

게다가 빠른 결정은 의료 응급시에 사람들의 생명을 구하는 데 중요하다. 그 중요한 이유는 골절, 뇌졸중, 혹은 심장 마비와 같은 응급 상황시 순식간에 생사가 엇갈릴 수 있기 때문이다. 따라서, 빠른 결정을 내릴 수 있는 사람만이 생명을 위협하는 상황에서 다른 사람의 생명을 구해줄 수 있다. 예를 들어 심장 마비를 겪고 있는 사람을 본 행인들은 911에 바로 전화해야 한다. 앰뷸런스가 오는 동안 주위에서 보고 있던 사람들은 종종 인공호흡을 해달라는 부탁을 받는다. 신속하고 과감하게 조치를 취하는 것은 심장 마비 희생자가 의식을 회복하도록 도우며 심각한 장기적 합병증을 예방해 준다.

결론적으로, 어떠한 의심의 여지도 없이 나는 순식간의 결정이 항상 옳지 않다는 진술에 반대한다. 그 이유는 즉시 내리는 결정은 일생일대의 기회를 잡도록 해주며 의료 응급시에 한 사람의 인생을 구할 수 있기 때문이다. 종합하여 볼 때, 나는 진심으로 "세월은 사람을 기다려주지 않는다"는 속담에 동의한다. 달리 말해, 때가 왔을 때 재빨리 행동하도록 준비가 되어 있어야 한다는 것이다.

어휘 Look before you leap (속담) 돌다리도 두들겨 보고 건너라   aphorism[ǽfərìzəm] 격언
split-second 일순간의, 순간적인   intuition[ìntjuːíʃən] 직감   swift[swift] 빠른, 신속한
seize[siːz] 잡다, 포착하다   brutally[brúːtəli] 잔인하게   countless[káuntlis] 셀 수 없는, 무수한
adversaries[ǽdvərsèri] 적, 반대자   dictate[díkteit] 지시하다   capitalize on ~ ~을 이용하다
stock[stɑk] 주식   bid[bid] 입찰하다   run one's own business 자기 사업을 경영하다
plot[plɑt] 작은 땅   on the spur of the moment 순간적인 충동으로   slip by (기회 등)사라지다, 없어지다
make up one's mind 결심하다, 결단을 내리다   advantageous[ǽdvəntéidʒəs] 유리한, 이로운
fraction of a second 순식간에   stroke[strouk] 뇌졸중   heart attack 심장 마비
on-looker 구경꾼   passerby[pǽsərbái] 통행인, 지나가는 사람   consciousness[kánʃəsnis] 의식
spare[spɛər] ~없이 지내다   complication[kàmpləkéiʃən] 합병증
Time and tide wait for no man (속담) 세월은 사람을 기다려주지 않는다

Actual Test Ⅱ

p.272

1. 방금 들은 강의의 논점들이 지문의 논점에 어떻게 의구심을 제기하는지를 설명하며, 전체 강의 내용을 요약하시오.

Note-taking 🎧 *Track 12*

읽기 노트

- Rural commu. short of doctors 시골 지역 의사 부족
  - no new graduates want 2 work 새로운 졸업생들 일하기 원하지 않음
    1. Low pay 적은 급료
       - debt in school → want ↑ paying job in city 학교 다니며 진 빚 → 도시의 보수 높은 직업 원함
    2. Lack access 2 experi. doc. 숙련된 의사들과 접촉 기회 부족
       - young doc.: no practical training 젊은 의사: 실무 경험 X
       - city: experienced doc. 도시: 노련한 의사
    3. Not appealing 매력적이지 X
       - city lifestyle: culture, entertain. 도시 생활: 문화, 오락
       - rural: slow, boring 시골: 느림, 지루함

듣기 노트

- Reasons to lure young docs 젊은 의사 유인 가능한 이유
  1. Gov't debt forgiveness 정부의 빚 면제
     - 4 doc. promise to work in rural area 시골 지역에서 근무 약속하는 의사에게
     - similar policy 4 teacher worked 교사들 대상으로 시행한 유사 정책의 성공
     - successful - waiting list 성공적 - 대기자 명단
  2. Can contact experi. doc. 숙련된 의사와 접촉 가능
     - phone, email, online chat 전화, 이메일, 온라인 채팅
  3. Hectic, intense lifestyle 바쁘고 긴장된 생활
     - city add stress 도시 스트레스 더함
     - quiet rural → offset stress, counterbalance 조용한 시골 → 스트레스 상쇄, 균형
     - appeals to grads. who grew up in countryside 시골서 성장한 졸업생들에게 매력적

Summary

The lecturer offers evidence that young doctors are attracted to working in the countryside. This contradicts the reading passage's view that a shortage of doctors in those regions is imminent because physicians do not want to work there.

First of all, the government has a policy of debt forgiveness for doctors who promise to work in the countryside for a certain period of time. So far, the program is so successful that a waiting list for these positions now exists. This shows that a doctor shortage in rural areas is unlikely because of financial considerations, contrary to what the reading passage asserts.

Furthermore, young physicians in the countryside have access to experienced urban doctors when they have questions or concerns. Modern technologies such as the telephone and email allow communication with more experienced doctors. Thus, the lecturer contradicts the reading passage's claims that young doctors without enough practical training do not want to work in rural areas because of lack of access to older physicians.

Finally, many doctors are attracted to the countryside because their lifestyles are so hectic and intense. They do not want to live in an urban environment that adds to their stress. As a result, many young physicians prefer to work in quiet rural areas that give them peace of mind and balance. In addition, those who grew up in the countryside usually choose to work in these familiar and quiet environments. Therefore, the lecturer abates the reading passage's fears that young doctors will find working in rural areas slow-paced, boring, and unappealing.

해석　교수는 젊은 의사들이 시골에서 근무하는 것에 끌린다는 증거를 제시한다. 이것은 의사들이 시골에서 일하기를 원치 않으므로 이러한 지역에서의 의사 부족 현상이 곧 대두할 것이라는 지문의 견해를 반박하는 것이다.

우선, 정부는 일정 기간 동안 시골에서 일하기로 하는 의사들에게 빚을 탕감해 주는 정책을 가지고 있다. 지금까지, 이런 프로그램은 아주 성공적이어서 현재 시골에서 일할 자리를 기다리는 대기 명단이 존재하고 있을 정도이다. 이것은 지문에서 주장하는 것과는 반대로, 재정적인 보답 때문에 시골 지역의 의사 부족 현상이 나타나지는 않을 것을 보여준다.

게다가, 시골 지역의 젊은 의사들은 질문이나 걱정이 있을 때 숙련된 도시의 의사들과 접촉할 수 있다. 전화나 이메일과 같은 현대 과학 기술은 더 숙련된 의사들과의 의사소통할 수 있게 해준다. 그러므로, 교수는 실제적인 훈련을 충분히 거치지 못한 젊은 의사들이 숙련된 의사들과 접촉할 수 있는 기회의 부족 때문에 시골 지역에서 일하기를 원하지 않는다는 지문의 주장을 반박한다.

마지막으로, 많은 의사들은 그들의 생활 방식이 너무 바쁘고 긴장돼 있어 시골 지역에 끌린다. 그들은 스트레스를 가중시키는 도시 환경에서 살고 싶어하지 않는다. 그 결과, 많은 젊은 의사들이 그들의 마음의 평안과 균형을 가져다 주는 조용한 시골 지역에서 일하기를 선호한다. 게다가, 시골에서 성장한 이들은 대개 이러한 친숙하고 조용한 환경에서 일하기를 선택한다. 그러므로, 교수는 젊은 의사들이 시골 지역에서 일하는 것을 느리고, 지루하고, 매력이 없다고 느낀다는 지문의 우려를 불식시킨다.

어휘　**shortage**[ʃɔ́ːrtidʒ] 부족　**imminent**[ímənənt] 임박한　**physician**[fizíʃən] 의사
debt forgiveness 채무 탕감　**waiting list** 대기 명단　**experienced**[ikspí(:)əriənst] 숙련된, 노련한
practical[prǽktikəl] 실용적인　**abate**[əbéit] 줄이다, 약하게 하다

스크립트 및 해석

Reading

미국의 농촌들은 의사 부족이라는 임박한 사태에 위협받고 있다. 현재 이러한 지역의 의사들 대부분은 중장년층이다. 그들이 은퇴할 때면, 이들을 대체할 만한 젊은 의사들이 부족하게 될 것이다. 유감스럽게도, 점점 다가오는 이 위기는 방지할 수 없을 것으로 보인다. 갓 졸업한 의대생들은 여러 가지 이유로 교외에서 일하기를 원하지 않는다.

젊은 의사들이 교외에서 일하는 것을 방해하는 가장 큰 요인 중 하나는 낮은 급료이다. 많은 의대 졸업생들은 학교를 다니면서 큰 부채를 지게 된다. 그리하여, 그들은 자신들의 부채에서 더 빨리 벗어나도록 도와주는 봉급이 높은 직업에 끌리게 된다. 도시의 근무지는 그들이 추구하는 바로 이러한 높은 보수를 제공한다. 그 결과, 대다수의 의사들은 낮은 봉급의 교외의 일자리를 회피하려 한다.

게다가, 교외에서 근무하는 많은 젊은 의사들은 숙련된 의사들과 접촉할 기회가 적다. 졸업한지 얼마 되지 않은 젊은 의사들은, 어려운 상황 속에서의 진단 능력에 자신을 가질 만큼 충분한 실습을 받지 않았다. 그러므로, 그들은 노련한 의사들 곁에 있으면서 그들로부터 배

우는 것을 선호한다. 도시에는 스승이자 안내자로서 역할을 해줄 수 있는 숙련된 의사들을 원하는 대로 고를 수 있을 정도로 많이 있다. 이러한 비공식적인 견습 기간은 젊은 의사들에게 매우 값진 것이며, 그들이 구해 낼 환자들에게도 매우 귀중한 것이다.

더욱이, 교외의 삶은 많은 젊은 의사들에게 전혀 매력적이지 않다. 그들 대부분은 문화, 오락 편의시설을 갖춘 대도시의 생활 방식을 즐기고 싶어한다. 교외 지역은 막 의대를 졸업한 의사들에게 종종 너무 느릿느릿하고 따분하게 느껴진다. 그 대신에, 그들은 인생에서 역동적인 시간을 보낼 수 있는 자극적이고 흥미로운 분위기를 추구한다.

impending[impéndiŋ] 임박한   physician[fizíʃən] 의사   elderly[éldərli] 나이가 지긋한
loom[lu:m] 어렴풋이 보이다   avert[əvə́:rt] 피하다   medical school 의대
accrue[əkrú:] 모으다   deterrent[ditə́:rənt] 방해물   remuneration[rimjù:nəréiʃən] 보수
practical training 실습   diagnose[dáiəgnòus] 진단하다   a wealth of 수많은
serve as~ ~으로 섬기다   mentor[méntɔ:r] 좋은 조언자   apprenticeship[əpréntisʃip] 견습생 기간
invariably[invέ(:)əriəbli] 늘, 반드시   appealing[əpí:liŋ] 마음을 끄는, 매력적인   amenity[əménəti] 오락, 편의시설
rural area 교외, 농촌   slow-paced 느릿느릿한   stimulating[stímjulèitiŋ] 활기를 띄게 하는
dynamic[dainǽmik] 활동적인

Listening

Although many people have discussed the possibility of a, um, doctor shortage in rural areas, this doesn't look likely. There are still lots of attractive reasons to lure young physicians to work in the countryside. First, the government is, you know, creating a policy of debt forgiveness for doctors who promise to work in outlying areas for a certain period of time. A similar policy has been tried before... to attract teachers to the inner city, and it worked, so the government has adopted a similar measure for recent medical school graduates to work in rural parts of the US. So far it looks successful... there's actually a waiting list for these positions!

And let's see... it's not like doctors in rural areas are completely cut off from the rest of the world! Young practitioners in the countryside can contact experienced urban doctors whenever they have questions or concerns about tricky diagnoses... it's as simple as making a phone call, sending out an email, or even logging onto online chat to obtain feedback! Just because you can't solicit advice face-to-face doesn't mean there's an isolation problem... doctors have more communication resources than ever before!

What's more, a physician's lifestyle is often hectic and intense. A city may just add stress to a doctor's frazzled nerves, after she's spent all day in a bustling hospital or office. Naturally, many young doctors gravitate to a quiet rural area to offset their stressful jobs. And doctors realize that for a balanced life and peace of mind, it's preferable to work in a slow-paced rural area to counterbalance their fast-paced working environment. On top of that, many med school graduates who grew up in the countryside often choose to work in a similarly quiet environment.

비록 많은 사람들이 교외의 의사 부족 현상에 대해 논의해 왔지만, 이런 상황은 일어날 것 같지 않아 보입니다. 젊은 의사들이 시골에서 일하도록 유인할 수 있는 매력적인 이유는 아직 많이 있습니다. 첫째로 정부는, 일정 기간이상 교외 지역에서 일하기를 약속하는 의사들에게 빚을 탕감해 주는 정책을 만들고 있습니다. 교사들을 도심으로 끌어들이기 위해 이와 흡사한 정책이 이전에 시행되었고, 이 정책은 효과가 있었습니다. 그래서 정부는 최근 의대 졸업생들이 미국의 교외 지역에서 근무하도록 이와 비슷한 정책을 채택했습니다. 지금까지는 성공적인 것 같습니다. 실제로 이런 근무처를 맡기 위한 대기자 명단까지 있을 정도죠!

그리고 의사들이 지방에 있다고 해서 세상에서 격리되는 것은 아닙니다! 교외의 젊은 개업 의사들은 까다로운 진단에 대하여 질문이 있거나 우려되는 바가 있을 때 숙련된 도시의 의사들에게 연락을 취할 수 있습니다. 전화를 걸거나, 이메일을 보내거나, 아니면 다른 의사의 소견을 받아보기 위해 인터넷상에서 온라인 채팅을 하는 것처럼 간단한 수단들이 있습니다. 어떤 경우에는 즉시 소견을 받을 수도 있거든요! 단지 직접 대면하여 조언을 부탁할 수 없다고 해서 고립이라는 문제가 생기는 것은 아니죠. 의사들에게는 어느 때보다도 정보를 교환할 수 있는 수단이 훨씬 많으니까요!

그뿐 아니라, 의사의 생활방식은 종종 몹시 바쁘고 긴장이 가득합니다. 도시 환경은 붐비는 병원이나 사무실에서 긴 하루를 보내 안 그래

도 몹시 곤두선 의사의 신경을 더 날카롭게 할 수도 있습니다. 자연히, 다수의 젊은 의사들은 스트레스가 많은 자신들의 직업을 상쇄 시키는 조용한 교외 지역에 마음이 끌립니다. 그리고 사려 깊은 의사라면, 균형 잡힌 생활과 마음의 평온을 위해서는, 삶의 속도가 느린 교외에서 근무하는 것이 그들의 빠른 속도의 근무 환경을 상쇄시키기 위해서 필요하다는 것을 깨달을 것입니다. 게다가, 교외에서 자란 많은 의대 졸업생들은 종종 자신들이 성장한 환경과 비슷한 조용한 환경에서 근무하기를 선택합니다. 교외의 의사들이 오래 걸리고 좌절스런 도시로의 통근을 하지 않아도 된다는 것은 말할 필요도 없겠죠!

lure[ljuər] 유혹하다　forgiveness[fərɡívnis] (빚 등의) 면제, 탕감　outlaying areas 외곽, 교외지역
inner city 도심　adopt[ədápt] 채택하다　cut off 차단시키다　practitioner[præktíʃənər] 개업 의사
tricky[tríki] 까다로운, 신중을 요하는　solicit[səlísit] 요청하다　isolation[àisəléiʃən] 고립
hectic[héktik] 몹시 바쁜　frazzle[frǽzl] 지치게 하다　bustling[bʌ́sliŋ] 부산스러운, 소란한
gravitate[ɡrǽvitèit] (사람이) 자연히 ~에 끌리다　offset[ɔ́(ː)fsèt] (장점이 단점을) 벌충하다, 상쇄하다
counterbalance[káuntərbæ̀ləns] 효과를 상쇄하다

2. 개인의 자유를 침해하는 것을 때로는 용인할 수 있다는 진술에 찬성하는지 반대하는지를 밝히고 구체적인 이유와 예를 들어 대답을 뒷받침하시오.

Outline

- Agree 찬성
  - 1. To protect public security
    - 많은 사람들의 안전을 보호하기 위해
    - – protects innocent people's lives
      - 무고한 사람들의 생명을 보호한다
    - – e.g. school bus drivers, pilots, firefighters are responsible for people's lives
      - 예) 학교 버스 기사, 조종사, 소방대원들은 사람들의 생명을 책임진다
  - 2. To protect public safety
    - 치안을 유지하기 위해
    - – many acts of random violence today
      - 오늘날 어디서 일어날 지 모르는 수많은 폭력
    - – e.g. airports conduct security check to protect public
      - 공항들은 사람들을 보호하기 위해 보안 검사를 실시한다

Model Essay

"Freedom does not come free" is a saying that holds great truth. Although the idea of taking away individual liberties is abhorrent to people, certain situations warrant this. Cases where people have jobs that put public security at risk or where people's safety is endangered warrant the infringement of people's freedom.

First, individuals' liberties can be violated when they have jobs that could endanger public security. This ensures employees undertake their work safely and responsibly and therefore protects innocent people's lives. For example, school bus drivers, pilots, and firefighters are in charge of many individuals' well-being. If they are under the influence of alcohol or drugs, they will not be able to perform their tasks safely. Thus, it is acceptable to infringe on their freedom and conduct random drug tests. This is necessary to ensure that these public workers are not compromising people's lives.

Protecting public safety is another instance when people's rights can be infringed upon. Especially given the situation today where an increase in random violence is occurring, measures must be taken to prevent these potential attacks from harming innocent people. To take an example, in order to ward off bombings and terrorist acts, airports around the world conduct security checks on people and their belongings and intrude on their personal space. Although this is obtrusive and a violation of one's freedom, it is nonetheless necessary in order to protect everyone from potential harm. Therefore, in these situations, government agencies and public institutions have the right to conduct searches and trespass one's privacy.

In conclusion, to prevent people from putting others at risk and to ensure the public's safety, some individual freedoms do need to be restricted. The government's responsibility to protect its citizens sometimes results in infringing upon a few people's rights. As danger and terrorism increase, it is the obligation of the government to do whatever it can to keep society safe.

해석 "자유는 거저 주어지지 않는다"는 말은 위대한 진실을 담고 있는 격언이다. 비록 사람들이 개인의 자유를 박탈하는 것에 질색할지라도, 특정 상황에서는, 이러한 행위가 정당화될 수 있다. 공공의 안전을 위협할 수 있는 업무를 담당하는 사람들이나 사람들의 안전을 위협할 소지가 있는 경우는 사람들의 자유에 대한 침해를 정당화한다.

첫째로, 개인이 대중의 안전을 위태롭게 할 수도 있는 직업을 가지고 있을 때 그 개인의 자유가 침해될 수도 있다. 이는 그들이 안전하고 책임감 있게 업무를 수행하게 하고, 따라서 무고한 사람들의 생명을 보호한다. 예를 들어, 학교 버스 기사, 비행기 조종사, 그리고 소방대원들은 많은 개인들의 안전을 책임지고 있다. 만일 그들이 술에 취하거나 마약을 복용한 상태에 있다면, 그들은 직무를 안전하게 수행하지 못할 것이다. 따라서, 그들의 자유를 침해하여 무작위 약물 검사를 실시하는 것은 용인할 수 있는 일이다. 이것은 이렇게 대중을 위하여 일하는 사람들이 사람들의 생명을 위협하지 않도록 보장하기 위해 필요한 것이다.

치안의 유지는 사람들의 권리가 침해당할 수 있는 또 하나의 사례이다. 특히 무작위의 범죄의 발생이 증가하고 있는 오늘날의 세상을 고려해볼 때, 이러한 공격으로부터 무고한 사람들이 해를 입지 않도록 조치를 취해야 한다. 예를 들면, 폭파와 테러 공격을 막기 위해 전 세계의 공항들은 사람들과 그들의 소지품을 검문하고 사적인 영역을 침범한다. 이는 비록 강제적이며 자유의 침해이지만, 그럼에도 불구하고 잠재적인 피해로부터 모두를 보호하기 위해서 필요하다. 따라서, 이러한 상황에서는 정부 기관이나 공공 기관은 수색하고 사생활을 침해할 권리를 지닌다.

결론적으로, 타인을 위험에 처하게 하는 것을 방지하고 대중의 안전을 보장하기 위해서 일부 개인의 자유를 제한할 필요가 있다. 정부는 시민들을 보호해야 할 책임이 있고, 그 결과 때로 몇몇 사람들의 권리를 침해하게 된다. 위험과 테러리즘이 증가함에 따라, 사회를 안전하게 유지하기 위해서 할 수 있는 것은 다 해야 하는 것이 정부의 의무이다.

어휘 abhorrent[əbhɔ́ːrənt] 질색인 warrant[wɔ́ːrənt] 정당화하다 endanger[indéindʒər] 위험에 빠뜨리다
infringement[infríndʒmənt] 침해 under the influence of~ ~의 영향 아래
liberty[líbərti] 자유 undertake[ʌ̀ndərtéik] ~을 맡다, ~의 책임을 지다 random[rǽndəm] 닥치는 대로의, 무작위의
ward off 피하다, 막다 security check (공중 납치 예방을 위한) 보안 검사 belongings[bilɔ́(ː)ŋiŋs] 소지품
intrude[intrúːd] 침입하다, 방해하다 obtrusive[əbtrúːsiv] 참견하는, 강요하는
nonetheless[nʌ̀nðəlés] 그럼에도 불구하고 trespass[tréspəs] 침해하다 obligation[àbləgéiʃən] 의무